# Network Topology in Command and Control:

## Organization, Operation, and Evolution

T. J. Grant
*R-BAR, The Netherlands*

R. H. P. Janssen
*Netherlands Defence Academy, The Netherlands*

H. Monsuur
*Netherlands Defence Academy, The Netherlands*

A volume in the Advances in Information Security, Privacy, and Ethics (AISPE) Book Series

| | |
|---|---|
| Managing Director: | Lindsay Johnston |
| Production Editor: | Jennifer Yoder |
| Development Editor: | Austin DeMarco |
| Acquisitions Editor: | Kayla Wolfe |
| Typesetter: | James Knapp |
| Cover Design: | Jason Mull |

Published in the United States of America by
Information Science Reference (an imprint of IGI Global)
701 E. Chocolate Avenue
Hershey PA 17033
Tel: 717-533-8845
Fax: 717-533-8661
E-mail: cust@igi-global.com
Web site: http://www.igi-global.com

Library of Congress Cataloging-in-Publication Data

Grant, T. J., 1947-
  Network topology in command and control : organization, operation, and evolution / T.J. Grant, R.H.P. Janssen, and H. Monsuur.
     pages cm
  Includes bibliographical references and index.
  Summary: "This book connects the fields of C2 and network science, featring timely research on topics pertaining to the C2 network evolution, security, and modeling"-- Provided by publisher.
  ISBN 978-1-4666-6058-8 (hardcover) -- ISBN 978-1-4666-6059-5 (ebook) -- ISBN 978-1-4666-6061-8 (print & perpetual access) 1.  Command and control systems. 2.  Electric network topology.  I. Title.
  UB212.G73 2014
  355.3'3041--dc23
                                        2014007809

This book is published in the IGI Global book series Advances in Information Security, Privacy, and Ethics (AISPE) (ISSN: 1948-9730; eISSN: 1948-9749).

# Advances in Information Security, Privacy, and Ethics (AISPE) Book Series

ISSN: 1948-9730
EISSN: 1948-9749

## MISSION

As digital technologies become more pervasive in everyday life and the Internet is utilized in ever increasing ways by both private and public entities, concern over digital threats becomes more prevalent.

The **Advances in Information Security, Privacy, & Ethics (AISPE) Book Series** provides cutting-edge research on the protection and misuse of information and technology across various industries and settings. Comprised of scholarly research on topics such as identity management, cryptography, system security, authentication, and data protection, this book series is ideal for reference by IT professionals, academicians, and upper-level students.

## COVERAGE

- Access Control
- Device Fingerprinting
- Global Privacy Concerns
- Information Security Standards
- Network Security Services
- Privacy-Enhancing Technologies
- Risk Management
- Security Information Management
- Technoethics
- Tracking Cookies

IGI Global is currently accepting manuscripts for publication within this series. To submit a proposal for a volume in this series, please contact our Acquisition Editors at Acquisitions@igi-global.com or visit: http://www.igi-global.com/publish/.

# Titles in this Series

*For a list of additional titles in this series, please visit: www.igi-global.com*

*Network Topology in Command and Control: Organization, Operation, and Evolution*
T. J. Grant (R-BAR, The Netherlands) R. H. P. Janssen (Netherlands Defence Academy, The Netherlands) and H. Monsuur (Netherlands Defence Academy, The Netherlands)
Information Science Reference ● copyright 2014 ● 330pp ● H/C (ISBN: 9781466660588) ● US $215.00 (our price)

*Cases on Research and Knowledge Discovery Homeland Security Centers of Excellence*
Cecelia Wright Brown (University of Baltimore, USA) Kevin A. Peters (Morgan State University, USA) and Kofi Adofo Nyarko (Morgan State University, USA)
Information Science Reference ● copyright 2014 ● 357pp ● H/C (ISBN: 9781466659469) ● US $215.00 (our price)

*Multidisciplinary Perspectives in Cryptology and Information Security*
Sattar B. Sadkhan Al Maliky (University of Babylon, Iraq) and Nidaa A. Abbas (University of Babylon, Iraq)
Information Science Reference ● copyright 2014 ● 443pp ● H/C (ISBN: 9781466658080) ● US $245.00 (our price)

*Analyzing Security, Trust, and Crime in the Digital World*
Hamid R. Nemati (The University of North Carolina at Greensboro, USA)
Information Science Reference ● copyright 2014 ● 281pp ● H/C (ISBN: 9781466648562) ● US $195.00 (our price)

*Research Developments in Biometrics and Video Processing Techniques*
Rajeev Srivastava (Indian Institute of Technology (BHU), India) S.K. Singh (Indian Institute of Technology (BHU), India) and K.K. Shukla (Indian Institute of Technology (BHU), India)
Information Science Reference ● copyright 2014 ● 279pp ● H/C (ISBN: 9781466648685) ● US $195.00 (our price)

*Advances in Secure Computing, Internet Services, and Applications*
B.K. Tripathy (VIT University, India) and D. P. Acharjya (VIT University, India)
Information Science Reference ● copyright 2014 ● 405pp ● H/C (ISBN: 9781466649408) ● US $195.00 (our price)

*Security Engineering Techniques and Solutions for Information Systems Management and Implementation*
Noureddine Boudriga (Engineering School of Communications, Tunisia) and Mohamed Hamdi (Engineering School of Communications, Tunisia)
Information Science Reference ● copyright 2014 ● 359pp ● H/C (ISBN: 9781615208036) ● US $195.00 (our price)

*Trust Management in Mobile Environments Autonomic and Usable Models*
Zheng Yan (Xidian University, China and Aalto University, Finland)
Information Science Reference ● copyright 2014 ● 288pp ● H/C (ISBN: 9781466647657) ● US $195.00 (our price)
Information Science Reference ● copyright 2010 ● 317pp ● H/C (ISBN: 9781605664149) ● US $180.00 (our price)

www.igi-global.com

701 E. Chocolate Ave., Hershey, PA 17033
Order online at www.igi-global.com or call 717-533-8845 x100
To place a standing order for titles released in this series, contact: cust@igi-global.com
Mon-Fri 8:00 am - 5:00 pm (est) or fax 24 hours a day 717-533-8661

# List of Reviewers

A. I. Barros, *Netherlands Organisation for Applied Scientific Research TNO, The Netherlands*

L. Breebaart, *Science & Technology Corporation, The Netherlands*

D. Eijndhoven, *B-Able Argent Consulting, The Netherlands*

P. Essens, *Netherlands Organisation for Applied Scientific Research TNO, The Netherlands*

P. C. van Fenema, *Netherlands Defence Academy, The Netherlands*

J. M. Jansen, *Netherlands Defence Academy, The Netherlands*

R.E. Kooij, *Delft University of Technology, The Netherlands*

M. Meijer, *Netherlands Ministry of Defence, The Netherlands*

D. M. Ooms, *Netherlands Defence Academy, The Netherlands*

P. V. Pearce, *Defence Science and Technology Laboratory, UK*

S. Rietjens, *Netherlands Defence Academy, The Netherlands*

L. J. M. Rothkrantz, *Delft University of Technology, The Netherlands*

W. Treurniet, *Netherlands Organisation for Applied Scientific Research TNO, The Netherlands*

A. J. van der Wal, *Netherlands Defence Academy, The Netherlands*

F. D. Wicker, *The Aerospace Corporation, Canada*

# Table of Contents

# Detailed Table of Contents

**Chapter 1**

*P.C. van Fenema, Netherlands Defence Academy, The Netherlands*
*S. Rietjens, Netherlands Defence Academy, The Netherlands*
*B. Besters, Netherlands Defence Academy, The Netherlands*

Operation Unified Protector (OUP) in Libya illustrated the urgent need for civil-military command in the sense of at least de-conflicting primary operational processes of military and international civilian actors. A military theater such as Libya is externally connected and surrounded by huge (additional) movements by air, sea, and land. This chapter provides insight into network structures and practices for achieving such de-confliction in the context of complex peace operations. Based on a case study and prior responsibilities of one of the authors, the chapter shows how NATO's Allied Movement Coordination Centre (AMCC) functioned as a linking pin between military and international civilian actors. Challenges it faced are addressed, including establishment of relationships with relevant actors, understanding their ways of working, and developing procedures to coordinate a heterogeneous network.

**Chapter 2**

*W. Treurniet, Netherlands Organisation for Applied Scientific Research TNO,*
*The Netherlands*

Given its nature, a crisis has a significant community impact. This applies in particular to emergencies: crises that arise quickly. Because of the complex and multifaceted nature of large-scale incidents, the response requires coordinated effort by multiple organizations. This networked collaboration is not solely restricted to professional organizations. In responding to an incident, the affected community can itself be an important source of information and capabilities. This chapter discusses how one can shape a trustworthy and decisive response organization in which relevant and useful capacities available in the community are incorporated. This discussion has two focal points. The first focal point is the role of the affected community in the case of an emergency. On the one hand, an emergency affects the fabric of the community, such as the critical infrastructure. On the other, a community has inherent internal resources that give it resilience and capacity to respond in a crisis. This needs to be reflected in the choice of emergency response planning model. The second focal point is the structure of the emergency response network. An emergency response network is a mixed-sector network. This means that coordination is needed among organizations and collectives with differing strategic orientations.

# Chapter 3

Decentralized, peer-to-peer command and control is a key principle of network-centric operations that has received a lot of scholarly attention. So far, robust networking, another principle, has remained rather underexposed in the academic debate. This chapter introduces theory on modular organizing to start a discourse on network robustness from an organizational design perspective. Above all, the chapter makes clear that the level of system decomposition influences the command and control process of composite military structures. When military organizations follow a fine-grained modularization approach, the structure of a task force deployed may become complex, asking for extra coordination mechanisms to achieve syntheses between the many contributing functional organizational components. In addition, it is argued that modularity's principle of near-decomposability has to be incorporated into the available mathematical models on network-centric operations. A point of concern, in this respect, is that the current modeling parameters make no clear distinction between the different types of actors—or nodes—in a military network structure, whereas in reality, technological, organizational, and human actors all live by their own specific rules.

# Chapter 4

This chapter proposes an approach to modelling the functions of C2 performed over a network of geographically distributed entities. Any kind of command and control (C2) organisation, hierarchical, networked, or combinations thereof, can be represented with this approach. The chapter also discusses why a theory of C2 needs to be expressed in functions in order to support design and evaluation of C2 systems. The basic principle of how to model functions performed by network is borrowed from Cares' network model of warfare, which is also used to model the context in which C2 is performed. The approach requires that C2 is conceived of as fulfilling a set of necessary and sufficient functions. Brehmer proposes such a theoretical model that is at a sufficiently high level of abstraction to illustrate the suggested approach. More detailed models will be required, however, for the approach to be of practical use.

# Chapter 5

Command and Control (C2) is an essential operating capability in which the commander exercises authority over assigned forces to accomplish the mission. Traditionally, military C2 was organized hierarchically with the commander issuing directives top-down and subordinates reporting progress upwards. Over the past two decades, developments in digital telecommunication technology have made it possible to link distributed computer systems into a network. These developments can be exploited to delegate decision-making authority down the organizational hierarchy. Subordinates can be empowered to share information and synchronize their actions with their peers, speeding up the response to changes in the situation. This is known as Network-Enabled Capabilities or information-age C2. Experience has shown that multiple factors must co-evolve to gain the full benefit of transforming C2 to become network enabled. In this chapter, the authors group these factors into five layers: geographical, physical, information, cognitive, and socio-organizational. They formalize the key entities in each layer, together with within- and across-layer relationships, into a conceptual ontology, known as the Formalized Layered Ontology for Networked C2 (FLONC). To ensure the ontology is militarily relevant, the authors show that a set of networks found in military operations can be extracted from the ontology. Finally, they compare the formalized ontology to related work on ontologies in C2. In further research, the ontology could be used in developing software to simulate and support network-enabled C2 processes. A case study based on the events of September 11, 2001 shows how this could be done.

## Chapter 6

*B. Drabble, Independent Researcher, USA*

This chapter describes an approach to modeling C2 and other types of networks as a series of nodes (people, groups, resources, locations, concepts, etc.). The nodes are linked by one or more weighted arcs describing the type and the strength of the dependency that one node has on another node. This model allows analysts to identify the most important nodes in a network in terms of their direct and indirect dependencies and to rank them accordingly. The same model also supports consequence analysis in which the direct, indirect, cascading, and cumulative effects of changes to node capabilities can be propagated across the networks. The chapter describes the basic modeling technique and two types of dependency propagation that it supports. These are illustrated with two examples involving the modeling and reasoning across insurgent networks and an Integrated Air Defense System. These show how aspects of the networks can be analyzed and targeted. Details are also provided on the mechanisms to link the analysis to a planning system through which plans can be developed to bring about desired effect(s) in the networks.

## Chapter 7

*R. H. P. Janssen, Netherlands Defence Academy, The Netherlands*
*H. Monsuur, Netherlands Defence Academy, The Netherlands*
*A. J. van der Wal, Netherlands Defence Academy, The Netherlands*

In modeling military (inter)actions and cooperation as networks, military units or actors may be represented as nodes. In analyzing military networked action, a key observation is that a node is not just part of one type of network but simultaneously belongs to multiple networks. To model the dynamical behavior of actors, one has to take into account the interdependence of the different networks. In this chapter, the authors present a method that is used to implement, analyze, and evaluate some specific principles that may be used by the actors in an organization to drive the process of constant change. It can be used to analyze the effect of these principles on the metrics for coordination, synchronization, robustness, and desired operational effectiveness of the network as a whole. To demonstrate the approach, the authors apply it to networks in which two basic principles are operational: reciprocity and a novel principle called covering.

## Chapter 8

*S. Deller, Textron Defense Systems, USA*
*A. Tolk, SimIS Incorporated, USA & Old Dominion University, USA*
*G. Rabadi, Old Dominion University, USA*
*S. Bowling, Bluefield State College, USA*

This chapter describes an approach to develop an improved metric for network effectiveness through the use of Cares' (2005) Information Age Combat Model (IACM) as a context for combat (or competition) between networked forces. The IACM highlights the inadequacy of commonly used quantifiable metrics with regards to comparing networks that differ only by the placement of a few links. An agent-based simulation is used to investigate the potential value of the Perron-Frobenius Eigenvalue ($\lambda$PFE) as an indicator of network effectiveness. The results validate this assumption. Another measurement is proven to be equally important, namely the robustness of a configuration. Potential applications from the domain of ballistic missile defense are included to show operational relevance.

## Chapter 9

*A. H. Dekker, University of Ballarat, Australia*

This chapter examines the connection between network theory and C2, particularly as it relates to self-synchronization, which requires a rich network structure. The richness of the network can be measured by the average degree, the average path length, and the average node connectivity. The chapter explores the connection between these measures and the speed of self-synchronization, together with other network properties, which can affect self-synchronization, resilience, and responsiveness. Two important network structures (random and scale-free) are described in the context of self-synchronization. Experimental data relating network topology to self-synchronization speed is also explored. In particular, the chapter notes the connection between average path length and self-synchronization speed, as well as the importance of good networking between sub-networks.

## Chapter 10

*J. Moffat, Defence Science and Technology Laboratory, UK*

This chapter focuses on understanding the nature of the information networks that can create Self-Synchronization of the force. The analysis takes place at a number of levels, which for simplicity, are called Levels 1, 2, and 3. At Level 1 ("linked"), the author considers the basic node and linkage topology. At Level 2 ("synched"), he considers the local interaction between intelligent nodes, sharing the information and awareness required for Self-Synchronization in the cognitive domain. At Level 3 ("cliqued"), the author considers how such local networking feeds through into emergent clustering effects in the physical domain. Structured experimental games coupled with information entropy-based measures of merit illustrate these ideas, as do models of fundamental information networking dynamics and their resultant emergent behaviour. It turns out that the tools, models, and concepts of Complexity Theory give deep insight into the topic of Self-Synchronization.

**Chapter 11**

Emerging information and communications technology has had significant importance for military operations during the last decades. Development within such technology areas as sensors, computers, and wireless communications has allowed for faster and more efficient collection, transmission, storage, processing, analysis, and distribution of data. This has led to new and improved military capabilities within command and control, intelligence, targeting, and logistics. However, the increased complexity and interdependencies of networked systems, the continuously growing amounts of data, changing non-technical requirements, and evolving adversary threats makes upholding cyber security in command and control systems a challenging task. Although some best-practice approaches have been developed, finding good solutions for protecting critical infrastructure and important information assets is still an open research question requiring an interdisciplinary approach. This chapter describes recent developments within emerging network technology for command and control, and suggests focus areas where further research is needed in order to attain sufficient operational effect from the employed systems. While a gradual and evolutionary progress of military cyber security has been seen, a long-term commitment is required within such areas as procurement, standardization, training, doctrinal, and legal development, in order to achieve military utility of command and control systems.

**Chapter 12**

To enable effective and efficient command and control in military operations it is necessary to have full awareness of all the actions in the field. In traditional C2 systems, human operators play key roles varying from observation in the field up to semantic interpretation of observed data in the Command and Control Centre. Networks are mainly used to transmit data between different components of the network. Observation by human operators will be replaced by sensor networks. The huge amount of incoming data is far beyond the capacity of operators, so the heterogeneous, multimodal data from the different sensor systems has to be fused, aggregated, and filtered. Automated surveillance sensor networks are discussed in this chapter. Sensors are modelled as a distributed system of smart agents. Methods and technology from Artificial Intelligence such as expert systems, semantic networks, and probabilistic reasoning is used to give a semantic interpretation of the sensed data from the environment.

# Foreword

## FROM COMBAT ADVANTAGE TO PREPAREDNESS FOR UNDEFINED CONNECTIVITY

I welcome the opportunity to introduce this important publication. As General Manager of the NATO Communications and Information Agency, I lead a team that is responsible for not only operating and defending NATO's global networks 24/7, but also helping to prepare, test, and promote the connectivity standards and methods for potential future missions, in partnership with key stakeholders such as NATO's Alliance Command Transformation.

In the Alliance, we have seen a clear evolution of the role of the network. The network has gone from a problem (struggling to achieve physical connectivity) to a critical source of combat advantage, as was demonstrated by the campaign in Afghanistan and the Afghanistan Mission Network (AMN). It is very telling that in 2009, in a letter to Ambassadors outlining the critical resources he needed to fulfill his mission, the then ISAF Commander, General Stanley A. McChrystal, listed as the second item (just after helicopters) a single network for the coalition of over 40 countries contributing to the mission.

Leveraging the groundwork laid by the concepts of network-centric warfare and the NATO Network Enabled Capability, the AMN was born. For those who witnessed and contributed to this (r)evolution, it was clear that the true breakthrough was in policy. For the first time—due to the intensity of the combat and the significant loss of soldier's lives—the need to share became (and will remain) the overriding paradigm.

The core challenge today remains preparedness; there were few who were able to predict the Libya operation. I am certain that few of us will be able to predict the next mission for which we have to build and connect networks. What is certain is that membership in these networks will remain volatile and non-traditional. In the case of Libya, not only did we have to interface with the civil sector, but also non-traditional state partners, like Qatar, whose jets flew armed sorties next to Swedish fighters. Furthermore, we will most likely have very limited time to establish these networks.

In the Alliance, this preparedness work is being taken forward under the umbrella of the Future Mission Network. Some of the important concepts being discussed in that framework are the same subjects you will find in this publication:

- Civil-military interaction – any disaster situation, but also preparing for ballistic missile defense (or even massive cyber-attacks) requires the ability to quickly interface with civilian actors and share information and a common picture of a rapidly unfolding situation;

- Implications for cyber defense – we are moving from protecting the boundaries of the network to managing the identity of the users who are on the network and focusing on protecting access to critical information on the network, knowing well that we may never fully control access to the actual network;
- Extreme mobility and the multiplicity of both access platforms as well as input sensors – the range and number of platforms on which data has to be made available, as well as the range and number of inputs is increasing dramatically;
- Standing joining instructions – in a rapidly evolving scenario, we will not have the luxury of months or years to build up a network as we did in Afghanistan. A key effort there is ensuring that the processes for joining a network are well-defined and known;
- Validation and verification – 60 years of standardization agreements in NATO have proven that nothing can replace the actual ability to rapidly validate technical interoperability, particularly in a situation of connecting to "non-traditional" or civil partners.

On a global scale, we also see a redefinition of the network. Networks are evolving from a "nice to have" to a core determinant of nations' wealth and prosperity. Similarly, as with operational networks, few of these networks are easy to define, or wholly owned by national governments. One example is smart electric grids: part private, part public. Perhaps, many years from now, the ability to protect critical networks in contested cyberspace will be regarded as having been the same kind of "game-changer" as was the technological ability of the Dutch East India Company to build ships more rapidly than their competitors.

Networks will remain first and foremost human. Building awareness and understanding of shared concepts is a first step to being able to establish the networks we will need in the future, particularly in an increasingly complex and multi-faceted reality. This is why I consider the work in this book essential reading, and I congratulate both the editors and the contributing authors.

*K. Gijsbers*
*NATO Communications and Information Agency, Belgium*

**K. Gijsbers** *became the first General Manager of the newly established NATO Communications and Information Agency on 1 July 2012. Prior to that, he was the CIO at the Ministry of Defence in The Netherlands. His main focus was on the rationalization of IT services throughout the organization. He was also responsible for the information security policy for the entire Dutch national government as a member of the national CIO Board and the national cyber board. During his tenure as CIO, he coordinated a major reorganization of the defence organization in order to implement a 15% budget cut (1 billion Euros). From 2006 to 2009, as Assistant Chief of Staff for Command, Control, Communications, Computers and Intelligence at NATO's Allied Command Transformation in Norfolk, VA, USA, he led NATO's network centric innovation as well as mentoring and overseeing NATO's Cooperative Cyber Defence Centre of Excellence (COE) in Estonia and the Command and Control COE in The Netherlands. In his career, he has commanded and supported troops both at home and around the globe, including Iraq, Afghanistan, Congo, and Kosovo. MGEN Gijsbers holds a Master's degree in Military Art and Science of the US Army Command and General Staff College. In 2001, he was knighted in the Order of Orange Nassau (with Swords), awarded by Her Majesty Queen Beatrix.*

# Preface

## INTRODUCTION

Network science and network-enabled Command and Control (C2) both emerged in the mid- to late-1990s, although their roots are much older. Network science is a modern branch of mathematics and Operations Research (OR), with its roots in graph theory going back nearly three hundred years to Leonhard Euler's solution of the *seven bridges of Königsberg* problem. C2 is a branch of the military sciences closely associated with leadership, with a history of thousands of years going back to the ancient Greeks, if not longer. With the introduction of telecommunications over the past 180 years – first the telegraph, then the telephone and radio, and, most recently, the computer and computer networking – C2 has gained a strong engineering flavor.

Lewis (2009, p. 9) defines network science as *"the study of the theoretical foundations of network structure/dynamic behavior and the application of networks to many subfields,"* listing these as social network analysis, collaboration networks, synthetic emergent systems, physical science systems, and life science systems. Brandes, Robins, McCranie, and Wasserman (2013, p.5) succinctly claim that *"theories about network representations and network theories about [real-world] phenomena"* both constitute network theory. There are two key elements in both definitions: theory and applications. From the theoretical viewpoint, a network is a set of nodes and a set of arcs linking these nodes to one another. From the application viewpoint, what networks, nodes, and arcs represent in the real world can vary widely. Vice versa, real-world applications can impose requirements on the mathematical representation and on how this representation is employed.

C2 is the process of monitoring, directing, and controlling assigned resources to achieve the mission, often in remote and perhaps dangerous environments (adapted from US DoD Joint Publication 1-02, 2013). Variants of this process are to be found in military operations, emergency management, disaster relief, and real-time process-control applications (e.g. transport, utilities, distribution, and logistics). C2 is invariably a team effort, often involving multiple organizations, supported by computers and telecommunications, each with their own doctrine, operating procedures, and norms of behavior. Human qualities, such as leadership, are essential to C2, and will remain so for the foreseeable future. C2 involves the interplay between humans and machines, demanding that it be studied from a *socio-technical systems* viewpoint (Trist & Bamforth, 1951).

In applying the network representation to C2, the nodes may model individual people, teams, organizational units, vehicles, ships, aircraft, satellites, computers, hubs, routers, and more. The arcs can link people who know each other or who have family, tribal, or national relationships in common, yielding a *social network*. Alternatively, they can designate superior-subordinate relationships between people, teams, and organizational units, yielding an *organizational structure* (often depicted as an *organigramme*). From an engineering viewpoint, arcs may model the wired or wireless links over which computers, hubs, and routers exchange digital messages, yielding a *telecommunications network*. Operationally, road, rail, water, sewage, electricity, and other types of *physical network* may all have an important role to play in C2.

Modern C2 systems link tens of thousands of computers and their users. With unmanned vehicles, sensors, and other devices being added daily, the number of C2 nodes is increasing exponentially. Modern network science provides the mathematical techniques for representing and analyzing networks with thousands and millions of nodes, i.e. for handling "big data." In the mid-1990s, Cebrowski and Garstka (1998) introduced some of the concepts from network science into military operations in advocating a new C2 approach, known initially as *Network-Centric Warfare* (NCW) and now known as *Network-Centric Operations* (NCO) in the US and *Network-Enabled Capabilities* (NEC) in Europe and NATO. Alberts and Hayes (1999, 2003, 2006, 2007) built extensively on these ideas at the conceptual level. Since 2004, network science techniques have been applied to C2, representing only the physical telecommunications network at first. Gradually, network science has been extended to the social networks of C2 users and their adversaries. Since 2009, network science has been applied to cognitive networks (i.e. the mental models in C2 users' minds). Until now, work on the application of network science to C2 has been focused on technical, information, and social networks.

The two disciplines—network science and C2—have developed separately, and have separate literatures. The academic communities are largely separate, with their own journals and conferences. There are books on C2, and books on network science, but no previous books have comprehensively applied network science to C2. There are scientific articles, some Masters and PhD theses, and at least one monograph (Cares, 2005) applying network science to C2, but these do not treat the subject comprehensively.

The objective of this book is to combine network science and C2 in a form that is accessible to readers from both disciplines. Prospective readers may be professional C2 users and developers or researchers in network science or C2. The book brings together researchers from the US, the UK, Australia, Sweden, and The Netherlands. Case studies range from engaging citizens in searching for missing children, through a major fire in a chemical factory and an insurgency scenario, to Operation Unified Protector in Libya and the events of September 11th, 2001. The book extends the applications all the way from the (cyber-) geography of C2, through physical, technical, information, and cognitive networks, to the socio-organizational level. A particular strength of the book is that it treats organizations (e.g. military units in a task force) and (civil-military) coalitions as networks. For both disciplines, the book will broaden the set of techniques available. It will aid C2 developers in designing and implementing truly network-enabled C2 systems. C2 users will learn how insights derived from network science affects the way they attack and defend C2 systems. Network science researchers will gain a detailed insight into how their techniques can be applied in multiple ways to critical, real-world systems. As each chapter provides extensive references and questions for readers to check their understanding, the book can also serve as a textbook for students at Bachelor and Masters levels.

This preface aims to place the contributions in this book into the context of the current state of the art, identifying what research has achieved so far and what directions future research should take. Following this introduction, the second section reviews the state of the art in network science, in C2, and in the application of the former to the latter. The third section presents a framework for analyzing the book's contributions. The fourth section briefly reviews each chapter using this framework. The fifth section identifies future research directions from this review. Finally, the sixth section draws conclusions and makes recommendations for further work.

# STATE OF THE ART

## Network Science

Lewis (2009) distinguishes three periods in the history of network science. After Euler's introduction of graph theory, it spent 200 years in the backwaters of arcane mathematics. It re-emerged in the 1950s when Paul Erdos investigated the mathematics of random graphs. In the 1960s and 1970s, graph theory was used by social scientists to study the behavior of humans in small groups, resulting in Stanley Milgram's introduction of the notion of the small-world network in his well-known "six degrees of separation" experiment. Graph theory became modern network science in the late 1990s when a number of scientists began to use networks as models of large-scale, real-world phenomena. Newman (2003) is a comprehensive survey of the advances in network theory, and Barabási (2003) is a readable introduction to network science for the general public.

In contemporary scientific research, applications of network science can be found in a wide variety of domains. For example, Newman (2003) surveys work on biological, technological, information, and social networks. However, this may be a modest view. According to the US National Research Council (2005), networks lie at the core of the economic, political, and social fabric of the 21$^{st}$ century. Transportation, power grids, social and economic interaction, business alliances, and military organizations and operations can all be represented in terms of networks and their analytical properties.

It is possible to analyze networks at several levels. At the level of individual nodes and arcs, one may identify measures such as the degree of a node (i.e. how many arcs are linked to it) or its centrality. In a communication network, where arcs represent communication links between C2 nodes, a central position enables fast communications. If a node has a high degree, then it may be classified as a hub in the network. In a social network, the degree measure can be indicative of a person's social status.

At the second level, analysis focuses on clusters of nodes. A cluster in which any one node can send a message to any other is known as a component. Ideally, a complete C2 network should be one giant component, allowing information to flow freely. However, if a C2 network is broken up in several components, the commander's intent will not reach all units, and situation reports from subordinate units may not reach the commander. A C2 network can be broken into multiple components by removing nodes or arcs through equipment failure, enemy action, or lack of interoperability. When targeting a hostile C2 network, one may seek the high-degree hubs, because eliminating these nodes quickly breaks the target networks into separate components. Analysis at the level of clusters can also be used to identify terrorist networks. For example, two clusters representing terrorist cells may be connected by just one node with a high betweenness measure. This node may then represent an information broker or courier between the two cells, making it an attractive target for counter-terrorist operations.

At the level of the network as a whole, one may look at the network's robustness or resilience to failure, at its topology, and at processes occurring through the network. Robustness relates to the number of alternative communication paths through the network. The network topology, whether it is a random graph, a small-world network, or a scale-free (or power-law) network, has an impact on robustness and other network properties. For example, scale-free networks have a hierarchy of hubs, making them vulnerable to targeted attack. Grant, Buizer, and Bertelink (2011) found that representative C2 networks, like the Internet and the World Wide Web, had a scale-free topology. Network processes relating to C2 include the spread of information, epidemiology (i.e. the spread of and recovery from infections), search for information, and network navigation. These processes are influenced by several analytical parameters that may be obtained at the various levels of analysis.

To analyze a network from this multi-level point of view, at least three network metrics are commonly used. The most important metric is the degree distribution of nodes in a network. Degree distribution reveals various properties. At the local atomic level, it may be used to assess whether or not links have been created at random. For example, a power-law degree distribution suggests that the network evolved using a preferential attachment scheme, in which a newly-created node is preferentially linked to a pre-existing, high-degree node (i.e. to a hub). However, as we have seen, such a scheme results in a network that is vulnerable to deliberate attack. Another commonly used metric is the average path length. If the path length is long, communication between nodes that are far apart is at risk of delay and/or failure because of the large number of intermediate nodes that signals must pass through. If path length is low, then nodes are closely tied together, and communication should be faster and less failure-prone. A third metric is the clustering coefficient, related to robustness. This measures the likelihood that two nodes that are linked to a common node, in addition are being linked themselves.

These metrics are also used to characterize and identify three types of network topology. The preferential attachment scheme has already been mentioned, resulting in scale-free networks. Random networks have low average path length and also a low clustering coefficient. Many real-world networks are small worlds, with a low average path length but high clustering.

In management and the military sciences, the concept of networked operations has attained considerable attention. Clearly, there is a dynamic interaction between the various structural properties of networks on the one hand, and new ways of networked operations and supporting technology on the other hand. Therefore, a very important issue is how possible ways of networked operations are affected by the topology and by the architecture of the information, physical and social networks that coexist between various organizational units. Classifying an existing C2 network into one of the three network classes may reveal important strengths, but also weaknesses.

Generally speaking, the demand for scientific and practical knowledge that can be used to *organize*, *operate,* and guide the *evolution* of networks is ubiquitous and growing. This also holds for the military domain. Often, important military advantages do not come from new technology alone, but also from new ways of organizing the fighting forces. The success of 21st century military operations and civil-military cooperation heavily depends on the integration of network science and C2.

## Command and Control

Command and Control (C2) is one of NATO's Essential Operating Capabilities. It is defined as *"the exercise of authority and direction by a properly designated commander over assigned and attached forces in the accomplishment of the mission"* (US DoD Joint Publication 1-02, 2013). A C2 system is *"an arrangement of personnel, equipment, communications, facilities, and procedures,"* and the functions of C2 include *"planning, directing, coordinating, and controlling forces and operations"* (ibid). These definitions show that C2 is not confined to the technical implementation. The definition hints at organization (*"authority and direction," "assigned and attached forces,"* and *"personnel"*), knowledge (*"mission," "procedures,"* and *"planning"*), and information (*"communications," "directing,"* and *"coordinating"*), as well as technology (*"equipment," "communications,"* and *"facilities"*).

Traditionally, military C2 was top-down and directive, emphasizing achievement of the commander's intent (the *"mission"*), with subordinates (the *"assigned and attached forces"*) periodically reporting their progress towards achieving this intent. This required a hierarchical organization, with communications passing up and down the hierarchy. Subordinate units report progress in the form of situation reports up the hierarchy, and commanders promulgate their intent down to their subordinates in the form of operation orders. In a hierarchical organization, subordinate units rarely communicate directly with one another. Instead, the commander carries the burden of synchronizing their activities, usually by deconfliction (e.g. by giving them mutually exclusive areas of responsibility). The technical systems supporting this traditional C2 process were designed to mirror the organizational hierarchy. This has been termed "industrial-age" C2 (Alberts, 2002).

There are several shortcomings of industrial-age C2. Firstly, commanders suffer from information overload. Secondly, commanders can form a bottleneck in the information flow, both in synchronizing their subordinates' activities and in summarizing the reporting from subordinates in a report to their own superior. Thirdly, only the commander has an overview of the situation, often hampering subordinates in gaining an understanding of the rationale behind their commander's intent. Fourthly, the concentration of information at the commander's location makes him/her an attractive target for the enemy.

Over the past two decades, developments in digital telecommunication technology have made it possible to link distributed computer systems into a network. In 1998, Vice Admiral Cebrowski and John Garstka published an article in the US Naval Institute Proceedings outlining the concept of NCW (Cebrowski & Garstka, 1998). In what follows, we use the term NEC and the associated NATO concepts. NEC is based on four tenets (Alberts, 2002):

**Tenet 1:** A robustly networked force improves information sharing.
**Tenet 2:** Information sharing and collaboration enhance the quality of information and shared situational awareness.
**Tenet 3:** Shared situational awareness enables self-synchronization.
**Tenet 4:** These, in turn, dramatically increase mission effectiveness.

As the name suggests, NEC focuses on networks. At the outset, networking was overwhelmingly seen as a technological capability. By "network," one meant the telecommunication network that linked the C2 systems electronically. Gradually, as scientific and practical knowledge built up, it became apparent that an exclusively technological view was too restrictive. Factors such as psychology and culture also had to be taken into account. NATO expressed the full set of factors as Doctrine, Organization, Training and Education, Materiel and Equipment, Leadership, Personnel, Facilities, and, depending on the author, Interoperability or Information, abbreviated "DOTMLPFI" (NATO, 2009).

A change in one of the DOTMLPFI factors meant that the others also had to change. In particular, experience shows that the greatest benefit could be gained from networking if the organizing principle changes from top-down direction to empowerment of the units at the edge of the hierarchy (becoming an "*edge organization*") (Alberts & Hayes, 2003). Empowerment means that awareness of the situation and decision making must be shared between the commander and his/her subordinates. Commanders give their subordinates goals to achieve ("*mission command*"), rather than directing how they should act. Moreover, subordinates are empowered to coordinate their activities directly with their peers; this is known as "*self-synchronization.*" Communications become predominantly peer-to-peer, running mostly across the hierarchy rather than predominantly up and down it. C2 systems must be networked to support the flow of messages up, down, and across the hierarchy. Modern technologies such as Internet protocols, Web-based systems, portals, Web 2.0, e-mail, chat (instant messaging), social media, and cloud computing are better suited to implementing these "information-age" C2 systems than the older, process-control technologies.

NATO (2009) defined five NEC Maturity Levels (NMLs) to measure the extent to which a military force or coalition was networked. When units are operating independently without interacting, then they are at the *stand-alone* level (NML 1). When they accept constraints to avoid interference with one another, they are at the *deconflict* level (NML 2). When the organizations cooperate including joint operational planning but their units execute these plans without interaction, they are at the *coordinate* level (NML 3). When organizations both plan and execute these plans collectively, then they are at the *collaborate* level (NML 4). At the highest *coherent* level (NML 5), organizations plan and execute missions as if they were a homogeneous force.

## Applying Network Science to C2

Around the same time that NEC was being developed in the C2 literature, mathematical network theory began increasingly to yield valuable results. It became clear that these results could be applied equally well to social, information, technological, and biological networks (Newman, 2003). This insight stimulated the NEC thought-leaders to group the DOTMLPFI factors into three domains (Alberts, Garstka, Hayes, & Signori, 2001). In their view, the *physical* domain represents the real world in which military units maneuver, weapon systems engage one another, and sensors capture data about the events taking place. In the *information* domain, information is created, manipulated, and transmitted, either as spoken or written natural language or as electronic bits and bytes. Invariably, technology is employed to store and transmit information. Traditionally, the technologies used were pen and paper, telephone, and radio, but modern Information and Communications Technologies (ICT) have now surpassed them. Information is received by the human C2 users, converted into knowledge, assessed, and acted upon in the *cognitive* domain (i.e. in the users' minds). It is in the cognitive domain that C2 decision making—usually modeled by Boyd's (1996) Observe-Orient-Decide-Act (OODA) loop—occurs. Alberts and Hayes (2003) observed that modern military endeavors are too complex to be understood by individuals. Empowered teams working peer-to-peer develop a shared understanding of the situation and of how to respond to this situation. They added a fourth, *social* domain.

In 2008, Van Ettinger and his NATO colleagues mapped three of the domains (social, cognitive, technical) to networks by means of the DOTMLPFI factors (Van Ettinger, 2008). The technical network covers the DOTMLPFI factors of Materiel (M) and Facilities (F). The cognitive network covers Doctrine (D), Organization (O), and Training (T), and the social network covers Leadership (L) and Personnel (P). In Van Ettinger's depiction, the three networks are shown as overlapping circles, with Interoperability/Information (I) providing the "glue" between them.

By contrast, Monsuur, Grant, and Janssen (2011) observed that the three networks were linked by military units and individuals. Being physically embodied, units and individuals appeared as nodes in the technical network. Units and individuals acquired, processed, and acted upon knowledge specific to the application domain. They also appeared, therefore, as nodes in the cognitive network. Since units and individuals communicated with one another, sharing awareness about the situation and synchronizing their actions, they also appeared as nodes in the social network. Monsuur et al termed these interlinking nodes as "*actors*," with nodes appearing in only one of the networks being termed "*objects*." Since the actors must appear in all three networks, it was easier to depict them as being layered on top of one another. Finally, Monsuur et al.'s article provided the basic mathematics for events occurring in one network to influence events in another. It was this article that was the inspiration for compiling this book.

Military interest in the application of modern network science started first and has gained the most intensive form in the United States. In 2003, the US Army proposed that network science should become a new research area. This gained form a year later by the establishment of the Network Science Center (NSC) at the US Military Academy West Point, supported by Dr. David S. Alberts at the US DoD's Command and Control Research Program (CCRP). The purpose of the NSC is to bring together military officers, civilians, and US Army cadets to research and develop significant contributions in the study of network representations of physical, biological, and social phenomena (NSC, 2014). Interdisciplinary undergraduate courses in network science were developed for the West Point cadets. NSC's collaborators include US Army research organizations, DARPA, the Naval Postgraduate School, and California State University San Bernardino.

In 2006, the US Army Research Laboratory (ARL) and the UK Ministry of Defence (MoD) formed the Network and Information Science International Technology Alliance (ITA). ITA's strategic goal is to produce fundamental advances in the information and network sciences that will enhance decision making for coalition operations (ITACS, 2014). The ITA consortium is led by IBM and comprises 24 partners, consisting of 8 major defense system integrators and 16 universities, almost equally divided between the US and the UK. In the first phase from 2006 to 2011, ITA adopted four technical areas, one of which was network theory focusing on wireless and sensor networks. The other three areas were not related to network science. In the second phase, due to end in May 2016, ITA has just two technical areas: coalition interoperable secure and hybrid networks, and distributed coalition information processing for decision making. Each area breaks down into three projects, and only the project on the performance of hybrid networks is directly related to network science.

In 2009, the US Army formed the Network Science Collaborative Technology Alliance (NS-CTA), comprising the ARL, CERDEC, and some 30 US industrial R&D laboratories and universities. The goal of the NS-CTA is to develop a deep understanding of the commonalities among intertwined social/cognitive, information, and communication networks, improving the ability to analyze, predict, design, and influence complex systems (NS-CTA, 2014). The CTA's research program divides into three academic areas focusing on communication, information, and social/cognitive networks. Research is tied together by two cross-cutting issues: trust in distributed decision making, and evolving dynamic integrated networks.

We regard the research done by the USMA's NSC, the US-UK ITA, and the NS CTA as the current state of the art for comparing the advances made by the contributions in this book.

## ANALYSIS FRAMEWORK

To analyze the contributions in this book, we extend the two elements in Lewis' (2009) definition of network science. His definition made a distinction between the theoretical foundations and applications. The same distinction can be made in C2. Since this book aims to combine network science and C2, our analysis framework is a two-by-two matrix with Lewis' two elements of network science forming the columns and the equivalent two elements of C2 as the rows.

We need to describe each element in more detail. Starting with network science, we can sub-divide the applications according to the domains found in NATO NEC theory: physical, information, cognitive, and social. We modify this scheme slightly in two ways. First, we split off the geographical elements underlying the physical domain into a separate geographical domain. What remains in the physical domain are the objects that can be placed in, or can move around, the geographical domain. This can include roads, buildings, vehicles, sensors, computer hardware, effectors, and other such man-made devices, as well as (groups of) people. Second, the social domain is extended to encompass both informal and formal groups and teams. To recognize this extension, we rename it the socio-organizational domain. Beyond the socio-organizational domain, we identify a coalition level in which multiple organizations (possibly civil as well as military) interact, whether that interaction take the form of deconfliction, coordination, or collaboration.

The theoretical foundations of network science can also be sub-divided. Taking our inspiration from network science surveys, such as Newman (2003), we can distinguish foci of theoretical attention on the properties of nodes and arcs, on network measures such as centrality and betweenness, on network topologies, and on processes occurring in networks, such as search and the spread of information.

Turning now to C2, we can sub-divide the application of C2 according to Boyd's (1996) OODA loop. C2 theory can focus on observation (covering sensing, detection, perception, and monitoring), on orientation (covering the processes needed to understand what has been observed, such as data fusion and intelligence analysis), to decision making, and acting upon these decisions. We note here that action in the C2 context has a strong communicative favor (e.g. sending situation reports and issuing orders). Physical action is largely performed by the resources that are assigned to the commander. Since the OODA loop is reactive in nature, we add the deliberative processes of planning and learning.

To sub-divide the theoretical foundations of C2, we identify a list of issues that recur in the C2 and NEC literature. Starting with individual C2 systems, these issues include providing the underlying infrastructure, gaining and maintaining Situation Awareness (SA), assessing the quality of information, agility in decision making, and designing a suitable command structure. Then we extend this list by considering issues relating to multiple C2 systems. Issues that arise include interoperability, information sharing, building up a Common Operational Picture (COP), collaboration, self-synchronization, and operational effectiveness (including C2 performance metrics).

Finally, we sound two cautionary notes. First, other researchers may choose to sub-divide network science and C2 in other ways. Second, we have used our judgment in placing the contributions and other initiatives within our analysis framework. This is, of course, necessarily subjective.

## ADVANCES TO STATE OF THE ART

The contributed chapters fell naturally into four groups. There were three contributions dealing with organizational issues, another three on how to model C2 networks, four on network theory, and finally two on C2 technology. Accordingly, the book is structured into four sections.

The first section of the book contains the three contributions on Organization. The first chapter is "De-Conflicting Civil-Military Networks" by Van Fenema, Rietjens, and Besters. Using Operation Unified Protector (OUP) in Libya as a case study, they provide insight in suitable network structures and practices for achieving de-confliction between civil and military partner organizations in complex peace operations. They identify several lessons learned, such as coordination depends on the personalities involved, on consistency between rotations, and agreeing on the objectives for the post-conflict environment. They recommend research into reaching agreement on network goals to coordinate civil and military operations. In the second chapter, "Shaping Comprehensive Emergency Response Networks,"

Treurniet discusses how professional organizations can incorporate the relevant and useful capacities of local communities in Emergency Response (ER). He shows how the social capital of communities provide substantial resilience, and contrasts two planning approaches for integrating community capacities into the ER organization. He recommends that ER organizations should strike a balance between directive and empathetic decision making and communication, and identifies the need for further research into effective mixed-sector ER network governance. In the third chapter, "Networked Operations: Taking into Account the Principles of Modular Organizing," de Waard introduces theory on modular organizing from the Organizational and Management (O&M) sciences to military forces, contrasting the US and Dutch armies' approaches. He shows that important organizational aspects remain underexposed by only concentrating on the relationship between the number of nodes and network effectiveness, arguing that near-decomposability is an important organizational design parameter. He makes several recommendations for further research, including the need to investigate cycling between centralized and decentralized organizational structures to increase coordination. He advocates applying the O&M debate on subgroup isolation and intergroup connectivity to the military domain, as well as elaborating on the effect of structural holes in organizational networks.

The second section of the book contains the three contributions on modeling. In the fourth chapter, "Modeling Command and Control in Networks," Jensen proposes an approach to modeling the functions of C2 performed over a network of geographically distributed entities, based on Brehmer's (2007, 2013) C2 theory. Her contribution suggests an approach that enables any C2 organization to be modeled. She recommends the use of empirical data to compare Brehmer's theory with other C2 theories, and the development of sub-theories of the functions of data collection, orientation, and planning. In the fifth chapter, "Formalized Ontology for Representing C2 Systems as Layered Networks," Grant presents a logical ontology for representing C2 systems from their underlying (cyber-) geography, through physical objects, information, and knowledge, to the socio-organizational constructs. Key contributions include dividing the ontology into layers, integrating cyberspace into the other four "kinetic" domains, and showing that a rich set of C2-relevant networks can be extracted from the ontology. Further research focuses on using the ontology to develop simulation software. In the sixth chapter, "Modeling C2 Networks as Dependencies: Understanding What the Real Issues Are," Drabble presents a C2 model focusing on capabilities, dependencies, and vulnerabilities. In this model, nodes representing people, groups, resources, locations, and concepts are linked by one or more directed arcs, weighted according to the strength of the inter-node dependency. Implemented systems based on this model allow analysts to rank and identify the most important nodes in a network, their critical vulnerabilities, and their susceptibility to feedback, and to identify the direct, indirect, cascading, and cumulative effects of changes in a network. Through an integrated planning capability, analysts can develop plans to alter the behavior of an opposition network to exploit its vulnerabilities, or to increase the resilience and robustness of their own networks. Drabble recommends the extension of this work to provide the abilities to track plan rationale so that the planner can be re-tasked if an effect can be achieved through a different node, and to update key information as the network changes over time.

The third section of the book contains the four contributions on Networks. In the seventh chapter, "Dynamical Network Structures in Multi-Layered Networks: Implementing and Evaluating Basic Principles for Collective Behavior," Janssen, Monsuur, and Van der Wal present a stochastic actor-based method that can be used to analyze the effect of the dynamic behavior of actors in a network on coordination, synchronization, robustness, and the desired operational effectiveness of a networked organization. They show that, in networked military action, a node is not just part of one network (e.g. a communication network or a social network), but simultaneously belongs to multiple networks. Therefore, to model the dynamical behavior of actors, one has to take into account the interdependency between networks. They recommend further work in simulating the use of several types of actors, of other measures of performance, and of basic principles other than reciprocity and covering. In the eighth chapter, "Improving C2 Effectiveness Based on Robust Connectivity," Deller, Tolk, Rabadi, and Bowling describe an approach to develop an improved metric for network effectiveness through the use of Cares' (2005) Information Age Combat Model (IACM) as a context for combat or competition between networked forces. The value of the Perron-Frobenius Eigenvalue metric, together with a robustness factor, is confirmed using an agent-based simulation, shifting the focus from the capabilities of the nodes to the capability of the network as a whole. Deller et al intend to check whether the results apply to even larger networks. In the ninth chapter, "C2, Networks, and Self-Synchronization," Dekker explores the connection between C2 and networks to address the question of which network topologies are the best for self-synchronization. He finds by experiment that low average path length, a high node connectivity, and good links between sub-networks all contribute to a network topology suitable for rapid self-synchronization. He recommends that, to avoid group-think, joint, combined, and coalition forces should make networking *between* components a higher priority than networking *within* components. Further research is needed to explore new classes of networks (e.g. entangled networks), beyond the well-studied random, scale-free, and small-world models, and to identify which organizational problems benefit best from self-synchronization. In the tenth chapter, "Complex Adaptive Information Networks for Defence: Networks for Self-Synchronization," Moffat focuses on understanding the nature of the information networks which can create self-synchronization of the force. The analysis is at three levels, covering the basic node and linkage topology (level 1), the local interaction between intelligent nodes sharing information and awareness (level 2), and how such local networking feeds through into emergent clustering effects in the physical domain (level 3). Moffat finds that the tools, modeling approaches, and concepts of complexity theory give a deep insight into self-synchronization.

The fourth and final section of the book contains the two contributions on C2 technology. In the eleventh chapter, "Cyber Security in Tactical Network Infrastructure for Command and Control," Sigholm describes recent developments in emerging network technologies for C2, including reconfigurable radio systems, emerging network topologies, technologies for situational awareness, security metrics, information asset protection systems, and autonomous network monitoring and control. He assesses their maturity using Technology Readiness Levels (TRLs). He concludes that a long-term commitment is required within such areas as procurement, standardization, training, doctrinal, and legal development, in order to achieve military utility of C2 systems. He recommends more detailed study of the requirements for tactical C2 network infrastructure to advance these technologies to a TRL that would permit transfer into systems and networks in support of a desired capability, within cost, schedule and risk constraints. In the twelfth and last chapter, "Smart Surveillance Systems," Rothkrantz argues that, in the near future, the huge amount of heterogeneous, multimodal data received from automated sensor networks will be far beyond the capacity of human operators to fuse, aggregate, and filter. He describes the development of a prototype based on a distributed system of smart agents communicating via blackboards and using Artificial Intelligence techniques such as expert systems, semantic networks, and probabilistic reasoning to give a semantic interpretation of the sensed data. The prototype has been tested using inputs from the Automated Identification System (AIS) monitoring ship movements in and around the Den Helder naval base in the Netherlands. The innovative aspect is the reduction of the role of human operators by using sensors and software agents to observe large areas. He recommends that the current decision support system should be developed as a fully automated system, fusing data from different sources and modalities and integrated with available radar or camera surveillance systems.

In Table 1, we have placed the contributions made by these chapters into the analysis framework introduced in section 3 above. The columns represent the theory and applications of network science, with the theory progressing from the levels of individual nodes and arcs ("nodes"), network measures, topologies, and processes. Network science applications progress from the underlying geography, through physical, information, cognitive, and socio-organizational domains, to coalitions. The rows represent the theory and application of C2. C2 theory covers the underlying infrastructure (hardware and communications network), issues relating to individual C2 nodes (such as Situation Awareness [SA], quality of information, agility), and the C2 organization or command structure, followed by issues relating to multiple C2 nodes (such as interoperability, information sharing, building a Common Operating Picture [COP], collaboration, and self-synchronization) and the overall issue of mission effectiveness. The C2 applications cover C2 models, the OODA processes, plus planning, and learning. The numbers in the table's cells refer to the chapter's number. The abbreviations NSC, ITA, and CTA refer respectively to the research areas (as we understand them from publically-available information) addressed by USMA West Point's Network Science Center, by the US-UK International Technology Alliance, and by the US Army Research Laboratory's Collaborative Technology Alliance. In addition, "Graph" indicates the pre-existing contributions of graph theory to C2 system design (e.g. for calculating bandwidth and for frequency management).

It is apparent from Table 1 that the contributions in this book have advanced the state of the art in the literature on the application of network science, as represented by the research done by West Point's Network Science Center, the US-UK International Technology Alliance, and ARL's Network Science Collaborative Technology Alliance. In particular, we have addressed a variety of new organizational issues, especially those relating to civil-military interaction (chapter 1), to involving the community in the area of operations (chapter 2), to modular organizations (chapter 3), to modeling C2 (chapters 4, 5, and 6), and to self-synchronization (chapters 9 and 10). Nevertheless, there are many "white areas" in Table 1, representing areas where future research is needed, as follows:

- The rows corresponding to the application of network science to individual C2 system nodes, covering C2 infrastructure, situation awareness, the quality of information, agility, and the organizational or command structure. Chapter 11 has made a start on applying network science to tactical network infrastructure in the physical and information domains.
- The columns corresponding to the application of the theory of network topologies and processes into all forms of C2. Chapters 7, 8, 9, and 10 have made a start on the application of topologies.
- The rows corresponding to the application of network science to C2 decision-making, acting, and learning. Chapter 7 has made a start on applying network science to learning.

## FUTURE RESEARCH DIRECTIONS

Because of the wide variety of contributions, we refer readers to the chapters in this book for their specific recommendations for further research. Despite these contributions and those from pre-existing research, there still exist at least three "white areas": the application of network science to individual C2 system

*Table 1. Mapping contributions to analysis framework*

| | | Network Science | | | | | | | | | |
|---|---|---|---|---|---|---|---|---|---|---|---|
| | | Theory: | | | | Applications: | | | | | |
| | | Nodes | Measure | Topology | Process | Geog | Phy | Info | Cogn | Socio-org | Coalition |
| **C2** | *Theory:* | | | | | | | | | | |
| | Infra | Graph | | | (Graph) | | 11 | 11 | | | |
| | SA | | | | | | | | | | |
| | Quality | | | | | | | | | | |
| | Agility | | | | | | | | | | |
| | Org | | | | | | | | | 3 | 2, 3 |
| | Interop | | | | | | ITA | ITA | | | 2 |
| | Info sharing | | | | | | NSC, ITA | NSC | NSC | NSC | 2 |
| | COP | | | | | | | | | | 2 |
| | Collab | | | | | | 1, 7 | | CTA | 7 | 1, 2 |
| | Self-syn | 10 | 9 | 7, 9, 10 | | | 10 | 1, 7 | CTA | CTA, 7 | 1, 2 |
| | Eff'ness | | 8 | 8 | | | | 7 | | 7 | |
| | *Appl:* | | | | | | | | | | |
| | Model | 5, 6 | 6 | | | 5 | 5 | 5 | 5 | 4, 5 | 5 |
| | Observe | 6 | 6 | | | | ITA, 12 | ITA, 12 | | 4 | |
| | Orient | 6 | 6 | | | | | | NSC, CTA | NSC, CTA, 4 | |
| | Plan | 6 | 6 | | | | | | | 4 | |
| | Decide | | | | | | | | | 4 | |
| | Act | | | | | | | | | 4 | |
| | Learn | | | 7 | | | | | | 4 | |

nodes and to decision-making, acting, and learning processes, and the specific application of network topologies and processes to C2 systems.

Twenty-first century operations increasingly rely on C2 networks to coordinate complex joint, combined, inter-agency, and civil-military endeavors. This trend will only intensify with the introduction of unmanned vehicles and networked devices such as sensor networks. Facing the corresponding socio-technical and organizational challenges, research on combining network science with C2 remains essential. To stimulate future research we pose a few high-level questions that need investigation. What are the competences required of organizational units to exploit networked operations to achieve the highest success? What are the precise characteristics of socio-technical C2 networks that enhance mission success? How should real-world experiments be designed to confirm whether or not the results of network analysis hold in actual (civil-) military environments? As well as addressing these application-oriented questions, fundamental research is also needed. For example, are there new classes of network, beyond the well-studied random, scale-free, and small-world models, that will meet the precise needs of C2?

Perhaps most importantly, new theory is needed to model networked C2 interacting with an intelligent networked opponent, because it takes one network to fight another (McChrystal, 2011).

## CONCLUSION

Network science and network-enabled Command and Control (C2) both emerged in the mid- to late-1990s. However, the two disciplines have developed separately, with separate conferences, journals, and books. The objective of this book has been to combine network science and C2 in a form that is accessible to readers from both disciplines. The chapters in this book have been contributed by researchers from the US, the UK, Australia, Sweden, and The Netherlands. These contributions cover applications ranging from the (cyber-) geography of C2, through physical, technical, information, and cognitive networks, to the socio-organizational level. Case studies range from engaging citizens in searching for missing children, through major fires in a chemical factory and an insurgency scenario, to Operation Unified Protector in Libya and the events of September 11th, 2001.

This preface has placed the contribution of each chapter into the context of the state of the art using an analysis framework based on the two disciplines' theory and applications. This shows that the book forms an advance on pre-existing research into the application of network science in C2. In particular, chapters in this book treat organizations (e.g. military units in a task force) and (civil-military) coalitions as networks.

Despite these advances, more research is needed. Each chapter makes its own recommendations for further research. Beyond this, the analysis framework clearly shows "white areas" where little or no work has been done to date: the application of network science to individual C2 system nodes and to decision-making, acting, and learning processes, and the specific application of network topologies and processes to C2 systems. Finally, this preface has posed a few high-level questions to stimulate other researchers, whether they are C2 designers and users or experts in network science.

*T. J. Grant*
*R-BAR, The Netherlands*

*R. H. P. Janssen*
*Netherlands Defence Academy, The Netherlands*

*H. Monsuur*
*Netherlands Defence Academy, The Netherlands*

## REFERENCES

Alberts, D. S. (2002). *Information-Age Transformation: Getting to a 21st century military*. Washington, DC: US DoD Command & Control Research Program.

Alberts, D. S., Garstka, J., Hayes, R. E., & Signori, D. T. (2001). *Understanding Information Age Warfare*. Washington, DC: US DoD Command & Control Research Program.

Alberts, D. S., & Hayes, R. E. (1999). *Network Centric Warfare: Developing and leveraging information superiority* (2nd ed.). Washington, DC: US DoD Command & Control Research Program.

Alberts, D. S., & Hayes, R. E. (2003). *Power to the Edge: Command Control in the information age*. Washington, DC: US DoD Command & Control Research Program.

Alberts, D. S., & Hayes, R. E. (2006). *Understanding Command and Control*. Washington, DC: US DoD Command & Control Research Program.

Alberts, D. S., & Hayes, R. E. (2007). *Planning: Complex endeavors*. Washington, DC: US DoD Command & Control Research Program.

Barabási, A.-L. (2003). *Linked: How everything is connected to everything else and what it means for business, science, and everyday life*. New York, NY: Plume.

Boyd, J. R. (1996). *The Essence of Winning and Losing. Unpublished lecture notes*. Maxwell Air Force Base.

Brandes, U., Robins, G., McCranie, A., & Wasserman, S. (2013). What is Network Science? *New Scientist, 1*(1), 1–15.

Brehmer, B. (2007). Understanding the Functions of C2 Is the Key to Progress. *The International C2 Journal, 1*(1), 211-232.

Brehmer, B. (2013). *Insatsledning*. [Command and control of missions]. Unpublished technical report. Swedish National Defence College.

Cares, J. (2005). *Distributed Networked Operations: The foundations of Network Centric Warfare*. Newport, RI: Alidade Press.

Cebrowski, A. K., & Garstka, J. H. (1998). Network-Centric Warfare: Its origins and future. In *Proceedings of the US Naval Institute*. Academic Press.

Grant, T. J., Buizer, B. C., & Bertelink, R. J. (2011). Vulnerability of C2 Networks to Attack: Measuring the topology of eleven Dutch Army C2 systems. In *Proceedings of 16th International Command & Control Research & Technology Symposium* (paper ID 087). Washington, DC: US DoD Command & Control Research Program.

ITACS. (2014). *US-UK International Technology Alliance Collaboration System*. Retrieved February 6, 2014, from https://www.usukita.org/

JP 1-02. (2013). *US Department of Defense Dictionary of Military and Associated Terms, Joint Publication 1-02, 8 November 2010 as amended through 15 December 2013*. Retrieved February 6, 2014, from http://www.dtic.mil/doctrine/dod_dictionary/

Lewis, T. G. (2009). *Network Science: Theory and applications*. Hoboken, NJ: John Wiley & Sons. doi:10.1002/9780470400791

McChrystal, S. A. (2011, March-April). It Takes a Network: The new frontline of modern warfare. *Foreign Policy, 1-6*.

Monsuur, H., Grant, T. J., & Janssen, R. H. P. (2011). Network Topology of Military Command & Control Systems: Where axioms and action meet. In *Computer Science, Technology, and Applications* (Vol. 3, pp. 1–27). Hauppauge, NY: Nova Science Publishers, Inc.

National Research Council. (2005). *Network Science: Report of the Committee on Network Science for Future Army Applications*. Washington, DC: The National Academies Press.

NATO. (2009). *Whitepaper on NNEC Maturity Levels. Unpublished working draft v2, 22 April 2009*. Brussels, Belgium: NATO.

Newman, M. E. (2003). The Structure and Function of Complex Networks. *SIAM Review, 45*(2), 167–256. doi:10.1137/S003614450342480

NS-CTA. (2014). *Network Science Collaborative Technology Alliance, US Army Research Laboratory*. Retrieved February 6, 2014, from http://www.ns-cta.org/ns-cta-blog/

NSC. (2014). *USMA West Point Network Science Center: About Us*. Retrieved February 6, 2014, from http://www.westpoint.edu/nsc/SitePages/About.aspx

Trist, E., & Bamforth, K. (1951). Some Social and Psychological Consequences of the Longwall Method of Coal Getting. *Human Relations, 4*, 3–38. doi:10.1177/001872675100400101

Van Ettinger, F. (2008). NATO Network Enabled Capabilities: Can it work? *Carre, 11*, 22–26.

# Acknowledgment

The editors would like to thank a number of people who have made this book possible. First, we acknowledge the effort expended by the authors in contributing and refining their ideas over several iterations. Many authors have also acted as reviewers of other authors' contributions. To them we owe double thanks. We designed the review process so that each contribution was reviewed double-blind by one peer author and by another researcher who had not been involved in the preparation of the book. Thanks too to the additional reviewers. We are especially honored that Major General (rtd) K. Gijsbers, General Manager of the NATO Communications and Information Agency, agreed to write the foreword of this book. His extensive operational experience makes him the right person to judge our scientific ideas. Throughout the whole process, we have been ably supported by our publishers, IGI Global. In particular, we are grateful for A. DeMarco's amicable guidance as the Editorial Assistant assigned to us by IGI Global.

*T. J. Grant*
*R-BAR, The Netherlands*

*R. H. P. Janssen*
*Netherlands Defence Academy, The Netherlands*

*H. Monsuur*
*Netherlands Defence Academy, The Netherlands*

# Chapter 1
# De-Conflicting Civil-Military Networks

**P.C. van Fenema**
*Netherlands Defence Academy, The Netherlands*

**S. Rietjens**
*Netherlands Defence Academy, The Netherlands*

**B. Besters**
*Netherlands Defence Academy, The Netherlands*

## ABSTRACT

*Operation Unified Protector (OUP) in Libya illustrated the urgent need for civil-military command in the sense of at least de-conflicting primary operational processes of military and international civilian actors. A military theater such as Libya is externally connected and surrounded by huge (additional) movements by air, sea, and land. This chapter provides insight into network structures and practices for achieving such de-confliction in the context of complex peace operations. Based on a case study and prior responsibilities of one of the authors, the chapter shows how NATO's Allied Movement Coordination Centre (AMCC) functioned as a linking pin between military and international civilian actors. Challenges it faced are addressed, including establishment of relationships with relevant actors, understanding their ways of working, and developing procedures to coordinate a heterogeneous network.*

## CLOUD COMPELLER

"**Man with lantern:** Who are you?

**Captain:** The Flying Cloud. 220 days out of New York and 50 days trying to find your blasted harbor.

**Man with lantern:** Nobody asked you to come.

**Captain:** Got anything in this hog-end of the world except fog?

**Man with lantern:** Sure, we've got gold, fountains of gold."

Ben Hecht (1894 – 1964), US screenwriter

DOI: 10.4018/978-1-4666-6058-8.ch001

## INTRODUCTION

Globalization has led to a soaring of trade and transportation over the past decades. This includes land, sea, and air transportation of people and goods. Massive transportation affects networked operations such as Operation Unified Protector (OUP) in Libya and their command and control. Stated differently, deliberately designed corridors within and outside the theatre can support mission success from a military[1] and humanitarian[2] perspective. In addition, crises and operations may trigger mass evacuations to areas adjacent to the theatre (van Fenema, 2012). Current operations often combine diverse civil and military organizations using the Comprehensive Approach as a method of pursuing high level goals (Crawshaw, 2007). Operations demand and secure corridors to focus on the area of operations.

New questions are raised such as: how joint and combined access to the theatre is assured (JCS, 2012); how restricted operations zone (ROZ) are organized (Docauer, 2011); how large numbers of civilians are evacuated; and who is capable, responsible and authorized for operationally de-conflicting multiple networks such that operational effectiveness is enabled. Answers to these questions depend on the type of operation, including changes during the operation (Rubbini & Vindua, 2012). De-confliction concerns the awareness of which actors should change their transportation pattern, which actors are denied access to the theatre, and which actors may contribute to the theatre. In addition to awareness, decision making must be authorized and decisions must be effectuated (Monsuur, Grant, & Janssen, 2011; Rietjens, Kampen, & Grant, 2010). Information processing underpins these processes, relying on geographical information, existing civil and military databases, and access to actors interested in using the theatre's air, sea and land domains.

Numerous studies have appeared on complex peace operations (C. H. de Coning, 2008, 2010), focusing on interagency cooperation, command and control, and cooperative planning (Stringer, 2010). Yet it seems that operational de-confliction is often assumed. *We define operational de-confliction as coordinating physical flows of people and goods within and or around theatre such that mutual interference is minimized.* This aspect of command and control increasingly has become a complex, multi-network challenge. The objective of this chapter is therefore to contribute to the understanding of operational de-confliction in complex peace operations. We focus in particular on operational de-confliction in networks consisting of military and a great variety of civilian actors. Operation Unified Protector (OUP) that took place in 2011 in Libya is used as a case study for this. Within this case study we focus specifically on the operational de-confliction of air movements to and from Libya as an example of Civil-Military Interaction.

The chapter is structured as follows. The next section (Conceptual Framework) provides an introduction to civil-military networks in complex peace operations and outlines the framework to analyze the case. We then describe the case OUP (Managing the Libyan Theater), and identify lessons learned and analyze the case (Lessons Learned and Conceptual Analysis). The final section (Conclusion: Mind the Gap) draws conclusions mainly from the perspective of AMCC.

## CONCEPTUAL FRAMEWORK

### Civil-Military Networks

In peace support missions, both military and civilian actors are dependent on each other in the execution of a variety of tasks (C. de Coning & Friis, 2011). This relates to the required capacity and expertise, such as military logistic capacity, that can be deployed to support a humanitarian organization in the delivery of food packages. Conversely, humanitarian organizations can assist the military in executing humanitarian operations like constructing a refugee camp or hospital. This is in accordance with the "altruistic self-interest principle" of Seiple (1996), who views civil-military coordination as a pragmatic strategy whenever partners consider themselves interdependent in reaching their objectives.

Interdependencies are partial, ambiguous and of a temporary nature. Involvement of network members in the particular area varies in terms of duration, intensity, and contributions. For military organizations, stakeholders (re)define mandates for expeditionary missions (Soeters & Manigart, 2008). Similarly, humanitarian organizations commit their resources for a limited period of time depending on their stakeholders' international assessment of mission needs (Kovács & Spens, 2007; Rietjens, Voordijk, & De Boer, 2007; Tatham & Rietjens, (under review); van der Laan, de Brito, van Fenema, & Vermaesen, 2009). The culture and doctrine of military organizations are rooted in part in the merits of coordinating efforts, and aim to achieve logical and clear structures to that end (Soeters, 2000; Soeters & Manigart, 2008).

Humanitarian organizations, on the other hand, are often driven by the 'humanitarian principles'. They are wary of anything interfering with their freedom of action and relationships with local communities. Stoddard (2006) refers to these principled organizations as being the 'Dunantists', whereas 'Wilsonian' organizations generally act more pragmatically and therefore interact more easily with military forces (Stoddard, 2006). Unsurprisingly, therefore, in many operational areas, the design of civil-military networks is essentially improvisational, pragmatic and ad hoc (Rietjens & Bollen, 2008). Meeting on the ground in an operational area, personnel from both sets of organizations typically appear to work out solutions and overcome differences to achieve the common good. As a result, the appropriate coordination mechanisms evolve over time in response to the specific circumstances of a particular operation. Many different terms are being used to address these coordination mechanisms in a civil-military

network. These terms include the integrated approach, whole of government approach, 3D-approach (Development, Diplomacy and Defence) and the Comprehensive Approach. This chapter uses the term Comprehensive Approach since this is the concept that is most widely used within NATO to describe its initiatives to pursue coordination and coherence within the civil-military network. Following de Coning and Friis (2011) we define the Comprehensive Approach as a process aimed at facilitating system-wide coherence across the security, governance, development and political dimensions of international peace and stability operations.

## Civil-Military Command

### Interdependence of Primary Operational Processes

Command and control has been defined as the *"responsibility for effectively using available resources, planning the employment of, organizing, directing, coordinating, and controlling military forces for the accomplishment of assigned missions. It also includes the responsibility for health, welfare, morale, and discipline of assigned personnel"* (Alberts & Hayes, 2005: 14). The Libya case we studied shows that in addition to military forces, international civilian activities partially continue in the theater. Libya represents a modern operation in which military interventions are precise and specific. Moreover, these operations occur amidst civil society (Curtis, 2005; Lind, 2004; Osinga, 2007). In this case, we interpret this phenomenon as interdependence between two types of primary operational processes: networked military operations, and international civilian activities. The former refer to the military missions initiated after the UN resolution. The latter represent on one hand regular international activities such as sea-based supply lines from and towards Libya, and on the other hand new international activities (mainly a variety of NGOs) for supporting the crisis. Using the same geographical environment, interdependence of these primary operational processes emerges. Simply put, when air strikes are planned, civilian actors want to know when not to get in. Conceptually, this activates coordination processes to manage these dependencies (Faraj & Xiao, 2006) and serve stakeholders having an interest in interdependence management (Neaga & Henshaw, 2011; Pestana, Rebelo, Duarte, & Couronné, 2012). In military terms, we can use the term command and control yet with the distinction of broadening its scope to civilian activities and limiting its scope by excluding the actual military command and control. We use the term civil-military command to define the process of coordinating *between* military and international civilian primary operational processes. To be precise, the word *coordination* in the military literature refers to the third level of network centric operations, on a five-level continuum of the absence of coordination (no mutual involvement) to coherence or 'edge' command and control (high mutual involvement) (Alberts & Nissen, 2009). This continuum qualifies the extent to which activities are coordinated and consists of the following levels (CCRP, 2010: xix):

Level 1 Conflicted C2
Level 2 De-Conflicted C2
Level 3 Coordinated C2
Level 4 Collaborative C2
Level 5 Edge C2

Considering the continuum's extremes, an example of the absence of coordination means that actors pursue activities that are interdependent (i.e. there are good reasons to coordinate) without considering each other's means (how each actor wants to achieve its goals), and ends (what each actor wants to achieve). On the other hand, high coordination would imply that actors strive for coherence across their activities (ends) (C. de Coning & Friis, 2011) and mutually adjust their means (Mintzberg, 1995; Van de Ven, Delbecq,

& Koenig Jr, 1976). Moving to the coherent side of the continuum is driven by opportunities to achieve meta-actor goals that appeal to all the actors involved.

This continuum from military theory differs from organization science perspectives where coordination has a more neutral meaning, i.e. the management of interdependence and a focus on 'how' aspects of coordination practices (Crowston, 1997; Faraj & Xiao, 2006). These perspectives commonly do not focus on what coordination achieves or could / should achieve in relation to actors' interests. In this chapter, our approach represents de-conflict from a military theory point of view because military and international civilian actors were not coherently enacting the Comprehensive Approach. The resulting outcomes of coordination – in this case de-conflict – should serve military and international civilian stakeholders' interests. Figure 1 illustrates this process. In this section we address each of the building blocks of civil-military command.

## Overarching Goals for Civil-Military Command

Once interdependencies and the associated need for command emerges, questions can be raised such as: what is the overarching goal associated with the management of dependencies? Which values are deemed important? For instance, in traffic control, de-conflict could be considered an overarching goal, operationalized by safety and efficiency. In regular command and control, mission accomplishment and continuity are essential. Our scope for the Libya case implies de-conflict of military operations and international civilian activities. No combined, synergetic effects are striven for (Rietjens, Soeters, & Klumper, 2010). Usually in the command and control and NNEC (NATO Network Enabled Capability) literatures, de-conflict represents a level of maturity immediately above level 1, i.e., conflicted, stand alone or disjointed operations (Alberts & Nissen,

*Figure 1. Civil-military command*

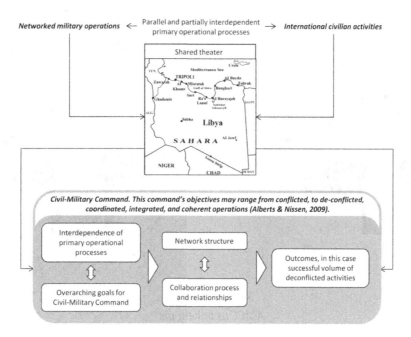

2009). Above level 2 (de-conflicton), level 3 aims for coordinated operations, level 4 for integrated operations, and level 5 for transformed / coherent operations. What exactly is the overarching goal of de-conflicton? It has been defined as:

*... the avoidance of adverse cross-impacts between and among the participants by partitioning the problem space. In order for entities to de-conflict their intents, plans, or actions, they need to be able to recognize potential conflicts and attempt to resolve them by partitioning across geography, function, echelon, and/or time. This involves limited information sharing and limited interactions. It requires that entities give up the freedom to operate without any constraints and thus, in effect, agree to delegate those decision rights that are necessary to ensure de-conflicton. It also requires that participating entities delegate their rights associated with operating without any constraints. Instead, participating entities agree not to act in a manner that violates any agreed upon constraint (CCRP, 2010: 52-53).*

De-confliction thus concerns important yet limited aspects of network actors' actions and their action space. In our case, level 2 is all stakeholders (civil and military actors in mutual relationship) strive for. Given this maturity level and goal for command, effectiveness and flexibility become paramount values, see for air space for instance (Seifert, et al., 2005). There is no joint striving for integrated effects. Next, we elaborate on the steps of civil-military command, covering network structure, collaboration process and relationships, and outcomes.

## Network Structure

While traditional command and control presupposed a hub and spoke network, current operations tend to feature a wide variety of network structures. Our typology, from a network theory perspective, is characterized by a structural hole (Monsuur, 2011; Monsuur, et al., 2011). That is, two networks co-exist that are operationally interdependent. This is depicted in Figure 2. On the left hand side,

*Figure 2. Networks with structural hole*

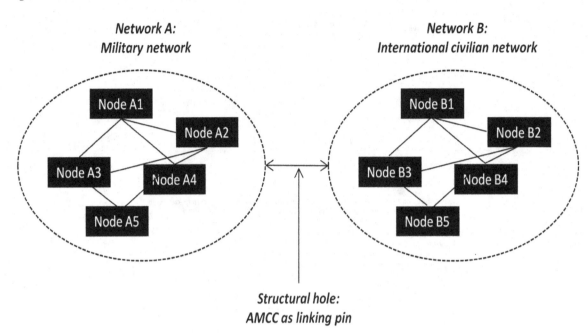

the figure shows the military network consisting of military nodes such as air force units. On the right hand side, the figure shows the international civilian network (e.g. airlines, UN, NGOs). The actors liaising between the two network clusters provide an exclusive communication channel (Burt, 1992). Theoretically speaking, they are very powerful because the networks depend entirely on them for managing interdependencies (Bollen & Soeters, 2010; Crowston, 1997). Reduction of the structural hole would mean that more nodes establish relationships, e.g. node A1 and node B2. This would, of course, change the coordination processes.

NATO's coordinating center liaises between the military operations and international civilian actors. A bi-polar network provides the linking pin with overview. Yet it makes the network potentially vulnerable to its failure. In contrast to military networks, elements are not hierarchically organized. Literature on governance distinguishes market, hierarchy and clan (Powell, 1990). In the Libya case, civilian actors have a clan type of

relationship with NATO yet mostly without long term relationships. The governance structure is lateral and often voluntary (Starkey, Barnatt, & Tempest, 2000).

## Collaboration Process and Relationships

The civil-military collaboration process concerns the interaction between network actors to shape their service to the two clusters. This can take the form of formal, procedure-based interaction, and/or informal, interpersonal cooperation. Communication theory proposes five different types of act: assertives (an actor commits to something), directives (actor receives an instruction to be followed), commissives (actor commits to future action), expressives (actors declare how they perceive something), and declarations (actors change a particular status) (Johannesson, 1995)). By interacting, the linking pin probes for network actors, their knowledge and interdependencies, expectations and contextual factors to be taken into account (Faraj & Sproull, 2000; O'Hair, Kelley, & Williams, 2011). He thus achieves a sufficient level of network awareness to coordinate between, in our case, the two clusters. Coordination theory refers to locating. Current collaboration processes are supported by electronic media and information technologies. The process is influenced by the way actors cooperate. Examples show that norms may differ or even if they are de-conflicted, the application may be inconsistent (Snook, 2000). The Libya network consists of a military and civilian cluster. Even within both clusters, actors and their norms differ (Grant, van Fenema, & van Veen, 2007). NATO's civil-military command addressed a new challenge that called for norm development. Over time, collaboration processes may lead to relationship development, with representatives of organizations getting to know each other (Pitsis, Kornberger, & Clegg, 2004).

## Outcomes

We started with primary operational process interdependencies. Looking at the network structure and collaboration process, a final part of our perspective is command outcomes. Reverting to the primary operational process, successful outcomes imply that military operations can proceed as planned within the military, and international civilian actors can access and exit the theater without being affected by military activities. These basic outcomes can be reinterpreted when considering NATO civil-military command a service with benefits and costs (Sirmon, Hitt, & Ireland, 2007). Benefits accrue to network actors, i.e. their continued operations or at least minimal level of disturbances. Since the network aims for de-confliction, synergetic effects are not expected or strived for. Furthermore, benefits could be interpreted as the volume of requests being processed which reflect the level of interdependencies between the two network clusters. This depends on the volume of traffic of international civilian actors and the pace of military operations. The costs of

NATO's civil-military command service can be determined by examining such parameters as the efficiency of cooperation, the number of mistakes, and the staffing of the liaising command cell.

## MANAGING THE LIBYAN THEATER: OPERATION UNIFIED PROTECTOR AND CIVILIAN ORGANIZATIONS

NATO on 31 March assumed sole command of air operations over Libya, as the number of countries supporting the international action has increased steadily since hostilities against forces loyal to Col Muammar Gaddafi began less than two weeks earlier.

*"The Alliance has the assets in place to conduct its tasks under Operation Unified Protector - the arms embargo, no-fly zone and actions to protect civilians and civilian centres," NATO says. "This is a very significant step, which proves NATO's capability to take decisive action," says secretary general Anders Fogh Rasmussen.*[3]

NATO's Operation Unified Protector (OUP) enforced United Nations Security Council Resolutions (UNSCR) 1970 and 1973 concerning the Libyan civil war. These resolutions were adopted on 26 February and 17 March 2011, respectively and imposed sanctions on the Gaddafi government. They authorized NATO to implement an arms embargo, a no-fly zone and to use all means necessary, short of foreign occupation, to protect Libyan civilians and civilian populated areas (Laity, 2012). As a result a multinational coalition force started a military intervention on 19 March in response to the same UN resolutions. On 27 March NATO decided to implement all military aspects of the UN resolutions and the formal transfer of command occurred on 31 March 2011, formally ending the national and Coalition operations such as the US-led Operation Odyssey Dawn. OUP encompassed all international operations in Libya. A peak of

8,000 soldiers were involved in the operation, 260 air assets (including fighter aircrafts, helicopters, air-to-air refuellers, unmanned aerial vehicles) and 21 naval assets such as frigates and aircraft carriers[4]. OUP officially ended on 31 October 2011, after the rebel leaders, formalized in the National Transitional Council, had declared Libya liberated on 23 October a military operation. The following statement of NATO's Secretary General confirms the complexity of OUP stemming from the many actors involved:

*Operation Unified Protector was one of the most remarkable in NATO's history. It showed the Alliance's strength and flexibility. European Allies and Canada took the lead; the United States provided critical capabilities; and the NATO command structure unified all those contributions, as well as those of our partners, for one clear goal. In fact, the operation opened a completely new chapter of cooperation with our partners in the region, who called for NATO to act and then contributed actively. It was also an exemplary mission of cooperation and consultation with other organizations, including the United Nations, the League of Arab States, and the European Union. Throughout, NATO proved itself as a force for good and the ultimate force multiplier.[5]*

Eighteen nations participated in OUP, each with different resources and mandates. Several countries including France, UK and Italy were able to conduct air to ground operations and contributed to strike missions (Coticchia, 2011). Other nations such as The Netherlands, Spain and Turkey deployed aircrafts to enforce the no-fly zone without attacking ground targets. At the same time some countries contributed Special Forces for operations on the ground in Libya (RUSI, 2011). In addition to their substance, also the size of the national contributions varied. The UK and France were the main contributors to the operation. At its peak, the UK had around 4,000 personnel, 37 aircraft and four ships committed to the intervention, while

France contributed 4,200 personnel, 40 aircrafts, 20 helicopters and one carrier (Coticchia, 2011). The military operations caused a great amount of air movements within the operational theatre. According to NATO official statistics over 26,500 sorties were carried out by sixteen countries. In addition to this large military presence, many international civilian organizations were present in the operational theatre. These organizations included commercial companies such as oil companies and international (humanitarian) organizations. Examples of the latter included the International Office for Migration (IOM), Médecins Sans Frontières (MSF) and the International Red Cross and Red Crescent (ICRC). These organizations also transported a wide variety of personnel and goods in and from the mission area. A large portion of their transportation happened overseas or overland. However, they also made a significant number of air sorties. For example, during OUP the World Food Program alone made 358 flights within the Libyan air space, while a Tunisian oil operator made 552 flights during that same period (NATO, 2011).

Late February 2011, the North Atlantic Council tasked its Supreme Headquarters Allied Powers Europe (SHAPE) to conduct an operational planning process. As a result SHAPE produced four different operational plans for Humanitarian assistance, Arms Embargo, No Fly Zone and No Fly Zone+. Roughly a month later OUP already started. The only player outside of NATO that was involved in this planning process was the European Union. Other organizations like the United Nations, the League of Arab States and the African Union were not involved in this process. Although the new Strategic Concept was in place and the concept Comprehensive Operational Planning Directive (COPD) was leading the planning process, no command and control (C2) structure or civil-military coordination guidelines were determined during the planning process. This led to an approach of de-confliction rather than harmonization as the latter would imply a joint planning process between NATO and non-NATO actors such as IOs and NGOs.

Meanwhile, UNSCR 1973 identified the need for humanitarian actors to have access to Libya for the purposes of providing humanitarian assistance. This requirement was confirmed by NATO's Secretary General[6] who nominated SHAPE as the primary point of contact to receive and de-conflict all requests from humanitarian actors and persons designated with special status. A copy of the letter of the NATO Secretary General is depicted in Figure 3.

The Allied Movement Coordination Centre (AMCC) was the designated unit at SHAPE to coordinate and de-conflict strategic movements of Allied Forces. During OUP this turned out to be a major challenge. As NATO's Joint Analysis and Lessons Learned Center (JALLC) reported, initially the AMCC consisted of only four military logisticians. One of the reasons the AMCC was so small in the beginning was the emphasis of several countries such as the US, UK and France on their own operations. These countries were already deployed. Also, during the first weeks of OUP several nations did not share their movement plans with the AMCC because of the high operational tempo and their direct contacts with Italy and Greece, the two countries that hosted many of the NATO resources that were dedicated to OUP (JALLC, 2012). This lack of awareness made it impossible for the AMCC to develop a well-coordinated deployment plan. In addition, during the operational planning phase in February 2011, only NATO and the European Union participated. The UN or other international organizations were not involved, which made it – again – difficult for the AMCC to get good situational awareness of all the (future) movements.

To address this issue, together with SHAPE's civil advisor, its civil-military cooperation branch, and several other stakeholders[7], the AMCC started to develop procedures to de-conflict all movements in and out of the operational theatre and to notify other actors of such movements. At the same time the AMCC installed a 24/7 de-confliction cell that was situated alongside SHAPE's operational team. The de-confliction concerned all air, sea and ground movements, but also locations of humanitarian actors and persons designated with special status. During the process of establishing this cell, the AMCC realized that many actors, within and outside NATO, played a role in this de-confliction process. Not only humanitarian organizations but also civil transport companies, the traffic control organization EUROCONTROL and governmental organizations were involved. Figure 4 provides an overview of workflows connecting civilian and military networks, centered on the role of AMCC as linking pin. The bold line represents the boundary between civilian and military networks.

Since guaranteeing civilian access to Libya was politically very sensitive, SHAPE was made responsible for it. The letter of NATO's Secretary General made this clear and since this letter was widely communicated, transferring this responsibility would confuse many civilian actors. Moreover, the expectation of NATO was that the operation would not take longer than the maximum of 90 Days.

To support the AMCC with identifying the humanitarian actors and persons designated with a special status, as stated in the letter of the NATO Secretary General, the UN posted a liaison officer (UNLO) at SHAPE. It was unprecedented that UN personnel participated in a NATO headquarters to support an ongoing operation. As has been indicated earlier, relationships between the military and IOs or NGOs incurs sensitivities given the diverse objectives of these organizations (Kitzen, Rietjens, & Osinga, 2012; Rietjens, Soeters, & van Fenema, 2013). It was therefore not allowed to communicate on this 'experiment' to the community outside of SHAPE. Collocation of NATO and UN personnel however facilitated open interpersonal interaction and the participants considered the cooperation as a great success.

*Figure 3. NATO Secretary General letter PO(2001)0094, dated 27 March 2011*

## ESTABLISHMENT OF A NATO POINT OF CONTACT FOR DE-CONFLICTION OF HUMANITARIAN ACTIVITIES IN LIBYA

1.     Following recent decisions by the North Atlantic Council to enforce an arms embargo into and from Libya as well as a No-Fly Zone over Libya pursuant to UN Security Council Resolutions 1970 and 1973, NATO operations are underway.  In this context, we are fully committed to permitting appropriate humanitarian access, as called for by the UN Security Council Resolution 1973.  We will also pay due attention to movement of persons and properties designated with special status.

2.     To this end, the Supreme Headquarters Allied Powers Europe (SHAPE) has established with immediate effect a point of contact to receive and de-conflict all requests from humanitarian actors and persons designated with special status.  This 24-hours a day, 7 days a week Centre can be reached as follows:

| | |
|---|---|
| NAME: | SHAPE Strategic Operations Centre |
| Email: | Shapesocwatch@shape.nato.int |
| PHONE: | 00-32-6544-2218 |
| FAX: | 00-32-6544-5354 |

3.     I would be grateful if you would be so kind as to convey this information to your capital for further distribution.

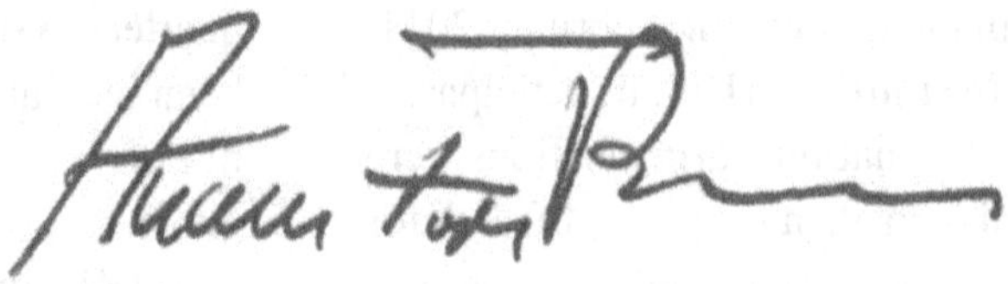

Anders Fogh Rasmussen

*Figure 4. Organizing civil-military networks during Libya 2011 operations (adapted from NATO powerPoint)*

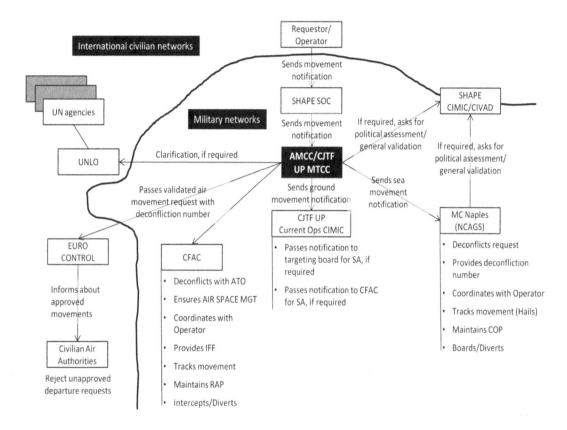

The access to Libya of persons designated with a special status had to be authorized by NATO's political experts. The civilian advisor at SHAPE was the linking pin within this process, while the role of UN's liaison officer was to advise on the status of humanitarian actors and to provide more specific information when needed. After working the process for some weeks the routine assessment of humanitarian actors and persons designated with special status was performed by the AMCC[8]. New requests that fitted earlier ones no longer demanded a formal procedure. Only in special occasions – e.g. requests from new organizations or nations – the official process of authorization was followed.

It seemed that all organizations that wanted to move into the no-fly zone by air, and even by sea or ground, had committed themselves to follow the NATO procedures. Humanitarian organizations, governmental organizations and diplomatic missions, realized that it would be very dangerous to enter this zone without permission. Conversely, NATO was very strict and careful not to hit a target that did not belong to the Gaddafi Forces. Such an incident could potentially harm the entire operation. This tension encouraged all stakeholders to work together. In hindsight, no catastrophic incident happened. In the seven months thousands of flights, mainly for reasons of humanitarian assistance and medical evacuation, were de-conflicted with operational NATO flights.

Figure 5 provides an overview of the total number of air movements that were de-conflicted by the AMCC in 2011. Starting early June (W(eek)22 in the Figure) and ending late October (W(eek)45 in the Figure) the graph shows a strong increase in

*Figure 5. Number of de-conflicted flights during Libya 2011 operations*

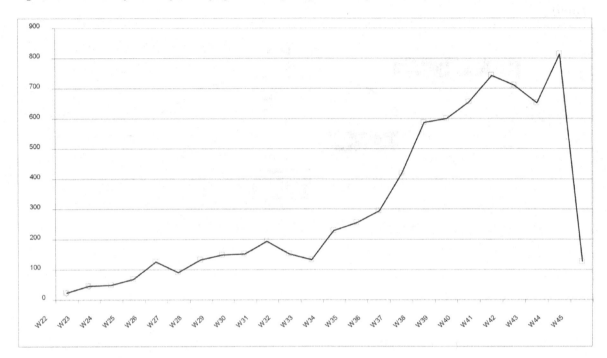

the number of de-conflicted flights. Subsequently, Table 1 illustrates the purpose of the flights that were de-conflicted.

## LESSONS LEARNED AND CONCEPTUAL ANALYSIS

### Shared Theater: Interdependence of Primary Operational Processes

The military activities comprising Operation Unified Protector introduced time-space interdependencies with international civilian actors moving from or towards Libya. These interdependencies could be characterized as 'pooled', in that the activities took part in the same geographical area (Grandori, 1997; Van de Ven, et al., 1976). Based on the OUP case, three command requirements are identified that shape such interdependence.

- **Means.** A first category concerns these task-based properties, and asks questions such as: what is the type of interdependen-

dence (here: pooled), and how uncertain are tasks (more uncertainty demands more information processing)? The literature tends to explore questions that could be summarized as 'how are interdependencies managed?' Such questions tend to focus on task execution (the means), not intentions (the ends to be achieved). Topics could include the interoperability of command and control systems, and procedures for common planning, task execution, and control.

- **Ends.** A second category of command requirements asks questions in the early stages of defining command requirements, such as: *to what end*, or: *how are interdependencies framed in relation to actors' own goals and operational processes*? In other words, to what extent do actors embrace joint goals for the way interdependencies are managed? In a heterogeneous network this is not an easy question. Civilian and military actors have different goals (Rietjens, Bollen, Khalil, & Wahidi, 2009; Yaziji & Doh, 2009). The intersection of their op-

*Table 1. Purpose of the flights that needed to be de-conflicted*

| Purpose | Total Flights | Percentage of Flights |
|---|---|---|
| Humanitarian assistance | 3576 | 48.4% |
| Medical evacuation | 1166 | 15.8% |
| Logistics | 959 | 13% |
| Governmental flights and diplomatic associated missions | 843 | 11.4% |
| Civilian personnel, including helicopter flights between Tunisia and oil platform | 842 | 11.4% |
| Grand total | 7386 | 100% |

erational processes, however, urges them to (re)consider these objectives in relation to their particular interdependencies. The letter shown in Figure 3 illustrates this topic from a NATO point of view. It communicates NATO's awareness of and commitment to civilian movements from and to Libya. Moreover, the management of these interdependencies is framed as a challenge of de-confliction. Our case does not represent an example of interest alignment for the purpose of a joint commercial (Gottschalg & Zollo, 2007), public (Uiterwijk, Soeters, & van Fenema, 2013), or civil-military undertaking (Rietjens, Soeters, et al., 2013). Rather, civilian and military actors experience the necessity to de-conflict operational processes in terms of their time-space demands, leaving mostly the content of activities untouched. NATO's lessons learned reflect on this issue:

*From the strategic analysis of the Comprehensive Approach of OUP even though all OUP documents address the Comprehensive Approach there is not any doctrine of standing operation procedures that define Comprehensive Approach, delineate commands roles and responsibilities or set up an organization to execute Comprehensive Approach. Which resulted in ad-hoc execution at all levels, no coherent measure of effectiveness, and no har-*

*monizing of efforts across all staff section. There also was a lack of knowledge of what non-NATO actors operations brought to the table and how harmonization of their efforts with NATO efforts could achieve strategic or operational objectives. The focus was more on de-confliction with the exception of Humanitarian Assistance planning but the non-NATO actors' objectives in that plan was not harmonized with other strategic objectives. Simply talking to non-NATO Actors is not the Comprehensive Approach SOPs and organizations needs to be developed at all levels on how to execute Comprehensive Approach and a culture that fosters cooperation with non-NATO actors, to understand the differences in organizational structure, culture and processes. So that NATO can harmonize and work towards unity of effort with non-NATO actors in order to achieve strategic goals (NATO, 2011: 4).*

It would be inappropriate, however, to consider this civil-military goal as less complex than more advanced forms of network cooperation that are in a more traditional sense aimed at achieving certain effects (Rietjens, Soeters, et al., 2010). Certainly, command and control of military operations – such as OUP – is important to realize political goals. Yet increasingly, military operations intersect with civilian activities. The overall political and military strategic success of a mission thus depends on civil-military command as well.

- **Network properties.** A third and final category of command requirements starts from network properties and asks the normative question: 'which properties are relevant for a network that can survive and perform well' (Cares, 2005). Or in a civilian context: 'How should firms organize to explore and search ... an altered performance landscape?' (Siggelkow & Levinthal, 2003: 650). Network properties that can vary include node and link types, flow, number of nodes, number of links, degree distribution, maximum degree, betweenness centrality, path horizon, and robustness. Particular values of these properties influence the extent to which a network can function. For instance, what are the consequences of removing nodes or links? This is a key question for (civil-) military networks.

## Network Structure and Collaboration Process and Relationships

Interdependencies between civilian and military networks led to new network structures and new routines (collaboration process and relationships). Following literature on innovation (Oshri, Pan, & Newell, 2005), we consider NATO's ad hoc initiative to de-conflict with civilian actors an exploration phase that was followed by exploitation. Exploration builds on weak, non-redundant networks, dyadic trust, and common knowledge (Kang, Morris, & Snell, 2007). Non-redundancy resembles a network with a structural hole (Figure 2). In this case, AMCC's took on the role of an exclusive liaison between military and international civilian networks. AMCC's exploratory role enabled organizational learning to develop new routines or modify existing ones. Actors accumulate experience, and articulate and codify knowledge (Zollo & Winter, 2002). Applied to our case, civil-military interfacing included both consultation and actual operational planning.

Consultation refers to building mutual understanding of operations and their mutual impact, and operational planning stands for a very pragmatic process of de-conflict activities. While the process seemed to have received ample attention during the exploration phase, the latter had been ignored for some time. This has been expressed in NATO's so-called lessons 22 and 33 (JALLC, 2012). These lessons state that the interaction between NATO and non-NATO actors was of crucial importance and in the end was a great success. This success was largely influenced by the many consultations the actors had during the early stages of the crisis. However, the lack of direct liaison authority with IOs and NGOs seriously complicated the military planning. It was not until the execution of OUP that the necessary mechanisms were in place to conduct liaison with these civilian actors. While the actual implementation of de-conflict was decentralized and carried out by NATO's subordinate commands, NATO concentrated the flight notifications and de-conflict planning at the AMCC. Such a deliberately centralized network node resembles similar approaches to de-conflicting military and civilian air space management (BFU, 2002; JCS, 2010). Centralization promotes consistency and situation awareness of a geographical area (air sectors for instance). In this case, the centralized NATO node connected with a wide range of civilian and military actors, often actors that playing a centralized role themselves in a civilian network such as EUROCONTROL (Figure 4). Civil-military command thus did not represent an example of self-synchronization. Interdependencies were explicitly coordinated by humans in a centralized fashion. The consistency achieved with centralization conflicts with notions of network robustness (Cares, 2004). On the other hand, in case centralized nodes fail, networks are likely to have (the capability of) backup in place for that particular node and its function in and between networks. Upon commencing its role, the AMCC searched for relevant civilian actors and commonly invested in developing some sort of relationships with these. These were, somewhat surprisingly, new network structures, which required new learning. While NATO HQ had invested in the Comprehensive Approach at a strategic conceptual and relational level, execution capabilities appeared lacking.

*Liaisons with United Nations organizations where done in the earliest stages of OUP but only at the NATO HQ and ACO JFC Naples was prohibited from this interaction. Only NATO HQ has a formal organization to execute the Comprehensive Approach but admitted that they had no SOPs. ACO [Allied Command Operations] used ad hoc methods to communicate with UN and other non-NATO actors and also had no SOPs for executing the Comprehensive Approach. Given the time constraints and guidance to focus on military option with the exception of the HA mission. True Comprehensive Approach collaboration [was] not done. Contact with UN and non-NATO was done more as de-confliction not as a unity of effort. Only the HA mission did ACO look at UN how NATO could support UN and non-NATO objectives but there was no formal organization to facilitate planning and communication with the UN and non-organization.*

*Recommendation: ACO create SOPs and establish Comprehensive Crisis Operations Management Center (CCOMC) as soon as possible as well as have all Operation commands establish a CCOMC in order to fully execute the Comprehensive Approach at all levels (NATO, 2011: 8).*

Reflecting on network relationships and command, one could argue that high level relationships and routine-concepts may be developed; yet actual operations require in addition operational relationships and routines.[9] This includes points of contact and SOPs.

*There was a good information sharing and liaison system at Political and Strategic level, while at the Operational AND Tactical level there seems be a big gap of these activities. Liaison and coordination arrangements are not easy to establish due to the IO/NGOs extreme reluctance to approach NATO operations to save their impartiality (NATO, 2011: 12).*

AMCC encountered gaps in this respect. Actors came from widely diverse domains related to air, sea and ground transportation (which is to be expected in a heterogeneous network), as well as their role (commercial, public, IO/NGO). AMCC had to switch to a learning mode, especially concerning international civilian actors. Previous contacts were lacking in particular concerning the commercial sector. From a network communication structure point of view, AMCC tended to liaise with representatives of military and international civilian networks when possible rather than individual network nodes (see also Figure 4). This economized communications. For instance, AMCC worked with UNLO at SHAPE to deal with UN agencies, with EUROCONTROL to coordinate with civilian air authorities, and with military units such as CFAC and CJTF UP.

When working with international civilian actors, AMCC had to develop an understanding of these professional practices and relate them to NATO practices (Bechky, 2003). AMCC developed ad hoc new routines, relating to the segmented military operational planning processes and products:

*There are many products published throughout NATO that gives advice on Comprehensive Assessment but none gives specifics on execution. OUP guidance was very specific on focusing on Military options with the exception of the HA mission. With four separate OPLAN [Operational Plans] OUP was segmented from the start which would make a Comprehensive Assessment of NATO and non-NATO contribution problematic at best. Also without SSA [SACEUR's Strategic Assessment] completed and an end state it is also difficult to assess contributions of NATO and non-NATO actors to achieving strategic goals (NATO, 2011: 9).*

Moreover, NATO had to develop how it was to work with civilian actors. Collaboration procedures were lacking and had to be geared towards the types of civilian actors involved.

*After a while it became clear that there was a need for fine tuning the procedures. Ships after all, move slowly and the de-confliction is therefore less urgent and anyway only intended to allow smooth passage and non-hailing / boarding for humanitarian actors. Badly de-conflicted air moves are potentially much more dangerous in terms of potential kinetic incidents. Ground moves can only be de-conflicted if their size and exact movements times can be trusted so that potentially temporary no firing zones can be created. All of this is depended on very clear and trusted contact between NATO and civilian actors. Making the forms easier to use and ensuring that notifications were passed on in real time made this possible. In terms of maritime movements it was noticed that commercial shipping was unnecessarily clogging the system and after a while those were dealt with in a different way (NAVWARN-system) (Rentenaar, (Forthcoming)).*

Thus, while AMCC centralized interfacing between civilian and military networks, a one-size-fits-all approach did not work in a satisfying manner. Routines were geared towards the specific properties of air and sea-related communities and de-confliction needs. This represents an informal approach to networking (De Toni & Nonino, 2010), jumpstarted by a formal letter of the NATO Secretary General. AMCC liaised with military and civilian stakeholders to develop shared understandings and procedures, rather than applying pre-structured formal procedures. Even finding out whom to contact within international

civilian networks (Figure 4) proved a challenge. Eventually, formal procedures were developed, implying with hindsight a switching between informal (noting the problem), formal (letter), informal (networking), and formal (procedures).

## Overarching Goals for Civil-Military Command and Outcomes

De-confliction may seem a technical task in which one actor should not be at a particular place at a particular time where another actor has work to do. Interdependencies could be managed in a technical sense of handling constraints. This assumes that actors, having their own objectives, are allowed in the shared theater in the first place. In the context of a military operation, however, some civilian movements jeopardized strategic military objectives. The overarching goal of civil-military command thus included in addition to de-confliction a check on potential clashes of interests.

*...it became clear that there exist a number of dual use goods such as oil, trucks, etc. that could be used by the regime as an instrument of power. Even though there was no official trade embargo those goods needed to be stopped from going into Qadhaffi-controlled Libya. The NATO enforced arms embargo together with the de-confliction-system proofed to be an effective instrument to achieve this. All of the above was incorporated in the 1st upgrade of the de-confliction standard operating procedure (Rentenaar, (Forthcoming)).*

In practice, however, responsibility for decision making on these dilemmas was not clearly identified and organizationally allocated. It seems that military involved in the actual de-conflicting process were allowed to make these decisions which in fact carried strategic importance. De-confliction of civil-military networks thus represents a multidimensional responsibility as actors' primary processes and de-confliction choices may have mutual impacts.

The exploration phase, commencing late March 2011, implied that the AMCC developed relationships with civilian actors and procedures. They acquired new experiences and knowledge (Zollo & Winter, 2002). This process occurred under strong time-pressure. Within a week it started already to routinely process for instance around four civilian flights per day until late May 2011. As far as we know, no examples of failed de-confliction have occurred. AMCC developed its boundary bridging role between networks (O'Mahony & Bechky, 2008). It faced a technical role of de-conflicting interdependence civil and military operations. This role was strategically well-embedded yet operationally-tactically disorganized. Moreover, de-confliction sometimes showed a less-technical face when civilian activities clashed with military strategic and operational objectives.

## CONCLUSION

The Libya case illustrated the need for de-conflicting primary operational processes of military and international civilian actors. The objective of this chapter has been to provide insight in network structures and practices for achieving such de-confliction in the context of complex peace operations. Our two main contributions are the conceptual development and contextualization of de-confliction drawing on organization and military theory, and the empirical illustration of de-confliction using a case study approach. Our study is conceptually limited in the sense that it only considers coordination theory from an organization and military perspective. Empirically, a single case study offers interesting yet limited insights in the complexities of de-confliction. We now elaborate on implications for practice and research.

*Beyond an ad hoc approach.* Operational de-confliction during the Libya operation was improvisational and ad hoc. As soon NATO and the IOs and NGOs were confronted with de-confliction issues, personnel worked out solutions overcoming differences for the common good. As such, de-confliction evolved over time in response to specific needs. There is merit in this ad hoc approach. Some argue that every crisis has unique characteristics in which strategies and structures need to reflect the specific and dynamically evolving circumstances. However, at an execution level, a tremendous responsibility devolved on the personnel involved as a result of the gap between the assigned mission and the requirements to fulfill this mission. They had to tailor their operations to the unexpected challenges they faced, rather than execute the sort of mission they were tasked, organized, and trained to perform. Overall, the coordination activities depended strongly on the personalities involved and the qualities they brought to the table, rather than on planning and standard operating procedures. Such an approach yields inefficient use of limited aid resources, delayed humanitarian relief efforts, enhanced inconsistency between rotations, and leads to conflicting objectives in the (post-) conflict environment (Peabody, 2005). This lack of coherence is one of the factors often cited as contributing to the poor success rate and lack of sustainability of international peace and stability operations (C. de Coning & Friis, 2011).

*Developing routines.* From NATO's side the AMCC obtained a central role in the civil-military network and encountered many obstacles in this respect. Actors came from widely diverse domains related to air, sea and ground transportation, as well as their roles (commercial, public, IO/NGO). This implies different professional practices epitomized by the way information is coded and shared, by diverse organizational cultures, and by idiosyncratic command and control routines. Practices associated with civilian actors had to be understood and related to NATO practices, a so-called transformational process (Carlile, 2004) for which little time was allocated. With support of SHAPE's civil advisor and a liaison of the United Nations, the AMCC developed ad hoc new routines that facilitated the segmented military operational planning processes and products. During the entire operation a large number of flights were de-conflicted (see Figure 5). There was no backup for the AMCC, in case this centralized node failed. Finally, AMCC's role revealed a gap between strategic and operational level concepts to network with civilian partners (Comprehensive Approach), and the actual ability to execute such tasks on a short notice. Bridging this doctrine-ability gap will require investments in training with representatives of key stakeholders to use concepts and refine them (Rietjens, van Fenema, & Essens, 2013).

*Deciding on goals.* Last, but not least, the overarching goals for Civil-Military Command should be reflected upon. Is de-confliction (NNEC level 2) a sufficiently ambitious goal for network coordination? Or should network partners reach out for level 3 (coordinated operations)? The latter would fit strategic and operational ambitions for comprehensively approaching the mission area, depending on the needs in the area and the type of mission required. However, achieving level 3 will also require substantial investments in mutual cooperation and the willingness to make compromises. Moreover, agreements on network goals alone may prove a daunting task given diverse interests of civilian and military organizations.

*Future research.* Our analysis suggests the importance of ex ante processes for enabling de-confliction. Specifically, we propose stakeholder-based research aimed at identifying organizations that are likely to participate in Civil-Military Networks. This includes understanding various stakeholders' interests, goals, expectations and resources. Network-level goals remain at present an ill-understood topic. Researchers can explore methods for analyzing and predicting interdependencies. Drawing on coordination theory, protocols, roles, and practices can be studied that underpin Civil-Military decision making and cooperation. In particular, those coordination mechanisms that offer long-term benefits should be studied, such as generic templates for organizing Civil-Military interfaces. Performance of Civil-Military command has received limited attention in this chapter. Future work may develop sophisticated tools for measuring and analyzing network achievements and relate these back to stakeholder expectations. This includes costs in a broad sense of coordinating between organizations. Finally, de-confliction may not be a desirable level of coordination given for instance dependencies and expectations concerning Civil-Military outputs. Researchers could explore how organizations participating in a network decide on their desired level and when / how they possibly switch over time.

## ACKNOWLEDGMENT

The authors thank Lieutenant Colonel Massimo Mattiacci (JFC Naples, J4 Division, M&T Operations Section Head) for his input.

## REFERENCES

Alberts, D. S., & Hayes, R. E. (2005). *Power to the Edge: Command and Control in the Information Age*. Washington, DC: CCRP Publication Series.

Alberts, D. S., & Nissen, M. E. (2009). Toward Harmonizing Command and Control with Organization and Management Theory. *C2 Journal, 3*(2), 1-59.

Bechky, B. A. (2003). Sharing Meaning Across Occupational Communities: The Transformation of Understanding on a Production Floor. *Organization Science, 14*(3), 312–330. doi:10.1287/orsc.14.3.312.15162

BFU. (2002). *Status Report (Midair collision 1st July 2002 near Überlingen/ Lake Constance).* Braunschweig (Germany), Bundesstelle für Flugunfalluntersuchung (BFU). Document # AX001-1/-2/02 (English version). Retrieved from http://www.bfu-web.de.

Bollen, M. T. I. B., & Soeters, J. M. M. L. (2010). Partnering with 'Strangers. In J. M. M. L. Soeters, P. C. van Fenema, & R. Beeres (Eds.), *Managing Military Organizations: Theory and Practice* (pp. 174–186). London: Routledge.

Burt, R. S. (1992). *Structural Holes: The Social Structure of Competition.* Cambridge, MA: Harvard University Press.

Cares, J. R. (2004). *An Information Age Combat Model.* Paper presented at the 9th International Command and Control Research and Technology Symposium (ICCRTS). Copenhagen, Denmark.

Cares, J. R. (2005). *Distributed Networked Operations: The Foundations of Network Centric Warfare.* Newport, RI: Alidade Press.

Carlile, P. R. (2004). Transferring, Translating, and Transforming: An Integrative Framework for Managing Knowledge Across Boundaries. *Organization Science, 15*(5), 555–568. doi:10.1287/orsc.1040.0094

CCRP. (2010). *NATO NEC C2 Maturity Model.* Washington, DC: CCRP. Retrieved from http://www.dodccrp.org/files/N2C2M2_web_optimized.pdf

Coticchia, F. (2011). The 'Enemy' at the Gates? Assessing the European Military Contribution to the Libyan War. *Perspectives on Federalism, 3*(3), 48–70.

Crawshaw, E. (2007). A Comprehensive Approach to Modern Conflict: Afghanistan and Beyond. *CONNECTIONS: The Quarterly Journal, 6*(2), 1–66.

Crowston, K. (1997). A Coordination Theory Approach to Organizational Process Design. *Organization Science, 8*(2), 157–175. doi:10.1287/orsc.8.2.157

Curtis, V. (2005). The Theory of Fourth Generation Warfare. *Canadian Army Journal, 8*(4), 17–32.

de Coning, C., & Friis, K. (2011). Coherence and Coordination: The Limits of the Comprehensive Approach. *Journal of International Peacekeeping, 15*(1-2), 243–272. doi:10.1163/187541110X540553

de Coning, C. H. (2008). Civil-Military Coordination Practices and Approaches within United Nations Peace Operations. In L. Olson, & H. Gregorian (Eds.), *Calgary Papers in Journal of Military and Strategic Studies, Civil-Military Coordination: Challenges and Opportunities in Afghanistan and Beyond* (Vol. 3, pp. 87–112). Calgary, Canada: Centre for Military and Strategic Studies.

de Coning, C. H. (2010). *Clarity, Coherence and Context: Three Priorities for Sustainable Peacebuilding. The Future of the Peacebuilding Architecture Project.* Norwegian Institute of International Affairs.

De Toni, A. F., & Nonino, F. (2010). The Key Roles in the Informal Organization: A Network Analysis Perspective. *The Learning Organization, 17*(1), 86–103. doi:10.1108/09696471011008260

Docauer, A. F. (2011). Efficient Airspace Use During Urban Air Operations. *Air Land Sea Bulletin,* (2), 4-7.

Faraj, S., & Sproull, L. (2000). Coordinating Expertise in Software Development Teams. *Management Science, 46*(12), 1154–1568. doi:10.1287/mnsc.46.12.1554.12072

Faraj, S., & Xiao, Y. (2006). Coordination in Fast-Response Organizations. *Management Science, 52*(8), 1155–1169. doi:10.1287/mnsc.1060.0526

Gottschalg, O., & Zollo, M. (2007). Interest Alignment and Competitive Advantage. *Academy of Management Review, 32*(2), 418–437. doi:10.5465/AMR.2007.24351356

Grandori, A. (1997). An Organizational Assessment of Interfirm Coordination Modes. *Organization Studies, 18*(6), 897–925. doi:10.1177/017084069701800601

Grant, T. J., van Fenema, P. C., & van Veen, M. (2007). *On Regarding 21st Century C2 Systems and their Users as Fallible ePartners.* Paper presented at the 12th International Command and Control Research and Technology Symposium (ICCRTS). Newport, RI.

JALLC. (2012). *Operation Unified Protector: Lessons for the Alliance.* Lisbon: JALLC.

JCS. (2010). *Command and Control for Joint Air Operations: Joint Chiefs of Staff, Joint Publication 3-30, 12 January 2010.* JCS.

JCS. (2012). *Joint Operational Access Concept (JOAC).* Retrieved from http://www.defense.gov/pubs/pdfs/JOAC_Jan%202012_Signed.pdf

Johannesson, P. (1995). Representation and Communication - A Speech Act Based Approach to Information System Design. *Information Systems, 20*(4), 291–303. doi:10.1016/0306-4379(95)00015-V

Kang, S.-C., Morris, S. S., & Snell, S. A. (2007). Relational Archetypes, Organizational Learning, and Value Creation: Extending the Human Resource Architecture. *Academy of Management Review, 32*(1), 236–256. doi:10.5465/AMR.2007.23464060

Kitzen, M., Rietjens, S. J. H., & Osinga, F. P. B. (2012). Soft Power, the Hard Way: Adaptation by the Netherlands' Task Force Uruzgan. In T. Farrell, F. P. B. Osinga, & J. A. Russell (Eds.), *Fighting the Afghanistan War.* Stanford, CA: Stanford University Press.

Kovács, G., & Spens, K. M. (2007). Humanitarian Logistics in Disaster Relief Operations. *International Journal of Physical Distribution and Logistics Management, 37*(2), 99–114. doi:10.1108/09600030710734820

Laity, M. (2012). The Latest Test for NATO. *RUSI Journal, 157*(1), 52–58. doi:10.1080/03071847.2012.664372

Lind, W. S. (2004, September-October). Understanding Fourth Generation War. *Military Review,* 12–16.

Mintzberg, H. (1995). The Structuring of Organizations. In H. Mintzberg, J. B. Quinn, & S. Ghoshal (Eds.), *The Strategy Process.* London: Prentice-Hall.

Monsuur, H. (2011). Cyber Operaties: een Operations Research perspectief. *Intercom,* (4): 37–38.

Monsuur, H., Grant, T. J., & Janssen, R. (2011). Network Topology of Military C2 Systems: Where Axioms and Actions Meet. In J. P. Bauer (Ed.), *Computer Science Research & Technology* (Vol. 3). Hauppauge, NY: Nova Science Publishers.

NATO. (2011). Strategic Analysis of the Comprehensive Approach in NATO Operation Unified Protector. *NATO Unclassified, draft 1 July 2011.*

Neaga, E. I., & Henshaw, M. (2011). A Stakeholder-Based Analysis of the Benefits of Networked Enabled Capability. *Defense & Security Analysis, 27*(2), 119–134. doi:10.1080/14751798.2011.578716

O'Hair, H. D., Kelley, K. M., & Williams, K. L. (2011). Managing Community Risks Through a Community-Communication Infrastructure Approach. In H. E. Canary, & R. D. McPhee (Eds.), *Communication and Organizational Knowledge: Contemporary Issues for Theory and Practice.* New York: Routledge.

O'Mahony, S., & Bechky, B. A. (2008). Boundary Organizations: Enabling Collaboration among Unexpected Allies. *Administrative Science Quarterly, 53*(3), 422–459. doi:10.2189/asqu.53.3.422

Oshri, I., Pan, S. L., & Newell, S. (2005). Trade-offs between Knowledge Exploitation and Exploration Activities. *Knowledge Management Research & Practice, 3*, 10–23. doi:10.1057/palgrave.kmrp.8500042

Osinga, F. P. B. (2007). On Boyd, Bin Laden, and Fourth Generation Warfare as String Theory. In J. Olson (Ed.), On New Wars. Oslo, Norway: Oslo Files on Defence and Security no 4/2007.

Peabody, D. (2005). The Challenges of Doing Good Work: The Development of Canadian Forces CIMIC Capability and NGOs. In *Proceedings of CDAI Conference*. CDAI.

Pestana, G., Rebelo, I., Duarte, N., & Couronné, S. (2012). Adressing Stakeholders Coordination for Airport Efficiency and Decision-Support Requirements. *Journal of Aerospace Operations, 1*(3), 267–280.

Pitsis, T. S., Kornberger, M., & Clegg, S. R. (2004). The Art of Managing Relationships in Interorganizational Collaboration. *M@n@gement, 7*(3), 47-67.

Powell, W. W. (1990). Neither Market nor Hierarchy: Network Forms of Organization. In L. L. Cummings, & B. M. Staw (Eds.), *Research in Organizational Behavior* (Vol. 12, pp. 295–336). Greenwich, CT: JAI Press.

Rentenaar, M. (Forthcoming). Blue on Blue: Civil-Military Interaction during the Libya Operations. In G. Lucius, & S. J. H. Rietjens (Eds.), *The Soldier's Handbook on Civil-Military Interaction in Peace Operations*. Berlin: Springer.

Rietjens, S. J. H., & Bollen, M. (2008). *Managing Civil-Military Cooperation: A 24/7 Joint Effort for Stability*. London: Ashgate. doi:10.1163/ej.9789004163270.i-253

Rietjens, S. J. H., Bollen, M. T. I. B., Khalil, M., & Wahidi, S. F. (2009). Enhancing the Footprint: Stakeholders in Afghan Reconstruction. *Parameters, 39*(1), 22–39.

Rietjens, S. J. H., Kampen, T., & Grant, T. J. (2010). Logistics Planning and Control: Lessons Learned in Afghanistan. In J. M. M. L. Soeters, P. C. van Fenema, & R. Beeres (Eds.), *Managing Military Organizations: Theory and Practice*. London: Routledge.

Rietjens, S. J. H., Soeters, J. M. M. L., & Klumper, W. (2010). Measuring Performance in Today's Missions: The Effects-based Approach to Operations. In J. M. M. L. Soeters, P. C. van Fenema, & R. Beeres (Eds.), *Managing Military Organizations: Theory and Practice*. London: Routledge.

Rietjens, S. J. H., Soeters, J. M. M. L., & van Fenema, P. C. (2013). Learning from Afghanistan: Towards a Compass for Civil–Military Coordination. *Small Wars & Insurgencies*. doi:10.1080/09592318.2013.778027

Rietjens, S. J. H., van Fenema, P. C., & Essens, P. (2013). 'Train as you Fight' Revisited: Preparing for a Comprehensive Approach. *PRISM, 4*(2).

Rietjens, S. J. H., Voordijk, H., & De Boer, S. J. (2007). Coordinating Humanitarian Operations in Peace Support Missions. *Disaster Prevention and Management, 16*(1), 56–69. doi:10.1108/09653560710729811

Rubbini, R., & Vindua, A. (2012). By Sea, Air, and Land. Plausible Responsibility to React Scenarios and Their Military Requirements. *Canadian Centre for the Responsibility to Protect*. Retrieved from http://ccr2p.org/wp-content/uploads/2013/01/SeaAirLand.pdf

RUSI. (2011). Accidental Heroes: Britain, France and the Libya Operation. *Interim RUSI Campaign Report, September 2011*.

Seifert, M., DiLego, T., Hitchings, J., Sterling, J., Hawks, K., & Griffith, D. (2005). JASMAD: Meeting Current and Future Combat Airspace Requirements. *Report AFRL-IF-RS-TP-2006-3*. Retrieved from http://www.dtic.mil/cgi-bin/GetTRDoc?AD=ADA451880

Seiple, C. (1996). *The US Military/NGO Relationship in Humanitarian Interventions*. Carlisle Barracks, PA: Peacekeeping Institute Centre for Strategic Leadership, U.S. Army War College.

Siggelkow, N., & Levinthal, D. A. (2003). Temporarily Divide to Conquer: Centralized, Decentralized, and Reintegrated Organizational Approaches to Exploration and Adaptation. *Organization Science, 14*(6), 650–669. doi:10.1287/orsc.14.6.650.24840

Sirmon, D. G., Hitt, M. A., & Ireland, R. D. (2007). Managing Firm Resources in Dynamic Environments to Create Value: Looking Inside the Black Box. *Academy of Management Review, 32*(1). doi:10.5465/AMR.2007.23466005

Snook, S. A. (2000). *Friendly Fire: The Accidental Shootdown of U.S. Black Hawks over Northern Iraq*. Princeton, NJ: Princeton University Press.

Soeters, J. M. M. L. (2000). Culture in Uniformed Organizations. In N. M. Ashkanasy, C. P. M. Wilderom, & M. F. Peterson (Eds.), *Handbook of Organizational Culture and Climate* (pp. 465–480). Thousand Oaks, CA: Sage.

Soeters, J. M. M. L., & Manigart, P. (2008). *Military Cooperation in Multinational Peace Operations: Managing Cultural Diversity and Crisis Response*. London: Routledge.

Starkey, K., Barnatt, C., & Tempest, S. (2000). Beyond Networks and Hierarchies: Latent Organizations in the U.K. Television Industry. *Organization Science, 11*(3), 299–305. doi:10.1287/orsc.11.3.299.12500

Stoddard, A. (2006). *Humanitarian Alert: NGO Information and its Impact on US Foreign Policy*. Sterling, VA: Kumarian Press.

Stringer, K. D. (2010, March-April). Interagency Command and Control at the Operational Level: A Challenge in Stability Operations. *Military Review*, 54–62.

Tatham, P., & Rietjens, S. J. H. (Manuscript submitted for publication). Integrated Disaster Relief Logistics: A Stepping Stone Towards Viable Civil-Military Networks? *Disasters*. PMID:21702893

Uiterwijk, D. J. W. B., Soeters, J. M. M. L., & van Fenema, P. C. (2013). Aligning National 'Logics' in a European Military Helicopter Program. *Defense & Security Analysis, 29*(1), 54–67. doi:10.1080/14751798.2013.760248

Van de Ven, A. H., Delbecq, A. L., & Koenig, R. Jr. (1976). Determinants of Coordination Modes Within Organizations. *American Sociological Review, 41*, 322–338. doi:10.2307/2094477

van der Laan, E., de Brito, M. P., van Fenema, P. C., & Vermaesen, S. (2009). Managing Information Cycles for Intra-organizational Co-ordination of Humanitarian Logistics. *International Journal of Services Technology and Management, 12*(4), 362–390. doi:10.1504/IJSTM.2009.025814

van Fenema, P. C. (2012). National Crisis Response Networks (NCRN) and Military Organizations: Revisiting the Katrina Case. In G. Kümmel, & J. M. M. L. Soeters (Eds.), *New Wars, New Militaries, New Soldiers: Conflicts, the Armed Forces and the Soldierly Subject* (Vol. 19, pp. 111–130). London: Emerald. doi:10.1108/S1572-8323(2012)0000019011

Yaziji, M., & Doh, J. (2009). *NGOs and Corporations: Conflict and Collaboration.* Cambridge, UK: Cambridge University Press. doi:10.1017/CBO9780511626708

Zollo, M., & Winter, S. G. (2002). Deliberate Learning and the Evolution of Dynamic Capabilities. *Organization Science*, *13*(3), 339–351. doi:10.1287/orsc.13.3.339.2780

## KEY TERMS AND DEFINITIONS

**Command and Control:** The "responsibility for effectively using available resources, planning the employment of, organizing, directing, coordinating, and controlling military forces for the accomplishment of assigned missions" (Alberts & Hayes, 2005: 14).

**Comprehensive Approach:** A process aimed at facilitating system-wide coherence across the security, governance, development and political dimensions of international peace and stability operations.

**De-Confliction:** Coordinating physical flows of people and goods within and or around theatre such that mutual interference is minimized.

## ENDNOTES

[1] NATO sea corridor mooted to help Libyan rebels (http://www.reuters.com/article/2011/04/15/us-nato-libya-shipping-idUSTRE73E55Y20110415).

[2] Robert Johansen proposes a "Humanitarian Corridor" in Libya (http://al.nd.edu/news/18814-nd-expert-humanitarian-corridor-could-save-lives-in-libya/).

[3] http://www.flightglobal.com/news/articles/libya-nato-assumes-sole-command-of-coalition-air-354992/

[4] http://www.nato.int/nato_static/assets/pdf/pdf_2011_11/20111108_111107-factsheet_up_factsfigures_en.pdf (accessed July 23, 2013).

[5] The Secretary General's Annual Report 2011 (NATO).

[6] Letter PO(2001)0094, dated 27 March 2011.

[7] E.g. CJTF UP at Naples, AC Izmir, MC Naples, CAOC PR.

[8] As of 1st June 2011 the Movement and Transport Coordination Cell (MTCC) of CJTF UP took over from the AMCC.

[9] At the same time, over the period preceding the operation, the relevance and urgency may not have been felt. This tends to lead to potential relationships and routines that cannot deliver when needed, as has been shown for homeland response in van Fenema, 2012, p. 111-130.

## APPENDIX:

## Questions

1.  Describe the key differences between military and humanitarian organizations in terms of principles, organizational culture and stakeholders.
2.  Why and under what conditions are their operational processes interdependent?
3.  Interdependence between military and humanitarian organizations leads to coordination demands. Why? What goals apply to the way these interdependencies are coordinated?
4.  To what extent was NATO ready to embark in a joint planning process with civilian organizations (humanitarian, governmental, international, business) in Libya?
5.  Describe the properties of de-confliction and harmonization. How do these concepts fit in the NNEC literature (NATO Network Enabled Capability)?
6.  What roles did NATO's Allied Movement Coordination Centre fulfill?
7.  Was the civilian-military network coordinated in a centralized or decentralized fashion? Explain, giving pros, cons, and conditions for each.
8.  To what extent are these coordination modes substitutes? "Personalities involved and the qualities they brought to the table" versus "planning and standard operating procedures". How could these modes work together?

*Table 2. Abbreviations*

| | |
|---|---|
| ADL | Allied Disposition List |
| AMCC | Allied Movement Coordination Centre |
| ATO | Air Tasking Order |
| CA | Comprehensive Approach |
| CFAC | Combined Force Air Command |
| CFAC | Combined Force Air Command |
| CIMIC | Civil-Military Interaction |
| CIVAD | Civil Advisor |
| CJTF UP | Combined Joint Task Force UNIFIED PROTECTOR |
| COP | Common Operational Picture |
| COPD | Comprehensive Operational Planning Directive |
| HA | Humanitarian Assistance |
| ICRC | International Committee of the Red Cross |
| IFF | Identification Friend or Foe |
| IOM | International Organization for Migration |
| IRM | International Relief Missions |
| JALLC | Joint Analysis and Lessons Learned Center |
| MC Naples (NCAGS) | Maritime Command Naples Naval Co-operation and Guidance for Shipping (http://www.shipping.nato.int/Pages/NCAGS.aspx) |
| MNDDP | Multinational Detailed Deployment Plan |
| MSF | Médecins Sans Frontières |
| MTCC | Movement and Transport Coordination Cell |
| NCAGS | Naval coordination and guidance for shipping cell |
| NED | NAC Execution Directive |
| NID | NAC Initiating Directive |
| NNEC | NATO Network Enabled Capability |
| OPLAN | Operation Plan |
| OPP | Operational Planning Process |
| PMR | Permanent Military Representative |
| RAP | Recognized Air Picture |
| ROZ | Restricted Operations Zone |
| SA | Situation awareness |
| SACEUR | Supreme Allied Commander Europe |
| SecGen | Secretary General (NATO) |
| SHAPE | Supreme Headquarters Allied Powers Europe |
| SOC | Strategic Operations Centre |
| UNLO | UN Liaison Officer |
| UNSCR | United Nations Security Council Resolutions |
| WFP | World Food Program |

# Chapter 2
# Shaping Comprehensive Emergency Response Networks

**W. Treurniet**
*Netherlands Organisation for Applied Scientific Research TNO, The Netherlands*

## ABSTRACT

*Given its nature, a crisis has a significant community impact. This applies in particular to emergencies: crises that arise quickly. Because of the complex and multifaceted nature of large-scale incidents, the response requires coordinated effort by multiple organizations. This networked collaboration is not solely restricted to professional organizations. In responding to an incident, the affected community can itself be an important source of information and capabilities. This chapter discusses how one can shape a trustworthy and decisive response organization in which relevant and useful capacities available in the community are incorporated. This discussion has two focal points. The first focal point is the role of the affected community in the case of an emergency. On the one hand, an emergency affects the fabric of the community, such as the critical infrastructure. On the other, a community has inherent internal resources that give it resilience and capacity to respond in a crisis. This needs to be reflected in the choice of emergency response planning model. The second focal point is the structure of the emergency response network. An emergency response network is a mixed-sector network. This means that coordination is needed among organizations and collectives with differing strategic orientations.*

## INTRODUCTION

Because of the complex and multifaceted nature of large-scale safety and security incidents such as floods and severe power outages, the response requires coordinated effort by multiple organizations. Some organizations are involved in the response because of their societal responsibilities. In the Dutch system for example, in principle, an emergency situation does not affect the regular allocation of responsibilities. Responsibilities in normal circumstances are still valid in an emergency situation (Brainich, 2012). Other organizations are involved because they can provide relevant information, knowledge or capabilities. In a densely populated and complex community, even a relatively small incident often requires the involvement of and collaboration among twenty or more organizations (Treurniet, van Buul-Besseling, & Wolbers, 2012). This collaboration is

DOI: 10.4018/978-1-4666-6058-8.ch002

not solely restricted to professional organizations. Scholars (Dupont, 2004; Dynes, 1994; Helsloot & Ruitenberg, 2004; Lindell, Perry, Prater, & Nicholson, 2006; Nakagawa & Shaw, 2004; Quarantelli & Dynes, 1985), policy-makers and practitioners stress that, in responding to an incident, the affected community can itself be an important source of information and capabilities. On the one hand, this acknowledges the limitedness of the potential of professional emergency response (ER). On the other, this reflects and recognizes the resilience of communities. The key question in this chapter is: what does this mean from the perspective of the response organization? How can one shape a trustworthy and decisive response organization, in which relevant and useful capacities available in the community are incorporated?

## Setting the Scene

In this chapter, a *crisis* is defined as an event in which safety or security are at stake because one or more vital community interests are affected while the regular structures and resources are not sufficient to maintain stability. The wording of this definition is derived from the one used by the Dutch government (Ministerie van Veiligheid en Justitie, 2013). Substantively, this definition is in line with those used by Boin, 't Hart, Stern, and Sundelius (2005, p. 2) and Stern (2003) although their formulations are more geared to national and international politics. Given its nature, a crisis has a significant community impact. The extent and the nature of this impact can be very diverse and compound. The impact is concrete if ecological or physical safety are at stake, in cases of environmental pollution or large-scale power outages. The impact is more abstract or psychological if territorial or economical security or social/political stability are at stake – as in a financial crisis, for example. The functioning of the community depends heavily on critical infrastructure facilities, such as transportation modes, telecommunication facilities, energy networks and provision of drinking water facilities (Luiijf & Klaver, 2006). This is worsened by the fact that these facilities are interdependent (Luiijf, Nieuwenhuijs, Klaver, Eeten, & Cruz, 2008). Furthermore, incidents can also have a big impact because the role of information within the community has changed. In particular, because of the widespread use of social media, community perceptions of an incident and public opinion can be influenced easily and strongly. An incident which in itself may be limited in nature can easily evoke strong feelings and lead to social unrest.

A framework to differentiate among several types of crises can be derived from Boin et al. (2005, pp. 16, 94, 95). The framework differentiates between crises based on rise rate and recovery rate. The rise rate denotes the speed at which a crisis unfolds, and the recovery rate denotes the speed at which a crisis is resolved. Table 1 outlines the framework.

This chapter focuses primarily on crises with a fast rise rate. Particularly in this type of crisis, it is difficult to gain rapid insights into the impact, especially over the longer term. In the chaos and

*Table 1. Crisis classification framework; after Boin et al. (2005)*

| Recovery rate vs. Rise rate | Fast | Slow |
|---|---|---|
| **Fast** | Fast-burning Crisis (e.g. large fire) | Long-shadow Crisis (e.g. earthquake, tsunami) |
| **Slow** | Cathartic Crisis (e.g. tracing and dismantling a threatening terrorist organization, gradually escalating international tension followed by a sudden resolution) | Slow-burning Crisis (e.g. climate change, population ageing) |

uncertainty, first responders often seem to have a tendency to under-estimate the size of an incident. As a consequence, the longer-term safety and security issues receive too little attention or too late. The longer-term dynamics of the incident take the ER organization by surprise.

Consider, for example, the chemical fire incident in Moerdijk, the Netherlands on 5 and 6 January 2011 (Inspectie Openbare Orde en Veiligheid, 2011). A complex mix of chemical substances caught fire in an industrial zone next to a port area. The dense plumes of smoke and pollution from water used to put out the fire had many environmental and societal consequences. To citizens it became unclear if they could safely continue their daily routine. Instead of responding empathically to the perceptions of risk emerging within local community, the crisis response organization tried to control those perceptions by emphasizing their own more technical view of the incident (Messemaker, Wolbers, Treurniet, & Boersma, 2013). The crisis response organization repeatedly stressed the fact that no hazardous substances were measured to the extent that they could endanger public health. In view of the thick, black smoke plume, this communication simply was at odds with the gut feelings of the public. Another recent example is an incident that occurred near the Ouwerkerk Creek (province of Zeeland, the Netherlands). In late July 2012 a dog died, showing symptoms of an infection from blue-green algae. The dog had been swimming in a creek near Ouwerkerk. Further investigation revealed the presence of the toxic algae in the dog's stomach as well as in the eastern part of the creek. A comprehensive crisis organization was set up. The committee evaluating this incident stated that, in the initial phase, the organizations involved in responding to this incident were primarily focused on ."... finding technical solutions to a technical problem, without having an eye for possible social impact of the incident" (Bos & Verberne, 2012, p. 7). The first week after the detection of the algae, the responding organizations had primarily been focusing on the development of an approach for controlling the toxic algae.

On the other hand, there are examples where incidents have been overstated, causing unnecessary social unrest and costs. A one recent Dutch example was an incidence of asbestos in the district of Kanaleneiland, Utrecht. On Sunday 22 July 2012 a red alert was raised because of the discovery of asbestos in an apartment building in Kanaleneiland. Residents of several apartment buildings were evacuated, parts of the district were closed, and a comprehensive crisis organization was set up. The incident attracted media attention and caused much anxiety among residents. The first conclusion of the evaluation committee reads: "The measures taken following the discovery of asbestos in Kanaleneiland were disproportionate in hindsight" (Jansen, Fernandes Mendes, Rook, Stordiau-van Egmond, & Zanten, 2012).

## Scope and Organization of the Chapter

This chapter proposes a preliminary answer to the question of how best to shape a trustworthy and decisive response organization, building upon the potential available within the community. It is argued that there is a mutual relation between the perceived scope and impact of an incident and the shaping of the ER network. The preliminary answer is based on combining scientific insights from several debates, including debates on crisis management, critical infrastructure protection and networked organizations. Illustrations of the theoretical insights with empirical findings from real emergencies in the Netherlands will be a recurring thread running throughout the chapter.

The remainder of this chapter consists of three main parts. The section *Emergency and community* discusses the role of the affected community in emergency situations. How does an emergency affect a community and what role can be expected of the affected community in responding to and recovering from an emergency? The section on

*Emergency Response Networks* discusses the structure of ER networks and how they make use of the potential available in the community. Furthermore, the section touches briefly upon the dynamics of proportionate shaping of ad hoc ER networks. The chapter concludes with a discussion of the implications for research and practice, and of the contribution to the body of knowledge, and provides recommendations both for practical application to the organization of ER in the Netherlands and for further related research.

## EMERGENCY AND COMMUNITY

This section discusses the role of the affected community when an emergency occurs. An emergency affects the supporting and enabling fabric of the community, such as the critical infrastructure. On the other side, a community has inherent internal resources which give it resilience and capacity to respond in a crisis. This is exemplified by a number of Dutch cases taken from the last two decades. Finally, it is shown that in choosing a planning model, one needs to take account of what resources and capacity a community itself may have to respond to an emergency situation.

### How an Emergency Impacts a Community

In the introductory section it is argued that a crisis, by definition, has a significant community impact. What kind of impact might this be? In this section this question is pursued by first discussing what we mean by community and subsequently discussing potential vulnerabilities.

In this chapter, the following definition of 'community'[1] is used: "The combination of social units and systems which perform the major social functions having locality reference[2]." This definition is adopted from Quarantelli and Dynes (1985, p. 158) and is also in line with Warren (1972). In other words, community is "the social system or

the organization of special activities which afford people daily local access to those broad areas of activity which are necessary in day-to-day living" (Quarantelli & Dynes, 1985, p. 158). Lindell et al. (2006) stress the interactions among the constituent parts of a community as they define communities as ecological networks in which the basic types of social units are *households*, *businesses*, and *government agencies*.

Five categories of major social functions can be distinguished: production-distribution-consumption, socialization, social control, social participation, and mutual support (Quarantelli & Dynes, 1985). To support these functions or agencies within a specific community, a number of critical sectors – or "systems," according to the definition of Quarantelli and Dynes (1985) – can be distinguished, including energy, transportation and drinking water. A more comprehensive instance of an overview of critical sectors will be given shortly.

Not much scientific material is available that focuses on the manifestations of how a crisis impacts a community. If we want to zoom in on the phenomenon of a fast-rising crisis or emergency, and how this kind of event impacts a community, the national and regional risk assessment methods adopted in the Netherlands provide valuable insights. The methods include a classification of crisis types that is based primarily on historical experience. At the regional level, for example, 25 different generic crisis types have been identified and classified in seven societal themes:

- Natural environment, such as floods, wild fires, extreme weather, and animal diseases.
- Built-up environment, such as fires and structural collapses.
- Technological environment, including incidents involving toxic substances and nuclear materials, for example.
- Critical infrastructures and facilities, such as energy supply, drinking water supply, telecommunications and food supply.

- Traffic and transportation, including aviation incidents and road and rail incidents.
- Health, including pandemics.
- Socio-cultural environment, including panic in crowds and public order disturbances.

As can already be concluded from the examples above, although the origins of crisis may fall under one specific societal theme, its impact can be multifaceted. A crisis has a societal impact in the sense that it affects or threatens one or more vital societal interests. In the Netherlands, six top-level vital interests have been distinguished: territorial security, physical safety, economical security, ecological safety, social and political stability, and cultural inheritance. As such, these six vital interests correspond to six societal domains that a crisis can have an impact on. This impact can be *direct* in the sense that one or more vital interests are threatened or harmed due to exposure to the original crisis event. The impact can also be *indirect* in the sense that the original crisis event affects another societal theme, causing this societal theme to affect one or more vital interests. The societal theme *critical infrastructures and facilities* plays a considerable role in second-order crisis impacts. The functioning of a community strongly depends on critical infrastructure facilities, such as transportation modes, telecommunication facilities, energy networks and drinking water facilities (Luiijf & Klaver, 2006). As an example, Table 2 lists the critical sectors, products and services distinguished in the Netherlands.

Consider the direct impact the flooding of a river can have on vital societal interests, for example Territorial security can be directly threatened as the flooded area cannot be used for a time for its intended purpose. Physical safety can be threatened as the flooding may cause fatalities, serious injuries and disruption to the provision of basic needs such as shelter. Economic security can be threatened because of the costs of relief, recovery and reconstruction, because of income loss, but also because economic activity is disrupted.

Ecological safety can be threatened because of structural disruption to scenic areas. Social and political stability can be threatened because of the disruption to daily living and because of the socio-psychological impact. Finally, cultural inheritance can be severely damaged or destroyed by a river flooding. In sum, a river flooding can have a direct impact on any of the vital interests of society.

Flooding of this kind can also have a number of second-order effects. Depending on the duration, the extent and the nature of the exposure to the water, the flooding may damage or disrupt objects that are vital to critical products or services. An example of such an object is an electricity generating station which obviously will fail in the event of a serious flooding. As a consequence, the critical product or service – e.g. the electricity supply – may fail or may be reduced in capacity, resulting in second-order societal effects[3].

## Community Resilience

In the previous subsection it is argued that a community is vulnerable and can be affected in a number of ways. One may say that, the more developed a community is, the more ways there are in which it can be affected by a crisis. The functioning of developed communities is highly dependent on a number of organizational structures and infrastructural facilities, i.e. the more visible and tangible part of the community structure (Little & Krannich, 1988, p. 30). Fortunately, this is not the whole story. Communities are inherently *resilient* as well in the sense that they exhibit the capability to cope with unanticipated dangers after they have become manifest, learning to 'bounce back' (Rosenthal, Boin, & Comfort, 2001, p. 16). The resilience of a community will be discussed in this section, with examples.

Internal to the community structure, *social capital* plays a dominant role. Putnam (1995) argues that social capital refers to networks, norms and social trust that facilitate coordination and

*Table 2. The 11 Dutch critical sectors and their 31 critical products and services (Luiijf & Klaver, 2006, p. 206)*

| Critical sector | Critical product or service |
|---|---|
| **Energy** | Electricity<br>Natural gas<br>Oil |
| **Telecommunications** | Fixed telecommunication networks services<br>Mobile telecommunication services<br>Radio communication and navigation<br>Satellite communication and GPS<br>Broadcast services<br>Internet access<br>Postal and courier services |
| **Drinking water** | Drinking water supply |
| **Food** | Food supply and food safety |
| **Health** | Healthcare |
| **Financial** | Financial services and financial infrastructure (private)<br>Financial transfer services (government) |
| **Retaining and managing surface water** | Management of water quality<br>Retaining and managing water quantity |
| **Public order and safety** | Maintaining public order<br>Maintaining public safety |
| **Legal order** | Administration of justice and detention<br>Law enforcement |
| **Public administration** | Diplomacy<br>Information provision by the government (e.g., weather service, citizenship registry)<br>Armed forces/defence (emergency support tasks)<br>Public administration |
| **Transport** | Road transport<br>Rail transport<br>Air transport<br>Inland navigation<br>Ocean shipping<br>Pipelines |

cooperation for mutual benefit. As such, social capital interconnects and thereby leverages the potential subsistent in the community, including physical, human and cultural capital. Despite the dominant role that social capital plays in community structures, until recently few attempts have been made to build the potential of this resource into disaster management planning (Nakagawa & Shaw, 2004). Nakagawa and Shaw (2004) elaborate the term social capital[4] by distinguishing three types of ties:

- *Bonding* social capital is the glue within a (sub)community and includes trust, social norms, participation within community activities and processes and formal as well as informal community memberships.
- *Bridging* social capital denotes the mutual linkage between sub-communities as well as the linkage between sub-communities and other types of non-governmental collectives.
- *Linking* social capital refers to the formal interaction with government officials.

Empirical research (Dynes, 1994; Helsloot & Ruitenberg, 2004; Nakagawa & Shaw, 2004; Quarantelli & Dynes, 1985) shows that, while some of the more concrete parts of the community fabric may severely be damaged and disrupted during an emergency, the more implicit part, of which the social capital is the dominant factor, appears to be very resilient and that some of the social ties will even be strengthened through the process of coping with the emergency.

Quarantelli and Dynes (1985) for example, discuss how the five major social functions they distinguish – production-distribution-consumption, socialization, social control, social participation and mutual support – are affected by a crisis. As shown in the previous sub-section, several types of crises dramatically change the *production-distribution-consumption* function. As a consequence, the focus of this function is shifted from luxury 'needs' towards more basic needs and ER equipment. *Socialization activities* – usually associated with higher regions of the Maslow hierarchy (Maslow, 1943), such as education and development – will be reduced and will be replaced by activities such as providing shelter and food. *Social control* is normally based on regular formal norms, such as speed limits and parking restrictions. These formal norms are set aside and, social control will be based instead on more informal norms such as willingness to help and to share. *Social participation* and *mutual support* show a dramatic increase in interaction and emergency support. Quarantelli and Dynes (1985, p. 164) conclude that:

*A notable aspect of all these activities is that they seldom involve conflict, disagreement, or dispute; they are clearly matters of high community consensus. (They may become point of controversy after the emergency is over, but that, in itself, is a sign that the community situation is returning to normal.)*

This view is supported by many other scholars, including Nakagawa and Shaw (2004) and Helsloot and Ruitenberg (2004). Helsloot and Ruitenberg (2004), for example, disprove three myths with respect to citizen responses to disasters:

1. *Citizens panic in a disaster.* It is argued that panic reactions are actually very rare, though they do occur in very specific circumstances where there is immediate and serious danger, a high level of uncertainty and few perceived means of escape.
2. *Citizens are helpless and dependent.* It is argued that, instead of being helpless and dependent, citizens tend to roll-up their sleeves and start to act. Where they need help or shelter, most victims go to relatives and friends on their own initiative.
3. *Looting occurs during and after a disaster.* It is argued that, in western cultures at least, looting rarely occurs after a disaster – at least not on a large scale.

From a different perspective, this view is also supported by Acquier, Gand, and Szpirglas (2008). They conducted an in-depth qualitative case study of an emergency experienced by a French public transportation company. Within the situation they studied, they argue that because the ER organization takes a *stakeholders perspective* on the emergency situation rather than *a technical and legal perspective*, this has a significant positive effect on the relationship between the ER organization and the affected community groups. Focussing attention on the affected or involved parts of the community rather than the incident itself, contributed to a smooth recovery from the emergency.

Not only the more informal part of social capital, i.e. *bonding* and *bridging*, plays an important role in ER. This also applies to the more formal public and private institutions and bodies, i.e. the *linking* social capital. From their empirical research Kapucu, Arslan, and Collins (2010) call for a greater focus on local-level capacity development in response to disasters. An emergency situation does not fundamentally change the responsibilities and capacities of community sectors – including the private ones – per se. In many countries the role of the public sector in ER has become too large. Dupont (2004, p. 77) argues that

*… the monopoly attributed to the state over the provision of security is more a historical distortion – or at least a temporary anomaly – than a durable condition.*

Indeed, there are many empirical indications that communities are generally able to cope with emergencies decisively and resiliently. In emergency situations, they may even exhibit more decisiveness and resilience than they appear to do in day-to-day life (Quarantelli & Dynes, 1985).

## ER with Focus on Community Recovery

The process of responding to an emergency situation must eventually lead to the recovery and reconstruction of the community. In the initial phase of responding to an emergency, however, the desired end-state will typically be far from concrete and specific. As time progresses, the desired end-state will become more elaborate and it is valuable to develop it in consent with the affected community itself. As Nakagawa and Shaw (2004, p. 12) put it: "Disaster recovery is not only about building houses but the reconstruction of the whole community as a safer place." A good example of aiming to "build back better" (Kennedy, Ashmore, Babister, & Kelman, 2008) is the recovery after the 2011 earthquake in Christchurch, New Zealand. In interaction with the affected community and based on more than 100,000 suggestions submitted by local people, a vision of the future for central Christchurch was developed (Christchurch Central Develop-

ment Unit, 2013), consisting of five key themes: green city; stronger built identity; compact core; live, work, play, learn and visit; accessible city; and embrace cultural values. The recovery of the Roombeek district (Enschede, the Netherlands) after the explosion at a fireworks depot in 2000 shows a similar pattern (Denters & Klok, 2010).

Taking advantage of community resilience in responding to an emergency and making use of its active role, has consequences for the selection of an appropriate ER planning approach (Dynes, 1994). A good example of a planning approach conceived with this in mind is one that is termed *Continuity, Coordination* and *Cooperation*. This approach builds on the assumption that emergencies do not significantly reduce the capacities of existing community structures to cope (Helsloot & Ruitenberg, 2004). In line with this assumption, it is a good thing in ER to respect the existing structures as much as is reasonably possible and to strive for cooperation and coordination. This is also reflected in a recent policy study of the United Nations Office for the Coordination of Humanitarian Affairs (2013, p. 2). This study

*… imagines how a world of increasingly informed, connected and self-reliant communities will affect the delivery of humanitarian aid. Its conclusions suggest a fundamental shift in power from capitals and headquarters to the people aid agencies aim to assist.*

The *Continuity, Coordination and Cooperation* planning approach is contrasted by Dynes (1994) and Messemaker et al. (2013) with a more directive planning approach denoted by the terms *Chaos, Command* and *Control*. The *Chaos, Command and Control* planning approach draws on the assumption that an emergency situation predominantly causes chaos in a community. This chaos leads to incapacity of existing structures to cope with the situation. So, an ER organization is needed to (Command and Control) restore order in a directive manner.

These two planning approaches are archetypes. In practice, neither of the two approaches are applicable in their purest form. Any emergency leads to a certain amount of chaos, insecurity and lack of safety and, as a consequence, some degree of directive command and control is necessary to restore stability decisively. At the same time it makes sense to make use of the potential available in the community and recognize the fact that in the end the community has to be able to deal with the emergency. So, an ER organization has to strike a balance between the two irreconcilable planning approaches.

To the author's knowledge, there is no prescription for finding a weighted optimum between the two planning approaches. This optimum is highly context-sensitive. It depends on what is needed for safety and security, and also on the competences required to perform specific tasks. It is worth mentioning that there is increasing evidence for a correlation between the planning approach and what type of crisis communication is used (Mannes, 2013; Messemaker et al., 2013). If *Chaos, Command and Control* is the dominant planning approach, the crisis communication tends to be rather technical-legal and also rather dragging and one-way. If *Continuity, Coordination and Cooperation* is the dominant planning approach, the crisis communication tends to be rather emotional-empathic and also rather up-to-date and more in tune with community feelings.

## Examples of Community Response in the Netherlands

In sum, in this section it is argued that, in responding to an incident, the affected community itself can be an important source of information and capabilities. Making use of the capacities of the community is effective because the extent to which community impact of an emergency can directly be effected by the responding organization is limited. After all, a distinguishing characteristic of a crisis is that regular structures and resources are not adequate to cope. In contrast, there is ample evidence that emergencies do not significantly reduce the capacities of individuals or social structures. More fundamentally, above all an emergency is an event impacting *the community,* and consequently *the community* eventually has to – and to a great extent can – deal with it.

An example of the practical value of community capacity can be found in the response in 2001 to a café fire in Volendam in the Netherlands. On 1 January, shortly after mid-night, a fierce fire raged in the café 't Hemeltje. Fourteen young people died and more than 200 were seriously injured. The first responders were faced with a severe challenge, due to the huge number of wounded people, the nature of their injuries and the low temperature outside. Fortunately an active First Aid Association flourished in Volendam. Although this association was not a formal part of the emergency services, members of the association played an active role that night. Through telephone calls, around seventy First Aid members came to the disaster site to contribute to the ER.

A less extreme example can be found in the aftermath of a fire in the rail traffic control centre that broke out on the 19 November 2011 in Utrecht. It was a Friday afternoon, and the rail services around the city could no longer run, due to the fire. There was a lot of mutual citizen support in the evacuation of passengers from stranded trains. Elderly and other less self-reliant people were looked after by fellow passengers. That evening, thousands of people were stuck at Utrecht Central Station. They had to find alternative means of transport or somewhere to sleep. Camp beds were set up in an adjacent trade fair centre. None of these camp beds were actually used. Via Twitter and other social media every stranded person was able to find another way of getting to their destination or was provided with a place to spend the night.

The role of the affected community in an emergency can further be illustrated by a fragment of an hitherto unpublished interview on this subject with a Dutch first responding officer:

*"Generally, in disaster-type incidents, fighting the cause of the incident is not problematic. Involved organizations know how to contact each other and are able to coordinate their activities. In the long term, incidents will however primarily be judged on the effect the incident has on the community.*

*How an incident affects the community can be illustrated with the lightning strike during a funeral in the village of Vorden on the 25 August 2006. A former member of the local marching band was being buried. During the ceremony, there was a performance of the marching band. Immediately after the funeral, a tree on the cemetery was unexpectedly struck by lightning and two members of the marching band lost their lives. This incident had a severe impact on the local community. In responding to this incident it was crucial to think from the perspective of the community right from the start. As an example, it was very important to take into account that there were many social ties with the victims and with the other members of the marching band, including family, neighbourhood and church membership ties. As a consequence, very soon – informally – the identity of the victims was generally known. It is very important to take this reality into account in responding to the incident; in the approach, in the allocation of tasks, in the organizations to be involved in the response and also in the crisis communication. In the heat of the moment it often happens that responders are very much focused on their own core tasks and activities and forget to think from the perspective of the affected community.*

*As said, in the long term, incidents will not be judged on the progression of fighting the cause of the incident. Instead they will primarily be judged on the effect the incident has on the community. The longer term image of the incident the community has is closely related to activities such as crisis communication, the settling of claims and psycho-social aftercare. Crisis communication and interaction with distinct target groups should*

*right from the start be taken into account as an integral part of approaching an incident. As an example, I once deliberately chose to organize a guided tour with journalists and photographers to give them a closer look on the process and progress of the fighting of a wildfire."*

## EMERGENCY RESPONSE NETWORKS

This section discusses the structure of the ER organizations. It is shown that ER organizations are typically *mixed-sector networks*. This means that coordination is needed among organizations and collectives *with differing strategic orientations*. What does this challenging context mean from the perspective of the response organization? What does it mean for its structure, its culture, its policy, its information infrastructure and its (internal and external) relationships (Whelan, 2012)? But it also raises issues for how it comes into being in the first place. Or – in other words – how should one shape a trustworthy and decisive response organization that draws on the potential available within the community and that takes account of the fact that in the end the community has to be capable of dealing with the emergency? The theoretical basis will be discussed in the first five subsections and will then be illustrated by examining the way in which crisis management is organized in the Netherlands.

### Emergencies and Networked Organizations

Because of the complex and multifaceted nature of large-scale incidents, the response requires coordinated effort by multiple organizations. An interesting characterization of this collaboration challenge can be found in the work of Hayes, who uses the term *endeavour* (Hayes, 2007). As Hayes defines it, an endeavour involves a large number of disparate entities whose activities are related to a broad range of effects, including safety, social, economic, political, and informational ones. Endeavours are formed because no single actor within the collective is capable of achieving its particular goals without appropriate activities and behaviours by other actors. A crucial distinction between endeavours and other types of collectives is that the actors involved in an endeavour do not have a single leader or commander.

In the literature, the term 'networked organization' is commonly used for this type of organization. In this chapter, the term 'networked organizations' is used not only to refer to networked organizations in the *strict sense* – being completely *informal* structures of relationships linking social actors, which may be persons, teams or organizations – but also to partial organizations as long as they have a dominant focus on emergent dynamics in collaboration and only a limited reliance on formal hierarchical structures (Ahrne & Brunsson, 2011, p. 88). Ahrne and Brunsson (2011) distinguish five types of mechanisms which can be selectively combined explicitly for the purposes of designing a networked organization, i.e. to strike a considered balance between a purely formal organization and a purely informal structure:

- **Membership:** confers a certain identity that differs from that of non-members. Membership of a network is not always explicitly registered (or *de jure*). Sometimes it is latent (or *de facto*), and develops gradually through the individual actions of its participants.
- **Hierarchy:** confers a right to oblige others to comply with central decisions. As Diefenbach and Sillince (2011) show, all types of (partial) organizations, including networked organizations, exhibit forms of hierarchy. They show that, either consciously or unconsciously, the more active or competent network members eventually begin to dominate discussions and deci-

sions in the network, resulting in certain types of hierarchy, albeit informal.

- **Rules and norms:** Rules, often known as standards in networked organizations, are primarily in written form whereas norms are handed down via socialisation and internalisation.
- **Monitoring:** the extent of belonging to the network. Ranking and rating mechanisms are well-known means of monitoring.
- **Sanctions:** In sanctioning, the monitoring is extended with penalties, certification, accreditation, prizes or awards.

This way of approaching the concept of networked organizations fits the way in which Whelan (2012) approaches networks. Networked organizations strike a balance between hierarchical organizations, controlled by administrative or bureaucratic means, and market forms of governance involving no organizational structure. Whelan (2012, p. 4) states that

*Network forms of governance involve repetitive exchanges between a set of autonomous but interdependent organisations in order to achieve individual and shared objectives. Network organisations are controlled not through administrative means or the law but through relationships based on reciprocity and trust. Networks are understood to balance the 'reliability' of hierarchies with the 'flexibility' of markets, providing them with a number of advantages as forms of organisation or governance.*

Research into networked collaboration has identified that the key problem in networked collaboration is that organizations depend on each other's expertise in order to coordinate tasks, but have little authority and control over the actions of other organizations (Kapucu et al., 2010; Provan, Fish, & Sydow, 2007; Whelan, 2012). Kapucu et al. (2010, p. 19) put it this way:

*Large, complex, and seemingly unsolvable problems, such as catastrophic disasters, are best approached from a cooperative effort combining resources and preventing duplication; however, organizing the cooperative effort is almost as difficult as the problems they are created to address.*

## Network Strategic Orientations and Matching Management Regimes

Earlier in this chapter it was argued that in emergency responses it makes sense to make use of the potential available in the community. To a large extent, this potential typically resides in private organizations and community networks. Examples of private organizations are electricity suppliers, which clearly play a crucial role in the event of a power outage, and providers of earthmoving equipment. Examples of community networks are neighbourhood associations and volunteer networks. As a consequence, a complicating aspect is that ER networks are compounded of organizations with fundamentally incompatible attitudes. Herranz (2008) uses the term *strategic orientation* to express this. He distinguishes three archetypical strategic orientations of a (networked) organization: *bureaucratic*, *entrepreneurial* and *community*. Governmental networks and public agencies are examples of organizational networks which are predominantly bureaucratically oriented. Networks of private companies primarily entrepreneurial in attitude. Volunteer organizations or neighbourhood associations are predominantly community-oriented. Table 3 characterises the three archetypical strategic orientations.

Note that *bureaucratic*, *entrepreneurial* and *community* are meant as archetypical characterisations. In a real-world situation the contrast between the three network types may not be as sharp as suggested here. Referring to the examples given above, an ER network typically exhibits all three types of strategic orientation. The organizational network of first responders, municipalities and government agencies involved has a predominantly

bureaucratic orientation. Legal order, fairness, stability, accountability and equitable treatment are important values in this part of the networked organization. Entrepreneurially oriented private organizations are often responsible for many of the critical products and services or may be involved as providers of capacity and expertise. Market focus, market share and business continuity are important values in this part of the networked organization. Citizens, volunteer organizations and also non-governmental collectives have a community nature and orientation. This part of the networked organization has a compassionate focus on civil society, on humanitarian aspects and on equitable outcomes for every individual affected.

In addition to the strategic orientation and building on a substantial body of literature, Herranz (2008) also distinguishes four archetypical network management regimes.

- *Reactive facilitation* is the most passive form of regime wherein network coordination relies primarily on social interactions rather than procedural mechanisms or financial incentives. The overall behaviour of the network emerges from the inter-nodal interaction rather than being deliberately planned.
- *Contingent coordination* applies some opportunistic directive influence to guide network behaviour. Reliance on emergent behaviour is still quite high.
- *Active coordination* implies a more deliberate design of the network, including its constituent partners as well as the interaction and incentive mechanisms among the partners.
- *Hierarchical-based directive administration* implies coordination with authoritative procedural mechanisms rather than reliance on social or incentive mechanisms.

Based on empirical research, Herranz (2008) makes a number of propositions as to which of

*Table 3. Characterisation of archetypical strategic orientations; after Herranz (2008, p. 10)*

| Strategic orientation vs. Values Dimension | Bureaucratic | Entrepreneurial | Community |
|---|---|---|---|
| **Ideology** | Legislated order (e.g., state-focused), fairness | Market focus, individualism, innovation, efficiency | Civil society focus, humanitarian, compassion |
| **Goals, preferences** | Stability, accountability, equitable treatment | Value maximization | Social balance, equitable outcomes |
| **Power and control** | Very centralized with more reliance on rules | Quasi-centralized with reliance on teams | Less centralized with interest groups |
| **Implicit structure** | Hierarchical, departmental | Quasi-autonomous units (often hierarchically structured) | Loosely coupled units |
| **Decision process** | Procedural, rationality, top-down | Technical, opportunistic, middle-out | Situational, participatory, bottom-up |
| **Decisions** | Follow from programs and routines | Follow from value-maximizing choice | Result from socially negotiated solutions/problems |
| **Information requirements** | Reduced by use of rules and procedures | Extensive and systematic | Ad hoc |

the network management archetypes is appropriate for each type of strategic orientation; see Table 4.

Recall the observation that an ER network typically exhibits all three of the strategic orientations. This implies that none of the four archetypical network management regimes distinguished by Herranz (2008) will fully meet the needs of a comprehensive ER network. Instead, well-designed ER network management shows characteristics of several regimes.

## Coherence of an Organization and its Environment

Taking this discussion on step further, there is a very close interplay between the comprehensive ER network and the whole community. This interplay is reflected in the way Karl Weick approaches *organizations* and *organizing*. Weick (1979, p. 166) shows that an organization and its environment are tightly linked together:

*Investigators who study organizations often separate environments from organizations and argue that things happen between these distinct entities.*

*This way of carving up the problem of organizational analysis effectively rules out certain kinds of questions. Talk about bounded environments and organizations, for example, compels the investigator to ask questions such as "How does an organization discover the underlying structure in the environment?" Having separated the "two" entities and given them independent existence, investigators have to make elaborate speculations concerning the ways in which one entity becomes disclosed to and known by the other. But the firm partitioning of the world into the environment and the organization excludes the possibility that people invent rather than discover part of what they think they see.*

This line of thinking has been brought a step closer towards the crisis management domain by the plea for the crisis management organization to adopt an *adaptive stance* made by Grisogono (2006), Grisogono and Radenovic (2007) and Spaans, Spoelstra, Douze, Pieneman, and Grisogono (2009). This adaptive stance starts from the fact that in crisis situations the regular structures fail to maintain stability while the power of the

*Table 4. Suitability mapping of network management regimes on strategic orientations, as proposed by Herranz (2008, pp. 25, 26)*

| Network Management Regime vs. Strategic Orientation | Reactive Facilitation | Contingent Coordination | Active Coordination | Hierarchically-Based Directive Administration |
|---|---|---|---|---|
| Bureaucratic | | | ✓ | ✓ |
| Entrepreneurial | | ✓ | ✓ | |
| Community | ✓ | ✓ | | |

response organization to limit or even influence the impact of a crisis on the community is also limited. The fact that there is a considerable level of uncertainty makes the situation even more complex. In such situations, a powerful way for the responding organization to gain success is to make use of the potential and the dynamics inherent to the community. Or, looking at it in a different way, the ER organization is a complex and in a practical sense unbounded endeavour (Hayes, 2007). By mindfully initiating actions and sensing the response of the community, the responding organization seeks to separate sensible, reasonable and helpful configurations from those which are not. As such, the most effective actions performed by the responding organizations are those that strike the right chord in the community.

## Shaping of Ad Hoc Networks

Not much has been published about the practical aspects of how one builds ad hoc and comprehensive organizations of this kind, in a dynamic way. Kapucu et al. (2010) focused on the inter-organizational and intergovernmental response to Hurricanes Katrina and Rita in 2005. One of the conclusions of this research is that more research is needed on development of ad hoc networks to respond to disasters. How should such organizations be shaped, given the dynamics of the environment as well as the various interests and goals of the stakeholders?

Topper and Carley (1999) studied the emergence of a networked organization in a specific case. They distinguish three theoretical perspectives on what they call integrated crisis management units (ICMUs).

- The first perspective assumes the *spontaneous emergence of a coordination group*, and suggests that, in the event of a severe crisis, communities and organizations will spontaneously reorganize and a coordination group will emerge.
- The second perspective assumes the *presence and maintenance of a centralized system*, typically designed into formal contingency plans.
- The third perspective assumes a *distributed structure of systems*. Centralized coordination will be limited as responding organizations coordinate their activities locally and laterally, typically making use of a common operational picture.

Topper and Carley (1999) subsequently operationalized these three theoretical perspectives in six social network measures: number of nodes, number of isolates, density, connectivity, graph efficiency, and 'betweenness centralization'. They did an in-depth quantitative study, using several sources of data, and found that the crisis organization started as a small, pre-existing centralized group. This centralized group kept its central role throughout the progress of the crisis response. At the same time, however, several groups of stake-holder organizations emerged on the periphery of the organization, leading to a combined distributed and centralized response.

Comfort and Kapucu (2006) scratch the surface of this subject by presenting a preliminary model of auto-adaptation in ER. Their paper argues that the concept of auto-adaptation fits the requirements for inter-organizational response to extreme events. They see an auto-adaptive system as moving through five distinct phases in its response to extreme events: (1) information search or scanning; (2) information exchange; (3) sensemaking, or selection of a plausible strategy of action, given the situation and resources available; (4) adaptation, or action taking to implement that strategy; and (5) evaluation of actions taken and modification of succeeding actions on basis of observed results. Shaping the organization, given the dynamics of the environment, would fit in phase 4 (adaptation) but this 'shaping' is hardly mentioned in the preliminary model of auto-adaptation.

## ER Networks in the Netherlands

How does the discussion on strategic orientations and network management work for a specific case, such as how ER is organized in the Netherlands? Following Brainich (2012), more than fifty *institutional chains* have been distinguished by the Dutch government, each playing a specific role during a crisis. By far the majority of these chains are *functional chains*, responsible for a specific functional domain such as electricity, social security, financial flows or food safety. There is one *general* (i.e. non-functional) *chain* specifically focused on ER and public order management. A distinctive characteristic of the general chain is that its main concern is taking care of the population. Most of the functional chains are made up of a mix of public and private organizations. The general chain is predominantly compounded of government institutions and government agencies.

If a crisis really affects a vital interest of the community – which will be typically the case because this is a distinctive characteristic of a crisis – the general chain should be one of the chains to be involved. In most crises, however, other chains will be involved as well. The general chain only has two concerns. The first (and main) one is population care, and the second is ensuring proper coordination among the chains involved. As *subsidiarity* is an important principle in the Netherlands, implying that a matter ought to be handled by the least centralized authority capable of addressing that matter effectively, decision making takes place as much as possible in the functional chains (Brainich, 2007, p. 9). Of course, given its responsibility for population care, as a last resort the general chain has the final say. Coordination between the chains can take place at two different levels. At the national level, coordination takes the form of interdepartmental alignment, because one of the departments is ultimately responsible for a functional chain. At the regional and municipality level, a regional or municipal administrative board and a regional operational team take care of the administrative and operational coordination respectively.

How does this work out on the ground? Consider, for example, a large electricity outage. The primary responsibility for coping with this incident resides with the functional electricity chain. As soon as vital interests of the community are threatened or even affected, the general chain comes into play. This general chain coordinates with the functional electricity chain, without taking over responsibilities. Legal regulations prohibit the functional electricity chain from distinguishing between individual electricity customers. So, the functional electricity chain is not allowed to provide emergency power generators selectively to individual customers. If the general chain – from the perspective of population care – decides that emergency power should be provided to a nursing home, for example, the general chain has the legal mandate to order the functional electricity chain to do so.

Looking at the way in which crisis response is organized in the Netherlands, it can be concluded that network management is predominantly of the *active coordination* type. The coordination mechanisms have been designed into the structure of the network as much as is reasonably possible. More specifically, the government can be seen as a network administrative organization (NAO), i.e. a separate administrative entity which is not an integral part of the network but is responsible for governing the network and its activities (Provan & Kenis, 2008; Whelan, 2012). This way of organizing crisis response is in line with the suggestion by Herranz (2008) that active coordination is suited to bureaucratically oriented networks as well as to ones that are more entrepreneurially oriented. Legislation and regulations as well as emergency orders and decrees can be used by the government (i.e. the general chain) to ensure fairness, stability and equitable treatment of the population and – if necessary – to temporarily curb value maximisation and business continuity of private organizations.

This description of the crisis response organization in the Netherlands is focused solely on the public and private professional response and does not include real integration of large-scale community response. A recent example of large-scale community response in the Netherland nicely illustrates the tension between strategic orientations and how these tension have been dealt with.

Two young brothers – Ruben and Julian – had been missing since the 6 May 2013. That day, they had been driving with their father through the south-eastern part of the country. The father was found on the 7 May. He had committed suicide. There was no clear clue as to where to look for the two boys. With so little to go on, police forces, reinforced with defence units conducted systematic search activities in several forests and rural areas.

On 9 May a citizen initiative was launched to carry out additional searches. Ten days later, a passer-by reported something suspicious to the police and the two boys were found in a ditch. Investigations showed that the boys had already been dead for a couple of weeks. From the 9 to 19 May search activities had been conducted by several citizen groups. The searches were coordinated via social media and a dedicated Website (JulianRubenNL, 2013). Through the use of these media, the citizen search activities were deliberately kept out of the way of the search activities of the professional forces. There was a separate section on the Website with questions to the public which arose from the police investigations. Moreover, the following statement was prominent on the Website: "We kindly ask you to keep the coordination in the hands of one person and not to initiate your own activities. If you want to search, please contact us, we will put you in contact with the person who has contacts with the Mayors and Police. […] Duplication of work would be a waste of effort. There are maps and we have a script that we can share."

In this particular case, the professional response organization did not discourage the citizen search initiatives. Some basic guidance on search techniques was provided and areas were explicitly assigned as "released for citizen search activities." Moreover, one particular person was assigned as the point of contact[5], and given the role of mediating between local people involved in the search and the professional response organization. In doing so, the citizen initiative – in itself a typical example of a network with a community-type strategic orientation – was enwrapped and made manageable for the professional response organization.

## FUTURE RESEARCH DIRECTIONS

In searching for an answer to the question of shaping comprehensive emergency response networks, this chapter is an attempt to combine several scientific debates and to substantiate this combination with empirical examples – mainly from Dutch emergency operations. The debate on community vulnerability and critical infrastructure protection is combined with the debate on community resilience. The debate on two archetypical ER planning approaches provides an initial outline of how the potential inherent in the community can be incorporated in the ER effort. After some subsequent discussion of mixed-sector networking, the chapter then focuses on how this works in terms of how ER is organized in the Netherlands.

It has been argued that it makes sense for an ER organization to make use of the potential available in the community and to strike a careful balance between being *directive* and being *empathic*. Further research is needed on what the implications of this challenge are for the decision-making process as well as for crisis communication. How should the potential available in the community be incorporated structurally into the decision-making process of the ER organization? Or – in other words – how should one orchestrate a complex and, in a practical sense, unbounded endeavour (Hayes, 2007), which an ER organization actually is?

Building on the propositions put forward by Herranz (2008) on mixed-sector networks and the suitability of network management regimes, it has also been argued that well-designed ER network management exhibits characteristics of several regimes. Other scholars have published some initial findings on emergence and adaptive development of ER networks (Comfort & Kapucu, 2006; Topper & Carley, 1999). Further research is needed to develop and underpin the logic of effective mixed-sector ER network governance.

## CONCLUSION

The main question in this chapter is how one can shape a trustworthy and decisive response organization, in which relevant and useful capacities available in the community are incorporated. The first focal point of this chapter is the role of the affected community in the event of an emergency. It is shown that an emergency affects the fabric of the community, including its critical infrastructure, and also that the more implicit capital of a community provides substantial resilience and ER capacity. This reality can be reflected in the choice of ER planning model. Two archetypical planning models are described. The *Chaos, Command and Control* planning approach is based on the assumption that an emergency situation predominantly causes chaos in a community, requiring directive intervention. The *Continuity, Coordination and Cooperation* planning approach seeks to build upon the capacities of the affected community, and assumes that emergencies do not significantly reduce their ability to cope. In practical situations an ER organization has to strike a balance between the two irreconcilable planning approaches and reflect this balance in its crisis communication.

The second focal point is the structure of the ER network. An ER network is a mixed-sector network. This means that coordination is needed among organizations and collectives with differing strategic orientations. Three different archetypical strategic orientations are distinguished – bureaucratic, entrepreneurial and community – and for each of these strategic orientations a limited number of network management regimes seems to be appropriate. Consequently, a well-designed ER network management regime shows characteristics of several regimes.

Combining the two above-mentioned focal points, there is a close interplay between the comprehensive ER network and the whole community. The most effective actions performed by the responding organizations are those that strike the right chord with the community.

In the Netherlands, network management is predominantly of the *active coordination* type. The government can be seen as an NAO. Citizen initiatives – in itself a typical example of a network with a community-type strategic orientation – are typically enwrapped and made manageable for the professional response organization.

Despite of the limitations of the research – as discussed in the previous section – some practical consequences and recommendations can already be formulated. The first is that it is a good thing for ER networks to bear in mind the community impact of an emergency. Right from the start, this impact can be used as a starting point for deciding which organizations and community networks to involve in the ER process. In interacting with these organizations and community networks, the professional emergency responders should seek to strike a balance between two archetypical planning approaches and choose the crisis communication approach accordingly. By initiating actions and paying heed to the response of the community, the responding organization seeks to separate sensible, reasonable and helpful configurations from those which are not. This emphasizes the need to invest in continuous monitoring of how the community reacts to the emergency and to action taken by the responding organizations.

The second consequence is that role of professional first responders in the Netherlands is more limited than often suggested. First of all, given the complexity of the community, the extent to which community impact of an emergency can directly be effected by the responding organization is limited. Second, the professional responders are part of the general chain, having two main concerns. The first one is population care and the second one is ensuring proper coordination among the involved chains. As *subsidiarity* is an important principle in the Netherlands, decision making takes place as much as possible in the functional chains.

## ACKNOWLEDGMENT

The author would like to thank Prof. Dr. Peter Groenewegen and Dr. Kees Boersma from the VU University Amsterdam | faculty of social sciences | department of organizational sciences for reviewing draft versions of this chapter and for providing valuable suggestions and comments. The author is grateful to the Netherlands Organisation for Applied Scientific Research TNO for sponsoring the writing of this chapter. A substantial part of this sponsoring can be attributed to three projects TNO contributes to. The first project is the EU Seventh Framework Project COBACORE on Community Based Comprehensive Recovery (Grant agreement no: 313308). The second one is a project on *Societal Impact of Interdependent Networks*, which is part of TNO's Enabling Technology Program *Models*. The third one is the project on *better utilization of information flows and cooperation*, which is part of TNO's research programme on *Society and Resilience*.

## REFERENCES

Acquier, A., Gand, S., & Szpirglas, M. (2008). From Stakeholder to StakeSholder Management in Crisis Episodes: A Case Study in a Public Transportation Company. *Journal of Contingencies and Crisis Management*, 16(2), 101–114. doi:10.1111/j.1468-5973.2008.00538.x

Ahrne, G., & Brunsson, N. (2011). Organization outside organizations: the significance of partial organization. *Organization*, 18(1), 83–104. doi:10.1177/1350508410376256

Bexley, E. (2007). *Social capital in theory and practice: Centre for the Study of Higher Education*. University of Melbourne.

Boin, A., Hart, P., Stern, E. K., & Sundelius, B. (2005). *The politics of crisis management: Public leadership under pressure*. Cambridge University Press. doi:10.1017/CBO9780511490880

Bos, J. H. G., & Verberne, E. M. J. (2012). *GRIP 3 Ouwerkerkse Kreek - Lessen uit de aanpak* [GRIP 3 Ouwerkerk Creek - Lessons from the approach]. The Hague, The Netherlands: Academic Press.

Brainich, E. (2007). *Rijksheren in het moderne crisismanagement* [Government lords in modern crisis management]. Haarlem, The Netherlands: Provincie Noord-Holland.

Brainich, E. (2012). Bestuurlijke Netwerkkaarten Crisisbeheersing. [Administrative Network Maps Crisis Management]. (Vierde druk, Ed.). Haarlem, The Netherlands: Provincie Noord-Holland.

Christchurch Central Development Unit. (2013). *Aspirations*. Retrieved 12 July 2013, from http://ccdu.govt.nz/plan/aspirations

Comfort, L. K., & Kapucu, N. (2006). Inter-organizational coordination in extreme events: The World Trade Center attacks, September 11, 2001. *Natural Hazards, 39*, 309–327. doi:10.1007/s11069-006-0030-x

Denters, B., & Klok, P. J. (2010). Rebuilding Roombeek: patterns of citizen participation in urban governance. *Urban Affairs Review, 45*(5), 583–607. doi:10.1177/1078087409356756

Diefenbach, T., & Sillince, J. A. A. (2011). Formal and Informal Hierarchy in Different Types of Organization. *Organization Studies, 32*(11), 1515–1537. doi:10.1177/0170840611421254

Dupont, B. (2004). Security in the age of networks. *Policing and Society: An International Journal of Research and Policy, 14*(1), 76–91. doi:10.1080/1043946042000181575

Dynes, R. R. (1994). Community Emergency Planning: False Assumptions and Inappropriate Analogies. *International Journal of Mass Emergencies and Disasters, 12*(2), 141–158.

Grisogono, A. M. (2006). *The implications of complex adaptive systems theory for C2*. Paper presented at the Command and Control Research and Technology Symposium. New York, NY.

Grisogono, A. M., & Radenovic, V. (2007). *The Adaptive Stance - Steps towards teaching more effective complex decision-making*. Paper presented at the Eighth International Conference on Complex Systems. New York, NY.

Hayes, R.E. (2007). It's an Endeavor, Not a Force. *The International C2 Journal, 1*(1), 145-176.

Helsloot, I., & Ruitenberg, A. (2004). Citizen Response to Disasters: a Survey of Literature and Some Practical Implications. *Journal of Contingencies and Crisis Management, 12*(3), 98–111. doi:10.1111/j.0966-0879.2004.00440.x

Herranz, J. (2008). The multisectoral trilemma of network management. *Journal of Public Administration: Research and Theory, 18*(1), 1–31. doi:10.1093/jopart/mum004

Inspectie Openbare Orde en Veiligheid. (2011). *Brand Chemie-Pack Moerdijk - Een onderzoek naar de bestrijding van (de effecten van) het grootschalig incident* [Fire Chemie-Pack Moerdijk - An investigation on fighting (the effects of) the large-scale incident]. The Hague: Ministry of Security and Justice, The Netherlands.

Jansen, G. J., Fernandes Mendes, H. K., Rook, M., Stordiau-van Egmond, A. M. E., & van Zanten, P. J. (2012). *Onderzoek asbestvondst Kanaleneiland* [Investigation Asbestos Discovery]. Utrecht, The Netherlands: Academic Press.

JulianRubenNL. (2013). *VERMIST / MISSING / FEHLT Julian & Ruben*. Retrieved from http://julian-ruben-vermist.Webklik.nl/page/vermist-julian-ruben

Kapucu, N., Arslan, T., & Collins, M. L. (2010). Examining Intergovernmental and Interorganizational Response to Catastrophic Disasters: Toward a Network-Centered Approach. *Administration & Society, 42*(2), 222–247. doi:10.1177/0095399710362517

Kennedy, J., Ashmore, J., Babister, E., & Kelman, I. (2008). The Meaning of 'Build Back Better': Evidence From Post-Tsunami Aceh and Sri Lanka. *Journal of Contingencies and Crisis Management, 16*(1), 24–36. doi:10.1111/j.1468-5973.2008.00529.x

Lindell, M. K., Perry, R. W., Prater, C., & Nicholson, W. C. (2006). Community Disaster Recovery. In *Proceedings of Fundamentals of emergency management* (pp. 308–345). FEMA.

Little, R. L., & Krannich, R. S. (1988). A model for assessing the social impacts of natural utilization on resource-dependent communities. *Impact Assessment, 6*(2), 21–35. doi:10.1080/07349165.1988.9725633

Luiijf, E. A. M., & Klaver, M. H. A. (2006). Protection of the Dutch critical infrastructures. *International Journal of Critical Infrastructures, 2*(2/3), 201–214. doi:10.1504/IJCIS.2006.009438

Luiijf, E. A. M., Nieuwenhuijs, A. H., Klaver, M. H. A., van Eeten, M., & Cruz, E. (2008). *Empirical Findings on Critical Infrastructure Dependencies in Europe*. Paper presented at the 3rd International Workshop on Critical Information Infrastructures Security. Frascati, Italy.

Mannes, P. (2013). *GRIP op CRISISCOMMU-NICATIE - Onderzoek naar de Maatschappelijke impact op Crisiscommunicatie*. [Grip on crisis communication - Research on the societal impact on crisis communication]. (Master Thesis). VU University, Amsterdam, The Netherlands.

Maslow, A. H. (1943). A theory of human motivation. *Psychological Review, 50*(4), 370. doi:10.1037/h0054346

Messemaker, M., Wolbers, J. J., Treurniet, W., & Boersma, F. K. (2013). *Shaping societal impact: between Control and Cooperation*. Paper presented at the 10th International ISCRAM Conference. Baden-Baden.

Ministerie van Veiligheid en Justitie. (2013). *Nationaal Handboek Crisisbesluitvorming* [National Handbook Crisis Decision-making]. Den Haag: Author.

Nakagawa, Y., & Shaw, R. (2004). Social Capital: A Missing Link to Disaster Recovery. *International Journal of Mass Emergencies and Disasters, 22*(1), 5–34.

Provan, K. G., Fish, A., & Sydow, J. (2007). Interorganizational Networks at the Network Level: A Review of the Empirical Literature on Whole Networks. *Journal of Management, 33*, 479–516. doi:10.1177/0149206307302554

Provan, K. G., & Kenis, P. (2008). Modes of Network Governance: Structure, Management, and Effectiveness. *Journal of Public Administration: Research and Theory, 18*(1), 229–252.

Putnam, R. D. (1995). Bowling alone: America's declining social capital. *Journal of Democracy, 6*(1), 65–78. doi:10.1353/jod.1995.0002

Quarantelli, E. L., & Dynes, R. R. (1985). Community Response to Disasters. In *Disasters and Mental Health Selected Contemporary Perspectives*. Academic Press.

Rosenthal, U., Boin, A., & Comfort, L. K. (2001). *Managing crises: Threats, dilemmas, opportunities*. Charles C Thomas Springfield.

Spaans, M., Spoelstra, M., Douze, E., Pieneman, R., & Grisogono, A. M. (2009). *Learning to be Adaptive*. Paper presented at the 14th International Command and Control Research and Technology Symposium (ICCRTS). New York, NY.

Stern, E. K. (2003). Crisis Studies and Foreign Policy Analysis: Insights, Synergies, and Challenges. *International Studies Review, 5*(2), 155–202. doi:10.1111/1521-9488.5020016

Tönnies, F. (2012). *Gemeinschaft und gesellschaft* [Community and Society]. Springer. doi:10.1007/978-3-531-94174-5

Topper, C. M., & Carley, K. M. (1999). A structural perspective on the emergence of network organizations. *The Journal of Mathematical Sociology*, *24*(1), 67–96. doi:10.1080/002225 0X.1999.9990229

Treurniet, W., van Buul-Besseling, K., & Wolbers, J. J. (2012). *Collaboration awareness - a necessity in crisis response coordination*. Paper presented at the 9th International ISCRAM Conference. Vancouver, Canada.

United Nations Office for the Coordination of Humanitarian Affairs. (2013). *Humanitarianism in the Network Age, including world humanitarian data and trends 2012. UN Office for the Coordination of Humanitarian Affairs*. OCHA.

Warren, R. (1972). *The Community in America*. Rand McNally.

Weick, K. E. (1979). *The social psychology of organizing*. Addison-Wesley Publishing Company, Inc.

Whelan, C. (2012). *Networks and National Security, Dynamics, Effectiveness and Organisation*. Surrey, UK: Ashgate Publishing Limited.

## ADDITIONAL READING

Alberts, D.S. (2007). Agility, Focus, and Convergence: The Future of Command and Control. *The International C2 Journal*, *1*(1), 1-30.

Allen, K. M. (2006). Community-based disaster preparedness and climate adaptation: local capacity-building in the Philippines. *Disasters*, *30*(1), 81–101. doi:10.1111/j.1467-9523.2006.00308.x PMID:16512863

Ekbia, H. R., & Kling, R. (2005). Network organizations: symmetric cooperation or multivalent negotiations? *The Information Society*, *21*(3), 155–168. doi:10.1080/01972240490951881

Okhuysen, G. A., & Bechky, B. A. (2009). Coordination in Organizations: An Integrative Perspective. *The Academy of Management Annals*, *3*(1), 463–502. doi:10.1080/19416520903047533

Powley, E. H. (2009). Reclaiming resilience and safety: Resilience activation in the critical period of crisis. *Human Relations*, *62*(9), 1289–1326. doi:10.1177/0018726709334881

Weick, K. E. (1988). Enacted Sensemaking in Crisis Situations. *Journal of Management Studies*, *25*(4), 305–317. doi:10.1111/j.1467-6486.1988. tb00039.x

## KEY TERMS AND DEFINITIONS

**Community:** The combination of social units and systems that perform the major social functions having locality reference.

**Crisis:** An event in which safety or security are at stake because one or more vital community interests are affected while the regular structures and resources are not sufficient to maintain stability.

**Emergency:** A crisis with a fast rise rate.

**Network Administrative Organization:** A separate administrative entity that is not an integral part of the network, but is responsible for governing the network and its activities.

**Networked Organizations:** Partial organizations with a dominant focus on emergent dynamics in collaboration and less reliance on formal hierarchical structures.

**Social Capital:** Networks, norms, and social trust that facilitate coordination and cooperation for mutual benefit.

**Society:** Social organization in which the ties can predominantly be characterized as indirect interactions, impersonal roles, formal values, and beliefs based on such interactions.

## ENDNOTES

[1] Note the difference between *community* and *society* (Tönnies, 2012). *Community* (in German: *Gemeinschaft*) is perceived to be a tighter, more enduring and more cohesive social entity, due to the presence of a "unity of will." *Society* (in German: *Gesellschaft*) on the other hand, is a group in which the individuals who make up that group are motivated to take part in the group purely by self-interest. To stress its more enduring nature, the word *community* is used deliberately.

[2] Note that the adjunct "locality reference" – present in the definition of Quarantelli and Dynes (1985) but also in the work of Lindell et al. (2006) – may not be that important anymore; at least not in the traditional sense of the word. Over the last decennia cyberspace has added a new dimension to 'locality'.

[3] Surprisingly enough, third order effects caused by interdependencies among critical infrastructures appear to be quite rare. While interdependencies exist everywhere, they rarely appear to be strong enough to trigger a reported serious cascading critical infrastructure outage. The majority of them are caused by interdependencies from the energy and telecom sectors (Luiijf et al., 2008).

[4] A structured and comprehensive discussion of the phenomenon social capital goes beyond the scope of this chapter. Nakagawa and Shaw (2004) and Bexley (2007) can be used for further reference.

[5] A point of contact mediating between the crisis management organization and a specific stakeholder group is what Acquier et al. (2008) call an *anchorage point*.

## APPENDIX

## Questions

1.  Suppose that the headline of an opinion article reads: "Down with the crisis communication plan!" What would be meant by this?

2.  How do you ensure that an emergency response organization communicates with the community in a consistent and coherent way?

3.  Explain why Hayes (2007) would characterize an emergency response organization as an *endeavour* rather than as a *force*?

4.  After the typhoon Haiyan struck the Philippines in 2013, Motoo Konishi (World Bank Country Director East Asia and Pacific) stated that "private sector recovery as well as private sector leadership in the recovery of the region is crucial" (The Philippine Star, 27 November 2013). Please explain how this statement can be underpinned.

# Chapter 3
# Networked Operations:
## Taking into Account the Principles of Modular Organizing

**E. J. de Waard**
*Netherlands Defence Academy, The Netherlands*

## ABSTRACT

*Decentralized, peer-to-peer command and control is a key principle of network-centric operations that has received a lot of scholarly attention. So far, robust networking, another principle, has remained rather underexposed in the academic debate. This chapter introduces theory on modular organizing to start a discourse on network robustness from an organizational design perspective. Above all, the chapter makes clear that the level of system decomposition influences the command and control process of composite military structures. When military organizations follow a fine-grained modularization approach, the structure of a task force deployed may become complex, asking for extra coordination mechanisms to achieve syntheses between the many contributing functional organizational components. In addition, it is argued that modularity's principle of near-decomposability has to be incorporated into the available mathematical models on network-centric operations. A point of concern, in this respect, is that the current modeling parameters make no clear distinction between the different types of actors—or nodes—in a military network structure, whereas in reality, technological, organizational, and human actors all live by their own specific rules.*

## INTRODUCTION

Since the mid 90s we have witnessed a change process within most Western militaries to improve organizational responsiveness, which is based upon fine-grained organizational cooperation, supported by the possibilities of modern-day information and communication technology (ICT). The United States and its European allies have respectively introduced Network Centric Warfare (NCW) and Network Enabled Capabilities (NEC) as the underlying concepts of their new doctrines. Both NCW and NEC propagate fundamental changes in the Command and Control (C2) process (Alberts, Garstka, & Stein, 2000). In the current dictionary of military and associated terms C2 is defined as: "The exercise of authority and direction by a properly designated

DOI: 10.4018/978-1-4666-6058-8.ch003

commander over assigned and attached forces in the accomplishment of the mission" (JP 1-02, p.47). Interesting about this definition is its quite traditional commander-centric focus, whereas NCW and NEC strongly broadcast the idea of peer-to-peer decision-making.

An important viewpoint in today's literature on NCW and NEC is that decentralized decision-making can only take shape when military organizations adopt a different type of organizational structure. Where the abovementioned definition makes clear that the paradigm of a centralized and hierarchical structure still dominates military practice, NCW/NEC advocates argue that Mintzberg's (1983) structural typology of the adhocracy better suits network-centric conditions (Alberts & Nissen, 2009). Especially, the ability to exploit network effects is more naturally incorporated into an adhocracy compared to a centralized hierarchy. However, since Mintzberg's adhocracy is a rather broadly defined organizational configuration, the NCW/NEC community has developed a toolkit, known as ELICIT, to translate the general organizational principles of the adhocracy into concrete organizational mechanisms that facilitate a decentralized C2 approach. As the title of Alberts and Hays (2003) book *Power to the Edge* indicates, simulation using the ELICIT toolkit shows that a structure – the edge organization – that avoids pre-assigned leaders and functional grouping offers more agility than the traditional hierarchy (Thunholm, et al., 2009).

Notwithstanding, the ELICIT program primarily concentrates on the relationship between organizational design parameters and decision-making. The connection between robust networking, which is also presented as one of NCW/NEC tenets (Alberts & Hayes, 2003), and specific organization design rules remains largely untouched. While, it could be argued that robust networking entails more than a decentralized, peer-to-peer process of decision-making. Kleindorfer and Wind (2009: 5) state that "A network may be defined mathematically as a set of nodes and arcs that connect specific pairs of these nodes. These interlinked structures serve as conduits for information, human resources and capital, material flows, and associated risks." Based on this definition it could be argued that the ELICIT program only lifts a corner of the networking veil. The principle of avoiding pre-assigned leadership and functional grouping relates to a certain degree to the composition of and interaction between nodes in a network. However, many important aspects of network robustness still remain unanswered. For example, ELICIT argues that functional grouping should be avoided, whereas many military task forces are by nature functionally grouped into specific task domains such as maneuver, combat support, combat service support, command and control, etc. Moreover many major military operations have a multi-national and multi-service character. The organizational dynamics of this reality of intra and inter organizational collaboration has not been explicitly addressed by the ELICIT program. This chapter aims to contribute to bridging this gap by digging into the principles of modular organizing.

The reason for focusing on the variable modular organizing is threefold. First, military transformation literature explicitly mentions modularity as the underlying organizational approach of military task force design (Dandeker, 2003). Second, organization and management theory (OMT) presents 'modular organizing' – or modularity – as a typical organizational design strategy to increase flexibility without jeopardizing operational performance. By using fixed, self-supporting, autonomous organizational modules and by controlling only the required output of these modules, a loosely coupled system is created that can be reconfigured into customized constellations (Sanchez, 2003; Schilling & Steensma, 2001; Worren, Moore, & Cardona, 2002). Third, as yet the military network modeling community makes no clear distinction between the different types of nodes in a network. Available insights from OMT on organizational modularity could offer some valuable preconditions for the modeling of military units within contemporary network-centric military task force structures.

This chapter is structured as follows. The first section discusses the theoretical underpinnings of modular organizing and relates these insights to current military deployment approaches and developments in the C2 domain. Based on modularity's key principle of near-decomposability, the second section contributes to the ruling debate on modeling parameters of NCW/NEC oriented doctrines. The final section concludes the chapter. This section also introduces avenues for further research and adds a brief summary of the limitations of this chapter's findings.

## BACKGROUND

Given the volatility of today's business environment, ambidexterity is according to OMT an important organizational quality to invest in (O'Reilly & Tushman, 2008). In short, ambidexterity means two-headedness in a sense that organizations should deliberately activate search activities to stimulate innovation and renewal while at the same time capabilities are needed that help to safeguard organizational alignment and stability (Benner & Tushman, 2003; He & Wong, 2004; Rivkin & Siggelkow, 2003). Modular organizing has emerged as a contemporary design approach facilitating ambidexterity.

### The Rules of Modular Design

Table 1 gives some definitions of modularity. All definitions stress that modularity is about independent or autonomous subsystems functioning together. According to Baldwin and Clark (1997) an ideal modular system relies on visible design rules and hidden design parameters. The latter refers to the autonomy of a subsystem or module. A module can be seen as a black box. Except for the restriction that its output has to comply with the general rules or specifications of the overall

system, the subsystem is entirely free in its own design. As Brusoni (2005: 1886) puts it "each module, at the extreme, could become the sole business of a specialist firm, which would have complete design authority over the specific module on which it focuses." In contrast with the hidden design parameters the visible design rules do affect subsequent design decisions. The design rules deal with the process of integrating the autonomous subsystems into a system that functions as a whole. It is best to determine the visible design rules in an early stage, because they form the backbone of the system's overall performance. Imperfect or incomplete modularization will only show at the end of the process after the modules have been connected.

Baldwin and Clark (1997) split the visible design rules into three categories: architecture, interfaces, and standards. The architecture specifies which modules will be part of the system and what their functions will be. Modularity theorists base their thinking in this area primarily on Simon's (1962) work on the architecture of complexity. Simon sees all complex systems –biological, technical, or social- as hierarchically nested entities. He explains that each system is composed of interrelated finer subsystems, which in turn consist of finer subsystems themselves, and so on until ultimately the level of elementary particles is reached. The architectural challenge in modular design is to find a structure that yields the best system decomposition, meaning to set the boundaries in such a way that interdependencies between subsystems are minimized and the system can almost be cleanly decomposed (Langlois, 2002).

Interfaces describe in detail how the modules will interact, including how they will fit together and communicate. The general aim is to reach a plug-and-play situation, in which modules can be clicked together, removed, replaced, and reconnected fairly easy by using standardized interfaces. This is where the contrast between traditional engineering and the modular approach comes to light. The traditional design methodology is char-

*Table 1. Definitions of modularity*

| Author | Definition |
|---|---|
| Sanchez & Mahoney (1996: 65) | *"Modularity is a special form of design which intentionally creates a high degree of independence or 'loose coupling' between component designs by standardizing component interface specifications."* |
| Baldwin & Clark (1997: 84) | *"Modularity is building a complex product or process from smaller subsystems that can be designed independently yet function together as a whole."* |
| Schilling (2000: 312) | *"Modularity is a general systems concept: it is a continuum describing the degree to which a system's components can be separated and recombined, and it refers both to the tightness of coupling between components and the degree to which the "rules" of the system architecture enable (or prohibit) the mixing and matching of components."* |
| Langlois (2002: 19) | *"Modularity is a very general set of principles for managing complexity. By breaking up a complex system into discrete pieces – which can than communicate with one another only through standardized interfaces within a standardized structure- one can eliminate what would otherwise be an unmanageable spaghetti tangle of systematic interconnections."* |

acterized by highly integrated and tightly coupled component designs. Sanchez and Mahoney (1996) state that traditional, tightly coupled component designs require intensive managerial coordination, since a change in the design of one component is likely to require extensive compensating changes in the design of many interrelated components. Unlike traditional engineering the modular approach specifically aims at minimizing the costs for coordinating. To be more concrete, Sanchez and Mahoney (1996: 65) explain that modularity "is a special form of design which intentionally creates a high degree of independence or 'loose coupling' between component designs by standardizing component interface specifications." Basically, by controlling only the required output of components, effective coordination can be achieved without the continual exercise of managerial authority.

Standards are for testing a module's conformity to the design rules and for measuring one module's performance relative to another. Their function is to counterbalance the performance advantages of synergistic specificity. Synergistic specificity has to do with the fact that some combinations of components function better together than other configurations, leading the system away from modularity and towards more integration. The move from stand-alone software products (e.g. Word Perfect and Excel) to integrated software packages (e.g. Microsoft Office) is a good example of this phenomenon (Schilling, 2000). Where an integrated system might achieve functionalities unobtainable through the combination of more independent components, the standardization process creates, what Sanchez and Mahoney (1996) call embedded coordination. In other words, standardization allows the mixing and matching of modules into different configurations and still achieve synthesis. ICT systems can fulfill this connecting role, as well as organizational mechanisms, such as standard operating procedures.

These principles of modularity have been adopted by many industries, mainly because they help to materialize the ruling demand of organizational ambidexterity. In short, the standardized interfaces allow the mixing and matching of independent modules into different constellations. This ease of recombining modules has led to the development of modular value networks between organizations, stimulating innovation and renewal in several ways. For example, it has pushed the invention and application of new technologies, the development of new products, and the upgrading of existing products (Langlois & Robertson, 1992; Loch, Terwiesch, & Thomke, 2001; Sanchez,

1995; Ulrich, 1995; Worren, et al., 2002). Apart from the potential to innovate, modular systems are also capable of obtaining economies of scale (Brusoni & Prencipe, 2006; Langlois, 2000). By relying on self-supporting, autonomous organizational modules specific operational advantages can be obtained, such as the localization of adaptation and trouble, and the reduction of costs for coordination (Orton & Weick, 1990; Weick, 1976). These advantages effectively seem to contribute to organizational efficiency and stability. Without disrupting the overall system, time delays can be absorbed, production sequences can be changed, and new equipment or production devices can be implemented.

## Modularity and Social Systems

Baldwin and Clark's (1997) modular design rules are derived from the development of the IBM System/360 family of mainframe computers. By speaking in terms of rules and parameters, they have adopted a strong 'engineering' approach to modular design. Yet, it is problematic to apply their technical insights coming from modular product design in a social systems' context. In this respect, one of the main causes for concern is that in reality Simon's (1962) concept of near-decomposability is difficult to achieve. Ethiraj and Levinthal (2004: 172) have analyzed modularity and innovation in complex organizational systems, and conclude from their research findings that suitable partitions, capturing the nearly decomposable structure of complex organizational systems, are not self-evident. This leads to situations in which firms end up with an organizational system characterized either by excessive integration or over-refined modularization. The fact that autonomous organizational modules are actually very difficult to create means that more emphasis is placed on the importance of interfaces. So far, modularity theory has primarily focused on the need for compatible technology to stimulate synthesis within inter-organizational value networks (Langlois &

Robertson, 1992). However, it is more and more being acknowledged that, to reach a satisfactory plug-and-play end-state within a modular social systems context, the coupling and de-coupling processes should not only be based on technological compatibility but also on organizational interoperability (Hellström & Wikström, 2005). Various scholars (e.g. Ancona & Caldwell, 1992; Hoegl, Weinkauf, & Gemuenden, 2004; Mohrman, Cohen, & Mohrman, 1995; Sinha & Van de Ven, 2005) have indeed found that in modular collaboration projects task interdependencies lead to situations in which teams become dependent on the input of other teams for the execution of their main tasks. It is common practice for teams to laterally coordinate, to, for example, synchronize technical data and attune activities to meet time schedules and stay within budget. Moreover, many complex modular projects are characterized by high levels of uncertainty, making it necessary to rely on lateral coordination mechanisms to effectively respond to changing or new circumstances.

## Modularity and the Military

Since the last two decades the international security environment has changed considerably. From a relatively stable security environment during the Cold War period Western armed forces are nowadays exposed to all kinds of different threats. Terrorism, the proliferation of NBC weapons and their means of delivery, ethnic and religious rivalry, territorial disputes, the abuse of human rights, the dissolution of states and other risks of a wider nature are security issues the international community currently has to deal with. The call for organizational flexibility has rocketed because of the shift from traditional, large-scale, mechanized operations to unpredictable crisis response deployment.

Within the Western military community modular organizing has become one of the anchor points to boost flexibility. In order to effectively respond to the diverse security environment Western armed forces nowadays configure packets of force that possess a customized range of military elements to meet the particular needs of a specific crisis situation (Dandeker, 2003). It could be argued that creating these tailor-made task forces is the military equivalent of what is taking place in the world of business to simultaneously stimulate renewal and organizational stability. With the modular design philosophy, Western military organizations aim for versatility and unconventional responses, but also try to retain the advantages of relatively fixed structures, such as sections, platoons, companies, and battalions (Bonin & Telford, 2004; De Waard & Kramer, 2008; Schilling & Paparone, 2005). The focus on modularity is strongly based on the hierarchical nested character of military organizations. The fact that military organizations are built upon standardized organizational elements offers the potential to mix and match these structures into various constellations.

## Unit Size

Existing research makes clear that unit size is an important variable for this military customization approach, especially for regular land forces (De Waard & Kramer, 2008). Maneuver brigades, consisting of 2000-2500 combat troops, are the basic operational building blocks of many armies. Using Mintzberg's (1983) terminology, the configuration of these brigades is divisional, which means that they have the capacity to conduct military operations or tasks autonomously. Their autonomy is based on the concept of combined arms, meaning that a fixed combination of combat (infantry, tanks), combat support (artillery, mortars, anti-tank systems, close air support), combat service support (supply, transportation, maintenance, and medical support), and command elements exists.

The maneuver brigades are hierarchically divided into sub-units that also possess all these functional elements, yet in smaller numbers. A brigade can be divided into battalions of approximately 800-1200 soldiers, and a battalion can be split up into companies of approximately 150 soldiers. By this way of organizing land forces have created building blocks that can conduct combat operations, from the operational to the tactical level, rather autonomously. The word 'rather' is used, because the smaller the unit becomes the smaller the combat, combat support, combat service support, and command elements will be. As a result, battalion or company-size units need extra capacity on these functional domains when operating independently for a longer period of time.

Below the company level the concept of combined arms is abandoned. This level is called the technical level and it consists of platoons (approximately 30 soldiers) that are made up of sections (approximately 10 soldiers). Military action materializes at this level and, therefore, platoons and sections can be typified as the land forces' operating core. The technical level relies heavily on unit cohesion based on standardized skills, drills and operating procedures for the execution of tasks. In a hostile and dangerous environment coordination by standardization helps to quickly react to changing circumstances and secures the effectiveness of the reaction itself. To safeguard the added value of this standardization process combat units at the technical level stay complete as much as possible.

## The Netherlands Army

Elaborating on the relationship between modularity, unit size and network robustness De Waard, Volberda, and Soeters (2013a) compare the deployment approaches of the Netherlands Army and the U.S. Army. The Netherlands Army is relatively small in size. To give an idea, the entire Netherlands Army consists of only two mechanized brigades and one air maneuver brigade. As a result, the strategic apex of the Netherlands Army has chosen a fine-grained capacity-driven deployment approach. The standing organization is considered a toolbox consisting of all kinds of modules with specific operational capabilities (De

Waard, Volberda, & Soeters, 2013b). Depending on the task, specific modules can be picked from the permanent organization and grouped into different constellations. Mostly, the largest building block of such a constellation is a maneuver battalion. Until today, because of sustainability issues, a complete army brigade has not been deployed by the Netherlands army. The minimum size of a unit depends on its functional domain. For example, infantry units will not be deployed below company level, whereas engineers can be deployed down to the level of sections. With this approach the Netherlands Army seems to focus on versatility. It offers the organization the potential to structurally adapt to different types of crisis response situations. To a certain extent it also enhances operational innovation, because the fine-grained selection and grouping process makes it possible to execute tasks that reach beyond the limits of traditional military formations and doctrine.

The fact that tailor-made task forces are formed on an ad hoc project basis, for very specific operational assignments, leads to situations in which units and individuals from different parts of the standing organization have to work closely together, without actually knowing each other very well. To overcome this problem the organization relies on three distinctive forms of lateral coordination. First, before actual deployment takes place, the Netherlands Army invests heavily in joint exercises and training programs to transform a tailor-made mixture of different functional units into a well-working machine. Second, additional staff capacity is deployed to take on the task of coordinating the different functional organizational elements. During the SFIR mission in Iraq this task was initially appointed to the battalion commander, as head of the largest unit deployed. The battalion commander, however, became so busy with this coordinating task that he was hindered in his main task of commanding his own battalion. During later rotations the organization therefore decided to also deploy a dedicated command and control element, comparable to a traditional brigade-staff, to take over this coordinating task. Based on the resulting positive experiences, the Netherlands Army now follows this approach in other missions as well. Third, liaison officers (LNOs) are appointed to take care of all kinds of interdepartmental boundary-spanning roles.

This situation confirms that when modularity's demand of near-decomposability is not sufficiently satisfied, a situation may develop in which the number of task-related interdependencies between organizational modules grows too large. Consequently, the organization has to start investing heavily in all kinds of coordination mechanisms to transform the mixture of interrelated organizational components into a functioning overall system. In this respect, De Waard and Kramer (2008) speak of the dilemma of satisfying two contradictory demands simultaneously, namely composition and operational flexibility. They explain that each type of flexibility takes a different approach towards the level of modularization. If the Dutch Armed Forces were only to address the demand of 'composition flexibility', it would be sensible to aim for a platform organization that is build up of a large number of smaller specialized units. This approach creates the opportunity to design a wide variety of task forces, needed to counter the unpredictable security environment. Opposed to that, if the Dutch Armed Forces were only focused on the demand of 'operational flexibility', it would be sensible to design a parent organization built upon a limited number of larger autonomous modules that could be deployed integrally for a specific operation. These integrally designed task forces are in a better position to deal with the challenges of a dynamic complex environment. Because they are fixed units, the preconditions for developing effective ways to coordinate and control their different sub-units, for example by creating an effective system of decentralization, are far better.

## The U.S. Army

Studying the design choices of the U.S. Army, as one of the biggest armies in the world, offers some interesting additional insights into the dynamics of system decomposition and modular organizing. In short, the U.S, Army is grouped into specialized brigades. Yet, where the Netherlands Army makes a distinction between a light air maneuver brigade and two mechanized brigades, it does not have – in comparison to the US Army - the numeric capacity to deploy these large units as a whole. As mentioned earlier the Netherlands Army uses its standing organization as a pool of military capabilities from which units can be picked and grouped into temporary customized task forces. Because of its size (42 active brigade combat teams (BCTs) and 28 national guard BCTs) the US Army does have the luxury to diversify into three distinctive types of brigades that can be deployed autonomously: (1) infantry BCTs, (2) heavy BCTs, and (3) medium 'Stryker' BCTs (Krepinevich, 2002). This subdivision provides the organization with a strong base of structural responsiveness, because the BCTs are tailored in advance for specific terrain and operational circumstances.

Operational performance also seems to benefit from this balance between the basic and the deployment structure. After all, the BCTs not only form the backbone of the permanent organization, they are also the standard unit of action for military operations. As a result, opposed to the Netherlands customization approach, no extra integration mechanisms are needed when these BCTs are deployed. In a RAND Corporation report on the pros and cons of the US Army's modular force structure one of the respondents hails the brigade-centric modular structure by saying that it helps "to maximize unit cohesion through habitual association among combat, combat support, combat service support units, creating relationships of mutual confidence and loyalty within companies, battalions, and brigades, which would, in turn,

make units more effective in combat" (Johnson, Kitchens, Martin, & Fischbach, 2012: 12).

Regarding the relationship between the U.S. Army BCT structure and organizational versatility two different viewpoints emerge. On one hand, because the U.S. Army complies with modularity's basic rule of near-decomposability only, a threshold level of inter- and intra-organizational coordination will occur, making it easier to focus managerial attention to external stimuli, rather than being busy with all kinds of internal adjustment problems. On the other hand, the U.S. Army approach carries the inherent risk of its BCTs becoming too independent and isolated. In this respect, unit size is an important contributing factor. The Netherlands Army follows a fine grained modularization approach, making it possible to create a wide range of organizational configurations out of the large number of available functional units. By contrast, the U.S. Army relies on larger standard building blocks, limiting the mixing and matching potential and thus the ability to offer customized organizational solutions.

## Modularization and Military C2

Although modularity's basic principle of near-decomposability also appears quite relevant for the military C2 process, it has hardly been addressed in the C2 research field up till now. Traditionally, C2 literature strongly relates to Boyd's Observe-Orient-Decide-Act (OODA) loop (Osinga, 2007). This cyclic model is in its most basic form about going through the OODA steps faster than the opponent in order to win. Yet, Osinga argues that Boyd's OODA loop is not only about information superiority and speed, in a broader sense it is perhaps even more about individual and organizational learning and adaptation. A key tenet of the OODA loop is situation awareness (SA), emphasizing that when commanders lose SA, or have none at all, the actions they take will most certainly fail for being based on wrong assumptions. Elaborating on its theoretical underpinnings,

Endsley (1995) argues that system capability is a stimulating or hindering factor in attaining SA. Yet, her actual explanation of system capability is rather basic. When attempting to open this black box, it could be argued that organizational structure probably is an important part of it. This then implies that organizational design choices can either have advantageous or disadvantageous effects on achieving SA. For example, it could be the case that the fine-grained modularization approach of the Netherlands armed forces creates many points of interdependency within a task force. As a result extra effort and time is needed to incorporate all relevant organizational actors into the C2 process. In contrast, one could say that the C2 process benefits from the U.S. Army approach of deploying standardized BCTs, because all relevant actors know each other and have had the opportunity to train together. So far, this relationship between structural complexity and the ease of decision-making has remained underexposed in the current C2 debate.

In addition, it is striking that the ruling C2 doctrine still takes a strong commander-centric view, considering it a process of objectives, task assignments and orders hierarchically cascading down the chain of command. The definition of C2, presented in this chapter's introduction, is a proof of that. Notwithstanding, the centralized character of command & control is increasingly debated, mainly because of the growing complexity of contemporary crisis response missions. Alberts and Nissen (2009) introduce two typical characteristics of today's complex endeavors that have pushed C2 from being commander-centric to more decentralized and less personalized. First, the number and diversity of actors is such that no longer a single chain of command exists. Moreover, the participants often have separate functions and responsibilities, leading to different, and sometimes even conflicting, perceptions of reality. Second, the operational context spans multiple domains, making it difficult to fathom networked cause and effect relationships, and

to predict the outcome of alternative courses of action. Under the title 'power to the edge' they encourage the exploration of new approaches to C2 more suitable for this growing complexity.

Power to the edge refers to a three-dimensional shift in the key variables of the C2 process. First, regarding the allocation of decision rights (ADR) the focus has to shift from a single actor to a collective effort. Second, regarding the patterns of interaction (PoI) a shift has to take place from constrained – highly formalized and tightly managed- to unconstrained. Third, the distribution of information (DoI) needs to develop from a tightly controlled information flow to a situation of widespread information sharing. On the whole, with this three-track shift, armed forces have to transform from autonomous entities that mainly focus on de-conflicting C2 interdependencies with other armed forces, into network actors trying to achieve synergetic situational awareness among all participating organizational elements. Fig. 1 schematically presents this general idea. It could be argued that most Western armed forces have steadily progressed towards coordinated or, at most, collaborative C2 systems. Making the last step is difficult because it implies radically breaking the status quo of old habits and daring to take an unconventional military path of far-reaching decentralization and self-control.

By recognizing that modern-day military deployments are fractal in nature, implicitly, the new power to the edge philosophy touches upon the level of organizational modularization (Alberts & Nissen, 2009). However, this cannot be truly fractal, because organizational modules are incapable of being reduced in granularity all the way down to Simon's (1962) atom while retaining the OODA capabilities that C2 requires. Most crisis response coalitions consist of different military and civilian organizations. Each participating organization has its own team structure, and these teams are then made up of individuals working together. Despite all sorts of differences, such as hierarchical position, expert power, claim on

*Figure 1. C2 approach space (adapted from Alberts & Nissen, 2009: 23)*

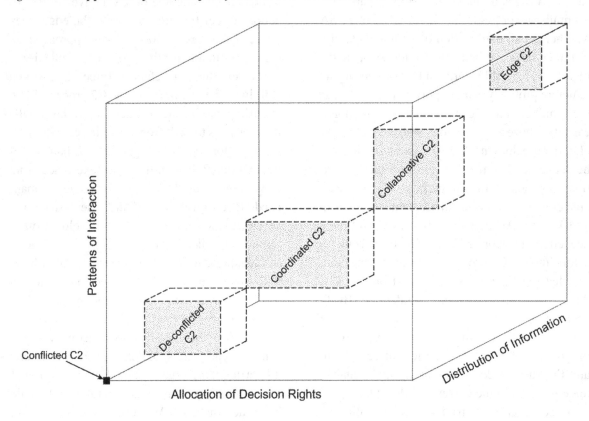

resources, reaction speed, physical location, and technological connectivity, all available organizational granules should be incorporated into the C2 process according to the new paradigm. Basically, a large variety of interconnected organizational elements is perceived as a source of versatility. As yet, the downside of fine-grained granular structures has not received a lot of attention in the debate on future C2 systems. The fact that it creates internal complexity, which most certainly will have a negative impact on the quality of intra- and inter-organization collaboration, deserves more attention.

## MILITARY NETWORK PARAMETERS

In line with the C2 paradigm shift a new generation of military network models that are network-centric has evolved (Deller, Bell, Bowling, Rabadi,

& Tolk, 2009). Inspired by research on networked systems in general, such as social, information, technological, and biological networks, the focal point has been to identify properties that are common to many of these systems, ultimately leading to mathematical rules that mirror those properties. In a broad sense, scientists from different fields describe a network as a set of nodes with connections between them. Yet, the number of nodes in a network, the specific characteristics of nodes in a network, and the interaction patterns between these nodes distinguishes one network from another (Newman, 2003). Based on these general insights Cares (2005) has made a start with identifying the key properties typical of an information age combat model. Three of these parameters modestly touch upon the organizational consequences of modularization.

First, regarding the *number of nodes* (N) the basic assumption is that networks of at least 100 nodes are capable of exploiting important network effects. Specifying a lower boundary in only numerical terms seems to comply with the ruling C2 argumentation that the number of network entities and the number of operational responses are positively related. However, just like NCW theorists this modeling rule makes no distinction between organizational and other types of nodes in a military network. Meaning that nodes in a mathematical model can be military units (e.g. HQ, infantry unit), as well technological assets (e.g. satellite, unmanned vehicle, submarine) but also individual persons (e.g. forward air controller, special forces agent). The fact that these different types of nodes live by different types of rules certainly deserves more attention. Especially from an OMT perspective it is worth investigating the specific characteristics of different types of organizational nodes and their interrelationships within a military task force structure.

Second, the *link to node ratio* (*l/N*) is presented as an important attribute of network-centric operations. The link to node ratio is based on the supposition that maximally connected networks needlessly incur extreme overhead. This has resulted in a specific rule, saying that complex networks should have about two links per node. Relating this parameter and its underlying rule to OMT offers a dual picture. On one hand, the belief that maximally connected networks need integration devices to counterbalance network complexity is supported. After all, available evidence indicates that additional staff capacity and training programs are necessary tools to transform a fine-grained, functionally-grouped military task force into a well-working machine. On the other hand, making a general rule for all nodes in a network –organizational, technological, or human- seems a bit too easy. It could be the case that the risk of excessive overhead is of primary concern when the number of task interdependencies between organizational nodes becomes too large. For technological nodes that rely on IT systems, such as computers, routers and transmitters, the capacity to efficiently process information is probably much better. This implies that different types of nodes ask for different rule-sets.

The third parameter, *degree distribution*, to some extent counters this critique, emphasizing that the total number of links should not be evenly distributed throughout a network. A skewed distribution is proposed, assuming that there are a very small number of highly connected nodes, a moderate number of moderately connected notes, and a very large number of minimally connected nodes. The rule of skewed distribution basically suggests that nodes in a network can play different roles. For example, some nodes act as central hubs, absorbing and transmitting information from and to a really large number of network entities. Many of the nodes merely pass through information to fixed neighbors or are at the end of the line only receiving information. Of course, all kinds of situations in between can also occur. With this rule a more realistic picture can be developed on how a military network functions. It is obvious that for example an HQ plays a central role in a military operation, whereas an infantry platoon conducting a routine patrol is in a more marginal C2 position. The same applies to technological nodes. A satellite, for example, is a key sensor in a military network. Front-level units rely on it for navigation, intra- and inter-organizational communication depends on it, and senior commanders use satellite footage and weather forecasts to plan their operations. Many of the other technological sensors are most likely of lesser importance. So the reality of hierarchical and other sorts of power differences between organizational nodes has to a certain extent been captured in the rule of skewed distribution.

Although, compared with the traditional combat models enormous progress has been made, the parameters discussed above still paint a very rough organizational picture of what actually happens in a complex task force structure. In line with Whelan (2012) it could be concluded that many relevant organizational dynamics still remain underexposed in the development of mathematical rules for network effectiveness. The main point of concern is that neither clear distinctions are made between the different types of nodes in a network nor the different types of relationships between the nodes are untangled. Yet, it is plausible that organizational, technological, and human nodes live by different sets of rules. This situation is problematic because available OMT insights make clear that the characteristics of an organizational element can have a profound effect on the smoothness of cooperation within a network. Especially an excessive level of modularization, which leads to a large number of small organizational granules in a network, can lead to internal complexity. Because no clear difference is made between organizational and technological nodes the modeling exercise becomes equivocal from an OMT perspective.

One side of the coin is captured in the first parameter –*number of nodes*-, which assumes that when the number of nodes in a network increases network effectiveness will rise (Alberts, et al., 2000). This is clearly in contrast with OMT insights indicating that a growing number of nodes leads to an increase in network complexity. The mainstream OMT viewpoint is that the relationship between the number of organizational elements in a network and network effectiveness is curvilinear. In other words, a tipping point exists where adding extra organizational parts to a network becomes dysfunctional. The optimal size of a network is difficult to specify, because different contingency factors have to be taken into account. Bigger is better is certainly not propagated (Provan & Kenis, 2007).

The other side of the coin is addressed with the *link to node* parameter, which does take into account the negative effects of network complexity. This parameter diagnoses network complexity as problematic when the average number of links per node in a network becomes too large. In this case, it is not the number of nodes in a network that leads to internal complexity, but the number of interactions between them. The link to node rule strongly complies with modularity's rule of near-decomposability, which OMT defines as breaking up the system in separate modules, whereas the interactions among the modules are weak but not negligible (Simon, 1962). However, from an OMT perspective it could be argued that parameter 2 loses much of its power, because parameter 3 – *degree distribution*- proposes a randomly skewed distribution of interactions between the nodes, based on the total number of network linkages ($l=2N$). That a skewed distribution of interactions is to be expected in a network-setting is not debated, but it is the randomness of this rule that weakens it. This again brings to the surface the importance of discriminating between different types of nodes and interactions in a network. For example, one way to deal with internal network complexity in military operations is implementing an ICT system that supports the development of a common operational picture (COP). To be more specific, a map of the area of operations is created on which real time relevant information can be uploaded. This map is accessible to many of the military actors and units taking part in an operation. In a way a COP is a means to easily interconnect a large number of organizational entities, without having the need to maintain a large number of dyadic linkages. This makes clear that certain technological nodes exist that are specifically designed to help coordinating a large number of organizational nodes and individuals. For modeling purposes it would be interesting to further analyze if such a COP is indeed a useful mechanism to counterbalance the organizational drawbacks of far-reaching organizational decomposition.

## FUTURE RESEARCH DIRECTIONS

Apart from the lessons drawn from modularity theory, adjacent OMT insights may be of value too and deserve attention from the military C2 and modeling communities. First, the topic of centralization versus decentralization is useful to discuss in more detail from an OMT perspective. With introducing the hybrid form, that takes a center position between the traditional hierarchy and the edge organization, the ELICIT program recognizes that centralization versus decentralization is not an either/or decision (Thunholm, et al., 2009). Although decentralization is an important attribute of network-centric operations, a certain level of centralized coordination is also deemed crucial to counter the multi-dimensional complexity of most of today's military operations. To investigate this challenge, of both centralizing without walking into the trap of micro-management, and de-centralizing without losing control, studying Mintzberg's (1983) typologies is not enough. More recent and concrete OMT studies have to be taken into account as well. For example, one could think of Siggelkow and Levinthal (2003), who conducted a simulation study on the balancing-act of centralization and decentralization. They conclude that pursuing a sequential approach is the best way to go, stating: "In environments that experience a series of shocks over time [.....] firms might cycle through different organizational structures, pulsating back and forth between decentralization to ignite new search, and centralization, to increase coordination" (2003: 665).

This idea of temporary decentralization followed by reintegration is valuable for the military context as well. To start with, most military operations are long-term endeavors, covering years rather than months. As a result, a rotation system, where fresh troops relieve their predecessors, is quite common. Much valuable operational information and knowledge can get lost when the hand-over/take-over process is not properly organized. A centralized intervention can avoid that such a knowledge gap develops. Next, as mentioned earlier, during deployment staff elements play a crucial coordinating role. A realistic problem is, however, that a far-reaching level of modularization creates such a tightly coupled complex organizational system that all staff effort has to be concentrated on de-conflicting the activities of individual network players. This situation is cap-

tured in parameter 2, assuming that many linkages between nodes in a network creates overhead. Yet, the added-value of a centralized staff structure is not made explicit in the parameters in any way. The positive influence a staff element can have on improving the situational awareness of the network as a whole, certainly has to be addressed in the mathematical models as well.

In addition, it is also useful to take notice of work from Topper and Carley (1999). In a number of emergency management case studies they found that many crisis organizations started as a small, pre-existing centralized group. This group kept its leading position throughout the crisis response effort. At the same time, however, several groups of stakeholder organizations emerged and submerged on the periphery of the standing organization, leading to a combined distributed and centralized response. This evolving organizational systems resembles Weick's (2004) concept of the skeleton organization. In short, Weick warns for the risk of over-designing organizations. He states: "If managers need to understand and coordinate variability, complexity, and effectiveness, then they need to create designs that mix together perceptual and conceptual modes of action or move back and forth between these modes or rely on multiple compounding of abstraction. Designs that fit these requirements are best achieved if design is recast as designing that uses transient constructs, bricolage, and improvisation" (Weick, 2004: 47). For the military network modeling community this may be a troubling statement, because it implies that defining general rules to forecast network performance is not the best way to go. It also makes clear that achieving desired effects, such as taking initiative, improvising, and self-organizing will only take place in organizational systems that are underspecified and left incomplete. At the same time, it could also be argued that the modeling community could play an important role in helping to determine the skeleton structure. After all, if a robust military skeleton network can be designed, the decentralized, peer-to-peer interaction processes will indirectly be facilitated.

The OMT discussion on subgroup isolation and intergroup connectivity appears to be an interesting second topic for the military domain. In a simulation study Fang, Lee, and Schilling (2010) differentiate between a nearly isolated subgroup structure, a semi-isolated subgroup structure, and a structure without subgroup identity. Fig. 2 shows these different forms. An interesting parallel can be drawn with the different deployment approaches of the U.S. Army and the Netherlands Army discussed earlier in this chapter. It could be argued that the U.S. Army has created a nearly isolated subgroup structure (a) with its brigade-centric organizational design. Opposed to that, the fine-grained modularization approach of the Netherlands Army has resulted in a task force structure that takes a position in between (b) and (c). On one hand identifiable subgroups are present (such as infantry, medical, and logistical units), on the other hand ad-hoc structures and individuals are also part of the task force (such as Civil-Military-Cooperation specialists, Foreign Affairs representatives, explosives specialists, Air Force and other liaisons).

Fang et al. (2010) have found that a semi-decomposable structure with a moderate level of task interdependency performs better than fully decomposed or fine-grained organizational structures that have either hardly any cross-group linkages or a large number of such linkages. What makes their findings even more interesting is that semi-decomposable structures yield the best long-term learning outcome under varying levels of problem complexity and environmental turbulence, mainly because these partly decomposed structures are best suited to transferring diverse ideas across organizational boundaries. These results corroborate with what has been discussed before in relation to the U.S. and Netherlands Army. Summarizing, regarding the U.S. Army deployment approach it was argued that the risk of designing units that may become too independent and isolated is prevalent. One of the key merits of the fine-grained mixing and matching strategy

of the Netherlands army was that it has boosted the organization's ability gain knowledge and keep learning.

Interesting would be to relate these insights on subgroup structures to modeling parameter 1. If the military community keeps looking at a military network structure as just an enormous set of nodes that need to be linked, important additional dynamics are missed out. In a network that purely consists of technological nodes a structure without subgroup identity, perhaps, does not have to be problematic. Yet, when a network is dominated by organizational elements that have to work efficiently together, only concentrating on the number of nodes could create a false sense of reality.

Third, the effect of structural holes (i.e. the absence of a link between the nodes B and C that are both linked to node A) in organizational networks is also worth further elaborating on. So far, the focus of the military C2 and network modeling community has been on determining the most effective military network structure, identifying all relevant nodes or agents involved. Moreover, one of the key assumptions within the NCW community is that the effectiveness of a networks will rise if number of actors increases (Alberts, et al., 2000). The combat modeling community does not agree with this viewpoint. The ruling opinion in this field of study is that a skewed distribution of interactions is more realistic, in which a small group of nodes has many interactions with other nodes, a moderate group of nodes has a moderate amount of interactions, and a large group of nodes has very limited interactions. The general idea of structural holes is to deliberately create disconnections in a network and invest in cooperation with 'non-redundant' partners to improve innovation in an organizational network (Burt, 1992). This not only implies that striving for a maximum number of connections is a suboptimal solution for a network structure. It also entails that, apart from a skewed distribution, a network should also have a type of design that accommodates struc-

*Figure 2. Subgroup identity (adapted from Fang et al., 2010: 630). Network (a) decomposable structure, (b) semi-decomposable structure, (c) fine-grained structure*

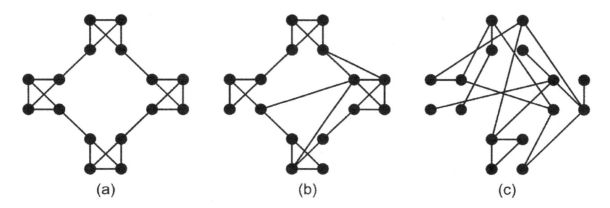

(a)              (b)             (c)

tural holes. A possible structure, derived from the work of Ahuja (2000: 449) and Burt (1992: 20) is presented in Fig. 3, where structural holes can be found between N10-11-12, and N13-15-16. It could even be argued that this structure has the potential to incorporate the issues of temporary centralization and semi-isolated subgroups discussed above.

Notwithstanding, it has to be taken into account that the structural holes theory is primarily about stimulating innovation, and military networks are above all focused on quick and decisive maneuvering. Therefore, creating disconnections and non-redundancy should only happen sporadically and be specifically aimed at unique actors to generate new knowledge, from which the network as a whole can operationally benefit. In this regard, De Waard, Volberda, and Soeters (2012) argue that relying on fixed military partners is a logical response of many Western armed forces to the unpredictability and hostility of most operational environments. At the same time this approach fosters rigidity, because standard collaboration configurations may be inappropriate for new conditions. Non-redundancy means in this regard that partners –military or non-military- have to be incorporated into the network that are new and offer distinctive capabilities or knowledge. This, basically, suggests that also the existence of new

players contributes to the power of a network. It would be interesting to investigate how this structural holes assumption could be translated into a modeling rule. Empirically a lot can be learned from the recent missions in Iraq and Afghanistan. During these missions cooperation with unfamiliar partners became part of the counter insurgency solution. One could think of NGO's, local contractors, private military corporations, judicial specialists, and police trainers. Questions like how these new partners were linked to the military network and what influence they had, may be a useful starting point.

A worthwhile and more applied academic exercise to conduct anyhow, would be to analyze in hindsight actual military deployments in terms of number and sorts of nodes involved. This could offer a better picture of how many organizational, technological, and human nodes on average take part in a complex military endeavor. It could also help to gain insight into the dominant interaction patterns within military network structures, and the distribution of interactions between the different types of participating nodes. Based on this information it becomes easier to apply mathematical modeling rules more precisely. Think of modularity's near-decomposability rule that is probably only applicable to a certain number of operational organizational elements. Undoubtedly,

*Figure 3. Structural holes (adapted from Ahuja, 2000; Burt, 1992)*

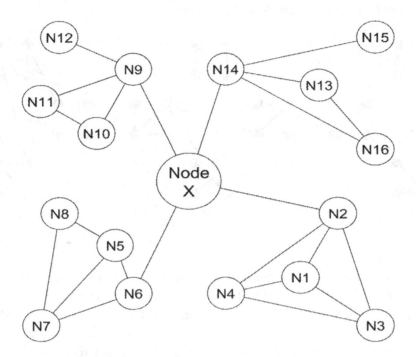

staff departments, individual agents, and technological systems in a network have to be captured in other mathematical equations. Moreover the randomness of, for example degree distribution, could be replaced by more pinpoint rules. Certain identifiable organizational, technological and human nodes in a military network will most likely have thick interaction patterns, while other specific nodes can be typified as minimally or moderately connected. For the best result of such an analysis a combined effort of military practitioners, C2 and network modeling specialists, and OMT scholars is preferable.

## CONCLUSION

On the whole, the goal of this chapter has been to enrich the ruling debate on military C2 and network modeling with OMT insights on modular organizing. Recapitulating, it could be concluded that this has been a worthwhile path to travel. One of the

key lessons to draw is that by only concentrating on the relationship between the numbers of nodes in a network and network effectiveness, important organizational aspects remain underexposed. To be more specific, this chapter has introduced modularity's rule of near-decomposability as an important organizational design parameter that deserves a more prominent position in the military command and control debate. Since most of today's crisis response operations are conducted by complex organizational systems, composed of military units from different arms, services, and countries, intra- and inter organizational collaboration has become a key attribute of network performance. If military organizations follow a fine-grained modular deployment approach, they should be aware of the fact that the internal complexity of the organizational system increases.

This chapter has used insights from the commercial business domain on organizational modularity. Applying this knowledge to a very specific topic, namely C2 in military networks, is debatable. After all, military organizations are not like any other organization. They have typical characteristics, in peacetime as well as during operations, that set them aside from others (Soeters, Van Fenema, & Beeres, 2010). This could imply that design solutions that work in a business setting do not necessarily have to be successful in a military context. For example, creating disconnections and non-redundancy may be beneficial to commercial organizations because it stimulates innovation. Yet, for a military task force this could be a risky strategy, increasing the vulnerability of the network to enemy attack. With this in mind, the reader should realize that introducing general modularity theory is just the first step to start a new discourse on the drivers of network robustness in contemporary military operations. Of course, this step has to be followed by empirical research, investigating whether or not these OMT insights are indeed useful for military organizations and networks.

Finally, to make progress on unraveling the key organizational foundations of command and control in a contemporary military context this chapter has suggested three directions for future research. First, it is important to take notice of recent OMT insights on the balancing-act of centralization and decentralization. Second, the OMT research stream on subgroup isolation and intergroup connectivity seems to be advantageous for the military domain as well. Third, the added value of structural holes in organizational networks is also worth further investigating from a military task force perspective.

## REFERENCES

Ahuja, G. (2000). Collaboration Networks, Structural Holes, and Innovation: A Longitudinal Study. *Administrative Science Quarterly, 45*(3), 425–455. doi:10.2307/2667105

Alberts, D. S., Garstka, J. J., & Stein, F. P. (2000). *Network Centric Warfare: Developing and Leveraging Information Superiority*. Washington, DC: CCRP Publication Series.

Alberts, D. S., & Hayes, R. E. (2003). *Power to the Edge: Command...Control...in the Information Age*. Washington, DC: CCRP Publication Series.

Alberts, D. S., & Nissen, H. E. (2009). Toward Harmonizing Command and Control with Organization and Management Theory. *The International C2 Journal, 3*(2), 1-59.

Ancona, D. G., & Caldwell, D. F. (1992). Bridging the boundary: External activity and performance in organizational teams. *Administrative Science Quarterly, 37*, 634–665. doi:10.2307/2393475

Baldwin, C. Y., & Clark, K. B. (1997, September-October). Managing in an Age of Modularity. *Harvard Business Review*, 84–93. PMID:10170333

Benner, M. J., & Tushman, M. L. (2003). Exploitation, Exploration, and Process Management: The Productivity Dilemma Revisited. *Academy of Management Review, 28*(2), 238–256.

Bonin, J. A., & Telford, E. C. J. (2004, March-April). The Modular Army. *Military Review*, 21–27.

Brusoni, S. (2005). The Limits to Specialization: Problem Solving and Coordination in 'Modular Networks'. *Organization Studies, 26*(12), 1885–1907. doi:10.1177/0170840605059161

Brusoni, S., & Prencipe, A. (2006). Making Design Rules: A Multidomain Perspective. *Organization Science, 17*(2), 179–189. doi:10.1287/orsc.1060.0180

Burt, R. S. (1992). *Structural holes: The social structure of competition*. Cambridge, MA: Harvard University Press.

Cares, J. (2005). Distributed Networked Operations: The Foundations of Network Centric Warfare. Lincoln, NE: iUniverse.

Dandeker, C. (2003). Building Flexible Forces in the 21st Century. In G. Caforio (Ed.), *Handbook of the Sociology of the Military* (pp. 405–416). New York: Kluwer.

De Waard, E. J., & Kramer, F. J. (2008). Tailored task forces: Temporary organizations and modularity. *International Journal of Project Management*, 26(5), 537–546. doi:10.1016/j.ijproman.2008.05.007

De Waard, E. J., Volberda, H. W., & Soeters, J. (2012). How to Support Sensing Capabilities in Highly Volatile Situations. *Journal of Management & Organization*, 18(6), 774–794. doi:10.5172/jmo.2012.18.6.774

De Waard, E. J., Volberda, H. W., & Soeters, J. (2013a). Drivers of Organizational Responsiveness: Experiences of a Military Crisis Response Organization. *Journal of Organization Design*, 2(2), 1–13.

De Waard, E. J., Volberda, H. W., & Soeters, J. (2013b). Engaging Environmental Turbulence: Drivers of Organizational Flexibility in the Armed Forces. *European Security*. doi:10.1080/09662839.2013.822367

Deller, S., Bell, M. I., Bowling, S. R., Rabadi, G. A., & Tolk, A. (2009). Applying the Information Age Combat Model: Quantitative Analysis of Network Centric Operations. *The International C2 Journal, 3*(1), 1-25.

Endsley, M. R. (1995). A Taxonomy of Situation Awareness Errors. In R. Fuller, N. Johnston, & N. McDonald (Eds.), *Human Factors in Aviation Operations*. Aldershot, UK: Ashgate Publishing Ltd.

Ethiraj, S. K., & Levinthal, D. A. (2004). Modularity and Innovation in Complex Systems. *Management Science, 50*(2), 159–173. doi:10.1287/mnsc.1030.0145

Fang, C., Lee, J., & Schilling, M. A. (2010). Balancing Exploration and Exploitation Through Structural Design: The Isolation of Subgroups and Organizational Learning. *Organization Science*, 21(3), 625–642. doi:10.1287/orsc.1090.0468

He, Z. L., & Wong, P. K. (2004). Exploration vs. Exploitation: An Empirical Test of the Ambidexterity Hypothesis. *Organization Science*, 15(4), 481–494. doi:10.1287/orsc.1040.0078

Hellström, M., & Wikström, K. (2005). Project Business Concepts Based on Modularity - Improved Manoeuvrability Through Unstable Structures. *International Journal of Project Management*, 23, 392–397. doi:10.1016/j.ijproman.2005.01.007

Hoegl, M., Weinkauf, K., & Gemuenden, H. G. (2004). Interteam Coordination, Project Commitment, and Teamwork in Multiteam R&D Projects: A Longitudinal Study. *Organization Science*, 15(1), 38–55. doi:10.1287/orsc.1030.0053

Johnson, S. E. P. J.E., Kitchens, K. E., Martin, A., & Fischbach, J. R. (2012). A Review of the Army's Modular Force Structure. RAND National Defense Research Institute.

Kleindorfer, P. R., & Wind, Y. (2009). The Network Imperative: Community or Contagion? In P. R. Kleindorfer, & Y. Wind (Eds.), *The Network Challenge: Strategy, Profit, and Risk in an Interlinked World*. Upper Saddle River, NJ: Wharton School Publishing.

Krepinevich, A. F. (2002). The Army and Land Warfare: Transforming the Legions. *Joint Force Quarterly,* (32), 76-82.

Langlois, R. N. (2000). Capabilities and Vertical Disintegration in Process Technology: The Case of Semiconductor Fabrication Equipment. In N. J. Foss, & P. L. Robertson (Eds.), *Resources, Technology, and Strategy*. London: Routledge.

Langlois, R. N. (2002). Modularity in Technology and Organization. *Journal of Economic Behavior & Organization, 49*(1), 19–37. doi:10.1016/S0167-2681(02)00056-2

Langlois, R. N., & Robertson, P. L. (1992). Networks and Innovation in a Modular System: Lessons From the Microcomputer and Stereo Component Industries. *Research Policy, 21*, 297–313. doi:10.1016/0048-7333(92)90030-8

Loch, C. H., Terwiesch, C., & Thomke, S. (2001). Parallel and Sequential Testing of Design Alternatives. *Management Science, 45*(5), 663–678. doi:10.1287/mnsc.47.5.663.10480

Mintzberg, H. (1983). *Structure in fives: designing effective organizations*. Englewood Cliffs, NJ: Prentice-Hall.

Mohrman, S. A., Cohen, S. G., & Mohrman, A. M. (1995). *Designing Team-Based Organizations: New Forms of Knowledge Work*. San Francisco, CA: Jossey-Bass Publishers.

Newman, M. E. J. (2003). The Structure and Function of Complex Networks. *SIAM Review, 45*(2), 167–256. doi:10.1137/S003614450342480

O'Reilly, C. A., & Tushman, M. L. (2008). Ambidexterity as a Dynamic Capability: Resolving the Innovator's Dilemma. *Research in Organizational Behavior, 28*, 185–206. doi:10.1016/j.riob.2008.06.002

Orton, J. D., & Weick, K. E. (1990). Loosely Coupled Systems: A Reconceptualization. *Academy of Management Review, 15*(2), 203–223.

Osinga, F. (2007). *Science, Strategy and War: The Strategic Theory of John Boyd*. London: Routledge.

Provan, K. G., & Kenis, P. (2007). Modes of Network Governance: Structure, Management, and Effectiveness. *Journal of Public Administration: Research and Theory, 18*(2), 229–252. doi:10.1093/jopart/mum015

Rivkin, J. W., & Siggelkow, N. (2003). Balancing Search and Stability: Interdependencies Among Elements of Organizational Design. *Management Science, 49*(3), 290–311. doi:10.1287/mnsc.49.3.290.12740

Sanchez, R. (1995). Strategic Flexibility in Product Competition. *Strategic Management Journal, 16*, 135–159. doi:10.1002/smj.4250160921

Sanchez, R. (2003). Commentary. In R. Garud, A. Kumaraswamy, & R. N. Langlois (Eds.), *Managing in the Modular Age*. Malden, MA: Blackwell Publishers.

Sanchez, R., & Mahoney, J. T. (1996). Modularity, Flexibility, and Knowledge Management in Product and Organization Design. *Strategic Management Journal, 17*, 77–91.

Schilling, M. A. (2000). Toward a General Modular Systems Theory and its Application to Interfirm Product Modularity. *Academy of Management Review, 25*(2), 312–334.

Schilling, M. A., & Paparone, C. R. (2005, August-November). Modularity: An Application of General Systems Theory to Military Force Development. *Defense Acquisition Review Journal*, 278-293.

Schilling, M. A., & Steensma, H. K. (2001). The Use of Modular Organizational Forms: An Industry-Level Analysis. *Academy of Management Journal, 44*(6), 1149–1168. doi:10.2307/3069394

Siggelkow, N., & Levinthal, D. A. (2003). Temporarily Divide and Conquer: Centralized, Decentralized, and Reintegrated Organizational Approaches to Exploration and Adaption. *Organization Science*, *14*(6), 650–669. doi:10.1287/orsc.14.6.650.24840

Simon, H. A. (1962). The Architecture of Complexity. *Proceedings of the American Philosophical Society*, *106*(6), 467–482.

Sinha, K. K., & Van de Ven, A. H. (2005). Designing Work Within and Between Organizations. *Organization Science*, *16*(4), 389–408. doi:10.1287/orsc.1050.0130

Soeters, J., Van Fenema, P. C., & Beeres, R. (2010). Introducing Military Organizations. In J. Soeters, P. C. Van Fenema, & R. Beeres (Eds.), *Managing Military Organizations: Theory and Practice*. London: Routledge.

Thunholm, P., Chong, N. E., Cheah, M., Kin Yong, T., Chua, N., & Ching Lian, C. (2009). Exploring Alternative Edge versus Hierarchy C2 Organizations using the ELICIT Platform with Configurable Chat System. *The International C2 Journal*, *3*(2), 1-52.

Topper, C. M., & Carley, K. M. (1999). A Structural Perspective on the Emergence of Network Organizations. *The Journal of Mathematical Sociology*, *24*(1), 67–96. doi:10.1080/0022250X.1999.9990229

Ulrich, K. (1995). The Role of Product Architecture in the Manufacturing Firm. *Research Policy*, *24*(3), 419–440. doi:10.1016/0048-7333(94)00775-3

Weick, K. E. (1976). Educational organizations as loosely coupled systems. *Administrative Science Quarterly*, *21*, 1–19. doi:10.2307/2391875

Weick, K. E. (2004). Rethinking Organizational Design. In R. J. Boland, & F. Collopy (Eds.), *Managing as Designing* (pp. 36–53). Stanford, CA: Stanford University Press.

Whelan, C. (2012). *Networks and National Security: Dynamics, Effectiveness and Organisation*. Surrey, UK: Ashgate Publishing Limited.

Worren, N., Moore, K., & Cardona, P. (2002). Modularity, Strategic Flexibility, and Firm Performance: A Study of the Home Appliance Industry. *Strategic Management Journal*, *23*, 1123–1140. doi:10.1002/smj.276

## ADDITIONAL READING

Beeres, R., Van der Meulen, J., Soeters, J., & Vogelaar, A. (2012). *Mission Uruzgan: Collaborating in Multiple Coalitions for Afghanistan*. Amsterdam: Amsterdam University Press.

Croser, C. (2006). Commanding the Future: Command and Control in a Networked Environment. *Defense & Security Analysis*, *22*(2), 197–202. doi:10.1080/14751790600775470

Ethiraj, S. K., & Levinthal, D. A. (2004). Bounded Rationality and the Search for Organizational Architecture: An Evolutionary Perspective on the Design of Organizations and Their Evolvability. *Administrative Science Quarterly*, *49*, 404–437.

Finkel, M. (2011). *On Flexibility: Recovery from Technological and Doctrinal Surprise on the Battlefield*. Stanford: Stanford University Press.

Huber, G. P. (2004). *The Necessary Nature of Future Firms: Attributes of Survivors in a Changing World*. London: Sage Publications.

Kenis, P., Janowicz-Panjaitan, M., & Cambré, B. (2009). *Temporary Organizations: Prevalence, Logic and Effectiveness*. Cheltenham: Edward Elgar. doi:10.4337/9781849802154

Kramer, F. J. (2007). *Organizing Doubt: Grounded Theory, Army Units and Dealing with Dynamic Complexity*. Copenhagen: Copenhagen Business School Press.

Moon, T. (2007). Net-centric or Networked Military Operations? *Defense & Security Analysis*, *1*(23), 55–67. doi:10.1080/14751790701254474

Moon, T., Fewell, S., & Reynolds, H. (2008). The What, Why, When and How of Interoperability. *Defense & Security Analysis*, *24*(1), 5–17. doi:10.1080/14751790801903178

Raisch, S., & Birkinshaw, J. (2008). Organizational Ambidexterity: Antecedents, Outcomes, and Moderators. *Journal of Management*, *34*(3), 375–409. doi:10.1177/0149206308316058

Ryan, M. (2003). Preparing for Complexity: The Case for an ExpEd.ary Task Force in the Australian Army of 2020. *Australian Army Journal*, *1*(2), 83–94.

Teece, D. J. (2009). *Dynamic Capabilities & Strategic Management: Organizing for Innovation and Growth*. Oxford: Oxford University Press.

Volberda, H. W. (1998). *Building the Flexible Firm: How to Remain Competitive*. Oxford: Oxford University Press.

## KEY TERMS AND DEFINITIONS

**Command and Control (C2):** The exercise of authority and direction by a properly designated commander over assigned and attached forces in the accomplishment of the mission (JP 1-02: 47).

**Modularity:** is building a complex product or process from smaller subsystems that can be designed independently yet function together as a whole (Baldwin and Clark, 1997: 84).

**Near-Decomposable Systems:** Are systems, in which the interactions among the subsystems are weak, but not negligible (Simon, 1962: 474).

**Network:** From an OMT perspective a network may be defined as a set of nodes and arcs that connect specific pairs of these nodes. These interlinked structures serve as conduits for information, human resources and capital, material flows, and associated risks (Kleindorfer and Wind, 2009: 5).

## APPENDIX

## Questions

1. What do modularity theorists mean by hidden design parameters?
2. In which categories can the visible design rules of modularity be split up?
3. What is synergistic specificity?
4. Why is it difficult to apply the visible design rules of modularity to modular organizational systems?
5. What is the key difference, from a modular design perspective, between the deployment approaches of the Netherlands and U.S. Armies?
6. How can military combat models be improved using theory on modular organizing?

# Chapter 4
# Modelling Command and Control in Networks

**E. Jensen**
*Swedish National Defence College, Sweden*

## ABSTRACT

*This chapter proposes an approach to modelling the functions of C2 performed over a network of geographically distributed entities. Any kind of command and control (C2) organisation, hierarchical, networked, or combinations thereof, can be represented with this approach. The chapter also discusses why a theory of C2 needs to be expressed in functions in order to support design and evaluation of C2 systems. The basic principle of how to model functions performed by network is borrowed from Cares' network model of warfare, which is also used to model the context in which C2 is performed. The approach requires that C2 is conceived of as fulfilling a set of necessary and sufficient functions. Brehmer proposes such a theoretical model that is at a sufficiently high level of abstraction to illustrate the suggested approach. More detailed models will be required, however, for the approach to be of practical use.*

## INTRODUCTION

The development in communication technology enables network centric warfare, i.e. geographically dispersed forces (consisting of entities) can share information, coordinate their actions, and act in concert to achieve specific goals (Alberts, Gartska & Stein, 1999). Not only the fighting per se, but also the commanding and controlling of it can be networked, or, in other words, performed collaboratively by a number of C2 entities connected by a network. Depending on the degree of collaboration, these C2 constellations are

considered more or less mature (NATO SAS-065 Research Task Group, 2010).

When reviewing the dominating theoretical models of command and control (C2) at the time, Brehmer (2005) and Grant and Kooter (2005) independently made quite similar observations. They found no theoretical models, networked or not, that could support a systematic design and evaluation of C2 systems. In addition there was, as observed by Pigeau and McCann (2002), little agreement on the definitions of the concepts, i.e., what the terms command, control and C2 referred to.

DOI: 10.4018/978-1-4666-6058-8.ch004

According to Brehmer (2010), there is a need for a general theory of C2 to organize the field, and for a suitable ontological framework. He claims that viewing C2 as a product of design provides such a framework. This places C2 science among what Simon (1996) called "the sciences of the artificial." This approach requires that the theoretical models proposed are models of *functions* (Brehmer, 2008).

In the scientific literature, there are, according to Nagel (1979), two categories of explanations that are referred to as functional explanations:

> *A functional explanation may be sought for a particular act, state, or thing occurring at a stated time…. Or, alternatively, a functional explanation may be given for a feature that is present in all systems of a certain kind, at whatever time such systems may exist. (p. 24)*

Simon (1996) refers to functional explanations of the second kind, when he discusses the science of design. This is also how the concept of function is used in engineering design (e.g., Pahl et al., 2007), and how Brehmer (2013, 2008) uses it.

Defining C2 science as a science of the artificial, or a design science, requires us to acknowledge that C2 systems are artefacts, that they are designed for a purpose. It suggests that C2 systems are probably best understood in terms of the logic that was used to construct them (Brehmer, 2008).

When analysing an artefact according to the logic of design, the system or artefact is considered from three different perspectives. These perspectives make three levels of analysis, hierarchically arranged according to the degree of abstraction. The levels are the system's purpose(s), its function(s) and its form (Brehmer, 2007).

Specifying the *purpose* of a system is to explain *why* the system exists (or needs to be constructed). Specifying the purpose of C2 is akin to defining C2. According to Alberts (2007) this purpose is to achieve focus and convergence of efforts within an organization in order to reach a common goal. Brehmer (2007) uses the terms direction and coordination instead of focus and convergence, but in a fairly similar way.

The next question is: *What* does the C2 system need to be capable of in order to fulfil its purpose? The answer is given by the system's necessary and sufficient *functions*. Functions are defined by their output, what they achieve, not how it is done (that is defined by the form). The set of functions and their relations constitute a theory of what is generally required for successful C2 (Brehmer, 2007). Brehmer suggests that the necessary and sufficient functions are data collection, orientation (or sensemaking in his earlier writings), and planning (Brehmer, 2013, 2007). Other C2 theorists may suggest another set of functions. If theories are to be compared, they need to be developed within the same ontological framework. Theories of C2 functions can only be compared with other theories of C2 functions, and not with theories based on other concepts.

A function may be thought of as an empty box. The box is labelled with what we want the content of the box to accomplish. Consider, as a simple example, an object that we want to split into two halves. The input to the function is the object to be split, and the desired output is two separate objects, i.e. the parts separated by the split. The function (the label on the box) is to split an object in two. Nothing is said about how this is supposed to be done. That is defined at the next level, the level of form.

Splitting an object in two can be done in several ways. It might be cut with scissors, torn apart, or chopped with an axe. These are possible *form* alternatives that might be chosen to fulfil the function of splitting an object in two. Which alternative is the most appropriate depends on the material of the object in question.

Defining the function splitting allows us to discuss splitting in general. It also enables us to compare and discuss splitting under different conditions in various contexts within the theory of splitting. We can, for example, study the output produced by one form under different conditions (i.e. varying the material of the object to be split). We can also study the output produced by different form alternatives under identical conditions (i.e. trying different tools and methods to split identical objects). These are all studies of the phenomenon of splitting. Theoretical models expressed in terms of functions allow us to treat different solutions to similar problems within one common framework.

A C2 system, according to Brehmer (2007) is not only a piece (or even a collection of pieces) of technology. It also consists of the personnel who use the equipment to fulfil the system's purpose, or more specifically the roles they occupy. The functions required for C2 are not fulfilled by simply putting people and equipment into the "function boxes." The personnel and the equipment need to do something to produce the desired output. These *processes* are also part of a C2 system's *form* according to Brehmer (2007).

## Objective and Scope

Brehmer's (2013, 2007) theoretical model of C2 is the only one I know of that is deliberatively created to be a function model. Alberts and Hayes (2006) list what they consider to be the necessary functions for successful C2 (p. 47), but the models they present of C2 do not contain these functions. They present other kinds of C2 models (Alberts & Hayes, 2006). Brehmer's (2013, 2007) model only considers the C2 functions as performed by hierarchically organized C2 entities. These functions may, however, be performed collaboratively by geographically distributed entities connected in a network. In this chapter I suggest a way to model the functions of C2, defined by Brehmer, as fulfilled by networked C2 constellations, and in a model of networked warfare.

My objective is to provide an example of a *functional* model of C2 that can be used to model various network constellations of C2, as well as showing how these networks of C2 functions can be integrated into a network model of warfare.

C2 is a function in a mission system. A mission or task is to be achieved by a specified force, in some context. The function of C2 within the mission system is to direct and coordinate the efforts of the force so that the mission is accomplished. This means that a model of C2 needs to include a representation of the context of these directed and coordinated efforts (Brehmer, 2005).

I have chosen to base my representation in the context of Cares' Information Age Combat Model (2005, 2004). It is a network model of warfare with a basic structure that I build upon and adapt to fit my present purpose.

Tolk (2012) presents Cares' model as an example of a combat model of networked forces that reflects the need for appropriate command and control, as well as communications. He also states that C2 structures other than traditional hierarchies are not well captured in existing combat models. I aim to suggest how this might be remedied.

## Chapter Outline

The chapter begins with a Background section that discusses traditional models of combat and how C2 is typically represented in such models. Brehmer's (2013, 2007) model of C2 and Cares' (2005, 2004) Information Age Combat Model IACM are both presented. This is followed by the main section on the modelling of C2 in networks, illustrated by combining Brehmer's and Cares' work. The IACM is expanded to include C2, the distinction between nodes and function is explained and how they relate to each other. I suggest how the different C2 approaches (NATO SAS-065 Research Task Group, 2010) could be modelled as networks of C2 nodes (or rather sub-nodes) that fulfil the C2 functions. The section ends with a discussion of the potential usefulness of this approach. The chapter closes with some words on future research directions and with concluding remarks.

## BACKGROUND

Combat and warfare are performed by military systems (of various sizes). C2 is part of (a function in) such systems. We therefore start here by looking at models of combat and warfare. The place for C2 within these models will be discussed later in the chapter.

## Models of Duelling Individuals

Boyd's OODA (Observe-Orient-Decide-Act) loop (Boyd, 1987) looks like a simple model of decision making, but was actually developed to analyse the results from dogfights between fighter aircraft. Boyd wanted to explain why American fighter pilots were more successful than their adversaries in the Korean War. This means that even if the OODA loop is mostly referred to as a model of C2, it was actually created as a model of duelling individuals.

In order to model the actual combat, the effects of the fighter interactions need to be represented. There is not much terrain or other contextual factors to consider in the air, but the situation is quite different for soldiers on the ground. Should we wish to model a shooting duel between two army soldiers, we would need to represent the terrain where the duel is fought. The terrain may both be an obstacle and shelter. In simulations of warfare today, the models tend to include effects of the terrain on the modelled entities (and maybe vice versa), and the results from entity-entity encounters (Tolk, 2012).

## Models of Forces

In his later work, Boyd developed the OODA loop into a more general model intended to apply to various forms of combat, and not only one-on-one fighter engagements (see Hammond, 2001). As mentioned above, Boyd's OODA loop mostly covers the decision making aspect of warfare, i.e. command and control, and has become the dominant model of C2. While the original OODA loop can be interpreted as a function model, the adapted version includes other kinds of elements that cannot be viewed as functions.

This kind of model represents *one* C2 entity and the force it commands. The NATO C2 Conceptual Model (Alberts & Hayes, 2006; NATO SAS-050 Research Task Group, 2007) is another example of such a model. Lanchester models (or some more recent alternative) are generally used to represent the *effects* of two forces engaged in combat on each other (Cares, 2005, 2004; MacKay, 2006).

## Models of Several Combatants

We might wish to model combat involving more than two duelling individuals without clustering the people belonging to either side into two fighting units (forces). This is absolutely necessary if we want to model networked forces.

One example of such a model is the Joint Warfare System (JWARS). The basic building blocks in JWARS are called the Battle Space Entities (BSE). BSEs are generally battalions in the case of manoeuvre units, flight groups for air operations, ships for maritime assets, and individual platforms for critical ISR systems (e.g. JSTARS, U2s) (Maxwell, 2000). This means that JWARS in an example of a platform-based model (Cares, 2005, 2004).

## Brehmer's Model of C2

The demand for C2 arises when a goal cannot be obtained by only one, or a few, person(s). The task for C2 is to break down the goal into sub-goals that may be assigned as tasks to be performed by different actors (commanded units).

If the goal is vast, only *one* division into sub-goals may be insufficient. The sub-goals may need to be broken down further in order to be obtainable for the intended actors. This will require C2 at an additional level. This is how C2 hierarchies evolve. The subordinate level is always considered as consisting of activity systems from the perspective of the commanding level, even if these activity systems may contain their own C2 systems, i.e., the next level in the C2 hierarchy. C2 hierarchies are thus hierarchically organized C2 systems.

Brehmer (2007, 2006, 2005) has been inspired by, and retained the simple structure of, the original OODA loop, but he has adapted it to represent the work of a C2 entity rather than the decision process of an individual engaged in a duel. Brehmer includes the effects produced by the military activity in his model, as did Boyd in his generalized OODA loop. C2 is not involved in the acting part of the loop, however. The role of C2 is to make the decisions, and tell the acting parties (the force) what to do. People involved in C2 are rarely able to observe events unfold first-hand, but have to rely on reports and sensor data. Data collection is therefore a more proper term for the information gathering involved in C2. The orientation taking place in C2 is a question of mental orientation rather than orienting oneself physically to engage an opponent. Brehmer (2007, 2006, 2005) has used the term sensemaking in his earlier writings for the task of identifying what needs to be done in order to bring about the desired outcome. In his later work he uses the term orientation instead, but with the same meaning as he previously assigned to sensemaking (Brehmer, 2013). When commanding a force consisting of a large number of acting units, it is not as simple as figuring out what needs to be achieved and then order it done. The commander needs to figure out how this might be achieved by the available force. What units should be assigned which tasks? This means that some planning is required as well, before orders can be given. The orders will eventually lead to some military activity, but they may be broken down further by lower levels of C2 in the hierarchy until the level of movement and fire is reached (Brehmer, 2007).

Brehmer (2013, 2009) has discussed the need to incorporate the demands of the situation into a theoretical model of C2. In a specific situation there will be a mission or task to be achieved by a specified force, in some context, within a limited amount of time. These factors put *demands* on the system (Figure 1.) (See also Jensen, 2012).

As mentioned above, the functions are defined by their output, i.e. what they are supposed to produce or deliver. The constraining factors put different demands on the functions that are required for C2 (Figure 1).

The *data collection* function collects and delivers data. *What* data need to be collected depends on the context of the mission.

The *orientation* function figures out *what* needs to be achieved. It delivers the identified required results, or effects. The demands on the orientation function depend on the nature of the received task. Is it a routine task or is it a complex or unfamiliar task? The latter puts heavier demands on orientation than the former.

The *planning* function determines *how* to obtain the required results with the available force. The product is a decision regarding *who* is to achieve what, expressed in orders to the subordinates. This could be rather tricky if the available force is small, badly equipped, inexperienced and/or exhausted. A large, experienced, well equipped and rested force offers more options, and may also be relied on to figure out the best course of action themselves.

*Time*, finally, is a factor that has to be considered in the fulfilment of all the functions required for C2. There is a limit on how much time they can be allowed altogether.

*Figure 1. The functions of a C2 system, their output, and the factors that put demands on this output*

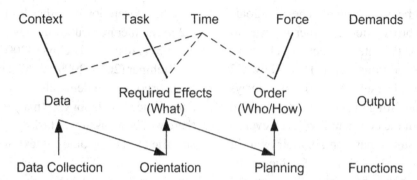

## The Information Age Combat Model

The development in information technology has made it possible to transfer large amounts of data over long distances. This means that a physical entity (platform) does not have to do all the sensing and deciding itself in order to act properly. Other entities may do the sensing and deciding, and then tell the acting entity what to do. Several entities may exchange data to such an extent that they can be said to do the observing for them all collectively. The sensing, observing or data collecting is not done by one single entity or platform, but by a network of entities.

Cares (2005, 2004) introduced the Information Age Combat Model (IACM) to serve as a means to model combat between distributed networked forces. The basic objects of the IACM are not platforms or other entities, but nodes corresponding, or contributing, to the necessary functions.

The IACM offers four types of nodes: sensors, deciders, influencers and targets. Links connect the nodes, and various relations might be modelled as links. *Sensors* make observations of other nodes, and forward the information to deciders. *Deciders* make decisions about the arrangements and actions of other nodes, and inform these nodes of the decisions concerning them. *Influencers* receive directions from deciders and interact with other nodes to affect the state of those nodes. *Targets* are nodes that are valuable and may be damaged

or destroyed by an adversary. All nodes belong to a "side" (e.g., blue, red, friend, foe, neutral, etc.) (Cares, 2005, 2004). A blue sensor (S) may, for example, detect a red target (T) and inform a blue decider (D) of the contact. The decider may then instruct a blue influencer (I) to engage the target (Deller et al., 2009).

The nodes may be defined to belong to an entity or a platform (Cares, 2005, 2004). Figure 2 could be a model of two soldiers engaged in a shooting duel. They are both possible targets that may be detected, or sensed, by their opponent. When they have detected the opponent they may decide to influence the opponent by firing at him or her.

Nodes may be clustered into aggregate nodes. The sensing capacity of all the soldiers and equipment belonging to an army platoon may be combined and represented by one single platoon sensor node. The same goes for the other types of nodes. This means that Figure 2 could also represent combat between two army platoons, or some other aggregates (Cares, 2005, 2004).

## MODELING C2 IN NETWORKS

## Expanding IACM to Include C2

There are deciders at the lowest echelons who can observe events unfold first-hand. They can be the targets of enemy fire, and have their own firing

*Figure 2. Duel between two independent agents*

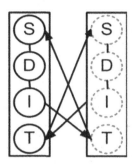

capacity. Their primary task, however, is to direct the efforts of those whom they command, in order to coordinate their united efforts. These deciders do not decide for themselves alone, but for a group. In other words, the deciding function is expanded and turned into a C2 function (Figure 3).

As mentioned above, IACM can also be used to model clusters of entities, such as army battalions. Figure. 4 could then represent the command and control of an army brigade, and the commanded battalions with all their sensing, influencing and C2 capabilities, together with the entities that might be targeted by an opponent.

So far the examples have been fairly traditional hierarchical platform-based models. The only thing I have contributed is to introduce the C2 node in exchange for the decision node where decisions are made for groups of individuals. The information and communication technologies have, however, made possible geographical distribution of the sensing, deciding, and influencing capabilities.

## Nodes and Functions

The IACM suggests that for the purpose of combat (or in the broader sense to produce military effects) a system has to fulfil the four functions of:

1. Sensing what is going on – the output is data;
2. Deciding what to do – the output is decisions;
3. Do as decided (influence the opponent) – the output is actions;
4. Be targeted by opponents – the output is effects (on the system).

The fourth function is one that you would not wish to fulfil, so you would strive to minimize that output.

*Figure 3. C2 at the lowest level of command*

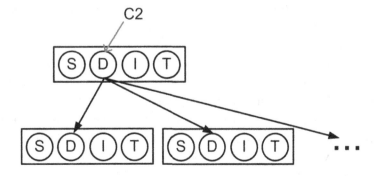

*Figure 4. Battalions and brigade C2*

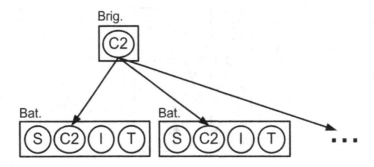

If these functions are all provided by a single platform, or entity, the nodes of that entity would fulfil the functions and the functions and nodes would completely overlap and render either concept superfluous. Combat is, however, no longer entirely platform based. For example, unmanned armed vehicles (UAVs) can be controlled from a distance by deciders, who may, in turn, receive contextual data from sensors (for example spotter planes) that are not mounted on the UAVs. Each spotter plane is a sensor node. But the required sensing function is done by all the involved sensors (spotter planes and other sensors). The nodes are, thus, abstract form elements according to the logic of design.

The functions of C2 can likewise be fulfilled by C2 nodes, and can be broken down into its functions data collection, orientation and planning. These functions can be fulfilled by data collection, orientation and planning nodes.

Sensors detect enemy units (and own, friendly, or neutral units too) and inform the data collection function. Sensors may collect other contextual data as well. Humans can serve as sensors, in which case the data may consist of anything within the range of human perception. The data collection function does not rely exclusively on sensor data. Information is gathered by other means as well such as maps, newspapers and other reading material, and by consulting experts on important subjects. The task or mission is received by the orientation function from the superior level or command. The planning function gives orders to the subordinates

who decide on how to use their influencing capacity to produce the requested effects.

Several entities involved with C2 may pool their data collection resources and freely share the collectively collected data among themselves. If two or more C2 units need to agree on what ought to be done, they could choose to do the orientation together in order to make the best use of their respective forces. They could choose to plan together as well, but then they might be considered as one distributed C2 unit.

## Modelling Different C2 Approaches

This provides a means to model the different C2 approaches identified by NATO SAS-065 Research Task Group (2010). In *conflicted* C2, no information is exchanged between the C2 units (involved organisations). There is no C2 network at all in place.

In *de-conflicted* C2, there is some exchange of data to establish constraints. I would consider this data exchange between data collection nodes belonging to different C2 entities, rather than data collection provided by networked data collection nodes.

In *coordinated* C2, the data exchange is more substantial. There is the question of whether data is gathered collectively in the interest of all involved (data collection (DC) nodes in a network fulfilling one common data collection function), or if every unit collects data mainly for its own purposes (or missions M1, M2, and M3) but is prepared to share

*Figure 5. Coordinated C2*

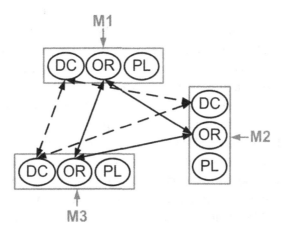

it (connected nodes that each fulfil separate data collection functions, i.e. the data is collected for different purposes) as in Figure 5. The involved C2 entities (or organisations) decide collectively on who is going to strive to achieve what. This means that the orientation function is performed collectively by the orientation (OR) nodes of the contributing C2 entities, while planning (PL) is performed (more or less) separately (Figure 5). The broken lines in Figure 5 represent limited exchange of data, while solid lines represent the function performed collectively by a network of distributed nodes.

In *collaborative* C2, all the functions are performed collectively to accomplish one shared mission (M). This means that there is *one* data collection function fulfilled by a network of interconnected data collection nodes, *one* orientation function fulfilled by a network of interconnected orientation nodes, and *one* planning function fulfilled by a network of interconnected planning nodes (Figure 6).

The edge approach in its extreme is not really a C2 approach. If decision rights are pushed to the very edge of an organisation, i.e. to those performing the actions, there will be a network of communicating deciders rather than a network of C2 entities that command deciders.

A C2 organisation may encompass a mixture of C2 approaches, and of hierarchies and networks.

*Figure 6. Collaborative C2*

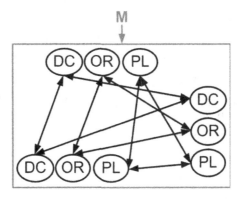

## Discussion

What has been outlined in this chapter is a possible approach to the analysis of C2 in networks. I propose a way to model the functions of C2 performed over a network of geographically distributed entities, whose capabilities are defined as nodes in the network. It allows modelling of all the C2 approaches proposed by NATO SAS-065 (2010). I am not aware of any similar theoretical model of C2 performed by networks, i.e. a theory of necessary and sufficient functions performed by networks, or structures combining hierarchies and networks.

Brehmer's (2013, 2007) theoretical model of C2 consists of only three functions: data collection, orientation, and planning. This is a model at the highest level of abstraction. The functions need to be broken down into sub-functions. We need to identify the sub-functions that are necessary and sufficient for successful data collection. There is so much involved in data collection (or orientation, or planning), that it has to be divided into more manageable chunks to enable a structured analysis. A comprehensive theory of C2 will require sub-theories for the respective C2 functions.

Observations of existing C2 systems may direct the search for these sub-functions. Stanton, Baber, & Harris (2008) present a model of C2 developed bottom-up from observations of communication and products in command teams in a variety of civilian and military contexts. Brehmer (2010) shows that Stanton, Baber, & Harris's (2008) more detailed model corresponds nicely to his own higher level model.

A system requirements analysis is a normative analysis that answers the question: What functions are necessary and what output from these functions is needed to meet the requirements? For a C2 theory to support the design of new C2 systems, it has to explain what the necessary functions are, what output is required to fulfil the system's purpose under different conditions. Identifying what the conditions are that might affect the outcome is also a task for C2 theory.

When designing a system, not only do you need to know what functions it needs to fulfil, you also need to know how these functions are related. This means that a C2 theory should describe the functional structure of a C2 system, i.e. the input-output relations among the functions.

A descriptive study of an existing system answers the question: What functions does the system fulfil, and how well does it fulfil these functions, i.e., what does it produce?

In an assessment of a system's performance, the results from a descriptive analysis are compared to the requirements identified in a normative analysis. The system's performance is assessed function-wise. The form (personnel and equipment) involved in fulfilling one function may fail to produce an output that meets the requirements. The personnel and equipment that are responsible for the functions that rely on this output for input may not be able to compensate for the insufficient input. The performance failure may propagate through the system and cause a sub-standard overall system output. Evaluating the system function-wise facilitates the localisation of the sources of insufficient performance.

The function-wise assessment allows for great freedom in defining system boundaries. All kinds of network solutions to C2 can be analysed. As mentioned above, the data collection function may, for example, be fulfilled by a network of data collectors (data collecting nodes).

Validation of simulation software is also facilitated by empirical work based on theories expressed in functions. If the input-output relations of the simulated function match the input-output relations reported in empirical studies, the piece of software (the function's form in this case) simulates the function well. It does not necessarily mean, however, that the process (the way the function is coded) at all mimics the behaviour of the real-world system. The fulfilment of a function can take various shapes (or forms).

## FUTURE RESEARCH DIRECTIONS

Brehmer's (2013, 2007) C2 theory mainly suggests the necessary and sufficient function at a high level of abstraction (or low level of resolution). He has discussed how they are logically related (Brehmer, 2007), and has recently presented an initial attempt at a comprehensive model of the functional structure, that states the input-output relations (Brehmer, 2013). He lists factors that could affect, and discusses how they might affect, the demands on C2 systems. They are, however, yet to be fully integrated with the theoretical model (Brehmer, 2013, 2009). Furthermore, there is a need to develop sub-theories of the functions data collection, orientation and planning.

It is likely that Brehmer's theory is not the final word on C2 theory. Competing theories may be conceived that claim a different set of necessary and sufficient functions. These competing theories should then be put to empirical tests. This will, however, be easier with the sub-theories, but these are yet to be developed. When these sub-theories have been developed, there will be the question of how these functions may be fulfilled by networks and how this might be modelled. In short, there will be work for many of us for quite some time.

## CONCLUSION

The chapter suggests an approach than enables modelling of any organisation of C2 (C2 approach). This is done by modelling C2 as a set of necessary functions that are performed collectively by nodes in a C2 network. The approach is inspired by Cares' (2005, 2004) IACM, and expands it to include C2. The necessary C2 functions in the suggested approach are from Brehmer's (2013, 2007) theoretical model of C2. Further work is required, however, to work out the details of the model sufficiently both to put it to empirical test and for practical use.

## ACKNOWLEDGMENT

I am indebted to Dr. Berndt Brehmer and Dr. Tim Grant for their comments on earlier versions of this chapter and to the anonymous reviewers for their insightful and useful comments on the submitted manuscript.

## REFERENCES

Alberts, D. S., Gartska, J. J., & Stein, F.-P. (1999). Network Centric Warfare: Developing and Leveraging Information Superiority (2nd Revised Ed.). Washington, DC: CCRP Publication Series.

Alberts, D. S., & Hayes, R. E. (2006). *Understanding Command and Control*. Washington, DC: CCRP Publication Series.

Alberts. (2007). Agility, Focus, and Convergence: The Future of Command and Control. *The International C2 Journal, 1*(1), 1-30.

Boyd, J. (1987). *A Discourse on Winning and Losing* (briefing slides). Maxwell Air Force Base, AL: Air University Library Document No. M-U 43947. Retrieved from http://www.ausairpower.net/APA-Boyd-Papers.html

Brehmer, B. (2005). The Dynamic OODA Loop: Amalgamating Boyd's OODA Loop and the Cybernetic Approach to Command and Control. In *Proceedings of the 10th International Command & Control Research & Technology Symposium (ICCRTS)*. US DoD Command & Control Research Program.

Brehmer, B. (2006). One Loop to Rule Them All. In *Proceedings of the 11th International Command and Control Research and Tecnhology Symposium*. Washington, DC: CCRP.

Brehmer, B. (2007). Understanding the Functions of C2 Is the Key to Progress. *The International C2 Journal, 1*(1), 211-232.

Brehmer, B. (2008). Command and Control is a Science of the Artificial. In *Proceedings of the 13th International Command and Control Research and Technology Symposium.* Washington, DC: CCRP.

Brehmer, B. (2009). From Function to Form in the Design of C2 Systems. In *Proceedings of the 14th International Command and Control Research and Technology Symposium.* Washington, DC: CCRP.

Brehmer, B. (2010). Command and control as design. In *Proceedings of the 15th International Command & Control Research & Technology Symposium (ICCRTS).* US DoD Command & Control Research Program.

Brehmer, B. (2013). *Insatsledning* [Command and control of missions]. Stockholm: The Swedish National Defence College.

Cares, J. R. (2004). *An Information Age Combat Model.* Office of the Secretary of Defense under. *Contract (New York, N.Y.)*, TPD-01–C-0023.

Cares, J. R. (2005). Distributed Network Operations: The Foundations of Network Centric Warfare. Lincoln, NE: iUniverse.

Deller, S., Bell, M. I., Bowling, S. R., Rabadi, G. A., & Tolk, A. (2009). Applying the Information Age Combat Model: Quantitative Analysis of Network Centric Operations. *The International C2 Journal 3*(1), 1-25.

Grant, T. J., & Kooter, B. M. (2005). Comparing OODA and Other Models as Operational View Architecture. In *Proceedings of the 10th International Command & Control Research & Technology Symposium (ICCRTS).* US DoD Command & Control Research Program.

Hammond, G. T. (2001). *The mind of war: John Boyd and American Security.* Washington, DC: Smithsonian Press.

Jensen, E. (2012). Operationalizing C2 Agility. In *Proceedings of the 17th International Command & Control Research & Technology Symposium (ICCRTS).* US DoD Command & Control Research Program.

MacKay, N. (2006). Lanchester combat models. *Mathematics Today, 42*(5), 170–173.

Maxwell, D. T. (2000). An Overview of the Joint Warfare System (JWARS). *Phalanx, 33*(3), 12–14.

Nagel, E. (1979). *The structure of science: Problems in the logic of scientific explanation.* Indianapolis, IN: Hackett Publishing Company.

NATO SAS-050 Research Task Group. (2007). *Exploring New Command and Control Concepts and Capabilities* (RTO Technical Report TR-SAS-050). Neuilly-sur-Seine Cedex, France: NATO Research and Technology Organisation.

NATO SAS-065 Research Task Group. (2010). *NATO NEC C2 Maturity Model.* Washington, DC: CCRP.

Pahl, G., Beitz, W., Feldhusen, J., & Grote, K. H. (2007). *Engineering Design: A Systematic Approach* (3rd ed.). London: Springer. doi:10.1007/978-1-84628-319-2

Pigeau, R., & McCann, C. (2002, Spring). Reconceptualizing command and control. *Canadian Military Journal*, 53-64.

Simon, H. A. (1996). *The Sciences of the Artificial* (3rd ed.). Cambridge, MA: MIT Press.

Stanton, N. A., Baber, C., & Harris, D. (2008). *Modelling command and control: Event analysis of systemic teamwork.* Aldershot, UK: Ashgate.

Tolk, A. (Ed.). (2012). *Engineering principles of combat modeling and distributed simulation.* Hoboken, NJ: Wiley. doi:10.1002/9781118180310

## ADDITIONAL READING

Alberts, D. S. (2011). *The Agility Advantage: A Survival Guide For Complex Enterprises and Endeavors.* Washington, DC: CCRP Publication Series.

Alberts, D. S., & Hayes, R. E. (2007). *Planning: Complex Endeavors*. Washington, DC: CCRP Publication Series.

Brehmer, B. (2009). Command without commanders. *Proceedings of the 14ᵗʰ International Command & Control Research & Technology Symposium (ICCRTS)*, US DoD Command & Control Research Program, Washington DC.

Jenkins, D. P., Stanton, N. A., Salmon, P. M., & Walker, G. H. (2009). *Cognitive Work Analysis: Coping With Complexity. Farnham*. Surrey, England: Ashgate.

Jensen, E. (2010). Mission design: Fitting the solution to the problem. *Proceedings of the 15th International Command and Control Research and Technology Symposium*. Washington, DC: CCRP.

Moffat, J. (2011). *Adapting Modeling & Simulation for Network Enabled Operations*. Washington, DC: CCRP Publication Series.

Naikar, N. (2013). *Work Domain Analysis: Concepts, guidelines and cases*. Boca Raton, FL: CRC Press. doi:10.1201/b14774

Naikar, N., Hopcroft, R., & Moylan, A. (2005). *Work domain analysis: theoretical concepts and methodology, DSTO-TR-1665*. Fishermans Bend, Australia: Air Operations Division, DSTO Defence Science and Technology Organisation.

Newman, M. E. J. (2003). The structure and function of complex networks. *SIAM Review, 45*(2), 167–256. doi:10.1137/S003614450342480

Newman, M. E. J. (2010). *Networks: An Introduction*. New York: Oxford University Press. doi:10.1093/acprof:oso/9780199206650.001.0001

Rasmussen, J., Pejtersen, A. M., & Goodstein, L. P. (1994). *Cognitive Systems Engineering*. New York: Wiley-Interscience.

Smith, E. A. (2006). *Complexity, Networking, and Effects-Based Approaches to Operations*. Washington, DC: CCRP Publication Series.

## KEY TERMS AND DEFINITIONS

**C2:** The function of a mission system that provides direction and coordination of the military activities.

**C2 Approach:** How C2 is organised, i.e. the extent to which C2 is performed by isolated C2 entities or performed collaboratively by networks of distributed C2 entities.

**C2 Network Node:** The C2 functions of can be fulfilled collaboratively by a number of C2 entities connected by a network. These entities are considered as nodes contributing to a C2 function. A C2 entity may act as a data collection, orientation and/or planning node in a C2 network.

**Data Collection:** One of the functions necessary for C2. You need to collect the data that are vital to accomplish the mission.

**Form:** While functions are abstract concepts, the form is how these functions are realised in the shape of equipment and procedures for using the equipment.

**Function:** Something that a system or artefact needs to accomplish to fulfil its purpose. There are a set of necessary and sufficient functions required to fulfil any conceivable purpose.

**Orientation:** Another of the functions necessary for C2. The output from this function is an understanding of what you need to achieve (the required effects) in order to accomplish the mission.

**Planning:** The third and final of the functions necessary for C2. The output from this function is a description (expressed in orders to subordinates) of how the force is to be applied to bring about the desired effects identified by the orientation function.

**Purpose:** Why a system or artefact exists (or needs to be constructed), i.e. what it is for.

## APPENDIX

## Questions

1. Why should theoretical models of C2 be models of functions?
2. What is meant by *function*? What is meant by *form*? How are the two concepts related?
3. How can the C2 functions be modelled if they are fulfilled by a network of interconnected entities?
4. What are the possible ways that C2 can be organised? How may these organisations be represented (or modelled)?
5. What is required of a C2 theory for it to be of practical use?

# Chapter 5
# Formalized Ontology for Representing C2 Systems as Layered Networks

**T. J. Grant**
*R-BAR, The Netherlands*

## ABSTRACT

*Command and Control (C2) is an essential operating capability in which the commander exercises authority over assigned forces to accomplish the mission. Traditionally, military C2 was organized hierarchically with the commander issuing directives top-down and subordinates reporting progress upwards. Over the past two decades, developments in digital telecommunication technology have made it possible to link distributed computer systems into a network. These developments can be exploited to delegate decision-making authority down the organizational hierarchy. Subordinates can be empowered to share information and synchronize their actions with their peers, speeding up the response to changes in the situation. This is known as Network-Enabled Capabilities or information-age C2. Experience has shown that multiple factors must co-evolve to gain the full benefit of transforming C2 to become network enabled. In this chapter, the authors group these factors into five layers: geographical, physical, information, cognitive, and socio-organizational. They formalize the key entities in each layer, together with within- and across-layer relationships, into a conceptual ontology, known as the Formalized Layered Ontology for Networked C2 (FLONC). To ensure the ontology is militarily relevant, the authors show that a set of networks found in military operations can be extracted from the ontology. Finally, they compare the formalized ontology to related work on ontologies in C2. In further research, the ontology could be used in developing software to simulate and support network-enabled C2 processes. A case study based on the events of September 11, 2001 shows how this could be done.*

DOI: 10.4018/978-1-4666-6058-8.ch005

## INTRODUCTION

## Background

Command & Control (C2) is one of NATO's Essential Operating Capabilities. It is defined as *"the exercise of authority and direction by a properly designated commander over assigned and attached forces in the accomplishment of the mission"* (US DoD Joint Publication 1-02, 2013). A C2 system is *"an arrangement of personnel, equipment, communications, facilities, and procedures"*, and the functions of C2 include *"planning, directing, coordinating, and controlling forces and operations"* (ibid.) These definitions show that C2 is not confined to the technical implementation. The definition hints at organization (*"authority and direction"*, *"assigned and attached forces"*, and *"personnel"*), knowledge (*"mission"*, *"procedures"*, and *"planning"*), and information (*"communications"*, *"directing"*, and *"coordinating"*), as well as technology (*"equipment"*, *"communications"*, and *"facilities"*).

Traditionally, military C2 was top-down and directive, emphasizing achievement of the commander's intent (the *"mission"*), with subordinates (the *"assigned and attached forces"*) periodically reporting their progress towards achieving this intent. This required a hierarchical organization, with communications passing up and down the hierarchy. Subordinate units report progress in the form of situation reports up the hierarchy, and commanders promulgate their intent down to their subordinates in the form of operation orders. In a hierarchical organization, subordinate units rarely communicate directly with one another (Van Fenema, Rietjens & Besters, 2014). Instead, the commander carries the burden of synchronizing their activities, usually by deconfliction, e.g. by giving them mutually exclusive areas of responsibility. The technical systems supporting this traditional C2 process were designed to mirror the organizational hierarchy. This has been termed "industrial-age" C2 (Alberts, 2002).

There are several shortcomings of industrial-age C2. Firstly, commanders suffer from information overload. Secondly, commanders can form a bottleneck in the information flow, both in synchronizing their subordinates' activities and in summarizing the reporting from subordinates in a report to their own superior. Thirdly, only the commander has an overview of the situation, often hampering subordinates in gaining an understanding of the rationale behind their commander's intent. Fourthly, the concentration of information at the commander's location makes him/her an attractive target for the enemy.

Over the past two decades, developments in digital telecommunication technology have made it possible to link distributed computer systems into a network. In 1998, Vice Admiral Cebrowski and John Garstka published an article in the US Naval Institute Proceedings outlining the concept of network-centric warfare (NCW) (Cebrowski & Garstka, 1998). Since then, NCW – now termed network-centric operations (NCO) in the USA and network enabled capabilities (NEC) in NATO, the UK, and the Netherlands – has been the subject of extensive research, concept development, experimentation, and operational application. (In this chapter, we will use NATO terminology.) NEC is based on four tenets (Alberts, 2002):

**Tenet 1:** A robustly networked force improves information sharing.

**Tenet 2:** Information sharing and collaboration enhance the quality of information and shared situational awareness.

**Tenet 3:** Shared situational awareness enables self-synchronization.

**Tenet 4:** These, in turn, dramatically increase mission effectiveness.

As the name suggests, NEC focuses on networks. At the outset, networking was overwhelmingly seen as a technological capability. By "network", one meant the telecommunication network that linked the C2 systems electronically. Gradually, as scientific and practical knowledge built up, it became apparent that an exclusively technological view was too restrictive. Factors such as psychology and culture also had to be taken into account. From a scientific viewpoint, C2 systems must be regarded as *socio-technical systems* (Trish & Bamforth, 1951). From an operational viewpoint, NATO express the full set of factors as Doctrine, Organization, Training & education, Materiel & equipment, Leadership, Personnel, Facilities, and, depending on the author, Interoperability or Information, abbreviated "DOTMLPFI" (NATO, 2009).

A change in one of the DOTMLPFI factors meant that the others also had to change. In particular, experience shows that the greatest benefit could be gained from networking if the organizing principle changes from top-down direction to empowerment of the units at the edge of the hierarchy (becoming an "*edge organization*") (Alberts & Hayes, 2003). Empowerment means that awareness of the situation and decision making must be shared between the commander and his/her subordinates. Commanders give their subordinates goals to achieve ("*mission command*"), rather than detailing how they should act. Moreover, subordinates are empowered to coordinate their activities directly with their peers; this is known as "*self-synchronization*". Communications become predominantly peer-to-peer, running mostly across the hierarchy, rather than predominantly up and down it. C2 systems must be networked to support the flow of messages up, down, and across the hierarchy. Technologies such as Internet protocols, web-based systems, portals, Web 2.0, e-mail, chat (instant messaging), social media, and cloud computing are better suited to implementing these "information-age" C2 systems than the older, process-control technologies.

Around the same time, mathematical network theory began increasingly to yield valuable results. It became clear that these results could be applied equally well to social, information, technological, and biological networks (Newman, 2003). This insight stimulated the NEC thought-leaders to group the DOTMLPFI factors into three domains

(Alberts, Garstka, Hayes & Signori, 2001). In their view, the *physical* domain represents the real world in which military units maneuver, weapon systems engage one another, and sensors capture data about the events taking place. In the *information* domain, information is created, manipulated, and transmitted, either as spoken or written natural language or as electronic bits and bytes. Invariably, technology is employed to store and transmit information. Traditionally, the technologies used were pen and paper, telephone, and radio, but modern information and communications technologies (ICT) have now surpassed them. Information is received by the human C2 users, converted into knowledge, assessed, and acted upon in the *cognitive* domain (i.e. in the users' minds). It is in the cognitive domain that C2 decision making – usually modeled by Boyd's (1996) Observe-Orient-Decide-Act (OODA) loop – occurs. Alberts and Hayes (2003) observed that modern military endeavors are too complex to be understood by individuals. Empowered teams working peer-to-peer develop a shared understanding of the situation and of how to respond to this situation. They added a fourth, *social* domain.

In 2008, Van Ettinger and his NATO colleagues mapped three of the domains (social, cognitive, technical) to networks by means of the DOTMLPFI factors (Van Ettinger, 2008). The technical network covers the DOTMLPFI factors of Materiel (M) and Facilities (F). The cognitive network covers Doctrine (D), Organization (O), and Training (T), and the social network covers Leadership (L) and Personnel (P). In Van Ettinger's depiction, the three networks are shown as overlapping circles, with Interoperability/Information (I) providing the "glue" between them.

By contrast, Monsuur, Grant and Janssen (2011) observed that the three networks were linked by military units and individuals. Being physically embodied, units and individuals appeared as nodes in the technical network. Units and individuals acquired, processed, and acted upon knowledge specific to the application domain. They also appeared, therefore, as nodes in the cognitive network. Since units and individuals communicated with one another, sharing awareness about the situation and synchronizing their actions, they also appeared as nodes in the social network. Monsuur et al termed these interlinking nodes as "*actors*", with nodes appearing in only one of the networks being termed "*objects*". Since the actors must appear in all three networks, it was easier to depict them as being layered on top of one another. Finally, Monsuur et al's article provided the basic mathematics for events occurring in one network to influence events in another.

This chapter extends in several ways Monsuur, Grant and Janssen's (2011) idea of representing C2 systems as layered networks. In what follows, we will talk about *layers*, rather than domains or networks. The word *domain* will be used to refer to the operational domains (land, sea, air, space, and cyberspace) or to the application domain (i.e. C2). The word *network* will generally refer to the representation of a real-world phenomenon (e.g. an organization) as a set of nodes together with a set of arcs linking those nodes. As will become apparent, we have found that there may be more than one network in a domain or layer, and there are also networks spanning across layers.

The first extension is related to the implicit limitation of the earlier work to military operations on land, at sea, in the air, and in space. Since then, cyberspace has become increasingly important. Kinetic operations are likely to be accompanied by cyber operations, with the planning process integrating kinetic and cyber action. Therefore, we have extended the scope of our research to find a representation unifying all five military spaces: land, sea, air, (outer) space, and cyberspace. The second extension flows out of this. By contrast with the continuous, three-dimensional physical space in which kinetic action occurs, cyberspace is virtual, discrete, and higher-dimensional. This necessitates splitting Van Ettinger's (2008) technical domain into two layers: a geographical layer and a physical layer. In the third extension, the

"glue" in Van Ettinger's model becomes another layer in its own right: the information layer. This leads synergistically to a useful distinction between the information held in the man-made part of the C2 system and the knowledge held in the minds of the human users. The fourth extension involves relaxing the privileged "actor" role that Monsuur et al (2011) gave to military units and individuals. Instead, humans are now simply another class of entities in the physical layer, and military units are an entity-class in the socio-organizational layer. The fifth and final extension is to formalize the entities in each layer as classes, together with the relations between these classes. The relations may be confined to within a layer or they may span across layers. We confirm the formalization by checking that each layer contains at least one network, with a set of nodes and a set of arcs. We characterize each network found, showing that it corresponds to one found in military practice. The resulting ontology is known as the Formalized Layered Ontology for Networked C2 (FLONC).

Our ultimate goal is to develop software that simulates the network-enabled C2 process, that supports parts of this process (e.g. planning military operations) or implements a complete C2 system. Hence, we need to formalize the layers, entity-classes, and relations in a way that will assist the future development of one or more information systems. To do so, we make use of an ontology represented in a formal (human- and) computer-readable language. The significance of making the FLONC ontology computer-readable is that this opens up the possibility for transforming it into a variety of information systems representations at some time in the future. For example, the FLONC ontology could be transformed into Structured Query Language (SQL) to implement the database underlying a C2 system, into Knowledge Query Modeling Language (KQML) to support C2 decision making using Artificial Intelligence (AI) techniques, into XML to implement standardized information exchange between C2 systems using

Internet and web-based technologies, or into a model for agent-based simulation of C2 processes.

Possible case studies that could be simulated include the Mission Execution Crew Assistant (MECA) scenario (Van Diggelen, Bradshaw, Grant, Johnson & Neerincx, 2009) and the events occurring in the air over the Continental US during September 11, 2001 (Grant, 2006). The MECA scenario involves self-synchronization between two man-robot teams (comprising a total of 12 agents) on the Martian surface to handle a life-threatening emergency. Despite the Martian setting, the military parallel of two cooperating platoons is obvious. The 9-11 scenario would be larger case study involving the implementation of some 30 agents representing the Al Qaeda terrorists, the hijacked aircraft, and the Federal Aviation Authority and US Air Force individuals and units involved. A subset of the 9-11 scenario is included in this chapter to illustrate the use of the FLONC ontology.

## Purpose and Scope of Chapter

The purpose of this chapter is to present a formalized logical ontology for representing C2 systems as layered networks. The FLONC ontology will be represented in a form that is both human- and computer-readable. More specifically, we intend to represent the ontology in future work using version 2 of the Web-based Ontology Language (OWL2) in the Protégé ontology editor, version 4. Figures in this chapter depict classes and their relations using Chen's (1976) Entity Relationship Diagram (ERD) graphical notation.

While the FLONC ontology covers all five military spaces and integrated kinetic and cyber action, only those parts of the ontology needed to represent C2 systems have been worked out. This includes an abstract representation of C2 system hardware, software, human users, information and knowledge relating to objects of interest within the C2 process, and the social and organizational structure of actors in the area of operations. The ontology provides high-level stubs for representing other kinds of systems, such as vehicles, sensors, weapons, etc. In short, the ontology provides a logical model of a networked C2 system, consisting only of classes and relations. An ontology author would have to add attributes and their facets (e.g. constraints) to complete the logical model. Information system developers would need to extend the stubs down to a more detailed level to obtain a complete model of the C2 system together with its "assigned and attached forces" and the environment in which they operate. Finally, implementers would have to create instances of all entity-classes, together with their relations, attributes, and facets in developing a working information system.

## Structure of Chapter

This chapter consists of seven sections. After this introductory section, the second section outlines the relevant aspects of ontology engineering, including the "Ontology Development 101" methodology used in this research. The third section determines the domain and scope of the ontology. The fourth section describes each layer informally, formalizes each layer in turn, then formalizes the relationships across layers, and finally extracts the militarily-relevant networks, together with their characteristics. The fifth section illustrates the use of FLONC to model a subset of the events of September 11, 2001. The sixth section describes related work on ontologies in C2. The seventh and last section draws conclusions, states the contributions and limitations of the work reported here, and recommends further research.

## ONTOLOGY ENGINEERING

## Defining Ontology

There are several ways in which domain concepts can be formalized (Pidcock, 2010). A *controlled vocabulary* is a list of terms that have been explicitly enumerated by some vocabulary registration authority so that each term is unambiguous and non-redundant. A *taxonomy* is a collection of controlled vocabulary terms organized into a hierarchical structure, with each term in one or more parent-child relationships to other terms. Typically, each term in a taxonomy has a single parent term, representing a more general concept, e.g. the terms *car*, *aircraft*, and *ship* all have *vehicle* as their parent. A *thesaurus* is a collection of controlled vocabulary terms organized into a network. In addition to parent-child relationships, terms may be related by associative relationships, e.g. the term *car* may be associated with the term *driver*. An *ontology* is a controlled vocabulary expressed in an ontology representation language. The language has a grammar for using vocabulary terms to express something meaningful about the domain. The grammar contains formal constraints specifying what is a well-formed statement, assertion, query, etc. The added value of an ontology is that it provides semantic interoperability between different users and that it retains the open world assumption.

In computer science, information science, artificial intelligence, and software engineering, an ontology is a "*formal, explicit specification of a shared conceptualization*" (Gruber, 1993). An ontology provides a shared vocabulary of the entities that exist in a domain, together with their properties and relationships. Common components of ontologies include *classes* (sets, types, collections), *individuals* (instances of these classes), *properties* (attributes, features, characteristics, parameters), *relations* (i.e. ways in which classes and individuals can be related to one another, such as abstraction, aggregation, and association), *constraints* (restrictions on what must be true for an assertion to be accepted), *rules* (if-then statements describing the logical inferences that can be drawn), and *events* (i.e. changes in properties or relations).

Generally, in the software world, ontologies are formalized by means of an ontology representa-tion language that is both human- and computer-readable. This enables the ontology not only to be shared between different people, but also between different computer systems (e.g. a database and a decision support tool) and between humans and computers. Being formal and computer-readable, the ontology can be validated. It can also be transformed into another computer language, e.g. a database schema in SQL, a rule-based expert system via KQML, or a web-based language such as XML. Being human-readable, the ontology can also be verified against the users' requirements.

In the research reported in this chapter, we kept in mind that we intend to use the Web-based Ontology Language (OWL) ontology representation language to formalize our representation of C2 systems as layered networks. The W3C standards organization oversees the specification of the OWL language (Smith, Welty & McGuinness, 2004). OWL is designed to facilitate ontology development and sharing via the Web, with the ultimate goal of making Web content more accessible to computers. OWL can be used to formalize an application domain by defining classes and their properties, to define instances and assert their property-values, and to reason about these classes and instances as permitted by OWL's formal semantics. The latest version is OWL version 2 (OWL2). OWL2 ontologies provide classes, properties, individuals (a.k.a. instances), and data values, and are stored and exchanged as semantic web documents. OWL2 ontologies can be created and maintained using software tools such as the open-source Protégé ontology editor and knowledge acquisition system, developed by Stanford and Manchester Universities.

## Applications of Ontologies

Since ontologies can be both human- and computer-readable, there are several different ways that they can be applied. Uschold & Jasper (1999) present a framework for classifying ontology applications. In their framework, humans can adopt a variety of roles. An *ontology author* creates and maintains ontologies. A *data author* creates and maintains operational data that is defined in terms of the vocabulary of the ontology. An *application developer* creates and maintains software applications that produce and consume operational data that is defined in terms of a shared ontology. An *application user* uses such software applications. A *knowledge worker* uses an ontology either to communicate with other knowledge workers or to search for information in a repository.

Uschold & Jasper (1999) identify three main classes of ontology application. Each class may have one or more subclasses (which they term "scenarios"). The main classes are:

- *Authoring*, in which an information artifact is created in a single language. It may then be converted into a different form for use in a variety of target systems. There are two subclasses: authoring an ontology, and authoring operational data. The benefits of using an ontology in authoring are knowledge reuse, improved maintainability, and long-term knowledge retention.

- *Common access to information*, in which information that is required by one or more persons or computer systems is expressed using an unfamiliar vocabulary. The ontology helps making the information intelligible by mapping between sets of terms. There are four subclasses: promoting common understanding among knowledge workers, accessing data via a shared ontology, accessing data via mapped ontologies, and interfacing systems via a common ontology. The benefits include interoperability and more effective (re-) use of knowledge resources.

- *Indexing for concept-based search*, in which an ontology assists a knowledge worker in locating information resources in a repository (e.g. documents in a library).

The prime benefit is faster access to important information resources.

In the research reported here we describe the authoring of an ontology. Since our ultimate aim is to develop software based on our ontology, we are seeking benefits primarily in software engineering. In particular, we focus on the future use of the ontology to assist the process of identifying requirements and defining the specifications for simulations, decision support tools, and C2 systems. In Uschold & Jasper's (1999) terminology, this is an authoring application. The intended users of these simulations, decision support tools, and information systems are military commanders and command staffs, themselves examples of knowledge workers. They would gain benefits through the common access to information, or, in military terminology, through interoperability and information sharing. This chapter also serves a secondary aim by presenting the ontology to fellow researchers working in the areas of C2 systems and network science, namely in promoting a common understanding of representing C2 systems as layered networks.

## Ontology Engineering Methodologies

Ontology engineering is the subfield of knowledge engineering that studies the engineering lifecycle, the development process, methods, and tools for creating ontologies (De Nicola, Missikof & Navigili, 2009). We concentrate here on methods and tools.

Ontology engineering methodologies draw heavily on the software engineering discipline and, in particular, on object-oriented analysis and design. Thus, De Nicola et al (2009) apply the Unified Process – itself closely connected to the object-oriented Unified Modeling Language (UML) – to ontology development in their Unified Process for ONtology building (UPON). The resulting UPON methodology is complex and designed for large-scale development by teams of ontology authors.

By contrast, Noy & McGuinness (2001) present the aptly-named "Ontology Development 101" methodology, intended for individual or small teams of ontology authors. This simple methodology consists of the following steps:

**Step 1:** Determine domain and scope of ontology. In step 1, the ontology author should determine what the ontology is going to be used for, what types of questions the ontology should provide answers for, and who will use and maintain the ontology.

**Step 2:** Consider reusing existing ontologies. In step 2, the ontology author should consider what other ontology authors have done, and whether existing sources can be refined and extended to serve the purposes determined in step 1.

**Step 3:** Enumerate important terms. In step 3, the ontology author should write down a list of all terms that the ontology is intended to make statements about or to explain to a user.

**Step 4:** Define classes and class hierarchy. In step 4, the ontology author identifies which of the important terms enumerated in step 3 represent classes. The author then structures these classes into an abstraction or inheritance hierarchy. Classes may be identified and structured into a hierarchy top-down, bottom-up, or by some combination of the two.

**Step 5:** Define properties of classes. In step 5, the ontology author considers each class in turn, and defines the properties of each class. These properties may be instance attributes (e.g. the registration number and color of a particular car), and/or relations between classes (e.g. the is-part-of relation, a.k.a. *aggregation*) or between class-instances.

**Step 6:** Define the facets of properties. In step 6, the ontology author determines the facets of each property of each class including its cardinality, value-type, domain, and range.

**Step 7:** Create instances. In step 7, the ontology author creates instances of each class, together with their properties, to model a particular domain.

An ontology can be developed to a variety of depths. A *conceptual* ontology is an abstract view consisting only of the high-level classes obtained from steps 1 to 4. This is useful in understanding the scope and general content of the ontology. A *logical* ontology adds all of the relations between the classes by performing steps 1 to 4 plus those parts of steps 5 and 6 specific to inter-class and -instance relations. This yields a more detailed model while remaining accessible to human understanding. A *physical* ontology is concerned with obtaining all the detail needed for computer understandability, e.g. for developing software. This depth is only reached when all seven steps have been completed. In the research reported in this chapter, we have developed a logical ontology.

## DOMAIN AND SCOPE OF ONTOLOGY

Step 1 of the Ontology Development 101 methodology is to determine the domain and scope of the ontology. In the Introduction we have already stated that the purpose is to formalize a logical ontology for representing C2 systems as layered networks. Our approach is to extend existing research by integrating cyberspace with the other four "kinetic" domains, by distinguishing the geographical and physical layers, by distinguishing information from knowledge, by relaxing the privileged role of military units and humans, and by extracting one or more networks from each layer. The ultimate goal is to develop software that simulates or supports the network-enabled C2 process.

The application domain – C2 – is clear. While the scope should cover all five operational domains – land, sea, air, space, and cyberspace – other aspects of the scope may not be obvious. In particular, we need to determine answers to the following questions:

- *What are the boundaries of the domain?* The boundaries, and hence scope, of the domain will be defined in several ways, as follows:
    - Research will focus for simplicity on the operational and tactical levels of C2. Hence, strategic C2 is outside the scope of this research.
    - All of the DOTMLPFI factors will be included, albeit distributed over five layers in the FLONC ontology. This implies that we must regard C2 systems as man-machine systems, with their users inside the system boundary.
    - A consequence is that we need to make a distinction between information held in the machine or technical part of the system and knowledge held in the minds of or shared socially among human users. In information science, a distinction is often made between data, information, knowledge, and wisdom (DIKW) (Rowley, 2007). A consequence of including both people (or the social domain) and machines (or technical domain) within the system boundary is that we need to draw a line somewhere within the DIKW "pyramid". Zins (2007) identifies five ways that this can be done. We adopt Zins' first model – the commonest – in which data and information are universal and external (i.e. held in the machine), while knowledge is subjective and internal (i.e. held in the human mind). We simplify this further

by making no distinction between data (i.e. isolated pieces of information) and information (i.e. "data in context"). Similarly, we make no distinction between knowledge and wisdom. The two remaining categories of information and knowledge will be in separate layers.
    - The separation of man from machine also fits with the inclusion of cyberspace, which refers both to the conceptual (i.e. virtual) space within ICT-based systems as well as to the technologies themselves (Dodge & Kitchin, 2001). Dodge and Kitchin emphasize the conceptual aspect, characterizing it as a set of contradictions. Thus, cyberspace is both spatial and spaceless, creates both place and placelessness, is both public and private, real and virtual, supports both listening and broadcasting, combines nature and technology, and is fixed and fluid. In designing the FLONC ontology we try to resolve these contradictions by separating them between layers. For example, the real nature of cyberspace is assigned to the physical, geographical, and information layers, while the virtual nature is found in the cognitive and socio-organizational layers. Spatiality is to be found in the geographical and physical layers, while the other layers are in themselves spaceless. Place is to be found in the socio-organizational layer, while the other layers are placeless. Whether a part of cyberspace is public or private depends on the size of the group that has access to the ICT system.
- *What is the ontology going to be used for?* The ontology is primarily intended to be used in the development of software for

simulating or supporting the C2 process. It also has a secondary role through the publication of this chapter of communicating certain ideas about C2 and networks to other researchers working in the fields of C2 theory and network science.

- *Who will use the ontology?* Since FLONC is a logical ontology, it will need to be enhanced before developing software for particular applications. This means that it will be used by ontology authors other than the author of this chapter. Moreover, it will be used by software developers and by the users of the resulting software, most likely C2 practitioners (i.e. commanders and command teams). In addition, it may be used by other researchers to develop their own ideas about C2 theory and practice and about networks that may be found in the C2 domain.

- *What questions should the ontology answer?* For the purposes of this research, the key questions that the ontology should answer are:
  - What militarily-relevant networks can be extracted from the ontology?
  - How are these networks connected to one another through the ontology?
  - What are the characteristics of these networks? Are they bipartite? Are they directed networks? Are they hierarchies? Can anything be said about their topologies, about processes occurring in these networks, or how they evolve?

## FORMALIZATION OF ONTOLOGY

### Informal Semantics

Step 3 of the Ontology Development 101 methodology is to enumerate the important terms in the application domain. We do this by describing the semantics of each layer informally. We identify five layers: geographical, physical, information, cognitive, and socio-organizational. One layer provides the basic functionality for the next. Each layer contains within it at least one militarily-relevant network, consisting of a set of nodes and a set of arcs.

### Geographical Layer

The purpose of the geographical layer is to represent the five spaces in which military (and civilian) activities can occur: land, sea, air, (outer) space, and cyberspace. These spaces may be conveniently represented as two-dimensional (e.g. land and sea), as three-dimensional (e.g. air and outer space), or as multi-dimensional (e.g. cyberspace). Time will be an additional dimension. Activity may be concentrated in one of these spaces, but more often it involves multiple spaces (i.e. operations are *joint*). In particular, virtual activity in cyberspace may be integrated with real (or "kinetic") activity in one or more of the other four spaces. Hence, the ontology must be capable of representing all five spaces and any combination of them.

Geography is the science that studies the lands, the features, the inhabitants, and the phenomena of the Earth. There are two main branches: physical geography and human geography. Tasks common to both branches include exploration, surveying, and cartography. Tools include surveying instruments, maps, geospatial coordinate systems, and geographical information systems. Techniques include spatial and demographic analysis. A recent development is the application of geography to cyberspace under the heading of *cybergeography*. The cybergeography literature concentrates on cyberspace in isolation from the other four spaces, on the social infrastructure within cyberspace, and on the cartography of cyberspace (Dodge & Kitchen, 2001). By contrast, we need to integrate cyberspace with the other four spaces, to relate social and physical infrastructures, and to find cartographical representations that apply to all five spaces.

Military geography is the application of geographical tools, information, and techniques to solve military problems. In planning a military operation, commanders first consider the geographical area within which operations will take place, the terrain and weather, and the actors and other objects of interest likely to be encountered in that area. The planning process then assesses the capabilities and intents of the actors, generates their possible courses of action, and wargames its own courses of action against those of other actors, finally developing Operation Orders for its best course of action. We assume that an analogy can be made for cyberspace, with the terrain consisting of computer hardware linked by telecommunications networks, and actors being software applications and human users operating in the physical, information, cognitive, and socio-organizational layers.

Geographical concepts that must be represented in the geographical layer include the idea of a space, with locations embedded in this space. Land, sea, air, and (outer) space are real spaces, with cyberspace being virtual. One or more frames of reference allows locations to be determined. Real spaces are continuous, while virtual locations are generally discrete. Location-pairs may be connected to one another by paths running through the space. The distance along these paths and the direction in which they run can also be determined from a suitable frame of reference.

## Physical Layer

The purpose of the physical layer is to represent the physical objects of interest involved in military (and civilian) activities, together with the physical links between them. Key objects of interest to the military include military units, vehicles, weapons, sensors, people, buildings, towns, airfields, etc. Interesting links between them might include roads running from one town to another, airways connecting one airfield to another, the presence of a particular person in a building, etc.

Objects have locations in the geographical layer, and links run along a geographical path. An object may have multiple locations only if each location is in a different space. For example, an airfield has one location on land and another location in the air, and a seaport has both land and sea locations. Objects and links in the physical layer are tangible, and may be natural (typically *humans*, because we are not interested here in animals or plants) or man-made (known here as *devices*). An additional form of link is an *interface* between devices and humans. We make no distinction whether the interface is an input (from human to device), or an output (from device to human), or both.

Devices may be part of another device. Moreover, one device may act upon itself or another device, causing it to move (i.e. change location), to change an attribute, or to create or delete a part-of relationship. For illustrative purposes, three types of device are distinguished: a facility with a fixed location, a transport that can change its location, and an ICT device (i.e. a piece of computing hardware) that can create, sense, store, copy, process, display, and/or delete information. An ICT device may also sense information about other devices. Note that an ICT device will generally have two locations: one in real space (i.e. on land, at sea, in the air, or in outer space) and the other in virtual space (i.e. cyberspace). Media that can carry information, such as paper, CD-ROMs, and USB sticks, are also regarded as ICT devices.

There are three corresponding types of link between devices, with an ICT link (i.e. telecommunications hardware) being able to transmit information from one ICT device to another. ICT links can be wired or wireless. Links between humans may be face-to-face or technology-mediated (e.g. typically telephone or radio, but also including older technologies such as pen and paper). Where it is necessary to represent digital communications between humans (e.g. email, chat, etc.), then this could be done by combining a (human-to-ICT device) interface at the sending end, with an ICT link, and with another (ICT device-to-human) interface at the receiving end. Note that ICT links will generally run along two paths, one in real space and the other in virtual space.

## Information Layer

The purpose of the information layer is to represent data, information, and software used in military (and civilian) activities. We make no distinction between a piece of information and how it is encoded (e.g. as software or as a mark on a piece of paper). Information can only exist if it is stored in an ICT device or transmitted over an ICT link.

Information is separated into *data* (typically representing a simple or complex variable, such as a sensed parameter of an object of interest, a set of such parameters, or a message to be transmitted across a link) and *programs* that process input data to obtain output data. Information has no inherent geographical location, but a location may be derived from the current location of the device in which it is stored. Since software can be readily copied, a piece of data or a program may be stored in multiple devices (and therefore in multiple locations) simultaneously.

## Cognitive Layer

The purpose of the cognitive layer is to represent pieces of knowledge held in the minds of humans engaged in military (or civilian) activities. This knowledge may be tacit or explicit, true or false, more or less certain, and based on direct observation, on messages from other humans, on information displayed by devices, or on inference from other pieces of knowledge. Knowledge can only exist if it is carried in the mind of a human or transferred across a human-to-human link. Like information, knowledge has no inherent geographical location, but a location may be derived from the current location of the human whose

mind is carrying it. Knowledge may be copied by transferring it to another human. Hence, a piece of knowledge may be known to several humans, and therefore in multiple locations simultaneously.

Just as information is separated into data and programs, so knowledge is separated into *beliefs* and *operators*. Taking our clue from the traditional definition of knowledge as "justified true belief" (Chisholm, 1982), we use the term "belief" to denote a piece of knowledge because this is more general than another term like (say) "assertion". Beliefs may be qualified by a degree of truthfulness, with justification for a belief being represented by the set of other beliefs that support it. We use the term "operator" in its mathematical sense (e.g. "+", "-", "*", "/", "sin", "cos", "log", etc are mathematical operators) to denote the equivalent in the cognitive layer of a program in the information layer. Other possible terms, such as "rule" or "procedure", would be too implementation-specific.

Humans may create knowledge in other ways than receiving knowledge transferred from other humans. In particular, new knowledge may be created by learning. A new belief may be learned by observing or assessing information displayed by an ICT device. A human may also deduce new knowledge by combining other pre-existing beliefs using an operator. Using induction (an operator for learning from examples), a human may create a new operator from a set of beliefs.

For C2 purposes, beliefs are sub-divided into *facts* and *goals*. Facts are beliefs that the human regards as being currently true or were true in the past. Typically, facts represent some element of the state of an object of interest. Goals are beliefs that the human intends to make true at some time in the future. Operators are sub-divided into *cases*, *rules*, *actions*, and *plans*. A case is the record of using an operator successfully in the past, together with the beliefs used as input and generated as output. A rule is an IF-THEN operator for deriving support for beliefs in the THEN part, given that all the beliefs in the IF part are true. An action is an operator that, when executed, will cause a change to occur in the physical layer. A plan is a sequence of one or more actions, designed logically so as to achieve a goal.

## Socio-Organizational Layer

The purpose of the socio-organizational layer is to represent the social and organizational relationships between humans engaged in military (or civilian) activities. Social relationships are more informal, while organizational ones are more formal. Whether formal or informal, these relationships are based on the membership of a group. A human becomes a member of a social or organizational group by filling (at least) one of the roles within the group. This requires the human to comply with the norms associated with this role. The literature on organizational norms distinguishes structural, functional, behavioral, and dialogical norms (Hübner, Sichman & Boissier, 2002) (Coutinho, Sichman & Boissier, 2005). Compliance with these norms may be rewarded, and violation may lead to punishment or even expulsion from the group. We need only to represent the behavioral and dialogical norms here, because we model structural and functional norms in other ways (as groups and roles and as goals and plans, respectively). Behavioral norms constrain the autonomy of group members by imposing obligations and prohibitions on their behavior. Dialogical norms constrain with whom group members may communicate and the message formats and protocols they should use. For example, a dialogical norm may stipulate that group members must share any knowledge they possess with other group members.

The most important role in a group is that of its leader. Behavioral norms associated with the leadership role typically state that the human filling that role is responsible for accepting tasks (i.e. goals) on behalf of the group, for generating plans to achieve these tasks, for assigning subtasks to other members of the group, for managing the resources (i.e. devices and humans) that the group owns, and for making decisions that affect the group. Dialogical norms define how the leader communicates decisions and subtask assignments to other group members and how the leader communicates with other groups.

One group may be associated with another. If this association requires the subgroup necessarily to adopt some or all of the roles and norms of the parent group, then the association is formal. When the requirement is optional, then the association is informal. When each subgroup has a single parent, then the set of associations models an organizational hierarchy. However, a set of associations generally forms a network. When the complete set is a network but some sub-networks are hierarchical, then this could represent a coalition of (hierarchical) organizations.

Some groups may attain the status of a community, characterized by social cohesion, personal intimacy, and moral commitment (Dodge & Kitchen, 2001). Such a group is regarded as being based in a *place*, where places are locations that are uniquely designated by shared social ties. For example, a family may be based at its home, an organizational team at its place of work, and an army unit at its barracks. As these examples show, a place in the geographical literature is implicitly assumed to have a fixed location. However, military operations are characterized by mobility. The place of work of a ship's crew is the ship, whose location can change. The same applies to aircrew, whose place of work is an aircraft. For this reason, instead of associating places directly with locations, we will say that a place is embodied in a device. If that device is a facility with a fixed location, such as a building or a town, then the meaning of the term place is as the geographical literature assumes. If the device is mobile, i.e. it is a transport, then the group of people who operate the transport are its *crew*. A synergistic effect of associating places with devices comes when we apply the association to ICT devices. In everyday terms, a place that associates a group with an ICT device is known as a (computer- or software-based) *system*, and the group is its set of *users*. In particular, we are interested in C2 systems and their users. Moreover, the group may be simultaneously based in one place (fixed or mobile) in real space and in another place in cyberspace. This opens up the possibility for encountering a group in cyberspace without discovering its real-space location and vice versa.

## Formalization by Layer

Steps 4 and 5 in the Ontology Development 101 method involve defining classes, the class hierarchy (i.e. inheritance), and the properties of these classes. In Step 5 we limit this to defining the inter-class relations. The resulting classes and relations are depicted formally as an Entity Relationship Diagram (Chen, 1976). We have extended Chen's graphic notation by including subclasses, as can be seen in Figure 1, where GeographicalSpace is specialized into the RealSpace and VirtualSpace subclasses.

Classes and relations are named according to the Smalltalk conventions (Goldberg & Robson, 1989). Classes have a name with an initial upper-case letter, e.g. Location. Instances of such a class are prefixed with "a" or "an", e.g. aLocation. If it is necessary to distinguish two or more instances, then their names will be suffixed with a unique number, e.g. aLocation1 and aLocation2 are distinct locations. If the name of the class or relation is formed from two or more words, then the name is formed by concatenating the words with the initial letter of each word in upper case, e.g. PhysicalObject. In some cases, we have enclosed names within curly brackets to indicate that we are referring to a set, e.g. {aLocation1, aLocation2} means the pair aLocation1 and aLocation2.

Relations are named so that they form a simple sentence when written together with typical instances of the classes that are related. For example, the binary directed relationship at: between physical objects and locations can be named as aPhysicalObject at: aLocation.

## Geographical Layer

Figure 1 shows the ERD for the geographical layer. In the geographical layer we identify four classes: GeographicalSpace (with its two subclasses RealSpace and VirtualSpace), FrameOfReference, Location, and Path.

The class GeographicalSpace represents a space that contains locations and paths. It has two subclasses: RealSpace with four instances (air, land, sea, outerSpace) and VirtualSpace with the single instance cyberspace.

The class FrameOfReference represents how distances and directions in a geographical space

*Figure 1. ERD for geographical layer*

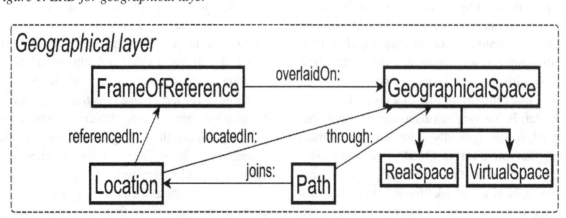

can be referenced. FrameOfReference can have multiple instances (e.g. Cartesian, polar, etc.) The classes GeographicalSpace and FrameOfReference are linked by the many-to-many relationship overlaidOn:, so that aFrameOfReference [is] overlaidOn: aGeographicalSpace. One or more frames of reference may be laid over one or more geographical spaces. For example, the Cartesian frame of reference may be laid over the air, land, sea, and outer space geographical spaces, but not over cyberspace.

As its name suggests, the class of Location represents unique locations in a geographical space. It can have multiple instances. The classes Location and FrameOfReference are linked by the many-to-many relationship locatedIn:, so that aLocation [is] locatedIn: aGeographicalSpace. One or more locations may be located in one or, more often, many frames of reference. This allows a particular location (i.e. an instance of Location) to be located in (say) both a Cartesian and a polar frame of reference for the land geographical space, enabling the conversion of locations, distances, and directions between frames of reference.

The class of Path represents permissible connections between one location and another through a particular space. A path is permissible if it could exist in the real world. For example, a

land path that crosses the sea would not be permissible, nor would an air path that led through a mountain. The Path class can have multiple instances. Classes Path and Location are related by the many-to-many relationship joins:, so that aPath joins: {aLocation1, aLocation2}.

In an implementation based on this ontology it may not be possible to model all paths explicitly because there could be infinitely many of them. Instead, some runtime procedure would have to be implemented to determine, when necessary, whether or not paths exist between two locations. In other words, instances of Path would be determined by lazy evaluation.

## Physical Layer

Figure 2 shows the ERD for the physical layer. In the physical layer we identify two root classes, each with an extensive tree of subclasses: PhysicalObject and PhysicalLink.

The class PhysicalObject represents objects of interest in the real world. This class is the root of a substantial tree of subclasses that may well be implementation-specific. Here we only sketch the beginnings of the tree. Given that most objects of interest in the C2 world are man-machine systems, the class PhysicalObject is subclassed into

*Figure 2. ERD for physical layer*

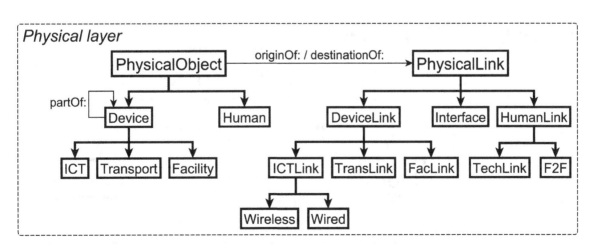

the classes of (man-made) Device and (natural) Human.

Device can itself be divided into a wide variety of subclasses, generally representing weapon systems, vehicles, sensors, effectors, etc., as needed by the ontology user. For illustrative purposes, we divide Device into Transport, Facility and ICTDevice classes. The Transport class represents devices that can change location (i.e. are mobile), while Facility represents devices with a fixed location. The ICTDevice class (shown in Figure 2 as "ICT") represents devices with computing and/or telecommunication capabilities, i.e. those employing information and communications technologies (ICT). In the ICT world, such devices are generally known as "hardware".

We also identify the abstract class PhysicalLink. As for the PhysicalObject class, the PhysicalLink class is the root of a tree of subclasses, again substantial and implementation-specific. Corresponding to the division of PhysicalObject into Device and Human subclasses, we divide the class PhysicalLink into DeviceLink, HumanLink, and Interface subclasses. As the class names suggest, these represent links between devices, between humans, and interfaces between humans and devices, respectively. Each of these three sub-

classes could be further divided as needed by the ontology user. For illustrative purposes we divide DeviceLink into TransportLink, FacilityLink, and ICTLink subclasses, with the last-named being further subclassed into WirelessICTLink and WiredICTLink. The HumanLink class could be subclassed into (say) F2FLink and TechLink, representing links between humans that are face-to-face or augmented using telecommunications technology (e.g. telephone and voice radio), respectively.

We identify three relationships in the physical layer. Physical objects are at the origin and destination of each link. To represent this, we identify aPhysicalObject originOf: aPhysicalLink and aPhysicalObject destinationOf: aPhysicalLink relationships. To represent the aggregation of devices into compound systems, we identify the aDevice1 partOf: aDevice2 relationship.

## Information Layer

Figure 3 shows the ERD for the information layer. In the information layer we identify a single class Information with its two subclasses Data and Program.

*Figure 3. ERD for information layer*

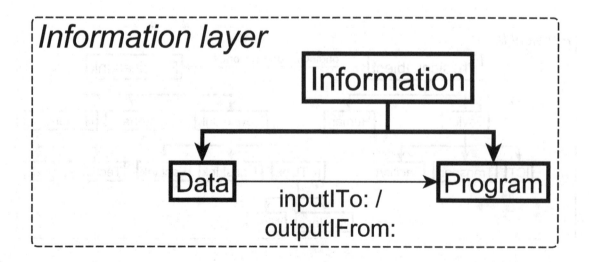

100

The class Information represents information that can be stored or transmitted using technical means. It is divided into two subclasses: Data and Program. The Data class represents pieces of data or information, such as a variable with its value (e.g. measured by a sensor), a tuple in a database, or a complex data structure modeling an object of interest with all its characteristics, behaviour, and history. Data instances may be time-stamped and may have some quality measure (e.g. probability, degree of belief, uncertainty, etc.) The Program class represents software that can input one or more Data instances, perform some process on them, and output one or more new Data instances. Processing may include displaying, storing, retrieving, and/or transmitting one or more Data instances. In terms of dataflow diagramming (Stevens, Myers & Constantine, 1974), Data instances are analogous to data-stores and Program instances are analogous to processes.

The classes Data and Program are linked by two many-to-many relationships: inputInformationTo: and outputInformationFrom:. The relationship aData [is] inputInformationTo: aProgram rep-

resents the input of data into a program, and the relationship aData [is] outputInformationFrom: aProgram represents data output or generated by a program.

## Cognitive Layer

Figure 4 shows the ERD for the cognitive layer. In the cognitive layer we identify the single class Knowledge with the two subclasses Belief and Operator, themselves further divided into sub-subclasses.

The class Knowledge represents knowledge that is held in the mind of humans. The Knowledge class is divided into two subclasses: Belief and Operator. These two subclasses are analogous to the Data and Program subclasses in the information layer. The Belief class is further divided into Fact and Goal sub-subclasses. The first represents a fact such as an observation, an assessment, or the current state or characteristic of an object of interest. The second represents a goal that should be made true at some time in the future.

*Figure 4. ERD for cognitive layer*

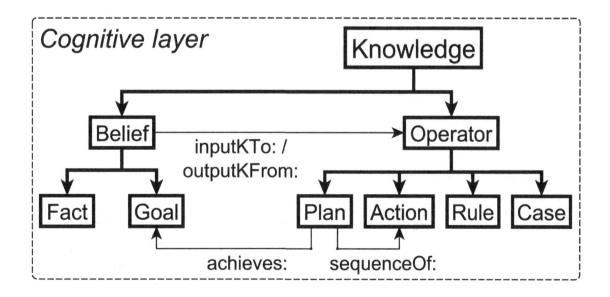

The Operator class represents operations on existing beliefs in order to derive or generate new beliefs. It is divided into four subclasses. The Action class represents actions or events that change one Fact into another. The Case class represents Actions that have occurred in the past. The Rule class represents Actions that occur conditionally in particular combinations of the state. The Plan class represents sequences of Actions that, when executed, will make a Goal become true. The relationship sequenceOf: represents a plan as a sequence of actions, so that aPlan [is] sequenceOf: {anAction}. The relationship achieves: indicates that a plan is intended to achieve a goal, so that aPlan achieves: aGoal.

The classes Belief and Operator are linked by two many-to-many relationships: inputKnowledgeTo: and outputKnowledgeFrom:. The relationship aBelief [is] nputKnowledgeTo: anOperator represents the input of a belief into an operator, and the relationship aBelief [is] outputKnowledgeFrom: anOperator represents the output or generation of a belief by an operator.

## Socio-Organizational Layer

Figure 5 shows the ERD for the socio-organizational layer. In this layer we identify four classes: Group, Role, Norm (with its two subclasses Behaviorial and Dialogical), and Place.

The class Group is used to model a unit in the structure of a formal or informal organization.

For example, an organization may be composed of departments and business units. At a lower level in the organizational structure, a department or business unit may be composed out of teams. Where the Group represents a coalition, it is composed out of organizations. To do so, one group may be associated with another. This is modeled by the associatedWith: relationship, in which aGroup1 [is] associatedWith: aGroup2. The associatedWith: relationship is transitive, forming a tree or network of associations, often visualized as an organigramme.

Associated with each Group is a set of one or more Roles. This is modeled by the many-to-one in: relationship, such that aRole [is] in: aGroup. Every group must have at least one role modeling the group leader, but may also have other roles. For example, a voluntary organization may have a treasurer role, a secretary role, as well as a chairperson role (i.e. the leader). A set of Norms is associated with each Role through the many-to-many has: relationship, so that aRole has: {aNorm}. These norms constrain how humans filling the associated roles should behave and communicate, represented by the subclasses BehavioralNorm and DialogicalNorm. For example, some of the behavioral norms for a treasurer (e.g. the norms concerning how to account for money) will differ from some of those for the secretary.

If a Group has sufficient social cohesion, it may be based in one or more Places. For example, a family Group would have a Place that it calls

*Figure 5. ERD for socio-organizational layer*

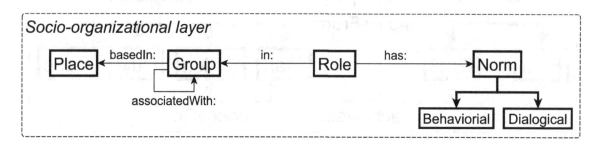

"home", and a Group of employees will have a Place that they call their "workplace". The relationship between Group and Place is modeled by the zero-to-many basedIn: relationship, such that aGroup [is] basedIn: aPlace.

## Formalization Across Layers

So far we have formalized each layer separately. Now we need to identify relations across layers, determining the order of layering. More specifically, we identify relations from classes in the physical layer to classes in the geographical layer, from classes in the information and cognitive layers to classes in the physical layer, and from classes in the socio-organizational layer to classes in the cognitive and physical layers. We formalize each interface in turn between one layer and the layers below it. Figure 6 shows the complete ERD for all five layers, together with the inter-layer relations linking them.

The physical layer is the lowest layer that has another layer below it, namely the geographical layer. There are two inter-layer relations between the physical and geographical layers. The first is the at: relation between the PhysicalObject class in the physical layer and the Location class in the geographical layer, so that aPhysicalObject [is] at: aLocation. The second inter-layer relation is the along: relation between the PhysicalLink class in the physical layer and the Path class in the geographical layer, so that aPhysicalLink [runs] along: aPath.

The information layer lies above the physical layer. This is determined by eight inter-layer relations. The ICTDevice class in the physical layer can be related to the Information class in the information layer by the senses:, stores:, processes:, and displays: relations, so that anICTDevice senses: / stores: / processes: / displays: anInformation. The senses: relation represents the creation of a piece of information by the ICTDevice sensing it from other PhysicalObjects. The stores: relation means that a piece of information is retained in

the ICTDevice. The processes: relation represents the creation of one or more new pieces of information (i.e. the outputs) by processing other, pre-existing pieces of information (i.e. the inputs). The displays: relation represents the ICTDevice displaying information so that it can be observed and assessed by a Human.

Similarly, the ICTLink class in the physical layer is related to the Information class in the information layer by the transmits: relation, so that anICTLink transmits: anInformation. This relation represents the transmission of the piece of information from the ICTDevice at the originOf: the ICTLink to the ICTDevice at the destinationOf: the ICTLink.

Finally, the Human class in the physical layer can be related to the Information class in the information layer by the observes:, assesses:, and enters: relations, so that aHuman observes: / assesses: / enters: anInformation. The observes: relation represents the Human observing a piece of information displayed by an ICTDevice and converting this information (by means of the remembers: relation – see below) into a piece of cognitive Knowledge in the Human's mind. The assesses: relation represents the Human evaluating a piece of information displayed by an ICTDevice to create a new piece of Knowledge by combining the displayed information with pre-existing Knowledge. The observes: and assesses: relations correspond to the Observe and Orient processes in Boyd's (1996) OODA loop. The enters: relation represents the Human entering a piece of Information into the ICTDevice, usually with the intention of causing an action to occur in one or more real or virtual spaces.

The cognitive layer also lies above the physical layer. This is determined by five inter-layer relations. The Human class in the physical layer can be related to the Knowledge class in the cognitive layer by the remembers:, adopts:, and learns: relations, so that aHuman remembers: / adopts: / learns: aKnowledge. The remembers: relation means that a piece of knowledge is retained in the Human's

*Figure 6. Complete ERD, including across-layer relations*

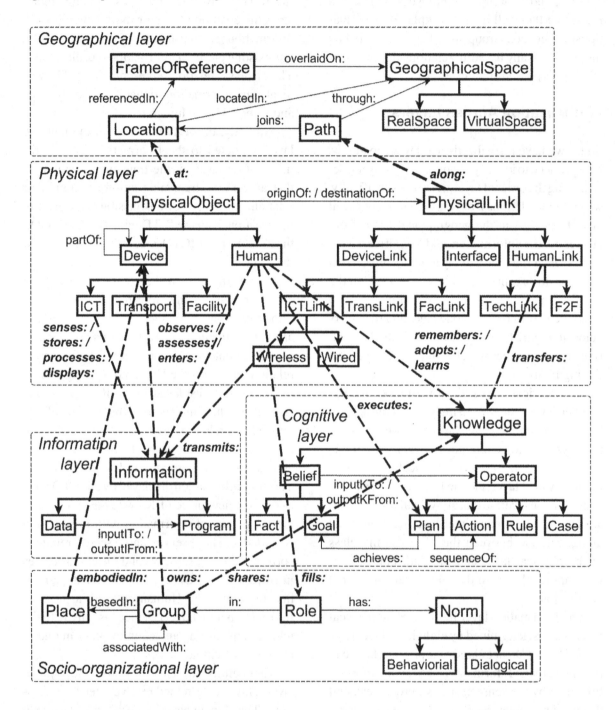

mind, usually as the result of observing or assessing Information displayed by an ICTDevice. The adopts: relation represents the Human retaining one or more pieces of Knowledge following its transfer from another Human through a HumanLink. The learns: relation represents the Human creating one or more new pieces of Knowledge from other, pre-existing pieces of Knowledge. If newly-created Knowledge is a decision, i.e. a commitment to act, then the remembers:, adopts:, or learns: relation corresponds to the Decide process in Boyd's (1996) OODA loop. Finally, the Human class in the physical layer can be related to the Plan class in the cognitive layer by the executes: relation, so that aHuman executes: aPlan. The executes: relation corresponds to the Act process in Boyd's OODA loop.

The socio-organizational layer lies above the cognitive and physical layers. This is determined by four inter-layer relations. The Place class in the socio-organizational layer is related to the Device class in the physical layer by the embodiedIn: relation, so that aPlace [is] embodiedIn: aDevice. The Group class in the socio-organizational layer is related to the Device class in the physical layer by the owns: relation, so that aGroup owns: aDevice. The Human class in the physical layer is related to the Role class in the socio-organizational layer by the fills: relation, so that aHuman fills: aRole. The Group class in the socio-organizational layer is related to the Knowledge class in the cognitive layer by the shares: relation, so that aGroup shares: aKnowledge.

## Identifying Networks

In this section we inspect the ERD to extract patterns that represent networks. There are two basic patterns and many compound forms of these basic patterns.

The first basic pattern depicts a class joined to itself by a relation. The class represents the nodes of the network, and the relation represents its arcs. This pattern often leads to hierarchies. For example, the class Device in the physical layer is joined to itself by the partOf: relation. This pattern represents a device hierarchy obtained by recursively disassembling a complex system into its component subsystems and parts. In the manufacturing, such a hierarchy is known as the complex system's "Product Breakdown Structure" (PBS). In maintenance and logistics, the same

hierarchy is known as the "Bill of Materials" (BoM). PBS looks at the hierarchy from the top down, and BoM from bottom up.

The second basic pattern consists of two classes joined by a relation. There are two interpretations of this pattern. In the first interpretation, one class represents the nodes and the other represents the arcs. For example, the class Location in the geographical layer is joined to the class Path. The equivalent network consists of a set of nodes representing locations and a set of arcs representing valid paths between locations. Applied to a road network, the nodes may be towns with the arcs being the roads connecting them.

In the second interpretation both classes represent nodes, albeit of different types. The relation(s) joining the classes represents the set of arcs. The resulting network is known as a *bipartite graph* (Newman, 2003). For example, the Data and Program classes in the information layer represent two types of node in an information network. In such a network, several pieces of Data may be input to a particular Program, which then outputs other pieces of Data. Any given piece of Data will typically be the output of one Program and the input to one or more other Programs. If one follows a path through an information network, then Data and Program nodes alternate. In software engineering, the Data and Program classes may be known as *datastores* and *processes*, respectively, with the entire network being termed a *dataflow diagram*. With two classes of node, a dataflow diagram is a bipartite graph. Moreover, the arcs are directional. In network science, such networks are known as *digraphs*, i.e. directed graphs (ibid.). Hence, a dataflow diagram is a bipartite digraph.

More complex variants of the two basic patterns can be found, e.g. tripartite graphs with three types of node. Moreover, a network can be found by transitively combining two relations that have a class in common. For example, to create the network of Humans who are members of Groups (a bipartite graph), one may combine transitively the aHuman fills: aRole and the aRole

[is] in: aGroup relations to derive the aHuman [is] memberOf: aGroup relation.

We first extract the networks to be found in each layer separately. Then we identify networks that span across the layers. To avoid a combinatorial explosion of possible networks, we confine ourselves to networks that can be found in military practice or doctrine, such as a map, a command structure, an order of battle, a plan, a telecommunications network, etc.

We identify one network in the geographical layer, consisting of the set of Location instances (the nodes) and the set of Path instances (the arcs). We name this the *geographical network*. This network would be visualized as a map of the area of operation.

We identify two networks in the physical layer. One network is represented by the set of instances of (leaf classes of) the PhysicalObject class (the nodes) and the set of instances of (leaf classes of) the PhysicalLink class (the arcs). We name this the *physical network*. The second network is represented by the set of Device instances (the nodes) and the set of partOf: relationships (the arcs). We name this network the *device breakdown structure*.

We identify one network in the information layer, consisting of the set of instances of the Information subclasses (the nodes) and the set of instances of the inputInformationTo: and outputInformationFrom: relationships (the arcs). We name this the *information network*. Note that the information network is a bipartite graph, with arcs running between unlike types (Data and Program). Moreover, the arcs are directed.

We identify three networks in the cognitive layer. The first network is represented by the set of instances of (leaf classes of) the Knowledge class (the nodes) and the set of instances of the inputKnowledgeTo: and outputKnowledgeFrom: relationships (the arcs). We name this the *knowledge network*. Note that, like the information network, the knowledge network is a bipartite graph, with directed arcs running between unlike

types (Belief and Operator). The second network is represented by the set of Goal and Plan instances (the nodes) and the set of achieves: relationships (the arcs). We name this network the *goal structure*. The third network is represented by the set of Plan and Action instances (the nodes) and the set of sequenceOf: relationships (the arcs). We name this network the *plan structure*.

We identify two networks in the socio-organizational layer. The first network consists of the set of Group nodes, with the associatedWith: relationships as arcs. This network represents the *organizational structure* of the set of groups. All or part of the network may be hierarchical, in which case it may be known as *command structure* and its depiction may be known as an *organigramme*. The second network has Groups and Places as its nodes, with the basedIn: relationships as its arcs. This network is a bipartite graph showing which Groups share Places,. We name this the *proximality network*.

Table 1 summarizes the networks we have identified within the five layers.

Next we identify selected networks spanning across layers. Many possible networks could be extracted, especially when an across-layer relation is combined transitively with a within-layer relation. We will restrict the selection to those networks that are important to C2 processes, such as situation awareness, information dissemination, mental models, a unit's order of battle and social network, and information and knowledge sharing within groups.

Situation awareness is aided by creating a map of the locations of objects of interest, which is then displayed to the users of a C2 system. We are not concerned here with how this information is visualized, but with how the underlying network of mappings between objects and locations is built up. This network consists of the PhysicalObject instances in the physical layer that are connected to Location instances in the geographical layer by means of the at: relation. The result is a bipartite graph which we call the *situation network*. This

*Table 1. Networks identified within layers*

| Layer | Network | Nodes | Arcs | Characteristics |
|---|---|---|---|---|
| Geographical | Geographical | Location | Path | |
| Physical | Physical | PhysicalObject | PhysicalLink | |
| Physical | Device breakdown structure | Device | part of: | |
| Information | Information | Information | inputInformationTo:, outputInformationFrom: | Bipartite, directed |
| Cognitive | Knowledge | Knowledge | inputKnowledgeTo:, outputKnowledgeFrom: | Bipartite, directed |
| Cognitive | Goal structure | Goal, Plan | achieves: | |
| Cognitive | Plan structure | Plan, Action | sequenceOf: | |
| Socio-organizational | Organization structure (a.k.a. command structure or organigramme) | Group | associatedWith: | May be hierarchy or contain sub-hierarchies. May be formal or informal |
| Socio-organizational | Proximality | Group, Place | basedIn: | |

would be visualized (in the information layer) by displaying the situation network over the underlying map. A C2 system user viewing this visualization would then gain situation awareness (in the cognitive layer).

Information is spread by means of computing hardware. A snapshot of where and what information is to be found in a set of ICT devices (e.g. a C2 system) can be represented as the bipartite graph of the ICTDevice instances in the physical layer that are related to Information instances in the information layer by the stores: relation. We call this the *information dissemination network*.

An analogous structure is the network of knowledge held in the mind of an individual C2 system user. This can be represented as the bipartite graph of the Knowledge instances in the cognitive layer that are related to a particular Human instance in the physical layer by the one-to-many remembers: relation. We call this the (user's) *mental model*. The inverse of this is the network obtained from the many-to-one remembers: relation, i.e. the set of Humans who know a particular piece of Knowl-

edge. The complete *cognitive model* is obtained from the many-to-many remembers: relation.

Next we consider two networks identifying the humans and non-human resources related to a particular group. We call the first the group's *social network* and the second the group's *Order Of Battle* (OOB). The social network is a bipartite graph relating Human instances in the physical layer to Group instances in the socio-organizational layer through the transitive combination of the fills: and in: relations, with the Role class as an intermediary. In military practice, an OOB consists of a unit's organization structure (usually hierarchical – see above) together with the human and device resources owned by each sub-unit. We simplify this for the purposes of this chapter by leaving out the human component, because this has already been covered by the unit's social network. In this simplified form, an OOB is the organizational structure of a unit, together with the (man-made) resources assigned to it. In network science terms, this would be a bipartite graph with two types of arc. One type of arc is based on the owns: relation linking Group instances in the socio-organizational layer to a set of Device instances in the physical layer through.

Finally, we identify another two networks modeling information and knowledge sharing. These represent the information and knowledge, respectively, shared by a Group. The *information sharing network* is the bipartite graph obtained between a Group instance in the socio-organizational layer and a set of Information instances in the information layer through the transitive combination of the owns: and stores: relations, with the ICTDevice class as an intermediary. The *knowledge sharing network* is the bipartite graph obtained between a Group instance in the socio-organizational layer and a set of Knowledge instances in the cognitive layer through the shares: relation.

Table 2 summarizes the across-layer networks that we have identified in this chapter.

## CASE STUDY: 9-11 REVISITED

## Setting the Scene

To illustrate the value of FLONC for software development, we show how the 9-11 scenario from Grant (2006) could be instantiated using the ontology. This case study is aimed at highlighting the difference between hierarchical and networked C2. To avoid the case study being overly long and complex, we limit the illustration to decision making by the FAA, the US National Command Authority (NCA), and the US Department of Defense (DoD) relating to just one of the four hijacked aircraft (American Airlines 11). Moreover, we will confine our modeling to the organizations involved and the information transmitted between them from the moment that a controller in FAA's Boston Center realized that AA11 was hijacked (at 08:25) to the moment that the F-15 fighters scrambled from Otis Air National Guard Base (ANGB) (at 08:46). Gaps in the source material also force us to simplify the

*Table 2. Networks identified across layers*

| Layers | Network | Nodes | Arcs | Characteristics |
|---|---|---|---|---|
| Physical-Geographical | Situation | PhysicalObject, Location | at: | Bipartite |
| Information-Physical | Information dissemination | Information, ICTDevice | stores: | Bipartite |
| Cognitive-Physical | Mental model | Human, Knowledge | remembers: (one-to-many) | Bipartite |
| Cognitive-Physical | Cognitive model | Human, Knowledge | remembers: (many-to-many) | Bipartite |
| Socio-organizational-Physical | Social | Group, Human (with Role as intermediary) | (transitive combination of) fills: and in: | Bipartite |
| Socio-organizational-Physical | Order Of Battle | Group, Device | (two types of arc:) owns: and associatedWith: | Bipartite |
| Socio-organizational-Information | Information sharing | Information, Group (with ICTDevice as intermediary) | (transitive combination of) owns: and stores: | Bipartite |
| Socio-organizational-Cognitive | Knowledge sharing | Knowledge, Group | shares: | Bipartite |

illustration by focusing mainly on the cognitive and socio-organizational layers.

Our source material is the 9/11 Commission Report (9/11 Commission, 2004), supplemented by the declassified timeline (9/11 Commission, 2005) from the US National Archives website. Additional material in a series of articles from Aviation Week & Space Technology provided insights into the events within the FAA (AWST, 2001) and NORAD (AWST, 2002a/b), as well as from the fighter pilots' viewpoint (AWST, 2002c). This source material does not provide information about the FAA's and NORAD's computing and communications infrastructure, other than that they were not interoperable. For this reason, we do not model the physical and information layers. The geographical layer will be neglected because it adds little to the scenario. While key persons are named in the notes to the 9/11 Commission report and in the declassified timeline, distinguishing them separately from the organizational units they worked in would make this case study too complex. We elide key persons with their organizational units. Therefore, the case study concentrates on groups and norms in the socio-organizational layer and on facts and rules in the cognitive layer.

The 9/11 Commission report (9/11 Commission, 2004, p.17-18) describes the protocols for the FAA to obtain military assistance from NORAD, as they existed on September 11, 2001. These protocols assumed that the aircraft pilot would notify the FAA controller of a hijacking by radio or by "squawking" a Secondary Surveillance Radar (SSR) transponder code of "7500". Controllers would notify their supervisors, who would in turn inform management all the way up to FAA Headquarters in Washington DC. FAA Headquarters had a hijack coordinator, who would contact the Pentagon's National Military Command Center (NMCC) to ask for a military aircraft to follow the flight, to report anything unusual, and to aid search and rescue in the event of an emergency. The NMCC would seek approval from the Office of the Secretary of Defense to provide military assistance. If approval was given, the orders would be transmitted down NORAD's chain of command. The protocols did not contemplate an intercept, assuming that the fighter escort would take up a position five miles directly behind the hijacked aircraft from where it could monitor the aircraft's flight path.

However, as the 9/11 Commission report states (9/11 Commission, 2004, p.18), the pre-existing FAA and DoD protocols for a hijacking *"presumed that:*

- *The hijacked aircraft would be readily identifiable and would not attempt to disappear;*
- *There would be time to address the problem through the appropriate FAA and NORAD chains of command; and*
- *The hijacking would take the traditional form: that is, it would not be a suicide hijacking designed to convert the aircraft into a guided missile.*

*On the morning of 9/11, the existing protocol was unsuited in every respect for what was about to happen."*

The actual events relating to AA11 are summarized in the 9/11 Commission report (9/11 Commission, 2004, p.32) as follows:

Figure 7 shows the organizational units from the FAA and the Defense Department (including the Pentagon and NORAD), plus the US President and Vice President, together with the information passing between them (9/11 Commission, 2004, pp.14-18). The units are shown as rectangles, linked together by superior-subordinate relationships (grey lines) with the superior unit higher up in the figure. For example, the FAA headquarters (HQ) is the FAA System Command Center's (SCC) superior, and the FAA Great Lakes and New England regions are the SCC's subordinates. Likewise, on the Defense Department side of the

*Table 3. American Airlines flight 11 (AA11), Boston to Los Angeles (from 9/11 Commission, 2004, p.32)*

| Time | Event |
|---|---|
| 07:59 | Takeoff |
| 08:14 | Last routine radio communication; likely takeover |
| 08:19 | Flight attendant notifies American Airlines of hijacking |
| 08:21 | Transponder is turned off |
| 08:23 | American Airlines attempts to contact the cockpit |
| 08:25 | Boston Center aware of hijacking |
| 08:37:52 | Boston Center notifies NEADS of hijacking |
| 08:46 | NEADS scrambles Otis fighter jets in search of AA11 |
| 08:46:40 | AA11 crashes into 1 World Trade Center (North Tower) |
| 08:53 | Otis fighter jets airborne |
| 09:16 | American Airlines headquarters aware that AA11 has crashed into WTC |
| 09:21 | Boston Center advises NEADS that AA11 is heading for Washington DC |
| 09:24 | NEADS scrambles Langley fighter jets in search of AA11 |

figure, Otis Air National Guard Base (ANGB) and Langley Air Force Base (AFB) are subordinate to the North Eastern Air Defense Sector (NEADS). The information passing between these units is shown as thick arrows starting at "AA11 hijacked!", running both up the FAA hierarchy and across to NEADS and Otis, then running up the Defense Department to the high-level teleconference, and finally running down the Defense Department to Otis, where the 102 Fighter Wing received the order to "Scramble!"

What actually happened between 08:25 and 08:46 on September 11, 2001, differed from the protocol. The 9/11 Commission report states (9/11 Commission, 2004, p.18, bold emphasis added) that *"Boston Center did not follow the protocol in seeking military assistance through the prescribed chain of command. In addition to notifications within the FAA, Boston Center took the initiative, at 8:34, to contact the military....At 8:37:52, Boston Center reached NEADS. This was the first notification received by the military – at any level that American 11 had been hijacked".* As the bolded text indicates, an FAA employee in Boston Center contacted a friend in NEADS

(AWST, 2002a), as well as informing his supervisor. Moreover, a similar across-organization report was generated by a controller in Boston Approach to a friend at Otis ANGB (ibid.). In both cases, the Boston controllers used their mobile telephones, rather than the FAA's communications infrastructure. By contrast, the request for military assistance that, according to the protocol, should have gone from the FAA hijack coordinator in FAA headquarters to the Pentagon's NMCC did not happen, as the 9/11 Commission report notes (9/11 Commission, 2004, p.19).

What is difficult to depict in Figure 7 is that the Battle Commander in NEADS telephoned his superior in NORAD seeking authorization to scramble the Otis fighters. His superior instructed the NEADS Battle Commander to "go ahead and scramble them, and we'll get authorities later" (9/11 Commission, 2004, p.20). In short, the scramble orders from NORAD progressed down the hierarchy to the 102 Fighter Wing at Otis *in parallel with* the reporting upward from NORAD to the President. Only after a protracted high-level teleconference did the formal authorization come down the hierarchy to back up what the NORAD

*Figure 7. Actual 9-11 reporting chain for AA11 (Grant, 2006, figure 4)*

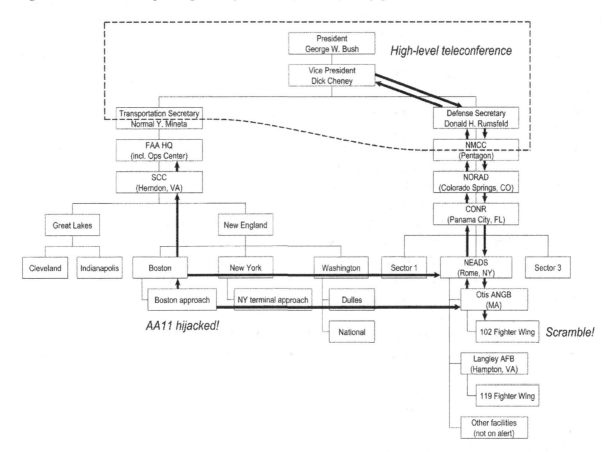

commander had done on his own initiative. By the time that this happened (at 10:30), all four hijacked aircraft had already crashed. Analysis of the corresponding timeline showed that the NORAD commander's use of his own initiative had saved around 70 minutes.

Inspection of Figure 7 shows that, in addition to following the protocol, FAA's Boston Center and Boston Approach had effectively performed self-synchronization by informing their friends in NEADS and Otis. What actually happened, then, was both hierarchical (vertical, industrial-age communication, according to the protocol) and networked (horizontal, information-age communication) in nature. Indeed, it was most fortunate that self-synchronization happened. If the two Boston controllers had not informed their

military contacts, then the reporting chain would have been interrupted when it reached the FAA hijack coordinator, delaying the US response for an indeterminate length of time. Moreover, the controllers' actions created the opportunity for the NORAD commander to use his initiative.

Our case study will contrast what should have happened according to the pre-existing (hierarchical) protocol to what actually happened on the day (partly hierarchical, partly networked).

## Organizations

For the purposes of this case study, there were four organizations involved in the events surrounding AA11: Al Qaeda, the FAA, the NAC, and the US DoD. Applying FLONC, each of these organizations would be modeled as an instance of the Group class. There would be associatedWith: relationships from the FAA and the US DoD to the NAC.

Al Qaeda's mission was to inflict a major terrorist attack on the United States. One of Al Qaeda's teams was assigned to hijack AA11. We shall call this team the "AA11 hijackers". Using FLONC, the AA11 hijackers would be modeled as an instance of the Group class, associatedWith: Al Qaeda. Each individual hijacker would be modeled as a Human, with Atta taking the leader Role within the AA11 hijacker Group. The other individual hijackers would also be modeled as Humans and take on the member Role.

The FAA's mission was to maintain a safe separation between airliners flying over the US and to minimize airport congestion. The FAA's units involved in the AA11 hijacking were the Boston Approach center, Boston Center, the SCC, and FAA HQ. Each of these units would be modeled as a Group, associatedWith: the FAA. Moreover, Boston Center would be associatedWith: the SCC, with this association being marked as subordinate-to-superior. Similarly, the SCC and FAA HQ would be associatedWith: each other as subordinate-to-superior.

The NAC's mission was to take strategic decisions in defense of the United States. The NAC would be represented as an instance of the Group class. It had no organizational structure, consisting of three Humans: President Bush, Vice President Cheney, and Secretary of Defense Rumsfeld. These Humans fill the Roles in the NAC Group of President, Vice President, and Secretary of Defense, respectively.

The US DoD's mission was to protect the United States. In this case study, we are specifically concerned with part of this mission, namely to defend the airspace of North America. Six units of the US DoD were involved in responding to the AA11 hijacking: the NMCC, NORAD, CONR, NEADS, Otis ANGB, and 102 Fighter Wing (102FW). These units would each be modeled as

a Group, associatedWith: the US DoD. Moreover, as for the FAA, the hierarchical organizational structure would be represented by additional associatedWith: relationships, appropriately marked subordinate-to-superior.

## Information Transmitted

For simplicity, we consider just four pieces of information (i.e. instances of the Fact class) needed between 08:25 and 08:46, as follows:

- The information broadcast by an AA11 hijacker over air traffic control frequencies, giving the clue that AA11 was hijacked.
- The fact that AA11 had been hijacked with violence.
- The request for authority to shoot down AA11.
- The order to scramble F-15 fighters from Otis ANGB.

Table 4 lists the key pieces of information passed from one organizational unit to another, together with a outline of the recipient's cognitive processing of the information received. We assume that the information was passed over the telephone or voice radio, i.e. instances of the TechLink class. The information content passed is one of the four Fact instances. To process the information received, the recipient uses Rule and Norm instances.

## Norms

Using dialogical Norms, it is straightforward to change the way in which information is routed between Humans filling a particular Role in a Group. This can be done for the two cases, as follows:

- *Should have happened.* The pre-9/11 protocol for FAA controllers (i.e. a particular Role filled by Humans within the FAA Group) could be expressed as the following Norm:

*Table 4. Information passed and recipients' responses*

| Time | Sender | Recipient | Information content |
|---|---|---|---|
| 08:24 | AA11 hijacker | Boston | Clue that AA11 had been hijacked |
| | Boston picked up the clue, using:<br>• A Rule for determining from the clue that a hijacking with violence was taking place.<br>• One or more (dialogical) Norms to determine who to inform: superior (SCC) and/or military friend (in NEADS). | | |
| 08:28 | Boston | SCC | AA11 has been hijacked with violence |
| | SCC used a Norm to determine who to inform, namely their superior (FAA HQ). | | |
| 08:32 | SCC | FAA HQ | AA11 has been hijacked with violence |
| | (FAA HQ took no effective action.) | | |
| 08:37 | Boston | NEADS | AA11 has been hijacked with violence |
| | NEADS used a Norm to determine who to inform, namely their superior (NORAD). | | |
| 08:38 | NEADS | NORAD | AA11 has been hijacked with violence |
| | NORAD used:<br>• A Rule to determine how to respond to the hijacking, namely to scramble fighters.<br>• A Norm to determine to whom the order should be given (namely NEADS). | | |
| 08:38 | NORAD | NEADS | Scramble F-15 fighters from Otis |
| | NEADS used a Norm to determine to whom the order should be given (namely 102FW). | | |
| 08:39 | NORAD | NMCC | Request authority to shoot down AA11 |
| | NORAD used:<br>• A Rule to determine that authority should be requested from the NAC to shoot down AA11.<br>• A Norm to determine to whom the request should be sent (namely NMCC) | | |
| 08:46 | NEADS | 102FW | Scramble F-15 fighters from Otis |
| | 102FW used a Rule to act on the order to scramble F-15 fighters, resulting in take-off at 08:53. | | |

**IF** you receive information that an aircraft has been hijacked **THEN** pass the information to your superior.

The FAA hijack coordinator (i.e. a Role specific to the FAA HQ Group) would also have had an additional Norm stating that:

**IF** you receive information that an aircraft has been hijacked **AND** violence has been used **THEN** pass the information to the NMCC **AND** request military assistance from them.

- *Actually happened.* In the actual event, the FAA Boston controllers acted as if they were obeying the following two Norms, both of which matched the situation:

**IF** you receive information that an aircraft has been hijacked **THEN** pass the information to your superior.

**IF** you receive information that an aircraft has been hijacked **AND** violence has been used **AND** you have a friend in the military **THEN** pass the information to your friend.

In summary, the case study has represented using the following classes from the FLONC ontology:

- **Physical layer:** Human and TechLink.
- **Cognitive layer:** Fact and Rule.
- **Socio-organizational layer:** Group and Norm.

## RELATED WORK

Step 2 of the Ontology development 101 methodology requires ontology authors to consider the reuse of existing ontologies. We sought C2 ontologies in the C2 literature and in ontology libraries, but found that there are few existing ontologies relevant to C2. Taking a wider viewpoint, there are a number of initiatives aimed at formalizing C2-related data, even if they do not use a formal language such as OWL (or even the term "ontology"). These initiatives are all stimulated by the need for interoperability between C2 systems from different military services and from different partners in international coalitions.

More generally still, there are existing standards and initiatives relating to geography. The current World Geodetic System (WGS), established in 1984 and last revised in 2004, is the accepted standard coordinate frame for the Earth, used in cartography, geodesy, and navigation. WGS 84 is the global coordinate system used by the Global Positioning System (GPS). While WGS 84 is formalized, it does not provide an ontology. Moreover, it is limited to one aspect (equivalent to the FrameOfReference) of the geographical layer.

By contrast, the Open Geospatial Consortium (OGC), established in 1994, is a worldwide standards organization comprising over 400 commercial, governmental, non-profit, and research organizations. The OGC's mission is to encourage the development and implementation of open standards for geospatial content and services, Geographical Information System (GIS) data processing, and data sharing in an Internet context. It has working groups covering eleven application domains, including Defense & Intelligence and Emergency Response & Disaster Management. The OGS standards baseline consists of more than 30 standards, many of which have been adopted as International Standards Organization (ISO) standards. While the OGS standards are themselves formalized using Unified Modeling Language (UML), they do not as yet incorporate an OGS-wide ontology. There is an associated Spatial Ontology Community of Practice (SO-COP) that is working towards the development of spatial ontologies for use by all in the Semantic Web. However, this initiative has not yet resulted in a definitive ontology.

There are three initiatives that appear to have made some progress in developing a C2-related ontology: the International Defence Enterprise Architecture Specification (IDEAS) group, the SAS-050 and SAS-065 projects of the System Analysis and Systems (SAS) panel of the NATO Science & Technology Organization, and the NATO-affiliated Multilateral Interoperability Programme (MIP). In addition, the international Simulation Interoperability Standards Organization (SISO) has investigated using the MIP ontology for linking simulations using their Coalition Battle Management Language (C-BML) to C2 systems.

The IDEAS group is a consortium of the Australian, Canadian, Swedish, UK, and USA defense ministries. They have been developing a formal ontology known as the Foundation Model to support the exchange and sharing of enterprise architectures. This Foundation Model provides a basic framework for expressing concepts that are frequently used in enterprise architecture, using types (classes), individuals (instances), and tuples (relationships) as the building blocks; see Figure 7. The IDEAS group expects that implementers will extend the Foundation Model for their own purposes. Associated with the IDEAS Model is the Business Object Reference Ontology (BORO) method for developing ontological or semantic models for large complex operational applications. Unfortunately, the IDEAS model is proprietary. Moreover, BORO is grounded in physical reality, suggesting that implementations of the Foundation Model are likely to focus on the physical layer. Beyond the wiki available on the IDEAS Group website, little has been published in the open scientific literature.

The SAS-050 project involved 35 representatives from nine NATO nations (Canada, Denmark, Germany, Italy, Portugal, Netherlands, Norway, UK, and USA) and two non-NATO nations (Australia and Sweden) (Alberts, 2006). SAS-050 was formed to explore new approaches to C2. The prime objective was to develop a conceptual model of C2, identifying the key variables and relationships among them. The resulting C2 Conceptual Reference Model (C2CRM) contained over 300 variables and "a selected subset of the possible relationships". The SAS-05 final report acknowledged that this model was not "finished". In particular, it noted that many of the concepts applying to individuals (e.g. awareness) had a team counterpart (e.g. shared awareness). Further work was needed to better understand these team concepts.

The subsequent SAS-065 project was aimed at developing a C2 Maturity Model for network-enabled operations. One of the products was a revised version of the C2CRM developed by SAS-050. C2CRM version 2.0 separated out the concepts applying to individuals from those applying to teams (Eggenhofer-Rehart, 2009). Table 4 shows a partial hierarchy of the variables, with the Quality of actions and Quality of decisions variables split down to the 2nd level. Clearly, the hierarchy is one of decomposition (aggregation). Variables are given a definition only at the lowest level of decomposition. Inspection shows that the C2CRM variables represent a mixture of classes and their attributes. For example, an action could be a class, with accuracy, appropriateness, completeness, consistency, correctness, efficiency, etc. as its attributes. Similarly, characteristics and behaviors are attributes of individuals and groups. Moreover, the first-level concepts are also a mixture of entities (e.g. individuals, groups, information), events (e.g. actions, decisions), and processes (e.g. decision making, sensemaking). Much work would need to be done before the C2CRM could be formalized as an ontology.

The Multilateral Interoperability Programme (MIP) has a long history. In 1976 NATO approved a military requirement for interoperability between automated data systems, leading to the start of the Army Tactical Command and Control Information System (ATCCIS) programme. Six NATO nations originated MIP in 1998, and in 2001 this was merged with ATCCIS. The name and scope of the data exchange standards developed by these programmes has also changed over the years. Originally known as the Generic Hub Data Model, the standards were progressively renamed Land Command & Control Information Exchange Data Model (LC2IEDM), then Command & Control Information Exchange Data Model (C2IEDM), to the current Joint Command, Control and Consultation Information Exchange Data Model (JC3IEDM).

MIP is now a consortium of 29 NATO and non-NATO nations plus NATO Allied Command Transformation (ACT) that meet quarterly to define interoperability specifications for sharing C2 information. Many of these nations have implemented the MIP standards in their national C2 systems, and NATO has ratified the JC3IEDM standard as STANAG 5525. The aim of JC3IEDM is to enable the "international interoperability of C2 information systems at all levels from corps to battalion (or lowest appropriate level) in order to support multinational (including NATO), combined and joint operations and the advancement of digitization in the international arena". This aim is achieved by specifying the minimum set of data that needs to be exchanged in coalition or multinational operations. Each nation, agency or community of interest is free to expand its own data dictionary to accommodate additional information exchange requirements.

The JC3IEDM high-level entities, shown in Figure 8, can be related to FLONC's five layers. The Location, Vertical-Distance, and Coordinate-System entities clearly related to the geographical layer. The entities Object-Type, Object-Item, Address, Capability, and Action relate to the physical layer. The entities Reporting-Data, Context, Reference, Rule-of-Engagement, and Candidate-Target-List relate to the information layer. There appear to be no entities that relate to the cognitive layer, probably because the Person entity is at a lower level (as a subclass of the Object-Item entity). The entities Affiliation and Group-Characteristic relate to the socio-organizational layer. At lower levels in the JC3IEDM, there is an extensive, domain-specific hierarchy of subclasses underlying the Object-Item high-level entity. These subclasses could form the starting point for ontology authors and implementers wishing to extend the Device class in our FLONC ontology.

## CONCLUSION

This chapter has presented a formalized logical ontology for representing C2 systems as layered networks, known as the Formalized Layered Ontology for Networked C2 (FLONC). There are five layers in FLONC: geographical, physical, information, cognitive, and socio-organizational.

The research reported here extends previous ideas on grouping NATO's DOTMLPFI factors into networks (Van Ettinger, 2008) (Monsuur, Grant & Janssen, 2011). It integrates cyberspace into the other four, "kinetic" domains, necessitating the representation of virtual, discrete, and higher-dimensional spaces. It makes a distinction between information held in ICT devices and knowledge held in human minds. It relaxes the privileged role of human individuals and military units in previous work. Humans are simply another class of entities in the physical layer, and units (i.e. groups) are an entity-class in the socio-organizational layer. The entity-classes in each layer, together with the relations between them, have been formalized. The resulting layered ontology has been validated by checking that each layer contains at least one militarily-relevant network. The ultimate goal of this research is to enable the development of software based on the FLONC ontology that can simulate or support network-enabled C2.

After introducing the background, this chapter outlines relevant aspects of ontology engineering, discusses key aspects of cyberspace, describes the formalization of the layers and the extraction of militarily-relevant networks, and compares related research. The networks identified include the geographical network of locations in an area of operations, the decomposition hierarchy of complex devices, the information and knowledge networks (i.e. dataflow and its cognitive equivalent), goal and plan structures, organizational structure (a.k.a. command structure), and the proximality network (i.e. where units are based). Additional networks can be identified from the relations running across the layers in FLONC. These include the situation network of objects of interest, the dissemination of information within a C2 system, each user's mental model, an overall cognitive model distributed over a set of users, units' social networks and order of battle, and information and knowledge sharing within and between groups. The use of the FLONC ontology is illustrated using the events of September 11, 2001, as a case study.

Finally, the FLONC ontology has been compared with related work on ontologies for C2. The IDEAS group's Foundation Model includes some comparable conceptual entities, but is proprietary, with little appearing in the open scientific literature. The C2 Conceptual Reference Model resulting from the SAS-050 and SAS-065 projects is a decomposition hierarchy of some 300 variables, together with a selected subset of relationships between them. Inspection shows that the variables are an unstructured mixture of classes and attributes and of entities, events, and processes. Much work would be needed to formalize C2CRM as an ontology. The Joint Command, Control and Consultation Information Exchange Data Model (JC3IEDM) resulting from the long-standing,

*Table 5. C2CRM version 2.0: partial hierarchy of variables*

| 1st level | 2nd level | Definition |
|---|---|---|
| C2 approach | | decomposed to 4th level) |
| Quality of actions | | (decomposed to 2nd level) |
| | Action accuracy | Extent to which actions executed are directed to the intended purpose |
| | Action appropriateness | Extent to which actions executed are the appropriate ones to achieve the intended purpose |
| | Action completeness | Extent to which actions executed encompass the full scope of the plan or order |
| | Action consistency | Extent to which actions executed are consistent with actions in an earlier timeframe |
| | Action correctness | Extent to which actions are executed without error |
| | Action efficiency | Extent to which actions executed are efficient in the use of resources |
| | Action precision | Extent to which actions executed are precisely related to the intended purpose |
| | Action synchronization | Purposeful arrangement of actions in time, space and purpose |
| | Action timeliness | Extent to which actions are executed at the time required by the plan or order |
| | Likelihood of success | Probability of mission accomplishment |
| Decision making | | (decomposed to 3rd level) |
| Quality of decisions | | (decomposed to 2nd level) |
| | Decision accuracy | Appropriateness of precision of decision (plan, directives) for a particular use |
| | Decision completeness | Extent to which relevant decisions encompass the necessary (1) depth: range of actions and contingencies included; (2) breadth: range of force elements included; and (3) time: range of time horizons included |
| | Decision consistency | Extent to which decisions are internally consistent with prior understanding and decisions |
| | Decision correctness | Extent to which a decision is consistent with ground truth |
| | Decision currency | Time taken to make a decision (start time - external signal) |
| | Decision precision | Level of granularity of decisions |
| | Decision relevance | Extent to which a decision is significant to the task at hand |
| | Decision timeliness | Extent to which currency of decision making is suitable to its use |
| | Decision uncertainty | Process of generating command intent |
| Individual entity characteristics and behaviours | | (decomposed to 4th level) |
| Sensemaking | | (decomposed to 3rd level) |
| Group entity characteristics and behaviours | | (decomposed to 3rd level) |
| Information | | (decomposed to 4th level) |
| Quality of information | | (decomposed to 3rd level) |
| High level measures of merit | | (decomposed to 3rd level) |

NATO-affiliated Multilateral Interoperability Programme is the most mature work. It offers a formalized hierarchy of entities, relations, and attributes in UML. It has been ratified by NATO as STANAG 5525, and is implemented in many nations' C2 systems. Moreover, it is publically available in OWL (Matheus & Ulicny, 2007).

FLONC distinguishes itself from this related work in three ways. First, it divides the ontology into layers. Second, a rich set of militarily-relevant networks can be extracted from the ontology. We claim this as the prime contribution of the research reported in this chapter. Third, it is a major step towards implementing these ideas in software.

## FURTHER RESEARCH

The research reported here is limited in several ways. First, the FLONC logical ontology comprises only classes and relations. Attributes and facets would have to be added to obtain an implementable ontology. Second, the abstraction hierarchy of PhysicalObjects and PhysicalLinks would have to be extended to fully represent the human and man-made resources (e.g. weapon systems, vehicles, sensors, weapons, computer terminals, radio handsets, communication links, routers, hubs, etc.) used in typical military operations. Third, the ontology has not been used in implementing software. This means that, while the ontology has been checked for consistency, it has

*Figure 8. IDEAS foundation model conceptual diagram (adapted from http://www.ideasgroup.org/dm2/)*

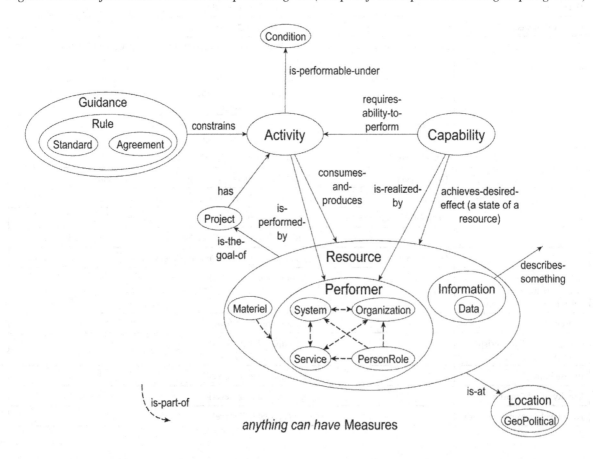

*Figure 9. JC3IEDM high-level entities (adapted from Matheus & Ulicy, 2007)*

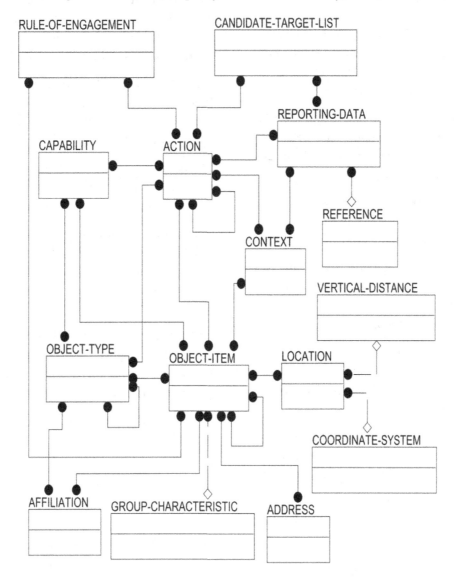

not been evaluated by prospective users, let alone verified in simulated or real operations. Fourth, the ontology separates information and knowledge into separate layers. This may raise conceptual problems in modeling autonomous man-made entities, i.e. devices that can be ascribed cognitive capabilities such as agency. Further research is needed to see how such intelligent agents can be incorporated in the FLONC ontology.

Further research could address these limitations one by one. It would be better to apply an iterative approach to the ultimate goal of using the FLONC ontology in implementing software, because this would more quickly elicit feedback from prospective users. The obvious starting point would be to use the ontology to develop and experiment with a simulation of network-enabled C2. One possibility would be to fill out the 9-11 case study described in Section 5. Another would be to develop a simulation of the MECA scenario (Van Diggelen et al, 2009).

# REFERENCES

9/11 Commission. (2004). *The 9/11 Commission Report: Final report of the national commission on terrorist attacks on the United States*. Washington, DC: US Government Printing Office.

9/11 Commission. (2005). *Staff Monograph on the Four Flights and Civil Aviation Security*. Retrieved 4 November 2005 from http://www.archives.gov/research/9-11-commission/

Alberts, D. S. (2002). Information-Age Transformation: Getting to a 21st century military. US DoD Command & Control Research Program.

Alberts, D. S. (Ed.). (2006). Exploring New Command and Control Concepts and Capabilities (Final Report, SAS-050). NATO Science & Technology Organization.

Alberts, D. S., Garstka, J., Hayes, R. E., & Signori, D. T. (2001). Understanding Information Age Warfare. US DoD Command & Control Research Program.

Alberts, D. S., & Hayes, R. E. (2003). Power to the Edge: Command Control in the information age. US DoD Command & Control Research Program.

AWST. (2001). Crisis at Herndon: 11 Airplanes Astray. Aviation Week & Space Technology, 155(25), 96–99.

AWST. (2002a). Exercise Jump-starts Response to Attacks. Aviation Week & Space Technology, 156(22), 48–52.

AWST. (2002b). NORAD and FAA Sharpen View Inside Borders. Aviation Week & Space Technology, 156(23), 50–52.

AWST. (2002c). F-16 Pilots Considered Ramming Flight 93. Aviation Week & Space Technology, 157(11), 71–74.

Boyd, J. R. (1996). The Essence of Winning and Losing. (Unpublished lecture notes). Maxwell Air Force Base.

Cebrowski, A. K., & Garstka, J. H. (1998). Network-Centric Warfare: Its origins and future. Proceedings of the United States Naval Institute. United States Naval Institute, 124, 1.

Chen, P. P.-S. (1976). The Entity-Relationship Model - Towards a unified view of data. *ACM Transactions on Database Systems*, 1(1), 9–36. doi:10.1145/320434.320440

Chisholm, R. (1982). Knowledge as Justified True Belief. In The Foundations of Knowing. University of Minnesota Press.

Coutinho, L. R., Sichman, J. S., & Boissier, O. (2005). Modeling Organization in MAS: A comparison of models. In *Proceedings of 1st Workshop on Software Engineering for Agent-oriented Systems* (SEAS05). SEAS.

De Nicola, A., Missikof, M., & Navigili, R. (2009). A Software Engineering Approach to Ontology Building. *Information Systems*, 34(2), 258–275. doi:10.1016/j.is.2008.07.002

Dodge, M., & Kitchen, R. (2001). Mapping Cyberspace. Routledge.

Eggenhofer-Rehart, P. (Ed.). (2009). C2 Conceptual Reference Model version 2.0 with suggestions for its application in conjunction with the NATO NEC C2 Maturity Model (N2C2M2). Appendix to NATO SAS-065 Final Report.

Goldberg, A., & Robson, D. (1989). Smalltalk-80: The language. Addison-Wesley Publishing Company.

Grant, T. J. (2006). Measuring the Potential Benefits of NCW: 9/11 as case study. In *Proceedings, 11th International Command & Control Research & Technology Symposium*. Washington, DC: US DoD Command & Control Research Program.

Gruber, T. R. (1993). A Translation Approach to Portable Ontology Specifications. *Knowledge Acquisition*, 5(2), 199–220. doi:10.1006/knac.1993.1008

Hübner, J. F., Sichman, J. S., & Boissier, O. (2002). A Model for the Structural, Functional, and Deontic Specification of Organizations in Multi-agent Systems. In *Proceedings, 16th Brazilian Symposium on AI* (SBIA 2002), (LNAI), (vol. 2507, pp. 118-128). Springer.

Matheus, C. J., & Ulicny, B. (2007). On the Automated Generation of an OWL Ontology based on the Joint C3 Information Exchange Data Model. In *Proceedings of the 12ᵗʰ International Command & Control Research & Technology Symposium* (ICCRTS). ICCRTS.

Monsuur, H., Grant, T. J., & Janssen, R. H. P. (2011). Network Topology of Military Command & Control Systems: Where axioms and action meet. Computer Science, Technology, and Applications, 3, 1–27.

NATO. (2009). Whitepaper on NNEC Maturity Levels. Working draft v2, dated 22 April 2009. NATO.

Newman, M. E. J. (2003). The Structure and Function of Complex Networks. *SIAM Review*, 45(2), 167–256. doi:10.1137/S003614450342480

Noy, N. F., & McGuiness, D. L. (2001). *Ontology Development 101: A guide to creating your first ontology*. Stanford Knowledge Systems Laboratory Technical Report KSL-01-5 and Stanford Medical Informatics Technical Report SMI-2001-0880.

Pidcock, W. (2010). *What are the Differences Between a Vocabulary, a Taxonomy, a Thesaurus, an Ontology, and a Meta-Model?* Retrieved from http://www.metamodel.com/article.php

Rowley, J. (2007). The Wisdom Hierarchy: Representations of the DIKW hierarchy. *Journal of Information Science*, 33(2), 163–180. doi:10.1177/0165551506070706

Smith, M.K., Welty, C., & McGuinness, D.L. (2004). *OWL Web Ontology Language Guide*. W3C Recommendation, 10 February 2004.

Stevens, W., Myers, G., & Constantine, L. (1974). Structured Design. *IBM Systems Journal*, 13(2), 115–139. doi:10.1147/sj.132.0115

Trist, E., & Bamforth, K. (1951). Some Social and Psychological Consequences of the Longwall Method of Coal Getting. *Human Relations*, 4, 3–38. doi:10.1177/001872675100400101

US DoD JP 1-02. (2013). *US Department of Defense Dictionary of Military and Associated Terms, Joint Publication 1-02, 8 November 2010 as amended through 15 December 2013*. Retrieved February 6, 2014, from http://www.dtic.mil/doctrine/dod_dictionary/

Uschold, M., & Jasper, R. (1999). A Framework for Understanding and Classifying Ontology Applications. In *Proceedings, 12ᵗʰ international workshop on Knowledge Acquisition, Modelling, and Management*, (vol. 99, pp. 16-21). Academic Press.

Van Diggelen, J., Bradshaw, J. M., Grant, T. J., Johnson, M., & Neerincx, M. (2009). Policy-Based Design of Human-Machine Collaboration in Manned Space Missions. In *Proceedings, 3ʳᵈ IEEE international conference on Space Mission Challenges for Information Technology 2009* (SMC-IT09). Pasadena, CA: SMC.

Van Ettinger, F. (2008). NATO Network Enabled Capabilities: Can it work? Carre, 11, 22–26.

Van Fenema, P., Rietjens, S., & Besters, B. (2014 This volume). De-conflicting Civil-Military Networks.

Zins, C. (2007). Conceptual Approaches for Defining Data, Information, and Knowledge. *Journal of the American Society for Information Science and Technology*, 58(4), 479–493. doi:10.1002/asi.20508

## ADDITIONAL READING

Alberts, D. S., & Hayes, R. E. (2006). Understanding Command and Control. Washington, DC: US DoD Command & Control Research Program.

Alberts, D. S., & Hayes, R. E. (2007). Planning: Complex endeavors. Washington, DC: US DoD Command & Control Research Program.

Alberts, D.S., & Nissen, H.E. (2009). Toward Harmonizing Command and Control with Organization and Management Theory. *International C2 Journal*, 3(2), 1-59.

Barabási, A.-L. (2003). Linked: How everything is connected to everything else and what it means for business, science, and everyday life. New York, NY: Plume.

BORO website. http://www.borosolutions.co.uk/research/, accessed 1 October 2013.

Brehmer, B. (2005). The Dynamic OODA Loop: Amalgamating Boyd's OODA loop and the cybernetic approach to Command and Control. In Alberts, D.S. (Ed.), Proceedings, 10th International Command & Control Research & Technology Symposium, Washington DC: US DoD Command & Control Research Program.

Dignum, V. (2004). A Model for Organizational Interaction: Based on agents, founded in logic. Unpublished PhD thesis, University of Utrecht, The Netherlands.

Ferber, J., Gutknecht, O., Jonker, C. M., Müller, J.-P., & Treur, J. (2000). Organization Models and Behavioral Requirements Specification for Multi-Agent Systems. In International Conference on Multi-Agent Systems (pp. 0387-0387). IEEE Computer Society.

Galbraith, J. R. (1973). Designing Complex Organizations. Reading, Massachusetts: Addison-Wesley.

Georgeff, M., Pell, B., Pollack, M., Tambe, M., & Wooldridge, M. (1999). The Belief-Desire-Intention Model of Agency. In Intelligent Agents V: Agents Theories, Architectures, and Languages (pp. 1–10). Berlin, Heidelberg: Springer. doi:10.1007/3-540-49057-4_1 doi:10.1007/3-540-49057-4_1

Grant, T. J. (2011). Combining Information Sharing and Seeking in Networked Coalitions. In Santos, M.A., Dugdale, J., & Medonça, D. (Eds.), Proceedings, 8th international conference in Information Systems for Crisis Response And Management (paper 253), Lisbon, Portugal: ISCRAM.

Grant, T. J., & Kooter, B. M. (2005). Comparing OODA and Other Models as Operational View Architecture. In Alberts, D.S. (Ed.), Proceedings, 10th International Command & Control Research & Technology Symposium (paper 196), Washington DC: US DoD Command & Control Research Program.

Horling, B., & Lesser, V. (2005). A Survey of Multi-Agent Organizational Paradigms. The Knowledge Engineering Review, 19(4), 281–316. doi:10.1017/S0269888905000317 doi:10.1017/S0269888905000317

IDEAS group website. http://www.ideasgroup.org/, accessed 1 October 2013.

Lewis, T. G. (2009). Network Science: Theory and applications. Hoboken, NJ: John Wiley & Sons. doi:10.1002/9780470400791 doi:10.1002/9780470400791

Mintzberg, H. (1979). The Structuring of Organizations: A synthesis of the research. Englewood Cliffs, NJ: Prentice-Hall.

Mintzberg, H. (1983). Structure in Fives: Designing effective organizations. Englewood Cliffs, N.J.: Prentice-Hall.

MIP website. https://mipsite.lsec.dnd.ca/Pages/Default.aspx, accessed 1 October 2013.

NATO SAS Panel main page. http://www.cso.nato.int/panel.asp?panel=6, accessed 1 October 2013.

Van Creveld, M. (1985). Command in War. Cambridge: Harvard University Press.

Wikipedia. (2013). Ontology (information science). http://en.wikipedia.org/wiki/Ontology_(information_science), accessed 1 October 2013.

Wikipedia. (2013). Ontology engineering. http://en.wikipedia.org/wiki/Ontology_engineering, accessed 1 October 2013.

## KEY TERMS AND DEFINITIONS

**Command and Control (C2):** US Department of Defense Joint Publication 1-02 defines C2 as *"the exercise of authority and direction by a properly designated commander over assigned and attached forces in the accomplishment of the mission"*. A C2 system is *"an arrangement of personnel, equipment, communications, facilities, and procedures"*, and the functions of C2 include *"planning, directing, coordinating, and controlling forces and operations"*.

**Cybergeography:** The application of geography to cyberspace. The cybergeography literature concentrates on cyberspace in isolation from the physical spaces of land, sea, air, and outer space, on the social infrastructure within cyberspace, and on the cartography of cyberspace (Dodge & Kitchen, 2001).

**DOTMLPFI:** NATO abbreviation for factors ("lines of development") relating to network-enabled capabilities: Doctrine, Organization, Training & education, Materiel, Logistics, Personnel, Facilities, and Information/Interoperability.

**FLONC:** Formalized Layered Ontology for Networked C2; described in this chapter.

**ICT:** Information and communication technologies.

**JC3IEDM:** Joint Command, Control, and Consultation Information Exchange Data Model. A data exchange standard for C2 systems, developed by the NATO-supported Multilateral Interoperability Project.

**Network:** A representation of real-world phenomena in the form of a set of atomic nodes and a set of arcs that link the nodes.

**Ontology:** An ontology provides a shared vocabulary of the entities that exist in a domain, together with their properties and relationships. Gruber's (1993) authoritative definition is a *"formal, explicit specification of a shared conceptualization"*.

**Ontology Engineering:** Ontology engineering is the subfield of knowledge engineering that studies the engineering lifecycle, the development process, methods, and tools for creating ontologies (De Nicola et al, 2009).

**OODA Loop:** Observe-Orient-Decide-Act; a cyclic decision-making process for dynamic and uncertain environments, developed by John Boyd over the period 1976 to 1996.

# APPENDIX

## Questions

1. Define ontology, as used in computer science, information systems, artificial intelligence, and software engineering. What does this have in common with the term ontology as it is used in philosophy?
2. In what ways are ontologies applied?
3. Describe an ontology development methodology.
4. What are the differences between a conceptual ontology and a logical ontology?
5. How can networks be identified from an ontology?
6. What are the limitations in modeling a real-world phenomenon as a network? How can these limitations be overcome?
7. In what ways does cyberspace differ from the other four "kinetic" domains of military operation?
8. This chapter describes the military operating environment in terms of five layers, based on ideas from the network-enabled C2 literature. Can you find other layering schemes in the scientific literature on cyberspace? Why would these other layering schemes not be appropriate for the purposes of this chapter?

# Chapter 6
# Modeling C2 Networks as Dependencies:
## Understanding What the Real Issues Are

**B. Drabble[1]**
*Independent Researcher, USA*

## ABSTRACT

*This chapter describes an approach to modeling C2 and other types of networks as a series of nodes (people, groups, resources, locations, concepts, etc.). The nodes are linked by one or more weighted arcs describing the type and the strength of the dependency that one node has on another node. This model allows analysts to identify the most important nodes in a network in terms of their direct and indirect dependencies and to rank them accordingly. The same model also supports consequence analysis in which the direct, indirect, cascading, and cumulative effects of changes to node capabilities can be propagated across the networks. The chapter describes the basic modeling technique and two types of dependency propagation that it supports. These are illustrated with two examples involving the modeling and reasoning across insurgent networks and an Integrated Air Defense System. These show how aspects of the networks can be analyzed and targeted. Details are also provided on the mechanisms to link the analysis to a planning system through which plans can be developed to bring about desired effect(s) in the networks.*

## OVERVIEW OF MODELING C2 NETWORKS AS INTER-CONNECTED NETWORKS

The purpose of this section is to provide a short overview of previous approaches to modeling C2 networks and identify the strengths of the approach proposed here. Several modeling approaches have addressed the need to understand how Command and Control (C2) and other types of networks are constructed and function. For the purpose of this chapter a network is defined as: "One or more nodes (people, organizations, resources, locations, concepts, etc.) that are linked by one or more weighted arcs describing the type and strength of the dependency that one node has on another node."

DOI: 10.4018/978-1-4666-6058-8.ch006

This allows a wide variety of different C2 networks to be modeled and studied, depending on how its nodes are instantiated. For example, instantiating a network's nodes as C2 Centers, Air Operations Centers, Airfields and their associated personnel would create a partial model of an Integrated Air Defense System (IADS). Whereas instantiating the nodes with distribution centers, headquarters buildings, repair centers and repair and installations crews would create a partial model of the C2 network of the local electrical power (EP) company. The dependency based approaches described in the following sections can be applied to model a wide variety of different networks, but more importantly they show how these networks are not standalone but are actually inter-dependent. For example, EP repair crews are dependent on transport links to travel to work sites and the transport network is dependent on EP for its traffic control systems, sensors and for communication between the nodes in its own C2 network.

The dependency based approach to network modeling builds on previous approaches by firstly fusing them into a coherent model and secondly significantly increasing the range of reasoning capabilities they can support. The "Five Ring"

Model developed by Col. John Warden (1995) represents the networks as a common set of fractal models where each ring can be decomposed into a lower model that is structured in the same way. Figure 1 displays the Center of Gravity (COG) for a country. Infrastructure is a ring in a Country COG, and this can be decomposed into an Infrastructure COG with the same five elements. For example, if the infrastructure COG is a countries EP system then the Leadership is the people who control the generation and distribution decisions, the Forces are the people running and repairing the network, etc. The Five Ring model provides a way to structure and decompose networks but it does not provide measures of the relative importance of the COGs or the rings within a COG. For example, in the COG model, are the countries Leadership elements more important than the Infrastructure elements and how are they dependent on one another? In order to address these issues Major Jason Barlow (1993) developed his National Elements of Value (NEV) model which is shown in Figure 2. This uses a different set of categories to those used in the Five Ring model and introduces the concepts of relative importance and linkages. Figure 2 shows that the Leadership has greater importance than Transportation (given

*Figure 1. John Warden's (1995) Ring model*

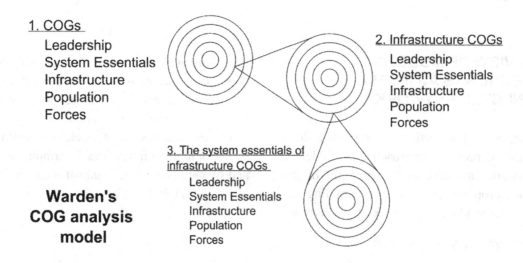

1. COGs
   Leadership
   System Essentials
   Infrastructure
   Population
   Forces

2. Infrastructure COGs
   Leadership
   System Essentials
   Infrastructure
   Population
   Forces

3. The system essentials of infrastructure COGs
   Leadership
   System Essentials
   Infrastructure
   Population
   Forces

**Warden's COG analysis model**

*Figure 2. Jason Barlow (1993) National elements of value model*

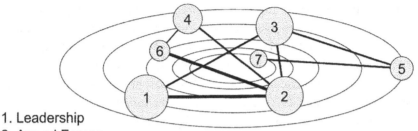

**Barlow's National Elements of Value (NEV) with interlinking and variable lines of influence**

1. Leadership
2. Armed Forces
3. Education
4. Alliances
5. Communications
6. Transportation
7. Industry

Size = importance of NEV (to entity)
Thickness = importance of connection

the relative size of the spheres) and that the linkage between Leadership and the Armed Forces is more important that the linkages between Leadership and Education (given the thickness of the arc). The approach developed by Dr. Joe Strange (1996) models networks as COGs with associated critical capabilities, vulnerabilities and requirements.

The COGs represent the strengths of the opponent to resist. Critical capabilities are those things a COG possesses to destroy something, or seize an objective, or prevent an opponent from achieving its mission. Critical requirements are the conditions, resources and means that are essential for a COG to achieve its critical capability. Critical vulnerabilities are the requirements, or components thereof, that are deficient, or vulnerable to neutralization or defeat in a way that will contribute to a COG failing to achieve its critical capability. The focus of the Strange model is to support decomposition and the identification of the key critical elements. But it does not provide an explicit model of the dependency and dependency strength between them which the NEV model does. The PMESII JFCOM model described by Mattis (2008) provides a structural

and decomposition scheme in which the COGs Political, Economic, Military, Social, Infrastructure and Information (PMESSI) are decomposed into a series of sub-networks or Target Systems. For example, the Military COG comprises Target Systems including Leadership, Armed Forces, Internal Security, Military Industrial Complex and Sustainment. The Infrastructure COG comprises Utilities, Transportation, Industry and Public Facilities. Analysis identifies system strengths and vulnerabilities to influence capabilities, perceptions, decision making, and/or behavior. Nodes are connected by arcs designating a relationship which can be behavioral, physical or functional but they do not specify any strength or relationship directionality values.

In each of these approaches the core idea is to represent networks as "systems of systems" in which an entity such as a country, Microsoft or Al-Qaeda is comprised of set of networks which are dependent upon one another. One aspect which has received less attention is the need to specify and reason with the strength of a dependency.

The approach described in this chapter fuses aspects of the NEV, PMESII and Strange models into a model where the focus is on the Capabilities, Dependencies and Vulnerabilities (CDV) of the nodes. It also embeds dependency type and strength information which explicitly models the mapping of how a capability is used to meet the needs of a dependency (e.g., the capability of IADS radars to provide search and tracking information and the dependency of C2 nodes on the information). In this example the dependency type is "physical provides physical" and the strength of the dependency is mapped to a scale from 1 to 10. Strength of 1 indicates a minor dependency and 10 indicates a critical one. Information on node CDV is collected from multiple sources including engineering models, intelligence models, open source materials, etc. Strength values are calculated based on the number of node options available to address the dependency and the criticality of the capability of the node in the network. This approach provides two essentials pieces of information. Firstly, it provides the mapping mechanism from one node in the network to another. For example, the CDV model posits that decision makers (leadership) in an electrical power (EP) system (a system essential) allocate the distribution of power to those who request EP. Hence, there is a linkage between customers and suppliers. That linkage is communication (a target system in infrastructure). Thus, in this example, two target systems, EP (a systems essential) and telecommunications (infrastructure), are linked via the need to address the dependency of the leadership for information. Note also that this shows linkages within a target system; in this case, decision makers and producers of EP. The second piece of information provided by the linkages is the strength of associations of those links. These strengths are not necessarily of equal magnitude in both directions. For example, the need for EP may be much stronger in the customer than the need to deliver power is from the supplier. Hence, loss of communication from customer to supplier is more devastating to the former than it is to the latter. The following section provides details of

the dependency models and it is illustrated using aspects of an IADS network. Later sections show how this model can be used to rank and identify the most important nodes in the networks. The model is also used to task a planning system to modify the behavior of the networks, identify the direct, indirect, cascading and cumulative effects of the plan and finally to understand what weaknesses the plan may contain.

The remainder of this chapter is structured as follows. The first section provides an overview of modeling C2 networks via dependencies using both nodes based and link based methods. The next section describes the propagation algorithms that allow direct and indirect dependency values to be calculated for each node in the network, and to identify the consequence(s) (in terms of a node's capability) to the network if one or more nodes are direct impacted. The next section describes two example applications. The first focuses on analyzing an insurgent network to identify its most important nodes and secondly to develop plans to disrupt the network's structure and functionality. The second application focuses on identifying which nodes should be targeted to increase the vulnerability of nodes in an IADS network. The Conclusion provides a summary of the chapter and describes future work and extensions to the modeling and reasoning capabilities described in this chapter.

## MODELING C2 NETWORK VIA DEPENDENCIES

C2 networks comprise a multitude of different nodes that function collaboratively to provide a set of individual and collective capabilities. For example, C2 Center nodes working collaboratively with sensor, communication and shooter[2] nodes have the ability themselves to provide "guidance and leadership." Functioning collectively with the other nodes, the network has the capability to provide the components and capabilities of an

IADS. The C2 center nodes can be decomposed into zonal, wing, etc. operations centers each of which has their own individual and collective capabilities which are required both within the C2 Center decomposition and without. Figure 3 shows the typical structure of an IADS and its interdependent sub-networks and nodes.

The directionality of the dependencies shows this to be a graph and not a simple decomposition. For example, the Shooters node is dependent on the Communications node to receive orders and the Communication node is dependent on the Shooters node for protection. However, the Shooters node can operate without receiving orders via the Communications node but the level of its capability to intercept targets is degraded.

Due to the directionality of the dependency links between nodes it is often the case that loops and more importantly feedback loops can occur in a network. For example, if several airfields are degraded then this impacts the capability of the Shooters node to provide protection which in turn impacts the Communications node. This impacts

the C2 Centers and its WOC[3] nodes which in turn impacts the airfields and aircraft. Hence, a small direct change to the output of a node may have a far greater impact due to indirect and feedback effects. Figure 3 also introduces the terms Target Set and Target System which are defined as follows:

1. **Target Set:** A grouping of target set(s) and/ or target instances that share a common attribute including:

   a. **Type:** Electrical Substations, Road Junctions, etc.

   b. **Location:** Electrical Transmission Infrastructure within 10 miles of London, etc.

   c. **Functionality:** Elements of the IADS Shooters node, etc.

2. **Target System:** A grouping of target set(s) that are so related that their destruction will produce some particular effect desired by the attacker. For example, IADS, electrical power, transportation, etc.

*Figure 3. IADS Structure and composition*

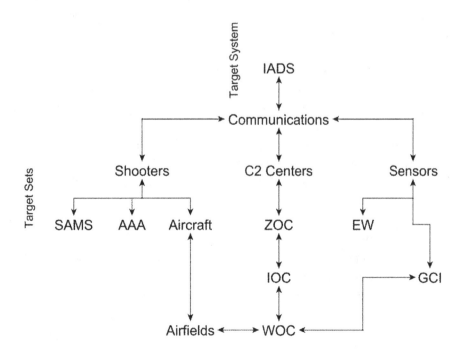

The capability of the C2 node shown in Figure 3 is to provide "orders, guidance and leadership" and the capability of the communications node is to provide information links between it and the other nodes in the IADS. The C2 and communications nodes each have one or more dependencies which are mapped to one or more capabilities of nodes within the IADS network and on the capability of nodes external to it. The dependency mapping specifies the link type and the strength of the dependency. The strength of these direct dependencies is used in various algorithms to calculate the importance of a network node based on its cumulative direct and indirect dependencies. For example, the C2 node is directly dependent on the communications node and it is directly dependent on an EP source. Hence there is an indirect or transitive dependency between the EP node and the C2 node. Due to the networks being represented as a graph with interdependent links, a node can be involved in multiple transitive dependencies. The cumulative value of a node's transitive dependencies can be used to identify the node as being a hub or having special value within the network. It also allows nodes to be compared in terms of their cumulative values, link types and dependency strengths. Two nodes may have similar cumulative values; however one score may comprise many low value strengths whereas the second is comprised of a few high value strengths. These differences allow algorithms and users to rank nodes to better identify which are the most important. If we consider the nodes in the example IADS network then what dependencies can be identified for them and which are met by the capabilities of nodes within the IADS network?

- C2:
  - Depends on sensors for information
  - Depends on communication to receive information and pass orders
  - Depends on Shooters for protection
- Sensors:
  - Depends upon C2 for orders

  - Depends upon communications to pass information and receive orders
  - Depends on shooters for protection
- Communications:
  - Depends on C2 for orders
  - Depends on shooters for protection
- Shooters:
  - Depends on sensors for information
  - Depends on C2 for orders
  - Depends on communications to receive orders

The IADS network is itself a node within a much larger network which contains networks describing other functions, nodes, dependencies, capabilities, etc. Figure 4 shows a partial PMESII model of CALIFON[4] which is composed of four separate COGs. The Military COG comprises two Target Systems one of which is the IADS network described in Figure 3 together with the dependency links to other COGs and Target Systems. For example, the dependency of the IADS Target System on the EP Target System in the Economy COG.

The bi-directionality of the link between the EP and IADS Target Systems indicates that each is dependent upon the other but for different reasons and purposes.

1. IADS
   a. Depends upon EP for main line power
   b. Depends upon Transportation for movement of units and re-supply
2. Transportation
   a. Depends upon EP for main line power
   b. Depends upon the IADS for protection
3. EP
   a. Depends upon IADS for protection
   b. Depends upon Transportation for movement of goods and services

Figure 4 and the dependencies listed here show that dependencies operate within a network and between networks and are referred to as *intra-*

*Figure 4. CALIFON Dependency network*

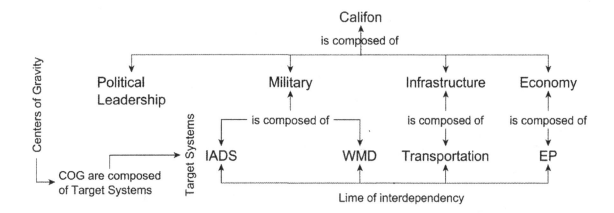

*dependencies* and *inter-dependencies* respectively. Models of C2 systems and networks have focused on military nodes. But it is their interdependencies that are often more important, because these dependencies tend to make the military nodes vulnerable. In addition, these dependency vulnerabilities tend to be the ones that are non-intuitive and tend to be overlooked by analysts looking for ways to improve and secure network operations. Networks developed for Wright Patterson AFB showed analysts that the dependency of several nodes on water/sewage links was addressed via an underground conduit that intersected the main runway. The vulnerability of the conduit to "seizure and occupation" and its capability to provide an access conduit could be used for unauthorized access to the base. Alternatively, increasing communications bandwidth, providing additional backups, etc. to improve a C2 network's robustness is of little use if a bases electrical supply upon which the communication network is dependent, is provided by a single sub-station located outside the base perimeter. The ability to reason across interdependent networks allows for the identification of indirect or transitive dependencies which can often lead to looping and feedback, where the direct impact on a node can be amplified to a far greater one. For example, if a power generation facility is directly damaged via an air strike then

this may reduce its output of EP by 50%. If the local railway network is dependent on that EP to power the trains that deliver the EP facility's fuel then the reduction in fuel deliveries may lead to an even larger reduction in EP output as the facility manages its dwindling fuel reserves. In this example, a change in the EP networks may impact the transportation network, which in turn may impact the EP network. The interdependency of the nodes in the transportation and the EP networks would be extracted from engineering materials, EP and rail company Websites, etc. In addition to these indirect effects there can be both cascading and cumulative effects which combined can have effects across networks and between them. Figure 5 describes the main elements of an EP network which shows the intra-dependency of the EP network on elements such as Repair Crews, Power Lines Transformers and on its own C2 systems which direct and guide its operation. This shows that C2 networks exist outside of military systems. They have similar dependencies and vulnerabilities on transport and communications networks as was described for military networks such as the IADS. Figure 5 also introduces the concept of the Repair Crews which are critical to the network function and comprises individual actors, groups and organizations which serve different roles in the network. The role of individu-

*Figure 5. Electric power network*

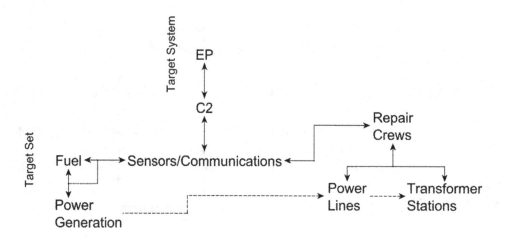

als and the functions they perform can often be overlooked whereas making them explicit nodes allows for their dependencies and vulnerabilities to be explicitly reasoned over.

A nodes capability or output can be affected **indirectly** via its dependencies as in the case of power facilities output of EP being dependent on fuel, transport links, personnel, etc., but it also the case that a capability can be a affected **directly** due to the exploitation of one of its inherent vulnerabilities. The generator halls of the power facility are directly vulnerable to *overpressure* which is a phenomenon that can be generated by any explosive or kinetic event, missile, bomb, etc. Alternatively, the supervisory and control system of the power facility is directly vulnerable to non-kinetic events such as a cyber-attack. These generate an *exploitation* type phenomenon to which the control system is vulnerable. Finally, vulnerabilities can also be inherited due to the nature of a dependency. For example a C2 Center being dependent on EP means it inherits the vulnerability to events/actions capable of generating an EMP phenomenon.

In summary a dependency based model allows networks to be modeled at different levels of granularity with nodes representing entities from Centers of Gravity to individual targets,

where each level can be decomposed into a more detailed level where available. Nodes are modeled by means of their capabilities, dependencies and vulnerabilities (CDV), with CDV values aggregated and abstracted to a higher level node as needed. Dependency on the capability of other nodes within and across networks is modeled using intra-dependency and inter-dependencies respectively. These record the dependency's type and the strength allowing algorithms to calculate the cumulative direct and indirect dependencies on a node. These algorithms can then rank a nodes importance either in terms of how dependent it is on other nodes or how dependent other nodes are on it. This contrasts with other approaches where the topology of the network is used to identify key nodes based on attributes including number of incoming and/or outgoing links, spanning node, etc. This approach uses semantic information regarding node type, CDV attributes, and type and strength of the dependencies to understand how networks actually function. This type of network modeling also allows for analyzing the direct, indirect, cascading and cumulative effects of changes to one or more nodes in the network. Analysts can use this to estimate the level of desirable or undesirable effects within the networks. In the case of an opposition network, additional actions may be needed to increase an effect or, in the case of their own network, actions may be needed to mitigate the effects and increase robustness. The following section provides details of the modeling methods and the analysis they support.

## Dependency Based Node Description

A node at any level within a dependency network is modeled using a structure as described in Figure 6. As described in the previous section a node's attributes are described by means of its CDV. A capability has a time profile and an identifiable function which defines the level of capability based on the level to which any dependencies it has are being addressed. In some cases quantities and units can be associated with a capability, as in the case of the capability of a thermal power plant to produce high voltage EP. However, sometimes

the capability may not be quantifiable, as in the case of a person's leadership or supervision skills. In the case of a non-quantifiable capability the granularity to which it can be measured is much courser and hence the ways in which it can be affected are much reduced. For example, it may be possible to reduce the output of the thermal power plant by 50% in order to impact a C2 Center, but you cannot degrade someone's knowledge of how to build IEDs by 50%. In this case, the only option would be to arrest the person to remove the source of the knowledge thereby reducing the availability of the knowledge in the network to zero. An alternative would be to remove the conduit through which the information is transferred. Without the conduit the information cannot be transferred to the network nodes that depend upon it. Again this would result in reducing the availability of the knowledge in the network to zero.

*Figure 6. Dependency node overview description*

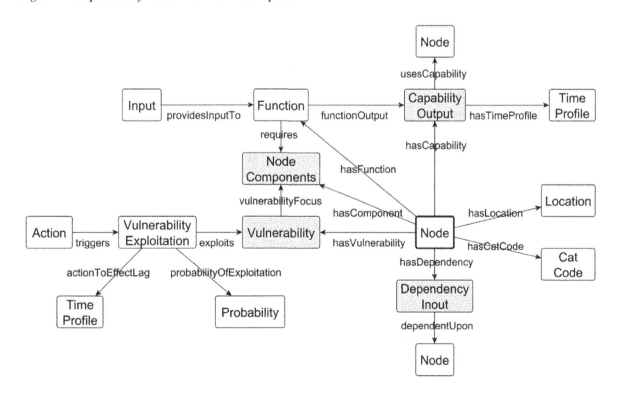

A nodes dependency is mapped to the capability(s)[5] of other node(s) and there is a dependency mapping for each capability or output that has identifiable dependencies. Vulnerability is defined for each phenomenon to which a node is susceptible. A partial overview of the vulnerability taxonomy is provided in Figure 7. This shows the three basic types of vulnerability phenomena that can be assigned to a node: physical, perceptual and behavioral. A node can be assigned a specific vulnerability (i.e. a leaf node), or to a class if all sub-classes and/or leaf nodes apply. The vulnerability was developed and refined with USTRATCOM planners and can be applied to both physical as well as human actor nodes that are elements of a network. The node itself has a *location* which can be dynamic or static and can be either known or unknown within the network. In addition a node can have *Node Components* which are themselves defined using the same node structure, making this a fractal model capable of modeling nodes from Centers of Gravity through to individual target instances.

Finally, sets of node CDV attribute values can be *aggregated*, *abstracted* and new CDV attributes *synthesized*, depending on the nodes they are collectively linked to, either directly or more importantly indirectly. For example, if the information is available via engineering sources, etc. then it may be possible for the amount of EP provided by dependent nodes to be *aggregated* to a C2 node to identify how much EP the C2 node may require. Again with access to the relevant information sources, the amount of fuel needed to supply the EP nodes can be *abstracted* in BTU[6] at the EP target system node, etc. The ability to *synthesize* new CDV attributes within a network allows the model to augment and expand those CDV attributes provided by human analysts or via data mining and extraction tools.

*Figure 7. Partial vulnerability taxonomy*

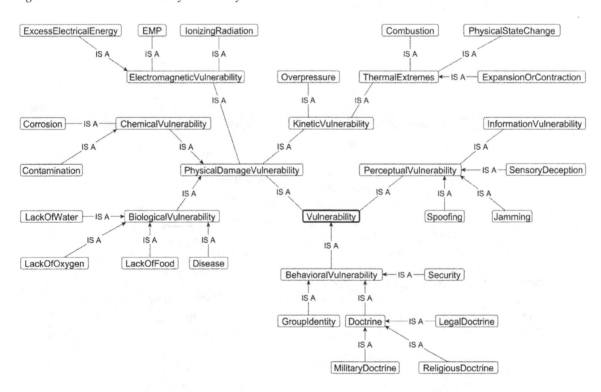

The structure shown in Figure 6 is used to model four distinct types of nodes as follows:

**Actor:** A person, group or organization composed of one or more persons.
**Physical:** A physical structure, resources or object.
**Concept:** An idea, goal, principle, method of organization or operating procedure.
**Composite:** A node composed of one or more of the above or other composite nodes.

The inclusion of a concept as a basic node type allows for the modeling of knowledge and information that a person, group or organization possesses, as well as the mechanisms for its access, storage, transmission or retrieval. One key aspect for the efficient function of C2 networks is access to knowledge or information upon which decisions, guidance, etc. are made. This can be in the form of procedures stored on computer systems or, as described earlier, by subject matter knowledge that an actor node possesses.

## Dependency Based Link Description

Nodes are linked by dependency arcs that specify the type of the dependency and also the strength of the dependency. The dependency type is based on the two nodes involved in the dependency, specified as either a dependee or a dependent. A dependee node is the one that has the dependency,

while the dependent node is the one that provides the capability to address the dependency.

Table 1 describes the permissible link types between dependent (row) and dependee (column). For example a Physical dependee node (column 2) can be dependent on an Actor dependent node (row 1) to operate the node (e.g. dependee airplane on a dependent pilot), maintain the node (dependee car on a dependent mechanic), etc. Associated with each dependency link is a strength value, either associated with the node in general or with a specific node output. For example, Figure 4 shows the generic dependency of the IADS (a dependee) on Electrical Power but without specifying specific dependent nodes (power plants, substations, etc.) and specific outputs (high voltage electrical power, rectified voltage, etc.). If appropriate information is available then the nodes in Figure 4 can be decomposed from Target Systems through to specific target instances. The result of the decomposition would be to add new nodes and links to the network. With the availability of appropriate information at the instance level a dependency would map for example, a specific C2 Center to the substations and power lines that address its EP dependency or to a node representing a group of potential insurgents with knowledge of manufacturing IEDs, etc.

In the case of a generic dependency the strength of the dependency is modeled using a scale where 1 represents a negligible dependency and 10 is critical. These dependency values can be gener-

*Table 1. Dependency types permissible between actors, physical and concept nodes*

|  | **Actor** | **Physical** | **Concept** |
|---|---|---|---|
| Actor | *Supports, Defends, Directs, Supervises, Opposes, Motivates* or *Moves.* | *Operates, Maintains, Repairs, Constructs, Damages, Destroyed, Moves* or *Accesses.* | *Formulates, Advocates, Opposes, Accepts, Rejects, AdoptsAsGoal, Votes* or *Implements* |
| Physical | *Protects, Supports, Motivates, Damages, Destroys* or *Moves* | *Supplies, Supports, Constructs, Destroys, Damages* or *Directs* | *Supports, Motivates* or *Instantiates* |
| Concept | *Motivates, Directs* or *Supports* | *Supports, Motivates,* or *Instantiates.* | *Motivates, Rebuts, Contradicts, Supports,* or *Subsumes* |

ated either by human analysts or generated using an algorithm called AutoLink (Drabble 2012) which takes into account network attributes. These include the number of nodes with similar capability, alternative nodes providing the capability, both within and external to the target set, ratio of nodes providing the capability to those dependent upon it, etc. AutoLink also uses WordNet (Fellbaum 1998) to provide a lexical database of English language concepts. Nouns, verbs, adjectives and adverbs are grouped into sets of cognitive synonyms (synsets), each expressing a distinct concept. Synsets are interlinked by means of conceptual-semantic and lexical relations. Autolink queries WordNet with a node's description and these searches for any nodes in the network that match any terms returned. For example, the WordNet query "SAM" returns the direct hyponyms "MANPAD" and "Stinger" which can then be searched for in the network. For each candidate node identified, Autolink examines the topology of the network to identify if the candidate node shares similar target set(s) to the queried node or whether they are linked directly or transitively. Based on this information and any geographic information that may be available Autolink creates a score as to how easily the candidate node could be used to substitute for the queried node. This score is then used to generate a dependency strength value between the candidate node and any node that relies on the candidate node, to address one of its dependencies. Autolink can be applied to generate strength values across the entire network or by an analyst seeking feedback on a particular strength value. An evaluation of Autolink identified a 90%+ correlation with the dependency strengths generated by human experts. However, while Autolink was able to generate its strength values in less than a few seconds, human expert took many minutes. For networks of more than a 100 nodes the human experts were unable to generate any coherent values whereas Autolink

generated values within seconds (Drabble, et al, 2006).

In the case of a specific node's capability or output, the strength of the dependency is modeled based on the additional units of output the dependee node can generate given the dependent node(s) input. For example, a dependee repeater node in the communications network supporting the IADS is dependent on EP provided by two dependent substations. If each substation is providing 50% of the repeaters EP need, then the repeater's output can be assumed to be zero with no power provided, 50% with half the EP being provided and 100% with all the required EP being provided. This assumes a linear relationship between the repeaters output and the level of EP supplied. The relationship between the dependee output and the dependent input can be modeled using five attributes:

- **Measure of Performance (MOP):** The range of output the node can produce. For example a thermal power plant can produce 100MW per hour, or a C2 Center can produce 1 Air Tasking Order per 24 hours.
- **Measure of Effect (MOE):** A mapping of the MOP to the scale in range 0-100 utils.
- **Base Operating Level Production (BOLP):** The output if no dependent input is being provided. For example, if all EP inputs to a C2 Center are reduced to zero it still may have some capability based on backup and other internal resources.
- **Strength of Dependency (SOD):** The MOE utils attributed to the input dependency.
- **Criticality of Dependency (COD):** The eventual output if the dependency is reduced to zero. In the BOLP case the C2 Center will be reduced to zero capability or output if the EP is reduced to zero. This can be despite the level of input from other dependent nodes.

Using the repeater example above, its MOP would be the range of megabytes the repeater can output (e.g., 0 – 200Mb per second) and assuming its MOE output range is linear then 0mb per second maps to 0 utils and 200mb per second maps to 100 utils. The BOLP Is the number of megabytes output if the value of all dependency inputs are reduced to zero. If we assume the repeater has not backup or other resources capable of providing EP then the BOLP would be zero. If for the purpose of this description we assume the repeater is only dependent on EP then its output is zero megabytes if all EP input is reduced to zero. Alternatively, if the repeater has a backup EP source then this could be modeled as a separate dependency or as a specified BOLP value. For example, if the backup source can provide 25% of the repeaters required EP then the BOLP would be set to 25 utils.

The SOD reflects the additional utils above the BOLP that can be attributed to the dependency and the SOD value is mapped to a range 0 – 1. For example, if the BOLP is zero and the repeater has a single EP source then the additional 100 utils (its maximum output) are mapped to the single EP source resulting in a SOD value 1.0. That is all 100 utils of repeater output are dependent on the single EP source giving a value of 1.0. If half or the repeater's output was attributed to the EP source the SOD value would be 0.5. Alternatively, if the repeater is equally dependent on two EP sources then SOD values of 0.5 and 0.5 respectively would reflect each providing 50% of the EP need. Values of 1.0 and 0.0 for the two EP sources would reflect the former as being the primary EP source and the latter is the backup.

The COD reflects the output in utils if the amount being provided by the dependent node is reduced to zero or is of zero value to the dependee node. For example, if the repeater is dependent on an electrical power node and a fiber optic cable node each with a SOD value of 0.5 with respect to the repeaters output, then the repeaters output will be reduced to zero if the EP input goes to

zero regardless of what is being provided by the fiber optic cable. Setting the COD value for the repeaters EP dependency to 0.0 would reflect this state as there would be zero repeater output if there is zero EP input. This assumes the BOLP of the repeater node is zero and hence has no way to compensate for the EP loss. There is a corresponding COD value for each SOD value that a capability or output has. In this case there would be a COD value for the fiber optic cable which would have the value 0.0 indicating the output of the repeater would be zero if the optic cable's output was reduced to zero, again irrespective of the level of EP provided.

The output based dependency propagation is based on previous research into modeling interdependent enterprises and groups working towards collective goals and objectives. Approaches such as those of Keating, Sousa-Poza, and Kovacic (2008), Jackson (1991) and White (2006) have taken a similar "systems of systems" view of an enterprise but their approaches focused on systems where all participants have agreed goals and purposes whereas this approach allows for potentially conflicting participant goals and actions. Rebovich (2005) developed a theoretical approach that emphasized studying systems of systems through how they interacted rather than each in isolation. However, the level of interaction was fairly simple and does not appear to scale to the size of problem that can be handled here. The FDNA approach of Garvey et al. (2005) offers similar dependency reasoning capabilities but it is primarily focused on understanding inter-dependencies within designs and finding ways of mitigating risk. The approach described here provides better link semantics, models both quantitative and non-quantitative outputs and allows for the inclusion of backups and alternative dependee and dependent nodes. The approach also allows for reasoning over aggregated dependee and dependent nodes, sub-networks and user selected sub-networks and clusters.

# DEPENDENCY AND CONSEQUENCE PROPAGATION

The node or output dependency models described in the previous section can be analyzed by a series of algorithms to identify and rank the most dependent nodes in a network or to identify the direct, indirect, cascading and cumulative consequence of changes to one or more network nodes. The following sections provide details of the Athena system (Drabble, et al, 2006) which contains these algorithms and provides a GUI for presentation of results and the development of networks. The fourth section provides examples of Athena's application to two different C2 networks.

## Node Based Dependency Propagation

Node based propagation uses the link dependency strengths to identify and rank nodes in terms of how dependent nodes are on them (dependent analysis) and how dependent they are on other nodes (dependee analysis). For example, the dependents of an Air Operations Center (AOC) are other C2 Centers, groups, organizations who are dependent on the AOCs capability to provide guidance, leadership, etc. The AOCs dependees are groups and organizations that provide it with information with which it can provide guidance, leadership, etc., and the communications infrastructure that allows information to pass into and out of the AOC. Athena builds a system-of-system model as a graph and calculates the transitive closure over its links based upon user made selections. The selections specify which nodes (COG, target systems, target sets or instances) in the network are to be included in the calculation. The degree of dependency is not fixed and Athena provides an analyst the means of varying those weights. Furthermore, those dependencies are not always reciprocal. For example, IADs are heavily dependent on EP but the EP network is less dependent on the IADS as an EP customer,

but is heavily dependent on the IADS to protect its infrastructure nodes. Figure 8 provides details of the node dependency propagation algorithm. Athena covers all of PMESII and can decompose down to the target level. However, an analyst may wish only to see the dependency links and weights at the target system level.

The major two obstacles the Athena technology had to overcome were the presence of loops in the graph and the presence of weights in the graph. In addition, the ability to provide a hierarchical view of the network based on COG, target system, etc. was another obstacle to be overcome. Related issues deal with whether the net is scaled, where a scale-free network is a network whose degree distribution follows a power law, at least asymptotically. Athena assumes scale free networks. The most notable characteristic in a scale-free network is the relative commonness of vertices with a degree that greatly exceeds the average. The highest-degree nodes are often called "hubs," and are thought to serve specific purposes in their networks, although this depends greatly on the domain. The scale-free property strongly correlates with the network's robustness to failure. Many networks are conjectured to be scale-free, including World Wide Web links, biological networks, and social networks. The ability to handle scale free networks allows Athena to determine the degree of criticality of any one node.

Figure 9 shows part of the insurgent scenario[7] and comprises the insurgent network (C2, logistics, intelligence, etc. sub-networks), communication, infrastructure and other dependent networks. The two menus show the definition of the link from a key insurgent to a safe house, the insurgent's dependencies, and which capabilities of the safe house are used to address the insurgent's dependencies. The lower menu shows the calculated strength of the dependency and the direct effect on the insurgent should the capabilities of the safe house be reduced by 100%. The propagation identifies a cumulative score for each of the node types selected by the user. In this example all node

*Figure 8. Node based dependency propagation*

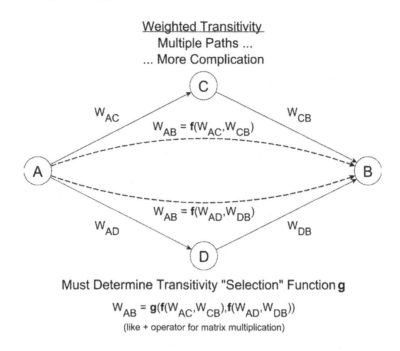

types are selected. This is a dependent analysis which identifies "Safe House 3" as the node that is depended upon most by other network nodes either directly or indirectly. The dependent score of 149 calculated for "Safe House 3" is not mapped to a specific scale. Rather it is used to compare different node rankings. For example, with scores of 119 and 112 respectively, Safe Houses 1 and 2 rank as roughly equivalent in terms of dependency. However, with a dependent score of 149, Safe House 3 ranks approximately 50% higher than the other safe houses. Hence, it is potentially of greater importance to the insurgent C2 network given the direct and indirect dependency of other nodes upon it.

Athena's propagation algorithms also provide analysis and ranking of the following:

- **Effects Analysis:** Ranks nodes based on the total change in the network if they were degraded 100%. Identifies which nodes have the greatest effect across the network

which is not always obvious from link count or type.

- **Vulnerability Analysis:** Ranks nodes based on how vulnerable they are in terms of their strength of dependencies. Identifies which nodes are "easiest" to affect indirectly.

- **Node Vulnerability:** For a selected node it identifies the percentage capability change if the dependee node is degraded by 100% and is applied to each node dependee.

- **Critical Node Vulnerabilities:** For a selected node identifies if there is a dependee node that can degrade the selected nodes capability by 100% and the percentage change to the dependee node to achieve the 100% degradation.

- **Cluster Analysis:** Identifies independent sub-networks whose links all have strength equal to or greater than a user specified value.

*Figure 9. Example node dependency network model*

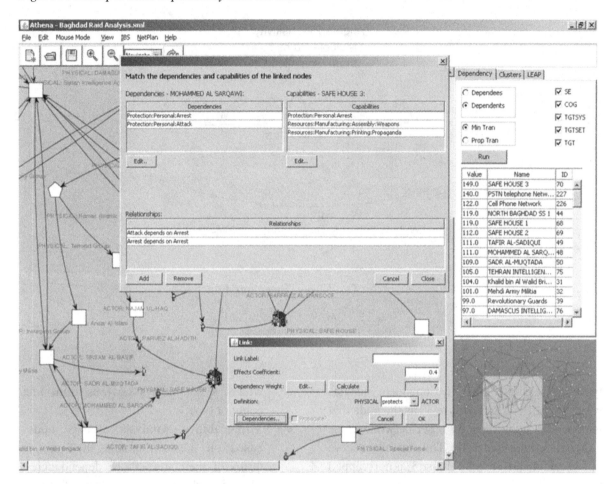

Athena's ability to handle loops and feedback can lead to Critical Node Vulnerabilities analysis identifying that a selected node is also one of its own dependencies. For example, if the insurgents C2 network was identified as being dependent of itself (due to feedback) with a value of 75%, then this would indicate that reducing the functionality of the node by 75% would in fact reduce it by 100%. The identification of these tipping points is especially useful to planners seeking to identify how robust their own networks are, or how much damage needs to be inflicted on an opposition network to bring about a desired level of degradation. Node based dependency propagation also supports a consequence analysis capability that allows analysts and planners to identify the

consequences of changes to one or more nodes in a network. LEAP (Linear Effects Analysis Propagation) identifies the direct and indirect percentage change to a node, based either on values suggested by an analyst or based on the effects of a plan (Drabble, et al, 2006). For example, if raids are proposed against insurgent safe houses, which result in 100% loss of their capabilities to provide protection from seizure or arrest, then what percentage change will occur across the insurgent networks and to any networks it is allied with or supporting etc.? Athena's analysis identifies the changes to impacted nodes and also measures the global effects across the network. This aids analysts in developing plans that have the desired effects on the focus nodes while at the same time minimizing the side effects of their actions. Details of linking dependency propagation to semi-automated plan development are detailed later in the chapter.

## Output Based Dependency Propagation

Output based dependency propagation uses the SOD and COD values specified for a node output to calculate the node's output based on a set of equations defined for the link. The generation and level of belief in the SOD and COD values is dependent on the quality of information available to the analyst. The default equation for a value is a linear one[8] and a separate equation is specified for each node output. The simplest example is a node output with a single dependency (hence one SOD and COD value respectively) and the equation is as follows:

(SOD * % being delivered) + 100(1 – SOD)

If a node's output has two dependencies, for example, two EP suppliers or being dependent on an EP node and fiber optic cable then the equation is as follows:

(SOD1 * % being delivered/2 + SOD2 * % being delivered/2) + 100(1 – (SOD1 + SOD2)/2)

The output equation can be generalized for any number of SOD values it has. To calculate the bandwidth output of a repeater node that has two EP sources (the BOLP for the repeater node is again assumed to be zero), the propagation algorithm needs to identify the Min value from the following three equations.

(0.5*100/2 + 0.5*100/2) + 100(1 – (0.5+0.5)/2)
=> 100 utils                                                    (1)

50+50 => 100 utils                                              (2)

50+50 => 100 utils                                              (3)

Equation 1 shows the bandwidth output is equally dependent on EP source 1 and source 2 and this is reflected by the two 0.5 SOD values. Associated with each SOD value is a percentage value indicating how much of the desired dependency is being supplied. Equation 1 shows the system operating at maximal output, hence 100% of the EP need is being supplied. This results in 100 utils which is the maximum bandwidth output of the repeater. Equation 2 is the COD constraint for EP source 1 where the first element is the number of utils of bandwidth output attributed to EP source 1 and the second is the number of utils attributed to source 2. As EP source 1 is providing enough EP to provide 50 utils of repeater output, this is added to the 50 utils that source 2 is providing, giving a value of 100 utils. If source 1 were to fail completely then the first value of Equation 2 would be set to zero with the bandwidth output being equivalent to only source 2's contribution. Equation 2 would become 0 +50 => 50 assuming EP source 2 is providing enough input to account for 50 utils of repeater output. Equation 3 is the COD constraint for EP source 2 and is essentially the reverse of Equation 2. In this example each equation has a value of 100 utils. Hence, the bandwidth output of the repeater node is 100 utils or its maximal MOE. This value is then propagated to any node that is dependent on the repeater's output and their value(s) updated. This propagation is able to handle loops and feedback in the same way as node based dependency propagation and terminates when no changes in output are detected. These equations can also be used to model a node's output under different circumstances.

- If the repeater node only needs to provide 70% of its maximal bandwidth output to meet the needs of dependent nodes, this is modeled by reducing the associated SOD values. For example, reducing the SOD 0.5 values in Equation 1 to 0.4 and 0.3 respectively.

- If one or more nodes reduces the amount they can provide then the percentage delivered is reduced accordingly. This can be due to damage to the dependee node or allocation of limited resources. This allows the analysis to discern whether the level of bandwidth output is by choice, or limited by a dependee input.

- If a dependee reduces the percentage being delivered then other dependee nodes can potentially be altered to compensate. For example, if EP source 1 can only deliver 40% of what is required then the SOD value for source 1 can be reduced to 0.2 and the SOD value for source 2 increased to 0.8. Similar analysis can also identify how a network might morph to provide a new source for an input if there is no immediate "backup" identified. For example, who might an insurgent network turn to if their leader is arrested to provide leadership?

- If an analyst wishes to identify how a specified level of output could be restored or maintained, then reducing the value 100 in Equation 1 to the required percentage of output would achieve this. For example, if Critical Node Vulnerability identifies that the communications network needs to maintain at least 70% of maximal output to avoid failing completely due to feedback, then what setting of SOD values would best provide the 70% level of output?

The modeling of outputs provides a more informative explanation of dependency over node based dependency as a node may have more than one output. It may not be immediately clear which output a node is dependent upon and why. Also using node output dependency allows for a wide range of descriptions of dependency to be modeled. For example, the description can be as simple as "the C2 center is dependent on two EP nodes which are assumed to be operating normally" can be mapped to two SOD values of 0.5, both of which are providing 100% of the required input. Alternatively, if information is available that one of the sources is the primary and the second is a backup then this can be mapped to two SOD values of 1.0 and 0.0 respectively. Finally, if actual megawatt values are available then these can be mapped to appropriate SOD, COD and percentage deliver values. The same scheme is used to model concept nodes which can be integrated into a network model to provide rationale for its structure and content. Figure 10 provides an overview of a concept node and its associated dependency links.

The output of a concept node is a *Boolean* value as to whether the concept is *valid* or *invalid*. The nodes supporting a *valid* or *invalid* concept can differ as can their associated SOD, COD, etc. values. For example, if the concept is a potential North Korean missile launch then the validity of the concept (i.e., they intend to launch) could be based on which people, groups, etc. who support it, infrastructure preparedness, etc. Alternatively if the concept is they do not intend a missile launch then the validity of this concept could be based on who does not support it, etc.

Treating concept nodes in the same way as actor and physical nodes, allows effects of actions and or events to be propagated across the network. For example, it allows analysts to identify the potential impact of flying B2s across South Korea as part of an exercise on the potential for a North Korean missile launch. If the *invalid* output of the launch concept node is heavily dependent on the opposition to the launch by a General and his standing in the Central Committee (a composite node comprising multiple actor nodes) is reduced due to his support for the concept that the South is not a threat. This may reduce support for the *invalid* output and potential raise the support for the *valid* output. The ability to handle concept nodes in this way allows analysts to document and record the rationale as to why C2 networks are configured the way they are and for that rationale to be re-evaluated as the network morphs over time.

*Figure 10. Concept node model*

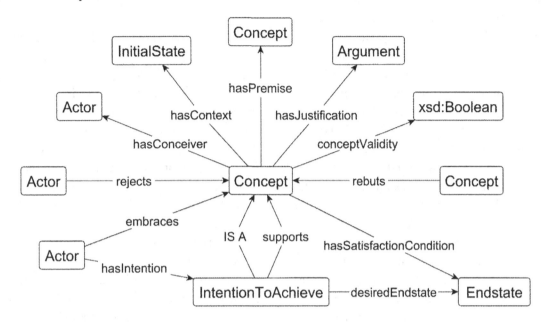

## APPLICATIONS OF DEPENDENCY BASED NETWORK ANALYSIS

The dependency based analysis approaches described in the previous sections have been integrated into two systems: Athena and Cassandra. Athena provides the technologies to firstly, identify the most dependent nodes in a network and secondly, to analyze the direct and indirect changes in network behavior from an external event or action. Cassandra provides the technologies to integrate Athena with various semi-autonomous plan development technologies. These planning systems are tasked via Athena and Cassandra's integration and mapping technologies are used to insert new links, actions and dependency strength values into the Athena networks. These new links, etc. specify where the effect(s) of a plan action will be focused and the resource(s) assigned to the task. Cassandra and Athena exchange information via (OBMIS) ontology based management information bridge (Drabble, McCrabb & Kinzig 2009, Drabble, Black & Kinzig 2009, Drabble & Kinzig 2010 and Drabble 2011) which is also used to ex-

change information with third party tools, systems and information sources. Cassandra and Athena have been evaluated against several scenarios and the following sections provide two of them.

### Scenario 1: Insurgent Command and Control

The insurgent C2 scenario was developed jointly with DARPA and former Special Operations Forces (SOF) operators and is based on several "seize and raid" plans conducted in Baghdad. The scenario contains several inter-dependent networks representing various aspects of the insurgent network (C2, logistics, intelligence, etc.), communication, EP, transport, housing, etc. Analysis of the network dependencies identified that targeting the key actors in the network would have the greatest impact on the leadership, planning and training capabilities of the C2 network. A user requested dependee analysis of the key actors identified several common familial links in their social/clan network and their links to several suspected safe houses. Athena was also able provide the analysts with the level of capability[9] change to the Safe House and the nodes that needed to be affected. The Athena interface can be used to task the planner to develop a plan to raid two of the Safe Houses and to create a cordon of road blocks to control ingress and egress from the area containing the two safe houses.

Figure 11 shows the GUI of the NETPlan[10] planning system which SOF planners used to decompose the tasks specified in Athena into executable actions and to track and maintain the constraints between them. The NETPlan GUI displays each resource as time line together with the actions assigned to the resources. Goals, deadline, decisions points can be specified and linked to actions within the plan. The pop-up menu in Figure 11 shows the precondition, effects, time constraints, etc. for the "Secure Safe House 3"action.

Once the plan is complete, OBMIS is used to map the resources specified in the NETPlan plan to one or more actor, physical or concept node in Athena network. The mapping takes into account partial text matches; similar CDV attributes, etc. It inserts an appropriate dependency link into the Athena network from the resource executing the action to the focus of the action. Figure 12 shows the insurgent network with the additional action dependencies (shown as annotated inks) between the SOF units and the Safe Houses they were tasked to raid. The pop-up menu shows the type of link "Actor damages Physical," the strength of dependency and the expected direct change to the node's capabilities (0.95 maps to 95% degradation). Analysis of the effects of the raid and other actions is shown middle right and shows the percentage degradation to the named nodes. The "Max Global Effects" value of 6.1% shows the cumulative effects on the networks outside the insurgent network. This is an efficient plan as it creates the required level of degradation in the targeted nodes without causing wide spread changes in other networks. A subsequent user instigated dependent analysis identified that a previously low ranking node had been significantly promoted.

The promoted node was an electrical substation that was being used to provide EP to the radio network used by the forces creating and manning the road blocks. Analysis showed that a 50% loss of electrical power to their radio network at the time of the raid would have a significant impact degrading the raids effectiveness by over 70%. Reasoning about dependencies within their own plans allowed SOF planners to identify how to make their plans more robust (hence more likely to succeed) and to guide the plan refinement process.

This example showed the development of plans to directly affect a node by means of its vulnerabilities. However, it is sometimes more efficient to focus on a node's dependencies. One scenario explored was to identify the methods used by the insurgent network to pass information and training knowledge between its members. While actors were identified as possessing specific knowledge, they needed a conduit through which to pass their knowledge and this potential conduit was identified as a local mosque. A similar raid plan could be constructed however, this would remove the mosque's capability to provide religious instruction and stop it being used as a food distribution center. Analysis of the dependencies of this conduit identified that its existence was dependent on the support of the mosque council. The level of support for radicalization by the mosque council was dependent on its radicalized leader. An alternative plan was constructed to de-radicalize the mosque by replacing its council leader. Without the support of the council the mosque could not function as conduit, thus impacting on the insurgent C2 network. Due to the non-quantifiable nature of the conduits output it meant the only option was to remove the conduit completely. By focusing on the dependencies of the conduit rather than the mosque node itself the plan was able to maintain the desirable capabilities of the mosque. Also by identifying any nodes with similar capabilities to the radicalized cleric the plan was able to suggest

*Figure 11. NETPlan planner GUI*

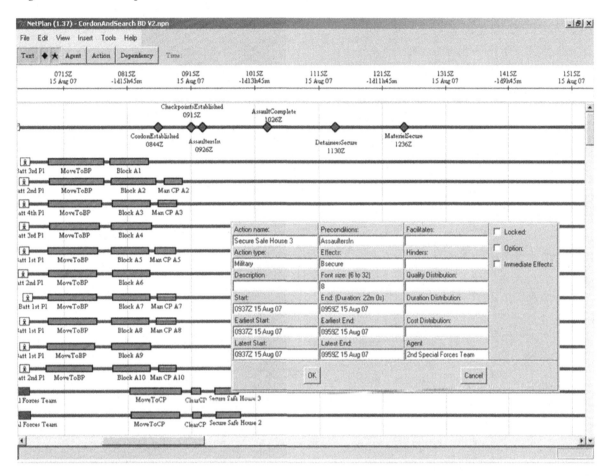

options that would stop the council turning to one of them as a replacement. This avoided the planning process becoming a "whack a mole" game where plan modifications were needed for each undesired replacement the council tried to turn to as their leader.

The planning tasks specified via Athena can be structured according to the needs of the user to either specify the type of action that should be employed or the type of resource that should be used. For example, a plan task could specify that an output is degraded by "seize and occupation." Hence, the planner needs to find the appropriate action(s) and resource(s). Alternatively, the plan task could specify the resources that should be used hence defining the effects that can be considered,

kinetic, non-kinetic, cyber, etc. This distinction gives rise to two different tasks specifications which can be used to create the desired network behavior.

- **VNOCPM:**

  ◦ **Verb:** One of the D or R verbs[11].
  ◦ **Noun:** Node to be affected.
  ◦ **Output:** Node output to be affected.
  ◦ **Change:** Percentage change to the output.
  ◦ **Phenomena:** Method of change.
  ◦ **OMM:** Constraints on option management.
  ◦ **Mechanism:** The chain of desired effects.

*Figure 12. Updated Athena network with action dependencies*

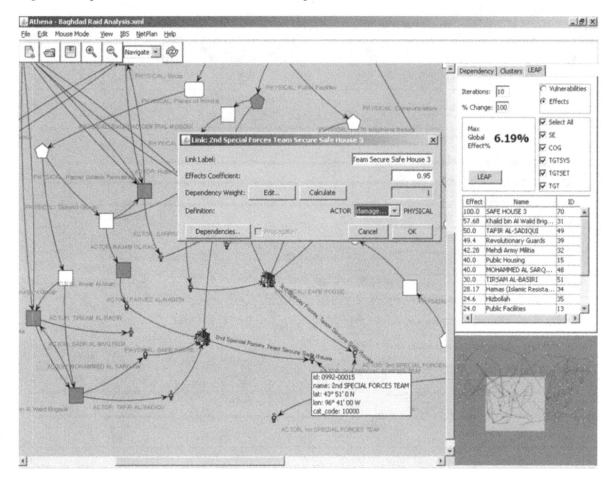

An example VNOCPM model would be: "Degrade Safe House Information Conduit output by 100% by "seizure and occupation" in order to Disrupt Insurgent Group 1's output of Weapons by 50%." This high level task is expanded to identify the node path(s) in the network that link the information conduit output to the production of weapons output. This ensures that firstly the dependency chain exists and secondly to add any additional nodes to the task that need to be affected directly by the plan. In this case disrupting the information conduit does not directly affect weapons production. However, it does stop the transfer of knowledge from the insurgents who possess the knowledge to those who need it and then use it to produce weapons.

- **VNOCDVM:**

  ◦ **VNOC:** Same definitions as above.
  ◦ **Device:** Node that creates the effect.
  ◦ **Vehicle:** Node(s) that deliver the Device.
  ◦ **Mechanism:** Same definition as above.

An example VNOCDVM model would be: "Degrade Safe House Information Conduit output by 100% by "SOF Team" in order to Disrupt IG1 output of Weapons by 50%. In this case the Device, a SOF team, is specified but the Vehicle (V) entry is left blank. If the user were to specify that the SOF team were to be inserted via air drop then this could be added to the V field as a type (e.g. rotary wing) or as a specific instance (e.g., a Blackhawk).

The task specifications use a series of "verbs" to convey the type of change needed and the level of the expected change. Athena is agnostic to the direction of change hence plans can be developed that negatively impact an opposing C2 network in the same way as plans to increase the robustness and resilience of our own C2 networks. Each of the D or R verbs is mapped to one or more actions and to one or more potential node output types. For example, the action "seize and arrest" on a "location" can "disrupt" a social "information conduit" but cannot be used to repair the same location. The information conduit output is vulnerable to "access," which can be exploited by a seizure and arrest action. Taxonomy is used to map generic output types (e.g., social conduit, EP generation, etc.) to vulnerabilities such as access, overpressure, bribery, etc. The selection of {node, action, verb} triplets to achieve a desired effect takes into account whether other outputs would be affected. For example, the "seizure" of a site being used as insurgent information conduit would not impact the location's ability to support medical programs, whereas dislocating it would. The verb, action outputs are set up once and maintained by the system as a library that can be accessed by the system or users. In some cases tasks may be a mixture of D and R verbs. For example de-linking the radical leader of the mosque council to impact the information conduit output and then re-linking a non-radical leader to head the mosques council to maintain its output of religious instruction.

## Scenario 2: Integrated Air Defense Example

The IADS scenario was developed to demonstrate vulnerability analysis and how actions against identified nodes could introduce new vulnerabilities or increase the susceptibility of other node vulnerabilities. The model was developed with AFRL Rome and through other UNCLASSIFIED information resources. Dependee and dependent analysis of the IADS network identified that two Air Operations Centers (AOCs) where the key nodes. However, due to the self-contained nature of the IADS network it was not possible to identify ways to affect the centers based on their dependencies on the EP, transport or other networks, as they possessed many backups and redundancies. Analysis of the AOC vulnerabilities identified their dependency on several SA-10 sites which addressed the AOC need for protection from air strikes (fragmentation and over pressure phenomena). A user instigated Critical Vulnerability analysis identified that a 70% reduction in the capability of the SAM network would be needed to degrade it to a point that the AOCs could be impacted. Several alternative Courses of Action were developed using NETPlan which comprised several sets of resources tasked with strike, AAR, SEAD and other support missions. These missions themselves are linked via dependencies which are mapped into the Athena network model when the plan nodes are imported using the process described previously. Using the techniques described previously the different Courses of Action were imported into the Athena IADS network model and the effects on the C2 Centers analyzed. These allowed planners to refine their plans to degrade additional sites that were needed to create the 70% reduction target. Athena also allows users to explore options if changes were desired at execution time. For example, could the desired effect be achieved if aircraft were lost, missions diverted, etc., allowing planners to identify some informal measures of plan robustness and to focus on which areas of the plan needed some form of mitigation strategy?

## CONCLUSION

This chapter provided an overview of dependency based network modeling and the two reasoning approaches it supports. Node based modeling reasons across networks based on the dependency of one node on another where the actual dependency on electrical power, leadership, manufacturing knowledge, etc. is recorded implicitly. Output based modeling reasons across networks in the same way as the node based approach however, it makes explicit which nodes outputs have a dependency and how the strength of the dependency maps to a change in the dependent node's output. Both these algorithms identify the most important nodes in the network and aid an analyst in identifying the true needs and dependencies of these nodes, both direct and indirect, and hence which ones they should concentrate on for further analysis.

These approaches can be used within the same network model where high level dependencies, as in the IADS C2 network on electrical power, can be modeled using node dependencies, whereas the dependency of a specific AOC on a transmission line can be modeled using output dependencies. The analysis and reasoning supported by the dependency network models allows analysts to rank and identify the most important nodes in a network, their critical vulnerabilities, and their susceptibility to feedback. The analysis also identifies the direct, indirect, cascading and cumulative effects of changes in a network. Through an integrated planning capability, analysts can develop plans to alter the behavior of an opposition network to exploit its vulnerabilities, or to increase the resilience and robustness of their own networks.

The approach is agnostic to the direction of change hence the algorithms described here are equally applicable to disaster and emergency management scenario where the aim is to direct resources to the most critical nodes to ensure functionality is restored as quickly as possible. The approach is being extended to provide the ability to track plan rationale, so that if an effect can be achieved through a different node, then the planner can be re-tasked. For example, if the financier of an insurgent network has just been identified, then a plan to arrest him may achieve the same effect as the current plan being developed to conduct raids to arrest one of the networks key leaders, but at far lower cost in terms of time and effort. Additionally, the ability to identify key information needs including node identity, node(s) addressing a dependency, etc., creating a prioritized list of requests, which can be updated as the network changes over time.

## REFERENCES

Barlow, J. (1993). Strategic Paralysis: An Air Power Strategy for the Present. *Airpower Journal*, *7*(4), 1–15.

Drabble, B. (2011). Dependency based collaboration: Ontology based information management. In *Proceedings of the Collaborative Technologies and Systems Conference (CTS 2011)* (pp. 579-586). Philadelphia, PA: IEEE.

Drabble, B. (2012). Information propagation through a dependency network model. In *Proceedings of the Collaborative Technologies and Systems Conference (CTS 2012)* (pp. 266-272). Denver, CO: IEEE.

Drabble, B., Black, T., Kinzig, C., & Whitted, G. (2009). Ontology based dependency analysis: Understanding the impacts of decisions in a collaborative environment. In *Proceedings of the Collaborative Technologies and Systems Conference (CTS 2009)*, (pp. 10-17). Baltimore, MD: IEEE.

Drabble, B., & Kinzig, C. (2010). The information triad: Collaborating across structured and non-structured information. In *Proceedings of the Collaborative Technologies and Systems Conference (CTS 2010)* (pp. 255-264). Chicago, IL: IEEE.

Drabble, B., McCrabb, M., & Haq, N. (2006). *Dependency Based Vulnerability Assessment* (Final Report, Defense Advanced Research Projects Agency, DARPA Order U051-16, Contract No: W41P4Q-06-C-003). Washington, DC: Academic Press.

Drabble, B., McCrabb, M., Whitted, G., & Kinzig, C. (2009). *Information Bridging Service* (Final Report, Contract Number: FA8650-07-C-4513). Air Force Research Laboratory (AFRL).

Fellbaum, C. (1998). *WordNet: An Electronic Lexical Database*. Cambridge, MA: MIT Press.

Garvey, P. R., & Pinto, C. A. (2005). Introduction to Functional Dependency Network Analysis, The MITRE Corporation and Old Dominion. In *Proceedings of Second International Symposium on Engineering Systems*. Cambridge, MA: The MITRE Corporation and the Old Dominion University.

Jackson, M. C. (1991). *Systems Methodology for the Management Sciences*. New York: Springer. doi:10.1007/978-1-4899-2632-6

Keating, C. B., Sousa-Poza, A., & Kovacic, S. (2008). System of Systems Engineering: An Emerging Multidiscipline. *International Journal of System of Systems Engineering*, *1*(1/2). doi:10.1002/9780470403501.ch7

Mattis, J. N. (2008). USJFCOM Commander's Guidance for Effects-based Operations. [JFQ]. *Joint Force Quarterly*, *51*, 105–109.

Rebovich, G. Jr. (2005). Enterprise Systems Engineering [*Systems Thinking for the Enterprise: New and Emerging Perspectives*. The MITRE Corporation.]. *Theory into Practice*, *2*.

Strange, J. (1996). *Centers of Gravity and Critical Vulnerabilities: Building on the Clausewitzian Foundation So That We Can All Speak the Same Language* (2nd ed.). Quantico, VA: Marine Corps University.

Warden, J. (1995). The Enemy as a System. *Airpower Journal*, *14*(1), 40–55.

White, B. E. (2006). Fostering Intra-Organizational Communication of Enterprise Systems Engineering Practices. In *Proceedings of NDIA, 9th Annual Systems Engineering Conference*. The MITRE Corporation.

## KEY TERMS AND DEFINITIONS

**CDV Modeling:** Modeling network nodes based on their capabilities, dependencies and vulnerability attributes. Where information is available use actual values to model the level of a CDV attribute that a node possesses.

**Dependency Based Network Analysis:** Identify and rank network nodes based on the cumulative strength of the direct and indirect dependencies on them. Use dependency type and strength to capture semantic information on how a network actually functions.

**Integrated Planning and Analysis:** Provide an integrated workflow for analysts to identify the most dependent nodes in a network and to develop plans to change or influence these nodes as desired. Support interoperability between the analysis and planning functions.

**Network Based Effects Analysis:** Identify and quantify the direct, indirect, cumulative and cascading effects of direct changes to the capability of one or more nodes in a network.

**Vulnerability Analysis:** Identify and quantify the phenomena that a single node or nodes is vulnerable to and the mechanisms that may be used to generate or produce the phenomenon.

## ENDNOTES

[1] The ideas were originally developed when the author was CTO of On Target Technologies, Inc.

2     Surface to Air Missiles (SAM), Anti-Aircraft Artillery (AAA) and aircraft.

3     WOC: Wing Operations Center, IOC: Intercept Operations Center and ZOC: Zone Operations Center.

4     CALIFON: Is an UNCLASSIFIED model used for evaluation and testing purposes.

5     A C2 Center may be dependent on several EP nodes as either a primary or backup provider.

6     BTU, British Thermal Units used for combing the different coal, oil, gas, etc. fuels needed by the power plants.

7     This is an unclassified scenario developed with DARPA.

8     Exponential, distribution and other types of equation can be user selected or a specialized function defined.

9     Capability to provide protection from seizure and arrest, manufacturing of weapons, etc.

10     NETPlan is a planning tool available from ActiveComputing: www.activecomputing. net.

11     The "D" verbs "*destroy, degrade, dislocate, demoralize, de-link,* etc. are used to negatively impact a node's capabilities and "R" verbs "*repair, remove, renovate, relink, relocate,* etc. positively impact a node's capabilities.

# APPENDIX

## Questions

1.  What is the difference between a dependent and dependee node in terms of analysis of a networks content and structure?
2.  What does the term CDV stand for and give examples of each?
3.  What is the difference between direct and transitive node dependency?
4.  What are the four different types of nodes that can modelled in a network and provide examples?
5.  If a node A has a dependency score of 100 and node B has a score of 200 what insight does this provide the analysts in terms of the node's importance?
6.  How can a direct effect on a node be amplified to create a greater capability impact?
7.  What mechanism is used to exploit the direct vulnerability of a node?
8.  What is meant by the term "Critical Vulnerability Analysis" and how does this impact the concept of looping or feedback?
9.  What are the main differences between the Warden Ring Model and the Barlow National Elements of Value Model?
10. What network or node attributes can be used to identify the weighting for a dependency strength on a link between a dependent and dependee node?

# Chapter 7
# Dynamical Network Structures in Multi–Layered Networks:
## Implementing and Evaluating Basic Principles for Collective Behavior

**R. H. P. Janssen**
*Netherlands Defence Academy, The Netherlands*

**H. Monsuur**
*Netherlands Defence Academy, The Netherlands*

**A. J. van der Wal**
*Netherlands Defence Academy, The Netherlands*

## ABSTRACT

*In modeling military (inter)actions and cooperation as networks, military units or actors may be represented as nodes. In analyzing military networked action, a key observation is that a node is not just part of one type of network but simultaneously belongs to multiple networks. To model the dynamical behavior of actors, one has to take into account the interdependence of the different networks. In this chapter, the authors present a method that is used to implement, analyze, and evaluate some specific principles that may be used by the actors in an organization to drive the process of constant change. It can be used to analyze the effect of these principles on the metrics for coordination, synchronization, robustness, and desired operational effectiveness of the network as a whole. To demonstrate the approach, the authors apply it to networks in which two basic principles are operational: reciprocity and a novel principle called covering.*

DOI: 10.4018/978-1-4666-6058-8.ch007

# INTRODUCTION

## Background / Motivation

Military operations have grown increasingly complex over the past years. Modern operations are non-conventional, involving missions like counterterrorism, peacekeeping and crisis management. Characteristics of these operations include the participation of many stakeholders, each with their own objectives and involving multiple chains of command, rapidly changing environments, short reaction times and increased uncertainty concerning the operating environment or theatre area. In addition to these complexities, the enemy or opponent operates in a networked manner. They are connected through complex social, informational and physical networks that dynamically adapt to the environment. Outmaneuvering such an intelligent opponent is a daunting task. As General McChrystal (2011) put it: "it takes a network to defeat a network."

Given these complexities and challenges, it is of paramount importance that the units of a defense organization are also connected through multiple social, informational and physical networks. This coupling enables military units to coordinate and synchronize their individual actions with one another to achieve greater operational effectiveness. These insights triggered the development of the concepts of Network Centric Warfare (NCW) in the mid-1990s, later named Network Centric Operations (NCO) in the US and Network Enabled Capabilities (NEC) within NATO. These concepts involve the use of complex, networked systems, consisting of many components that are heterogeneous in functionality and capability with both nonlocal and non-linear interactions and effects, cf. Alberts et al., 1999; Cares, 2005; Monsuur, Grant and Janssen, 2011. It is now widely accepted that C2 systems are socio-technical in nature. In addition to the technical infrastructure in the form of supporting computing and telecommunication networks, the analysis also centers on the inter-relationship between doctrine, organization, training, material, leadership, personnel, facilities (DOTMLPF). This view induces a transformation of C2 systems from a rigid, hierarchical organizational structure towards an agile networked organizational form. In this case one assumes that information sharing, collaboration and self synchronization ultimately lead to increased mission effectiveness (an element of the so-called NEC value chain). As described in McChrystal (2011), lessons learned from recent operations show that, in addition to being connected, the organizational form also has to be dynamic. To be agile and be able to react adequately to varying conditions, a constantly changing, adapting operational social and information network has to be the hallmark of a modern defense organization or crisis management team. As also illustrated by other research (for example, see Alberts, 2011), various heterogeneous networked units are needed to ensure agility and mission effectiveness. This process of constant change, if restricted to social and information networks, has several characteristics (see McChrystal, 2013). First of all, change is not centrally orchestrated and units may, to a degree, be considered as autonomously acting agents. Change is neither meant to create the most efficient bureaucratic model nor is it a process of optimizing for variables that have become irrelevant. Secondly, as is the case with the competitors, there is neither an organizational end-state, nor advance knowledge of the next state. Finally, change has to be guided by a few basic principles. Meanwhile, one has to constantly monitor the health of the network by how well each unit shares a common understanding of the battlefield and the strategy to defeat an enemy or manage a crisis situation. This self-monitoring of the network as an enabler of C2 is necessary to be able to act both reactive and proactive. Finding the right basic principles that drive the process of change will be a learning process.

In this chapter, we present a method that can be used to implement, simulate, analyze and evalu-

*Figure 1. Controlling the process of dynamically changing network structures*

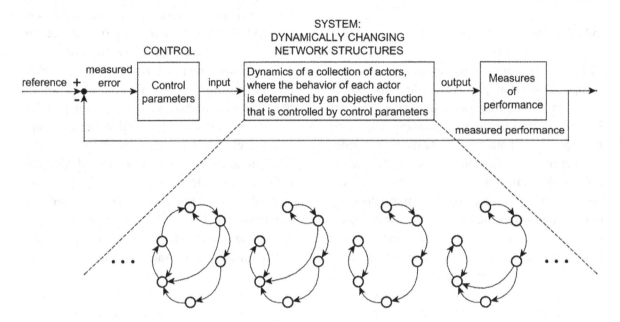

ate the three characteristics of constant change of organizational form mentioned above. In this so-called stochastic actor-based approach, actors are used to mimic individual units of the organization. To guide the process of constant change, actors are endowed with some specific basic behavioral principles. By simulating their actions, we can analyze the effect of these principles, and combinations thereof, on metrics for the ability of coordination, synchronization, robustness and desired operational effectiveness of the network as a whole. We refer to Figure 1 to explain and clarify our approach, using a classical control paradigm.

Although not centrally orchestrated, individuals of an organization use, or should be trained to use, some basic principles to decide whether or not links to others have to be created or severed. We assume that we have some knowledge regarding good basic principles that one may use, but this has to be fine-tuned by some control system. This control system is also able to measure the performance/health of the networks in terms of operational effectiveness. It may take appropriate actions via the feedback loop if necessary. As is

indicated in Figure 1, it is important to note that there will be no simple end state of this process. Social and information networks will always be exposed to change. The outcome of the system therefore is an ongoing sequence of dynamically changing network structures. The role of the control system is a designers' role. It directs this chain of dynamically changing networks into some desirable direction. The health of the organization is then represented by the mean performance of this collection of dynamically changing network structures.

To describe the basic principles that actors may utilize, we use the language of networks, as it adequately represents social, informational and physical connections between organizations, teams and units. We refer to Acebrón et al., 2005; Barabási, 2003; Boccaletti et al., 2006; Goyal, 2007; Jackson, 2009; Janssen and Monsuur, 2010, 2012; Van der Wal, 2010; Watts, 1999; Wasserman and Faust, 1994 for discussions, with examples that range from biological, social, information networks to terrorist networks. As is the case in NEC, social, information and physical networks taken together represent the current state of an organization. For individual, autonomously acting units or actors, these multi-layered networks constitute the framework for the investigation of their possible moves. In these layered structures, units operate simultaneously within their social, information and physical networks. This makes it possible to also analyze and evaluate the interaction between principles that drive the process of constant change in social networks and principles that drive the change at information networks. It also enables the formulation and evaluation of certain social norms or guiding principles that interrelate the various networks in which an actor operates. For example, it may be a (social or cultural) norm or principle that in order for information to be exchanged and a connection to be established between units in an information network, the two actors must be socially connected. This means that the social network structure simultaneously enables, but also restricts the exchange of information in the information network. This illustrates the idea that a network may be seen as a strategic asset of an actor since it is a source of both opportunities and constraints. We therefore postulate that each unit or actor has incentives to manage and optimize its networks. One therefore should have insight into the qualities of some specific guiding principles.

To illustrate our method for the implementation and evaluation of some specific guiding principles for change, we restrict ourselves to study two such principles. The first one is stated in terms of bi-directional connections to other units in the *information domain* or network. The second one is stated in terms of social status of a unit or actor in the *social domain*. Performing well in both domains (the information and the social network) may add to the operational effectiveness or health of the organization. The first principle mentioned above counts for an individual unit or actor the number of bi-directional connections to other units, i.e. the number of reciprocated links. The ability of an individual unit to communicate through many direct connections increases its

informational value, and as such increases the robustness and operational effectiveness of the overall C2 structure. For the second principle we introduce the novel notion of covering that will be discussed in detail later in the chapter. Using this notion, a unit or actor is able to assess whether or not its position in the social network is outperformed by another one in terms of social connections to others within the network. The guiding principle is that a unit will change its links to minimize the number of units by which it is outperformed. This adds to the value of the combined, multi-layered C2 network structure. Not taking into account these kinds of incentives of individual actors may also lead to unexpected and unexplained changes in social C2 network structures.

Organizations take shape as a result of autonomous actors seeking to achieve their individual objectives. To implement these guiding principles, we use stochastic actor-based models (Snijders et al., 2010). In these models, actors evaluate their network structure and try to change it according to some objective function. These functions are linear combinations of several characteristics of the network, like the two measures or principles we described above. Iterating this process of change, initiated by individual actors leads to a chain of dynamically changing network structures or organizational forms. As a consequence, actors' actions have implications for robustness and operational effectiveness. Therefore, we have investigated the characteristics of the collection of dynamically changing network topologies. For example, we may look at the robustness of such dynamically changing networks by asking ourselves: "how many nodes have to be eliminated to be sure to disintegrate networks of this collection of dynamically changing networks, making communication impossible?" An analysis of this kind may be used to assess the quality of specific guiding principles for change of organizational forms. In demonstrating our method, we consider the global equivalents of the two guiding principles used by individual units or actors. More specifically, we will consider the effect of the weights set by the control system in Figure 1 for each of the guiding principles in the objective function, on the chain of dynamically changing networks. By describing our method in detail, it will be possible to model military networked action by using stochastic actor-based models that also incorporate multi-layered networks.

## Overview

The purpose of this chapter is to present a method that can be used to implement, analyze, and evaluate some specific principles that can be used by individual units or actors of the organization to guide the process of constant change networks are exposed to. In the second section, we introduce stochastic actor-based models. To the set of existing effects or characteristics that are used in the objective function of actors, we add a new characteristic called covering, which is introduced in the third section. Then, we study the interaction between the well-known reciprocity characteristic and our new notion of covering. We consider the effect of weights assigned to each guiding principle. Characteristics of the sequence of dynamically changing networks are fully examined and explained. Then, we extend the stochastic actor-based models to also incorporate multi-layered networks: actors are active in social as well as information networks. By doing so, we are able to evaluate social (or security) norms concerning the creation and deletion of links between actors in a network. Implementation of other explicitly formulated basic principles and avenues for further research are discussed in the conclusion.

## STOCHASTIC ACTOR-BASED MODELS FOR NETWORK DYNAMICS

In this section, we focus on the 'control' and 'system' part of Figure 1. As we will make extensive use of the language of networks, we first present some graph-theoretical preliminaries.

## Graph Theoretic Preliminaries

A *directed graph* or a *network G* is a pair $(V,E)$ where $V = \{v_1, v_2, \ldots, v_n\}$ is a finite set of $n \geq 2$ *vertices* representing *nodes* or *actors*, and $E$ is a set of *edges*, which is a subset of $\{(a,b): a, b \in V, a \neq b\}$, the set of *ordered* pairs of $V$. An element $(a,b)$ of $E$ is called a *link* from $a$ to $b$. This link $(a,b)$ is an *outgoing link* for actor $a$ and an *incoming link* for actor $b$. A network $G$ is completely described by its *adjacency matrix*: the *adjacency matrix x* of $G$ is the $n \times n$-matrix with $x_{ab} = 1$ if $(a,b) \in E$ and $x_{ab} = 0$ if $(a,b) \notin E$. So, $x_{aa} = 0$ for all actors $a$. For example, the network $G$ in Figure 2 has the adjacency matrix

$$\begin{pmatrix} 0 & 1 & 0 & 0 & 1 & 1 \\ 0 & 0 & 1 & 1 & 0 & 0 \\ 0 & 1 & 0 & 1 & 0 & 0 \\ 0 & 1 & 1 & 0 & 1 & 0 \\ 1 & 0 & 0 & 1 & 0 & 0 \\ 1 & 0 & 0 & 0 & 0 & 0 \end{pmatrix}$$

Note that, in contrast to most approaches in Network Centric Operations, where links are always bi-directional, we use directed links. This is due to our assumption that the actors are autonomously initiating links to other actors, seeking to satisfy their own objectives.

The link $(a,b) \in E$ from actor $a$ to actor $b$ is called a *reciprocated link* if, in addition, $(b,a) \in E$. In terms of the adjacency matrix, the link from actor $a$ to actor $b$ is a *reciprocated link* if and only if $x_{ab} = 1$ and $x_{ba} = 1$, i.e. the product $x_{ab} \cdot x_{ba} = 1$. In that case we call the actors $a$ and $b$ *neighbors*. The *degree* of an actor $a \in V$, denoted by degree($a$), is the number of neighbors of actor $a$: degree($a$) $= \Sigma_{v \in V} x_{av} \cdot x_{va}$.

*Figure 2. A network G (left) and the corresponding network G^{rec} (right)*

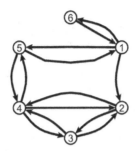 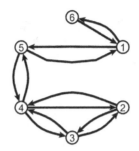

Given a network $G = (V,E)$, the network $G^{rec}$ is the subnetwork $(V,E^{rec})$ where $E^{rec}$ is the smallest subset of $E$ containing all reciprocated links: $E^{rec} = \{(a,b): a, b \in V, a \neq b, (a,b) \in E, (b,a) \in E\}$. See Figure 2 for an example of networks $G$ and $G^{rec}$. The adjacency matrix of the network $G^{rec} = (V,E^{rec})$, denoted by $x^{rec}$, is a symmetric matrix with the entries $x^{rec}_{ab} = x_{ab} \cdot x_{ba}$ and zero entries on the main diagonal. For example, the network $G^{rec}$ in Figure 2 has the adjacency matrix

$$\begin{pmatrix} 0 & 0 & 0 & 0 & 1 & 1 \\ 0 & 0 & 1 & 1 & 0 & 0 \\ 0 & 1 & 0 & 1 & 0 & 0 \\ 0 & 1 & 1 & 0 & 1 & 0 \\ 1 & 0 & 0 & 1 & 0 & 0 \\ 1 & 0 & 0 & 0 & 0 & 0 \end{pmatrix}$$

This means that $a$ and $b$ are connected in $G^{rec}$ if, and only if, $a$ has a link to $b$ and $b$ has a link to $a$ in $G$.

## Stochastic Actor-Based Models

Networks, social as well as information networks, gradually change over time. Friendship, trust or cooperation links are established, but can also be severed due to the actions of autonomously operating actors. The method that we introduce to analyze dynamically changing networks is a stochastic actor-based approach for network dynamics (Snijders et al., 2010). A wide variety of interaction mechanisms, called effects or principles, can be incorporated in these stochastic actor-based models. These principles steer the process of change by influencing the creation and annihilation of links as indicated in the system part of Figure 1. Such a principle can express the desire of an actor to ascertain a favorable position within the network of connections. In most applications found in the literature, data on the temporal network structure at several points in time is used to develop hypotheses about the social processes that might produce the observed structural properties. For this kind of analysis, a computer program has been developed, called Simulation Investigation for Empirical Network Analyses or SIENA (Snijders et al., 2010). In terms of the problem described in the Introduction, this boils down to inferring from observed organizational forms at several points in time, the underlying principles that might have driven the process of change. In this chapter, we follow a reverse route. Proposed guiding principles for change are implemented in objective functions of actors. By iterating the process of change and use of these interactions, we may investigate global metrics of the set of dynamically changing networks or organizational forms. We used these metrics to evaluate the level of synchronization or operational effectiveness of the networked organization.

*Figure 3. Current network (a) and the three possible resulting networks (b) if the focal actor is actor 1*

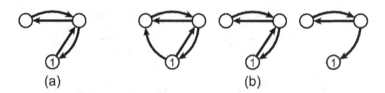

(a)                                        (b)

The process of dynamically changing networks is a Markov process. This means that only the current state of the network determines probabilistically its further evolution. To describe the model in more detail, we highlight a few important assumptions for each iteration of the model. First of all, at some point in time, a so-called focal actor is chosen according to some probability distribution over the set of all actors. We assume that this distribution is the uniform distribution, which means that no actor is preferred to act firstly, i.e. the focal actor is chosen at random. This actor is allowed to change his set of outgoing links to other actors, or leave the network as it is. More precisely, given a total of $n$ actors, the focal actor has a set of $n$ admissible actions: he can do nothing, or can change the state of precisely one of his possible connections to other actors, i.e. he can add an outgoing link if that link does not exist or he can remove that outgoing link if it exists. A focal actor cannot add or remove incoming links. In Figure 3, if actor 1 is the focal actor, he can move to any of the three networks in Figure 3 (b) by adding or deleting at most one (outgoing) link.

The focal actor uses an objective function to evaluate each of these possible resulting network configurations. This objective function expresses how likely it is to change the current network in a particular way. On average, each actor moves in the direction of higher values of his objective function, resulting in a more favorable network structure. This may be seen as mimicking the use of the basic principles mentioned in the Introduction, subject to some random influences. Note that

the approach using stochastic actors implies that changes are sequentially, excluding simultaneous dynamics that require coordination or negotiation.

## The Objective Function

Each actor has an objective function which, in general, is a linear combination of several effects related to network properties. One effect can be the number of neighbors the actor has, reflecting the tendency of actors to try to reciprocate incoming links. Another effect may express the tendency to form triplets. In social networks, for example, actors may like to form triplets, meaning that neighbors of neighbors become neighbors. A focal actor then counts the number of these triplets he is involved in. Quite another example of an interaction is related to structural equivalence with respect to outgoing links (cf. Burt, 1982), which is the tendency to keep and create links to other actors who make the same choices as the focal actor. We refer to Snijders et al (2010) for these and many more examples of effects that can be used in objective functions. The same objective function is applied to all actors. Furthermore, in this chapter, we assume that all effects are stated in terms of (endogenous) network characteristics only

Now, suppose that actor $a$ is the focal actor and that the current network is represented by an adjacency matrix $x$. The objective function is $f_a(\beta, x)$, where $\beta = \{\beta_k\}$ is a set of control parameters, one for each principle. This function is a linear combination of several effects: $f_a(\beta, x)$

$= \Sigma_k \beta_k \bullet s_{a,k}(a,x)$. An example of an effect is the number of reciprocated links of the focal actor: $s_{a,rec}(a,x) = \Sigma_{v \in V} x_{av} \bullet x_{va}$. As mentioned before, the first step in a stochastic actor-based model is the selection of the focal actor who gets the opportunity to make a change. We assume that this choice is made with equal probabilities for all actors, i.e. the probability that one particular actor will be the focal actor equals $1/n$ if $n$ is the total number of actors. Next, the focal actor, say $a$, may initiate a new link $(a,b)$ if $(a,b) \notin E$, sever an existing link $(a,b)$ if $(a,b) \in E$, or do nothing. So, the focal actor can choose from a set $C$ consisting of $n$ possible new states of the network. Note that this set $C$ of adjacent network structures includes the current state since the focal actor may decide to do nothing. The objective function ranks these $n$ networks with respect to the desirability from the point of view of the focal actor, and as a result measures how likely it is to change the current network in a particular way. To be more precise, the transition probability of going to some new state $y \in C$ is given by

$$\frac{\exp(f_a(\beta, y))}{\sum_{x' \in C} \exp(f_a(\beta, x'))},$$

where $\beta$ is a set of control parameters. Consider again the network of Figure 3 and take the case where only one characteristic is measured, namely the number of reciprocated links. Then the objective function is given by $f_a(\beta, x) = \beta_{rec} \bullet s_{a,rec}(a,x)$. If actor 1 is the focal actor, the probabilities of transition to the $n = 3$ possible new network states are given by

$$\frac{e^{\beta_{rec} \cdot 1}}{e^{\beta_{rec} \cdot 1} + e^{\beta_{rec} \cdot 1} + e^{\beta_{rec} \cdot 0}} = \frac{e^{\beta_{rec}}}{2e^{\beta_{rec}} + 1},$$

$$\frac{e^{\beta_{rec} \cdot 1}}{e^{\beta_{rec} \cdot 1} + e^{\beta_{rec} \cdot 1} + e^{\beta_{rec} \cdot 0}} = \frac{e^{\beta_{rec}}}{2e^{\beta_{rec}} + 1} \text{ and}$$

$$\frac{e^{\beta_{rec} \cdot 0}}{e^{\beta_{rec} \cdot 1} + e^{\beta_{rec} \cdot 1} + e^{\beta_{rec} \cdot 0}} = \frac{1}{2e^{\beta_{rec}} + 1}.$$

After the choice is made, again a focal actor is selected at random, that evaluates all adjacent network structures. The network transitions can thus be interpreted as the transitions of a Markov process, since the probabilities of transition to the new possible network states are completely determined once the current network state is known.

## Characteristics of Dynamically Changing Networks

Given the Markov process described in the previous section, an interesting question is: what are the characteristics of the dynamically changing networks in this process of constant change? Are these networks robust? What is the overall operational effectiveness of an organization represented by such network structures? Just as an example, regarding the level of total reciprocity of outgoing links of all actors, we have the following simulation result in case $n = 3$. See Figure 4 (left), where we have plotted the analytical calculated expected or mean total number of reciprocated links in the sequence of changing networks as a function of the parameter $\beta_{rec}$ in case the network consists of three actors and the objective function $f_a(\beta_{rec}, x) = \beta_{rec} \bullet s_{a,rec}(a,x)$. The total number of reciprocated links is less than or equal to six, since each actor has at most two (incoming) links that can be reciprocated. For example, in Figure 4 (right) the number of reciprocated links in a run with 250 iterations of the stochastic actor-based approach in a network of 3 actors is plotted as a function of the iteration number, where $\beta_{rec} = 1$. The average value of the number of reciprocated links in these 250 network structures equals 3.2240. The expected value equals 3.2241 which is an analytic result. We further note that the parameter $\beta_{rec}$ can also be negative, implying that the focal actor tries to avoid networks where links are reciprocated.

*Figure 4. (left) Expected number of reciprocated links as a function of $\beta_{rec}$ in a network of 3 actors. (right) Number of reciprocated links as a function of the iteration k in a typical run of the stochastic actor-based approach in a network of 3 actors ($\beta_{rec} = 1$)*

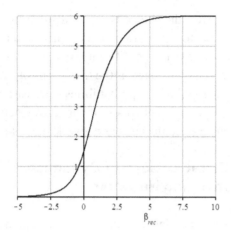
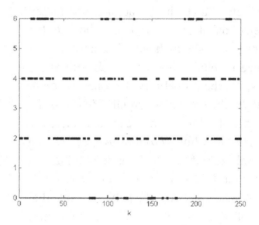

If more than one effect is used, one may study the consequences of applying several principles simultaneously. An actor that uses such objective functions prevents focusing on just one principle. We will extensively study the interaction between two competing characteristics: the reciprocity and a new characteristic, called covering, introduced in the third section, which quantifies the central position of an actor in the network. As a new feature, we also will extend this approach to multi-layered networks and will study a social norm or restriction for link formation and deletion. This norm may also be interpreted as a principle for network change. Using these simulation results, we are also able to perform some testing of hypotheses concerning the control parameters $\beta = \{\beta_k\}$, which can be compared to the results obtained with e.g. the SIENA software.

## A NEW PRINCIPLE TO EVALUATE NETWORKS: COVERING

In this section the novel principle of covering to evaluate networks is introduced. This notion originated from the study of the theory of vot-ing and tournament solutions, see Miller (1980). Consider a tournament with several participants, where everyone plays against everyone. Then a participant, say $a$, is said to outperform another participant $b$, if $a$ has defeated $b$, and in addition has defeated all participants that were defeated by $b$. In that case we say that $a$ covers $b$. We have altered this definition of covering so that it also is applicable to social networks. Using this notion, an actor is able to assess whether or not its position in a network is outperformed by another one in terms of connections to other actors within the network. Covering can be implemented as a guiding principle within network dynamics as stochastic actor-based modeling in the sense that a random individual actor may change its local network structure to minimize the number of actors by which it is outperformed. Although we restrict ourselves in this book chapter to the notion of covering, we note that it is a special case of the notion of $W$-covering as described in the Appendix and in Janssen and Monsuur (2013).

## The Notion of Covering

To the existing set of network measures or effects, we add a new effect, by introducing the concept of covering. Actors may use this effect to benchmark their position and act accordingly. We give three reasons to introduce this new effect.

First of all, a network may be seen as a strategic asset of an actor. It may have positive features, but an actor may also (temporarily) be locked in a subdued position, which reveals a possible negative side of a network of relations. For a focal actor such an unattractive and subdued situation may be characterized by the existence of another actor that outperforms the focal actor in the sense that all neighbors of the focal actor are also neighbors of the other actor and the latter actor has at least one extra neighbor. In a network this means that the other actor has more possibilities to communicate compared to the communication possibilities of the focal actor. As an example, consider the situation of a network $G$ consisting of six actors, as in Figure 2. A link directed from an actor, i.e. actor 1, to another actor that is reciprocated (which means that there is also a link directed from the other actor to actor 1) means that the two actors are neighbors. So, the actors 1 and 5 are neighbors and therefore can share and verify first-hand information, whereas the actors 5 and 2 or actors 1 and 2 cannot. Now we state that actor 6 is in an unfavorable position when compared with the position of actor 5: each neighbor of actor 6 is also neighbor of actor 5, but actor 5 has actor 4 as an extra neighbor to share information with. Therefore, using this benchmark to evaluate his position, actor 6 is outperformed by actor 5. In this case we say that actor 6 is *covered* by actor 5. By using the same argument, we may conclude that actor 6 is also covered by actor 1. In the situation of a network $G$, actor 6 is not covered by three actors: actors 2, 3, and 4. So the covering effect can be used to inform the actor to what extent he is locked in an unfavorable position by counting the number of actors by which he is not covered.

Note that at first glance, it seems that having a lot of reciprocated links is a guarantee for a node not to be covered, or *uncovered*. But this is not true: even when an actor has many reciprocated links, it can still be covered.

In actor-based models actors take rational decisions to obtain a more positively evaluated network configuration of relations. Commonly, it is assumed that the rational actions of an actor do not negatively affect the interests of other actors. A second and related motivation for introducing the notion of covering is that it challenges this tacit assumption. For example, consider network $G$ in Figure 2 in which actor 2 is covered by actor 4 and therefore is in a subdued position relative to actor 4. To escape from this unpleasant situation, actor 2 can reciprocate the link initiated by actor 1. As a result, actor 2 is not covered anymore by actor 4. Note that this is the only way in which actor 2 can become uncovered. However, this action by actor 2 results in actor 5 being covered by actor 2, whereas originally actor 5 was not covered by any actor. So, even if the set of all neighbors of a node $a$ does not change, the creation of a link between two other nodes $b$ and $c$ may result in $a$ being covered. This observation will play an important role in interpreting simulation results for stochastic actor-based models later on.

A third consideration for introducing the covering effect is that it connects three levels of analysis for networks. First of all, one may study a network at the atomic level of individual actors. For example, the positioning of an actor in a network can be studied using the notion of centrality. A second level of analysis is the evaluation of the network by considering clusters of actors, for example the clusters of structurally equivalent actors. An actor may also evaluate a network by looking at a cluster of actors; for example, it may have a preference to be connected to the cluster of similar nodes (assortativity). Our notion of covering connects these two levels of analysis, as it informs an individual actor whether or not his cluster of neighbors is sufficiently unique such that, at the atomic level, he is not outperformed by other actors. A third level of analysis is the study of the network as a whole. All effects, including the covering effect, have implications for the structure of the dynamically changing networks, for example in terms of degree distribution or level of reciprocity. This will be investigated later on.

The definition of covering is in terms of the link structure of the network $G$, see Monsuur and Storcken (2004). We refer to Janssen and Monsuur (2012) for a comprehensive study of the notion of covering. In the following, we review the key concepts of covering.

In terms of the link structure of $G$ let $a$ and $b$ be actors in $V$, $a \neq b$. Then $a$ covers $b$ in $G = (V, E)$ or equivalently, $b$ is covered by $a$ in $G = (V, E)$, if

1.  For all actors $v$ in $V$, $v \notin \{a, b\}$: $(b, v) \in E^{rec}$ implies $(a, v) \in E^{rec}$, and
2.  At least one actor $v \notin \{a, b\}$ exists such that $(a, v) \in E^{rec}$ while $(b, v) \notin E^{rec}$.

Actor $b$ in $V$ is called covered in $G = (V, E)$ if for at least one actor $a$ in $V$, $a \neq b$, $b$ is covered by $a$ in $G = (V, E)$. An actor is called uncovered in $G = (V, E)$ if he is not covered in $G = (V, E)$.

To elucidate this definition, note that all links mentioned in the definition are reciprocated links, i.e. the actors are neighbors. We say that actor $a$ covers actor $b$ if all neighbors of $b$ (minus $a$ if $(a, b) \in E^{rec}$) are also neighbors of $a$ (minus $b$ if $(a, b) \in E^{rec}$) and actor $a$ has at least one extra neighbor. Note that we do not require that $(a, b) \in E^{rec}$. Intuitively speaking, $a$ outperforms $b$. For example, actor 4 covers actor 3 in network $G$ in Figure 2. In network $G$ the actors 2 and 4 are uncovered. If the network is a social network or a network of alliances, then it is also clear that $a$'s position is more advantageous: every (social) reciprocated link of $b$ can be covered by one of $a$ and $a$ has at least one extra reciprocated link. More technical remarks about the notion of covering can be found at the end of this chapter.

Note that 'actor $a$ covers actor $b$' is *not* equivalent to 'degree($a$) > degree($b$)'. For example, in network $G$ in Figure 2 we have degree(actor 4) > degree(actor 1) while actor 4 does not cover actor 1. Of course, degree($a$) > degree($b$) in case actor $a$ covers actor $b$. This implies that an actor with the highest degree *of all actors in the network* certainly is uncovered.

## The Covering Effect in the Objective Function

Actor $i$ prefers networks in which he is uncovered. In such a network he has some unique information compared to any other actor and as a result he will be more valuable for other actors to link to. The least preferred topology is a network in which he is covered by all other actors. In that case, he is outperformed by all actors. The most preferred topology is a network in which he is not covered by any other actor. Intermediate situations are characterized by the number of other actors that do cover the focal actor. This means that an actor $i$ may evaluate a network by considering the number of actors that do not cover him. An actor may try to improve his situation by creating a reciprocated link to some actor that possibly reduces the number of actors that cover him.

Let $i$ be an actor in $V$. Then the covering effect is defined by $s_{\{i, uncov\}}(x) = |\{j \in V: j \text{ does not cover } i \text{ in } G\}|$, the number of actors that do not cover actor $i$.

Let us, for illustrative purposes, consider the case of $n = 3$ actors, where $2^6 = 64$ networks are possible. If no distinction between the actors is made, the number of possible networks reduces to 16 (see Figure 5). In this figure, the number of uncovered actors in a network is also given. A line between two network structures means that a state transition is possible between these two network states by an action of one of the three actors.

Using this figure, a few remarks can be made. First of all, from a global point of view, in every network (except for the completely connected

*Figure 5. All possible network structures for 3 actors, with the number of uncovered actors. The lines indicate possible transitions as a result of one of the actors' creation or deletion of a link*

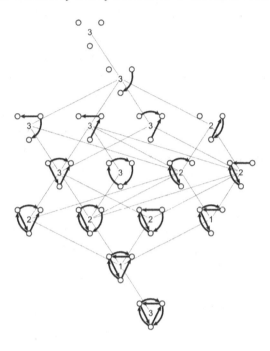

network), it is socially desirable that some actors delete links. To illustrate this we note that for each network in Figure 5 (except for the completely connected network), the deletion of a link always reduces the total number of uncovered nodes increases, or at least it does not decrease. Secondly, actors cannot always escape from the status of being covered. For example, take the fourth network at the third row, where the actor without links is covered. But, irrespective of his action, this actor remains covered. Only if one of the other actors deletes a link does he become uncovered. Thirdly, in many networks actors exist that are in a position to 'harm' others. For example, consider the third network of the fourth row. Then the actor that is covered by two other actors can create a link, so that he is covered by just one actor. By doing so, the third actor becomes covered. This illustrates the issue of the negative externalities, as discussed in Jackson (2009).

## INVESTIGATIONS INTO CHARACTERISTICS OF DYNAMICALLY CHANGING NETWORKS

Having dealt with the preliminaries, we now are able to illustrate our tool for the implementation, analysis and evaluation of some specific principles for the process of constant change that may be used by individual actors of the organization. We present outcomes of a simulation study for $n = 15$. The reason to restrict the value of $n$ to 15 is that this already gives sufficient insight into the peculiarities of the effects and their interaction. In this simulation study, we use two effects driving the Markov transitions. These are implemented as an objective function that is used by actors in the stochastic actor based simulation model. As mentioned previously, actors evaluate the choices they can make by means of such an objective function. The two effects that we consider are: the number of actors that do not cover the focal actor $i$, $s_{\{i,uncov\}}(x)$, and the number of reciprocated links of the focal actor $i$, $s_{\{i,rec\}}(x)$, where $x$ is the adjacency matrix. So the objective function of a focal actor $i$ equals

$$f_i(\beta_1,\beta_2,x) = \beta_1 \cdot s_{i,uncov}(x) + \beta_2 \cdot s_{i,rec}(x),$$

where $\{\beta_1,\beta_2\}$ is the set of control parameters. The probability of moving to some adjacent network depends on this objective function. For example, let the focal actor be actor 1 in a network of three actors in Figure 3. Then the value of the objective function of actor 1 in the current network (a) equals $\beta_1\bullet1+ \beta_2\bullet1$, whereas this value for actor 1 in the three networks of Figure 3 (b) equals respectively $\beta_1\bullet1+ \beta_2\bullet1$, $\beta_1\bullet1+ \beta_2\bullet1$ and $\beta_1\bullet0+ \beta_2\bullet0$. So the transition probability to the rightmost network of Figure 3 (b), is given by

$$\frac{e^{(\beta_1\cdot0+\beta_2\cdot0)}}{e^{(\beta_1\cdot1+\beta_2\cdot1)} + e^{(\beta_1\cdot1+\beta_2\cdot1)} + e^{(\beta_1\cdot0+\beta_2\cdot0)}} = \frac{1}{2e^{\beta_1+\beta_2}+1}.$$

The results of our simulation are represented by the figures in the next subsection. In these figures, we measure the consequences of the use of the two principles driving the change. In terms of block diagram of Figure 1, these figures show the performance of the system for different combinations of the control parameters $\beta_1$ and $\beta_2$. The chosen measures of performance of the system are respectively the expected *total* number of reciprocated links and the expected *total* number of uncovered actors. These expected values were estimated by averaging respectively the *total* number of reciprocated links and the *total* number of uncovered actors of the separate dynamically changing network structures. Note that the chosen measures of performance are formulated in terms of global counterparts of the chosen principles that drive the decisions of the individual actors: the total number of reciprocated ties and the total number

of uncovered actors. The reason for this choice, is the assumption that there is a positive correlation between sufficiently high values of these metrics and the ability of coordination, synchronization, robustness and desired operational effectiveness of the network as a whole. It gives insight into good balancing weights $(\beta_1,\beta_2)$ for these two competing principles that drive the change. Generally also other measures of performance can be chosen.

To summarize, in this section, we investigate the characteristics of the dynamically changing networks if we use the covering effect. We also study how this effect competes and interacts with the reciprocity effect, depending on the choices of the parameters $(\beta_1,\beta_2)$. Later on in this section, we also point out a reverse route.

## The Case $n = 15$

The results of our stochastic actor-based simulations are presented in Figs. 6 and 8. In this subsection, we will interpret these simulation results and discuss their implications. In our simulation, we took over $10^8$ iterations in the stochastic actor-based model. This clearly makes possible to identify the set of dynamically changing network structures. For a large number of combinations of $\beta_1,\beta_2$ we averaged the number of reciprocated links and uncovered actors over the set of these dynamically changing networks. This set was large enough to let the standard deviation become small enough to replace the confidence intervals for the expected total number of reciprocated ties and the expected total number of uncovered actors by the realized averages.

In Figure 6 (left), we note that for $\beta_1 = 0$, the number of uncovered actors strongly depends on the choice of $\beta_2$. For example, if also $\beta_2 = 0$, meaning that the actor chooses his action at random, the number of uncovered actors already is equal to approximately 10. If $\beta_2 = 2$, so the actor balances the covering effect with a strong reciprocity effect, at $\beta_1 = 0$ we only have approximately 3 uncovered actors, which grows fast to 15 (the total number of

*Figure 6. Expected number of uncovered actors (left) and expected number of reciprocated links (right) as a function of $\beta_1$ for different values of $\beta_2$ in dynamically changing networks of 15 actors*

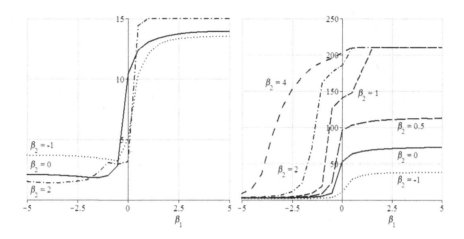

actors) if $\beta_1$ slightly increases. The fact that at $\beta_1$ = 0 the number of uncovered actors is relatively small for $\beta_2 = 2$, can be ascribed to the negative externalities discussed previously: adding links creates the possibility of (unintended) covering. In Figure 6 (right) we note that for $\beta_2 \leq 0.5$, the number of reciprocated links stabilizes at a value of approximately 115. For example, if $\beta_2 = 0$ this stabilizes at 72.6. This is due to the fact that for larger values of $\beta_1$, most actors are already uncovered (left part of the figure), meaning that the covering effect no longer drives the network formation process. As a result, the actor makes a random choice which matches Figure 8 (right) (take $\beta_2 = 0$). Note that in Figure 6 (right) the network dynamics strongly reacts on the addition of reciprocity: the number of reciprocated links reaches its maximum level if we increase $\beta_1$.

To understand and appreciate the unexpected dynamics of Figure 8 (left) (in particular the graph for $\beta_1 = 0$), we consider Figure 7 and Figure 8 (right).

In Figure 7 randomly generated networks are considered, where for each pair of actors, the probability of a reciprocated link is $p$. Starting from $p$ = 0, where all actors are uncovered, the expected number of uncovered actors in such a randomly

generated network decreases very fast. This is due to the fact that adding only a few links already creates covering of the actors without links. Then the expected number of uncovered actors increases for $p > 0.03$, as actors can easily escape from their covered position. If $p$ increases further, the expected number of uncovered actors decreases again. This decrease in number of uncovered actors is due to the negative externalities. Only if $p$

*Figure 7. The expected number of uncovered actors for randomly generated networks (n = 15) as a function of the probability p of existence of a reciprocated link*

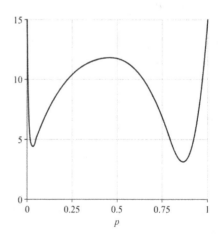

*Figure 8. Expected number of uncovered actors (left) and expected number of reciprocated links (right) as a function of $\beta_2$ for different values of $\beta_1$, in dynamically changing networks of 15 actors*

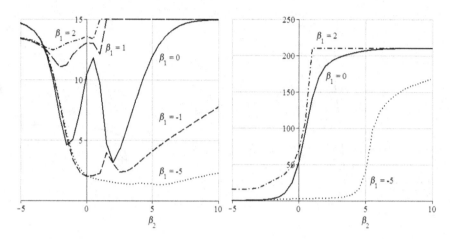

is close to 1, the number increases very fast to 15. Regarding the expected number of reciprocated links in these randomly generated networks, we note that this expected number increases with increasing values of $p$: it is equal to $n(n-1)p$. We next observe that also in Figure 8, for increasing values of $\beta_2$, the expected number of reciprocated links increases. Although there is no one-to-one match between dynamically changing networks using an objective function (where the deletion of links is a possible action) and randomly generated networks, we observe the following pattern: if we increase $\beta_2$, the number of reciprocated links increases, which may be seen as corresponding to an increase in $p$ in randomly generated networks. This increase in $p$ gives the behavior of uncovered actors as in Figure 7, which closely corresponds to the behavior of the expected number of uncovered nodes in Figure 8. For example, if $p = 0.87$, the expected number of uncovered actors in randomly generated networks reaches a minimum of 3.15. The expected number of reciprocated links in randomly generated network for this value of $p$ equals 182.7. In Figure 8 (with $\beta_1 = 0$), this corresponds to $\beta_2 \approx 2$. Then in Figure 8, we observe, at approximately the same value for $\beta_2$ the minimal expected number of uncovered actors: 3.16. The

other (local) minima of Figure 7 and Figure 8 are related similarly.

## Estimating Parameters

Up until now, we assumed full knowledge of the set of control parameters in the objective function of actors or units in an organization. In the previous subsection, we mapped out the interaction between our two guiding principles for various values of these parameters. But, given these results, we now may follow a reverse route: Given some specific characteristics for dynamically changing network structures, what are the corresponding values for the control parameters that might have produced these characteristics? This corresponds to an empirical point of view, where the stochastic actor-based model contains parameters that have to be estimated from observed data. Snijders et al. (2010) proposes the method of moments as is implemented by their Sienna computer simulation. From the point of view of the feedback loop in Figure 1, this also is an interesting problem, especially if these specific characteristics have proven to be successful regarding the mission of the organization.

*Figure 9. The expected number of reciprocated links (horizontal axis) versus the expected number of uncovered actors (vertical axis) for all possible combinations of ($\beta_1$, $\beta_2$) [-5,10] x [-5,10] (left) and ($\beta_1$, $\beta_2$) [0,2] x [0,2] (right) in a network of 15 actors*

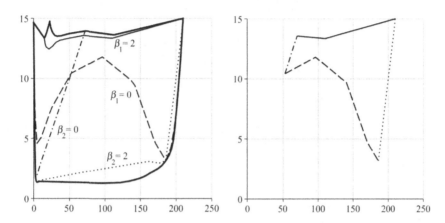

For Figure 9, we computed the expected number of reciprocated links and the expected number of uncovered actors for a few combinations of $\beta_1$ and $\beta_2$, for $n = 15$. If only the two effects described so far are used, we may propose an inversion method to estimate the values of the two parameters. Simply look up the observed values of the expected number of reciprocated links and the expected number of uncovered actors, and read the corresponding values of the parameters from Figure 9. If there are no corresponding values, apparently the actor must have included other effects as well to evaluate the possible network configurations.

This reverse problem of estimating parameters from observed dynamically changing network structures, may also be of interest to the study of other quantities such as, e.g. the resilience of network structures, cf. Monsuur et al. (2012). In Figure 9, one may choose a proven 'good' point in terms of number of reciprocated links and number of uncovered actors. Using the estimation procedure described above, we find the corresponding set of parameters in the objective function. Knowledge of these parameters may be used to train actors to use this objective function. If, for some reason, the network is disturbed or damaged, the actors will respond to recreate a network with similar characteristics.

## STOCHASTIC ACTOR-BASED MODELS FOR MULTI-LAYERED NETWORKS

By modeling military organizations as networks, military units or actors can be represented as nodes. An important observation is that a military unit or actor is not part of just one single network, but instead can be modeled as operating simultaneously in multiple networks. See, for example, Figure 10, where three actors are represented that operate simultaneously in two networks. Failing to take into account that the actors' behavior depends on their positions in both networks, may therefore render any analysis of their behavior incomplete and may lead to wrong conclusions. To model the behavior of these autonomously acting nodes, we have to take into account that they belong to more than one network. For example, it may be the case that military units connected by a social network may not share important information because of security regulations. This illustrates that military networked action may be viewed as

*Figure 10. Three actors belonging to both a social network and an information network*

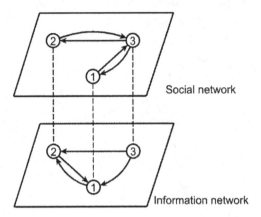

being constrained by e.g. policies, norms, values, regulations, procedures, and rules of engagement.

In this section, we introduce an extension of the stochastic actor-based modeling approach. It can be used to describe, analyze and evaluate multi-layered network dynamics. It takes into account that an actors' behavior cannot fully be understood if not all relevant networks are taken into consideration simultaneously. To illustrate this extension, we restrict ourselves to two networks, namely the social network and the information network. Figure 10 illustrates a situation in which three actors belong to both networks.

The two-layered network in Figure 10 is represented by two adjacency matrices, namely $x_1$ being the adjacency matrix of the social network and $x_2$ being the adjacency matrix of the information network. As in the one-layered actor-based model, the first step in a multi-layered stochastic actor-based model is the choice of the focal actor who gets the opportunity to make a change. Again we assume that this choice is made with equal probabilities for all actors, i.e. the probability that one particular actor will be the focal actor equals $1/n$ if $n$ is the total number of actors. Let actor $i$ be the focal actor. Suppose that the guiding principle for change in the social network represented by $x_1$ is the number of actors that do not cover the focal actor $i$, $s_{\{i,uncov\}}(x_1)$ and that the guiding principle

in the information network $x_2$ is the number of reciprocated links of the focal actor $i$, $s_{\{i,rec\}}(x_2)$. The objective function of the focal actor $i$ is a linear combination of both guiding principles or effects

$$f_i(\beta, x) = f_i(\beta_1, \beta_2, x_1, x_2) = \beta_1 \cdot s_{i,uncov}(x_1) + \beta_2 \cdot s_{i,rec}(x_2),$$

where $\beta = \{\beta_1, \beta_2\}$ is a set of control parameters and $x = \{x_1, x_2\}$ represents the state of both networks in terms of their adjacency matrices. If more effects are taking into account, the objective function of the focal actor $i$ is again a linear combination of all effects. As in the one-layered actor-based model, the transition probability of going to some new state $y \in C$ is given by

$$\frac{\exp(f_i(\beta, y))}{\sum\limits_{x' \in C} \exp(f_i(\beta, x'))}.$$

where $C$ is the set of all adjacent network structures of the current state including itself. So, if actor 1 in Figure 10 is the focal actor, then the probability of not acting is given by

$$\frac{e^{(\beta_1 \cdot 1 + \beta_2 \cdot 1)}}{(e^{(\beta_1 \cdot 1 + \beta_2 \cdot 1)} + e^{(\beta_1 \cdot 1 + \beta_2 \cdot 1)} + e^{(\beta_1 \cdot 0 + \beta_2 \cdot 1)}} =$$
$$+ e^{(\beta_1 \cdot 1 + \beta_2 \cdot 0)} + e^{(\beta_1 \cdot 1 + \beta_2 \cdot 2)})$$
$$\frac{e^{\beta_1 + \beta_2}}{2e^{\beta_1 + \beta_2} + e^{\beta_2} + e^{\beta_1} + e^{\beta_1 + 2\beta_2}}.$$

So far, no restrictions have been imposed on the actions of the focal actor. If some actions of the focal actor are prohibited, these actions are removed from the set $C$ of adjacent network structures. This e.g. can be used to illustrate the implementation of a social norm. As an example we assume that information is exchanged and a connection is established between units in an information network *only if* the two actors are socially connected. In terms of our two networks, we impose the restriction that a link from a node $a$ to another node $b$ in the information network is only possible if a link from node $a$ to node $b$ already exists in the social network. This restriction excludes, for example, the situation in Figure 10: the link between actor 1 and 2 is not present in the social network. To investigate the consequences of this restriction, we have applied our extension of the stochastic actor-based modeling approach to the case where we have $n = 15$ actors.

In Figure 11 (left), we have plotted the results for the unrestricted case, where all link deletion and creation possibilities are allowed, and for the restricted case, where no link in the information network is possible without a corresponding link in the social network. Measuring the expected or average number of uncovered nodes in the social network as a function of $\beta_1$, with $\beta_2 = 1$ fixed, yields the two curves in Figure 11 (left). As illustrated by this figure, imposing restrictions on acting will generally influence the characteristics of the dynamically changing networks. In this constrained dynamics, the action of a an actor to delete a link to another actor in the social domain is not feasible if a link between them is present in

the information domain, and also adding a link in the information domain is not allowed if no social link is present.

Compared to the unconstrained case, the dynamics for the constrained case is more complicated. From Figure 11 (left) even a discontinuity at $\beta_1 \approx 0.7$ may be conjectured, where in the dynamically changing networks for larger values of $\beta_1$ typically all actors are uncovered. More detailed analysis of these cases also showed that the social network is completely connected. In Figure 11 (right), we present a plot of a typical run for values of $\beta_1$ that are greater than 0.7. As may be seen from the first 2000 iterations, it occasionally happens that all actors are uncovered. But to reach the situation that all actors are uncovered and remain so in further iterations, apparently the social network has to pass through a phase where almost all nodes are covered. If this stable situation is reached, the dynamics in the information domain, the second layer, will be as described in the fourth section (with $\beta_1 = 0$): the norm does not constrain link creation anymore in the information domain.

This first exploration of our proposed stochastic actor-based method for multi-layered networks already illustrates some intriguing phenomena, as shown in Figure 11. This method offers an excellent tool for describing the dynamics of multi-layered networks. It takes into account that actors simultaneously operate in multiple networks and that the evolution of these networks does not take place in isolation but influence each other, depending on the constraints imposed.

## CONCLUSION

In modeling military (inter)actions and cooperation as networks, military units or actors may be represented as nodes. In analyzing military networked action a key observation is that a node is not just part of one type of network, but simultaneously belongs to multiple networks.

*Figure 11. (left) Expected number of uncovered actors as a function of $\beta_1$ (n = 15, $\beta_2$ = 1 fixed). (right) Number of uncovered actors as a function of the iteration k in a typical run of the stochastic actor-based approach (n = 15, $\beta_1$ = 1.5, $\beta_2$ = 1)*

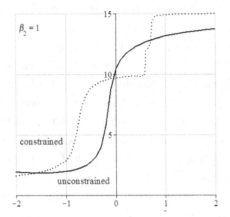 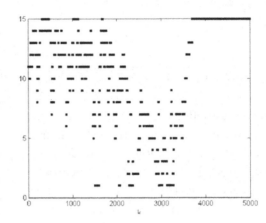

Here, we have presented a method that may be used to implement, analyze and evaluate some specific principles that may be used by the actors in an organization to drive the process of constant change. Our method is a stochastic actor-based approach. It can be used to analyze the effect of these principles on the applicable metrics for coordination, synchronization, robustness and desired operational effectiveness of the network constellation as a whole. To illustrate our approach, we apply it to networks in which two basic principles are operational: *reciprocity* and a novel principle called *covering*. An actor is covered by another actor if all its neighbors are also neighbors of that other actor, which in addition has at least one extra neighbor. For a particular actor in a network, covering captures the idea of being outperformed by another actor in terms of the possibility of information gathering. The results presented here clearly illustrate the influence on the dynamically changing networks caused by this novel covering interaction. Although we restricted our discussion to two basic principles when demonstrating our method, other basic principles which are summarized in, for example, Snijders et al. (2010), can be applied to the stochastic actor-based models that also incorporate multi-layered networks.

## FUTURE RESEARCH DIRECTIONS

In further research, other basic guiding principles or social norms will be investigated, for single networks as well as for multi-layered networks. In terms of the block diagram of Figure 1, other measures of performance of the system can also be investigated. In this chapter the chosen measures of performance are formulated in terms of global counterparts of the chosen principles that drive the decisions of the individual actors: the total number of reciprocated ties and the total number of uncovered actors. Another measure of performance is the largest eigenvalue $\lambda$ of the adjacency matrix corresponding to $G^{rec}$. This largest eigenvalue $\lambda$, the Perron-Frobenius eigenvalue, is used in warfare models as a quantification of *global* network effects, see Cares (2005). In Deller et al. (2009) one may find a computer simulation illustrating that a higher value for $\lambda$ gives a higher probability for success in a battle between two homogeneous adversaries.

The correlation between two measures of performance of the system can also be investigated in further research. For example, in Figure 12 (left), we show the number of reciprocated links in the information network for the same run of the stochastic actor-based model shown in Figure 11 (right). In each iteration $k$ not only the number of reciprocated links in the information network was calculated, but also the largest eigenvalue $\lambda$ of the adjacency matrix corresponding to $G^{rec}$. For each iteration $k$ the combination of this eigenvalue $\lambda$ and the number of reciprocated links is plotted in Figure 12 (right). Clearly, this figure shows the strong positive correlation between the largest eigenvalue $\lambda$ and the number of reciprocated links. As this Perron-Frobenius eigenvalue is commonly used in warfare models as a quantification of global network effects, we can conclude that the number of reciprocated links can indeed serve as a measure of performance of the system in Figure 1 because of this positive correlation.

Other possible lines of research are the use of several types of actors. For example, what is the effect of a few actors that differ in their guiding principles that drive the change? Regarding the notion of covering, one could also explore the consequences of using the $W$-covering as explained hereafter.

## TECHNICAL REMARKS ABOUT COVERING AND W-COVERING

We note that in Definition 1, the first condition is logically equivalent to $(a,v) \notin E^{rec}$ implies $(b,v) \notin E^{rec}$. So if actors $a$ and $v$ are no neighbors, then certainly actors $b$ and $v$ are no neighbors. In terms of the adjacency matrix $x$ of $G$ we can now say that actor $a$ covers actor $b$ in $G = (V, E)$ if the following two requirements hold:

1.  For all actors $v$ in $V$, $v \notin \{a, b\}$, $x_{bv} \bullet x_{vb} \leq x_{av} \bullet x_{va}$, and
2.  At least one actor $v \notin \{a, b\}$ exists such that $x_{av} \bullet x_{va} - x_{bv} \bullet x_{vb} = 1$.

Condition 1. can be replaced by saying that the number of actors $v$ in $V$ such that $x_{bv} \bullet x_{vb} > x_{av} \bullet x_{va}$ equals $x_{ba} \bullet x_{ab}$ and condition 2. can be replaced by the expression $\Sigma_{v \notin \{a, b\}} (x_{av} \bullet x_{va} - x_{bv} \bullet x_{vb}) \geq 1$. Since $x_{aa} = x_{bb} = 0$ and $x_{ab} \bullet x_{ba} = x_{ba} \bullet x_{ab}$, this is equivalent to $\Sigma_{v \in V} (x_{av} \bullet x_{va} - x_{bv} \bullet x_{vb}) \geq 1$. In summary, we may present the following alternative definition of covering:

Definition 3 (in terms of the adjacency matrix $x$ of $G$). Let $a$ and $b$ be actors in $V$, $a \neq b$. Then $a$

*Figure 12. (left) Number of reciprocated links as a function of the iteration k in a typical run of the stochastic actor-based approach (n = 15, $\beta_1$ = 1.5, $\beta_2$ = 1). (right) The largest eigenvalue $\lambda$ of the adjacency matrix corresponding to $G^{rec}$ versus the number of reciprocated links in a typical run of the stochastic actor-based approach (n = 15, $\beta_1$ = 1.5, $\beta_2$ = 1)*

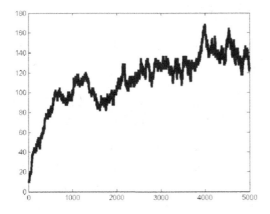
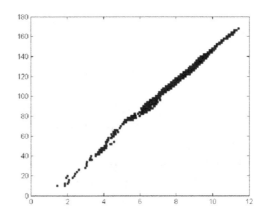

covers $b$ in $G = (V, E)$ or equivalently $b$ is covered by $a$ in $G = (V, E)$, if

1. $\Sigma_{v \in V}$ IndicatorFunction$(x_{bv} \bullet x_{vb} > x_{av} \bullet x_{va}) = x_{ba} \bullet x_{ab}$, and

2. $\Sigma_{v \in V} x_{av} \bullet x_{va} - \Sigma_{v \in V} x_{bv} \bullet x_{vb} \geq 1$

where IndicatorFunction$(x_{bv} \bullet x_{vb} > x_{av} \bullet x_{va}) = 1$ if $x_{bv} \bullet x_{vb} > x_{av} \bullet x_{va}$ and 0 otherwise.

This definition of covering in terms of the adjacency matrix $x$ of $G$, which can also be formulated in terms of the adjacency matrix $x^{rec}$ of $G^{rec}$, can easily be implemented in software. The reduction of the network $G$ to the network $G^{rec}$ is not strange: one of the effects that is used very frequently is the reciprocity effect, where each actor actively is trying to increase reciprocated links, to make $G$ look more like $G^{rec}$.

Note that the statement actor $a$ covers actor $b$ is not equivalent to the requirement degree$(a) >$ degree$(b)$. So the condition $\Sigma_{v \in V} x_{av} \bullet x_{va} > \Sigma_{v \in V} x_{bv} \bullet x_{vb}$ does not imply that actor $a$ covers actor $b$.

We note that Definitions 1 and 2 of covering can be regarded as a special case of $W$-covering as was introduced in Janssen and Monsuur (2013). Although we restrict ourselves in this chapter to the notion of covering from Definition 1, for completeness we present here the notion of $W$-covering.

Definition 4 Fix a network $G = (V, E)$. Let $W$ be a subset of $V$. Let $a$ and $b$ be actors in $V$, $a \neq b$. Then $a$ $W$-covers $b$ in $G = (V, E)$ or equivalently, $b$ is $W$-covered by $a$ in $G = (V, E)$, if

1. For all actors $v$ in $W \backslash \{a, b\}$, $(b, v) \in E^{rec}$ implies $(a, v) \in E^{rec}$, and

2. At least one actor $v$ in $W \backslash \{a, b\}$ exists such that $(a, v) \in E^{rec}$ while $(b, v) \notin E^{rec}$.

Actor $b$ in $V$ is called $W$-covered in $G = (V, E)$ if for at least one actor $a$ in $V$, $a \neq b$, $b$ is $W$-covered by $a$ in $G = (V, E)$. An actor is called $W$-uncovered in $G = (V, E)$ if he is not $W$-covered in $G = (V, E)$.

In the case $W$ is the set of all nodes $V$, the $W$-cover relation of Definition 4 coincides with the cover relation of Definitions 1 and 3. To explain what the notion of $W$-covering tries to capture, we assume that there is a subset $W$ of essential or important nodes. Their importance is affirmed by the fact that all nodes derive value by being linked to these nodes. This value of being linked to nodes in $W$ may be due to presumed exogenous attributes or status of these nodes, but may also be due to their high centrality or their high number of links. At this level of analysis, some nodes are essential or important, others are not. Whether or not a node, say $a$, belongs to $W$, it may be outperformed by another node, say $b$, with respect to the value and status implied by their network positions. This happens if the neighbors of node $a$ belonging to $W$ (except possibly for node $b$ if node $b$ is a neighbor of node $a$) are also neighbors of node $b$, while $b$ has at least one additional neighbor in $W$. This illustrates the idea that not every link adds to a node's status or position in a network, motivating the focus on links toward essential nodes; its position within the network remains outperformed. In the context of social networks, the predicate *key player* is assigned to nodes in $W$ if all nodes of $W$, and also all nodes in $V \backslash W$ are $W$-uncovered. More details about $W$-covering and its applications can be found in Janssen and Monsuur (2013).

# REFERENCES

Acebrón, J. A., Bonilla, L. L., Peréz Vicente, C. J., Ritort, F., & Spigler, R. (2005). The Kuramoto model: A simple paradigm for synchronization phenomena. *Reviews of Modern Physics, 77*, 137–185. doi:10.1103/RevModPhys.77.137

Alberts, D. S. (2011). *The agility advantage: A survival guide for complex enterprises and endeavors. The Command and Control Research Program*. CCRP.

Alberts, D. S., Garstka, J. J., & Stein, F. P. (1999). Network centric warfare: Developing and leveraging information superiority (2nd ed.). DoD Command and Control Research Program. Washington, DC: CCRP.

Barabási, A.-L. (2003). *Linked: How everything is connected to everything else and what is means for business, science and everyday life.* New York: Plume.

Boccaletti, S., Latora, V., Moreno, Y., Chavez, M., & Hwang, D.-U. (2006). Complex networks: Structure and dynamics. *Physics Reports, 424*(4-5), 175–308. doi:10.1016/j.physrep.2005.10.009

Burt, R. S. (1982). *Toward a Structural Theory of Action.* Academic Press.

Cares, J. (2005). *Distributed networked operations: The foundations of network centric warfare.* Newport, RI: Alidade Press.

Deller, S., Bowling, S.R., Rabadi, G.A., & Tolk, A. (2009). Applying the information age combat model: Quantitative analysis of network centric operations. *International C2 Journal, 3*(1), 1-25.

Goyal, S. (2007). *Connections: An introduction to the economics of networks.* Princeton, NJ: Princeton University Press.

Jackson, M. O. (2009). *Social and economic networks.* Princeton, NJ: Princeton University Press.

Janssen, R. H. P., & Monsuur, H. (2010). Networks, information and choice. In *Collective decision making: Views from social choice and game theory* (pp. 211–230). Berlin: Springer. doi:10.1007/978-3-642-02865-6_14

Janssen, R. H. P., & Monsuur, H. (2012). Stable network topologies using the notion of covering. *European Journal of Operational Research, 218*, 755–763. doi:10.1016/j.ejor.2011.12.001

Janssen, R. H. P., & Monsuur, H. (2013). Identifying stable network structures and sets of key players using a W-covering perspective. *Mathematical Social Sciences, 66*, 245–253. doi:10.1016/j.mathsocsci.2013.05.005

McChrystal, S. A. (2011, March-April). It Takes a Network: The new frontline of modern warfare. *Foreign Policy.*

McChrystal, S. A. (2013). *Lesson from Iraq: It Takes a Network to Defeat a Network.* Retrieved from http://www.linkedin.com/today/post/article/20130621110027-86145090-lesson-from-iraq-it-takes-a-network-to-defeat-a-network

Miller, N. R. (1980). A new solution set for tournaments and majority voting: further graph-theoretical approaches to the theory of voting. *American Journal of Political Science, 24*, 68–96. doi:10.2307/2110925

Monsuur, H., Grant, T. J., & Janssen, R. H. P. (2011). Network topology of military command and control systems: Where axioms and action meet. In *Computer Science Research and Technology* (pp. 1–27). New York: Nova Science Publishers.

Monsuur, H., Kooij, R. E., & Van Mieghem, P. F. A. (2012). Analysing and modelling the interconnected cyberspace. In *Cyber warfare: Critical perspectives* (pp. 165–183). The Hague: Asser Press.

Monsuur, H., & Storcken, T. (2004). Centers in connected undirected graphs: An axiomatic approach. *Operations Research, 52*, 54–64. doi:10.1287/opre.1030.0082

Snijders, T. A. B., Van de Bunt, G. G., & Steglich, C. E. G. (2010). Introduction to stochastic actor-based models for network dynamics. *Social Networks, 32*(1), 44–60. doi:10.1016/j.socnet.2009.02.004

van der Wal, A. J. (2010). Self-organization and emergent behaviour: distributed fuzzy decision making through phase synchronization. In *Computational Intelligence, Foundations and Applications* (pp. 263–268). Singapore: World Scientific Publishing. doi:10.1142/9789814324700_0038

Wasserman, S., & Faust, K. (1994). *Social network analysis: Methods and applications*. Cambridge, UK: Cambridge University Press. doi:10.1017/CBO9780511815478

Watts, D. J. (1999). *Small worlds: The dynamics of networks between order and randomness*. Princeton, NJ: Princeton University Press.

## KEY TERMS AND DEFINITIONS

**Control Theory:** An interdisciplinary branch of engineering and mathematics that deals with the behavior of parameterized dynamical system. When one or more system variables need to follow a certain reference over time, a control system manipulates the parameters of the system to obtain the desired effect.

**Covering:** A measure to evaluate the position of an actor in a network. Using this notion, an actor is able to assess whether or not its position in a network is outperformed by another one in terms of connections to other actors within the network. We say that actor $a$ covers actor $b$ if all neighbors of $b$ (minus $a$ if $b$ is a neighbor of $a$) are also neighbors of $a$ (minus $b$ if $b$ is a neighbor of $a$) and actor $a$ has at least one extra neighbor.

**Dynamically Changing Network:** A network that changes as a function of time, by creating and destroying links between the nodes in the network.

**Information Network:** A network of entities, i.e. computers, interconnected by communication channels that allow sharing of data and information.

**Network Theory:** As part of graph theory, it concerns itself with the study of graphs as a representation of relations between discrete objects.

**Stochastic Actor-Based Model:** A model for network dynamics that can represent a wide variety of influences on network change, based on stochastic decisions of nodes.

**W-Covering:** A measure to evaluate the position of an actor in a network with respect to being linked to nodes in a subset $W$ of essential or important nodes.

## APPENDIX

## Questions

1. Consider a group of people, including yourself. Draw at least two different networks to which everyone belongs.
2. Identify at least two measures of performance for the networks you drew in answer to question 1.
3. Consider a group of people, including yourself. What does it mean to be *covered* by someone? What other people in the group *cover* you? Whom do you *cover*?
4. Why is the process of dynamically changing networks as described in this chapter a Markov process?
5. See Figure 4. Why is the expected number of reciprocated links in a network of 3 actors exactly 3/2 when $\beta_{rec} = 0$?
6. While inspecting Figs. 6, 8, and 11, one might be tempted to conclude that the system evolves via a Markov chain of states into a well-defined end state. Why is this not necessarily true? Is there such a thing as "the" end state?

# Chapter 8
# Improving C2 Effectiveness Based on Robust Connectivity

**S. Deller**
*Textron Defense Systems, USA*

**A. Tolk**
*SimIS Incorporated, USA & Old Dominion University, USA*

**G. Rabadi**
*Old Dominion University, USA*

**S. Bowling**
*Bluefield State College, USA*

## ABSTRACT

*This chapter describes an approach to develop an improved metric for network effectiveness through the use of Cares' (2005) Information Age Combat Model (IACM) as a context for combat (or competition) between networked forces. The IACM highlights the inadequacy of commonly used quantifiable metrics with regards to comparing networks that differ only by the placement of a few links. An agent-based simulation is used to investigate the potential value of the Perron-Frobenius Eigenvalue ($\lambda_{PFE}$) as an indicator of network effectiveness. The results validate this assumption. Another measurement is proven to be equally important, namely the robustness of a configuration. Potential applications from the domain of ballistic missile defense are included to show operational relevance.*

## INTRODUCTION

The application of network theory enables us to investigate alternatives to the traditional hierarchical organizations of Command and Control (C2) processes and systems. Traditional hierarchical organizations were the result of centralized command and control cultures and the significant costs, both in time and money, of distributing the necessary information to enable sound decision-making. The increased desire for peer-to-peer negotiation and self-synchronization and the incredible reduction in these costs during the past decade has made non-hierarchical organizations viable alternatives. It also introduced a significant

DOI: 10.4018/978-1-4666-6058-8.ch008

challenge: what should we measure to determine which organization can be more effective?

The effectiveness of a C2 network is more than just the sum of its nodes and arcs, which can be measured by the *link-to-node ratio* (*l*/N). A maximally-connected network, where every node is connected to every other node (i.e., $l = (N-1)!$), not only remains prohibitive in monetary cost; it is undesirable due to the inability of a node to manage or process the overwhelming information flow represented by the arcs. However, a minimally-connected network may not be desirable due to either insufficient capability or capacity or an increased vulnerability of the network. Additionally, the *link-to-node ratio* metric cannot discriminate between alternative network organizations that have the same numbers of nodes and links, but differ solely in their arrangement. The mere counting of a link does not account for its significance, or lack thereof.

The *degree distribution* metric is a measurement of whether the number of links connected to each node is uniformly distributed throughout a network. Adaptive, complex networks have a small number of highly connected nodes (i.e., a skewed degree distribution). Such highly connected nodes can be clustered together or can be distanced from each other, and is expressed as a *clustering coefficient* calculated from the proportion of a node's direct neighbors that are also direct neighbors of each other. This represents a measurement of a network's cohesion and self-synchronization. The *characteristic path length* is a related metric, and is measured as the median of the mean of the lengths of all the shortest paths in the network. While these metrics begin to account for link significance, they are insufficient in discriminating between network configurations that vary in the placement of just a single link.

Jain and Krishna (2002) introduced the relationship between the Perron-Frobenius Eigenvalue ($\lambda_{PFE}$) of a graph and its autocatalytic sets, and used graph topology to study various network dynamics. Cares (2005) employed a similar approach

to describe combat (or competition) between distributed, networked forces or organizations. His Information Age Combat Model (IACM) focused on the $\lambda_{PFE}$ as a measure of the ability of a network to produce combat power. Cares proposed that the greater the value of the $\lambda_{PFE}$, the greater the effectiveness of the organization of that networked force.

Deller, et al (2009, 2012) confirmed this proposal by constructing an agent-based simulation that enabled networked organizations to compete against each other in the context of Cares' IACM. The results of the agent-based simulation indicated that the value of the $\lambda_{PFE}$ was a significant measurement of the performance of a networked force. However, the effectiveness of the $\lambda_{PFE}$ measurement was dependent on the existence of unique $\lambda_{PFE}$ values for the configurations under consideration. When alternative organizations had a shared $\lambda_{PFE}$ value, additional measurements were required to enable discrimination. Of the additional metrics considered, *robustness* proved the most effective in improving the value of the $\lambda_{PFE}$ as a quantifiable metric of network performance. Ultimately, the best indicator of network effectiveness was a metric that combined both the $\lambda_{PFE}$ and robustness values.

## THE INFORMATION AGE COMBAT MODEL

Cares designed the IACM to facilitate his investigation into how a networked force organizes. It is not intended to be a combat simulation or a tool to test weapon platforms. Instead, the basic objects of the IACM are generic nodes defined by the simple functions they perform, not by any performance specifications they were built or designed to. For example, Sensor nodes receive signals about observable phenomena of other nodes in the model. The types of signals received are not relevant; just that the Sensor "sensed" something about that node and passed that information on to a Decider node.

Decider nodes direct the actions of other nodes in the model. Likewise, the types of actions are not relevant; just that those other nodes take direction from that particular Decider (i.e., fall within that Decider's "command and control"). Nodes that interact with other nodes to affect the state of those nodes are called Influencers. Again, the types of interactions are not relevant, just that they may occur. Finally, those nodes that can be acted upon, but perform no sensing, deciding, or influencing functions are included as Target nodes. For the purpose of this discussion, all nodes belong to one of two opposing sides, conventionally termed BLUE and RED.

The links that connect these nodes represent the various physical and communicative interactions between them. Since these nodes perform a single function (e.g., "sense, "direct," etc.), information flow between the nodes is necessary for activity to occur, and generally takes the form of a combat cycle (see FigureFigure 1). In its simplest form, this cycle consists of a Sensor detecting an opposing node and passing that information to the Sensor's controlling Decider. The Decider may then direct one of its assigned Influencers to initiate action on the opposing node, such as exerting physical force, psychological or social influence, or some other form of influence. The effect of this action is subsequently detected by the Sensor and the cycle may be repeated until the desired outcome has been achieved. While the four links forming this cycle are just a small subset of the all the possible node-to-node permutations, they collectively represent the most important activity in the model and are the focus of this study.

All links in the model are directional, and have different meanings depending on which nodes they go "from" and "to". For example, a link from a Decider to any friendly node (whether it be a Sensor, Influencer, Target or other Decider) represents the conveyance of the Decider's direction (such as engagement or repositioning), but the links from an opposing Sensor and Influencer represent the Decider being detected and acted

*Figure 1. Basic combat cycle*

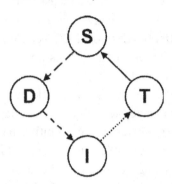

upon. Some links have two meanings, such as those from an Influencer to an opposing Sensor. These links represent two different interactions: detection and engagement. Both interpretations are valid and the context of the model will make clear which is intended.

Other links have ambiguous meanings, such as those connecting Sensors of the same side. These can be defined as either the Sensors detecting each other or coordinating with each other. Links from a Sensor to other Sensors, Influencers, or Targets of the same side can be defined direct coordination but are not included in this discussion as it is assumed that the information detected must be routed through a friendly Decider. Additionally, links from an Influencer to other nodes of the same side represent fratricide and are not included either.

A collection of nodes and links can be described though the application of graph theory (Chartrand, 1984). A concise description of any graph is provided by the adjacency matrix A, in which the row and column indices represent the nodes, and the matrix elements are either one or zero according to the rule: $A_{ij} = 1$, if there exists a link from node $i$ to node $j$ and $A_{ij} = 0$, otherwise. Consequently, each unique network configuration of nodes and links has a unique mathematically-equivalent matrix portrayal. This enables the application of mathematical tools to analyze these networks, such as the Perron-Frobenius theorem. This theorem guarantees the existence of a real, positive principal (maximum) eigenvalue of $A_{ij}$ if $A_{ij}$ is an irreducible nonnegative matrix. Since all the nodes on each side are connected to all the opposing Sensor and Influencer nodes, the matrix is strongly connected and, therefore, irreducible. This eigenvalue, $\lambda_{PFE}$, is a measure of the selective connectivity within the network (i.e., networks with the same number of links may have different $\lambda_{PFE}$ values depending on the placement of the links). The full range of mathematical values for a $\lambda_{PFE}$ of any adjacency matrix goes from 0 (for a network with no links at all) to n, where n = the total number of nodes (for a maximally connected network). Clearly, the $\lambda_{PFE}$ is a quantifiable metric with which to measure the different ways to organize a networked force.

The $\lambda_{PFE}$ is also an indicator of the effectiveness of that network's organization. This was determined through the construction of an agent-based simulation representing the IACM and the conduct of a series of force-on-force engagements to investigate the correlation of each opposing network's $\lambda_{PFE}$ value with its corresponding probability of winning the engagement (Deller, et al, 2012). The opposing forces had equal assets and capabilities, but differed in their connectivity arrangements (i.e., where the links existed). These differences in connectivity often, but not necessarily, lead to unequal $\lambda_{PFE}$ values.

The consideration of different $\lambda_{PFE}$ values for the opposing forces reflects the first challenge in modeling the IACM. The IACM as originally described by Cares (2005) uses a single adjacency matrix to reflect the collective nodes and links of both BLUE and RED forces. This is sufficient when focusing on one side's organizational effectiveness while holding the other side constant. But BLUE and RED are each seeking separately to maximize their own organizational effectiveness, while at the same time minimizing the organizational effectiveness of the opposing force. This dynamic interaction cannot be accounted for with a single $\lambda_{PFE}$ value, so we calculate separate values ($\lambda_{BLUE}$ and $\lambda_{RED}$) to measure the potential effectiveness of each opposing configuration independent

of the asset arrangement of the opposing force. Note, however, that these calculations required the adjacency matrices include a Target node to enable the complete depiction of any combat cycles the network configurations may contain. Any Target nodes included will be linked to all opposing Sensors (to enable potential detection) and Influencers (to enable potential action). While the number of Target nodes included affects the $\lambda_{PFE}$ value, it does so because of the additional volume of nodes and links, not because of a difference in their configuration. Consequently, the use of a single Target node representative of all the enemy forces capable of being targeted can be assumed in order to focus on the aspect of the network that determines the $\lambda_{PFE}$ value ordering.

The agent-based paradigm was utilized for this purpose because the resulting models provide both the ability to account for small unit organization and the autonomy of action that was necessary for our investigation. An additional advantage of utilizing an agent-based simulation was the ability to work around the ambiguities of link interpretation in the IACM described earlier. For details on the construct of the agent-based simulation see Deller, et al (2012).

The design of this experiment was intended to isolate the effect of the $\lambda_{PFE}$ value by keeping as many variables between the forces as equal or constant as possible. The opposing forces consisted of the same number of Sensors, Deciders, and Influencers, differing only in how they were arranged (i.e., linked). Within each force, the numbers of Sensors and Influencers were equal to preclude any bias towards configurations that have more of one or the other, because the potential value of a Sensor may not truly equal the potential value of an Influencer. Consequently, the composition of each force followed an X-Y-X-1 (Sensor-Decider-Influencer-Target) template, with the sole target being representative of all the opposing nodes. Additionally, the performance capabilities of all Sensor and Influencer nodes within the agent-based simulation were identical (i.e., the sensing range equaled the influencing range, and the speeds of movement for both types of nodes were the same).

The goal of this experiment was to gain a "first order" understanding of the IACM, therefore two key scoping decisions were made. First, each Sensor and Influencer would only be connected to one Decider (but any given Decider could be connected to multiple Sensors and Influencers). Second, the connectivity within any X-Y-X-1 force was limited to only those links necessary to create combat cycles (i.e., Target to Sensor, Sensor to Decider, Decider to Influencer, and Influencer to Target). These are the essence of the $\lambda_{PFE}$. Whereas the other link types can significantly enhance both the $\lambda_{PFE}$ value and the performance of any given network configuration, the present model provides a baseline for assessing what the potential effects of that inclusion may be.

There are many ways in which nodes can be connected for specific values of X and Y. The number of possible configurations grows rapidly even for small values. Consider a tiny network consisting of three Sensors and three Influencers distributed between two Deciders. There are only four different permutations of the allocation of these Sensors and Influencers between these De-ciders. However, because the nodes of the IACM are generic two of these four permutations are, in effect, isomorphic and therefore can be excluded (i.e., the only meaningful difference between these two possible configurations is whether the Decider that is linked to two Sensors is the same Decider that is linked to two Influencers. While this 50% reduction in combinations to be considered is trivial for this tiny network, it quickly becomes a crucial step in reducing the search space of the problem. Considering a slightly larger force of just five Sensors and five Influencers allocated across three Deciders yields 36 different permutations which, fortunately, can be reduced to eight meaningfully different configurations by applying the same logic.

As the size of the force is increased it is obvious that the contrast between the number of possible configurations and the number of meaningfully different configurations becomes extremely large very quickly. This disparity is further compounded by the comprehensive design of the experiment, where each configuration was tested against every possible configuration. Since a 7-3-7-1 network has 42 meaningfully different configurations this required 1,764 (i.e., $42^2$) unique engagements. Had we not reduced the search space, we this would have required 50,625 (i.e., $225^2$) unique engagements. The numbers of meaningfully different configurations for all X-Y-X-1 forces where X <

*Table 1. The numbers of meaningfully different configurations of all X-Y-X-1 networked forces where X < 11 and Y < 8*

| | | | Number of Deciders (Y) | | | |
|---|---|---|---|---|---|---|
| | | 3 | 4 | 5 | 6 | 7 |
| Numbers of Sensors (X) and Influencers (X) | 3 | 1 | | | | |
| | 4 | 2 | 1 | | | |
| | 5 | 8 | 2 | 1 | | |
| | 6 | 19 | 9 | 2 | 1 | |
| | 7 | 42 | 27 | 9 | 2 | 1 |
| | 8 | 78 | 74 | 30 | 9 | 2 |
| | 9 | 139 | 168 | 95 | 31 | 9 |
| | 10 | 224 | 363 | 248 | 105 | 31 |

11 and Y < 8 based on the unique values for the distributions of Sensors and Influencers across the Deciders are summarized in Table 1.

As previously mentioned, each of these configurations has a unique adjacency matrix that represents the connectivity, or lack thereof, between each of the nodes. If we segment the adjacency matrix into parts by grouping the types of nodes together (as depicted in FigureFigure 2), we see that 14 of the 16 sections (the shaded areas in the figure) are homogenous, i.e. either all "1" or "0," due to the absolute absence or existence of any links between those types of nodes. The two unshaded sections reflect the connectivity of each Sensor and Influencer to and from a particular Decider, and vary by configuration based on the allocation of Sensors and Influencers across the Deciders. The effect of this near uniformity is to constrain the variance between the $\lambda_{PFE}$ values to just a narrow portion of the full range of possible $\lambda_{PFE}$ values. In the example case of a 7-3-7-1 network the full range of possible $\lambda_{PFE}$ values varies between 0 (no connections) and 18 (maximally connected), but the actual range of $\lambda_{PFE}$ values for the 42 meaningfully different configurations varies from 1.821 to 2.280.

Although the variation between the $\lambda_{PFE}$ values is small, it is of significant utility because the values of other common statistical measures as defined by Cares (2005) remain constant between these configurations. The 42 meaningfully different configurations of a 7-3-7-1 network all have a link-to-node ratio of 1.556, regardless of where the links are placed. The characteristic path length and clustering coefficients are also constant across every configuration. These metrics can provide valuable insight regarding large, complex networks, but cannot discriminate between near-identical configurations of a smaller network, even

*Figure 2. An adjacency matrix for one of the 42 meaningfully different configurations of a 7-3-7-1 network*

**To**

| From | S | S | S | S | S | S | S | D | D | D | I | I | I | I | I | I | I | T |
|------|---|---|---|---|---|---|---|---|---|---|---|---|---|---|---|---|---|---|
| S | 0 | 0 | 0 | 0 | 0 | 0 | 0 | 1 | 0 | 0 | 0 | 0 | 0 | 0 | 0 | 0 | 0 | 0 |
| S | 0 | 0 | 0 | 0 | 0 | 0 | 0 | 1 | 0 | 0 | 0 | 0 | 0 | 0 | 0 | 0 | 0 | 0 |
| S | 0 | 0 | 0 | 0 | 0 | 0 | 0 | 1 | 0 | 0 | 0 | 0 | 0 | 0 | 0 | 0 | 0 | 0 |
| S | 0 | 0 | 0 | 0 | 0 | 0 | 0 | 1 | 0 | 0 | 0 | 0 | 0 | 0 | 0 | 0 | 0 | 0 |
| S | 0 | 0 | 0 | 0 | 0 | 0 | 0 | 1 | 0 | 0 | 0 | 0 | 0 | 0 | 0 | 0 | 0 | 0 |
| S | 0 | 0 | 0 | 0 | 0 | 0 | 0 | 0 | 1 | 0 | 0 | 0 | 0 | 0 | 0 | 0 | 0 | 0 |
| S | 0 | 0 | 0 | 0 | 0 | 0 | 0 | 0 | 0 | 1 | 0 | 0 | 0 | 0 | 0 | 0 | 0 | 0 |
| D | 0 | 0 | 0 | 0 | 0 | 0 | 0 | 0 | 0 | 0 | 1 | 1 | 1 | 1 | 1 | 0 | 0 | 0 |
| D | 0 | 0 | 0 | 0 | 0 | 0 | 0 | 0 | 0 | 0 | 0 | 0 | 0 | 0 | 0 | 1 | 0 | 0 |
| D | 0 | 0 | 0 | 0 | 0 | 0 | 0 | 0 | 0 | 0 | 0 | 0 | 0 | 0 | 0 | 0 | 1 | 0 |
| I | 0 | 0 | 0 | 0 | 0 | 0 | 0 | 0 | 0 | 0 | 0 | 0 | 0 | 0 | 0 | 0 | 0 | 1 |
| I | 0 | 0 | 0 | 0 | 0 | 0 | 0 | 0 | 0 | 0 | 0 | 0 | 0 | 0 | 0 | 0 | 0 | 1 |
| I | 0 | 0 | 0 | 0 | 0 | 0 | 0 | 0 | 0 | 0 | 0 | 0 | 0 | 0 | 0 | 0 | 0 | 1 |
| I | 0 | 0 | 0 | 0 | 0 | 0 | 0 | 0 | 0 | 0 | 0 | 0 | 0 | 0 | 0 | 0 | 0 | 1 |
| I | 0 | 0 | 0 | 0 | 0 | 0 | 0 | 0 | 0 | 0 | 0 | 0 | 0 | 0 | 0 | 0 | 0 | 1 |
| I | 0 | 0 | 0 | 0 | 0 | 0 | 0 | 0 | 0 | 0 | 0 | 0 | 0 | 0 | 0 | 0 | 0 | 1 |
| I | 0 | 0 | 0 | 0 | 0 | 0 | 0 | 0 | 0 | 0 | 0 | 0 | 0 | 0 | 0 | 0 | 0 | 1 |
| T | 1 | 1 | 1 | 1 | 1 | 1 | 1 | 0 | 0 | 0 | 0 | 0 | 0 | 0 | 0 | 0 | 0 | 0 |

if the only link changed has a significant impact on the effectiveness of that network.

Identical configurations of the same network always have the same $\lambda_{PFE}$ value, but it is also possible for meaningfully different configurations to share the same $\lambda_{PFE}$ value. In our example, the 42 meaningfully different configurations of a 7-3-7-1 networked force had only 13 unique $\lambda_{PFE}$ values. When this occurs, the $\lambda_{PFE}$ loses its utility as an indicator of potential performance between these configurations. Note that the numbers of unique $\lambda_{PFE}$ values (shown in Table 2 for all X-Y-X-1 forces where X < 11 and Y < 8) increase at a significantly smaller rate than the numbers of meaningfully different combinations (shown in Table 1). This disparity has a significant impact on the analysis approach and results.

The initial experiment consisted of all possible force-on-force engagements of the 42 meaningfully different configurations of two 7-3-7-1 networked forces (BLUE and RED). These configurations had the same numbers of assets but differed only in the way nodes were connected, which will enable us to study the impact of connectivity on the network performance. To test the performance of each of these 42 configurations against each other required 1,764 different engagements were required with 30 replications of the agent-based simulation, each with a random distribution of the BLUE and RED nodes across the battlespace. The possible outcomes of each replication was a BLUE win, a RED win, or an undecided result.

The results showed that the greater the $\lambda_{PFE}$ value for either BLUE or RED, the more likely that force would win the engagement. This trend is clear in FigureFigure 3, where the probability of a BLUE win for any particular configuration is averaged over all RED configurations. Note that the vertical groupings reflect those BLUE configurations that shared each of the 13 unique $\lambda_{PFE}$ values. A linear regression model confirms the visual evidence with a coefficient of determination ($R^2$) of 0.896 for the following equation: y = 1.0162(x) − 1.5780, where y = the average probability of a BLUE win for that configuration and x = the $\lambda_{PFE}$ value of a configuration.

The correlation between p(Win) and the $\lambda_{PFE}$ value remains true for the 8-3-8-1 force as well. Adding just the one Sensor and Influencer increased the number of meaningful combinations to 78, with 24 unique $\lambda_{PFE}$ values, with 6,084 different engagements to be tested (see FigureFigure 4). This linear regression resulted in a coefficient

*Table 2. The numbers of unique $\lambda_{PFE}$ values for the meaningful configurations for all X-Y-X-1 forces where X < 11 and Y < 8*

| | | Number of Deciders (Y) | | | | |
|---|---|---|---|---|---|---|
| | | 3 | 4 | 5 | 6 | 7 |
| Numbers of Sensors (X) and Influencers (X) | 3 | 1 | | | | |
| | 4 | 2 | 1 | | | |
| | 5 | 4 | 2 | 1 | | |
| | 6 | 8 | 4 | 2 | 1 | |
| | 7 | 13 | 8 | 4 | 2 | 1 |
| | 8 | 20 | 13 | 8 | 4 | 2 |
| | 9 | 27 | 20 | 13 | 8 | 4 |
| | 10 | 38 | 27 | 20 | 13 | 8 |

of determination ($R^2$) equal to 0.876 for the following equation: $Y = 0.9484(x) - 1.5633$, where y = the average probability of a BLUE win for that configuration and x = the $\lambda_{PFE}$ value of a configuration.

The correlation between p(Win) and the $\lambda_{PFE}$ value decreased significantly for a 9-5-9-1 force, however. The additional Sensor, Influencer, and Decider nodes increased the number of meaningfully different configurations to 95, and resulted in 9,025 different engagements to be tested. Surprisingly, the additional assets reduced the number of unique $\lambda_{PFE}$ values to 13 (13.68%). This is a dramatic reduction from 30.77% (24 of 78) for the 8-3-8-1 force, and 30.95% (13 of 42) for the 7-3-7-1 force. The impact of this reduction in unique $\lambda_{PFE}$ values is a greater variety of p(Win) across for each $\lambda_{PFE}$ value (see FigureFigure 5); hence the reduction in R2 to a value of 0.519 for the resulting equation: $Y = 0.5861(x) - 0.7736$, where y = the average probability of a BLUE

win for that configuration and x = the $\lambda_{PFE}$ value of a configuration. Note that the highest p(Win) value does not belong to the configuration with the highest $\lambda_{PFE}$ value, indicating that there is some other correlating factor in effect.

The most significant difference between the configurations sharing a common $\lambda_{PFE}$ value concerns the balance of Sensors and Influencers for each Decider within that configuration. This balance defines the "robustness" of the configuration, which was a term used by Barabasi (2002) to describe a network's resilience to failure due to the loss of some of its nodes. Robustness can be defined here as the minimum number of nodes lost that would make the configuration ineffective (i.e., unable to destroy any more enemy nodes). Mathematically this can be expressed as: Robustness $= [\min(S_1, I_1)] + [\min(S_2, I_2)] + \ldots + [\min(S_n, I_n)]$, where $S_n$ = the number of Sensors assigned to Decider $n$ and $I_n$ = the number of Influencers assigned to Decider $n$.

*Figure 3. The average probability of a BLUE win by $\lambda_{PFE}$ for 42 configurations of a 7-3-7-1 BLUE network*

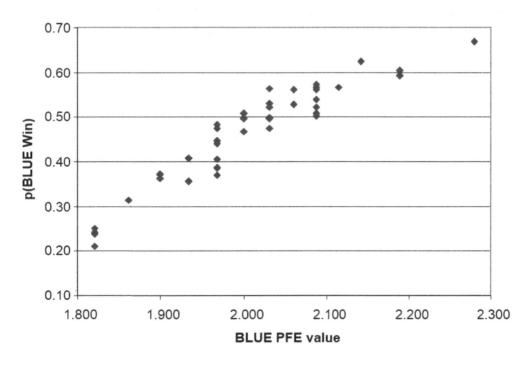

*Figure 4. The average probability of a BLUE win by $\lambda_{PFE}$ for 78 configurations of an 8-3-8-1 BLUE network*

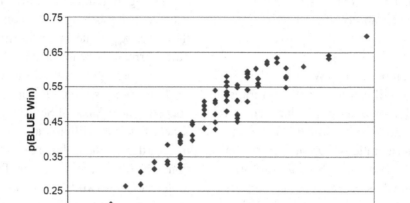

For example, a Decider has three Sensors but only one Influencer. This imbalance reduces the minimum number of nodes that can be lost before a portion of the force is rendered combat ineffective (i.e., unable to contribute due to the lack of combat cycles). If the sole Influencer is lost, then all three Sensors are combat ineffective as the information collected by the Sensors cannot be acted on. Essentially, the robustness value reflects the rate of the reduction of the $\lambda_{PFE}$ value over time. The quicker a force can be rendered completely ineffective, the lower the robustness value. Configurations that were more robust generally had a greater probability of winning, while less robust configurations generally had a lower probability of winning (see FigureFigure 6).

Since the robustness value varied between configurations sharing the same $\lambda_{PFE}$ value it be-

*Figure 5. The average probability of a BLUE win by $\lambda_{PFE}$ for 95 configurations of a 9-5-9-1 BLUE network*

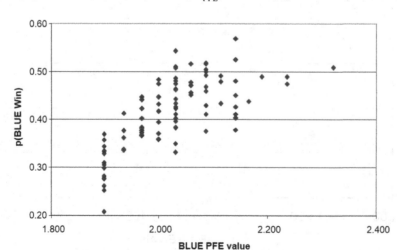

*Figure 6. The robustness values of the 95 configurations of a 9-5-9-1 BLUE network*

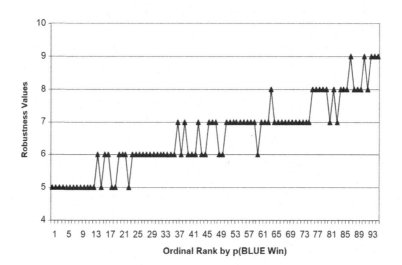

came a useful discriminator. For example, 20 of the 95 configurations of a 9-5-9-1 network share a $\lambda_{PFE}$ value of 2.031, but their robustness values varied between 6 and 9. Of these 20, only one configuration had a robustness value of 9, and it was the one that scored the highest p(Win) value, 0.5425, which was significantly higher than the other 19 configurations. While there was a strong correlation between robustness and p(Win), it was not absolute: 3 of the configurations outperformed others that had a robustness value one greater. A regression analysis of both the $\lambda_{PFE}$ value and the robustness value yields a significant increase in the coefficient of determination ($R^2$) from a value of 0.621 to 0.805 and provides the following equation: $y = [(-0.0307)(x_1) + 0.0615(x_2)] + 0.0678$, where y = the average probability of a BLUE win for that configuration, $x_1$ = the $\lambda_{PFE}$ value of a configuration, and $x_2$ = the robustness value of a configuration.

## APPLICATION FOR PRACTITIONERS

Due to the high costs and high risk of real system tests, the use of modeling and simulation instead of live tests and exercises has been recommended

by Ender et al. (2010) and Garrett et al. (2011). Although the authors are not aware of any study on the efficiency of the ballistic missile defense system based on the principles of IACM, several studies have been provided that evaluate so called 'kill chains' or 'kill cycles' that have to be established in order to have efficient solutions (Holland and Wallace 2011). This study establishes a good use case for the approaches discussed in this chapter.

The challenges to design a reliable and secure defense system against ballistic missile attacks have been recognized and evaluated nationally (Fogleman 1995, Gompert and Isaacson 1999) as well as internationally (Yost 1982) for more than a decade. Recent political changes introduced additional constraints that require a high degree of interoperability between the systems and the detailed integration of command and control processes (Frühling and Sinjen 2010).

The general technical challenge remained the same since described in detail by Weiner (1984). The overall task is to destroy a hostile ballistic missile before it hits the target to be protected. To be able to do this, radars and other sensor means have to search for threats and detect them. Once a hostile missile is detected, it needs to be tracked and a decision has to be made whether to target it or not. If the decision is positive, an interceptor has to be launched and guided into the target, followed an assessment if the engagement was successful or not.

Radar systems are space based, air based, and land based, with famous land based radar systems constructed close to the periphery of the alliance. The Cobra Dane Radar in Alaska, the Thule Radar in Greenland, and the Fylingdales Radar in the United Kingdom being examples. The US command centers Strategic Command (STRATCOM) and Northern Command (NORTHCOM) provide the Command, Control, Battle Management, and Communications (C2BMC) for the control. The interceptors are land-based Terminal High Altitude Area Defense (THAAD) Fire Units, sea-based Aegis Cruisers and Destroyers, and the land-based Patriot systems. Europe, Israel, and Japan are contributing their own components to support local concepts. The Missile Defense Agency, Army, Air Force, and Navy share responsibilities for operation, management, maintenance, and ongoing developments.

Holland and Wallace (2011) define a kill chain as a series combining all six main tasks to be conducted by the radar system, the control system, and the missile system. The proposed chain is displayed in Figure 7.

As identified by Garrett et al. (2011), the ballistic missile defense system is actually a system of systems in which the various components themselves are systems with established governance rules and that support the common objective of missile defense, but that are operationally independent. Overall, they fulfill the distinguishing characteristics compiled by Tolk, Adams, and Keating (2011):

- Operational independence of the systems,
- Managerial independence of the systems,
- Geographic distribution,
- Emergent behavior,
- Evolutionary development.

To establish a kill chain, components providing radar functionality to search and detect, control functionality to track, target, and assess, and missile functionality to engage are required to be interconnected via interoperable interfaces. Holland and Wallace (2011) identify scenario graphs to address what they refer to as integration readiness level: are the various components able to connect with each other in order to establish a kill chain, and are there redundancies to increase the stability of the ballistic missile defense operation. They use corresponding adjacency matrixes to identify which radar system connects with which control systems and which missile system.

This motivates, however, to map the ballistic missile defense components to the IACM components, eventually adding some extensions as discussed before: The hostile ballistic missile is the target T, the sensor provides the radar functionalities S, the decision nodes model the control functionalities, and the engaging interceptor missile system represents the influencer. The IACM interpretation of the kill chain is shown in the following figure.

This interpretation allows to apply the IACM insights described before to evaluate effectiveness and efficiency of the ballistic missile defense system. If each likely attack must be met by at

*Figure 7. Kill Chain for the Ballistic Missile Defense System*

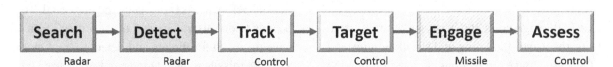

*Figure 8. IACM Interpretation of the kill chain*

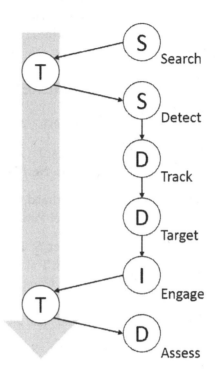

least one kill chain. However, each additional kill chain increases the likelihood of a defense success, and the more kill chains can cover a target, the higher the defense success gets. The number of possible kill chains, however, can be captured by computing the eigenvalue $\lambda_{PFE}$ of the resulting adjacency matrix resulting from the interpretation of interoperable components within the IACM.

The engagement step itself must also be interpreted as a kill cycle within the IACM. An interceptor fire unit comprises its own command and control center (D), a fire control radar (S), and the interceptor missile (I) to engage a hostile ballistic missile (T). In particular in combined operations in which several nations are fighting within a coalition, mutual support – like easily possible between two Aegis cruisers or two Patriot systems – is not the rule. The Israeli Arrow Weapon System, e.g., can be integrated into the kill chain using the C2BMC, but in the engage-

ment cycle itself the fire unit components are not interchangeable, which is often a problem between services and sometimes even within the services as well. The kill cycle for the engagement step maps one-to-one to the basic combat cycle shown in FigureFigure 1 in the beginning of the chapter, although it should be pointed out that the tracking of the hostile ballistic missile by the fire control radar is a process, not an event. For high-level analysis as targeted within most contributions to this book, this level of detail is often negligible and it can be assumed that each fire unit can and will operate independently. Cross fire unit support can only increase the overall efficiency and has no negative effects on the overall performance of ballistic missile defense.

## CONCLUSION

As recommended in the NATO Code of Best Practice for C2 Assessment (2002), the use of an orchestrated set of tools and methods is best practice when addressing complex questions like this one. The benefit of IACM based scenarios is that they allow us to analyze a broad volume of the solution space to identify a smaller fraction of particular interest. This smaller area can then be evaluated using detailed simulation systems, such as described by Lynch, Diallo, and Tolk (2013), which is based on the concepts theoretically introduced by Garrett et al. (2011).

The application of the IACM also shifts the focus of the assessment of a networked force from the capabilities of the nodes (generic in the IACM) to the capability of the network as a whole. The results of the agent-based simulation indicated that the value of the $\lambda_{PFE}$ was a significant measurement of the performance of a networked force. We also learned that the $\lambda_{PFE}$ value alone was insufficient indicator when the ratio of unique $\lambda_{PFE}$ values for the configurations under consideration decreased. Other quantifiable network metrics, such as the link-to-node ratio, degree distribution, clustering coefficient, and characteristic path length, were unable to consistently discriminate between these configurations that differed by a single link, regardless of the significance of that link. The addition of a robustness factor was necessary to aid in predicting the network performance. By utilizing both the $\lambda_{PFE}$ value and the robustness value, the coefficient of determination for the numerous configurations of three different networked forces showed a strong degree of correlation with the average probability of a Win.

We expect that these results will apply to even larger networks as well given that the only difference in the context of the IACM is a larger, possibly much larger, adjacency matrix. The mathematics of the application of graph theory remain the same. It is possible, however, that larger networks may have a smaller ratio of unique $\lambda_{PFE}$ values. If so, the consideration of the robustness factor along with the $\lambda_{PFE}$ value becomes even more necessary.

## REFERENCES

Barabási, A. (2002). *Linked*. Perseus Publishing.

Cares, J. (2005). *Distributed Networked Operations*. New York: iUniverse.

Chartrand, G. (1984). *Introductory Graph Theory*. Dover Publications.

Deller, S. T., Bell, M. I., Bowling, S. R., Rabadi, G., & Tolk, A. (2009). Applying the Information Age Combat Model: Quantitative Analysis of Network Centric Operations. *The International Command and Control (C2). Journal, 3*(1), 1–25.

Deller, S. T., Rabadi, G., Tolk, A., & Bowling, S. R. (2012). Organizing for Improved Effectiveness in Networked Operations. *Military Operations Research Journal, 17*(1), 5–16. doi:10.5711/1082598317105

Ender, T., Leurck, R. F., Weaver, B., Miceli, P., Blair, W. D., West, P., & Mavris, D. (2010). System-of-Systems Analysis of Ballistic Missile Defense Architecture Effectiveness through Surrogate Modeling and Simulation. *IEEE Systems Journal, 4*(2), 156–166. doi:10.1109/JSYST.2010.2045541

Fogleman, R. R. (1995). Theater Ballistic Missile Defense. *Joint Force Quarterly, 9*, 75–79.

Frühling, S., & Sinjen, S. (2010). *Missile defense: challenges and opportunities for NATO*. NATO Defense College, Research Paper, 60: 1-5.

Garrett, R. K., Anderson, S., Baron, N. T., & Moreland, J. D. (2011). Managing the interstitials, a system of systems framework suited for the ballistic missile defense system. *Systems Engineering, 14*(1), 87–109. doi:10.1002/sys.20173

Gompert, D. C., & Isaacson, J. A. (1999). *Planning a ballistic missile defense system of systems*. RAND Report IP-181, 1-14.

Holland, O. T., & Wallace, S. E. (2011). Using Agents to Model the Kill Chain of the Ballistic Missile Defense System. *Naval Engineers Journal, 123*(3), 141–151. doi:10.1111/j.1559-3584.2011.00336.x

Jain, S., & Krishna, S. (2002). *Graph Theory and the Evolution of Autocatalytic Networks*. Retrieved from http://arXiv.org/abs/nlin.AO/0210070

Lynch, C. J., Diallo, S. Y., & Tolk, A. (2013). Representing the ballistic missile defense system using agent-based modeling. In *Proceedings of the Military Modeling & Simulation Symposium* (pp. 3-12). San Diego, CA: Society for Computer Simulation International.

*NATO Code of Best Practice for C2 Assessment*. (2002). Command and Control Research Program (CCRP) Press.

Tolk, A., Adams, K. M., & Keating, C. B. (2011). Towards Intelligence-based Systems Engineering and System of Systems Engineering. In *Intelligence-based Systems Engineering* (pp. 1–22). Springer. doi:10.1007/978-3-642-17931-0_1

Weiner, S. (1984). Systems and technology. In *Ballistic Missile Defense* (pp. 49–97). Brookings Inst Press.

Yost, D. S. (1982). Ballistic Missile Defense and the Atlantic Alliance. *International Security, 7*(2), 143–174. doi:10.2307/2538436

## ADDITIONAL READING

Tolk, A. (2012). *Engineering Challenges for Combat Modeling and Distributed Simulation*. John Wiley and Sons. doi:10.1002/9781118180310

## KEY TERMS AND DEFINITIONS

**Ballistic Missile Defense System:** A system of operationally independent systems that support the common objective of missile defense.

**Command and Control (C2):** The exercise of authority and direction by a properly designated commander over assigned and attached forces in the accomplishment of the mission.

**Information Age Combat Model (IACM):** A model, proposed by Cares (2005), of search, detection and attrition processes that is specifically designed to capture complex local behaviors, interdependencies and the skewed distribution of networked performance.

**Kill Chain:** A series of tasks that execute the following functions: search (sensor), detect (sensor), track (decision), target (decision), engage (influencer) and assess (decision).

## APPENDIX

## Questions

1. What other connectivity measures for matrices could be applied?
2. How will this observation change if connections are no longer sure (p=1.0) but only likely (0 < p < 1), e.g. when detection probabilities or communication probabilities are modeled in the IACM?
3. Can Kill Chains as described for the BDMS example be expressed in form of matrices?
4. Can we determine the value of a Sensor relative to an Influencer?
5. How many assets can organizational optimization offset (i.e. a smaller, more optimally organized force defeating a larger force)?

# Chapter 9
# C2, Networks, and Self–Synchronization

**A. H. Dekker**
*University of Ballarat, Australia*

## ABSTRACT

*This chapter examines the connection between network theory and C2, particularly as it relates to self-synchronization, which requires a rich network structure. The richness of the network can be measured by the average degree, the average path length, and the average node connectivity. The chapter explores the connection between these measures and the speed of self-synchronization, together with other network properties, which can affect self-synchronization, resilience, and responsiveness. Two important network structures (random and scale-free) are described in the context of self-synchronization. Experimental data relating network topology to self-synchronization speed is also explored. In particular, the chapter notes the connection between average path length and self-synchronization speed, as well as the importance of good networking between sub-networks.*

## INTRODUCTION

The past few decades have seen an increasing awareness of the importance of C2 networks. There has also been an exploration of non-traditional designs for C2 networks, both in terms of network topology and in terms of network-enabled styles of operation, in order to achieve greater effectiveness in the face of modern threats (Alberts & Hayes, 2003, 2006). The application of network theory has obvious benefits here. But what can network theory tell us about C2 network design? What measures and metrics from network theory characterize "good" networks? There has also

been an increasing awareness of the importance of *agility* in military forces. Agility can be broken down into the attributes of *robustness*, *resilience*, *responsiveness*, *flexibility*, *innovation*, and *adaptation* (Alberts & Hayes, 2003, p. 128). Which networks make a military force more agile?

At the same time, recent decades have seen important advances in network theory, and the concept of self-synchronization has become a meeting-point, approached both from inside the network science community (Watts & Strogatz, 1998; Watts, 2003; Strogatz, 2003) and the military community (Alberts & Hayes, 2003, 2006; Orr & Nissen, 2006; Brehmer, 2009). Detailed

DOI: 10.4018/978-1-4666-6058-8.ch009

mathematical analysis of network attributes has been conducted (Bollobás, 2001; Chung & Lu, 2003), and this has been complemented by experiments studying the ability of human beings to self-synchronize in practice (Kearns *et al.*, 2006; Thunholm *et al.*, 2009). Computer simulation experiments (Watts & Strogatz, 1998; Dekker 2005, 2006, 2007a, 2007b, 2010a, 2011; Gateau *et al.*, 2007) have further illuminated this meeting-point between network theory and military science.

In this chapter, we explore the connection between C2, networks, and self-synchronization, in order to address the question of which network topologies are best. In particular, we examine how several network measures and attributes relate to the ability of a networked system to self-synchronize. We do this by surveying the relevant theoretical literature as well as reporting the results of some experiments with an abstract model of synchronization. We begin with the factors that influence an organization's choice between a centralized and a decentralized structure, and continue with evidence for the importance of networks with low average path length, high average node connectivity, and a priority on networking across a whole force, rather than simply within subnetworks.

## NETWORK TOPOLOGY AND PROBLEM TYPE

Much of Command and Control (C2) consists of addressing challenging resource allocation problems – often under conditions of uncertainty and risk. It is true that there is a core part of C2 which is essentially creative, and involves outlining a conceptual framework or way of thinking about the problem at hand (Builder *et al.*, 1999). However, a large part of C2 involves the allocation of people and platforms (on the one hand) to places and tasks (on the other). A good network topology will facilitate this process.

In studying C2-related resource allocation problems, we can divide them into three categories, which we will call "easy," "difficult," and "fiendish." An example of an "easy" problem is finding the largest number in a set. The effort required to solve such an "easy" problem will be at most proportional to the size of the problem, since the problem can be solved by a single scan through the set. Technically, such problems are known as linear-time or sub-linear-time problems.

"Difficult" problems include finding the Minimum Spanning Tree (MST) of a network (Cormen *et al.*, 1990). Figure 1 shows an example. If the network is understood to be a network of cities connected by roads of various lengths, then the minimum spanning tree is the shortest network of cables which will connect all the cities, on the assumption that the cables must be strung alongside the roads. This problem can be solved with a computer, but large instances require minutes (or even hours) of computation. In general, the effort required to perfectly solve "difficult" problems will be proportional to some more-than-linear polynomial function of the problem size. Technically, such problems (together with the "easy" class) are known as polynomial-time problems.

"Fiendish" problems (technically, NP-hard problems) include the Travelling Salesman Problem (TSP), which requires finding the shortest loop visiting all nodes in the network exactly once (Cormen *et al.*, 1990). Again, Figure 1 provides an example. Perfectly solving "fiendish" problems requires effort proportional to some exponential function of the problem size, which makes problem instances of even moderate size impossible to solve. Typically, the best that can be hoped for is finding reasonably good solution, and doing so may fall into either the "easy" or "difficult" categories.

In a more military context a similar distinction arises. The Assignment Problem (AP) – the simple assignment of units to tasks, where each task requires one unit, and each unit can carry out only one task – is a "difficult" problem, requiring

*Figure 1. An example network (on the left), with the corresponding minimum spanning tree (MST) in the center and a good (though possibly not optimal) travelling-salesman (TSP) solution on the right*

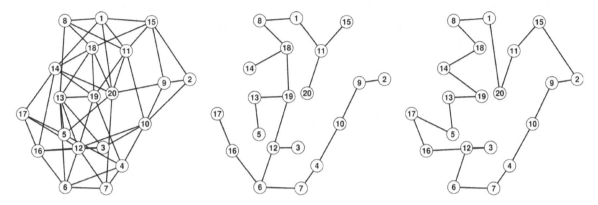

effort proportional to the cube of the problem size (Christofides, 1975). On the other hand, the Weapon–Target Allocation (WTA) problem is "fiendish" (Malcolm, 2004; Johansson & Falkman, 2009). In the WTA, multiple weapons may be assigned to a single target, and there may be synergistic benefits in doing so. For example, electronic-warfare weapons may be synergistic with kinetic-energy weapons (US Army, 2009). However, this additional complexity makes a perfect solution unobtainable for anything but very small problem instances, and commanders must instead concentrate on finding a "good enough" answer within the time window dictated by circumstances. This applies particularly in the more complex land environment where, according to Moltke, "even the mediocre is quite an achievement" (Van Creveld, 1985). Figure 2 compares the solution efficiency of the "easy," "difficult," and "fiendish" problems we have listed.

Problems in the intermediate "difficult" class lend themselves to centralized decision-making, particularly when the time window dictated by circumstances allows for a perfect or near-perfect solution to be found (Dekker, 2003; 2006). A centralized headquarters or other C2 node is often best able to solve resource allocation problems of this kind. A classic example is the 72-hour cycle

in the US Air Force for producing detailed Air Tasking Orders (Alberts & Hayes, 2003, p. 47). The availability of a suitable centralized platform also supports centralized decision-making, particularly when the platform has access to a high-quality information source. An AWACS (Airborne Warning and Control System) aircraft is a good example of how a centralized C2 node provides a "knowledge edge" (Clancy, 1995).

At higher tempos, however, as in the prosecution of time-sensitive targets, a significant degree of decentralization becomes necessary (Dekker, 2003). Low network bandwidth also necessitates some degree of decentralization and the adoption of "mission command." Improvements in information technology can facilitate the work of a centralized headquarters, by making problems in the "difficult" class more tractable. However, improved information technology can also support decentralization by helping soldiers, pilots, and sailors manage information without being distracted from focusing on their immediate threats. The ability of computer technology to partially automate decision-making also supports decentralization (Dekker, 2003).

Improved communications technology can facilitate communication to and from a centralized headquarters, and can consequently encourage

*Figure 2. Efficiency (inverse of effort required) for five different problems, arbitrarily scaled to give the same value for a problem size of 10. The "fiendish" Travelling Salesman Problem and Weapon–Target Allocation problem are effectively impossible to solve perfectly for even moderately-sized instances. The "difficult" Assignment Problem and Minimum Spanning Tree problem are solvable for large instances, but require substantial effort*

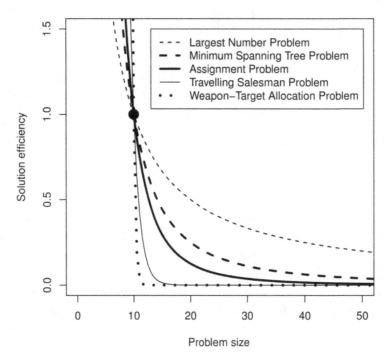

centralized decision-making, and facilitate the monitoring of subordinates through video feeds and blue force tracking. However, improved communications technology can also facilitate communication between subordinate units, and allow a form of decentralized decision-making where problems are solved in a collaborative, distributed fashion, rather than in a centralized location. This process is called self-synchronization, and allows the creation of what have been called "edge organizations" (Alberts & Hayes, 2003; 2006).

## EDGE ORGANIZATIONS

Metaphorically, an "edge organization" is like the circular saw blade in Figure 3. The "cutting edge" carries out the task at hand, while the "center"

provides broad direction. This "cutting edge" corresponds to what Mintzberg (1980) calls the "operating core." The "edge" metaphor avoids the power differential reflected in the "top/bottom" language of organizational hierarchies. As Alberts & Hayes (2003, p. 5) put it, "*power to the edge* involves the empowerment of individuals at the edge of an organization." This empowerment involves greater and more rapid access to information, as well as a greater ability to make decisions, than is usual in traditional hierarchies. Both these changes require interaction, and hence network links, between entities within the "edge." The "edge" metaphor also de-emphasizes the organizational stovepipes and personal "empires" associated with middle management: "in an edge organization, virtually everyone is at the edge

*Figure 3. The "Edge" metaphor. The "cutting edge" carries out the task at hand, while the "center" provides broad direction. The "edge" must be held together by strong yet flexible bonds. In particular, communication links are needed within the "edge" to facilitate self-synchronization*

because they are empowered" (Alberts & Hayes, 2003, p. 176).

Edge organizations can also be described in terms of the "C2 Cube" (Alberts & Hayes, 2006; NATO, 2010), redrawn in Figure 4. At the bottom left of this diagram are tightly controlled organizations where individual units interact very little, have little information, and have few decision rights. This makes sense for problems that lend themselves to centralized decision-making, where units only need to carry out their portion of the overall plan. At the top right are edge organizations, where units interact more, have more information, and are given more decision rights. This makes sense for "fiendish" problems, or high-tempo situations.

Figure 4 also shows two other extreme cases of organizational design. At the back of the cube are unfortunate "aware but powerless" organizations, where units have good information, but no authority to act on it. At the lower right are independent teams, where units are authorized to act independently, but do not interact with each other. Independent teams are a common structure with Special Forces organizations and other organizations with highly trained staff operating in situations where communication between units is difficult or unnecessary.

There are a number of approaches to non-hierarchical networking of an organization. The "more interaction" and "more information" axes of Figure 4 require improvements to network connectivity. Directly connecting every entity to every other entity would be the ultimate "edge structure," maximizing the interaction between nodes. However, this is generally prohibitively expensive, both in terms of the dollar cost of installing network infrastructure, and in the human cost of managing so many connections. An obvious compromise is the Erdős–Rényi random network (Bollobás, 2001), usually called simply a "random network." In this kind of network, shown on the left of Figure 5, a manageable number of direct links is provided at random. The number of

*Figure 4. The "C2 Cube." In edge organizations (top right), units interact more, have more information, and are given more decision rights than in tightly controlled organizations (bottom left). The two cylinders show two other extreme cases: "aware but powerless" organizations (back), where units have good information, but no authority to act on it; and the more common case of independent teams, where units are authorized to act independently, but do not interact with each other*

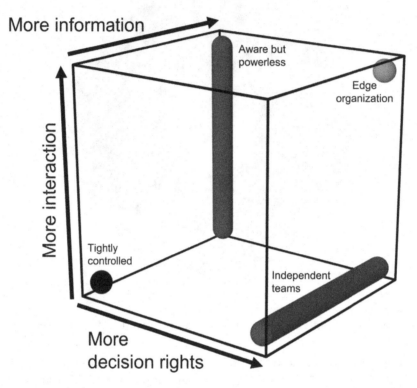

links attached to specific nodes (i.e. the *degrees* of those nodes) follows a Poisson distribution with an average degree of $2m/n$, where $m$ is the number of links and $n$ the number of nodes. This degree distribution can be approximated by a bell curve, and indeed approaches a bell curve as the average degree becomes large. For the random graph on the left of Figure 5, the degrees range from 1 to 12, with 70% of the nodes having degrees in the range 4 to 8 (inclusive). Thus most nodes have only a moderate number of direct connections, which should not pose an excessive information management burden if each node has appropriate information management technology. In practice, rather than being totally random, connections would be provided between nodes that are required

to interact, with any additional links made in some way without an obvious pattern.

As we will see later, the ability of such a network to self-synchronize depends on the speed at which information can flow through the network. In particular, it depends on the average path length or average network distance between pairs of nodes. The lower the average path length, the faster information will flow, and the more up-to-date information nodes will have access to.

The average path length is surprisingly low for random networks: about $\log n / \log d$, where $n$ is the number of nodes and $d$ the average degree (Chung & Lu, 2003). For the random graph on the left of Figure 5, the average path length is 2.77 (compared to $\log n / \log d = 2.57$). An organization structured like a random network

*Figure 5. Random (left) and scale-free (right) networks each with 100 nodes and average degree 6. Labels show the degree of each node (the degree ranges are 1–12 and 3–67 respectively), and node areas are roughly proportional to the degree. The average path lengths are 2.77 for the random network and 2.21 for the scale-free network*

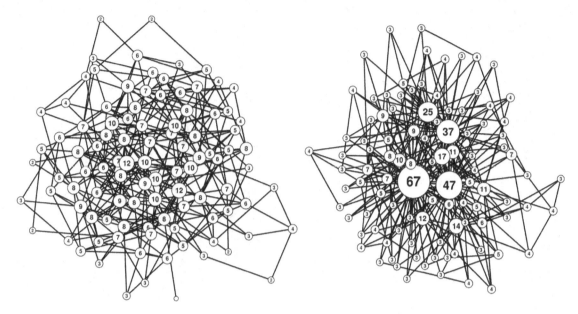

therefore has the potential to be agile and respond rapidly to changing circumstances – but only if it can self-synchronize. The network on the left of Figure 5 has no "center" at all, and thus limited opportunity for centralized direction.

Another widely studied network structure is the scale-free network, in which the distribution of node degrees follows a power-law distribution (Albert & Barabási, 2002; Barabási, 2002). The network on the right of Figure 5 provides an example, where 51% of nodes have degree 3, 43% of nodes have degree 4 to 12 (with an average of 5.6), and six highly-connected "hub" nodes have degrees 14, 17, 25, 37, 47, and 67. In a real-life network, such highly-connected nodes may be shared information-storage nodes, high-value shared sensors, or major C2 nodes. As we will see later, these nodes may represent network vulnerabilities, unless there is sufficient duplication of key nodes to provide redundancy. Scale-free networks are not simply a theoretical concept: in

a study of eleven Dutch Army C2 systems with between 44 and 171 nodes, Grant *et al.* (2011) found that all of them were approximately scale-free. Similarly, Jarvis (2005) analyzed the email network of a US/UK naval exercise, and found that it was scale-free.

Scale-free networks have even shorter average path lengths than random networks with the same average degree. Alternatively, they may have the same average path length with a lower average degree. The two networks in Figure 5 have the same average degree, but the average path length for the scale-free network is 20% shorter.

Another structure, perhaps more realistic for organizational networks, is a hierarchy supplemented by random cross-links, as shown in Figure 6. The random cross-links give a structure very similar to a pure random network, and with a similar average path length. One might ask whether the hierarchical backbone still provides value in such a supplemented network, and this depends

*Figure 6. Adding random links to a hierarchy gives a result very similar to a pure random network. Here, a 100-node hierarchy, with the black node at the top, and with hierarchical links as thick lines (left) is supplemented by random links (right) so as to have the same average degree as the networks in Figure 5. Labels show the degree of each node, as in Figure 5. The average path length is 7.35 for the pure hierarchy, but 2.75 for the supplemented hierarchy, which is virtually the same as for the random network in Figure 5*

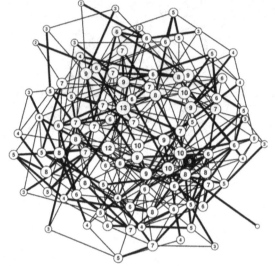

on the rationale behind the original hierarchy. For example, if the original hierarchy corresponded to a decomposition of a "difficult" or "fiendish" problem into appropriate sub-problems (e.g. by assigning geographical areas of responsibility), then retaining the hierarchical backbone will provide continued value (Dekker, 2007b).

## SELF-SYNCHRONIZATION

In recent years, there has been considerable literature on self-synchronization, examining theoretical issues, organizational issues, and empirical data. A number of experimental studies have shed light on the relationship between network properties and self-synchronization. Kearns *et al.* (2006), for example, studied networks of human subjects attempting to collaboratively solve the network coloring problem (Gibbons, 1985). In this case, "synchronization" meant finding an agreed way

of assigning colors to people, such that linked people had different colors. Each participant had a purely local view of the color assignment, and could only infer what was going on elsewhere in the network from the color choices of his or her neighbors. For classes of networks where subjects usually found a correct solution (those where only two different colors were required), the time taken (in minutes) to find a solution was approximately 20 times the average path length of the network used (Kearns *et al.*, 2006; Dekker, 2010b).

Thunholm *et al.* (2009) conducted experiments using ELICIT, the Experimental Laboratory for Investigating Collaboration, Information-sharing and Trust (Ruddy, 2007). This is a tool for exploring organizational concepts, in which a team of 17 people plays the role of an intelligence analysis cell, discovering and communicating "factoids" concerning a fictional terrorist plot. In this case, "synchronization" meant using the factoids to decide when, where, and how the terrorist attack

*Figure 7. The three organizational structures studied by Thunholm et al. (2009), with average path lengths L = 2.85, 2.15, and 1, respectively. The average synchronization time was 26.3 + 5.7 L minutes (Dekker, 2011)*

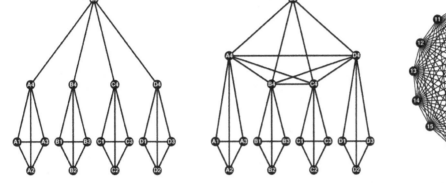

**(a) Traditional Hierarchy     (b) Hybrid Organization     (c) Edge Organization**

would occur. Thunholm *et al.* considered the three organizational network structures in Figure 7 – a traditional hierarchy (with cross-links within teams at the "bottom"), a hybrid organization (which added cross-links between team leaders), and an "edge organization" (which linked all participants to each other). In these experiments, the time required for the teams to synchronize was, on average, 26.3 + 5.7 L minutes, where L was the average path length (Thunholm *et al.*, 2009; Dekker, 2011).

An agent-based experiment where agents solved a factorization task also found a synchronization time proportional to the average path length (Dekker, 2011), as did a hybrid human/agent experiment involving an assignment task (Dekker, 2012). This relationship between synchronization time and average path length is due to the fact that the ability of a network to self-synchronize depends on the speed at which information can flow through the network, which in turn depends on the number of network "hops" between nodes. As noted above, random networks have an average path length of approximately log *n* / log *d*, and this sets a limit on how fast a large network with a reasonable restriction on node degrees can

self-synchronize. The relationship between synchronization time and average path length is not necessarily linear, however, as we will now see.

One of the simplest possible models of self-synchronization is the networked Kuramoto oscillator model (Kuramoto, 1948; Strogatz, 2000; Dorogovtsev *et al.*, 2008; Kalloniatis, 2008, 2010; Dekker 2007a, 2010a, 2011). Drawn from the physical sciences, this model is a simple system of *n* networked oscillators $O_1 \ldots O_n$, each with a natural frequency $f_i$ (assumed to come from a unimodal and symmetric distribution) and a phase angle $\theta_i$. Figure 8 shows an example. The dynamics of the model are given by a differential equation, which specifies changes in the phase angles $\theta_i$ such that (for the constant *k* sufficiently high) the $\theta_i$ align with each other:

$$\theta_i' = f_i + k \sum_j^{i \leftrightarrow j} \sin\left(\theta_j - \theta_i\right)$$

The sum here is taken over all oscillators $O_j$ connected to $O_i$ in the network topology. The equation describes a negative feedback process: differences between $\theta_i$ and $\theta_j$ act to bring $\theta_i$ and $\theta_j$ closer together. At the point of synchronization, not

*Figure 8. The Kuramoto oscillator model, where the $\theta_i$ are oscillator phase angles which become similar as the network synchronizes*

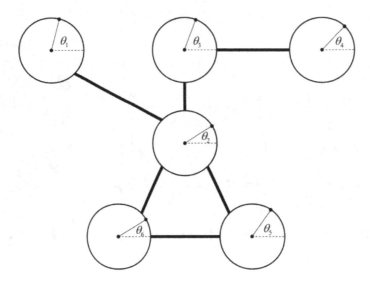

only are the phase angles similar, but the rotational velocities (rate of change of phase angles) are all the same. The number $k$ represents an overall tendency to self-synchronize, and the synchronization time will be roughly inversely proportional to $k$ (provided $k$ is above a threshold value). However, since we are interested primarily in the effect of network topology, we will not discuss the impact of $k$ further, except to note that there are always organization-wide factors (such as organizational culture) which can improve self-synchronization. More significantly for our purposes, experiments with the Kuramoto oscillator model show that the synchronization time is roughly proportional to the fourth power of the average path length, rather than the linear relationship observed in the other experiments we have discussed.

However, there is a very close relationship between the form of self-synchronization displayed in the Kuramoto model, and the form of self-synchronization displayed in collaborative problem-solving. Lee & Lister (2008) demonstrate this relationship in the case of the graph coloring problem studied by Kearns *et al.* (2006). We have also demonstrated this relationship for

the case of the Assignment Problem (Dekker, 2013a). In both collaborative problem-solving and the Kuramoto model, self-synchronization requires the network as a whole to "settle down" into a high-quality (or minimum-energy) state. The negative feedback process in the Kuramoto model closely resembles the negative feedback mechanism in networked collaborative problem-solving, where participants discuss and eliminate conflicts between the choices they have made, in order to gradually produce an overall solution of high quality. The Kuramoto model can therefore be used to explore how well particular network topologies facilitate self-synchronization.

The relationship between synchronization time and the average path length is fundamentally the same for the Kuramoto model and for collaborative problem-solving – it takes time for information to flow along paths in the network. This remains true whether the time factor is expressed as a differential equation (as above), or whether the time factor is expressed using explicit time delays (indeed, approximating the differential equation by a difference equation converts one form of time-dependence to the other). Common to both

*Figure 9. Self-synchronization begins in random networks with multiple loose clusters of locally synchronized nodes (left), while scale-free networks synchronize from the central core outwards (right). The diagrams are the result of solving two instances of the Kuramoto model (for the networks in Figure 5), and the numbers in each node (and the shade of grey) represent the rotational velocity $\theta_i$ of the corresponding oscillator. Node sizes are as in Figure 5*

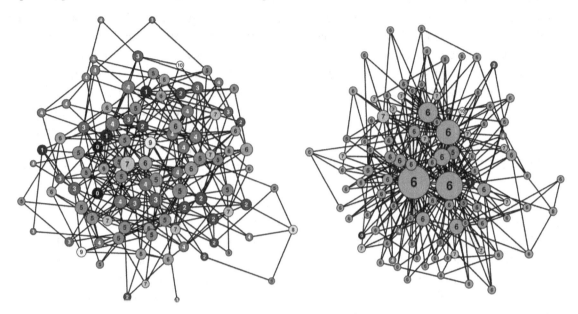

the Kuramoto model and collaborative problem-solving is the fact that networks with low average path length facilitate self-synchronization, although the precise relationship between synchronization time and average path length may be different.

Figure 9 shows the behavior of the networked Kuramoto oscillator model for the two networks in Figure 5. The statistical software R (Maindonald & Braun, 2007) was used to solve the differential equation above for a random vector of natural frequencies $f_i$ and a random vector of initial angles $\theta_i$. The numbers in each node of Figure 9 (and the shade of grey) represent the rotational velocity $\theta_i$ of the corresponding oscillator at a point in time half-way to complete synchronization. These rotational velocities are scaled to a 0–10 range for clarity.

Since synchronization time for the Kuramoto model is roughly proportional to the fourth power of the average path length, the scale-free network

in Figure 9 self-synchronizes about 2.4 times as rapidly as the random network, and this is reflected in a visibly greater number of nodes with the consensus rotational velocity coded as "6."

Figure 9 also illustrates the fact that scale-free networks self-synchronize from the central core outwards, as other researchers have previously demonstrated (Dorogovtsev *et al.*, 2008). Only a few nodes on the right of Figure 9, mostly on the periphery, have a rotational velocity different from the consensus value coded as "6." For random (Erdős–Rényi) networks, in contrast, synchronization begins with multiple loose clusters of locally synchronized nodes (Dorogovtsev *et al.*, 2008). For example, there is a cluster of nodes coded "4" at the top left of Figure 9. Only later do these clusters merge to share a single consensus rotational velocity. This effect is exaggerated in a network which is composed of well-connected components which are themselves only poorly linked together. Here the high-quality networking *within* a cluster speeds self-synchronization among cluster members, but actually interferes with self-synchronization *between* clusters (Dekker, 2013b). Essentially, within-cluster networking can promote a kind of "group-think," by generating so much message traffic that messages from the outside are ignored. To avoid this, joint, combined, and coalition forces should make networking between components a higher priority than networking within components. If this is impossible, they should have other ways of achieving overall consensus.

## A "FLOCKING" EXAMPLE

The Kuramoto model is a rather over-simplistic model of self-synchronization. A somewhat more realistic abstract model of self-synchronization is the flocking model of Reynolds (1987), which he called "boids." We have generalized this model to higher dimensionality (Dekker, 2013b), so that agents travel through an abstract four-dimensional space, of which Figure 10 and Figure 11 are three-dimensional projections. In this model, "synchronization" means the alignment of velocity vectors, and self-synchronization results from agents aligning their velocity vectors with those of their neighbors in the network. As with the Kuramoto model, we can use this flocking model to explore how well particular network topologies facilitate self-synchronization.

As in the Kuramoto model, self-synchronization for the "flocking" model in scale-free networks happens from the central core outwards, while self-synchronization in random networks begins with multiple loose clusters of locally synchronized nodes. As in other abstract models of self-synchronization, the average path length $L$ is the best predictor of how long a network will take to self-synchronize, because the average path length determines the speed at which information can flow through the network. As Figure 12 shows, for average path lengths greater than 3, the time required to self-synchronize was proportional to $L^{2.23}$ (Dekker, 2013b). This almost-quadratic relationship is thus intermediate between the fourth power observed in the Kuramoto model and the linear relationship seen in the other experiments we have mentioned: studies of collaborative network coloring (Kearns et al., 2006; Dekker, 2010b); experiments with the ELICIT tool (Thunholm et al., 2009; Dekker, 2011); an agent-based experiment where agents solved a factorization task (Dekker, 2011); and a hybrid human/agent experiment involving an assignment task (Dekker, 2012). Regardless of the exact power, however, the general rule is that networks with a greater average path length take longer to self-synchronize.

However, Figure 12 also shows an important exception to this general rule. The lower left of the diagram actually shows a peak in synchronization time at an average path length of 2.17, which corresponds to random networks with an average degree of 12. When self-synchronization begins in these networks, the multiple loose clusters of locally synchronized nodes are sufficiently well-connected internally to promote "group-think," and thus to resist converging on an overall consensus.

This phenomenon occurs even more dramatically for the network on the left of Figure 13, which has an average degree of 6.2 and average path length of 4.28. Adding more links to each cluster (for an average degree of 19.2 and an average path length of 2.89) actually *slows down* self-synchronization by 43% (Dekker, 2013b). Self-synchronization within clusters can be detrimental to overall self-synchronization.

Some authors suggest that the suitability of a network for self-synchronization can be measured using spectral graph theory (Biggs, 1993), rather than average path length. In particular, it has been suggested that the ratio of the Laplacian eigenvalues $\lambda_2$ and $\lambda_N$ is a good predictor of synchronizability (Chen & Duan, 2008). However, we have found this not to be the case. For the networks in Figure 12, the Laplacian eigenvalue ratio has a correlation of 0.71 with median self-

*Figure 10. Early signs of self-synchronization in the "flocking" model, for the scale-free network from Figure 5. Each agent (represented by a cone) has a four-dimensional velocity vector, which is shown by the direction the cone is pointing plus (for the fourth dimension) the shade of grey of the cone*

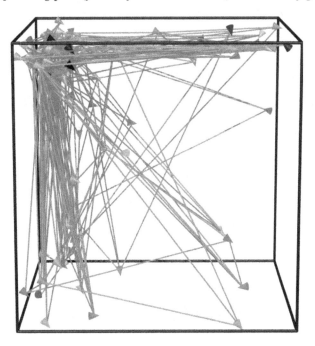

*Figure 11. Final state of self-synchronization in the "flocking" model, for the scale-free network from Figure 10. All agents have the same four-dimensional velocity vector, as indicated by cone direction and grey-shade*

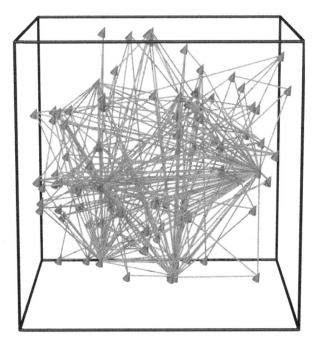

*Figure 12. Self-synchronization times for 68 different networks (all with 120 nodes). The solid curve shows how the time to synchronize is proportional to $L^{2.23}$ for average path lengths $L \geq 3$, and the correlation here is 0.93. However, for $L < 3$, there is a significant deviation from the curve. (Diagram redrawn from Dekker, 2013b)*

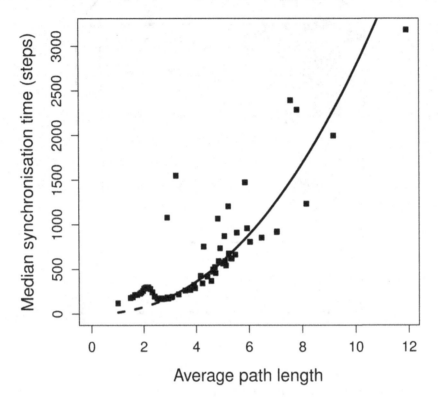

synchronization time (as opposed to a correlation of 0.93 for average path lengths $L \geq 3$, and 0.83 for all average path lengths). Furthermore, combining the Laplacian eigenvalue ratio with the average path length does not give a better predictor than the average path length alone.

## SELF-SYNCHRONIZATION AND AGILITY

For an "edge organization" to put less weight on "control from the top" and more weight on self- synchronization, a number of attributes are necessary. As a group, these attributes are often referred to as *agility*. Individually, they include *robustness, resilience, responsiveness, flexibility,*

*innovation,* and *adaptation* (Alberts & Hayes, 2003, p. 128).

Some of these attributes are largely cultural. *Innovation,* for example, is "the ability to do things in new ways or to undertake new things to do" (Alberts & Hayes, 2003, p. 149). This depends heavily on the quality of staff training, the extent to which staff are empowered to "think outside the box," and the extent to which the organization takes advantage of "lessons learned." However, innovation is also related to network structure. Improved networking – reflected in a network topology with a higher average degree – makes it much easier to assemble a team of entities into a mission package to carry out a new task, or to carry out an old task in an unusual way. If entity A must cooperate with entity B, and requires network

*Figure 13. A loosely clustered network (left), with 120 nodes arranged in six clusters of 20, giving an average degree of 6.2 and average path length of 4.28. Adding more links to each cluster (right) reduces the average path length to 2.89, but actually increases the synchronization time by 43%*

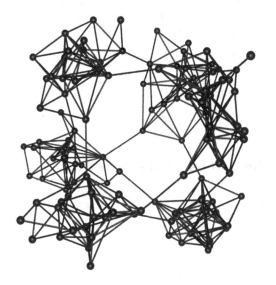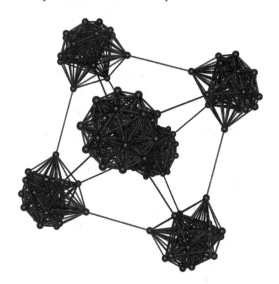

connectivity to do so, the number of candidate Bs is precisely the degree of entity A. Each network link represents a potential working relationship.

In a similar way, flexibility, the "capability to achieve success in different ways" (Alberts & Hayes, 2003, p. 143) and adaptation, "the ability to alter force organization and work processes when necessary" (Alberts & Hayes, 2003, p. 153) depend partially on the ability of an organization to restructure itself, which in turn depends partly on the number of network links (i.e., on the average degree).

## Responsiveness

*Responsiveness* is the ability of a force "to act (or react) effectively in a timely manner" (Alberts & Hayes, 2003, p. 139). This depends on the time it takes to transfer information across the network. As we have seen in looking at self-synchronization, the time to transfer information across the network depends in turn on the average path length $L$ of the network. Indeed, the average time required to send information between a pair of network

nodes will be $Lt + (L-1)T$, where $t$ is the average time required to send information across a single network link, and $T$ the average time required for intermediate nodes to process messages and pass them on. When $t$ is large compared to $T$, this reduces to approximately $Lt$; when $t$ and $T$ are approximately equal, this reduces to approximately $(2L-1)T$; and when $t$ is small compared to $T$, this reduces to approximately $(L-1)T$. The last case is the most likely, particularly where slow organizational processes produce unnecessary delays in passing on a message. In all cases, the time taken is a linear function of $L$. If we assume that the recipient also requires time $T$ to process the message, and include that within the transmission time, then the total transmission time in all cases becomes $L(t+T)$. In other words, the total transmission time is the product of the average path length and the time consumed by each stage along the path.

During the September 11 attacks of 2001, for example, airline authorities were first notified of a hijacking at 08:19, by flight attendant Betty Ong (NCTAUUS, 2004, p. 5). This information filtered through airline and FAA entities until at 08:38, the Northeast Air Defense Sector of NORAD was notified; this was the first notification received by any US military entity (NCTAUUS, 2004, p. 20). US Air Force F-15 fighters were scrambled at 08:46, but without clear instructions (NCTAUUS, 2004, p. 20). The President of the United States was given the first incomplete information on what appeared to be an accident at 08:55 (NCTAUUS, 2004, p. 35). Presidential authority to shoot down aircraft if needed came at 10:20, just over two hours after the original call by Betty Ong (NCTAUUS, 2004, p. 41). This delay reflects a network where information travelled along a path with multiple "hops," and where each entity required some minutes (the time $T$) to absorb information and to formulate a response (including the decision on who else to notify).

To improve responsiveness, Alberts & Hayes (2003, p. 82) recommend centralized information repositories with a "post before processing" policy. A centralized information repository accessible to most nodes significantly reduces the average path length $L$, while "post before processing" significantly reduces the delay factor $T$.

It may be the case that the delay factor $T$ is itself dependent on network topology. For example, high-degree nodes may become overloaded by the message traffic they are required to process. There are two possible responses to this. First, increased automation of message handling reduces overload on the human beings within a node (although the technology itself may still be overloaded). Second, network topologies with *both* low average path length and low to moderate degree will be particularly responsive. For example, a 120-node random network with average degree 6 has an average path length of around 2.9. The small-world networks described by Watts & Strogatz (1998) are another alternative. These networks result from replacing some links in a regular grid network by random cross-links. This can reduce the average path length of a 120-node network to around 3.8, while retaining an average degree of 4. The two

120-node networks recorded in the Foster Census of symmetric graphs have average path lengths of only 4.91 and 5.08, in spite of every node having degree 3 (Conder & Dobcsányi, 2002). Such networks may offer effective alternatives to simply adding links until the desired low average path length is achieved, although further work would be required to explore this possibility, particularly since robustness and resilience are difficult to achieve with very low degrees.

## Robustness and Resilience

*Robustness* is "the ability to retain a level of effectiveness across a range of missions" (Alberts & Hayes, 2003, p. 128), while *resilience* is "the ability to recover from or adjust to misfortune, damage, or a destabilizing perturbation in the environment" (Alberts & Hayes, 2003, p. 135).

These two attributes are related to the *node connectivity* of a network, which is based on the number of node-independent paths between two nodes – that is, on the number of paths between nodes A and B which have no intermediate nodes in common. The node connectivity is the minimum count of such paths, considered over all pairs of nodes A and B (Dekker & Colbert, 2004a). Consequently, the node connectivity represents the least number of node failures or node removals required to break a network into two disconnected pieces. As Alberts & Hayes (2003, p. 135) put it, "the loss of a single node or link is absorbed by a robustly networked force" – that is, one with a node connectivity of two or more. In simple simulations of military combat, the advantage lies with a robustly networked force having a high node connectivity (Dekker, 2004). Furthermore, because node connectivity is a worst-case measure, it particularly indicates resilience in the face of an intelligent enemy who targets the removal of nodes in a way which does the most damage. For infrastructure networks, a high node connectivity therefore improves resistance to terrorist attack (Dekker & Colbert, 2004b; Dekker, 2005).

*Figure 14. Resistance of some 120-node networks to random attack (left) and targeted attack (right). The vertical axis shows the percentage of pairs of surviving nodes which remain connected by some path. The targeted attacks were conducted by always removing the node with the highest betweenness score (Wasserman & Faust, 1994). The thin line corresponds to one of the 120-node symmetric graphs in the Foster Census (Conder & Dobcsányi, 2002)*

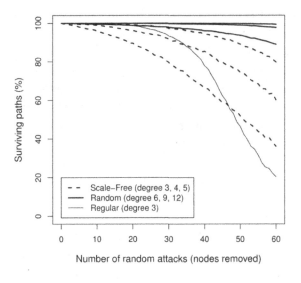 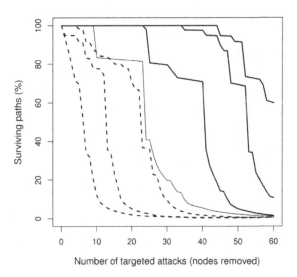

While node connectivity is a standard network measure (Gibbons, 1985), it is overly influenced by even a single poorly-connected node. A better indication of overall network connectivity is the *average node connectivity* (Dekker, 2007a), which is the average count of node-independent paths, considered over all pairs of nodes A and B. The random and scale-free networks in Figure 5 have average node connectivity 4.66 and 3.42 respectively. The value for the scale-free network is lower because the large number of links between the "hub" and the "edge" reduce the average path length, but also reduce the number of node-independent paths.

As shown on the left of Figure 14, both random and scale-free networks are resistant to random node failures, and to random attacks on nodes. However, the extent of resistance to attack depends on the average degree, with networks of higher average degree being more robust, since they have more links.

On the other hand, the right of Figure 14 shows that scale-free networks are vulnerable to targeted attacks on the high-degree nodes in the central "hub," since these can take many links out of action at once (Albert & Barabási, 2002; Barabási, 2002; Barabási & Bonabeau, 2003). For example, just two node removals from the scale-free network in Figure 5 can eliminate 38% of the links. Four node removals can eliminate 57% of the links, and cause multiple nodes to become disconnected. In Figure 14, targeted attacks were conducted by always removing the node with the highest betweenness score (Wasserman & Faust, 1994). If "catastrophic failure" is defined as 50% of the surviving pairs of nodes no longer having a functioning path between them, then the scale-free networks of degree 3, 4, and 5 experience catastrophic failure after 7, 13, and 23 attacks respectively. In contrast, the random networks of degree 6 and 9 only experience catastrophic failure after 41 and 53 attacks respectively.

The "clustered" network in Figure 13 is even more fragile in the face of targeted attacks, experiencing catastrophic failure after just 6 targeted node removals. This is because the network consists of six clusters, with 12 bridging links, so that the removal of 6 appropriately chosen nodes will separate the network into two separate parts of roughly equal size.

It is possible to improve robustness by intelligent non-random placement of links. This takes advantage of the fact that triangles within a network can be wasteful way of obtaining robustness, because the third side of the triangle connects nodes that already have a good indirect connection. A better combination of robustness and average path length can be obtained when a network contains no triangles, squares, or other small cycles. The thin line in Figure 14 corresponds to one of the 120-node symmetric networks in the Foster Census already mentioned above (Conder & Dobcsányi, 2002). This network is free from small cycles, and has degree 3 and average path length 5.08 (somewhat worse than the 3.59 for the scale-free network of degree 3 in Figure 14). It only experiences catastrophic failure after 24 attacks, compared to 7 attacks for the scale-free network of degree 3. This robustness is due partly to the average node connectivity being as high as possible (equal to the degree of 3) and partly to the high degree of symmetry, which guarantees that all links have equal importance. The "entangled networks" of Donetti *et al.* (2005) are a possible half-way house to such symmetric networks.

The vulnerability to targeted attack is of concern, given the existence of scale-free C2 networks in the real world (Grant *et al.*, 2011; Jarvis, 2005). This vulnerability makes centralized information repositories and C2 nodes a point of weakness. To counter this, doctrine should allow the network to function even in the absence of centralized C2 nodes, or the centralized C2 nodes should be hardened to an extent that makes targeted attack infeasible, or there should be "failover" provisions to replace the centralized C2 nodes by other nodes. Centralized information repositories should be replicated, creating a distributed information storage sub-network, capable of withstanding the loss of one or more information storage nodes (Ceri & Pelagatti, 1984; Mullender, 1993). Centralized high-value sensors should also be backed up by alternate (possibly more limited) sensors.

While the presence of multiple node-independent paths is often thought of in terms of resilience to possible node loss, such redundant paths also improve overall information flow. Having multiple information pathways reduces the impact of any one node failing to pass on information in a timely way. In hierarchies, such redundancy is often provided by "informal networks," which communicate information and requests for assistance horizontally (Warne *et al.*, 2005). This avoids the need for slow and possibly unreliable communication channels that go up several levels in the hierarchy, across, and down again. Having multiple node-independent paths thus contributes to self-synchronization, and experiments show that this effect is separate from the effect of average path length (Dekker, 2007a, 2011).

## CONCLUSION

This chapter has examined the connection between network theory and C2, particularly as it relates to self-synchronization (Alberts & Hayes, 2003; 2006). We have seen that, if an organization has been set up to solve problems falling *between* the extreme categories of "easy" and "fiendish" – problems such as the Assignment Problem (AP) – then centralized decision-making may be appropriate, at least if time pressure is not severe. A classic example is the 72-hour cycle in the US Air Force for producing detailed Air Tasking Orders (Alberts & Hayes, 2003, p. 47). In other situations, some degree of decentralization or mission command becomes appropriate. Taken to its logical conclusion, such decentralization leads to an "edge organization," in which entities coordinate their activities (to solve the overall organizational problem) through a process of self-synchronization.

"Edge organizations" operate on a metaphor of center/edge, rather than the hierarchically oriented metaphor of top/bottom, and rely on empowerment of individuals at the "cutting edge" to achieve their goals. In particular entities at the "cutting edge" are authorized to share information and to coordinate their activities through self-synchronization. Achieving these two goals requires a rich network structure, well beyond merely a hierarchical tree. The richness of the network can be measured by the *average degree*, which reflects the total number of links; the *average path length*, which measures the speed at which information can flow through the network (and hence the speed of self-synchronization and the overall responsiveness); and the *average node connectivity* (Dekker, 2007a), which measures the extent to which redundant paths exist (and hence the overall resilience). Redundant pathways also contribute to self-synchronization, independently from the effect of the average path length. In real life, "informal networks" are one way of providing redundant pathways (Warne *et al.*, 2005).

Two frequently studied network structures are Erdős–Rényi or random networks (Bollobás, 2001) and power-law or scale-free networks (Albert & Barabási, 2002; Barabási, 2002). Examples of both are given in Figure 5. Random networks have a low average path length: about $\log n / \log d$, where $n$ is the number of nodes and $d$ the average degree (Chung & Lu, 2003). They also have considerable similarity between the nodes, in terms of network linkages. Scale-free networks, in contrast, have a relatively small number of highly-connected "hub" nodes. In real life, these may be shared information-storage nodes, high-value shared sensors, or major C2 nodes. The scale-free structure achieves even faster information flow (and hence faster self-synchronization) than random networks with the same average degree, but at the cost of less robustness. In particular, the "hub" nodes are potentially vulnerable to enemy attack. More realistic C2 networks may combine elements of both these kinds of network, together with elements of a traditional tree structure.

Both simulation experiments and experiments with human beings support the connection between average path length and self-synchronization speed (although they differ on whether the relationship is linear or nonlinear). The Kuramoto-model and "flocking" experiments described here also support the relationship between average path length and self-synchronization speed. In addition, they highlight the fact that scale-free networks self-synchronize from the central core outwards, while random networks self-synchronize from multiple loose clusters of locally synchronized nodes (Dorogovtsev *et al.*, 2008). Networks without a clear central "core" may therefore suffer from a kind of "group-think," where locally synchronized clusters have difficulty aligning to an overall consensus. To avoid this, joint, combined, and coalition forces should make networking *between* components a higher priority than networking *within* components, or they should have other ways of achieving overall consensus.

In summary, network theory points out several different ways in which the topology of an organizational network can affect the ability of an organization to self-synchronize, and hence to engage in collaborative, decentralized solution of the problems which it was set up to address. The *average path length* and *average node connectivity* are two independent network measures relevant to self-synchronization. A low average path length, a high node connectivity, and good links between sub-networks all contribute to a network topology suitable for rapid self-synchronization.

## FUTURE RESEARCH DIRECTIONS

Although analysis and experimentation to date has confirmed the importance of the *average path length* and *average node connectivity*, the vulnerability of scale-free networks to targeted attack, and the importance of self-synchronization;

real-world experimentation is still required to confirm that these principles hold in actual military environments, in the midst of the fog and friction of genuine conflict. There will be a need for new and more detailed simulation experiments exploring the effect of network topology, but also for additional empirical studies of network effects in real operations, in the spirit of Jarvis (2005).

As mentioned above, it is important to further explore the relationship between network topology and information overload. This may result in identifying categories of network (such as, perhaps, networks of high degree) which exacerbate information overload.

It is also important to further explore new classes of network, beyond the well-studied random, scale-free, and small-world models. The "entangled networks" of Donetti *et al.* (2005) are one intriguing example which may repay further study. Further empirical analysis in real C2 networks, along the lines of Grant *et al.* (2011), is also essential.

Finally, although the potential benefits of self-synchronization are becoming clear, further work is required on identifying which organizational problems benefit best from such an approach, and which organizational problems are best suited to traditional C2 structures. The work by Kalloniatis *et al.* (2010) represents one step in this direction.

## REFERENCES

Albert, R., & Barabási, A.-L. (2002). Statistical mechanics of complex networks. *Reviews of Modern Physics*, *74*, 47–97. doi:10.1103/RevModPhys74.47

Alberts, D. S., & Hayes, R. E. (2003). *Power to the Edge*. Washington, DC: CCRP Press. Retrieved from www.dodccrp.org/files/Alberts_Power.pdf

Alberts, D. S., & Hayes, R. E. (2006). *Understanding Command and Control*. Washington, DC: CCRP Press. Retrieved from www.dodccrp.org/files/Alberts_UC2.pdf

Army, U. S. (2009). *Electronic Warfare in Operations: U. S. Army Field Manual FM 3-36*. Washington, DC: HQ, Department of the Army.

Barabási, A.-L. (2002). *Linked: The New Science of Networks*. Cambridge, MA: Perseus Publishing.

Barabási, A.-L., & Bonabeau, E. (2003). Scale-Free Networks. *Scientific American*, *288*, 50–59. doi:10.1038/scientificamerican0503-60 PMID:12701331

Biggs, N. (1993). *Algebraic Graph Theory* (2nd ed.). Cambridge, UK: Cambridge University Press.

Bollobás, B. (2001). *Random Graphs* (2nd ed.). Cambridge, UK: Cambridge University Press. doi:10.1017/CBO9780511814068

Brehmer, B. (2009). Command Without Commanders. In *Proceedings of the 14th International Command and Control Research and Technology Symposium (ICCRTS)*. Washington, DC: CCRP Press. Retrieved from www.dodccrp.org/events/14th_iccrts_2009/papers/041.pdf

Builder, C. H., Bankes, S. C., & Nordin, R. (1999). *Command Concepts: A Theory Derived from the Practice of Command and Control*. Santa Monica, CA: RAND.

Ceri, S., & Pelagatti, G. (1984). *Distributed Databases: Principles and Systems*. New York, NY: McGraw-Hill.

Chen, G., & Duan, Z. (2008). Network Synchronizability Analysis: A Graph-Theoretic Approach. *Chaos (Woodbury, N.Y.)*, *18*, 037102. doi:10.1063/1.2965530 PMID:19045476

Christofides, N. (1975). *Graph Theory: An Algorithmic Approach*. New York, NY: Academic Press.

Chung, F., & Lu, L. (2003). The Average Distance in a Random Graph with Given Expected Degrees. *Internet Mathematics, 1*(1), 91–113. doi:10.1080 /15427951.2004.10129081

Clancy, T. (1995). *Fighter Wing: A Guided Tour of an Air Force Combat Wing.* New York, NY: Berkley Books.

Conder, M., & Dobcsányi, P. (2002). Trivalent Symmetric Graphs up to 768 Vertices. *Journal of Combinatorial Mathematics and Combinatorial Computing, 40,* 41–63.

Cormen, T., Leiserson, C., & Rivest, R. (1990). *Introduction to Algorithms.* Cambridge, MA: MIT Press.

Dekker, A. H. (2003). Centralisation and Decentralisation in Network Centric Warfare. *Journal of Battlefield Technology, 6*(2), 23–28.

Dekker, A. H. (2004). Simulating Network Robustness: Two Perspectives on Reality. In *Proceedings of SimTecT 2004.* Simulation Industry Association of Australia.

Dekker, A. H. (2005). Simulating Network Robustness for Critical Infrastructure Networks. Proceedings of the 28th Australasian Computer Science Conference (ACSC), Newcastle, Australia, January. *Conferences in Research and Practice in Information Technology, 38,* 18–22.

Dekker, A. H. (2006). Centralisation vs Self-Synchronisation: An Agent-Based Investigation. In *Proceedings of the 11th International Command and Control Research and Technology Symposium (ICCRTS).* Washington, DC: CCRP Press. Retrieved from www.dodccrp.org/events/11th_IC-CRTS/html/papers/030.pdf

Dekker, A. H. (2007a). Studying Organisational Topology with Simple Computational Models. *Journal of Artificial Societies and Social Simulation, 10*(4).

Dekker, A. H. (2007b). Using Tree Rewiring to Study Edge Organisations for C2. In *Proceedings of SimTecT 2007.* Simulation Industry Association of Australia.

Dekker, A. H. (2010a). Average Distance as a Predictor of Synchronisability in Networks of Coupled Oscillators. In *Proceedings of the 33rd Australasian Computer Science Conference (ACSC).* Brisbane, Australia: ACSC.

Dekker, A. H. (2010b). Mimicking Human Problem-Solving with Agents: Exploring Model Calibration. In *Proceedings of SimTecT 2010.* Simulation Industry Association of Australia.

Dekker, A. H. (2011). Analyzing C2 Structures and Self-Synchronization with Simple Computational Models. In *Proc. 16th International Command and Control Research and Technology Symposium (ICCRTS).* Washington, DC: CCRP Press. Retrieved from www.dodccrp.org/events/16th_iccrts_2011/ papers/010.pdf

Dekker, A. H. (2012). Analyzing Team C2 Behaviour using Games and Agents. In *Proc. 17th International Command and Control Research and Technology Symposium (ICCRTS).* Washington, DC: CCRP Press. Retrieved from www.dodccrp. org/events/17th_iccrts_2012/post_conference/ papers/006.pdf

Dekker, A. H. (2013a). Epistemological Aspects of Simulation Models for Decision Support. *International Journal of Agent Technologies and Systems, 5*(2), 55–77. doi:10.4018/jats.2013040103

Dekker, A. H. (2013b). Self-Synchronisation in C2 Networks. In *Proc. 20th International Congress on Modelling and Simulation (MODSIM 2013).* Adelaide, Australia: MODSIM.

Dekker, A. H., & Colbert, B. (2004a). Network Robustness and Graph Topology. In *Proc. 27th Australasian Computer Science Conference (ACSC).* Dunedin, New Zealand: ACSC. Retrieved from crpit.com/confpapers/CRPITV26Dekker.pdf

Dekker, A. H., & Colbert, B. (2004b). Scale-Free Networks and Robustness of Critical Infrastructure Networks. In *Proc. 7th Asia-Pacific Conference on Complex Systems*. Cairns, Australia: Academic Press.

Donetti, L., Hurtado, P., & Muñoz, M. (2005). Entangled Networks, Synchronization, and Optimal Network Topology. *Physical Review Letters*, *95*, 188701. doi:10.1103/PhysRevLett.95.188701 PMID:16383953

Dorogovtsev, S. N., Goltsev, A. V., & Mendes, J. F. F. (2008). Critical phenomena in complex networks. *Reviews of Modern Physics*, *80*(4), 1275–1353. doi:10.1103/RevModPhys.80.1275

Gateau, J. B., Leweling, T. A., Looney, J. P., & Nissen, M. E. (2007). Hypothesis Testing of Edge Organizations: Modeling the C2 Organization Design Space. In *Proceedings of the 12th International Command and Control Research and Technology Symposium (ICCRTS)*. Washington, DC: CCRP Press. Retrieved from www.dodccrp.org/events/12th_ICCRTS/CD/html/papers/093.pdf

Gibbons, A. (1985). *Algorithmic Graph Theory*. Cambridge, UK: Cambridge University Press.

Grant, T. J., Buizer, B. C., & Bertelink, R. J. (2011). Vulnerability of C2 Networks to Attack: Measuring the topology of eleven Dutch Army C2 systems. In *Proc. 16th International Command and Control Research and Technology Symposium (ICCRTS)*. Washington, DC: CCRP Press. Retrieved from www.dodccrp.org/events/16th_iccrts_2011/papers/087.pdf

Jarvis, D. A. (2005). A Methodology for Analyzing Complex Military Command and Control (C2) Networks. In *Proc. 10th International Command and Control Research and Technology Symposium (ICCRTS)*. Washington, DC: CCRP Press. Retrieved from www.dodccrp.org/events/10th_ICCRTS/CD/papers/099.pdf

Johansson, F., & Falkman, G. (2009). An empirical investigation of the static weapon-target allocation problem. In *Proceedings of the 3rd Skövde Workshop on Information Fusion Topics* (pp. 63–67). Skövde, Sweden: University of Skövde.

Kalloniatis, A. (2008). A New Paradigm for Dynamical Modelling of Networked C2 Processes. In *Proc. 13th International Command and Control Research and Technology Symposium (ICCRTS)*. Washington, DC: CCRP Press. Retrieved from www.dodccrp.org/events/13th_iccrts_2008/CD/html/papers/180.pdf

Kalloniatis, A. (2010). From incoherence to synchronicity in the network Kuramoto model. *Physical Review E: Statistical, Nonlinear, and Soft Matter Physics*, *82*(6), 066202. doi:10.1103/PhysRevE.82.066202 PMID:21230718

Kalloniatis, A., Macleod, I., & Kohn, E. (2010). Agility in an Extended Space of Constructible Organisations. In *Proc. 15th International Command and Control Research and Technology Symposium (ICCRTS)*. Washington, DC: CCRP Press. Retrieved from www.dodccrp.org/events/15th_iccrts_2010/papers/069.pdf

Kearns, M., Suri, S., & Montfort, N. (2006). An Experimental Study of the Coloring Problem on Human Subject Networks. *Science*, *313*(11), 824–827. doi:10.1126/science.1127207 PMID:16902134

Kuramoto, Y. (1948). *Chemical Oscillations, Waves, and Turbulence*. Berlin, Germany: Springer.

Lee, S., & Lister, R. (2008). Experiments in the Dynamics of Phase Coupled Oscillators When Applied to Graph Colouring. In *Proceedings of the 31st Australasian Computer Science Conference (ACSC)*. Wollongong, Australia: ACSC.

Maindonald, J., & Braun, J. (2007). *Data Analysis and Graphics Using R: An Example-Based Approach* (2nd ed.). Cambridge, UK: Cambridge University Press.

Malcolm, W. P. (2004). *On The Character and Complexity of Certain Defensive Resource Allocation Problems*. Report DSTO-TR-1570. Edinburgh, Australia: DSTO.

Mintzberg, H. (1980). Structure in 5's: A Synthesis of the Research on Organization Design. *Management Science, 26*(3), 322–341. doi:10.1287/mnsc.26.3.322

Mullender, S. (1993). *Distributed Systems* (2nd ed.). New York, NY: ACM Press.

National Commission on Terrorist Attacks Upon the United States (NCTAUUS). (2004). *The 9/11 Commission Report*. US Government. Retrieved from govinfo.library.unt.edu/911/report

NATO. (2010). *NATO NEC C2 Maturity Model*. Washington, DC: CCRP Press. Retrieved from www.dodccrp.org/files/N2C2M2_Web_optimized.pdf

Orr, R. J., & Nissen, M. E. (2006). Hypothesis Testing of Edge Organizations: Simulating Performance under Industrial Era and 21$^{st}$ Century Conditions. In *Proceedings of the 11$^{th}$ International Command and Control Research and Technology Symposium (ICCRTS)*. Washington, DC: CCRP Press. Retrieved from www.dodccrp.org/events/11th_ICCRTS/html/papers/057.pdf

Reynolds, C. W. (1987). Flocks, Herds, and Schools: A Distributed Behavioral Model. *Computer Graphics, 21*(4), 25–34. doi:10.1145/37402.37406

Ruddy, M. (2007). ELICIT – The Experimental Laboratory for Investigating Collaboration, Information-sharing and Trust. In *Proceedings of the 12$^{th}$ International Command and Control Research and Technology Symposium (ICCRTS)*. Washington, DC: CCRP Press. Retrieved from www.dodccrp.org/events/12th_ICCRTS/CD/html/papers/155.pdf

Strogatz, S. (2000). From Kuramoto to Crawford: exploring the onset of synchronization in populations of coupled oscillators. *Physica D. Nonlinear Phenomena, 143*, 1–20. doi:10.1016/S0167-2789(00)00094-4

Strogatz, S. (2003). *Sync: The Emerging Science of Spontaneous Order*. New York, NY: Hyperion.

Thunholm, P., Ng, E.-C., Cheah, M., Tan, K.-Y., Chua, N., & Chua, C.-L. (2009). Exploring Alternative Edge versus Hierarchy C2 Organizations using the ELICIT Platform with Configurable Chat System. *International C2 Journal, 3*(2).

Van Creveld, M. (1985). *Command in War*. Cambridge, MA: Harvard University Press.

Warne, L., Bopping, D., Ali, I., Hart, D., & Pascoe, C. (2005). The Challenge of the Seamless Force: The Role of Informal Networks in Battlespace. In *Proceedings of the 10$^{th}$ International Command and Control Research and Technology Symposium (ICCRTS)*. Washington, DC: CCRP Press. Retrieved from www.dodccrp.org/events/10th_ICCRTS/CD/papers/215.pdf

Wasserman, S., & Faust, K. (1994). *Social network analysis: Methods and applications*. Cambridge, UK: Cambridge University Press. doi:10.1017/CBO9780511815478

Watts, D. J. (2003). *Six Degrees: The Science of a Connected Age*. London, UK: William Heinemann.

Watts, D. J., & Strogatz, S. H. (1998). Collective dynamics of 'small world' networks. *Nature*, *393*, 440–442. doi:10.1038/30918 PMID:9623998

## KEY TERMS AND DEFINITIONS

**Average Degree (of a Network):** The average of the *degrees* of the nodes. If there are a total of $N$ nodes and $M$ links in a network, the average degree of the network will be $2M/N$.

**Average Node Connectivity (of a Network):** The average, over all pairs of distinct nodes $X \neq Y$, of the number of distinct paths between $X$ and $Y$ (paths having no intermediate nodes in common). See *node connectivity*.

**Average Path Length (of a Network):** The average of the *path lengths* between all pairs of distinct nodes $X \neq Y$.

**Degree (of a Node in a Network):** The number of network links which connect to that node.

**Node Connectivity (of a Network):** The minimum, over all pairs of distinct nodes $X \neq Y$, of the number of distinct paths between $X$ and $Y$ (paths having no intermediate nodes in common). See *average node connectivity*.

**Path Length (Between Nodes X and Y in a Network):** The shortest number of network links that must be traversed to get from $X$ to $Y$. If $X = Y$, this is 0, otherwise it will be at least 1.

**Random Network:** A network in which every pair of nodes $X$ and $Y$ in a network has an equal probability of being directly connected by a link. In a random network, the node *degrees* follow a Poisson distribution. Such networks also have a low *average path length*.

**Scale-Free Network:** a network in which the node *degrees* follow (at least approximately) a power-law distribution, with the number of nodes with degree $d$ being proportional to $d^{-\gamma}$, for some constant $\gamma$. Such networks have a low *average path length*, and a small number of "hub" nodes of very high degree.

**Small-World Network:** a network created by starting with a regular grid (often a grid rich in triangles) and replacing (or "rewiring") some links by random links. Such networks have a low *average path length*, while retaining much of their original structure.

**Symmetric Network:** a network in which all the links are mathematically equivalent. A simple example is the network formed by the edges of a cube. In such a network, all the nodes have the same *degree*. In addition, the *node connectivity* will always be equal to this value, making symmetric networks quite robust.

## APPENDIX

## Questions

1. Referring to a textbook on algorithms, name some other "fiendish" (NP-hard or NP-complete) problems. Which of them are likely to arise in a military context?

2. Referring to the "C2 Cube" in Figure 4, what might an organization be like if its units have high levels of interaction and decision rights, but low levels of information?

3. Referring to the hierarchy on the left of Figure 6, assume that the central headquarters takes 40 hours to make a decision, and it takes each other unit 5 hours to process a decision from above and pass it on (in modified form) to subordinate units. How long does it take before every unit knows what to do? Referring to the network on the right of Figure 6, let the time taken to reach a decision by self-synchronization be $TL$, where $L$ is the average path length. For which values of $T$ is self-synchronization in this network faster than centralized decision-making in the hierarchy?

4. Draw the formal hierarchy of some organization of which you are part (perhaps a class group, a work group, or a social club). Add links corresponding to informal working relationships. Estimate the average path length $L$ (if informal working relationships form cross-links across the whole organization, use the random-network formula $L = \log n / \log d$, where $d$ is the average degree). Is the network capable of rapid self-synchronization? Are there any "clusters" which would slow down self-synchronization?

5. Consider the network you drew in Question 4. Are there any people the removal of whom disconnects the network into two (or more) parts?

# Chapter 10

# Complex Adaptive Information Networks for Defence:
## Networks for Self–Synchronization

**J. Moffat**
*Defence Science and Technology Laboratory, UK*

## ABSTRACT

*This chapter focuses on understanding the nature of the information networks that can create Self-Synchronization of the force. The analysis takes place at a number of levels, which for simplicity, are called Levels 1, 2, and 3. At Level 1 ("linked"), the author considers the basic node and linkage topology. At Level 2 ("synched"), he considers the local interaction between intelligent nodes, sharing the information and awareness required for Self-Synchronization in the cognitive domain. At Level 3 ("cliqued"), the author considers how such local networking feeds through into emergent clustering effects in the physical domain. Structured experimental games coupled with information entropy-based measures of merit illustrate these ideas, as do models of fundamental information networking dynamics and their resultant emergent behaviour. It turns out that the tools, models, and concepts of Complexity Theory give deep insight into the topic of Self-Synchronization.*

## INTRODUCTION

Modern military operations now cover a broad spectrum of missions that are beyond conventional warfare and span the range from peace-keeping and counter-terrorism to large-scale disaster response. Major coalition interventions resemble *complex endeavours* (Alberts & Hayes, 2007). They include military and non-military participants with multiple 'chains of command' and different objective functions, a lack of understanding of cause-effect relationships and unpredictability of effects. In such an uncertain environment, Network Enabled (or Network Centric) approaches are necessary in order to allow the necessary force adaptability and agility to emerge.

### Synchronization of the Force

A key aspect of the Network Centric value-chain consists of a force's ability to Self-Synchronize, that is, *the ability of a well-informed force to or-*

DOI: 10.4018/978-1-4666-6058-8.ch010

*ganize and synchronize complex warfare activities from the bottom up* (Cebrowski & Garstka, 1998). This definition comprises two aspects;

- Synchronization, as an output characteristic of the C2 processes that arrange and continually adapt the relationships of actions (including moving and tasking forces) in time and space in order to achieve the established objective(s). […] Synchronization takes place in the physical domain (Alberts, Garstka et. al., 2001).
- Self, as being a result generated by the system itself without the need for guidance from outside (Atkinson & Moffat, 2005).

Synchronization has been a fundamental concept in warfare throughout history, of course, but achieving it is becoming more challenging due to increased complexity, growing heterogeneity, and a faster pace of events (Alberts, Garstka et. al., 2001). Thus, we consider the dynamic aspect of Self-Synchronization a key one in the context of modern operations. We also consider that its application is beyond the physical domain of the battlespace and covers the cognitive and social domains of awareness, shared awareness, decision making and task sharing. The experience of a number of case studies (NATO, 2006; NATO, 2010) indicates that it can only be sustained where there is high trust and the group involved is 'hardened' – i.e. it has most likely trained together and each member understands the group as well as the task. Typical examples might be special force units or teams of medical experts.

## Aim of this Chapter

This Chapter focuses on understanding the nature of the information networks which can create and sustain Self-Synchronization of the force.

Our analysis takes place at a number of levels which for simplicity we call Levels 1, 2 and 3. At Level 1 we consider the basic node and link 'topol-ogy' of the information network. At Level 2 we consider the local interaction between 'intelligent' nodes, sharing the awareness required for decision making in the cognitive and social domains. At Level 3 we consider how these feed through into emergent effects in the physical domain.

## Chapter Structure

As a result, the Chapter structure follows the classification of networks at these three levels. At Levels 1 and 2 we begin by discussing the standard networks (Random, Small World and Scale Free) and then go into more detail on the node and link structure (the 'infostructure') of information networks which are required to underpin the possible range of approaches to military Command and Control (C2).

## Approaches to Command and Control

Consistent with the five levels of operational capability defined by the NATO Network Enabled Capability Feasibility Study (NC3A, 2005) a range of approaches to C2 have been developed by a diverse group of experts drawn from across the NATO nations and endorsed by NATO. These approaches extend from Conflicted C2 through De-conflicted C2 to Coordinated C2, Collaborative C2 and Edge C2 (NATO, 2010). To illustrate what they mean we can characterise them by three first order variables:

- The degree to which decision rights are allocated by entities to the collective.
- The patterns of information networking and interaction among entities.
- The degree to which information is distributed across these information networks.

The regions in the resultant three dimensional 'C2 approach space' within which these classes of C2 approach are located are shown in Figure

*Figure 1. C2 approaches and the C2 approach space (NATO, 2010)*

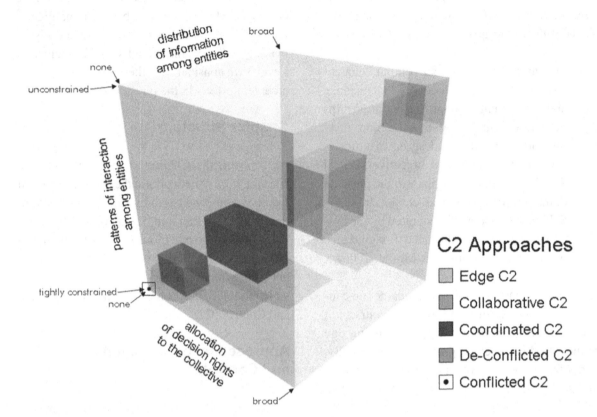

1. They lie sequentially along the diagonal vector of this space, with Conflicted C2 at the origin and Edge C2 in the upper right hand corner.

The axes are not independent of each other; as we move along this vector, the approach to C2 becomes more Network Enabled and the domain focus changes from *entity* based networking to *task* based networking. For example, as we move up the left hand side of Figure 1, the frequency of interactions among entities increases and thus their focus shifts from the information domain (from sparse to rich exchange of information) to the cognitive domain (toward higher degrees of situational awareness) and to the social domain (towards higher degrees of shared awareness and understanding and increased sharing of resources).

Later in the Chapter we will look in detail at the topology of the information sharing networks

generated by a counter-terrorism game for each of these C2 approaches. We will also develop entropy based metrics to describe their direct information interaction at Level 2.

Finally, we will analyse the Level 3 emergent behaviour of a locally networked and Self-Synchronizing force by describing in detail joint work carried out with Brunel University UK (Professor G Rodgers). Professor Rodgers was the joint originator of the 'Rodgers-D'Hulst' mechanism which describes the local clustering and reclustering of traders in making deals, leading to volatility in the stock price. This has been applied by others to the combining and splitting of Self-Synchronized locally networked terrorist and insurgent groupings (Bohorquez, Gourley et al., 2009). We are assuming that this local networking (e.g. by radio contact or messaging) induces a high level of shared awareness and correlated action across the collective and thus leads to Self-Synchronization of these cognitively aware actors (as opposed to the self-organization of inert objects).

## INFORMATION SHARING NETWORK STRUCTURE AT LEVEL 1

We can think of nodes or vertices as representing the individual entities of a system. They share information through links or edges. The set of these nodes or vertices and links or edges is referred to as a graph or network. From (Albert & Barabasi, 2002), it is clear that a key classification property of a network at this level is its distribution of degree; i.e. the distribution of the number of edges per node of the network, which is a measure of the relative *richness* of node connections. If $k_i$ is the degree of node $i$ of the network, then its richness is defined as

$$\frac{k_i}{\sum_{\text{all nodes } j} k_j}.$$

In addition it is possible to investigate the *average path length* (the mean number of edges in the shortest path between two randomly chosen nodes) and the *clustering coefficient* (a measure of how well linked the neighbours of a given node are). All of these are useful measures of network connectivity, and lead to a first level classification of networks into three main types; *random networks, small worlds, and scale free networks.* This classification of networks has only recently emerged from the academic research community.

*Node Fitness and Richness:* Other characteristics of networks which can be investigated at this level are the *growth* of new nodes over time, and how these new nodes connect to the existing network. For example, we can consider the *preference for attachment* of edges to nodes in terms of both node '*fitness*' (an attribute of nodes to be discussed later in relation to scale free networks) and node

'*richness*' (defined above as proportional to the number of edges already terminating at that node).

*Vulnerability:* We also wish to consider the *vulnerability of the network to node or link loss* (in terms of the possible breakup of the network into disconnected components which cannot 'communicate'). We will see that this can be radically different for various network topologies, and has important implications later in the Chapter.

*Loops in the Network:* Finally, it is of interest to consider the number of loops there are in the network, of a given length; a loop being a number of edges or links which start and finish at the same node. This is another good measure of network structure.

### Random Networks

The first category of network, and the earliest studied, consists of *random networks,* developed by Erdos and Renyi. A random network is built in the following way. Firstly a fixed set of $N$ nodes is given. Each pair of nodes is examined in turn, and a link is made between the two nodes with probability $p$. Thus in this case, the number of nodes remains constant, and the number of links is a random variable with mean value

$$\frac{N(N-1)p}{2}.$$

An example might be an array of cheap, simple sensors with an equally simple set of information sharing protocols. Due to the random and uncorrelated nature of link connection, the resultant distribution of degree is well approximated by a Poisson distribution (for large $N$ and small $p$), with a well defined mean value which then defines a scale for the network. Since this mean value defines a fixed scale, such networks can never be scale independent.

Research on random networks has focused on what happens to the connectedness, and other properties of the network, as we let the number of nodes $N \to \infty$. Among the questions studied by Erdos and Renyi are; is a typical random graph connected? Does it contain a triangle of linked nodes? This relates to the idea of the fraction of transitive triples used in sociological studies (Wasserman & Faust, 1994); a transitive triple is such a triangle. How does the average path length vary as the number of nodes $N$ increases?

The other key question in random graph theory is; how do the properties of a given network of $N$ nodes change as we vary the link probability $p$ from 0 (all nodes isolated) to 1 (all links in place)? The greatest discovery of Erdos and Renyi is that many properties of random graphs appear suddenly as $p$ is varied, as in a phase change or tipping point, rather than gradually. Thus for a given link probability $p$, either almost all random graphs have a certain property (such as connectedness) or almost no random graph has the property. There is no gradual transition. For many properties of random graphs, this means that there is a critical link probability determining this phase shift.

Ultimately, the reason for this is that such phase shift effects in random graphs are equivalent to the phenomenon of percolation in Complexity Theory, as discussed in (Moffat, 2003). If we define the neighbours of a node to be all the other nodes which are linked directly to it by a single link, then clearly, as the size of the graph (i.e. the total number of nodes $N$) goes to infinity, the number of neighbours can also go to infinity. Thus such phase change effects are equivalent to percolation in an infinite dimensional lattice. (In a finite dimensional lattice, each node only has a finite number of nearest neighbours).

In terms of the connectedness and average path length of random graphs, a key discriminant is the average degree per node, denoted $\langle k \rangle$. From the nature of random graphs we have that $\langle k \rangle = p(N-1)$ since there are $N$-$1$ other nodes each of which can be linked to our node with a probability $p$. For a fixed $N$, increasing the link probability $p$ increases the average degree per

node $\langle k \rangle$. How does this change the nature of the random graph? The key results are

- If $\langle k \rangle < 1$, a typical graph is composed of isolated trees (i.e. branching graphs with no loops).
- If $\langle k \rangle > 1$, a giant cluster of connected nodes appears (here is the phase change effect we discussed earlier in terms of percolation).
- If $\langle k \rangle > ln(N)$ almost every graph is totally connected (i.e. there are no isolated nodes).
- The average path length scales with the number of nodes as

$$l \propto \frac{\ln(N)}{\ln(\langle k \rangle)}.$$

If we consider a node $v$ of a graph, and its nearest neighbours, we can consider the *local clustering coefficient* of the graph at node $v$. Firstly we consider the set of nodes on the graph which are only one link away from $v$. This is the set of neighbours of $v$. The clustering coefficient for the node $v$ is the ratio of the actual number of links between these neighbours divided by the total number of possible links. Since a link between two neighbours of $v$, together with the links between the neighbour nodes and $v$ itself make a triangle, the local clustering coefficient is a measure of the number of triangular links between the node $v$ and its neighbouring nodes on the graph. The *clustering coefficient* $C$ across the entire graph or network is the mean of the local values across all nodes. For a random graph, the clustering coefficient for a node is just $p$, and hence the clustering coefficient of the graph is also $p$. We also know that $\langle k \rangle = p(N-1)$, thus we have that (for a random graph);

$$C = p = \frac{\langle k \rangle}{N-1}$$

## Small World Networks

A network is called a *small world* if the average path length is small, but the clustering coefficient $C$ is high. More formally (Watts, 1999), a network is a small world if the average path length $l$ is of the same order as the equivalent random graph (i.e. a random graph having the same number of nodes, and the same average degree per node) but where the clustering coefficient $C$ is much greater than for the equivalent random graph.

Real networks such as the World Wide Web and the Internet tend to have a small world character; i.e. a low value of the average path length but a much higher clustering coefficient than that associated with a random graph. This led Watts and Strogatz to propose a network model which achieves such characteristics by explicit construction.

Their model (Watts, 1999) has its roots in social systems in which most people have very local relationships (e.g. local friends), but also have a few friends who are a long distance away, in other countries for example. In a one parameter model of such a network, they start with an ordered lattice of $N$ nodes forming a ring. We assume that every node is linked to its first $K$ neighbours ($K/2$ on each side) and that $N$ is significantly bigger than $K$. In order to capture the idea of 'distant friends' we assume that each of the edges of this network is 'rewired' with a probability $p$ such that self connections and duplicate edges are excluded. This process introduces $pNK/2$ long range edges which connect nodes that otherwise would be part of different local communities.

By varying $p$, the network varies from complete order ($p=0$) with only local connections, to a fully random graph ($p=1$). For a fairly large span of values of $p$, the Watts-Strogatz model network shows the desired characteristics of low average path length $l$ and high clustering coefficient $C$ (Albert & Barabasi, 2002; Watts, 1999).

In developing a model which relates the average path length to the main driving parameters of the system ($p$, K, N), they use the approach of a *scale invariant metamodel*, as discussed in (Moffat, 2003). This leads to a relationship,

$$ l \propto \frac{N^{\frac{1}{d}}}{K} f(pKN) $$

where $f(x)$ is a normalised 'scaling' function.

This scale invariant metamodel has been confirmed by extensive computer simulations and renormalisation group techniques (Newman & Watts, 1999). Note the collapse of three variables $p, K, N$ into one composite variable $x$. This is a usual and welcome characteristic of this metamodel approach and its use of renormalisation group approaches.

The number of loops in the network is determined by the adjacency matrix; the matrix of 0s and 1s corresponding to which node is attached to which. It turns out that the *spectral density* (i.e. the distribution of eigenvalues for the adjacency matrix), is directly related to the loop structure of the network; its $k$th moment is precisely the number of paths with $k$ links returning back to the same node in the graph (i.e. the number of loops of length $k$). When the rewiring probability $p$ is low, the spectral density function of the Watts-Strogatz model has several spikes, reflecting the regular lattice-like nature of the network. As $p$ increases to 1, the spectrum smooths out and tends to the semicircular distribution characteristic of a random graph (Albert & Barabasi, 2002). Thus the loop structure tends towards that of a random network for high values of the rewiring probability $p$.

## Scale Free Networks

A network is said to be *scale free* if the distribution of degree follows a power law and the network exhibits properties of scale invariance. This means that a few nodes are hubs with many ingoing and outgoing links, while most nodes have much sparser connection to the rest of the network. In general, neither random graphs nor the Watts-Strogatz network models have this as a natural property. Since it is an emergent property of many real networks such as the World Wide Web and the Internet, research has focused on how such scale free networks evolve, while still retaining other characteristics such as being a small world. It turns out that the two key factors required to create a scale free network are *growth* and *preferential attachment*. These are described as follows.

*Growth:* At each timestep, a new node is added to the network. This node comes with a fixed number $m$ of new links which are attached to $m$ of the existing nodes.

*Preferential Attachment:* When choosing which node a new link should attach to, the probability of choice is proportional to the richness of each of the existing nodes.

Numerical simulation and theoretical modelling indicates that a network which has the growth and preferential attachment assumptions above, will evolve to have a scale free structure. Each of these two properties is required to achieve the scale free emergent topology of the network (Albert & Barabasi, 2002).

For this basic network evolution model, we find that $\gamma = 3$, where $\gamma$ is the exponent characterising the power law which describes the degree distribution. It also has low average path length, in the sense that the average path length $l$ is proportional to the logarithm of the number of nodes. It can further be shown that for such a scale free network, built using growth and preferential attachment, correlations $(k,l)$ develop spontaneously between connected pairs of nodes with degree values $k$ and $l$. It is possible to generalise the basic model in a number of ways. Thus far, research has focused on the question of whether such generalisations preserve or destroy the emergent property of a power law distribution of degree.

*Local Modification:* In the basic scale free network evolution model, there is only one driver of the topology of the system, namely that of preferential attachment. In real networks, there are also other 'local' changes which go on which modify the resultant degree distribution of the network. The two main ones studied in the literature thus far are *internal edges* and *rewiring*. Internal edges refers to the phenomenon of adding edges to the existing network over time, as well as adding new nodes (and hence new edges for these new nodes). With rewiring, we do not add an edge (either to a new node or between existing nodes). What we do is to take an existing edge and then reassign its ending node within the existing network.

*Explanation for preferential attachment assumption:* There have been a number of attempts in the literature to develop some deeper mechanism which has the effect of assuming preferential attachment. Of these, the simplest is to assume that at each timestep a new node is added to the network, and this node connects (by two new edges) to both node ends of a randomly chosen edge. Existing nodes with high richness of edges are more likely to be chosen and in fact this assumption is exactly equivalent to preferential attachment. It generates the same scale free topology as the basic Barabasi model, with an exponent of 3.

*Node Fitness and Richness:* When adding new edges to a network, or rewiring existing nodes, so far, the attractiveness of a node has been taken to be proportional to its 'richness' (i.e. the number of links between that node and the rest of the network). In addition to richness, we can also allocate a *fitness* to the node, which is an absolute measure of its attractiveness which does not change over time. (In contrast, the richness of a node will change as edges are added to or rewired away from a node). As a generalisation of the Barabasi evolution model, we can thus consider the following.

Each node $i$ of the existing network has a fitness value $\eta_i$ chosen from some distribution $\rho(\eta)$. At each timestep a new node is added to the network. Each new node connects to $m$ existing nodes, and the probability of connecting to node $i$ is linearly proportional to the product of the fitness and richness of that node. In general this gives rise to a degree distribution which is a weighted sum of different power laws.

## Relation to Bose-Einstein Statistics

There is a direct connection between evolving networks of the Barabasi type and the characteristics of a Bose gas, as described by Bose-Einstein statistics. This is not surprising, as the following explanation shows. Consider the set of nodes of the existing network as a set of urns, with the number of balls in each urn corresponding to the degree of the node. A new node is generated. The making of an edge between the new node and one of the existing nodes corresponds to increasing the degree of the existing node by one. We model this by throwing a ball into that urn. In wiring up the edges from the new node to the set of existing nodes, we are thus throwing balls into a set of urns, with the chance of throwing into a particular urn being proportional to the number of balls already in that urn (assuming preferential attachment applies so that the attraction of a node is in proportion to the number of edges that node already possesses).

It can be shown that if we proceed in this way, the frequency distribution of balls across the urns follows a Bose-Einstein distribution. The Bose-Einstein distribution explicitly allows for the possibility of most urns being nearly empty, and one urn containing most or all of the balls. This is termed a Bose-Einstein 'condensation', in which most elements of the system revert to a state of very low energy. For a network, this implies that one node has almost all the edges, and all the other nodes only have one (leading to a star network topology). In this case one node sits at the centre and all other nodes simply link to it. This is termed a 'winner takes all' result. In recent academic research work on network dynamics, the idea of considering Bose-Einstein statistics has been extended to include both the richness and fitness of a node.

## Network Vulnerability

From the way that random networks are constructed, it is clear that the removal of any node at random will have about the same effect as the removal of any other node, since all nodes have the same expected connectivity (i.e. degree value). Thinking of a large random network in terms of a percolation problem in Complexity Theory, as discussed earlier, we can also see that if we now define $p$ to be (equivalently) either the probability of removing a node at random, applied to each node, or the proportion of nodes randomly removed from the network, then there is a critical value of $p$, denoted $p_c(N)$, (a function of the network size $N$ in general) such that if $p < p_c(N)$ then the network is connected. However, if $p > p_c(N)$ then the network is disconnected. Disruption of a random network is thus due to an effect which can target equally every node of the network. By contrast, if we have a scale free network, then this topology is more robust than a random network to random node removal since most nodes only have a few links. A scale free network will still be connected at a higher proportion of nodes removed than the equivalent random network. However, if the richest nodes (i.e. those having the highest degree and hence highest connectivity to the rest of the network) are preferentially taken out, then a scale free network will disconnect faster than the equivalent random network. Disruption of a scale free network is thus most likely to be due to effects which preferentially target the richest nodes.

## Cascading Failures

We can consider, in addition to this static consideration of the disconnection of the network, the case in which removal of a node places additional strain on other nodes (due to load shedding in an electrical supply network, or information shedding in an information network for example). This has been analysed by Watts for example, in an analogy to the 'sandpile model' of self-organised criticality in Complexity Theory (discussed in Moffat, 2003) using the following network model. We assume that each node is a simple cellular automaton with only two states, either on or off, and that this state is determined by the states of neighbour nodes in the network. For example, the node is only on if a threshold fraction of neighbouring nodes are on. In this model, the probability that a perturbation in an initially 'all off' state can spread to the entire network can be connected to the existence of a 'giant cluster' of vulnerable nodes. (Watts, 2000) has shown that generalised random networks with a power law degree distribution are less vulnerable than normal random networks to such a perturbation.

From this review it is clear that complex networks lie within the more general realm of complex systems with many similar characteristics including:

- *Percolation effects* and phase change in network characteristics;
- *Scale invariant metamodels* for the emergent behaviour of networks;
- *The use of cellular automata techniques* to consider the clusters and cascades which occur in complex networks where the attributes of node states are defined in terms of the attributes of neighbouring node states.

In consequence, the tools, approaches and concepts of Complexity Theory can be applied to understanding the structure and evolution of such complex networks.

## SELF-SYNCHRONIZATION IN THE COGNITIVE DOMAIN AT LEVEL 2

In order to understand what 'Self-Synchronization in the Cognitive Domain' means we first had to define it and then explore its dynamics through a programme of experimentation. The basic idea was first defined in (Manso & Manso, 2010) and exploits the previous development of entropy based metrics in (Moffat 2003). The corresponding metric variables are called *Cognitive Self-Synchronization* (CSSync), and *Cognitive Entropy* (CE). The programme of experimentation used the ELICIT structure which we now discuss a little further.

## The ELICIT Model

ELICIT (Experimental Laboratory for Investigating Collaboration, Information-sharing, and Trust) is a game based model developed by the US DoD which allows real players to interact and share information in order to achieve a task related to counter-terrorism. The aim is to compare the performance of different ways of sharing information (e.g. using a hierarchical network as opposed to a more richly linked network). In each case the agents/actors receive information facts that have been separated into four categories; the *who*, *what*, *where* and *when* of a possible terrorist related attack. The information is represented by individual 'factoids' which can be shared with other players, or posted or pulled from Websites. The goal of the players is to build awareness of each of the knowledge categories in order to prevent the occurrence of the terrorist incident. Receiving, sharing, posting and pulling information is constrained by the underlying network topology (Ruddy, 2007; Ruddy & Nissen, 2008).

## Experimental Results

In our case, the experiments were carried out using teams of cadets from the Portuguese Military Academy in Lisbon. The experimental structure consisted of playing each of the five C2 approaches of Figure 1 several times (either 3 or 4 games for each C2 approach) and assessing whether the game outcomes were consistent with the NATO NEC C2 Maturity Model hypotheses. 18 games were played in total. The detailed work and results of these experiments are presented in (Manso & Manso, 2010) and (Manso & Moffat, 2011) and an overview of the instantiation of each C2 approach is described here. The assessment was based on measurement of variables defined in the NATO NEC C2 Maturity Model (NATO, 2010) and the NATO C2 Reference Model (NATO, 2006).

## Cognitive Entropy

In thermodynamics, entropy is defined through considering the phase space of a dynamical system. Each point of this phase space represents a description of the system in terms of the location and momentum of each of its constituent particles at a given time. As time passes the system then traces out a curve in phase space with different curves corresponding to different initial conditions. The emergent behaviour of this classical system gives rise to regions of phase space, each corresponding to similar macro- level behaviour. The number and variation in size of these regions reflects the overall complexity of the system. This process is known as 'coarse graining' of the phase space since it carves the phase space into separate chunks. The entropy of such a coarse grained region is essentially given by a count of all of the different micro-configurations constituting that region; i.e. it is a measure of the volume V of that region in phrase space. Boltzmann's formula for entropy is thus given by *k logV* where *k* is Boltzmann's constant (see for example Penrose, 2010) with the logarithm ensuring that entropy is additive in nature. A system starting in a low entropy state will tend to wander into larger coarse grained volumes of phase space. That is why thermodynamic entropy tends to increase over time.

For information networks we also consider system complexity. However, information rather than time is now the key variable and we consider not the complexity of phase space but instead the *Kolmogorov Complexity* since this is an informa-

tion based measure of 'descriptive complexity' (Cover & Thomas, 1991).

Given a dataset $D$, we have a likelihood or probability of D denoted $p(D)$, and then $-\log p(D)$ is the expected description length of dataset D. We have: $-\log p(D)$ = expected description length of dataset $D$ = Kolmogorov Complexity of D.

More generally, we have that

$$-\sum_{i=1}^{N} p(D_i) \log p(D_i)$$

is the expected description length across a sequence of datasets, and it is equal to the composite information entropy for these datasets. From this equation we can see that:

a.  If $p(D_j) = 1$ for some dataset, and is zero on the others, then information entropy has a minimum value of 0, and the expected description length is also zero. Knowledge in this case is a maximum, corresponding to the most succinct description, and corresponding to Gell-Mann's idea of repeated patterns in the data leading to the ability to succinctly describe the data (Gell-Mann, 2002).

b.  If, on the other hand

$$P(D_i) = \frac{1}{N} \quad (1 \leq i \leq N)$$

then the expected description length is

$$-\sum_{i=1}^{N} \frac{1}{N} \log \frac{1}{N} = \log N.$$

Thus the information entropy has a maximum value as does the expected description length and knowledge is a minimum, corresponding to Gell-Mann's idea of a very lengthy description with no pattern.

We wish to measure the descriptive complexity of the awareness of a group of individuals – that is, the result of their cognitive process – over time. The formulation will be presented based on our ELICIT experimental results. We thus apply the Kolmogorov Complexity formulation to ELICIT as the game unfolds over time $t$, in the cognitive domain.

For our experiments each ELICIT game was played by teams of 17 military cadets (that is, N=17) and we define four 'solution spaces' corresponding to the four parts of the overall solution (who, what, where and when). When, in particular, is further decomposed into when-hour, when-day and when-month.

For a given solution space, each player at time $t$ will have a description of the solution at time $t$ (including the null case where no solution is given) – we call this an ID in ELICIT. For each solution space, there are $K$ possible choices, and a particular choice is represented by $k \, (1 \leq k \leq K)$.

For example the 'who' choices would correspond to $K$ different possible terrorist organizations. For each solution space $i$ at time $t$, we thus define

$S(i,t,k) =$ Number of IDs for solution space $i$ at time $t$ of type $k$.

For example, if we consider the 'who' solution space, and there are $M$ identical IDs by various players for a 'who' of type $k$, then $S(i,t,k) = M$. The probability of this description is defined as

$$p(i,t,k) = \frac{S(i,t,k)}{17}$$

where the number of players is 17. Note that $-\log p(i,t,k)$, (the expected description length) in this case will be small and positive where there are several coincident IDs, falling to zero if all 17 players give the same ID.

The total number of positive IDs is given by

$$\sum_{k=1,S(i,t,k)\neq0}^{k=K} S(i,t,k)$$

The number of players who do not make a positive ID for solution space $i$ is then given by

$$17 - \sum_{k=1,S(i,t,k)\neq0}^{k=K} S(i,t,k).$$

This equation also provides an indication of the level of uncertainty of a group towards any possible ID, assuming that uncertainty is related to unwillingness to make a positive ID.

For the null case (no ID given) we define the probability of this description as

$$p(i,t,k = \varnothing) = \frac{1}{17}$$

where $\varnothing$ denotes the null set. In this case the expected description length of each null ID is

$$-\log(\frac{1}{17}) = \log 17$$

and is thus as large and positive as it can be. Thus if many players do not supply an ID (an event which requires a long description length to lay out), then we assume the cognitive entropy has increased significantly. For example, at the beginning of the game, when there are no positive IDs, there are 17 such null IDs, each with a description length of log(17).

We now define the cognitive entropy CE for solution space $i$ at time $t$ as

$$CE(i,t) = -\left\{ \left\{ 17 - \sum_{k=1,S(i,t,k)\neq0}^{k=K} S(i,t,k) \right\} \frac{1}{17} \log \frac{1}{17} + \sum_{k=1,S(i,t,k)\neq0}^{k=K} p(i,t,k) \log p(i,t,k) \right\}$$

This expression goes beyond simple variability measures by representing the expected description length (or cognitive entropy) for our solution space corresponding to each of the possible values of $p(i,t,k)$ including all of the null IDs (each taken separately in the summation). In addition, it also provides an indication of the level of uncertainty of the group towards any possible ID since it refers to the number of individuals that did not provide a positive ID.

## Cognitive Self-Synchronization

Cognitive Self-Synchronization (CSSync) measures the amount of coherence across a group at a particular time $t$ in terms of determining the knowledge problem (finding the *who*, *what*, *where* and *when* of a potential terrorist attack before it happens). Note that our emphasis here is on the synchronization of the positive IDs made by the subjects. Treating these subject identifications as a measure of uncertainty, the function we use to represent CSSync, based on Cognitive Entropy and Kolmogorov Complexity, is the following:

$$CSSync_{\mathrm{Pr}\,oblemSpace}(i,t) = 1 - \frac{CE(i,t)}{Max\_Disorder_{\mathrm{Pr}\,oblemSpace}}.$$

CSSync is measured for each identification input field $i$ (i.e. each *ProblemSpace i*). Note that $Max\_Disorder_{ProblemSpace}$ refers to the maximum entropy value (described before) and is used to normalize CSSync to a value between 0 and +1. The values at the boundaries may be interpreted as follows:

- CSSync=0 means the system is fully disordered.
- CSSync=1 means the system is fully synchronized.

We assume that any group of players operating in ELICIT has an initial state of maximum disorder (maximum entropy), that is:

$$Max\_Disorder_{ProblemSpace} = -\sum_{i=1}^{N} \frac{1}{N} \log \frac{1}{N} = \log N$$

In our case (N=17),

$$Max\_Disorder_{\mathrm{Pr}\,oblemSpace} = \log 17$$

Thus

$$CSSynch_{\mathrm{Pr}\,oblemSpace}(i,t) = 1 - \frac{CE(i,t)}{\log 17}$$

The measure for the overall CSSync(t) at time $t$ is simplified to be the equally weighted sum of the partial CSSync values, that is:

$$CSSync(t) = 0.25 * \sum_{i=ProblemSpace} CSSync(i,t)$$

We are essentially assuming that the four solution spaces are independent so that we can add the entropies from each of them to give an overall entropy for the state of the game at time $t$. Formally this is not strictly true since the solution spaces are linked, but the sum of the entropies is always an upper bound and the sum usually works well in practice as a measure of merit.

As the game progresses, individuals share information and collaborate and, as a result, subjects develop awareness and make identification attempts, some of which are equivalent. In such a scenario, the cognitive entropy decreases (equivalently, the cognitive synchronization increases) and the group is said to be *converging* to a common understanding of the problem. Ultimately, if all 17 subjects provide the same identification for all of the problem spaces, we may conclude that the system was able to converge and fully Self-Synchronize at some time $t$ (assuming no external influence is exerted, as is the case in ELICIT). In such a scenario we have a description length of zero for all problem spaces, with $CE(i,t) = 0$ for all $i$. and $CSSync(t) = 1$.

We now bring together the ideas of varying C2 approaches, experimentation based on these approaches using ELICIT gaming, and the evaluation of game outcomes using Cognitive Entropy and Cognitive Self-Synchronization.

*Figure 2. C2 approaches as ELICIT information network topologies*

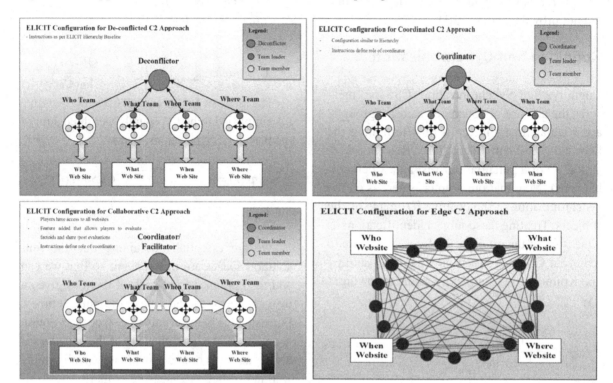

The network topology for the four non-trivial C2 approaches is shown in Figure 2. The Conflicted C2 case (not shown) assumes no interconnection between the four isolated teams. Small light circular nodes are team members, small dark circular nodes are team leaders (where present) and large circular dark nodes are coordinators across teams (where present). As we progress to higher levels of C2 approach, the coordinator's role becomes more dynamic and proactive. Rectangles represent Websites potentially accessible by team members to post or pull information, with networked cross-coupling between these Websites increasing at higher C2 approaches.

*Problem Difficulty*: a more difficult problem should generate more Cognitive Entropy than an easier one. The difficulty of the ELICIT problem set was analysed in (Alston, 2010) and was characterized as tame (an unambiguous solution may be found) and simple (all information is available and is unambiguous). Nevertheless, the way the information is distributed, the dynamics generated by subjects and the amount of information actually accessible (usually below 80%) results in a difficult problem to solve from the subjects' perspective. Future work should take this concept of problem difficulty further in terms of its likely effect on CE and CSSync.

For the work discussed here, we focus on the available experimentation data which resulted from positioning a system at a specific C2 approach and then measuring its effects in terms of CE and CSSync. Additionally, we will present results for the 'energy' or effort required to sustain a given level of C2 approach during the game.

## Measurements of Cognitive Self-Synchronization

A key result of the analysis is that Cognitive Self-Synchronization increases monotonically with higher C2 approaches. The CSSync average values

*Figure 3. Average values of Cognitive Self-Synchronization for each of the C2 approach network topologies*

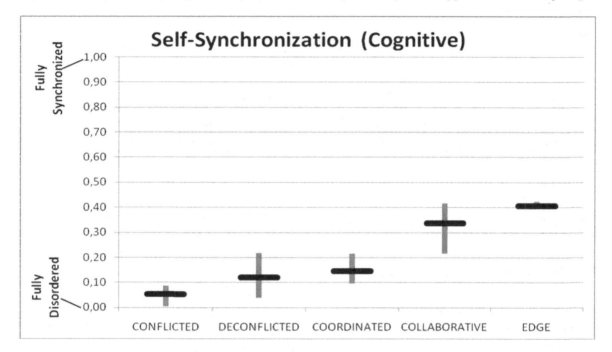

per C2 approach, including their maximum and minimum values, are shown in Figure 3.

We can conclude the following:

- On average, the CSSync increases as the C2 approach increases in level. Edge C2 and Conflicted C2 have respectively the highest and the lowest value for CSSync.
- Edge C2 has the lowest variability between Min and Max (0.02), therefore giving the most consistent results across games.

Based on the data collected, it seems that a direct relation exists between the C2 approach adopted and the resultant Self-Synchronization achieved in the cognitive domain (CSSync). From the data we have available, we may interpret this as a result of moving up in terms of the C2 approach. A collective thus progressively removes constraints that inhibit information sharing, interaction, allocation of decision rights and the development of shared awareness and, at the same time, sets enablers that influence an increase in their members' proactiveness.

This in turns contributes to more information sharing, better levels of shared awareness and increased CSSync. This is confirmed when increasing the C2 approach from Conflicted C2 through the other C2 approaches to Edge C2. The latter case is of particular interest

Collaborative C2 and Edge C2 are equivalent in terms of 'Network access' (i.e., access to other subjects and Websites) and the change in outcome is due to changing the organizational structure from a well-defined organization to an organization without pre-defined roles and with fully distributed decision rights ('power to the edge'). Both organizations succeeded in making most information accessible to all members. Yet, for the Edge organization, subjects displayed a significant increase in activity during the game (see 'effort spent' below) and were able to reach the best scores for CSSync.

Within the constraints of the ELICIT experiments (which are limited to information sharing,

*Table 1. Enablers and inhibitors for each C2 approach affecting CSSync within the constraints of the ELICIT experiments*

| CSSync Category | CSSync Inhibitors | CSSync Enablers |
|---|---|---|
| Shared Information Resources | None or a few shared (mainly kept within own entities) | Shared across members. All information accessible across entities. |
| Patterns of Networked Interaction | Non-existent or highly constrained | Unconstrained / broad and rich across entities and subjects |
| Allocation of Decision Rights | None / fixed task-role based | Distributed (to all subjects) |

awareness and problem solving), the enablers and inhibitors for each C2 approach affecting CSSync are presented in Table 1.

## The Cost of Self-Synchronization

Finally we consider the associated cost to Self-Synchronize. In determining CSSync, the matter of how much it 'costs' is also a relevant one. In ELICIT, we will account as a cost the amount of activity (i.e., energy) that a given organization expends during a run. Activity in ELICIT is measured when any of the following actions occurs:

- A factoid is shared by a player with another player.
- A factoid is posted by a player to a Website.
- A player performs a pull from a Website.
- A player performs an identification (an ID).

Each transaction corresponding to any of the above mentioned activities will be measured as having a unitary activity or energy cost of +1. Effort is expressed per hour to normalize the values across the different ELICIT games. The total resulting activity cost (per hour) measured per C2 approach is presented in Figure 4.

The various bands of shading in Figure 4 show the main contributors to the total effort in each case. At higher C2 approach levels, the increasing number of pulls from Websites is the dominant feature. Maintaining the Edge C2 approach dur-

ing the game required the greatest expenditure of effort, followed by Collaborative C2. High Cognitive Self-Synchronization thus requires significant activity to sustain it.

This correlation is confirmed by a linear regression across the 18 game outcomes from which it is clear that a direct and proportional relation exists between effort spent and CSSync. It would be worth exploring in future work higher values for CSSync and their implications in terms of effort and C2 approach adopted.

Overall, the results indicate that the ability to Self-Synchronize in the cognitive domain (as measured by an information entropy based measure of merit) shows a steady improvement with the C2 approach adopted in the game. This improvement in cognitive Self-Synchronization with C2 approach is also directly related to the level of activity (the energy or activity 'cost') required to sustain that C2 approach.

## SELF-SYNCHRONIZATION IN THE PHYSICAL DOMAIN AT LEVEL 3

The phenomenon of self-organised 'herding' in financial markets and its impact on the volatility of stock prices led to the *Rodgers-D'Hulst mechanism* of coalescence and fragmentation and its analysis as an underlying explanation of the herding phenomenon (D'Hulst & Rodgers, 2000). When used by (Bohorquez, Gourley et al., 2009),

*Figure 4. Effort expended per C2 approach*

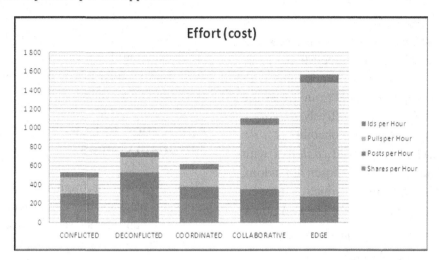

this coalescence and fragmentation mechanism is applied to the dynamically adapting 'attack strength' of a terrorist or insurgent group.

Following the same line of thought as (Bohorquez, Gourley et al., 2009) we define the attack strength $s_i$ of a given terrorist or insurgent attack unit $i$ as the *minimum* number of people typically injured or killed as the result of an event involving attack unit $i$. In other words, a typical event (an attack or a 'clash') involving group $i$ will lead to the death or injury of *at least* $s_i$ people, and hence a *severity* of at least $s_i$. The sum of the attack strengths over all of the attack units is assumed to be a constant $N$, thus

$$\sum_i s_i = N$$

The question then is how this total distribution of attack strengths is partitioned. At one extreme there could be a very large number of attack units ($N$) each with an attack strength of 1. At the other extreme there could be one completely coalesced attack unit with attack strength $N$. In general, the real distribution will lie between these. The Rodgers-D'Hulst coalescence and fragmentation mechanism assumes that these attack strengths adapt in the following way (Johnson, Spagat et al., 2005).

## Clustering and Fragmentation

Consider an arbitrary attack unit $i$ with attack strength $s_i$. At any one instant in time, labelled $t$, we assume that this attack unit may either;

1. Fragment (i.e. break up) into $s_i$ attack units of attack strength equal to 1. This feature aims to mimic a terrorist or insurgent group which decides, as a group, to split itself up in order to mislead or confuse the enemy through pursuing a number of distributed attacks at the same time.

2. Coalesce (i.e. combine) with another attack unit $j$ of attack strength $s_j$, hence forming a single attack unit of attack strength $s_i + s_j$. This feature mimics two insurgent groups deciding via radio communication or locally networked messaging to meet up and join forces in order to carry out a larger scale attack.

To implement this fragmentation/coalescence process at a given timestep, we choose an attack unit $i$ at random but with a probability which is proportional to its attack strength $s_i$. With a probability $\nu$, this attack unit $i$ with attack strength $s_i$ fragments into $s_i$ attack units with attack strength 1. A justification for choosing attack unit $i$ with a probability which is proportional to its attack strength is as follows. Attack units with higher attack strength will either run across the enemy more and/or be more actively sought by the enemy. By contrast, with a probability $(1 - \nu)$ the chosen attack unit $i$ instead *coalesces* with another attack unit $j$ which is chosen at random, but again with a probability which is proportional to its attack strength $s_j$. The two attack units of attack strengths $s_i$ and $s_j$ then combine to form an attack unit of attack strength $s_i + s_j$. The justification for choosing attack unit $j$ for coalescence with a probability which is proportional to its attack strength, is as follows. It is presumably risky to combine attack units, since it must involve significant message passing between the two units in order to coordinate their actions; as we discussed earlier in terms of the characteristics of Coordinated C2. Hence it becomes increasingly less worthwhile to combine attack units as the attack units get smaller.

It turns out that infrequent fragmentation (a low value of $\nu$) is sufficient to yield a steady state process in which the number of attack units with attack strength $s$, plotted against the value $s$ gives a power-law distribution with exponent $\alpha = 2.5$. If we assume that any particular attack unit could be involved in an event in a given time interval, with a probability $p$ which is independent of its attack strength (Johnson, Spagat et al, 2005), then we have, given our definition of attack strength;

$$P(attack\ of\ severity \geq x) = P(attack)$$
$$P(attack\ strength\ x)$$
$$\propto px^{-2.5}$$

This definition of attack severity, as greater than a given level of effect, reflects the uncer-tainty of outcome of any given incident. (Johnson, Spagat et al, 2005) also indicate that this exponent value is an attractor over time in the sense that the distribution of terrorist attack severity, defined as above, converges to a power law with exponent $\alpha = 2.5$.

## Application to ELICIT Counter-Terrorism Games

These processes of fragmentation and coales-cence are mechanisms whereby insurgent units can adapt their interactions over time in response to the variety of attack tasks which they wish to carry out. In joint work with Brunel University, a summary of which appears in (Wyld & Rodg-ers, 2007) we have taken these ideas further by applying them to the type of information defined tasks carried out in the counter-terrorism ELICIT games described earlier.

We thus wish to analyse the ability to reconfig-ure information sharing between units in an agile way in order to complete these counter-terrorism tasks. Temporary clusters of tasked units form and dissipate over time as these links are made and broken, forming an Edge organization sustained by Edge C2. Our earlier analysis indicates that such Edge organizations have the highest levels of Cognitive Self-Synchronization but also require the highest levels of effort to sustain them over time. To capture the fundamental dynamics we developed a simple model of the process as follows.

We define a task vector as

- A complete set of information categories $m$;
- That subset $s$ required to complete a par-ticular knowledge based task.

For example, the who, what, where and when of a potential terrorist attack is a task vector which has to be completed to perform a knowledge based task in ELICIT. More generally, given two actors who have different tasks, and hence different task vectors to be completed, we assume that if they have more similar tasks, they are more likely to form an informal link and share information. This may come about by the use of 'tags', which are social cues attached to individual actors and observable by others (Hales & Edmonds, 2005). To reflect this, we define the *link strength* between the two actors as proportional to the inner product of their task vectors.

We define the following adaptive mechanism for this knowledge network. We start with a set of isolated actors, each of which has a task vector, with $m$ entries, $s$ of which are non-zero, and the rest zero, corresponding to the information requirements for each actor's specific task. We can thus define a maximum of $\binom{m}{s}$ different types of task corresponding to where we place the zero and non-zero information categories. In our modeling of the adaptation process for this network, we assume that at the start, the task vectors are allocated randomly to the actors.

We assume that these actors must share information in order to perform their tasks, and they do this by forming links with other actors. However, as discussed in (Perry & Moffat, 2004), excessively broad sharing can be counterproductive. We thus assume that information tends to be shared with actors with similar tasks (and hence similar task vectors). It follows that informal links to allow this information sharing should occur preferably between such actors. As these links accumulate across the network, they will form *clusters*. A cluster is a set of actors who are connected by unbroken paths of one or more links and can thus share information across the whole cluster. This is similar in approach to the clustering examined in (Perry & Moffat, 2004).

At each timestep, our model chooses whether to create a new informal link which we term 'exploration', or to destroy a cluster of existing information links ('dissipation'). The precise pro-

cess in the model is based on the Rodgers-D'Hulst mechanism described earlier, and works as follows.

With probability $p$, the model chooses to attempt to create a new informal link. In this case, two actors are chosen at random, and their link strength $f$ (i.e. the inner product of their task vectors) is calculated. This link strength is proportional to the similarity of the tasks of the two actors and takes a value between 0 and 1 when suitably normalized. It is then used as the probability that an informal link is formed between the actors. Alternatively, with probability $(1-p)$, the model chooses to attempt to dissipate an existing cluster of links, and we consider two models of this process.

## Model 0

In our first model of the dissipation process ('Model 0') we assume that a link is chosen at random. This link will have a link strength, denoted $f$. With probability $(1-f)$ all links in the cluster containing this link are destroyed.

## Model 1

In our second model of the dissipation process ('Model 1') a link is chosen with probability proportional to $(1-f)$ where $f$ is the link strength of the chosen link (thus weak links are preferentially chosen). With probability $(1-f)$ all links in the cluster containing this link are then destroyed.

These models of dissipation follow the simple non-causal approach of (Moffat, 2003) in order to minimise the number of additional contextual assumptions made.

## Theoretical and Experimental Results for Model 0

We first considered the case of a network model where every data vector has length 6, and three

*Figure 5. Proportion of the link strengths $\frac{1}{3}$, $\frac{2}{3}$ and 1 (middle, top and bottom respectively on the vertical axis) plotted against the cluster size considered (horizontal axis)*

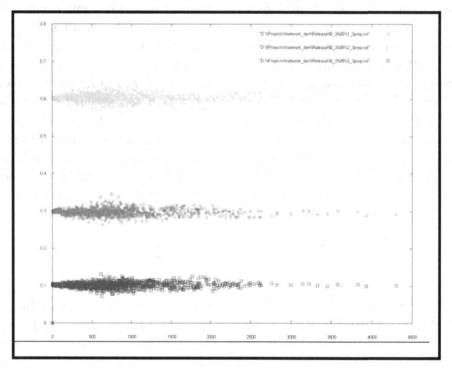

of the entries have to be filled to complete a task (thus $m = 6$, $s = 3$). In this case the link strengths (the inner product of different task vectors) can only take the values

$$\frac{1}{3}, \frac{2}{3} \text{ and } 1.$$

There are just these three options for the strength of possible links between different actors. The proportions of these link strengths in the model as the cluster size varies is shown in Figure 5. There is no change as we increase the size of the clusters considered. Other plots varying the model assumptions show similar results.

In the case we have considered here, the three possible link strengths,

$$\frac{1}{3}, \frac{2}{3} \text{ and } 1$$

have the proportions 0.3. 0.6 and 0.1 respectively in a given cluster of actors, as shown in Figure 5. If we increase the number of possible tasks, we will have a larger number of possible link strengths, and we can look at this more refined distribution. We thus analysed a much larger task vector of length 32, and with 16 entries required for task completion (i.e. $m = 32$, $s = 16$) in order to allow a more general distribution of link strengths. It turns out that the model results are very close to the theoretical prediction, Similar results are also achieved for Model 1.

If we now consider the distribution of cluster sizes across the network, we wish to test the key theoretical prediction that this should approximate to a power-law distribution with an exponent of 2.5 (as expected from the Rodgers-D'Hulst mechanism). Figure 6 shows the distribution of cluster sizes for an informal network with task

*Figure 6. Log-log plot of cluster size distribution as the size of the network increases. The straight line is the corresponding power-law with exponent 2.5*

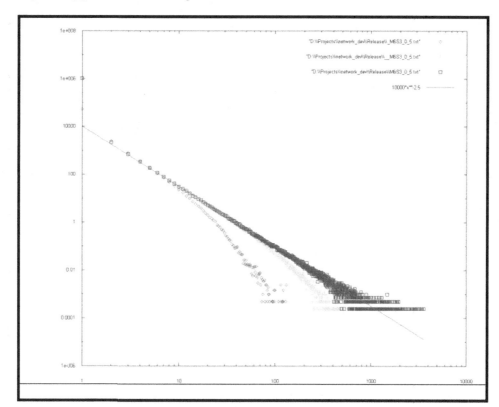

vectors corresponding to $m = 6$ and $s = 3$ and with a probability of exploration $p = 0.5$. The first plot (shown as open diamonds) corresponds to a network of total size (number of actors) equal to $2^{16}$; the middle plot (shown as crosses) to a network size of $2^{18}$ and the right hand plot (open squares) to a network size of $2^{20}$. Considering these very large numbers of actors is analogous to taking the thermodynamic limit of a classical dynamical system, and reveals the underlying power-law behaviour as the limiting case. From the results we can see that the constraint on size of the system produces 'exponential roll off', where the curve falls away from the true power law line.

Figure 6 shows that the distribution of cluster sizes does approximate to a power-law with an exponent of 2.5 (the straight line shown in Figure

6), and the approximation improves as the network increases in size. Similar results are obtained when the other parameters of the network model are varied (Wyld & Rodgers, 2007).

In general the characteristics of Models 0 and 1 cluster dissipation are very similar. For example, Figure 7 superimposes the distribution of cluster sizes for the two models under the same set of task and exploration assumptions ($m = 6$, $s = 3$ and $p = 0.5$). The two distributions are essentially the same.

## The Effect of these Assumptions on the Clustering of the Actors

The mechanisms of informal networking we have so far considered seem quite plausible, and, as expected, lead to a distribution of clusters of

*Figure 7. Superposition of the cluster size distributions for Models 0 and 1. The straight line is a power-law distribution with the exponent 2.5*

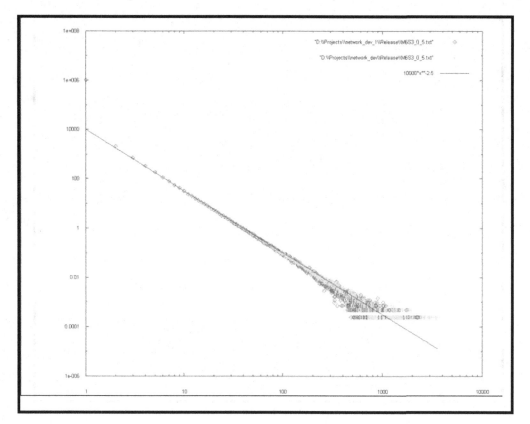

actors which follows a good approximation to a power-law with an exponent of 2.5. However, further investigation of the nature of these clusters of interlinked actors indicates that they tend to be very 'ramified' (i.e. spindly) and 'tree like' with very few loops or cycles. The emergent informal networks thus tend to have low clustering coefficients and a high average path length (i.e. the opposite of the properties of a small world network). This implies that a single cut of a link would tend to disconnect the entire cluster. Edge-like organizations with such dynamics would be highly adaptable but also highly vulnerable to attack of their information links.

## Small World Clusters

We close this Chapter by discussing the properties which might be required to produce clusters showing characteristics similar to the theoretical small world networks and thus potentially less vulnerable to such attacks.

Thus far, we have considered only a task vector for each agent, and a number of information categories of that task vector to be filled. We now enrich that representation, following the ideas of the ELICIT game, by assuming that each agent has both a task vector and an 'available information' vector. Both of these now represent factoids of information. The information vector is defined in the same way as the task vector, with the same number of information categories. If a category of information is known to the actor, a 1 is placed in the appropriate category. Otherwise it is 0. Actors can thus have incomplete information. Actors can also have unneeded information,

In Model 2, our mechanism for dissipation and exploration now becomes the following.

*Dissipation:* If an actor's task vector equates to its information vector, the actor has succeeded in gathering the information to complete the knowledge task, and the actor breaks all links with other actors in its cluster ('simple disconnection'). The actor is then given a new task vector and a reset information vector.

*Exploration:* Otherwise, choose an actor at random. With probability $C$ proportional to the degree of the actor, the actor shares information with one of its linked neighbours, (i.e. all 1s on their information vectors are shared between the two actors). With probability $1-C$ choose another actor at random to make a link with. The probability of making this link is proportional to the link strength between the two chosen actors.

In addition to these mechanisms, it might be necessary to allow neighbours of linking actors also to form links, thus including more 'triangular' social relationships among actors. This may be the key to forming the desired small world characteristics.

## CONCLUSION

This Chapter has focused on understanding the nature of the information networks which can create Self-Synchronization of the force. The work reported here sustains a classification of such complex information networks at three levels. At Level 1 ('linked') we consider the basic node and linkage topology. At Level 2 ('synched') we consider the local interaction between intelligent nodes, sharing the information and awareness required for Cognitive Self-Synchronization. At Level 3 ('cliqued') we consider how such local networking feeds through into emergent clustering effects in the physical domain.

We have also shown that complex information networks are complex systems, and the tools, modelling approaches and concepts of Complexity Theory can all be successfully applied. Structured experimental ELICIT games coupled with information entropy based measures of merit are one example of a successful Complexity based approach. Simple models of fundamental information networking dynamics using task vectors and examining the resultant emergent behaviour are another.

Throughout the Chapter we have indicated where these ideas could be taken further.

## REFERENCES

Albert, R., & Barabasi, A. (2002). Statistical mechanics of complex networks. *Reviews of Modern Physics*, 74.

Alberts, D., Garstka, J., Hayes, R., & Signori, D. (2001). *Understanding Information Age Warfare*. Washington, DC: US DoD CCRP.

Alberts, D., & Hayes, R. (2007). *Planning: Complex Endeavors*. Washington, DC: US DoD CCRP.

Alston, A. (2010, June). *Assessing the difficulty and complexity of ELICIT factoid sets*. Paper presented at the 15th ICCRTS. Santa Monica, CA.

Atkinson, S., & Moffat, J. (2005). *The Agile Organization - From Informal Networks to Complex Effects and Agility*. Washington, DC: US DoD CCRP.

Bohorquez, J., Gourley, S., Dixon, A., Spagat, M., & Johnson, N. (2009). Common Ecology Quantifies Human Insurgency. *Nature, 462*, 911–914. doi:10.1038/nature08631 PMID:20016600

Cebrowski, A., & Garstka, J. (1998). Network-Centric Warfare: its origin and future. *Proceedings of the US Naval Institute*, 28–35.

Cover, T., & Thomas, J. (1991). *Elements of Information Theory*. New York: Wiley. doi:10.1002/0471200611

D'Hulst, R., & Rodgers, G. (2000). Exact Solution of a Model for Crowding and Information Transmission in Financial Markets. *International Journal of Theoretical and Applied Finance*, *3*(4), 609–616. doi:10.1142/S0219024900000784

Gell-Mann, M. (2002). *Personal communication*. Santa Fe Institute, New Mexico, USA.

Hales, D., & Edmonds, B. (2005). Applying a Socially Inspired Technique (Tags) to Improve Cooperation in P2P Networks. *IEEE Trans Sys, Man and Cybernetics Part A, Systems and Humans*, *35*(3), 385–395. doi:10.1109/TSMCA.2005.846399

Johnson, N., Spagat, M., Restrepo, J., Bohórquez, J., Suárez, N., Restrepo, E., & Zarama, R. (2005). From Old Wars to New Wars and Global Terrorism. *Cornell University Library reference arXiv:Physics/0506213* retrieved 28 May 2013.

Manso, M., & Manso, B. (2010, June). *N2C2M2 Experimentation and Validation: Understanding Its C2 Approaches and Implications*. Paper presented at the 15th ICCRTS. Santa Monica, CA.

Manso, M., & Moffat, J. (2011). *Defining and Measuring Cognitive Entropy and Cognitive Self-Synchronization* Paper presented at 16th ICCRTS. Quebec, Canada.

Moffat, J. (2003). *Complexity Theory and Network Centric Warfare*. Washington, DC: US DoD CCRP.

NC3A. (2005). *NATO NEC Feasibility Study Executive Summary v 2.0*. NATO Communications and Information Agency.

NATO. (2006). Exploring New Command and Control Concepts and Capabilities. NATO RTO SAS Task Group 050 Final Report prepared for NATO. *US DoD CCRP*. Retrieved 28 May 2013, from www.dodccrp.org

NATO. (2010). *NATO NEC C2 Maturity Model*. Washington, DC: US DoD CCRP.

Newman, M., & Watts, D. (1999). Renormalization Group Analysis of the Small-World Network Model. *Elsevier Physics Letters A*, *263*, 341–346. doi:10.1016/S0375-9601(99)00757-4

Penrose, R. (2010). *Cycles of Time*. London, UK: The Bodley Head.

Perry, W., & Moffat, J. (2004). *Information Sharing Among Military Headquarters, The Effects on Decision-Making*. Santa Monica, CA: The RAND Corporation.

Ruddy, M. (2007, June). *ELICIT – The Experimental Laboratory for Investigating Collaboration, Information-sharing and Trust*. Paper presented at 12th ICCRTS. Newport, RI.

Ruddy, M., & Nissen, M. (2008). *New Software Platform Capabilities and Experimentation Campaign for ELICIT*. Paper presented at 13th ICCRTS. Seattle, WA.

Wasserman, S., & Faust, K. (1994). *Social network analysis: Methods and applications*. Cambridge, UK: Cambridge University Press. doi:10.1017/CBO9780511815478

Watts, D. (1999). *Small Worlds, The Dynamics of Networks between Order and Randomness*. Princeton, NJ: Princeton University Press.

Watts, D. (2000). *Santa Fe Working Paper 00-12-062*. Santa Fe Institute.

Wyld, A., & Rodgers, G. (2007). Models for Random Graphs with Variable Strength Edges. *Physica A*, *374*, 491–500. doi:10.1016/j.physa.2006.07.002

## KEY TERMS AND DEFINITIONS

**Cognitive Entropy:** A measure of the number of distinguishably different solutions held by individuals working in a team or group to solve a common problem.

**Complexity Theory:** The study of systems of large numbers of units whose interactions are local, non-linear and may involve feedback.

**Edge Organization:** A team or group consisting of a number of components that can interact in complex ways without centralized control.

**Entropy:** A measure of the number of distinguishable ways in which a system can be arranged while having the same macro-level emergent behavior.

**Infostructure:** The information network and associated resources linking together a military unit or force.

**Self-Synchronization:** Synchronization which emerges from the local interactions of the military units or forces, and is not imposed from outside.

**Synchronization:** The meaningful arrangement of military units, forces or effects in time and space.

## ENDNOTES

- © British Crown copyright 2014/DSTL – Published with the permission of the Controller of Her Majesty's Stationery Office

# APPENDIX

## Questions

1.  What are the key forms (topologies) of information sharing networks?
2.  How are these different topologies represented in the ELICIT counter-terrorism game?
3.  How do we measure the outcomes of these games?
4.  Why is entropy a good approach to measuring these outcomes?

# Chapter 11
# Cyber Security in Tactical Network Infrastructure for Command and Control

**J. Sigholm**
*Swedish National Defence College, Sweden*

## ABSTRACT

*Emerging information and communications technology has had significant importance for military operations during the last decades. Development within such technology areas as sensors, computers, and wireless communications has allowed for faster and more efficient collection, transmission, storage, processing, analysis, and distribution of data. This has led to new and improved military capabilities within command and control, intelligence, targeting, and logistics. However, the increased complexity and interdependencies of networked systems, the continuously growing amounts of data, changing non-technical requirements, and evolving adversary threats makes upholding cyber security in command and control systems a challenging task. Although some best-practice approaches have been developed, finding good solutions for protecting critical infrastructure and important information assets is still an open research question requiring an interdisciplinary approach. This chapter describes recent developments within emerging network technology for command and control, and suggests focus areas where further research is needed in order to attain sufficient operational effect from the employed systems. While a gradual and evolutionary progress of military cyber security has been seen, a long-term commitment is required within such areas as procurement, standardization, training, doctrinal, and legal development, in order to achieve military utility of command and control systems.*

## INTRODUCTION

During the last couple of decades we have witnessed a rapid development within information and communications technology, something that has affected and reshaped our society in many ways. The advent of the Internet during the 1990s and its subsequent proliferation through mobile technology during the 2000s, including high-capacity mobile terminals and high-speed wireless communications, has resulted in a pervasive network where content is increasingly be-

DOI: 10.4018/978-1-4666-6058-8.ch011

ing generated by end-users at the network edge. The ongoing miniaturization of components, and the integration of computational elements and physical entities, has given rise to cyber-physical systems, supporting and facilitating a multitude of human processes. The ability to mine large data sets, to fuse information from heterogeneous sources, and to perform real-time positioning of individual network nodes, has paved the way for a variety of new network-based services. Whereas most of these do indeed make our lives easier and facilitate our every-day tasks, some may be more questionable in terms of privacy.

The development of information and communications technology has also had a significant influence on military organizations. During the last few years, the concept of "cyber" has become extremely popular throughout many sectors, not least within the military domain. Armed forces of many countries have scrambled to update their doctrines and strategies on the topic (Ventre, 2012), and assertions have been made that the "cyber threat" is one of our time's most potent and alarming dangers (Bumiller & Shanker, 2012). A relevant question to ask is if this development thus constitutes a technical revolution, something that will profoundly change the way wars are fought and crises are responded to. Will cyberspace be the battlefield of tomorrow, leaving nations without an effective cyber defense vulnerable to attacks? Or has the fear of cyber warfare been blown out of proportion, perhaps at the expense of more relevant conventional military capabilities? Although the answer to these questions may vary depending on who you ask, we can say with certainty that the idea of information technology having a revolutionary effect on how wars are fought is not new.

The conduct and outcome of the first Iraq War in the early 1990s served as an eye-opener for many of those who had previously had little reason to stay updated on the latest development in military use of advanced technology. This was the first major conflict in which the Global

Positioning System (GPS) came to active use, allowing for guided munitions to strike against targets with what appeared as surgical precision. This stood in stark contrast to the razing of entire cities and mass bombings as witnessed during World War II and the Vietnam War. The broadcasting of aerial video sequences showing specific government buildings, military installations and critical infrastructure in crosshairs being struck seconds later, in combination with reports of surprisingly low casualty figures, contributed to the sense that warfare had taken a revolutionary leap. This change was captured by the concept of "revolution in military affairs" (RMA), which predicted that military operations would forever be transformed by the ability to exploit technical advances in innovative ways to achieve victory, opening "a whole new era of warfare." (Boot, 2006) While not everyone was convinced of this at the time, it was difficult to analyze the first Iraq War without recognizing that the application of information and communications technology in support of a superior command and control capability had contributed to the successful outcome for the allied forces. There also seemed to be a near-universal agreement that a significant change in contemporary war-fighting was likely underway.

The concept of what constitutes "a revolution", military or otherwise, often differs depending on the circumstances in which it is being used, but commonly involves dramatic events that imminently attract attention. However, the term is more commonly used than defined, and one could quite easily compile a long list of events in recent history which would qualify as being social, political, technological or scientific revolutions. The difference between revolutionary and evolutionary changes can also be discussed. Whereas both concepts contain measures of wide-ranging (scope) and significant (magnitude) transformations, the main difference lies in how rapidly (speed) the change occurs (Shimko, 2010). However, when it comes to RMA, it has been suggested that the issue of speed should perhaps not be overly dwelled upon

(Liaropoulos, 2006). While rapid technological advances were undoubtedly a key component of the RMA envisioned during the 1990s, they were only part of the equation. Technology by itself does not bring about a revolution, it merely creates the opportunity (Singer, 2009). Hence, in order to bring about a revolution, technology needs to be accompanied by a military doctrine and an organization reform that supports the realization of the revolutionary potential. A frequently used example is the German development of tanks and mechanized infantry during World War II, employed in the revolutionary and very successful maneuver warfare approach. Although the Germans were not the only ones with access to such technology, it was the combination of availability, use, and military organization that provided the distinct advantage on the battlefield.

During the mid to late 1990s much of the focus of the discourse amongst military theorists and academics was on the nature of the ongoing changes in contemporary warfare. One of the outcomes of the Iraqi War was the concept of network-centric warfare (NCW), a term first coined by the U.S. Admiral Arthur Cebrowski. It proposed that all available sensors, platforms and weapons systems should be jointly interlinked through a global information grid, contributing to a dominant battle space knowledge through extensive information sharing, and thus speeding up the OODA (observe, orient, decide, and act) loop (Cebrowski & Garstka, 1998). Critics of the RMA/NCW concepts put forward that these were too occupied with the possible benefits that exploiting commercial information and communications technology for military purposes could bring (Mukunda & Troy, 2009). The cost of this narrow focus was a lack of development of accompanying doctrine and a compatible organization (Shimko, 2010). A further push towards facilitating information flows between agencies of the U.S. government came as a result of the 9/11 2001 terror attacks in New York and Washington D.C. Following the attacks, there was a significant shift within the intelligence community, moving from "need to know" to "responsibility to share," with the goal of enabling rapid coordination of crisis response through shared situational awareness (Stern, 2009). This new paradigm has indeed improved intelligence sharing through such novel services as Intellipedia – an online system for collaborative data sharing similar to that of the publicly available service Wikipedia – enabling actors and stakeholders inside and outside of government to access information necessary to play their parts in a crisis scenario (Vogel, 2009). However, as the circles of individuals with clearance to access classified intelligence has rapidly been extended, the risk of damaging information leaks has simultaneously increased. This has become apparent through several recent events, such as the "Afghan War Diary" and "Cablegate" leaks published by Wikileaks in 2010, and the vast number of classified documents leaked to the press by ex-NSA contractor Edward Snowden in 2013.

So, how do we approach the challenge of protecting our networks, infrastructure and other relevant resources from the threat of cyber-attacks? Much of the existing research related to network technologies for professional environments focuses on the technical aspects. This includes studies of the efficiency of a certain communications protocol, the performance of a given weapons system or the level of protection that certain fortification procedure affords. Less focus has been put on human-centered issues of security, such as addressing the institutional and cultural challenges of crisis management and other scenarios requiring efficient command and control. The purpose of this chapter is thus not only to assess the impact that emerging network technologies may have on the command and control of future crisis management and contingency operations, but also to study consequences arising from the use of technology by human beings, and preconditions for the use of this technology to provide utility in a professional environment. The scope is limited to emerging tactical communications technology and networking information infrastructure for command and control, and The Swedish Armed Forces are used as a reference.

The methodology used in this chapter is Technology Assessment (TA), a practice intended to enhance societal understanding of the broad implications of science and technology and, thereby, to improve decision-making (Sclove, 2010). Technology Assessment is thus useful both when studying possible future effects of emerging technologies, but also when making decisions on resource allocation for technology development, and as a subset of high-level risk management. A key part of performing Technology Assessment involves determining the Technology Readiness Level (TRL) of evolving technologies, a measure used during technology development to define maturity and suitability for application into a system or subsystem (U.S. Department of Defense, 2011). Originally pioneered by NASA in the 1980's, Technology Readiness Level is now widely endorsed throughout government and private sectors in many parts of the world, including adoption by such organizations as the U.S. Department of Defense (DoD), the European Space Agency (ESA), the European Defense Agency (EDA), and NATO.

The rest of this chapter is structured as follows. the following section presents the nature of modern conflicts and the challenging environments in which crisis management operations are carried out. The next section focuses on recent technical developments in tactical communications, and then describes emerging security challenges and the various, sometimes contradicting requirements that society and professional organizations have on information and communications technology. The later sections present the assessed Technology Readiness Levels (TRL) for tactical Command & Control (C2) network infrastructure and cyber security, discusses the major obstacles that need to be overcome, and suggests possible future research directions.

## CHALLENGING ENVIRONMENTS

The nature of modern conflicts are changing, and state-on-state disputes are becoming less frequent while non-state conflicts and one-sided violence against civilians were by far the most common during the last decade (SIPRI, 2013). Furthermore, most of the developed world has experienced heavy strains on public finances during recent years due to a widespread economic recession, leading to constraints on political and military capacities to address global and regional security challenges. Budget austerity measures have resulted in reduced military spending. Armed forces of many countries are thus faced with a new reality – having to achieve effect to meet their mandates with less available resources and an uncertain political backing. These conditions have led to a focus on smaller and quicker missions and concepts such as "pooling & sharing" of military capabilities. The main idea is that increased flexibility, effectiveness and inter-organizational multilateral collaboration will result in a boost of the collective capacity-building and offset the budget cut-backs. To achieve this goal, an increased reliance is put on advanced information and communication based systems to support command and control, intelligence gathering, targeting, logistics, tactical communications and other functions enabling network-centric capabilities through fusion of sensor data from multiple systems and platforms within a coalition of actors.

A paradigm that has emerged during the recent years is the commitment by the international community to the Responsibility to Protect doctrine. An example of a military operation based on this doctrine is the NATO-led intervention "Operation Unified Protector" in Libya in 2011. During the initial stage of the operation, stopping the offensive against the civilian population of Benghazi and establishing a no-fly zone, hostile targets could relatively easily be identified and engaged. However, as the conflict developed, putting a higher focus on ground forces, targeting became increasingly difficult as light civilian vehicles were used to transport military units, and heavy assets were being hidden in urban areas to prevent being targeted (Traynor & Norton-Taylor, 2011). To engage these time-sensitive targets while adhering to the principle of distinction between combatants and civilians (in some cases deliberately used as "human shields") the use of advanced command and control systems was required. This included information from airborne sensor platforms such as the Swedish JAS Gripen fighter aircraft, deployed with reconnaissance capabilities which "outstripped other combat assets with the quality of its tactical ISR (intelligence, surveillance and reconnaissance)." (Johnson & Mueen, 2012)

Other challenging scenarios for collaborative crisis management operations, requiring information and communication technology resources to rapidly establish tactical communications networks, include addressing natural and man-made disasters. According to the U.S. National Oceanic and Atmospheric Administration (NOAA), the extreme weather year of 2012 (including hurricane Sandy) ranked as the second most expensive year for natural disaster losses in U.S. history since 1980, with total costs exceeding $60 billion, second only to 2005, when four hurricanes (including Hurricane Katrina) made landfall along the Gulf coast (NOAA, 2012). On a global scale, 2012 was not as bad as record year 2011, where the costs of damages due to natural disasters amounted to $400 billion, primarily due to major earthquakes in Japan and New Zealand, and severe floods in Thailand (Munich Re, 2012). All in all, natural disasters have cost the world a staggering $3.8 trillion since 1980, according to the World Bank. It has also found that annual costs are on the rise, from around $50 billion a year in the 1980s to $200 billion a year today, a consequence of growing global economic development as well as a rising number of disasters (World Bank, 2013). While not every disaster can be linked to climate change, some predictions suggest that that flood damage alone could cost coastal cities worldwide

$1 trillion every year by 2050 (Hallegatte, Green, Nicholls, & Corfee-Morlot, 2013). The capability to mitigate such events, and the potential conflicts they may give rise to, are thus an increasingly urgent challenge in several regions of the world. Response operations from both affected and supporting nations will likely include military as well government and civilian actors and stakeholders, creating requirements on collaboration as well as information sharing across organizations.

Disaster scenarios are especially demanding for command and control. The situation in such an environment is usually chaotic, with large amounts of dead and wounded, substantial material destruction, and significant parts of previously existing infrastructures left disabled. This is especially apparent to disaster response units, such as police, firefighters or defense forces, who during a mission cannot rely on working power grids, wire line or mobile telephony services or mass media broadcasts. Although the circumstances of each disaster are different, there is commonly an extensive initial information deficit, generating a great need for communications. Victims and families are desperately trying to get in contact with each other, overloading what little communication resources that may still be available. Information exchange is also required for efficient coordination of the disaster response operation – a key in minimizing suffering and maximizing saved lives. As time is a critical factor in these situations, the ability to rapidly establish a collaborative tactical network, enabling real-time situational awareness and supporting timely resource distribution, may in many cases make the difference between life and death.

## Collaborative C2 Networks

While some progress has been done in the area during the last few years, many organizations that may be tasked with missions requiring extensive inter-organizational collaboration, unfortunately still lack the capability of fully participating in shared command and control networks. There are several reasons for this inability, where the main challenges have traditionally been centered on interoperability issues due to heterogeneity in the employed information and communications technology based equipment. The advent of such emerging technologies as Software Defined Radio (SDR) based Mobile Ad-hoc Networks (MANETs) have gradually enabled the capability to interconnect disparate radio networks by loading multiple waveforms and signaling specifications in software. In combination with Cognitive Radio (CR) technology, which gives improved spectral utilization by intelligent frequency allocation, these technologies can now increasingly provide end-to-end communications in challenging and dynamic environments, such as extended disaster areas. However, it is not always purely technical challenges that are the greatest hurdles that need to be overcome. While advanced information and communication technology is indeed a great resource, and many times a requirement for establishing a collaborative command and control network, the technology is used by humans who have different traditions, cultures, experiences, and levels of education. Furthermore, the users may belong to organizations with varying command structures, doctrines, professional practices and economic or political incentives. Overcoming this type of social heterogeneity, or at least finding a way to balance the various requirements, is still quite a tough challenge (Törnqvist, Sigholm, & Nadjm-Tehrani, 2009).

A recent example is the problems that the Swedish contingent was faced with during the above mentioned Operation Unified Protector in Libya in 2011. Although the Swedish soldiers and officers proved to be well-prepared for the mission, and their technical systems had a high degree of NATO compatibility and interoperability, a key challenge turned out to be the lack of access to NATO secret command and control networks and cryptographic keys required for information exchange. The cumbersome bureaucratic procedures that the Swedish contingent was faced with

when (as a non-NATO country) requesting access to these resources, and the lack of experience of dealing with such a process, resulted in a delay of 58 days before the contingent could be integrated with the common operational command and control system and thus reach full operational capability (Egnell, 2012). Overcoming this type of non-technical heterogeneity, or at least finding a way to balance the various requirements, is a challenge which is important to address in order to achieve a high degree of efficiency in future collaborative missions.

One of the major challenges in realizing effective collaboration among a group of heterogeneous organizations is thus how to achieve inter-organizational interoperability, so that the physical information and communications systems can communicate and exchange mission information, and that the collaborating players can interact using their equipment. Many times collaborating parties come from organizations which may also have different communication cultures, organizational structures, ways of sharing information and reaching decisions. Other previous examples include such incidents as the Hurricane Katrina, which hit the coast of Louisiana, U.S.A, in 2005, killing almost 1900 people (1200 directly) and causing property damages of at least $108 billion (Blake & Gibney, 2011). There were a large amount of various governmental agencies responding to the disaster, including the police, military units, fire fighters and medical services. Among the non-governmental organizations the American Red Cross alone assembled approximately 250 000 volunteer rescue workers (Becker, 2008). Dividing the work load and organizing the information dissemination between all these people proved itself to be a greater challenge than anyone had previously realized. Many post-disaster studies have tried to find a solution for future similar scale disasters. One of the outcomes of this work has been the development of the Incident Command System (ICS), a hierarchical network organizational model for emergencies, and its subsequent adoption by

*Table 1. Components of a conversation space (Denning, 2006)*

| Category | Characteristics | Examples |
|---|---|---|
| **Physical systems** | Media and mechanisms by which people communicate, share information, and allocate resources | Telephone, power, roads, meeting places, supplies, distribution systems |
| **Players** | Players included and their roles, core competencies, and authorities | Citizens, fire department, policy department, highways department, federal emergency management agency |
| **Interaction practices** | Rules of the "game" followed by the players to organize their cooperation and achieve their outcomes | Situational awareness, sharing information, planning, reaching decisions, coordination, unified command and control, authority, public relations |

the U.S. Federal Emergency Management Agency (FEMA) as the preferred approach for disaster response operations (Moynihan, 2007).

Although a higher degree of preparation would likely have made post-Katrina response more effective, a conclusion drawn after the incident was that response quality did not depend primarily on pre-incident planning or investments in technical equipment, but rather on the quality of the network which came together to provide relief (Denning, 2006). This so-called Hastily Formed Network (HFN) describes a multi-organizational collaborative environment where a shared communications network is used to interact and fulfill a common, urgent goal. The ways in which the parties interact through the given network, in combination with the acknowledged rules and protocols, defines the conversation space (see Table 1). These types of networks are formed when an incident occurs where response is required from several different organizations (players), and where collaboration is an important factor for success. HFNs also have to handle insufficient resources and a lack of supporting infrastructure (Nelson, Steckler, & Stamberger, 2011).

## Cyber Threats

As earlier mentioned, the ability to rapidly establish a tactical C2 network is crucial in enabling efficient disaster response and crisis management operations. While preparing for such extreme events is an obviously difficult task, it is likewise challenging to prepare for the cyber threats that the operations may be faced with. Antagonists, motivated by various incentives, may try to disrupt the employed networks, to eavesdrop on communications, or to manipulate information (Asplund, Nadjm-Tehrani, & Sigholm, 2009). An example of such an attack is the sabotage of the C2 radio network used by the Swedish police during the riots of the EU summit in Gothenburg in 2001 (Stenumgaard, 2011). Besides such traditional approaches as jamming and eavesdropping, the attackers also employed more sophisticated techniques. By recording orders sent from commanders to subordinate units, manipulating them, and retransmitting them on the network, the attackers managed to create a great deal of confusion and disorganization.

When it comes to cyber security in general, not only is the target hard to anticipate, but the method of attack and the extent of the resulting consequences are often difficult to fully evaluate. This is due not only to the employment of new technology, but also in part to the retention of outdated methods of managing risks and vulnerabilities. Moreover, the initial classification of a cyber-attack as a criminal act or as a military aggression can be problematic. Since the identity of the attacker is commonly unknown, and since information flowing through computer networks is oblivious to geographical boundaries, an attack emanating from a node physically located in a certain country could in reality be initiated by a person in the same country as the victim, or equally by a government-sanctioned entity in an unidentified hostile nation. Hence, although the cyber environment has an obvious physical dimension (routers, switches, antennas and fiber optical cables are present in a given geographic location), the main challenge of attributing a cyber-attack to a specific individual or organization is the ease with which the attackers can obfuscate their trails by hopping through a chain of compromised nodes. This commonly makes tracing the originating source unfeasible, as the systems leveraged by the attacker need to be investigated forensically in a sequential chain, oftentimes by responding agencies in several different countries or legal jurisdictions. The investigation also needs to be done in a timeframe short enough to prevent the perpetrator from covering up any digital tracks that may have been left, such as implicating logs or software.

The growing prevalence of malicious activities in cyberspace makes it a volatile domain. As major information security vulnerabilities and data breaches make international headlines, addressing the problems of advanced persistent threats, fraud, insider attacks and other cyber-related security incidents is becoming increasingly important for organizations within the public as well as the private sector. As many of the information assets that are sensitive, valuable or critical from a national security perspective are located within the private sector, while the legal mandate to act against antagonists targeting these assets lies within the public sector, an interdependency is created which results in new challenges for the counterintelligence community responsible for addressing cyber espionage.

This type of espionage, committed by advanced actors with large resources leveraging modern information and communications technology, is growing in frequency and scale. The 2013 edition of the Verizon Data Breach Investigations Report (Verizon, 2013) reveals that, while organized

criminal groups are still the top actor category when it comes to causing data breaches, state-affiliated groups have now taken the number two spot. Actors within the latter category, commonly labeled as an Advanced Persistent Threats (APT), are not motivated by short-term financial gain but are rather in pursuit of data that furthers specific national interests, such as military or classified documents, results from research and innovation, insider information or trade secrets, and technical resources such as source code. The "Mandiant APT1 Report" (Mandiant Corp., 2013) is another example of a study of the prevalence of this form of cyber espionage. It asserts that, over the last few years, over 140 organizations across the globe have been victims of advanced hostile cyber operations committed by a single antagonistic organization based in mainland China. However, the Mandiant report has been criticized for having a confirmation bias in linking the attacks to the People's Liberation Army (Carr, 2013). While China is often accused of being the most active source of cyber espionage in the world today, disclosures (Lam, 2013) made by whistleblower Edward Snowden in June 2013, a former member of the U.S. intelligence community, demonstrate that the U.S. government has also been conducting extensive so-called Offensive Cyber Effects Operations (OCEO) in order to further national objectives around the world (Greenwald, 2013).

The lack of adequate security measures against these types of highly sophisticated cyber operations is being reported as an increasingly urgent problem in many parts of the world (Smith, 2013; Sood & Enbody, 2013). Whereas military organizations, government agencies and high-security corporations traditionally have a high level of operational security awareness and thus may be somewhat better off in regards to these threats, the most heavily affected organizations are those that are not accustomed to having information security considerations and risk management being an important part of their everyday business concerns. Most organizations in public as well as private sectors continue to rely mainly on passive-reactive measures, such as firewalls and anti-virus software, to block out malicious traffic and software from their networks (Cole, 2013). In most cases regular system patching is seen as enough to correct discovered vulnerabilities in installed software. While these approaches are effective against some threats, they fail to stop advanced attacks from an APT leveraging zero-day exploits, and provide no knowledge of what such an adversary does once the network is penetrated.

Moreover, much of the information security work being done within companies and government agencies is heavily compliance-driven, with a focus on living up to such information security management system standards as ISO/IEC 27000-series, as required by regulatory bodies. The day-to-day efforts are centered on mitigating the continuous flow of discovered software vulnerabilities, patching servers, cleaning up infected clients, and getting back to business as usual. This has been perceived as the best approach to maintain business continuity, and to maintain the trust of customers and the general public. The main line of thought is that, if you admit to being hacked, nobody would want to do business with you or trust your ability to safeguard their sensitive data. Many cyber-incidents have thus been classified or otherwise concealed from public knowledge.

However, this practice is slowly changing. The severity of data breaches caused by high-capability adversary entities, in combination with increasing legal obligations to report incidents, has resulted in a more positive attitude towards open sharing of cyber threat data, both to raise awareness and to learn from collective experience. Public disclosures of cyber espionage incidents, such as the one committed against the New York Times in early 2013 (Perlroth, 2013), have resulted in an increased inter-organizational information exchange to promote common Situational Awareness (SA) regarding the adversaries' activity, and to help prioritize cyber defense resources. A major

benefit of this approach is that one organization's detection can become another's prevention.

The challenges described above give rise to new prerequisites for the counterintelligence community in the cyber domain, especially in regards to methodology, tools, and information management. An open question is thus how the community best should respond to these changes and the challenges that lie ahead.

## THE EVOLUTION OF TACTICAL COMMUNICATIONS

Wireless radio communications has developed from broadcast technology, found in classic walkie-talkies, to the hub-and-spoke configuration also called star networks, employed in modern mobile telephony services (see Fig. 1). Some point-to-point broadcast radios have also been given the capability to perform basic signal relaying or repeating, in order to extend their range. However, the next major step in wireless network evolution is the configuration where each node may communicate with any node it happens to come into contact with, on an ad-hoc basis. This type of network, usually called MANET (Mobile Ad-Hoc Network), consists of nodes that in themselves constitute the network, in a self-organizing fashion. The fact that no infrastructure is needed in order to deploy a MANET makes it highly interesting to individuals and organizations who operate in areas with no preexisting communications infrastructures are available, where coverage from existing networks is poor, or in scenarios where one does not want to rely on external services. In parallel with the evolution in network topologies, the data rates have improved greatly by using advanced modulation techniques, achieving high spectral efficiency. This allows for new services, such as real-time video, to be transmitted in environments where this was not previously possible.

One of the consequences of the ongoing Swedish defense transformation, where fewer people

*Figure 1. The evolution of tactical communications*

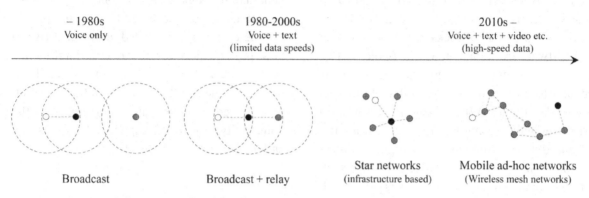

must be able to solve more complex tasks, is the requirement of adequate support tools. Enabling efficient command and control networks is thus of increasing importance. Collaboration is required between military branches to make good use of limited resources, but also to allow for work with external parties, such as other national government agencies, or to share information with coalition partners or NGOs during international operations. The need for an adequate information and communications technology platform supporting collaboration for public safety professions led to the standardization of the TErrestrial Trunked RAdio (TETRA) mobile radio system in the mid-1990s by the European Telecommunications Standards Institute (ETSI), previously also known for the GSM standard. In the Nordic countries the TETRA standard has been employed to create national dedicated radio networks for emergency management services and government agencies, such as the Swedish RAKEL network and the VIRVE network in Finland. These networks provide many benefits, such as inter-agency communication, allowing for collaboration, but they also have some drawbacks such as requiring a fixed infrastructure and new specialized hardware in order to interoperate.

In emerging information and communications systems for inter-organizational collaboration (see Fig. 2) technical interoperability issues are being addressed by the integration of bridging technologies. This allows for establishing hybrid networks, consisting of both modern and legacy systems, so that several different information and communications systems can be connected. One of the largest developments within the area of tactical communications during the last decade has been the advent of Software Defined Radio (SDR) technology, which in turn has allowed for Reconfigurable Radio Systems (RRS), promising decreased lifecycle costs and longer durability for the equipment. RRS has the capability to rapidly interconnect disparate radio networks by merely loading the required waveform (see below) and signaling specifications in software. In combination with Cognitive Radio (CR) technology, which gives improved spectral utilization by intelligent frequency allocation, RRS equipment has the potential of providing a platform for reliable end-to-end communications in challenging and dynamically changing environments. These emerging technologies are described in more detail below.

## Software Defined Radio (SDR)

A software defined radio is a wireless communication system that, instead of using traditional hardware components, implements the functionality these components provide in software running on a computer or in an embedded system (Grayver, 2012). As shown in Table 2, SDRs can be divided into four different system categories, depending on the operational area. Systems that are capable of handling a combination of bands, standards, services or channels are commonly referred to as multimode systems.

Fig. 3 illustrates the conceptual design of a simple SDR transceiver. In an ideal setup, an antenna is connected directly to analog-to-digital converters (A/D–D/A) for receiving and transmitting signals, with software running on an attached processor taking care of everything else. However, some additional components are usually needed, especially for multimode systems. As can be seen in the figure, the main hardware components are the antenna, the radio frequency (RF) front end module (containing amplifiers, filters and mixers), and the analog-to-digital conversion module. All other functions are done in software, including baseband processing, error correction, encryption-decryption, network routing, presenting a graphical user interface etc. The parameterization control bus supplies the modules with control parameters, that describe the standard, band, channel and service that is currently in use. The function of the SDR thus changes into the desired waveform, the set of radio and communication functions that occur from the user's input to the RF output and vice versa. Parameterization decreases the size of the required application software and also limits the hardware reconfiguration time.

## Cognitive Radio (CR)

Cognitive radio is a term that, in short, describes an "intelligent" radio platform (Grayver, 2012). A CR has the ability to continuously monitor and analyze its operational radio environment, to determine which frequencies and services that are currently in use and which parts of the spectrum are available, and adjust its operational parameters to select the frequencies and protocols

that are optimal for data transmission in the local environment.

In a sense, CR may be compared to a driver in a car traveling on a multiple-lane freeway, reacting to what other drivers are doing. If traffic is heavy in one lane, it might probably be a good idea to shift to another lane that is not so busy. The driver must still adhere to certain rules, preventing cars from bumping into one another etc. In other words, a benefit of CR is that it allows for efficient use of the available frequency space, even though there are many users and services in the same geographical area. A practical example of this, frequently experienced by end users living in apartment buildings, is the limited frequency space assigned for the IEEE 802.11 (Wi-Fi) standards. In a densely populated residential area users may find dozens of wireless networks sharing the same "channels", commonly leading to reduced network quality and performance. By using CR the wireless equipment could dynamically identify and select frequencies that are not used by neighbors, or avoid those that are suffering from interference from microwave ovens, cordless phones or other similar equipment emitting radio signals. In this way problems of collisions and interference may be mitigated.

When considering large military or disaster response operations, cognitive radio may help remedy some of the problems associated with spectrum management. When many different organizations gather in an area, all with their own wireless communications equipment, the radio spectrum will quickly get very crowded, as was experienced during the 2010 Haiti earthquake response operation (Wentz, 2010). Besides overload of common frequency bands for mobile telephony, Wi-Fi, VHF and satellite connections, the wide variety of used radio transmitters can cause severe interference. The lack of an efficient regulatory body for frequency coordination in a disaster area may further add to the chaotic situation, as was the case in Haiti (Wentz, 2010). By deploying CR-based equipment, a responding organization

*Figure 2. Emerging tactical information infrastructures(© 2013 Martin Ek. Used with permission.)*

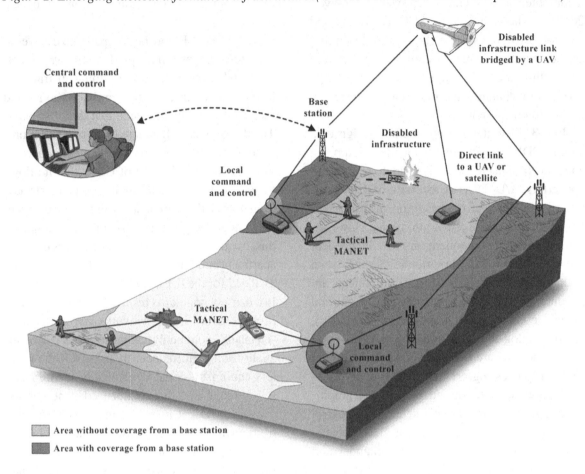

can make use of so-called "white spaces", parts of the radio spectrum that has been reserved for such services as analog TV broadcasting, but that is currently not used. In cases of extreme volatility in the wireless environment, technologies such as orthogonal frequency division multiplex (OFDM) and multi-carrier code division multiple access (MC-CDMA) can be leveraged to limit interference caused by CR users who opportunistically utilize regulated spectrum. In this way communications may be enabled even in wireless environments which are subject to intended or unintended

*Table 2. Conceptual categories of Software Defined Radios based on operational area*

| | |
|---|---|
| **Multistandard** | Supports more than one communication protocol standard. This can include protocols within a standards family (e.g. ULTRA-FDD and ULTRA-TDD for the UMTS 3G mobile cellular standards family), or protocols across several standards (e.g. GSM, LTE, WLAN, TETRA or P25) |
| **Multiband** | Supports more than one frequency band used by a protocol standard (e.g. GSM 900/1800 or IEEE 802.11 b/g) |
| **Multiservice** | Supports several different services (e.g. voice, video and data) |
| **Multichannel** | Supports the use of more than one simultaneous channel within a frequency band |

*Figure 3. Conceptual design of a simple SDR transceiver*

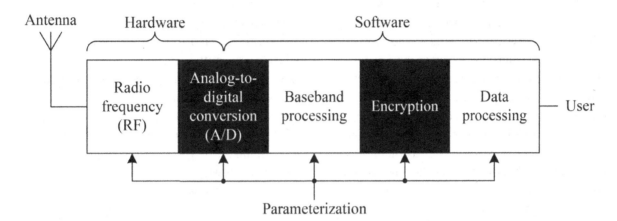

jamming, or where multiple actors are otherwise required to share a given set of frequencies.

## Reconfigurable Radio Systems (RRS)

RRS is a fairly recent concept defined by European standardization organization ETSI (mentioned above), based on technologies such as Software Defined Radio (SDR) and Cognitive Radio (CR) (Iacobucci, 2013). Even though the RRS concept is relatively new, reconfigurability in radio development is well-known within the military domain as it has been used for radio intelligence purposes since the 1980s. Early features that were developed included automatic modulation mode recognition and basic bit stream analysis. Although such military needs as command and control, communications and intelligence were traditionally driving factors for R&D of state-of-the-art wireless technologies, progression in this area is now mainly fueled by the rapidly growing demand for mobile communications on the consumer side. There are already more than 4 billion mobile phone users globally, and some estimates suggest that by 2020 there will be 7 trillion wireless devices serving 7 billion users (Sørensen & Skouby, 2009). This prediction does not assume

that every user will personally control 1000 devices, but rather that most communications by this time will be machine-to-machine communications (e.g. between wirelessly networked cyber-physical systems). To meet this demand, and to deliver robust services in environments with many users and limited available frequency space, new flexible and intelligent methods for spectrum allocation, management and control are needed.

By combining these technologies, an RRS-based radio network can achieve efficient and dynamic self-adaptation to a constantly changing radio environment. In this way, available radio frequencies can be shared by multiple services, thus greatly improving spectrum utilization and service quality. These advantages are also attractive in communications in other areas than strictly commercial ones, such as for military or government purposes.

## Mobile Ad-Hoc Networks (MANETs)

As mentioned earlier, wireless devices such as mobile phones, laptop computers, tablets or professional radios are usually either connected to a fixed network infrastructure or communicating directly in a broadcast manner. The infrastructure that devices connect to could be a cell tower, a

Wi-Fi access point, a mesh network or a satellite in orbit. Communication based on fixed infrastructures or long-range broadcasting is effective, fairly straightforward to implement, and allows for high-speed data transfers (at least on the downlink). However, setting up the required infrastructure takes time and can be expensive, and mobile broadcast-type communications usually have a fairly limited range and capacity. There are also situations where user-required infrastructure does not exist or has been disabled, cannot be set up as quickly as required, or is subject to such adverse actions as jamming or communications surveillance by foreign intelligence units. Examples of scenarios where these conditions could apply are military operations, disaster response missions, and monitoring of natural events in dynamic environments. To provide the required communications services to users in these scenarios another approach is required.

Mobile ad-hoc network (MANET) is an emerging information infrastructure that has received quite a lot of attention by researchers during the last decade or so, mainly due to the appealing properties of self-configuration and self-organization (see e.g. Lakhtaria, 2012, and references therein). MANETs are networks that are made up of a set of autonomous nodes, interconnected via wireless links, where the nodes act as clients, servers and routers simultaneously. However, in contrast to the closely related Wireless Mesh Networks (WMN), MANET nodes are non-stationary and may move independently in any direction. As the nodes move in and out of range from each other, the network topology changes dynamically without the need of any central administration.

When considering communications systems based on fixed-wire or stationary wireless networks it is common to abstract away parts of the network topology. This includes functions concerned with medium-specific interfaces, the maintaining of reliable node-to-node links, and managing message propagation across the network. The lower network layers, such as the physical, data-link and network layers, are thus in concert assumed to provide for reasonably reliable transfer of data sequences from one node to another, connected to the same network. Thus, when a transmitting network node performs a send action, the recipient node is expected to perform a receive action, as intermediary faults due to network failure are relatively unlikely to occur due to assumed redundancy (Grant, Buizer, & Bertelink, 2011).

However, when considering highly dynamic network topologies such as MANETs, this abstraction is not as useful. Solving higher level requirements of the network, such as interoperability and end-to-end security can often not be done if ignoring the effects of topology changes. In MANET-based networks, data is transmitted from one node to another, by letting other nodes on the path between the sender and receiver relay the message one hop at a time. A message sent between two nodes, moving along different edges of a MANET out of range from one another, is thus relayed by intermediate nodes in a hop-by-hop fashion until it reaches its destination. The nodes in a MANET can thus be said to make up the network infrastructure by themselves, allowing for seamless communication over large geographic distances in areas with no previously existing fixed infrastructure. Nevertheless, any available infrastructure that does in fact exist, and is available for use, may be leveraged to extend network range, to uplink nodes to the Internet or to other networks, or to bridge between network partitions (as previously illustrated in Fig. 2). The nodes in a MANET communicate in a broadcast manner, establishing links to any other node that is within range and organize themselves arbitrarily.

The benefits of using MANET-based information and communications systems are that they are very flexible and robust, and they can also be used in areas where no traditional communications infrastructure is available. Scenarios where these systems offer leverage over traditional centralized or point-to-point communication methods are during operations in undeveloped areas, or extended areas hit by natural or man-made disasters. In these situations it is not practical, or economically feasible, to deploy interim cover-all solutions, such as container-based mobile telephony systems, microwave links and satellite communication equipment. They could however work in complement to each other, e.g. traffic generated in a MANET network, destined for an external recipient, may be handed over to available infrastructure at a bridging point for subsequent termination.

The main focus of MANET research during the last few years has been on finding solutions to the many challenges that these networks are faced with, including network survivability, routing, partitions and delay tolerance, upholding information security, and protection against various attacks. Military MANETs will likely also have different requirements than corresponding civilian networks, especially relating to information security when dealing with classified information. However, the complexity of the proposed solutions and the general immaturity of the research area have unfortunately in many cases turned out to be a hindrance for successful real-world deployment of the technology. Examples of some remaining challenges to be overcome are related to finding realistic radio and mobility models for simulations, mitigating MANET susceptibility to targeted attacks, and achieving true scalability in large MANETs.

## THE FUTURE OF TACTICAL COMMUNICATIONS

Traditionally, tactical information and communications equipment has commonly been researched and developed through specific military projects, resulting in customized solutions intended for use in combat situations. The main benefits of this development process have been that the customer (the acquiring military organization) gets a product that is developed according to given

specifications and has qualities such as increased durability, resistance to jamming and interference, and that supports certain cryptographic security mechanisms. On the negative side, the resulting products are usually expensive in relation to comparable commercial products, and the systems are often non-interoperable. The history book is filled with examples of large military information and communications technology and C2 development projects that have turned out badly, where the U.S. Joint Tactical Radio System (JTRS) project may be one of the most recent additions (Gallagher, 2012).

During the last couple of decades, the enormous roll-out of commercial cellular technology has led to a large supply of cheap phones. Although top-of-the-line smartphones may be quite pricy, the fact that well over a billion new units are shipped every year creates a huge second-hand market. The total number of mobile subscriptions globally is 6.6 billion, with 4.5 billion actual subscribers (as many people have several subscriptions) (Ericsson, 2013). The average global mobile penetration is thus approximately 63%. Although 2G and 3G technologies still dominate globally, the number of Long Term Evolution (LTE) subscriptions is growing fast and is, at the time of writing, predicted to be the next generation technology standard of choice for 4G telephony and mobile data services, with a 65% world coverage by 2019. Data traffic usage in mobile networks is currently seeing an exponential growth, and it is estimated that more than 50% or all traffic in mobile networks will come from video by 2019 (Ericsson, 2013).

In the light of this rapid development, a relevant question to ask is if the large investments in R&D of specialized solutions for tactical communications, such as the previously mentioned JTRS project, are defendable, if equivalent or at least acceptable results can be achieved by adapting commercial off-the-shelf equipment to military needs. A common objection is that the goal for the commercial telecommunications industry is not to create robust and dependable communications systems, but simply to make as much money as possible. However, even if this statement is true, it is not a valid reason to immediately and without further thought disqualify the use of civilian information and communications technology for military purposes. A plausible solution could be to focusing future research on hybrid solutions, where different types of equipment types (civilian or military) and standards are used depending on the situation.

## Technical Security Challenges

As previously mentioned, the capability to participate in inter-organizational collaboration, sharing of resources and dividing tasks in a joint mission, is assumed to be important for future defense forces. In a perfect world the collaborating parties, interconnected by interoperable information and communications systems, may achieve this by opening up their networks, systems and databases to each other and providing full access to all resources. However, this utopian scenario is not very realistic in a real-world situation. The need for control over sensitive or classified data disqualifies completely open systems (i.e. without any security functions) as an option, in national as well as international collaboration situations. This is especially true on the battlefield, where the threat of adversary action is also present.

In the TETRA standard there are several mechanisms to provide system security (Roelofsen, 2000). Many of these are similar to the ones present in the GSM system, providing confidentiality, integrity and authentication. Besides standard cryptographic algorithms for ensuring end-to-end confidentiality for individual calls, there is also an advanced scheme for authentication. This is used both so that the network can know that all connected mobile stations (phones) are legitimate, but also so that the mobile stations know that the network they are connecting to is trusted, and not a "fake base station" set up by an adversary. However, a remaining problem in TETRA networks is the lack of protection against interference or intentional jamming attacks. Although the time division slot structure theoretically allows for slow frequency hopping (Politis, Tsagkaropoulos, & Kotsopoulos, 2007), this is not part of the TETRA standard in common use. One of the main reasons for this is that the available frequency region is too small for frequency hopping to give any major improvements (Stenumgaard, 2011).

MANET-based communications systems also introduce some new demands in order to ensure network survivability, such as frequent network topology changes, resource constraints due to limited energy supplies in individual nodes and shared capacity levels across the network. The fact that information "jumps" between nodes in a MANET makes it very important to ensure that no intermediate nodes are compromised (physically or through illicit software). Furthermore, the network faces challenges such as disconnectivity and lack of central management, as well as traditional information security threats existing in infrastructure-based tactical communications systems such as TETRA networks.

In military scenarios attaining situational awareness is important. Commanders need to have access to a good picture of the current situation, where own and enemy resources are located, the status of important infrastructure, how the mission is progressing etc. Creating such a common operational picture requires that data be collected, processed and communicated both internally and externally through various sensors. The resulting information set is a highly valuable asset, which must be protected from adversary access or manipulation. There may also be a non-negligible security threat from inside the organization itself, from spies or infiltrators who convey this information to external parties, either through malign intent, carelessness, or as a consequence of inadequate information management procedures. Leaks may also be caused by broken, misconfigured or "hacked" computer equipment that exposes the information assets.

Countering the above mentioned threats, while maintaining the ability to share information with collaborating parties, requires that internal as well as external communications are adequately secured in such a way that leaks can be prevented, or at least stopped in an early stage. However, solving this problem is non-trivial. Some of the more common technical methods of information asset protection are illustrated in Fig. 4 by an adversary trying to access the "golden egg." A traditional approach, well used in many private and professional networks, is the firewall. A firewall allows or blocks incoming (or outgoing) connections or data flows based on a pre-defined rule set. While a firewall is almost always useful to achieve a basic level of network protection, configuring it for a collaborative scenario may be problematic as it may be either too strict or too lenient in its view of legitimate traffic, and it may be too static or require too much manual interaction.

Another approach is therefore using an Intrusion Prevention System (IPS), a system which tries to identify and block malicious activity by means of "intelligent" algorithms performing real-time traffic analysis (Sigholm, 2010; Koch, 2011). While this security measure might be effective against intrusions, it does not protect against authorized insiders or already infected nodes sending information out of the network. For this reason, a Data Leakage Prevention (DLP) system may be used, focusing on denying exfiltration of sensitive information (Sigholm & Raciti, 2012). A DLP aims to take a holistic approach to data protection, including information residing in a computer system (data in use), information on network-attached storage systems (data at rest), and information leaving the organizational boundary via some communications protocol (data in motion). As a final protective measure, if the information has already left the network, a Digital Rights Management (DRM) system can be used to assure that only authorized entities are allowed read access to the information asset (Gollmann, 2010). However, while DRMs may be effective

for short-term access control, they are commonly vulnerable to encryption circumvention or brute-force attacks by an antagonist with sufficient time and computing resources (Hauser & Wenz, 2003).

## Cyber-Attacks and Cyber Warfare

The growing importance of cyberspace to modern society, and its increasing use as an arena for dispute, is becoming a national security concern for governments and armed forces globally. Furthermore, the fast-paced technical advancement, and the rapid development of new military doctrines, public policy and various legislation makes the area quite volatile and subject to constant change. The special characteristics of cyberspace, such as its asymmetric nature, the lack of attribution, the low cost of entry, the legal ambiguity, and its role as an efficient medium for protest, crime, espionage and military aggression, makes it an attractive domain for nation-states as well as non-state actors in cyber conflict. Cyberspace has been identified by many armed forces as a new fifth arena, besides land, sea, air, and space in which military operations can be performed (e.g. Netherlands Ministry of Defence, 2012). These operations, called cyberspace operations (or cyber operations), include both offensive and defensive measures, and may be performed independently or as a complement to conventional warfare.

As the concept of cyber warfare is becoming gradually more relevant for many nation-states, the need of quickly achieving a military cyberspace operation capability has become a top priority for armed forces and intelligence agencies around the world. This is seen as a requirement both to defend against cyber-attacks, but also to provide freedom of action to carry out own offensive cyberspace operations. Although large nations such as China and Russia have been focusing on achieving a cyber capability for a long time, the country that has probably seen the greatest development in this area during recent years is the U.S. with the establishment of its Cyber Command. The U.S.

*Figure 4. Methods for information asset protection*

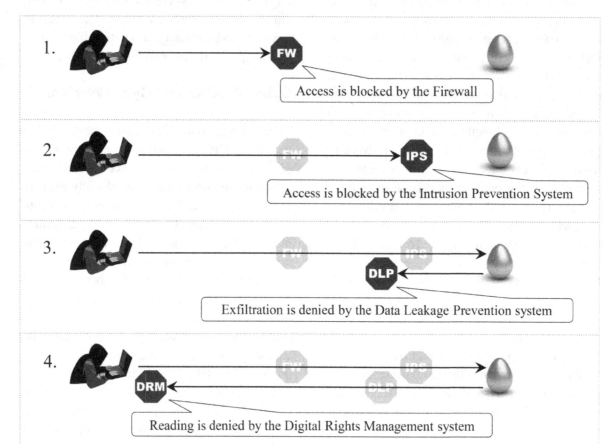

Department of Defense recently approved a major expansion of its cyber security force by increasing the size of the Cyber Command to include close to 5,000 troops and civilians (Nakashima, 2013). Nevertheless, it is hard to evaluate the capabilities that different armed forces have in the cyber domain. This is due to the fact that official numbers of employees in various units and programs often remain undisclosed, and that the number of people associated with cyber-related tasks does not give a clear indication of their actual ability to contribute to operational effect.

Cyber-attacks are deliberate aggressions where computer and network resources, rather than bullets, are used to disrupt, damage or distort an opponent's information and communications infrastructure. These attacks can be directed against civilian objects and installations as well as military targets, such as public websites or industrial production systems. In contrast to large-scale terror attacks, a cyber-attack can often be carried out in a relatively cost-effective manner, and thus be an attractive approach to forcing one's will upon an enemy or opponent. From an attacker's point of view a significant advantage over, for instance, a suicide bomb or some similar conventional asymmetric violence, is that a cyber-attack is almost impossible for the victim to trace or attribute to the originating attacker. In the unlikely event that attribution for a cyber-attack is established, such an aggression may also be considered as more acceptable by the international community than a conventional attack.

In December 2011, the Swedish Civil Contingencies Agency (MSB) presented a unified national strategy for the protection of critical societal functions (MSB, 2011). It initially identified a number of sectors containing functions that must continue to function during a crisis in order to ensure a functional society. This includes such services as power production, IT and communications, transportation, financial services, health care, water supply, etc. There are of course several threats aimed towards these vital societal functions, both in the form of large-scale accidents and severe natural disasters threatening restrict public access to goods, services and other societal services. Moreover, the public's demand on increased availability and improved service levels has resulted in that a large amount of IT systems, databases, and communications systems related to critical infrastructures, public as well as private, are now linked, causing complex system interdependencies. The vulnerability of our increasingly network-dependent society has thus become a current and important issue for nations with a well-developed and pervasive IT infrastructure, and where the general population has a high level of IT maturity. In this aspect, Sweden is thus likely to be one of the more exposed countries in the world.

Cyber warfare and cyber terrorism is a research subject that has been heatedly debated by researchers, military experts, and security professionals during the last few years. It has also been a rather emotionally charged subject, in which expert opinions on the realism of the threat have been divided. Whereas some experts claim that cyber terror is one of our times most potential and alarming dangers (Thibodeau, 2010; BBC, 2012), others mean that the risk of cyber warfare has been greatly exaggerated (Schneier, 2010; Weimann, 2004), perhaps at the expense of more plausible and possible cyber problems (Dunn Cavelty, 2012). There have not yet been any reported cases of cyberterror attacks, and it has been argued that cyberterrorism does not

exist (Lewis, 2010). In reports that have been published on cyber terrorism, the so-called terrorists are regularly "ordinary" hackers, or other actors, mistaken for terrorists (Weimann, 2004). However, if terrorists would manage to conduct such attacks in cyberspace, the consequences might be significant and thus cannot completely be ignored.

Already in the early 2000s, the Swedish Defence Research Agency (FOI) described how vulnerable industrial control systems could easily be targeted by directed cyber-attacks (Grennert & Tham, 2001; Lindahl & Wedlin, 2003). Since then several reports have been released on plausible methods of how such an attack could be carried out, e.g. by distributing USB thumb drives containing specifically crafted malware. Recently it was also discovered that members of the international hacker collective "Anonymous" had gained access to industrial control systems of sawmills and hydroelectric plants in mid-Sweden with administrative privileges (Hielle, 2013). Previous threats have primarily come to be associated with the phenomena of corrupted websites or blocked Internet connections, such as in the case of the cyber-attacks against Estonia in 2007. While those types of attacks can certainly cause extensive damage, many experts have asserted that Sweden is quite well equipped to deal with such relatively unsophisticated attacks, e.g. distributed denial of service (DDoS) attacks, due in part to a high level of expertise within national internet service providers and computer emergency response teams.

Other, perhaps somewhat more sensitive targets of these hackers that have been identified are facilities like the newly built Facebook datacenter in Luleå, in Northern Sweden (Eklund, 2013). Such targets might perhaps not be considered critical to the general needs of society, but the information stored could be used in more serious subsequent attacks. The fact that vulnerabilities exist in parts of our critical infrastructure should be beyond question. The attacks previously brought to light may not primarily been directed at Swedish targets, but it is well known that the digital arena is not bound by national borders. There is still a substantial uncertainty as to the extent of the existing vulnerabilities, which real threats that can exploit these and have the resources and knowledge to do so, which information assets that may be exposed, how effective the implemented security measures are and what actual risk that these factors together result in regarding the infrastructures in question.

In 2010 an advanced, and at the time uniquely crafted, malware called "Stuxnet" was discovered (Farwell & Rohozinski, 2011). This specially designed computer virus was created with the intended purpose of infiltrating computer systems responsible for the monitoring and control of industrial process (SCADA) systems. What distinguishes Stuxnet from previous computer viruses is, in addition to its complexity, the supposed purpose as a cyber-weapon, probably the most advanced such to date that has come to public knowledge (Falliere, Murchu, & Chien, 2011). Results from the analysis of the Stuxnet source code and its distribution patterns suggest that the virus was likely created to sabotage the reprocessing of enriched uranium at the Iranian facility at Natanz (Langner, 2011). Although this virus did not directly pose a threat to Sweden, the fact that the attack method was made publicly available, including access to the source code, can potentially create problems in the future. By downloading a copy of the Stuxnet source code, and providing it with new directives, the virus could be made to attack and seriously injure civilian as well as military assets. We have also seen some subsequent examples of this, through the Stuxnet-related malware Duqu, Flame and Gauss.

As mentioned above, cyber threats have also become a concern and priority for the armed forces in the industrialized world. The effects of an unknown antagonist launching a cyber-attack that could "trojanize" military systems, enslaving them in networks of compromised computers (so-called "Botnets") under alien command, must be considered to be very serious. Although this might not be a very likely scenario in the present, one could at least in theory by using this approach achieve complete control of an opponent's command and control systems and other net-based resources, in something that would resemble a kind of digital invasion. This possibility raises questions as how these cyber threats affect the officer's use of technology, and the degree of confidence one can attribute the information presented in the command and control systems.

## DISCUSSION

The rapid progression within the area of information and communications technology makes accurate predictions of technology advancements difficult to perform. Implementing new technologies in an organization is a complex process, and even though it may sometimes be tempting to forgo the process of fully evaluating the effects and risks associated with adopting a given technology, the process may prove valuable in ensuring that the technology is in accordance with the needs and requirements of the organization, of the employees, or of society in a wider perspective. Technology Assessment is a tool that can help us understand the impact that emerging technologies may have. Table 3 presents an assessment of the Technology Readiness Levels of six categories of emerging technology relevant for tactical command and control network infrastructure and cyber security. In addition to the previously discussed reconfigurable radio systems, the assessment includes emerging network topologies, technologies for situational awareness, security metrics, information asset protection systems, and autonomous network monitoring and control. The contemporary levels are extrapolated in a 10 and 20 year future perspective (2024, 2034) illustrating the rate of which each technology is maturing. The listed technologies are also interrelated and research and development progress in one technology area may thus influence development of one or more of the others.

As discussed earlier in this chapter the number of global users of information and communications technology will likely increase rapidly during the next 20 years. This is also true when it comes to machines interacting with each other via networks, where the growth according to many predictions will be even more substantial. This development is mainly fueled by demands from the civilian society, where many developing regions of the world are just starting to get connected. In a

couple of decades, citizens of the most developed nations will likely be used to having access to "all information, all the time." Challenges that will arise from this are related to such aspects as information control and management, information security, privacy and physical limitations such as spectrum management in densely populated areas. The trend of system interdependencies and increased network complexity will likely continue to be a challenge. Solving this problem requires good models of system behavior in daily opera-

*Table 3. Assessed Technology Readiness Levels of technology for tactical C2 network infrastructure and cyber security*

| Category | Technology Year | 2014 | 2024 | 2034 |
|---|---|---|---|---|
| Reconfigurable radio systems (RRS) | Mobile ad-hoc networks (MANETs) | 5 | 7 | 9 |
| | Software defined radio (SDR) | 8 | 9 | 9 |
| | Cognitive radio (CR) | 4 | 7 | 9 |
| Emerging network topologies | Reactive networks | 4 | 7 | 9 |
| | Semantic networks | 5 | 8 | 9 |
| | Cloud-based networks | 9* | 9 | 9 |
| | Quantum networks | 3 | 4 | 7 |
| Technologies for situational awareness | Security information and event management systems (SIEM) | 8 | 9 | 9 |
| | Automated incident & digital forensics analysis | 3 | 5 | 7 |
| | Tools for data mining and Big Data analysis | 7 | 8 | 9 |
| | Secure inter-organizational information exchange | 5 | 8 | 9 |
| Security metrics | Automated information asset evaluation and classification | 4 | 6 | 7 |
| | Automated network discovery and topology analysis | 7 | 9 | 9 |
| | Tools for simulation and modeling of computer network attacks | 5 | 7 | 9 |
| Information asset protection systems | Firewalls | 9 | 9 | 9 |
| | Intrusion detection/prevention systems (IDS/IPS) | 7 | 8 | 8 |
| | Data leakage prevention systems (DLP) | 7 | 8 | 8 |
| | Digital rights management systems (DRM) | 9* | 9 | 9 |
| Autonomous network monitoring and control | Remote administration and monitoring | 9* | 9 | 9 |
| | Smart grids | 7 | 9 | 9 |
| | Smart sensors for surveillance and monitoring | 4 | 6 | 8 |
| | Survivable networks (self-repairing) | 3 | 4 | 6 |
| | Dynamic security networks | 4 | 6 | 8 |
| | Privacy enhancing technologies (PET) | 5 | 8 | 9 |

* Although this technology is currently assessed as TRL 9, an ongoing development is still occurring.

tions as well as during extreme circumstances, and conducting thorough risk analyses.

Due to such factors as greenhouse gas emissions, world population growth, increasing urbanization and overexploiting of natural resources, natural and man-made disasters are likely to remain a challenge in the assessed timeframe. The capability to conduct effective disaster response, mitigation and recovery will thus continue to be a high-priority capability for governments in most parts of the world. Facing these challenges requires the capability to partake in efficient inter-organizational collaboration, increasingly relying on emerging tactical command and control network infrastructures for information exchange, coordination of common efforts, and distribution of resources and assets. While efficient multi-organizational collaboration can be supported by such frameworks as Hastily Formed Networks (HFNs), one of the key issues in achieving mission success in an HFN is maintaining a high level of pre-incident technical and social education and training within each organization, both when it comes to operating own technical equipment and how to interact with other organizations in the network by establishing communities of practice. Furthermore, the aspect of security in these commonly chaotic environments needs to be considered thoroughly, allowing for required information sharing, contributing to situational awareness and a common operational picture, while simultaneously safeguarding highly valuable, possibly classified information, also residing in the systems. The presence of adverse actors seeking to exploit the uncertainty and confusion that a disaster brings should also be taken into account, including protection against cyber-attacks and cyber espionage.

When it comes to command and control networks, many of the technology trends seen in the consumer market in a 10 and 20 year perspective will likely also be applicable. A reason for this is the increasing reliance on commercial of-the-shelf (COTS) equipment used in military and profes-

sional environments. However, several of the emerging technologies that are not mature enough as of today (e.g. the previously mentioned JTRS RRS-based tactical communications system) will have high readiness levels in this time frame. This requires a continued monitoring of requirements on these technologies and the systems and subsystems in which they may be applied. It is also hard, if not impossible, to predict the advent of disruptive technologies that may lead to a revolution in development and use, instead of the easier to predict evolutionary development. Organizations wanting to embrace the revolutionary potential of such technologies should nevertheless remember to simultaneously focus on accompanying doctrine and organizational development.

## CONCLUSION

In this chapter we have reviewed some of the recently emerging information and communications technologies for tactical command and control networks from a cyber security perspective. We have also assessed the maturity of these technologies by way of Technology Readiness Levels, in order to appraise their respective maturity and suitability for application into tactical C2 systems. As with most assessments the resolution is quite coarse, but it gives an indication of how fast research and development is moving in each technology field, as seen from a contemporary perspective.

Based on the described technologies, a consequence study can be made to analyze how they may contribute to future capabilities, what cyber security threats that may arise as a result of emerging technologies, and what areas that may require more resources for research and development in the coming years. A revision of risk management of command and control networks in relation to the ongoing technology development may be called for, as well as a review of strategies for protection of networked critical societal functions.

This chapter has been limited to assessment of emerging technologies for tactical network infrastructure. Future work includes studies of the requirements to advance the identified, still immature technologies from their current respective readiness levels to a level that permits transfer into systems and networks, in support of a desired capability, and within cost, schedule and risk constraints.

# REFERENCES

Asplund, M., Nadjm-Tehrani, S., & Sigholm, J. (2009). Emerging Information Infrastructures: Cooperation in Disasters. In R. Setola, & S. Geretshuber (Eds.), *LNCS)* (Vol. 5508, pp. 258–270). Lecture Notes in Computer Science Berlin: Springer-Verlag.

BBC. (2012, October 12). *US prepares first-strike cyber-forces.* Retrieved from http://www.bbc. co.uk/news/technology-19922421

Becker, J. C. (2008, May 6). *The Opportunities and Limits of Technology in Non Profit Disaster Response.* Paper presented at the 5th International Conference on Information Systems for Crisis Response and Management (ISCRAM 2008). Washington, DC.

Blake, E. S., & Gibney, E. J. (2011, August). The deadliest, costliest and most intense United States tropical cyclones from 1851 to 2010 (and other frequently requested hurricane facts). *NOAA Technical Memorandum NWS NHC-6.* Miami, FL: National Oceanic and Atmospheric Administration.

Boot, M. (2006). *War Made New: Technology, Warfare, and the Course of History, 1500 to Today.* New York: Gotham Books.

Bumiller, E., & Shanker, T. (2012, October 11). Panetta Warns of Dire Threat of Cyberattack on U.S. *The New York Times.*

Carr, J. (2013, February 19). *Mandiant APT1 Report Has Critical Analytic Flaws.* Retrieved from http://jeffreycarr.blogspot.nl/2013/02/mandiant-apt1-report-has-critical.html

Cebrowski, A. K., & Garstka, J. H. (1998). Network-Centric Warfare: Its Origins and Future. *Proceedings of the United States Naval Institute. United States Naval Institute, 124*(1).

Cole, E. (2013). *Advanced Persistent Threat: Understanding the Danger and How to Protect Your Organization.* Waltham, MA: Syngress - Elsevier.

Denning, P. J. (2006). Hastily Formed Networks. *Communications of the ACM, 49*(4), 15–20. doi:10.1145/1121949.1121966

Dunn Cavelty, M. (2012). The Militarisation of Cyberspace: Why Less May Be Better. In *Proceedings of the 4th International Conference on Cyber Conflict (CYCON 2012)* (pp. 141-153). Tallinn, Estonia: NATO CCD COE Publications.

Egnell, R. (2012). *The Swedish Experience in Operation Unified Protector: Overcoming the Non-NATO Member Conundrum.* Stockholm: Stockholm Center for Strategic Studies.

Eklund, N. (2013, January 7). *Hackerhot mot Facebooks nya datacenter i Luleå (Hacker-threat against Facebook's new datacenter in Luleå).* Retrieved from http://sverigesradio.se/sida/artikel. aspx?programid=83&artikel=5383951

Ericsson. (2013, November). *Ericsson Mobility Report: On the pulse of the Networked Society.* Retrieved from http://www.ericsson.com/ mobility-report

Falliere, N., Murchu, L. O., & Chien, E. (2011). *W32 Stuxnet Dossier.* Retrieved from http://www. symantec.com/connect/blogs/w32stuxnet-dossier

Farwell, J. P., & Rohozinski, R. (2011). Stuxnet and the Future of Cyber War. *Survival, 53*(1), 23–40. doi:10.1080/00396338.2011.555586

Gallagher, S. (2012, June 19). *How to blow $6 billion on a tech project*. Retrieved from http://arstechnica.com/information-technology/2012/06/how-to-blow-6-billion-on-a-tech-project/

Gollmann, D. (2010). Computer security. *Wiley Interdisciplinary Reviews: Computational Statistics*, *2*(5), 544–554. doi:10.1002/wics.106

Grant, T. J., Buizer, B. C., & Bertelink, R. J. (2011). Vulnerability of C2 Networks to Attack: Measuring the topology of eleven Dutch Army C2 systems. In *Proceedings of the 16th International Command & Control Research & Technology Symposium (ICCRTS 2011)*. Quebec, Canada: ICCRTS.

Grayver, E. (2012). *Implementing Software Defined Radio*. New York: Springer.

Greenwald, G. (2013, June 7). Obama orders US to draw up overseas target list for cyber-attacks. *The Guardian*.

Grennert, J., & Tham, M. (2001). Influencing Conflicts with IT-Weapons: The Possibility of Non-State Actors Influencing the Course of a Conflict. *User Report FOI-R--0263--SE*. Stockholm, Sweden: Swedish Defence Research Agency.

Hallegatte, S., Green, C., Nicholls, R. J., & Corfee-Morlot, J. (2013). Future flood losses in major coastal cities. *Nature Climate Change*, *3*(9), 802–806. doi:10.1038/nclimate1979

Hauser, T., & Wenz, C. (2003). DRM Under Attack: Weaknesses in Existing Systems. In E. Becker, W. Buhse, D. Günnewig, & N. Rump (Eds.), *LNCS)* (Vol. 2770, pp. 206–223). Lecture Notes in Computer Science Berlin: Springer-Verlag. doi:10.1007/10941270_14

Hielle, L. P. (2013, January 5). *Anonymous-medlem: Jag kunde styra sågverk (Anonymous-member: I had control over sawmills)*. Retrieved from http://sverigesradio.se/sida/artikel.aspx?programid=83&artikel=5384724

Iacobucci, M. S. (2013). *Reconfigurable Radio Systems: Network Architectures and Standards*. West Sussex, UK: John Wiley & Sons, Ltd. doi:10.1002/9781118398401

Johnson, A., & Mueen, S. (Eds.). (2012, March). Short War, Long Shadow: The Political and Military Legacies of the 2011 Libya Campaign. *Whitehall Report 1-12*. The Royal United Services Institute (RUSI).

Koch, R. (2011). Towards next-generation intrusion detection. In *Proceedings of the 3rd International Conference on Cyber Conflict (ICCC 2011)*. Tallinn, Estonia: NATO CCD COE Publications.

Lakhtaria, K. I. (Ed.). (2012). *Technological Advancements and Applications in Mobile Ad-Hoc Networks: Research Trends*. Hershey, PA: IGI Global. doi:10.4018/978-1-46660-321-9

Lam, L. (2013, June 14). Edward Snowden: US government has been hacking Hong Kong and China for years. *South China Morning Post*.

Langner, R. (2011). Stuxnet: Dissecting a Cyberwarfare Weapon. *IEEE Security & Privacy Magazine*, *9*(3), 49–51. doi:10.1109/MSP.2011.67

Lewis, J. A. (2010, June 24). Cyberwarfare and Its Impact on International Security. *UNODA Occasional Papers*. New York, NY: United Nations.

Liaropoulos, A. (2006). Revolution in Warfare: Theoretical Paradigms and Historical Evidence - the Napoleonic and First World War Revolutions. *The Journal of Military History*, *70*, 363–384. doi:10.1353/jmh.2006.0106

Lindahl, D., & Wedlin, M. (2003, December). IT Weapons in a Laboratory Environment. *User Report FOI-R--1056--SE*. Linköping, Sweden: Swedish Defence Research Agency.

Mandiant Corp. (2013, February 18). *APT1: Exposing One of China's Cyber Espionage Units*. Retrieved from http://intelreport.mandiant.com

Moynihan, D. P. (2007). *From Forest Fires to Hurricane Katrina: Case Studies of Incident Command Systems. Networks and Partnerships Series.* Washington, DC: IBM Center for The Business of Government.

MSB. (2011, December). A Functioning Society in a Changing World. *Report.* Swedish Civil Contingencies Agency. Retrieved from https://www.msb.se/RibData/Filer/pdf/26084.pdf

Mukunda, G., & Troy, W. J. (2009). Caught in the Net: Lessons from the Financial Crisis for a Networked Future. *Parameters, 39*(2), 63–76.

Munich Re. (2012, January 4). *Review of natural catastrophes in 2011: Earthquakes result in record loss year.* Retrieved from http://www.munichre.com/en/media_relations/press_releases/2012/2012_01_04_press_release.aspx

Nakashima, E. (2013, January 27). *Pentagon to boost cybersecurity force.* Retrieved from http://articles.washingtonpost.com/2013-01-27/world/36583575_1_cyber-protection-forces-cyber-command-cybersecurity

Nelson, C. B., Steckler, B. D., & Stamberger, J. A. (2011). The Evolution of Hastily Formed Networks for Disaster Response: Technologies, Case Studies, and Future Trends. In *Proceedings of the 2011 IEEE Global Humanitarian Technology Conference (GHTC)* (pp. 467-475). Seattle, WA: IEEE.

Netherlands Ministry of Defence. (2012, September). *The Defence Cyber Strategy.* The Hague, The Netherlands: Ministry of Defence.

NOAA. (2012, December 20). *Preliminary Info on 2012 U.S. Billion-Dollar Extreme Weather/Climate Events.* Retrieved from http://www.ncdc.noaa.gov/news/preliminary-info-2012-us-billion-dollar-extreme-weatherclimate-events

Perlroth, N. (2013, January 31). Hackers in China Attacked The Times for Last 4 Months. *The New York Times,* p. A1.

Politis, I., Tsagkaropoulos, M., & Kotsopoulos, S. (2007). Video Transmission over TETRA. In P. Stavroulakis (Ed.), *Terrestrial trunked radio - TETRA: A global security tool* (pp. 133–190). Berlin: Springer-Verlag. doi:10.1007/3-540-71192-9_5

Roelofsen, G. (2000). TETRA Security. *Information Security Technical Report, 5*(3), 44–54. doi:10.1016/S1363-4127(00)03006-5

Schneier, B. (2010, July 7). *Threat of 'cyberwar' has been hugely hyped.* Retrieved from http://Ed.cnn.com/2010/OPINION/07/07/schneier.cyberwar.hyped/

Sclove, R. (2010). *Reinventing Technology Assessment: A 21st Century Model. Science and Technology Innovation Program Report.* Washington, DC: Woodrow Wilson International Center for Scholars.

Shimko, K. L. (2010). *The Iraq Wars and America's Military Revolution.* New York, NY: Cambridge University Press. doi:10.1017/CBO9780511845277

Sigholm, J. (2010). Reconfigurable Radio Systems: Towards Secure Collaboration for Peace Support and Public Safety. In *Proceedings of the 9th European Conference on Information Warfare and Security (ECIW)* (pp. 268-274). Thessaloniki, Greece: ACPI Ltd.

Sigholm, J., & Raciti, M. (2012). Best-Effort Data Leakage Prevention in Inter-Organizational Tactical MANETs. In *Proceedings of the 2012 IEEE Military Communications Conference (MILCOM)* (pp. 1143-1149). Orlando, FL: IEEE.

Singer, P. W. (2009). *Wired for War: The Robotics Revolution and Conflict in the 21st Century.* New York, NY: Penguin Books.

SIPRI. (2013). *Stockholm International Peace Research Institute. Yearbook 2013: Armaments, Disarmament and International Security.* Oxford, UK: Oxford University Press.

Smith, D. (2013). Life's certainties: death, taxes and APTs. *Network Security*, (2): 19–20. doi:10.1016/S1353-4858(13)70033-3

Sood, A. K., & Enbody, R. J. (2013). Targeted Cyberattacks: A Superset of Advanced Persistent Threats. *IEEE Security & Privacy Magazine*, *11*(1), 54–61.

Sørensen, L., & Skouby, K. E. (Eds.). (2009, July). User Scenarios 2020 - A Worldwide Wireless Future. Outlook, 4.

Stenumgaard, P. (2011, May). Interference susceptibility of civilian wireless consumer technology. *User Report FOI-R--3216--SE.* Linköping, Sweden: Swedish Defence Research Agency.

Stern, E. K. (2009). Crisis Navigation: Lessons from History for the Crisis Manager in Chief. *Governance: An International Journal of Policy, Administration and Institutions*, *22*(2), 189–202. doi:10.1111/j.1468-0491.2009.01431.x

Thibodeau, P. (2010, March 24). *Cyberattacks an 'existential threat' to U.S., FBI says.* Retrieved from http://www.computerworld.com/s/article/9173967/Cyberattacks_an_ existential_ threat_to_U.S._FBI_says

Törnqvist, E., Sigholm, J., & Nadjm-Tehrani, S. (2009). Hastily Formed Networks for Disaster Response: Technical Heterogeneity and Virtual Pockets of Local Order. In *Proceedings of the 6th International Conference on Information Systems for Crisis Response and Management (ISCRAM2009).* Gothenburg, Sweden: ISCRAM.

Traynor, I., & Norton-Taylor, R. (2011, April 5). *Nato lacking strike aircraft for Libya campaign.* Retrieved from http://www.guardian.co.uk/world/2011/apr/05/nato-lacking-strike-aircraft-libya

U.S. Department of Defense. (2011, May). *Technology Readiness Assessment (TRA) Guidance.* Washington, DC: U.S. Department of Defense.

Ventre, D. (2012). *Cyber Conflict: Competing National Perspectives.* Hoboken, NJ: John Wiley & Sons. doi:10.1002/9781118562666

Verizon. (2013, April). *2013 Data Breach Investigations report.* Retrieved from http://www.verizonenterprise.com/DBIR/2013/

Vogel, S. (2009, August 27). For Intelligence Officers, A Wiki Way to Connect Dots. *The Washington Post.*

Weimann, G. (2004, May). Cyberterrorism: How Real is the Threat?. *Special Report.* Washington, DC: United States Institute of Peace.

Wentz, L. (2010). Haiti Information and Communications Observations: Trip Report for Visit 18 February to 1 March 2010. *Center for Technology and National Security Policy.* Washington, DC: National Defense University.

World Bank. (2013, November). Building Resilience: Integrating Climate and Disaster Risk into Development. *The World Bank Group Experience.* Washington, DC: World Bank Publications.

## ADDITIONAL READING

Blumenthal, U., Haines, J., Streilein, W., & O'Leary, G. (2012). Information Security for Situational Awareness in Computer Network Defense. In C. Onwubiko, & T. Owens (Eds.), *Situational Awareness in Computer Network Defense: Principles, Methods and Applications* (pp. 86–103). Hershey, PA: IGI Global. doi:10.4018/978-1-4666-0104-8.ch006

Bordetsky, A. (2012). Patterns of Tactical Networking Services. In A. Bento, & A. K. Aggarwal (Eds.), *Cloud Computing Service and Deployment Models: Layers and Management* (pp. 311–329). Hershey, PA: IGI Global. doi:10.4018/978-1-4666-2187-9.ch018

Denning, D. E. (2011). Cyber Conflict as an Emergent Social Phenomenon. In T. J. Hold, & B. H. Schell (Eds.), *Corporate Hacking and Technology-Driven Crime: Social Dynamics and Implications* (pp. 170–186). Hershey, PA: IGI Global.

Ghosh, S. (2009). *Net Centricity and Technological Interoperability in Organizations: Perspectives and Strategies.* Hershey, PA: IGI Global. doi:10.4018/978-1-60566-854-3

Guan, J., Xu, C., Zhang, H., & Zhou, H. (2012). Mobility Challenges and Management in the Future Wireless Heterogeneous Networks. In G.-M. Muntean, & R. Trestian (Eds.), *Wireless Multi-Access Environments and Quality of Service Provisioning: Solutions and Application* (pp. 18–51). Hershey, PA: IGI Global. doi:10.4018/978-1-4666-0017-1.ch002

Malik, A. A., Mahboob, A., Khan, A., & Zubairi, J. (2011). Application of Cyber Security in Emerging C4ISR Systems. In J. A. Zubairi, & A. Mahboob (Eds.), *Cyber Security Standards, Practices and Industrial Applications: Systems and Methodologies* (pp. 223–258). Hershey, PA: IGI Global. doi:10.4018/978-1-60960-851-4.ch012

Pomponiu, V. (2011). Securing Wireless Ad Hoc Networks: State of the Art and Challenges. In J. A. Zubairi, & A. Mahboob (Eds.), *Cyber Security Standards, Practices and Industrial Applications: Systems and Methodologies* (pp. 1–22). Hershey, PA: IGI Global. doi:10.4018/978-1-60960-851-4.ch001

Ramsay, G. (2012). Terrorism and the Internet: Do We Need an International Solution? In P. C. Reich, & E. Gelbstein (Eds.), *Law, Policy, and Technology: Cyberterrorism, Information Warfare, and Internet Immobilization* (pp. 352–375). Hershey, PA: IGI Global.

Ruiz, M. E., & Redmond, R. (2012). Cyber Command and Control: A Military Doctrinal Perspective on Collaborative Situation Awareness for Decision Making. In C. Onwubiko, & T. Owens (Eds.), *Situational Awareness in Computer Network Defense: Principles, Methods and Applications* (pp. 29–47). Hershey, PA: IGI Global. doi:10.4018/978-1-4666-0104-8.ch003

Tatham, P., & Kovács, G. (2011). Developing and Maintaining Trust in Hastily Formed Relief Networks. In G. Kovács, & K. M. Spens (Eds.), *Relief Supply Chain Management for Disasters: Humanitarian, Aid and Emergency Logistics* (pp. 173–195). Hershey, PA: IGI Global. doi:10.4018/978-1-60960-824-8.ch010

Yang, J., Lee, J., Rao, A., & Touqan, N. (2009). Interorganizational Communications in Disaster Management. In V. Weerakkody, M. Janssen, & Y. K. Dwivedi (Eds.), *Handbook of Research on ICT-Enabled Transformational Government: A Global Perspective* (pp. 240–257). Hershey, PA: IGI Global. doi:10.4018/978-1-60566-390-6.ch013

## KEY TERMS AND DEFINITIONS

**Advanced Persistent Threat:** An adversarial actor with substantial resources, advanced operational and logistical capabilities, and an ongoing intention to commit long-term espionage, sabotage or other forms of offensive cyber operations leveraging modern information and communications technology. The goal of an APT is to penetrate computers, networks and digital information assets to allow for subsequent exfiltration of intellectual property or information with an economic, political or military value.

**Cyber Security:** Whereas information security is concerned with safeguarding the confidentiality, integrity and availability of information assets, including the infrastructure that stores or transmits information, cyber security is also about protecting the people using information and communications technology resources and any other resources that can be reached via cyberspace and that are vulnerable to threats.

**Cyber War:** Occurs when cyber-attacks reach the threshold of hostilities commonly recognized as war by the international community and as defined by international law.

**Cyber-Attacks:** A subset of cyberspace operations employing the hostile use of cyberspace capabilities, by nation-states or non-state actors acting on their behalf, to cause damage, destruction, or casualties in order to achieve military or political goals.

**Cyber-Physical Systems:** Systems created by the integration of computing hardware and software, and functions for communications and control, with natural or human-made systems that are governed by the laws of physics. The main purpose of cyber-physical systems are to allow for efficient monitoring (from physical to cyber) and control (from cyber to physical) of objects and artifacts in the physical world around us.

**Cyberspace Operations:** Military activities employing cyberspace capabilities in order to achieve strategic objectives or effects in or through cyberspace.

**Hastily Formed Network:** A framework in support of rapid response multi-organizational collaboration. A shared communications network is used for interaction, information sharing, and resource allocation to fulfill a common, urgent goal.

**Reconfigurable Radio System:** A re-programmable, software-controlled wireless device that can sense its radio environment and, accordingly, perform dynamic resource allocation, such as adaptation of its transmission waveform, channel access method, spectrum use, and networking protocols. A reconfigurable radio system is an example of a cyber-physical system, with integrated capabilities of control, communications, and computing.

## APPENDIX

## Questions

1.  Which (if any) of the technologies listed in Table 3 would you say could have the potential to be revolutionary (in a 10-20 year perspective) for use in tactical C2 networks or for furthering the capability to conduct effective cyberspace operations?

2.  Give examples of some advantages and challenges of deploying a tactical C2 network based on Reconfigurable Radio System technology, using a Mobile ad-hoc network topology, in comparison to a C2 network with traditional radio devices using a broadcast topology.

3.  What is the main difference between information security and cyber security? Put this into the context of a commander, using a tactical C2 network to view the location and status of subordinate units and resources, and to disseminate orders to them.

4.  Name two cyber threats that Data Leakage Prevention (DLP) system could offer protection against, but that an Intrusion Prevention System (IPS) would be less likely to catch.

5.  Imagine that you are in charge of cyber security for a military unit, deployed alongside a large number of other military and civilian organizations, in response to a major natural disaster. A Hastily Formed Network is used to share various information between the collaborating organizations, such as C2 information in support of resource allocation a common operational picture, digital maps etc. The area of operations is quite extensive, requires a high degree of mobility, and lacks (functioning) communications infrastructure. Describe what communications technology and network topology that you would prefer, and list your three main cyber security concerns for you unit.

# Chapter 12
# Smart Surveillance Systems

**L. J. M. Rothkrantz**
*Delft University of Technology, The Netherlands*

## ABSTRACT

*To enable effective and efficient command and control in military operations it is necessary to have full awareness of all the actions in the field. In traditional C2 systems, human operators play key roles varying from observation in the field up to semantic interpretation of observed data in the Command and Control Centre. Networks are mainly used to transmit data between different components of the network. Observation by human operators will be replaced by sensor networks. The huge amount of incoming data is far beyond the capacity of operators, so the heterogeneous, multimodal data from the different sensor systems has to be fused, aggregated, and filtered. Automated surveillance sensor networks are discussed in this chapter. Sensors are modelled as a distributed system of smart agents. Methods and technology from Artificial Intelligence such as expert systems, semantic networks, and probabilistic reasoning is used to give a semantic interpretation of the sensed data from the environment.*

## INTRODUCTION

In the military domain many C2 networks are used. These networks are used to convey information from sender to receiver. In case of hierarchical networks the command and control centre is at the top of the network. To get full context awareness it is necessary to process the incoming information. Operators in those centres are confronted with a tsunami of messages and are supposed to process the incoming data 24 hours, 7 days in a week. Obviously, there is a need of automated systems to support operators during their work.

A special type of C2 networks are surveillance networks. The use of sensor networks has been proposed for military surveillance and environmental monitoring applications. Those systems deploy a heterogeneous set of sensors to observe the environment. For example, unmanned vehicles (UAV's) such as the ScanEagle (see Figure 1) are able to survey an environment with their high tech video camera system. The recordings are transmitted to the ground station which is connected to the control room via a C2-network. To navigate the drones and to inspect the video recordings many operators are needed in the ground station. In general, observed data has to be processed automatically, and finally has to be displayed in a control room.

DOI: 10.4018/978-1-4666-6058-8.ch012

*Figure 1. ScanEagle launched from Zr.Ms.Rotterdam*

In the control room observed data is monitored by human operators. They are supposed to give a semantic interpretation to the observed data. In case of suspicious or unwanted behaviour they start an alert procedure. The increase of surveillance cameras in the military domain requires an exponential growth of the number of human operators which is far beyond available human and financial resources. So there is a need to automate the semantic interpretation process of sensor data. Most distributed networks of video sensors are wireless connected and suffer from limited bandwidth, storage and processing capacity. To transfer the data from point to point, the data has to be filtered and aggregated to short messages. Information captured from different sensors from different complexity and modality has to be fused.

Most networks support smart search agents. Those agents are able to search automatically and independently for relevant information. Smart agents are also used to control the information flow and to secure the network. Nowadays, agents can be designed that are able to read coded text in different formats. The automated processing of pictures and video is more complex (VSAM, 1996). Video footage of surveillance cameras is still processed by human operators. A surveillance system must be able to detect and track objects in the field of views (FOV) of the cameras, classify these objects and detect some of their activities. It

should also be capable of generating a description of the events happening within its field of view. But the ultimate challenge is to give a semantic interpretation of the observed events. That is why human operators are usually needed in control and command centres. But as stated before, constantly monitoring by human operators is no longer an option.

In this chapter smart agents are defined in C2 networks. They are modelled after human model and replace the role of human operators. A great advantage of such agents is that they can easily by defined in great numbers, they are able to operate continuously with a high quality of performance all the time. Another advantage of the use of such agents is that they are not localized on specific places as human operators in control stations, but are able to operate throughout the whole network. The use of agents transforms C2 networks into smart networks with a hierarchical structure of locally processing independent units, solving the common drawbacks of human operators.

As a proof of concept an automatic surveillance project will be discussed in this chapter. The project is about the AIS-Automated Identification System (Vessel tracking, 2013) which will be used to monitor ship movements. Since the increase of terroristic attacks, also in Europe there is a need for a surveillance system along the coast of Europe to detect intruders and suspicious ship movements. AIS was designed for the safety of ships. Visibility of ships, even in bad weather conditions is necessary to prevent collisions. At this moment even small military ships and unmanned surface vehicles will be equipped with AIS transponders. This increases the context awareness of the C2 network. Ships and their movements will be displayed in real time automatically. How to handle such a huge amount of data, to monitor these data and generate a semantic interpretation, is the main research topic of this chapter.

Currently, ship movements are monitored by human operators in control rooms. To automate this surveillance system some questions have to be discussed. The first question is about the topology of the surveillance network, to design a central or decentralized system. Because of the multiple sensors and limited bandwidth of the surveillance network, local processing of observed data is needed. Questions about this local data processing will be solved by designing a network of smart agents running on the surveillance network. The next question is where to store the recorded data. To this end, a system of distributed blackboards will be introduced.

The developed system should be able to perform:

- Automatic identification, localization and tracking of ships in a parallel way, using observed AIS data.
- Store recorded tracks in a database.
- Visualize recorded tracks.
- Automatically analyse recorded tracks.
- Monitor and control fishing fleet movements.
- Investigate accidents.
- Protect critical infrastructure, such as military harbours and installation against piracy, terrorist attacks and intruders.
- Generate alerts and alarms after probabilistic/deterministic reasoning/processing.

The outline of this chapter is as follows. In the next section we give an overview of related projects and research. Then we present different aspects of sensor surveillance networks. Finally we report about a surveillance network implemented by researchers of the Netherlands Defence Academy (Scholte, 2013; Rothkrantz & Scholte, 2013). At the end of the chapter there is a general conclusion.

## RELATED WORK

The Defence Advanced Research Projects Agency (DARPA) Information Systems Office is funding research into Video Surveillance and Monitoring technology under BAA 96-14, Image Understanding for Battlefield Awareness (VSAM, 1996). The objective of the VSAM project is to develop automated video understanding technology for use in future urban and battlefield surveillance and monitoring applications. Under BAA 96-14, one Integrated Feasibility Demonstration (IFD) contract was awarded to a team composed of Carnegie Mellon University and the David Sarnoff Research Center (Collins et al., 1999). The Defender and Agile Programs formed the foundation of DARPA sensor surveillance. In 2013 DARPA launched a device for a ground sensor (video) based on Android technology for surveillance purposes and network processing. This device is related to the concept of smart dust (Rothkrantz et al., 2010).

Sensor networks in distributed wireless communication technology and its applications in military surveillance have been discussed by He et al. (2004). They developed a new data aggregation algorithm called AIDA for wireless sensor networks. A surveillance network of smart cameras for a military area was developed by Hameete et al (2012).

AMASS (2010) (Autonomous Marine Surveillance System) is a European project which draws on the latest technology to provide a reliable, round-the-clock maritime monitoring solution. A line of buoys located offshore ensures comprehensive coverage of territorial waters. Each buoy is equipped with the latest visual and acoustic sensors. When a suspicious vessel is detected, images can be transmitted directly to a control centre on shore. This provides authorities with unprecedented observation capabilities an enables them to take swift appropriate action.

The goal of the European project Intelligent Surveillance and Border Security (I2C, 2010) is to design an integrated system for interoperable sensors & information sources for common abnormal vessel behaviour detection & collaborative identification of threat.

Indra (2009) designs, builds and integrates state of-the-art border surveillance systems for coastal and terrestrial supervision use. These systems can be integrated with existing systems and networks to improve the performance with respect to detection and coordination.

The Northrop Grumman MQ-4C Triton (2013) is an unmanned area vehicle (UAV) under development for the United States as a surveillance aircraft. Developed under the Broad Area Maritime Surveillance (BAMS) program, this system is intended to provide continuous maritime surveillance for the US Navy.

The Maritime Surveillance System from Saab (2013) represents the new vision of Maritime Surveillance for detection, identification, monitoring and control of the territorial sea, economic zones and environmentally sensitive areas.

Two NATO Centres of Excellence (CJOS, CSW) have taken the challenge of exploring maritime security issues and searching for global solutions. They jointly organized the Maritime Security Conference 2011 and a second jointed Conference 2012 in Halifax (MSC 2011, 2012).

The Automatic Identification System (AIS-Wik, 2013) is an automatic traffic system used for identifying and locating vessels by electronically exchanging data with other nearby ships. It was developed in the 1990s as a high intensity, short range identification and tracking network. But since 2005 AIS receivers were deployed at satellites by companies as exactEarth. The use of satellites enables operators to receive a huge amount of AIS messages. Correlating optical and radar imagery with AIS data results in rapid identification of all types of vessels. Satellite-based radar and other sources can contribute to maritime surveillance by detecting all vessels in specific maritime areas of interest. This is a particularly useful attribute when trying to coordinate a long-range rescue effort or when dealing with Vessel Traffic Services issues, collision avoidance, fishing fleet monitoring and control, maritime security, pirate surveillance, search and rescue, and accident investigation.

## ASPECTS OF SENSOR AND OPERATOR SURVEILLANCE SYSTEMS

### Large Scale Surveillance Systems

The Atlantic Wall was an extensive system of coastal fortifications built by Nazi Germany between 1942 and 1945 along the western coast of Europe and Scandinavia. It was designed as a defense against an anticipated Allied invasion of the mainland continent from Great Britain (Hakim, 1995). Field Marshal Erwin Rommel improved the Atlantic wall by adding reinforced pillboxes built along the beaches. From those pillboxes the sea was monitored by human observers. All the local command post along the sea were connected to each other and finally to the central command post in Berlin. Nowadays, there is no longer a need for protection against a large scale invasion. Instead, a new, daunting task is the protection against (the invasion by) terrorist, criminals and illegal persons. Given the large area that has to be protected, observation by human operators along the Atlantic coast is no option. Human operators have to be replaced by sensor surveillance systems. To be more precise, in the next section we propose a mixture of sensors of varying complexity and human observers. Smart sensors are able to process observed data locally and can be placed in distributed sensor networks. In the next section we will introduce a hierarchy of C2 sensor networks. Some sensors are components of a centralized network and transmit recorded data to communication centres for further processing and interpretation. As an application we introduce a huge sensor network of AIS data.

Nowadays ship movements along the coast of Europe and the North Sea are monitored by the AIS system. Vessels fitted with AIS transceivers and transponders can be tracked by AIS base stations located along coast lines or, when out of range of terrestrial networks, through a growing number of satellites that are fitted with special AIS receivers. Information provided by AIS equipment, such as unique identification, position, course and speed, can be displayed on a screen or an ECDIS (AIS, 2013), compare Figure 2. The International Maritime Organization's International Convention for the Safety of Life at Sea requires AIS to be fitted aboard international voyaging ships with gross tonnage (GT) of 300 or more tons, and all passenger ships regardless of size. Currently ship movements are monitored by human operators in control rooms (Vessel tracking, 2013).

## Decision Making

Klein (1999) claims that there is a difference between human and automated observation and reasoning. He states that human operators generate a hypothesis using their experience when confronted with relevant patterns. When people need to make a decision they can quickly match the situation to the patterns they have learned during training in the past. If they find a clear match, they can carry out the most typical course of action. In that way, people can successfully make extremely

rapid decisions. Human operators are unable or not willing to consider alternatives simultaneously. They stick to the first hypothesis and give it up only if many contradictory data becomes available that supports an alternative hypothesis. This perspective took advantage of new developments in cognitive psychology and Artificial Intelligence such as knowledge representation, concepts of scripts, schemas, and mental models, to contrast expert versus novice behaviour.

An automated surveillance system should be able to reason about many hypotheses in parallel. Computational methods, such as Bayesian reasoning and classifiers, are used to make an optimal choice. According to Klein this automated way of reasoning is quite different from the human way of reasoning called Naturalistic Decision Making (NDM). Both methods have in common that experience, historical data are needed to develop human way of reasoning or to train automated systems. Moreover, they don't allow innovative thinking. Human experts come up with solutions experienced in the past, while in computational systems possible solutions are defined a priori

*Figure 2. A graphical display of AIS data*

by the designer. Recently new ways of creative thinking based on computational methods have been developed. In such a bottom up approach, most salient and relevant features are combined in an innovative way (Rothkrantz et al., 2009).

Klein states in (1987, 1999) that the U.S. Navy became interested in naturalistic decisions following the 1988 USS Vincennes shoot-down incident, in which a U.S. Navy Aegis cruiser destroyed an Iranian commercial airliner, mistaking it for a hostile attacker. Both the Army and the Navy wanted to help people make high-stakes decisions under extreme time pressure and under dynamic and uncertain conditions. The first NDM conference, in 1989, assembled researchers studying decision making in field settings. In a chapter that emerged from that meeting, Lipshitz & Strauss (1997) identified no less than nine NDM models that had been developed in parallel. One of these was Hammond's cognitive continuum theory (Hammond et al., 1987), which asserts that decisions vary in the degree to which they rely on intuitive and analytical processes. Conditions such as amount of information and time available, determine where decisions fall on this continuum and whether people rely more on patterns or on functional relationships.

A second account of decision making was Rasmussen's (1985) model of cognitive control, which distinguished skill-based, rule-based, and knowledge-based behaviour operating within the context of a decision ladder that permitted heuristic cut-off paths.

## Actor-Agent Community in C2 Networks

A surveillance network of human operators is composed of several layers of communication (see Figure 3)

- overlapping clouds of actors (human sensors, perception devices).

- corresponding clouds of representative agents.
- C2 centre and clouds of services.

In the first layer human observers observe the surrounding world and communicate with each other within that layer. The observed information will be communicated to the control room, outside world or stored in a database via a communication layer. In the communication layer the information will be processed by a process of filtering, aggregation and fusion. It is important to note that human observers are trained observers, who are sensitive to specific features. Observed data from sensors is under human control and will be processed and interpreted by human operators.

A sensor surveillance system is composed of several layers and components (Klapwijk et al., 2006) (see Figure 4):

- a human communication layer
- a virtual communication layer
- a layer of virtual coordinating agents.

At the highest level the real world is observed by sensors and human observers. Sensors are designed to observe specific features and events. Human observers have specific role and task in the observation process. Both are modelled as agents. (In the agent community there is no difference between actors and agents.) The observation area is covered by different sets of actor-agents with overlapping field of views. Human observers are assumed to report their observations to the surveillance system via handhelds. Sensors are wired or wireless connected to the surveillance system and report by means of communication devices.

The communication devices link the observation layer and communication layer. Within the communication layer there is the communication between special agents taking care of fusion, filtering, aggregation, linking and storage. Because agents are defined as autonomous objects they live their own life in the communication layer with

*Figure 3. Surveillance network of human operators*

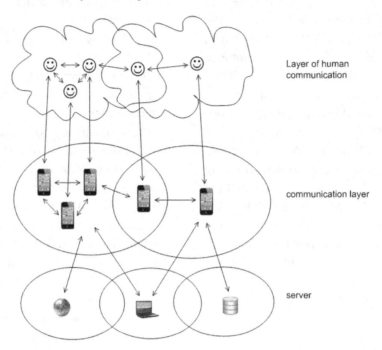

limited human control. In the kernel of the network is a layer of coordinating agents. This layer is connected to human operators in the control room. It is important to notice that a sensor surveillance system as an actor-agent community is beyond human control. Currently hybrid systems are used under full or limited human control. This will be discussed in more details in our case study.

Every human observer has a digital counterpart, a personal 'guardian angel' taking care of his wellbeing and taking care of the communication with other parts of the system. It is important to notice that human observers are not aware of the communication of personal agents, and have only partly control of the communication between agents. Nowadays, a decentralised approach is very common in military missions. Seals can be dropped in a hostile area to perform their mission without central control. Communication with a central control room will reveal their position to the enemy. The innovative aspect is that a sensor surveillance network is populated by agents. In the actor-agent community, agents and human

operators are both modelled as agents and can play similar roles.

According to its definition, agents are autonomous pieces of software, able to perceive the world, reason about it and take appropriate actions. Agents extract knowledge from the surrounding world. This information is placed on blackboards, shared by a cluster of agents. Every blackboard has special functions to combine, aggregate, update, communicate or delete information. In a surveillance network there can be one central blackboard or a hierarchical network of distributed blackboards. From bottom to the top there is a fusion of low sensor information up to high semantic information. The concept of an actor agent community and a network of blackboards was first introduced by Rothkrantz (Tatomir et al., 2006; Fitrianie et al., 2009).

## Centralized, Decentralized, Multimodal Surveillance Systems

A sensor surveillance network can be composed of different kinds of sensors ranging from radar,

*Figure 4. Surveillance network of agents*

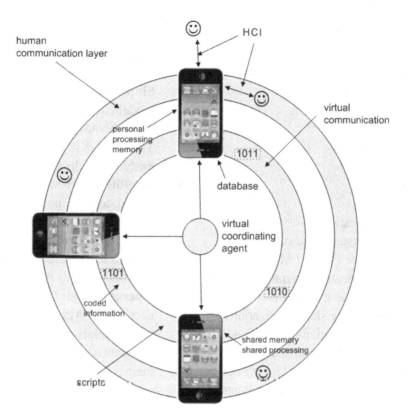

sonar to camera systems. To localise, for example, a submarine a sonar system can be used. Another option is to connect the submarine to a floating GPS system. However, GPS doesn't function below the sea level. To navigate, locally a network of floating smart dust can be used (Rothkrantz, 2010). To obtain visual information from above the water surface information from a drone equipped with camera can be used. Such a sensor network may cover a huge area. If wireless networks are involved, such a network has to handle the limitations in bandwidth and storage capacity. Here, a central approach has its limitations and a distributed system is more appropriate.

Every individual sensor monitors its own area and has a limited span of control. In our case study to be discussed later, the information extracted by the sensor is processed locally and send to the local blackboard which is shared by the global blackboards. Semantic interpretation of observed

events starts with observations of sensors that are remote in place and time and are from different modality. The fusion of observed data from multiple sensors is performed at the blackboard systems. Observation and processing of data is a distributed process. Due to the huge amount of sensors, central processing by human operators is no option anymore. The important question therefore is: do local optimal systems also result in globally optimal systems? A similar paradigm shift is observed in C2 systems in general. Until recently, in C2 system centralised decision making was favoured. In the NEC approach, the decision making process is distributed over the network.

Drones and satellites are able to survey fully automatically. But launching a missile from a drone is still under human control. In fact more than 200 operators, including maintenance staff, navigation staff, etc. are involved to keep one drone operational. In this chapter it is demonstrated that a first step to a fully automated surveillance system is a decision support system. In case of coordinated actions, the man is still in the loop. A dedicated orchestration between global and local decision making is needed. This process is facilitated by the hierarchical blackboard structure.

## CASE AIS-SYSTEM

### Introduction

The Automatic Identification System (AIS) is an automatic tracking system used on ships and by Vessel Traffic Service (VTS) (AIS-Live). It uses UHF radio communications to transmit and receive data. Ships are able to detect their position, course and speed using ship's navigational sensors such as global navigational satellite and gyrocompass. Together with the ships name and cargo information, these data can be broadcasted at regular intervals via a VHF transmitter built into AIS transponders. The signals can be received by other ship transponders or land based VTS systems. The data can be displayed on computer screens and will be used for navigation and collision avoidance.

Shipboard AIS transponders have a horizontal range of about 70 km. This is enough to avoid collisions between ships. But for surveillance of ship movements data from large areas are needed. Signals of AIS transponders are able to reach satellites. Currently a network of satellites with AIS transponders takes care of the distribution of AIS data over large areas. AIS position data are now available on the Internet and public domain. This raises a serious question concerning safety of navigation and security of military harbours and transport. Of course, ship movements can be detected by an observer with a binocular, as in the old days of the Atlantic Wall. But, his range of sight will be limited by weather conditions. Ships can also turn off their AIS transponders, but then they are still visible by radar which makes their behaviour suspicious.

The AIS system can be viewed as a huge network of nodes composed in 3 layers:

- **Ship layer:** At the lowest level ships are modelled as moving nodes. They are linked at neighbouring nodes in a region of 70km. The network is very dynamic; links will be enabled and disabled continuously.
- **Satellite layer:** Moving satellites are connected to ship nodes within their reach. Satellites are connected to ground stations. The data will be processed at these ground stations and distributed via communication networks such as the World Wide Web.
- **Operator level:** Operators are able to connect to the AIS system via WWW. They have to select a region of their interest, and AIS data of ship tracks will be displayed on their computer screen.

It is almost impossible to monitor ship movements 24 hours, 7 days in a week in all possible sea regions for the detection of unwanted behaviour such as violating traffic rules, entering forbidden areas or attacking ships or installations. Command centre need aggregated data to take their decisions. So there is a need to automate the surveillance process at the operator level. The research questions are:

- How to handle huge amounts of data streams in huge, dynamic networks? In some areas thousands of ships can be detected and their tracks should be visualized.
- How to design monitoring agents modelled after human operator mode? Such an agent should be able to monitor data from computer screens, reason about these data, and give a semantic interpretation. Eventually, it should be able to generate an alert to a command centre staffed by human operators.

The proposed solution is to introduce smart agents in the AIS surveillance network. The AIS network is split up in overlapping regions. The ship movements in a region can be displayed on a computer screen. As soon as a ship appears in a region a smart agent will be attached to it as a surveillance agent. We notice that this agent based approach is different from the analysis of a human operator. A human operator usually starts with a global scan of the screen and if a salient feature is detected the operator zooms in, and the situation will be analysed. Our agents track the vessels, and the attached vectors of features will be analysed continuously. Every region has a specific set of unwanted/suspicious behaviour and, as a consequence, a context sensitive surveillance system. In case unwanted behaviour will be detected, the surveillance agent will send a message to the control room, usually via some intermediate steps in the hierarchical network connecting ships, ground stations, sensors, satellites, etc. Because the regions are overlapping, a surveillance agent can move from one region to the other, following the route of a ship. As a proof of concept, the design and implementation of a surveillance system around the military harbour of Den Helder will be presented.

## Automated Surveillance

Each Automatic Identification System (AIS) position report gives basic kinematic data: the geographical position and speed vector of a vessel. These can be used to directly trigger simple inference rules or nodes in a network. For example whether a speed limit is violated or whether a vessel is currently in a restricted area. Using multiple (sequential) reports we can derive more complex events (or features) from these basic parameters over time. Important events are change in speed and course, as these may be indicative of more complex events, e.g. anchoring (deceleration at open sea) or departure of a Traffic Separation Scheme (TSS) (change in course). Changes in course or speed can be inferred using the derivative of either the speed or course function.

The ultimate research challenge is to give a semantic interpretation of the kinematic data. At this moment detection of behaviour and intent takes place in the mind of the operator in the control room, the hierarchical top of the surveillance network. To design an automatic system for assessment of situation awareness after human model, we have to analyse the cognitive model of an operator. Situation awareness consists of three steps. First the operator observes information on his computer display, then he interprets the information so that he understands what it means, and finally he places the meaning of the information in a wider context and forms a mental picture of the situation that is occurring.

The cognitive model of an operator is similar to the BDI (Belief-Desire-Intention) model that has been developed for agents as described in (Rao, 1995).

In the phase called situation awareness the operator tries to form beliefs about what is going on, based on the information displayed on the computer screen. He then defines a set of goals or desires based on those beliefs. With these goals in mind he plans and performs actions (intentions) to achieve those goals. The agent never stops monitoring the system. This means the steps that have been described can be performed in parallel. It might be that the operator, during one of the steps of the process, observes some very important information and might stop the process. Then he begins the process anew based on the new information. An alternative model is based on the OODA loop (Boyd, 1976) as described in the next section.

## A Human Based AIS Surveillance System

In this section the knowledge extraction from the operator will be described. This knowledge will be the basis of a decision support system. The focus is on the area of the military harbour of Den Helder (Scholte, 2013).

The basic input of the AIS-based-surveillance system is the identity of the ship, position, and kinematic data such as speed and heading. These data are updated with some sample rate. From these input features more advanced features can be computed, such as trajectories, curvature of trajectories, acceleration, etc. All these detected features can be displayed on the annotated map around the military harbour. An operator is monitoring a computer screen with a map of the area around the harbour. On the map the ship movements sensed by the AIS system, are displayed (see Figure 5). The map is annotated with the following Region of Interest (ROI):

- The main traffic routes, which are identified by logging AIS data for some time. These routes are marked by buoys, transmitting light and radio signals. Ships are supposed to sail within traffic routes. At special crossings they are permitted to take another traffic route.

- Critical infrastructure, such as oil rigs or other strategic locations, entrance of the military harbour, areas around windmill parks.
- Special areas such as fishing grounds that require a permit, shallow areas (bathymetric data), nature reserves.

In general the ROI's are no-go areas or areas with limited access. Ships entering this area or intent to enter this area show deviant, suspicious or unwanted behaviour. But the list of unwanted behaviour is not limited to entering forbidden areas. Based on interviews with human operators the following classes of salient and possible unwanted behaviour have to be considered:

- Sudden change of directions, sharp U-turns. There is a risk that these sudden movements will not be detected by other ships in time.
- Deviant sailing behaviour such as continuous change of heading, change of speed or even stopping. Such a snake-like behaviour, could be caused by mechanical prob-

*Figure 5. Map of the harbour of Den Helder*

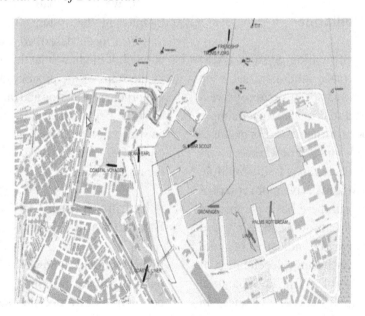

lems or by personal factors of the captain (drunk/ill/incompetent captain).

- Intent of intrusion in ROIs. Some critical infrastructures are surrounded by special forbidden areas.
- Intent of collision. Every ship is surrounded by a personal space which should not be intruded.
- Leaving traffic separation corridors at unexpected place and time or sailing outside usual corridors. The sea maps are annotated with traffic separation corridors, computed using historical data.
- Violating traffic rules, such as surpassing speed limit, entering military areas without permission or anchoring close to oil platforms.
- Sailing at unexpected/forbidden place and time.
- Switching off the AIS system at unexpected place and time.

Finally all these unwanted behaviours will be filtered and results in an alert that will be sent to the operator room if the probability that a behaviour or combination of behaviours is suspicious, passes a threshold.

A human operator is supposed to monitor all the displayed ship tracks continuously. He has special characteristics to perform this task. In the first place he is able to focus his attention on the place where the action is, and adapt the level of attention. Secondly, he is able to zoom in and zoom out and include context information. Thirdly, he is able to fuse events distributed in place and time. And last but not least he is able to handle incomplete, ambiguous data updated with different sample rates. To perform this challenging tasks a human operator has a high qualified perception system, which is very sensitive to small movements and unusual events. He has a short term and long term memory, a well developed reasoning system and is able to monitor and evaluate his own actions.

In fact, a human operator is difficult to emulate as a digital agent.

To design an automated system to survey a large area covered by the AIS system, it is necessary to split up the area in smaller parts, analyse these parts in parallel and again and again combine the results, to come up with a context awareness of the whole area. In the next section the implementation of such an automated system will be presented.

## Design of an AIS Surveillance System

The task of the surveillance system is to detect unwanted behaviour automatically. Just like the operator based system, the input of the automated system is the kinematic AIS data, such as position, speed, track, heading and the identity of the ship. As mentioned before the challenge of an automated system is to give a semantic interpretation of the kinematic data. One of the problems to solve is that observed data is distributed in place and time. Usually a sequence of events is observed. As soon as the first events are observed, the system has to come up with a tentative interpretation and a prediction of possible future events. For example, in case of a terrorist attack in the harbour aimed at exploding an oil reservoir, the system registers the intrusion of a ROI of a critical infrastructure. But to take appropriate defence action it is necessary to detect the intent to intrude a ROI long before. Such events can only be detected with some probability. Two approaches will be presented, a rule based system and a Bayesian system.

### Rule Based System

In (Rothkrantz & Scholte, 2013) the authors present a decision support system. The decision support system is modelled after human operator model. Operators in the control room of the Coast Guard at Den Helder were interviewed. They were requested to answer open questions and to give an interpretation of selected screen dumps of AIS data. It shows that an operator is triggered by unusual events, generates a hypothesis about the possible ongoing situation, validates this hypothesis by new data and generates an action. This procedure is very similar to the well-known OODA loop (Boyd, 1976). The knowledge/expertise of the human operator has to be extracted from the experts by interviews and comments of operators confronted with simulated suspicious events. The knowledge of the operator is represented as if-then rules. A well-known expert system shell CLIPS (Boullart et al., 1992) was used to implement the knowledge rules and to design a reasoning procedure. Features extracted from the AIS system are fed into the expert system and the system generates possible actions.

The knowledge elicitation task was again realised by interviewing the experts in the human control room. These experts were requested to report about their past experience using the OODA loop model. While monitoring the computer displays with AIS data, they reported about salient triggers, which hypothesis was generated, how they are evaluated and which action has to be generated. A list of triggers, hypothesis, evaluation and actions was generated and corresponding IF-THEN rules. The system was implemented using CLIPS, an expert system toolkit.

- IF <trigger> THEN Suggest <hypothesis

- <hypothesis> confirmed by <validation tests>
- If <validation tests> THEN DO <action>

Operators act according to a processing information model, as shown in Figure 6. We distinguish two types of processes: a rule-based flow, and a knowledge-based flow. Note the absence of a skill-based track. An operator cycles through his set of Region Of Interest (ROI). In some cases he might see unexpected behaviour from a contact. This abnormality is either a violation he recognizes, or a possible violation that is not instantly recognizable for which more information is required. In the former case, the operator associates a rule with the violation after which a corresponding action is triggered. For example, a vessel is observed speeding in the port and subsequently the harbour police is informed to fine the vessel. In the latter case, things are more complex. An abnormality is observed, but it is unclear to the operator which or even if a violation has been committed by the contact. This urges the operator to gather more information on the situation.

Another approach is to annotate the tracks of ships as displayed in Figure 8. The onset and offset of detected behaviour can be indicated, using markers or different colours for behaviour and intensities. A sequence of behaviours has a special semantic interpretation in general. In general a

*Figure 6. Simplified model of traffic monitoring operator cognitive processes*

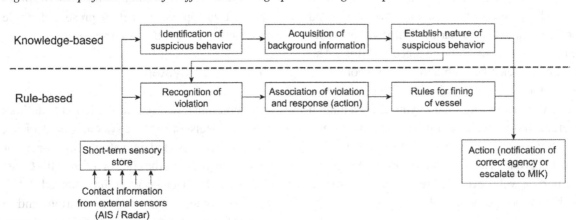

sequence of unwanted behaviours is even more unwanted. Let us consider special sequences of behaviours. The data process starts with sampling data. At discrete time steps a vector of AIS data will be sensed such as position, speed, heading. From that data some feature vectors will be extracted or computed such as change of speed, change of heading TSS, ROI. A semantic interpretation can be given to a sequence of time stamped features. We consider two examples:

Example 1: Let us consider a ship leaving his trajectory (TSS) and taking a sharp turn. Then it enters an ROI with restricted entrance permission. Finally the AIS system is switched of. This string of features is a typical example of illegal fishing.

Example 2: Let us consider a vessel approaching the harbour. Before it enters the harbour it stops and appears to be drifting at sea. No signal from the vessel is received that anything is wrong. Given the string of features an alert will be generated, because the vessel behaviour us suspicious. Later it turned out that the vessel arrived 2 hours early and its pilot was not available yet.

From the given examples it is clear that it is not always possible to give a unique semantic interpretation of the observed sequence of features. The situation can be very ambiguous or the observed data is not complete. Such sequences of behaviours can be modelled by finite state diagrams or analysed using probabilistic models. A sequence of behaviours can be analysed using a rule based system. First a list of all possible scenarios was defined and possible sequences of behaviours. But usually the system is forced to come up with a semantic interpretation after the onset of the first features. The main goal of the AIS surveillance system is to detect unwanted behaviour as soon as possible. So after the onset of the first behaviour, all possible scenarios are triggered and listed in priorities. After observation of the next scenarios, the first list of possible scenarios has to be reduced and eventually a new scenario gets

the highest priority and will eventually generate an alert. In this way the system is able to reason with incomplete, ambiguous data. Considering possible solutions in parallel is not feasible for human operators, as stated by Klein (1987, 1999). In section 3 we cited Klein reporting the incident with the Airliner. If an Airliner and a missile are far away there is a low recognition rate. So it is no option to shoot down every moving object to guarantee that a ship will not be hit by a missile.

One of the disadvantages of using a rule-based system is that IF-THEN rules are always deterministic. Either the IF-condition of the rule is fulfilled or it is not. A certain event or variable value may be an indication for more than one situation. For example, a ship at high speed approaching the harbour wants to embark as soon as possible, or has hostile intents. The rule based system doesn't satisfy the requirements, and a more flexible model is needed. This flexibility can be achieved using a probabilistic model. Basically this models the probability that a situation is occurring, or that it is not occurring based on the information displayed on the computer screen and the reasoning process of the operator. Usually a huge data corpus is needed to compute the Conditional Probability Tables (CPT) in Bayesian networks. But unwanted behaviours are rare events. So it is impossible to gather data by logging data for some time. Military experts have to set the values in the Conditional Probability Tables.

## Bayesian Reasoning

Bayesian belief networks are often used in reasoning systems (GeNie and Smile, 2013). They have proven themselves in a number of applications. Wiggers et al., (2011) present a successful application of Bayesian networks in the detection of missiles. In a Bayesian belief network one can indicate the effect that an event has on another event. Bayesian networks can be visualized as directed graphs. Given some evidence (some facts should be specified as being either true or false with a certain probability) the probability of the events one is interested in (the query events) can be calculated. One can also state that it is not completely certain that an event has happened, but is has happened with a certain probability. This probability is then taken into account when the probability of the queried event is calculated.

In Figure 7 a Bayesian model of automated detection of unwanted behaviour has been displayed. At every sampled point $t_n$, kinematic parameters, position and identify will be observed. The position parameter will be matched to the ROI's to compute the distance to the ROI's. Next, the onset of one or more of the unwanted behaviours will be computed from the observed parameters. Finally the probability of an onset of an alert has to be computed. The relationship between the variables related to unwanted behaviour and the generation of an alert is defined by the CPT-tables. Usually in Bayesian networks discrete variables are used. The entries of the CPT-tables between variables have to be computed or set by experts. A functional

relation between variables corresponding to the probabilities of connecting variables has to be computed or defined. In Figure 7 the probabilistic function between connecting variables is indicated by Pi's. These functions are defined as follows:

**P1:** Let $T(t_n)$ be the trajectory of a ship. The curvature $C(t_n)$ can be computed with alpha $(t_n)$ as corresponding angle. If alpha increases from zero to 90 degrees, the probability that the ship is turning increases from 0-1, modelled as a sigmoid function such that P1 (30 degrees) is 0.5. Similarly, the probability that the ship is making a U-turn is also modelled as a sigmoid function but with a lower slope, such that P1(90 degree) is 0.5.

**P2:** Let $T(t_n)$ be the trajectory of a ship, where n is between 1 and N. Let M be the number of times that the acceleration or heading passes some given threshold. Then P2 is defined as a cumulative Poisson distribution. If a ship stops then P2 will be set to 1 immediately.

*Figure 7. Model of a Bayesian network to detect abnormal sailing behaviour*

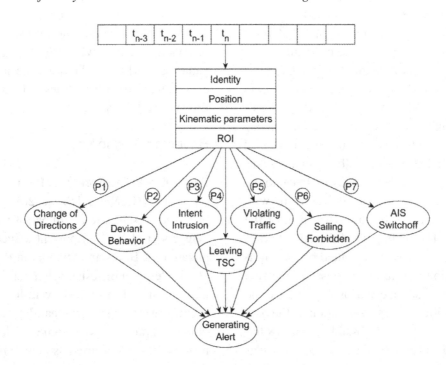

**P3:** Let $T(t_n)$ be the trajectory of a ship and $d(t_n)$ the distance between the ship and a critical infra-structure, then P2 is defined as exp(-$d_n$).

**P4:** A ship is assumed to sail within well-defined traffic separation trajectories. If a ship leaves this trajectory, P4 will be set to 1, and is set to 0 if the ship turns back to the trajectory.

**P5:** If a ship violates the traffic rules, P5 will be set to 1.

**P6:** P1 is related to a ROI with no entrance allowed. But even in case the ship is sailing in open areas, it could show suspicious behaviour if this happens at unexpected times and place. Special ROI have to be defined given place and time. Then P6 is similar to the computation of P1

**P7:** If a sailing ship turns off his AIS system, then P7 is set to 1.

To compute the probability of the generation of an alert, the probabilities of the observed unwanted behaviours have to combined using a noisy AND-OR approach as an inference method. A first prototype has been implemented and reported in (Rothkrantz & Scholte, 2013) using Genie as a Bayesian reasoning tool.

The Bayesian inference procedure can be executed at every time step $t_n$. The computed probabilities of the generation of an alert at successive time steps are related. This has been studied using the Dynamic Bayesian network version of Genie. Up to now, the duration and intensity of a sequence of unwanted behaviours has not been considered. Recently Scholte (2013) defined a probabilistic version of the observed unwanted behaviours. The probabilities of the observation will increase if the intensity and the duration of the observed behaviours increase. The implemented prototype has been tested and compared to the performance of human operators. It proved that the automatic system generated a lot of false positives caused by the fact that all options were analysed in parallel. The number can be reduced by decreasing the thresholds of generating an alert, but then there is a danger that the number of false negatives increases.

## Experiment Speed and Course Change Detection

To test the designed surveillance system a list of scenarios has been designed, representing one of the classes of unwanted behaviours as defined before. In the database of logged data, examples of such scenarios are looked up and the system has been tested. A scenario of speed and course change detection will be discussed. Many other scenarios are tested.

Consider a vessel executing a turn. Starting from the last point (the most recently received position update), we can calculate the course change using the numerical approximation given in the following Equation:

$$C(t)' = \frac{C(t) - C(t-1)}{\delta t}$$

where $C(t)$ = course at point t, n=last data point, $\delta t$=time between data points.

However, there need to be some form of smoothing or thresholding on the data. Consider a vessel that intends to travel in a straight line. Due to factors such as tide, wind or sea state, the observed track is not straight when looking at a small number of consecutive data points. This may lead to the triggering of events even though the vessel maintains its course. Therefore we expand upon the Equation above by introducing a sliding window over which the delta values are averaged:

$$C(t)' = \frac{C(t) - C(t-1)}{\delta t}$$

where $C(t)$ = course at point t, n=last data point, m=window size (in seconds).

This means that we average the cumulative change in course (or speed) between two consecutive data points over the entire window. By using a windowed function, noise in the "signal" caused by environmental factors such as tide, wind or sea state, is suppressed.

Change in course or speed is detected when the above mentioned windowed derivative exceeds a certain threshold. This concept can be translated into a simple algorithm of which the pseudo code given below. Note that this algorithm uses a specified window over which the mean is calculated, as mentioned above.

**Algorithm:** Detecting course and speed changes in a vessel's track over time.

**Data:** Vessel track

**Result:** Detected changes in course $C$ or speed $S$/* We assume point index 1 is the most recent point */

1    Select track points over period $m$ $-\rightarrow$ pointList; /* this is the buffer window */
2    $n$ = length(pointList);
3    $\delta C(1)$ = pointList(1).course - mean(pointList(2).course to pointList(n). course) /m;

4    $\delta S(1)$ = pointList(1).speed - mean(pointList(2).speed to pointList(n). speed) / m;

The algorithm described above was used to detect changes in course and speed of vessels. As an example of how this behaves with real data, Figure 8 shows the track of the "MV Nestor."

A moving window size (m = 60s) was used, a course change threshold Tc was set at 0.08deg/s and a speed change threshold Ts = 0.01kts/s. The total track length is 39736s; or approximately 11 hours. The "Nestor" (mmsi = 244688000) is a vessel used for sea fishing trips. Depicted in the Figure 8 is the vessel returning to its port of call, Den Helder. Note that the first AIS position report is the most recently received one and the last the oldest. The course and speed parameters are quite noisy. This is to be expected as wind, tide and sea state have a large impact on these parameters. The noisy characteristics can also be found in the derivatives of both parameters.

Similar output can be observed when looking at vessels with a more stable course and speed, e.g. those that are in a Traffic Separation Scheme (TSS).

*Figure 8. Track data for the "MV Nestor"*

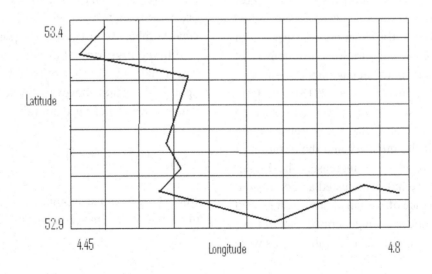

## CONCLUSION

In this chapter surveillance networks are researched and one application is presented. The application was focused on surveillance of a military harbour and its environment using the AIS system. It shows that it was possible to give a semantic interpretation of sensed kinematic data distributed via the AIS network. The designed system can be used as a fully automated system or as a decision support system in the control room by human operators. In surveillance networks smart sensors survey the environment. They replace human observers. It is no option to have human observers anytime, anywhere. The sensors are modelled after a human observer. A well-known model to emulate human observation is the OODA loop. The sensors are distributed over a large area. The agents in the network are not localized in space and time but distributed and moving round the network all the time. To convey the observed information to the control room it is necessary to fuse data recorded by different sensors, to aggregate the information and to give a semantic interpretation of the recorded information. For that reason a hierarchical structure of distributed blackboards has been introduced. The human way of observation and reasoning is implemented in the smart sensors. This is why sensors are modelled as software agents moving around in the surveillance network. At the end the information is conveyed to the control room and displayed on computer screens in a user friendly way. Again it is no option to have human operators monitoring those screens 24/7 hours. Special agents have been designed that are able to monitor the screens, to reason about the observed information and to generate an alert in case unusual events or unwanted or suspicious behaviours have been detected.

The innovative aspect of this chapter is the reduction of the role of human operators. They are replaced by sensors and software agents which are able to observe, reason and behave in a human like way. This type of surveillance networks enables surveillance of large areas as the Atlantic Coast, critical infrastructures and special objects.

One aspect has not been discussed in the chapter, the security of the network. The introduction of a virtual space of agents enables a smart surveillance system. But unfortunately it offers intruders of the network the option to design agents destroying the positive effects of the surveillance network. To prevent a battlefield of agents in the virtual space, it is necessary to secure the network for intruders and to design counterattacks if intruders are detected.

## FUTURE RESEARCH DIRECTIONS

In this chapter a prototype has been described of a surveillance system using AIS data. The focus of the system was to detect abnormal behaviour of ships in and around the military harbour at Den Helder, The Netherlands. As a next step, the prototype has to be developed to a full operational system and should include all the AIS areas along the Atlantic Coast. In the introduction of this chapter we mentioned at least 7 functionalities of the Surveillance system. The current prototype is limited to detection of unwanted behaviour. Similar systems can be developed that send personal alerts to ships in possible danger due to upcoming bad weather conditions. Other possible applications are to the detection of illegal fishing, or the analysis of ship accidents. Another interesting application is to use the system as a surveillance system for all open waters. For their own safety more and more small ships install AIS systems, and this enables surveillance systems to monitor them

The current AIS based system should be integrated with available radar or camera surveillance systems. The fusion of data from different sources and modalities is a special research challenge. At the end, the current decision support system should be developed as a full automated system.

The current system has been preliminary tested at the control room of the Coast Guard at Den

Helder. A full human computer interaction test has to be performed in the near future.

## REFERENCES

*AIS - Live Ships Map - Vessel Traffic and Positions*. (2013). Retrieved January 01, 2014, from http://www.marinetraffic.com

*AIS-Wik*. (2013). Retrieved January 01, 2014, from http://en.wikipedia.org/wiki/Automatic_Identification_System

*AMASS, Autonomous Marine Surveillance System*. (2010). Retrieved January 01, 2014, from http://www.amass-project.eu

Boullart, L., Krijgsman, A., & Vingerhoeds, R. A. (1992). *Application of Artificial Intelligence in Process Control*. Elsevier Science Limited.

Boyd, J. R. (1976). *Destruction and Creation*. US Army Command and General Staff College.

Collins, R., Lipton, A., & Kanade, T. (1999). A System for Video Surveillance and Monitoring, In *Proc. American Nuclear Society (ANS) Eighth International Topical Meeting on Robotics and Remote Systems*. ANS.

Fitrianie, S., & Rothkrantz, L. J. M. (2009). Computed Ontology-based Situation Awareness of Multi-User Observations. In *Proceedings of International Conference on Information Systems for Crisis Response and Management*, (pp. 13-21). Academic Press.

GeNie and Smile. (2013). *A Bayesian network toolkit*. Retrieved January 01, 2014, from http://genie.sis.pitt.edu/

Hakim, J. (1995). *A History of Us: War, Peace and all that Jazz*. New York: Oxford University Press.

Hameete, P., Leysen, S., van der Laan, T., Lefter, I., & Rothkrantz, L. J. M. (2012). Intelligent Multi-Camera Video Surveillance. *International Journal on Information Technologies and Security*, *4*, 51–62.

Hammond, K. R., Hamm, R. M., Grassia, J., & Pearson, T. (1987). Direct comparison of the efficacy of intuitive and analytical cognition. *IEEE Transactions on Systems, Man, and Cybernetics*, *17*(5), 753–770. doi:10.1109/TSMC.1987.6499282

He, T., Blum, B. M., Stankovic, J. A., & Abdelzaher, T. (2004). AIDA: Adaptive Application-Independent Data Aggregation in Wireless Sensor Networks. *ACM Transactions on Embedded Computing Systems*, *3*(2), 426–457. doi:10.1145/993396.993406

*I2C, Intelligent surveillance and border security*. (2010). Retrieved January 01, 2014, from http://www.i2c.eu/

*Indra*. (2009). Retrieved January 01, 2014, from http://www.indracompany.com/en/sectores/transporte-y-trafico

Klapwijk, P., & Rothkrantz, L. J. M. (2006). Topology based infrastructure for crisis situations. In *Proceedings of the 3rd International Conference on Information Systems for Crisis Response and Management* (pp. 288-297). Academic Press.

Klein, G. (1999). *Sources of Power: How People Make Decisions*. Cambridge, MA: MIT Press.

Klein, G., & Klinger, D. (1987). Naturalistic Decision Making. *Human Systems IAC GATEWAY*, *11*(3).

Lipshitz, R., & Strauss, O. (1997). Coping with Uncertainty: A Naturalistic Decision-Making Analysis. *Organizational Behavior and Human Decision Processes*, *69*(2), 149–163. doi:10.1006/obhd.1997.2679

*MSC - COE maritime security conference.* (2011). Retrieved January 01, 2014, from http://maritimesecurityconference.org

*MSC - COE maritime security conference.* (2012). Retrieved January 01, 2014, from http://maritimesecurityconference.org

*Northrop Grumman MQ-4C Triton.* (2013), Retrieved January 01, 2014, from http://www.northropgrumman.com/triton

Rao, A. S., & Georgeff, M. P. (1995). BDI agents: From theory to practice. In V. Lesser & L. Gasser (Eds.), *Proceedings of the first international conference on multi-agent systems.* MIT Press.

Rasmussen, J. (1985). The role of hierarchical knowledge representation in decision making and system management. *IEEE Transactions on Systems, Man, and Cybernetics, 15*(2), 234–243. doi:10.1109/TSMC.1985.6313353

Rothkrantz, L. J. M. (2013). Crisis Management Using Multiple Camera Surveillance Systems. In *Proceedings of the 3rd International Conference on Information Systems for Crisis Response and Management* (pp. 617-626). Academic Press.

Rothkrantz, L. J. M., & Scholte, K. (2013). A Surveillance System of a Military Harbour Using an Automatic Identification System. In B. Rachev & A. Smrikarov (Eds.), *International Conference on Computer Systems and Technologies* (pp. 95-102). Academic Press.

Rothkrantz, L. J. M., Takapoui, R., Datcu, D., & Yang, Z. (2010). AUV Localisation using floating smart dust. In *Contributions in Military-Technology.* Swedish National Defence College.

Rothkrantz, L. J. M., Yang, Z., Jepson, M., Datcu, D., & Wiggers, P. (2009). A bottom-up approach of fusion of events in surveillance systems. In B. Rachev & A. Smrikarov (Eds.), *Proceedings of the 2009 International Conference on Computer Systems and Technologies* (art. 29). Academic Press.

*Saab - Maritime surveillance. State of the art.* (2013). Retrieved January 01, 2014, from http://www.saabgroup.com

*ScanEagle, Ministry of Dutch Defence.* (2013). Retrieved January 01, 2014, from http://www.defensie.nl

Scholte, K. (2013). *Detecting suspicious behavior in Marine traffic using the Automatic Identification System.* (Unpublished doctoral dissertation). Delft University of Technology, Delft, The Netherlands.

Tatomir, B., Klapwijk, P., & Rothkrantz, L. J. M. (2006). Topology based infrastructure for medical emergency coordination. *International Journal of Intelligent Control and Systems, 11*(4), 228–237.

*Vessel tracking and Automatic Transmitter Identification System (marine).* (2013). Retrieved January 01, 2014, from http://en.wikipedia.org/wiki/Automatic_Identification_System

VSAM Home page, Carnegie Mellon University. (1996). *Video Surveillance and Monitoring Homepage.* Retrieved January 01, 2014, from http://www.cs.cmu.edu/~vsam/OldVsamWeb/vsamhome.html

Wiggers, P., Mertens, B., & Rothkrantz, L. J. M. (2011). Dynamic Bayesian Networks for Situational Awareness in the Presence of Noisy Data. In *Proceedings of International Conference on Computer Systems and Technologies* (pp. 411-416). Academic Press.

## KEY TERMS AND DEFINITIONS

**Agent Technology:** The design of software packages which are able to perceive the environment, to reason about that and to plan and execute appropriate actions and evaluate the effect if those actions.

**AIS:** Automatic Identification System.

**Artificial Intelligence:** The intelligence exhibited by machines or software, and the branch of computer science that develops machines and software with intelligence.

**Bayesian Reasoning:** A way of probabilistic reasoning based on Bayes' rule.

**C2 Networks:** Command and control structures that are robust and match natural usage patterns.

**Decision Support Systems:** A computer-based information system that supports business or organizational decision-making activities.

**Rule Based Systems:** A reasoning system based on if-then rules reasoning mechanism.

**Surveillance Systems:** Is a system to monitor the behavior or activities of people for the purpose of protecting them and others.

## APPENDIX

## Questions

1.  In the introduction we defined 7 requirements for a surveillance system based on AIS. We defined some rules to detect abnormal behaviour.
    a.  Define some rules to detect an accident using the developed surveillance system based on AIS.
    b.  Define some rules to detect possible threats of critical infrastructure using the surveillance system.
2.  In this chapter a surveillance system has been described to detect abnormal behaviour of ships. Describe a system based on AIS generating personal alerts in case of a bad weather forecast to ships in danger given their position, type of ships and maximum speed.
3.  Describe a system based on AIS to detect ships involved in illegal fishing.
4.  In the military domain ships are usually localised, identified and tracked using a radar system. What are the advantages and disadvantages of the current system based on AIS instead of radar data?
5.  The developed AIS system is based on a bottom u approach and sensors re modeled as agents. How is it possible to control the system from the control centre?
6.  The world map is composed of many areas surveyed by AIS systems (http://www.marinetraffic.com). List some requirements to fuse the local systems to a global system?

# Compilation of References

9/11 Commission. (2004). *The 9/11 Commission Report: Final report of the national commission on terrorist attacks on the United States*. Washington, DC: US Government Printing Office.

9/11 Commission. (2005). *Staff Monograph on the Four Flights and Civil Aviation Security*. Retrieved 4 November 2005 from http://www.archives.gov/research/9-11-commission/

Acebrón, J. A., Bonilla, L. L., Peréz Vicente, C. J., Ritort, F., & Spigler, R. (2005). The Kuramoto model: A simple paradigm for synchronization phenomena. *Reviews of Modern Physics, 77*, 137–185. doi:10.1103/RevModPhys.77.137

Acquier, A., Gand, S., & Szpirglas, M. (2008). From Stakeholder to StakeSholder Management in Crisis Episodes: A Case Study in a Public Transportation Company. *Journal of Contingencies and Crisis Management, 16*(2), 101–114. doi:10.1111/j.1468-5973.2008.00538.x

Ahrne, G., & Brunsson, N. (2011). Organization outside organizations: the significance of partial organization. *Organization, 18*(1), 83–104. doi:10.1177/1350508410376256

Ahuja, G. (2000). Collaboration Networks, Structural Holes, and Innovation: A Longitudinal Study. *Administrative Science Quarterly, 45*(3), 425–455. doi:10.2307/2667105

*AIS - Live Ships Map - Vessel Traffic and Positions*. (2013). Retrieved January 01, 2014, from http://www.marinetraffic.com

*AIS-Wik*. (2013). Retrieved January 01, 2014, from http://en.wikipedia.org/wiki/Automatic_Identification_System

Albert, R., & Barabási, A.-L. (2002). Statistical mechanics of complex networks. *Reviews of Modern Physics, 74*, 47–97. doi:10.1103/RevModPhys.74.47

Alberts, D. S., & Hayes, R. E. (2003). *Power to the Edge*. Washington, DC: CCRP Press. Retrieved from www.dodccrp.org/files/Alberts_Power.pdf

Alberts, D. S., & Hayes, R. E. (2006). *Understanding Command and Control*. Washington, DC: CCRP Press. Retrieved from www.dodccrp.org/files/Alberts_UC2.pdf

Alberts, D. S., & Nissen, M. E. (2009). Toward Harmonizing Command and Control with Organization and Management Theory. *C2 Journal, 3*(2), 1-59.

Alberts, D. S., Gartska, J. J., & Stein, F.-P. (1999). Network Centric Warfare: Developing and Leveraging Information Superiority (2nd Revised Ed.). Washington, DC: CCRP Publication Series.

Alberts. (2007). Agility, Focus, and Convergence: The Future of Command and Control. *The International C2 Journal, 1*(1), 1-30.

Alberts, D. S. (2002). *Information-Age Transformation: Getting to a 21ˢᵗ century military*. US DoD Command & Control Research Program.

Alberts, D. S. (2011). *The agility advantage: A survival guide for complex enterprises and endeavors. The Command and Control Research Program*. CCRP.

Alberts, D. S. (Ed.). (2006). *Exploring New Command and Control Concepts and Capabilities (Final Report, SAS-050)*. NATO Science & Technology Organization.

Alberts, D. S., Garstka, J. J., & Stein, F. P. (2000). *Network Centric Warfare: Developing and Leveraging Information Superiority*. Washington, DC: CCRP Publication Series.

Alberts, D. S., Garstka, J., Hayes, R. E., & Signori, D. T. (2001). *Understanding Information Age Warfare*. US DoD Command & Control Research Program.

Alberts, D. S., & Hayes, R. E. (1999). *Network Centric Warfare: Developing and leveraging information superiority* (2nd ed.). Washington, DC: US DoD Command & Control Research Program.

Alberts, D. S., & Hayes, R. E. (2005). *Power to the Edge: Command and Control in the Information Age*. Washington, DC: CCRP Publication Series.

Alberts, D. S., & Hayes, R. E. (2007). *Planning: Complex endeavors*. Washington, DC: US DoD Command & Control Research Program.

Alston, A. (2010, June). *Assessing the difficulty and complexity of ELICIT factoid sets*. Paper presented at the 15th ICCRTS. Santa Monica, CA.

*AMASS, Autonomous Marine Surveillance System*. (2010). Retrieved January 01, 2014, from http://www.amass-project.eu

Ancona, D. G., & Caldwell, D. F. (1992). Bridging the boundary: External activity and performance in organizational teams. *Administrative Science Quarterly, 37*, 634–665. doi:10.2307/2393475

Army, U. S. (2009). *Electronic Warfare in Operations: U. S. Army Field Manual FM 3-36*. Washington, DC: HQ, Department of the Army.

Asplund, M., Nadjm-Tehrani, S., & Sigholm, J. (2009). Emerging Information Infrastructures: Cooperation in Disasters. In R. Setola, & S. Geretshuber (Eds.), *LNCS)* (Vol. 5508, pp. 258–270). Lecture Notes in Computer ScienceBerlin: Springer-Verlag.

Atkinson, S., & Moffat, J. (2005). *The Agile Organization - From Informal Networks to Complex Effects and Agility*. Washington, DC: US DoD CCRP.

AWST. (2001). Crisis at Herndon: 11 Airplanes Astray. *Aviation Week & Space Technology, 155*(25), 96–99.

AWST. (2002a). Exercise Jump-starts Response to Attacks. *Aviation Week & Space Technology, 156*(22), 48–52.

AWST. (2002b). NORAD and FAA Sharpen View Inside Borders. *Aviation Week & Space Technology, 156*(23), 50–52.

AWST. (2002c). F-16 Pilots Considered Ramming Flight 93. *Aviation Week & Space Technology, 157*(11), 71–74.

Baldwin, C. Y., & Clark, K. B. (1997, September-October). Managing in an Age of Modularity. *Harvard Business Review*, 84–93. PMID:10170333

Barabási, A.-L. (2002). *Linked: The New Science of Networks*. Cambridge, MA: Perseus Publishing.

Barabási, A.-L. (2003). *Linked: How everything is connected to everything else and what it means for business, science, and everyday life*. New York, NY: Plume.

Barabási, A.-L., & Bonabeau, E. (2003). Scale-Free Networks. *Scientific American, 288*, 50–59. doi:10.1038/scientificamerican0503-60 PMID:12701331

Barlow, J. (1993). Strategic Paralysis: An Air Power Strategy for the Present. *Airpower Journal, 7*(4), 1–15.

BBC. (2012, October 12). *US prepares first-strike cyber-forces*. Retrieved from http://www.bbc.co.uk/news/technology-19922421

Bechky, B. A. (2003). Sharing Meaning Across Occupational Communities: The Transformation of Understanding on a Production Floor. *Organization Science, 14*(3), 312–330. doi:10.1287/orsc.14.3.312.15162

Becker, J. C. (2008, May 6). *The Opportunities and Limits of Technology in Non Profit Disaster Response*. Paper presented at the 5th International Conference on Information Systems for Crisis Response and Management (ISCRAM 2008). Washington, DC.

Benner, M. J., & Tushman, M. L. (2003). Exploitation, Exploration, and Process Management: The Productivity Dilemma Revisited. *Academy of Management Review, 28*(2), 238–256.

Bexley, E. (2007). *Social capital in theory and practice: Centre for the Study of Higher Education*. University of Melbourne.

BFU. (2002). *Status Report (Midair collision 1st July 2002 near Überlingen/ Lake Constance).* Braunschweig (Germany), Bundesstelle für Flugunfalluntersuchung (BFU). Document # AX001-1/-2/02 (English version). Retrieved from http://www.bfu-web.de.

Biggs, N. (1993). *Algebraic Graph Theory* (2nd ed.). Cambridge, UK: Cambridge University Press.

Blake, E. S., & Gibney, E. J. (2011, August). The deadliest, costliest and most intense United States tropical cyclones from 1851 to 2010 (and other frequently requested hurricane facts). *NOAA Technical Memorandum NWS NHC-6.* Miami, FL: National Oceanic and Atmospheric Administration.

Boccaletti, S., Latora, V., Moreno, Y., Chavez, M., & Hwang, D.-U. (2006). Complex networks: Structure and dynamics. *Physics Reports, 424*(4-5), 175–308. doi:10.1016/j.physrep.2005.10.009

Bohorquez, J., Gourley, S., Dixon, A., Spagat, M., & Johnson, N. (2009). Common Ecology Quantifies Human Insurgency. *Nature, 462,* 911–914. doi:10.1038/nature08631 PMID:20016600

Boin, A., Hart, P., Stern, E. K., & Sundelius, B. (2005). *The politics of crisis management: Public leadership under pressure.* Cambridge University Press. doi:10.1017/CBO9780511490880

Bollen, M. T. I. B., & Soeters, J. M. M. L. (2010). Partnering with 'Strangers. In J. M. M. L. Soeters, P. C. van Fenema, & R. Beeres (Eds.), *Managing Military Organizations: Theory and Practice* (pp. 174–186). London: Routledge.

Bollobás, B. (2001). *Random Graphs* (2nd ed.). Cambridge, UK: Cambridge University Press. doi:10.1017/CBO9780511814068

Bonin, J. A., & Telford, E. C. J. (2004, March-April). The Modular Army. *Military Review,* 21–27.

Boot, M. (2006). *War Made New: Technology, Warfare, and the Course of History, 1500 to Today.* New York: Gotham Books.

Bos, J. H. G., & Verberne, E. M. J. (2012). *GRIP 3 Ouwerkerkse Kreek - Lessen uit de aanpak* [GRIP 3 Ouwerkerk Creek - Lessons from the approach]. The Hague, The Netherlands: Academic Press.

Boullart, L., Krijgsman, A., & Vingerhoeds, R. A. (1992). *Application of Artificial Intelligence in Process Control.* Elsevier Science Limited.

Boyd, J. (1987). *A Discourse on Winning and Losing* (briefing slides). Maxwell Air Force Base, AL: Air University Library Document No. M-U 43947. Retrieved from http://www.ausairpower.net/APA-Boyd-Papers.html

Boyd, J. R. (1976). *Destruction and Creation.* US Army Command and General Staff College.

Boyd, J. R. (1996). *The Essence of Winning and Losing. (Unpublished lecture notes).* Maxwell Air Force Base.

Brainich, E. (2012). Bestuurlijke Netwerkkaarten Crisisbeheersing. [Administrative Network Maps Crisis Management]. (Vierde druk, Ed.). Haarlem, The Netherlands: Provincie Noord-Holland.

Brainich, E. (2007). *Rijksheren in het moderne crisismanagement* [Government lords in modern crisis management]. Haarlem, The Netherlands: Provincie Noord-Holland.

Brandes, U., Robins, G., McCranie, A., & Wasserman, S. (2013). What is Network Science? *New Scientist, 1*(1), 1–15.

Brehmer, B. (2005). The Dynamic OODA Loop: Amalgamating Boyd's OODA Loop and the Cybernetic Approach to Command and Control. In *Proceedings of the 10th International Command & Control Research & Technology Symposium (ICCRTS).* US DoD Command & Control Research Program.

Brehmer, B. (2006). One Loop to Rule Them All. In *Proceedings of the 11th International Command and Control Research and Tecnhology Symposium.* Washington, DC: CCRP.

Brehmer, B. (2007). Understanding the Functions of C2 Is the Key to Progress. *The International C2 Journal, 1*(1), 211-232.

Brehmer, B. (2008). Command and Control is a Science of the Artificial. In *Proceedings of the 13th International Command and Control Research and Technology Symposium.* Washington, DC: CCRP.

Brehmer, B. (2009). Command Without Commanders. In *Proceedings of the 14ᵗʰ International Command and Control Research and Technology Symposium (ICCRTS)*. Washington, DC: CCRP Press. Retrieved from www.dodccrp.org/events/14th_iccrts_2009/papers/041.pdf

Brehmer, B. (2009). From Function to Form in the Design of C2 Systems. In *Proceedings of the 14th International Command and Control Research and Technology Symposium*. Washington, DC: CCRP.

Brehmer, B. (2010). Command and control as design. In *Proceedings of the 15ᵗʰ International Command & Control Research & Technology Symposium (ICCRTS)*. US DoD Command & Control Research Program.

Brehmer, B. (2013). *Insatsledning*. [Command and control of missions]. Unpublished technical report. Swedish National Defence College.

Brusoni, S. (2005). The Limits to Specialization: Problem Solving and Coordination in 'Modular Networks'. *Organization Studies, 26*(12), 1885–1907. doi:10.1177/0170840605059161

Brusoni, S., & Prencipe, A. (2006). Making Design Rules: A Multidomain Perspective. *Organization Science, 17*(2), 179–189. doi:10.1287/orsc.1060.0180

Builder, C. H., Bankes, S. C., & Nordin, R. (1999). *Command Concepts: A Theory Derived from the Practice of Command and Control*. Santa Monica, CA: RAND.

Bumiller, E., & Shanker, T. (2012, October 11). Panetta Warns of Dire Threat of Cyberattack on U.S. *The New York Times*.

Burt, R. S. (1982). *Toward a Structural Theory of Action*. Academic Press.

Burt, R. S. (1992). *Structural Holes: The Social Structure of Competition*. Cambridge, MA: Harvard University Press.

Cares, J. (2005). Distributed Networked Operations: The Foundations of Network Centric Warfare. Lincoln, NE: iUniverse.

Cares, J. R. (2004). *An Information Age Combat Model*. Paper presented at the 9th International Command and Control Research and Technology Symposium (ICCRTS). Copenhagen, Denmark.

Cares, J. R. (2005). Distributed Network Operations: The Foundations of Network Centric Warfare. Lincoln, NE: iUniverse.

Carlile, P. R. (2004). Transferring, Translating, and Transforming: An Integrative Framework for Managing Knowledge Across Boundaries. *Organization Science, 15*(5), 555–568. doi:10.1287/orsc.1040.0094

Carr, J. (2013, February 19). *Mandiant APT1 Report Has Critical Analytic Flaws*. Retrieved from http://jeffreycarr.blogspot.nl/2013/02/mandiant-apt1-report-has-critical.html

CCRP. (2010). *NATO NEC C2 Maturity Model*. Washington, DC: CCRP. Retrieved from http://www.dodccrp.org/files/N2C2M2_web_optimized.pdf

Cebrowski, A. K., & Garstka, J. H. (1998). Network-Centric Warfare: Its Origins and Future. *Proceedings of the United States Naval Institute. United States Naval Institute, 124*(1).

Ceri, S., & Pelagatti, G. (1984). *Distributed Databases: Principles and Systems*. New York, NY: McGraw-Hill.

Chartrand, G. (1984). *Introductory Graph Theory*. Dover Publications.

Chen, G., & Duan, Z. (2008). Network Synchronizability Analysis: A Graph-Theoretic Approach. *Chaos (Woodbury, N.Y.), 18*, 037102. doi:10.1063/1.2965530 PMID:19045476

Chen, P. P.-S. (1976). The Entity-Relationship Model - Towards a unified view of data. *ACM Transactions on Database Systems, 1*(1), 9–36. doi:10.1145/320434.320440

Chisholm, R. (1982). Knowledge as Justified True Belief. In *The Foundations of Knowing*. University of Minnesota Press.

Christchurch Central Development Unit. (2013). *Aspirations*. Retrieved 12 July 2013, from http://ccdu.govt.nz/plan/aspirations

Christofides, N. (1975). *Graph Theory: An Algorithmic Approach*. New York, NY: Academic Press.

Chung, F., & Lu, L. (2003). The Average Distance in a Random Graph with Given Expected Degrees. *Internet Mathematics, 1*(1), 91–113. doi:10.1080/15427951.2004.10129081

Clancy, T. (1995). *Fighter Wing: A Guided Tour of an Air Force Combat Wing*. New York, NY: Berkley Books.

Cole, E. (2013). *Advanced Persistent Threat: Understanding the Danger and How to Protect Your Organization*. Waltham, MA: Syngress - Elsevier.

Collins, R., Lipton, A., & Kanade, T. (1999). A System for Video Surveillance and Monitoring, In *Proc. American Nuclear Society (ANS) Eighth International Topical Meeting on Robotics and Remote Systems*. ANS.

Comfort, L. K., & Kapucu, N. (2006). Inter-organizational coordination in extreme events: The World Trade Center attacks, September 11, 2001. *Natural Hazards, 39*, 309–327. doi:10.1007/s11069-006-0030-x

Conder, M., & Dobcsányi, P. (2002). Trivalent Symmetric Graphs up to 768 Vertices. *Journal of Combinatorial Mathematics and Combinatorial Computing, 40*, 41–63.

Cormen, T., Leiserson, C., & Rivest, R. (1990). *Introduction to Algorithms*. Cambridge, MA: MIT Press.

Coticchia, F. (2011). The 'Enemy' at the Gates? Assessing the European Military Contribution to the Libyan War. *Perspectives on Federalism, 3*(3), 48–70.

Coutinho, L. R., Sichman, J. S., & Boissier, O. (2005). Modeling Organization in MAS: A comparison of models. In *Proceedings of 1st Workshop on Software Engineering for Agent-oriented Systems* (SEAS05). SEAS.

Cover, T., & Thomas, J. (1991). *Elements of Information Theory*. New York: Wiley. doi:10.1002/0471200611

Crawshaw, E. (2007). A Comprehensive Approach to Modern Conflict: Afghanistan and Beyond. *CONNECTIONS: The Quarterly Journal, 6*(2), 1–66.

Crowston, K. (1997). A Coordination Theory Approach to Organizational Process Design. *Organization Science, 8*(2), 157–175. doi:10.1287/orsc.8.2.157

Curtis, V. (2005). The Theory of Fourth Generation Warfare. *Canadian Army Journal, 8*(4), 17–32.

D'Hulst, R., & Rodgers, G. (2000). Exact Solution of a Model for Crowding and Information Transmission in Financial Markets. *International Journal of Theoretical and Applied Finance, 3*(4), 609–616. doi:10.1142/S0219024900000784

Dandeker, C. (2003). Building Flexible Forces in the 21st Century. In G. Caforio (Ed.), *Handbook of the Sociology of the Military* (pp. 405–416). New York: Kluwer.

de Coning, C. H. (2008). Civil-Military Coordination Practices and Approaches within United Nations Peace Operations. In L. Olson, & H. Gregorian (Eds.), *Calgary Papers in Journal of Military and Strategic Studies, Civil-Military Coordination: Challenges and Opportunities in Afghanistan and Beyond* (Vol. 3, pp. 87–112). Calgary, Canada: Centre for Military and Strategic Studies.

de Coning, C. H. (2010). *Clarity, Coherence and Context: Three Priorities for Sustainable Peacebuilding. The Future of the Peacebuilding Architecture Project*. Norwegian Institute of International Affairs.

de Coning, C., & Friis, K. (2011). Coherence and Coordination: The Limits of the Comprehensive Approach. *Journal of International Peacekeeping, 15*(1-2), 243–272. doi:10.1163/187541110X540553

De Nicola, A., Missikof, M., & Navigili, R. (2009). A Software Engineering Approach to Ontology Building. *Information Systems, 34*(2), 258–275. doi:10.1016/j.is.2008.07.002

De Toni, A. F., & Nonino, F. (2010). The Key Roles in the Informal Organization: A Network Analysis Perspective. *The Learning Organization, 17*(1), 86–103. doi:10.1108/09696471011008260

De Waard, E. J., & Kramer, F. J. (2008). Tailored task forces: Temporary organizations and modularity. *International Journal of Project Management, 26*(5), 537–546. doi:10.1016/j.ijproman.2008.05.007

De Waard, E. J., Volberda, H. W., & Soeters, J. (2012). How to Support Sensing Capabilities in Highly Volatile Situations. *Journal of Management & Organization, 18*(6), 774–794. doi:10.5172/jmo.2012.18.6.774

De Waard, E. J., Volberda, H. W., & Soeters, J. (2013a). Drivers of Organizational Responsiveness: Experiences of a Military Crisis Response Organization. *Journal of Organization Design*, 2(2), 1–13.

De Waard, E. J., Volberda, H. W., & Soeters, J. (2013b). Engaging Environmental Turbulence: Drivers of Organizational Flexibility in the Armed Forces. *European Security*. doi:10.1080/09662839.2013.822367

Dekker, A. H. (2005). Simulating Network Robustness for Critical Infrastructure Networks. Proceedings of the 28ᵗʰ Australasian Computer Science Conference (ACSC), Newcastle, Australia, January. *Conferences in Research and Practice in Information Technology, 38*, 18–22.

Dekker, A. H. (2006). Centralisation vs Self-Synchronisation: An Agent-Based Investigation. In *Proceedings of the 11ᵗʰ International Command and Control Research and Technology Symposium (ICCRTS)*. Washington, DC: CCRP Press. Retrieved from www.dodccrp.org/events/11th_ICCRTS/html/papers/030.pdf

Dekker, A. H. (2010a). Average Distance as a Predictor of Synchronisability in Networks of Coupled Oscillators. In *Proceedings of the 33ʳᵈ Australasian Computer Science Conference* (ACSC). Brisbane, Australia: ACSC.

Dekker, A. H. (2011). Analyzing C2 Structures and Self-Synchronization with Simple Computational Models. In *Proc. 16ᵗʰ International Command and Control Research and Technology Symposium (ICCRTS)*. Washington, DC: CCRP Press. Retrieved from www.dodccrp.org/events/16th_iccrts_2011/papers/010.pdf

Dekker, A. H. (2012). Analyzing Team C2 Behaviour using Games and Agents. In *Proc. 17ᵗʰ International Command and Control Research and Technology Symposium (ICCRTS)*. Washington, DC: CCRP Press. Retrieved from www.dodccrp.org/events/17th_iccrts_2012/post_conference/papers/006.pdf

Dekker, A. H. (2013b). Self-Synchronisation in C2 Networks. In *Proc. 20ᵗʰ International Congress on Modelling and Simulation (MODSIM 2013)*. Adelaide, Australia: MODSIM.

Dekker, A. H., & Colbert, B. (2004a). Network Robustness and Graph Topology. In *Proc. 27ᵗʰ Australasian Computer Science Conference* (ACSC). Dunedin, New Zealand: ACSC. Retrieved from crpit.com/confpapers/CRPITV26Dekker.pdf

Dekker, A. H., & Colbert, B. (2004b). Scale-Free Networks and Robustness of Critical Infrastructure Networks. In *Proc. 7ᵗʰ Asia-Pacific Conference on Complex Systems*. Cairns, Australia: Academic Press.

Dekker, A. H. (2003). Centralisation and Decentralisation in Network Centric Warfare. *Journal of Battlefield Technology*, 6(2), 23–28.

Dekker, A. H. (2004). Simulating Network Robustness: Two Perspectives on Reality. In *Proceedings of SimTecT 2004*. Simulation Industry Association of Australia.

Dekker, A. H. (2007a). Studying Organisational Topology with Simple Computational Models. *Journal of Artificial Societies and Social Simulation, 10*(4).

Dekker, A. H. (2007b). Using Tree Rewiring to Study Edge Organisations for C2. In *Proceedings of SimTecT 2007*. Simulation Industry Association of Australia.

Dekker, A. H. (2010b). Mimicking Human Problem-Solving with Agents: Exploring Model Calibration. In *Proceedings of SimTecT 2010*. Simulation Industry Association of Australia.

Dekker, A. H. (2013a). Epistemological Aspects of Simulation Models for Decision Support. *International Journal of Agent Technologies and Systems, 5*(2), 55–77. doi:10.4018/jats.2013040103

Deller, S., Bell, M. I., Bowling, S. R., Rabadi, G. A., & Tolk, A. (2009). Applying the Information Age Combat Model: Quantitative Analysis of Network Centric Operations. *The International C2 Journal, 3*(1), 1-25.

Deller, S., Bowling, S.R., Rabadi, G.A., & Tolk, A. (2009). Applying the information age combat model: Quantitative analysis of network centric operations. *International C2 Journal, 3*(1), 1-25.

Deller, S. T., Bell, M. I., Bowling, S. R., Rabadi, G., & Tolk, A. (2009). Applying the Information Age Combat Model: Quantitative Analysis of Network Centric Operations. *The International Command and Control (C2). Journal, 3*(1), 1–25.

Deller, S. T., Rabadi, G., Tolk, A., & Bowling, S. R. (2012). Organizing for Improved Effectiveness in Networked Operations. *Military Operations Research Journal, 17*(1), 5–16. doi:10.5711/1082598317105

Denning, P. J. (2006). Hastily Formed Networks. *Communications of the ACM, 49*(4), 15–20. doi:10.1145/1121949.1121966

Denters, B., & Klok, P. J. (2010). Rebuilding Roombeek: patterns of citizen participation in urban governance. *Urban Affairs Review, 45*(5), 583–607. doi:10.1177/1078087409356756

Diefenbach, T., & Sillince, J. A. A. (2011). Formal and Informal Hierarchy in Different Types of Organization. *Organization Studies, 32*(11), 1515–1537. doi:10.1177/0170840611421254

Docauer, A. F. (2011). Efficient Airspace Use During Urban Air Operations. *Air Land Sea Bulletin,* (2), 4-7.

Dodge, M., & Kitchen, R. (2001). *Mapping Cyberspace.* Routledge.

Donetti, L., Hurtado, P., & Muñoz, M. (2005). Entangled Networks, Synchronization, and Optimal Network Topology. *Physical Review Letters, 95*, 188701. doi:10.1103/PhysRevLett.95.188701 PMID:16383953

Dorogovtsev, S. N., Goltsev, A. V., & Mendes, J. F. F. (2008). Critical phenomena in complex networks. *Reviews of Modern Physics, 80*(4), 1275–1353. doi:10.1103/RevModPhys.80.1275

Drabble, B. (2011). Dependency based collaboration: Ontology based information management. In *Proceedings of the Collaborative Technologies and Systems Conference (CTS 2011)* (pp. 579-586). Philadelphia, PA: IEEE.

Drabble, B. (2012). Information propagation through a dependency network model. In *Proceedings of the Collaborative Technologies and Systems Conference (CTS 2012)* (pp. 266-272). Denver, CO: IEEE.

Drabble, B., & Kinzig, C. (2010). The information triad: Collaborating across structured and non-structured information. In *Proceedings of the Collaborative Technologies and Systems Conference (CTS 2010)* (pp. 255-264). Chicago, IL: IEEE.

Drabble, B., Black, T., Kinzig, C., & Whitted, G. (2009). Ontology based dependency analysis: Understanding the impacts of decisions in a collaborative environment. In *Proceedings of the Collaborative Technologies and Systems Conference (CTS 2009),* (pp. 10-17). Baltimore, MD: IEEE.

Drabble, B., McCrabb, M., & Haq, N. (2006). *Dependency Based Vulnerability Assessment* (Final Report, Defense Advanced Research Projects Agency, DARPA Order U051-16, Contract No: W41P4Q-06-C-003). Washington, DC: Academic Press.

Drabble, B., McCrabb, M., Whitted, G., & Kinzig, C. (2009). *Information Bridging Service* (Final Report, Contract Number: FA8650-07-C-4513). Air Force Research Laboratory (AFRL).

Dunn Cavelty, M. (2012). The Militarisation of Cyberspace: Why Less May Be Better. In *Proceedings of the 4th International Conference on Cyber Conflict (CYCON 2012)* (pp. 141-153). Tallinn, Estonia: NATO CCD COE Publications.

Dupont, B. (2004). Security in the age of networks. *Policing and Society: An International Journal of Research and Policy, 14*(1), 76–91. doi:10.1080/1043946042000181575

Dynes, R. R. (1994). Community Emergency Planning: False Assumptions and Inappropriate Analogies. *International Journal of Mass Emergencies and Disasters, 12*(2), 141–158.

Eggenhofer-Rehart, P. (Ed.). (2009). C2 Conceptual Reference Model version 2.0 with suggestions for its application in conjunction with the NATO NEC C2 Maturity Model (N2C2M2). Appendix to NATO SAS-065 Final Report.

Egnell, R. (2012). *The Swedish Experience in Operation Unified Protector: Overcoming the Non-NATO Member Conundrum.* Stockholm: Stockholm Center for Strategic Studies.

Eklund, N. (2013, January 7). *Hackerhot mot Facebooks nya datacenter i Luleå (Hacker-threat against Facebook's new datacenter in Luleå).* Retrieved from http://sverigesradio.se/sida/artikel.aspx?programid=83&artikel=5383951

Ender, T., Leurck, R. F., Weaver, B., Miceli, P., Blair, W. D., West, P., & Mavris, D. (2010). System-of-Systems Analysis of Ballistic Missile Defense Architecture Effectiveness through Surrogate Modeling and Simulation. *IEEE Systems Journal, 4*(2), 156–166. doi:10.1109/JSYST.2010.2045541

Endsley, M. R. (1995). A Taxonomy of Situation Awareness Errors. In R. Fuller, N. Johnston, & N. McDonald (Eds.), *Human Factors in Aviation Operations.* Aldershot, UK: Ashgate Publishing Ltd.

Ericsson. (2013, November). *Ericsson Mobility Report: On the pulse of the Networked Society.* Retrieved from http://www.ericsson.com/mobility-report

Ethiraj, S. K., & Levinthal, D. A. (2004). Modularity and Innovation in Complex Systems. *Management Science, 50*(2), 159–173. doi:10.1287/mnsc.1030.0145

Falliere, N., Murchu, L. O., & Chien, E. (2011). *W32 Stuxnet Dossier.* Retrieved from http://www.symantec.com/connect/blogs/w32stuxnet-dossier

Fang, C., Lee, J., & Schilling, M. A. (2010). Balancing Exploration and Exploitation Through Structural Design: The Isolation of Subgroups and Organizational Learning. *Organization Science, 21*(3), 625–642. doi:10.1287/orsc.1090.0468

Faraj, S., & Sproull, L. (2000). Coordinating Expertise in Software Development Teams. *Management Science, 46*(12), 1154–1568. doi:10.1287/mnsc.46.12.1554.12072

Faraj, S., & Xiao, Y. (2006). Coordination in Fast-Response Organizations. *Management Science, 52*(8), 1155–1169. doi:10.1287/mnsc.1060.0526

Farwell, J. P., & Rohozinski, R. (2011). Stuxnet and the Future of Cyber War. *Survival, 53*(1), 23–40. doi:10.1080/00396338.2011.555586

Fellbaum, C. (1998). *WordNet: An Electronic Lexical Database.* Cambridge, MA: MIT Press.

Fitrianie, S., & Rothkrantz, L. J. M. (2009). Computed Ontology-based Situation Awareness of Multi-User Observations. In *Proceedings of International Conference on Information Systems for Crisis Response and Management,* (pp. 13-21). Academic Press.

Fogleman, R. R. (1995). Theater Ballistic Missile Defense. *Joint Force Quarterly, 9,* 75–79.

Frühling, S., & Sinjen, S. (2010). *Missile defense: challenges and opportunities for NATO.* NATO Defense College, Research Paper, 60: 1-5.

Gallagher, S. (2012, June 19). *How to blow $6 billion on a tech project.* Retrieved from http://arstechnica.com/information-technology/2012/06/how-to-blow-6-billion-on-a-tech-project/

Garrett, R. K., Anderson, S., Baron, N. T., & Moreland, J. D. (2011). Managing the interstitials, a system of systems framework suited for the ballistic missile defense system. *Systems Engineering, 14*(1), 87–109. doi:10.1002/sys.20173

Garvey, P. R., & Pinto, C. A. (2005). Introduction to Functional Dependency Network Analysis, The MITRE Corporation and Old Dominion. In *Proceedings of Second International Symposium on Engineering Systems.* Cambridge, MA: The MITRE Corporation and the Old Dominion University.

Gateau, J. B., Leweling, T. A., Looney, J. P., & Nissen, M. E. (2007). Hypothesis Testing of Edge Organizations: Modeling the C2 Organization Design Space. In *Proceedings of the 12th International Command and Control Research and Technology Symposium (ICCRTS).* Washington, DC: CCRP Press. Retrieved from www.dodccrp.org/events/12th_ICCRTS/CD/html/papers/093.pdf

GeNie and Smile. (2013). *A Bayesian network toolkit.* Retrieved January 01, 2014, from http://genie.sis.pitt.edu/

Gibbons, A. (1985). *Algorithmic Graph Theory.* Cambridge, UK: Cambridge University Press.

Goldberg, A., & Robson, D. (1989). *Smalltalk-80: The language.* Addison-Wesley Publishing Company.

Gollmann, D. (2010). Computer security. *Wiley Interdisciplinary Reviews: Computational Statistics, 2*(5), 544–554. doi:10.1002/wics.106

Gompert, D. C., & Isaacson, J. A. (1999). *Planning a ballistic missile defense system of systems.* RAND Report IP-181, 1-14.

Gottschalg, O., & Zollo, M. (2007). Interest Alignment and Competitive Advantage. *Academy of Management Review, 32*(2), 418–437. doi:10.5465/AMR.2007.24351356

Goyal, S. (2007). *Connections: An introduction to the economics of networks.* Princeton, NJ: Princeton University Press.

Grandori, A. (1997). An Organizational Assessment of Interfirm Coordination Modes. *Organization Studies, 18*(6), 897–925. doi:10.1177/017084069701800601

Grant, T. J. (2006). Measuring the Potential Benefits of NCW: 9/11 as case study. In *Proceedings, 11th International Command & Control Research & Technology Symposium.* Washington, DC: US DoD Command & Control Research Program.

Grant, T. J., & Kooter, B. M. (2005). Comparing OODA and Other Models as Operational View Architecture. In *Proceedings of the 10th International Command & Control Research & Technology Symposium (ICCRTS).* US DoD Command & Control Research Program.

Grant, T. J., Buizer, B. C., & Bertelink, R. J. (2011). Vulnerability of C2 Networks to Attack: Measuring the topology of eleven Dutch Army C2 systems. In *Proc. 16th International Command and Control Research and Technology Symposium (ICCRTS).* Washington, DC: CCRP Press. Retrieved from www.dodccrp.org/events/16th_iccrts_2011/papers/087.pdf

Grant, T. J., van Fenema, P. C., & van Veen, M. (2007). *On Regarding 21st Century C2 Systems and their Users as Fallible ePartners.* Paper presented at the 12th International Command and Control Research and Technology Symposium (ICCRTS). Newport, RI.

Grayver, E. (2012). *Implementing Software Defined Radio.* New York: Springer.

Greenwald, G. (2013, June 7). Obama orders US to draw up overseas target list for cyber-attacks. *The Guardian.*

Grennert, J., & Tham, M. (2001). Influencing Conflicts with IT-Weapons: The Possibility of Non-State Actors Influencing the Course of a Conflict. *User Report FOI-R--0263--SE.* Stockholm, Sweden: Swedish Defence Research Agency.

Grisogono, A. M. (2006). *The implications of complex adaptive systems theory for C2.* Paper presented at the Command and Control Research and Technology Symposium. New York, NY.

Grisogono, A. M., & Radenovic, V. (2007). *The Adaptive Stance - Steps towards teaching more effective complex decision-making.* Paper presented at the Eighth International Conference on Complex Systems. New York, NY.

Gruber, T. R. (1993). A Translation Approach to Portable Ontology Specifications. *Knowledge Acquisition, 5*(2), 199–220. doi:10.1006/knac.1993.1008

Hakim, J. (1995). *A History of Us: War, Peace and all that Jazz.* New York: Oxford University Press.

Hales, D., & Edmonds, B. (2005). Applying a Socially Inspired Technique (Tags) to Improve Cooperation in P2P Networks. *IEEE Trans Sys, Man and Cybernetics Part A, Systems and Humans, 35*(3), 385–395. doi:10.1109/TSMCA.2005.846399

Hallegatte, S., Green, C., Nicholls, R. J., & Corfee-Morlot, J. (2013). Future flood losses in major coastal cities. *Nature Climate Change, 3*(9), 802–806. doi:10.1038/nclimate1979

Hameete, P., Leysen, S., van der Laan, T., Lefter, I., & Rothkrantz, L. J. M. (2012). Intelligent Multi-Camera Video Surveillance. *International Journal on Information Technologies and Security, 4,* 51–62.

Hammond, G. T. (2001). *The mind of war: John Boyd and American Security.* Washington, DC: Smithsonian Press.

Hammond, K. R., Hamm, R. M., Grassia, J., & Pearson, T. (1987). Direct comparison of the efficacy of intuitive and analytical cognition. *IEEE Transactions on Systems, Man, and Cybernetics, 17*(5), 753–770. doi:10.1109/TSMC.1987.6499282

Hauser, T., & Wenz, C. (2003). DRM Under Attack: Weaknesses in Existing Systems. In E. Becker, W. Buhse, D. Günnewig, & N. Rump (Eds.), *LNCS)* (Vol. 2770, pp. 206–223). Lecture Notes in Computer ScienceBerlin: Springer-Verlag. doi:10.1007/10941270_14

Hayes, R.E. (2007). It's an Endeavor, Not a Force. *The International C2 Journal, 1*(1), 145-176.

Hellström, M., & Wikström, K. (2005). Project Business Concepts Based on Modularity - Improved Manoeuvrability Through Unstable Structures. *International Journal of Project Management, 23*, 392–397. doi:10.1016/j.ijproman.2005.01.007

Helsloot, I., & Ruitenberg, A. (2004). Citizen Response to Disasters: a Survey of Literature and Some Practical Implications. *Journal of Contingencies and Crisis Management, 12*(3), 98–111. doi:10.1111/j.0966-0879.2004.00440.x

Herranz, J. (2008). The multisectoral trilemma of network management. *Journal of Public Administration: Research and Theory, 18*(1), 1–31. doi:10.1093/jopart/mum004

He, T., Blum, B. M., Stankovic, J. A., & Abdelzaher, T. (2004). AIDA: Adaptive Application- Independent Data Aggregation in Wireless Sensor Networks. *ACM Transactions on Embedded Computing Systems, 3*(2), 426–457. doi:10.1145/993396.993406

He, Z. L., & Wong, P. K. (2004). Exploration vs. Exploitation: An Empirical Test of the Ambidexterity Hypothesis. *Organization Science, 15*(4), 481–494. doi:10.1287/orsc.1040.0078

Hielle, L. P. (2013, January 5). *Anonymous-medlem: Jag kunde styra sågverk (Anonymous-member: I had control over sawmills).* Retrieved from http://sverigesradio.se/sida/artikel.aspx?programid=83&artikel=5384724

Hoegl, M., Weinkauf, K., & Gemuenden, H. G. (2004). Interteam Coordination, Project Commitment, and Teamwork in Multiteam R&D Projects: A Longitudinal Study. *Organization Science, 15*(1), 38–55. doi:10.1287/orsc.1030.0053

Holland, O. T., & Wallace, S. E. (2011). Using Agents to Model the Kill Chain of the Ballistic Missile Defense System. *Naval Engineers Journal, 123*(3), 141–151. doi:10.1111/j.1559-3584.2011.00336.x

Hübner, J. F., Sichman, J. S., & Boissier, O. (2002). A Model for the Structural, Functional, and Deontic Specification of Organizations in Multi-agent Systems. In *Proceedings, 16th Brazilian Symposium on AI* (SBIA 2002), (LNAI), (vol. 2507, pp. 118-128). Springer.

*I2C, Intelligent surveillance and border security.* (2010). Retrieved January 01, 2014, from http://www.i2c.eu/

Iacobucci, M. S. (2013). *Reconfigurable Radio Systems: Network Architectures and Standards.* West Sussex, UK: John Wiley & Sons, Ltd. doi:10.1002/9781118398401

*Indra.* (2009). Retrieved January 01, 2014, from http://www.indracompany.com/en/sectores/transporte-y-trafico

Inspectie Openbare Orde en Veiligheid. (2011). *Brand Chemie-Pack Moerdijk - Een onderzoek naar de bestrijding van (de effecten van) het grootschalig incident* [Fire Chemie-Pack Moerdijk - An investigation on fighting (the effects of) the large-scale incident]. The Hague: Ministry of Security and Justice, The Netherlands.

ITACS. (2014). *US-UK International Technology Alliance Collaboration System.* Retrieved February 6, 2014, from https://www.usukita.org/

Jackson, M. C. (1991). *Systems Methodology for the Management Sciences.* New York: Springer. doi:10.1007/978-1-4899-2632-6

Jackson, M. O. (2009). *Social and economic networks.* Princeton, NJ: Princeton University Press.

Jain, S., & Krishna, S. (2002). *Graph Theory and the Evolution of Autocatalytic Networks.* Retrieved from http://arXiv.org/abs/nlin.AO/0210070

JALLC. (2012). *Operation Unified Protector: Lessons for the Alliance.* Lisbon: JALLC.

Jansen, G. J., Fernandes Mendes, H. K., Rook, M., Stordiau-van Egmond, A. M. E., & van Zanten, P. J. (2012). *Onderzoek asbestvondst Kanaleneiland* [Investigation Asbestos Discovery]. Utrecht, The Netherlands: Academic Press.

Janssen, R. H. P., & Monsuur, H. (2010). Networks, information and choice. In *Collective decision making: Views from social choice and game theory* (pp. 211–230). Berlin: Springer. doi:10.1007/978-3-642-02865-6_14

Janssen, R. H. P., & Monsuur, H. (2012). Stable network topologies using the notion of covering. *European Journal of Operational Research*, *218*, 755–763. doi:10.1016/j.ejor.2011.12.001

Janssen, R. H. P., & Monsuur, H. (2013). Identifying stable network structures and sets of key players using a W-covering perspective. *Mathematical Social Sciences*, *66*, 245–253. doi:10.1016/j.mathsocsci.2013.05.005

Jarvis, D. A. (2005). A Methodology for Analyzing Complex Military Command and Control (C2) Networks. In *Proc. 10th International Command and Control Research and Technology Symposium (ICCRTS)*. Washington, DC: CCRP Press. Retrieved from www.dodccrp.org/events/10th_ICCRTS/CD/papers/099.pdf

JCS. (2010). *Command and Control for Joint Air Operations: Joint Chiefs of Staff, Joint Publication 3-30, 12 January 2010*. JCS.

JCS. (2012). *Joint Operational Access Concept (JOAC)*. Retrieved from http://www.defense.gov/pubs/pdfs/JOAC_Jan%202012_Signed.pdf

Jensen, E. (2012). Operationalizing C2 Agility. In *Proceedings of the 17th International Command & Control Research & Technology Symposium (ICCRTS)*. US DoD Command & Control Research Program.

Johannesson, P. (1995). Representation and Communication - A Speech Act Based Approach to Information System Design. *Information Systems*, *20*(4), 291–303. doi:10.1016/0306-4379(95)00015-V

Johansson, F., & Falkman, G. (2009). An empirical investigation of the static weapon-target allocation problem. In *Proceedings of the 3rd Skövde Workshop on Information Fusion Topics* (pp. 63–67). Skövde, Sweden: University of Skövde.

Johnson, A., & Mueen, S. (Eds.). (2012, March). Short War, Long Shadow: The Political and Military Legacies of the 2011 Libya Campaign. *Whitehall Report 1-12*. The Royal United Services Institute (RUSI).

Johnson, N., Spagat, M., Restrepo, J., Bohórquez, J., Suárez, N., Restrepo, E., & Zarama, R. (2005). From Old Wars to New Wars and Global Terrorism. *Cornell University Library reference arXiv:Physics/0506213* retrieved 28 May 2013.

Johnson, S. E. P. J. E., Kitchens, K. E., Martin, A., & Fischbach, J. R. (2012). A Review of the Army's Modular Force Structure. RAND National Defense Research Institute.

JP 1-02. (2013). *US Department of Defense Dictionary of Military and Associated Terms, Joint Publication 1-02, 8 November 2010 as amended through 15 December 2013*. Retrieved February 6, 2014, from http://www.dtic.mil/doctrine/dod_dictionary/

JulianRubenNL. (2013). *VERMIST / MISSING / FEHLT Julian & Ruben*. Retrieved from http://julian-ruben-vermist.Webklik.nl/page/vermist-julian-ruben

Kalloniatis, A. (2008). A New Paradigm for Dynamical Modelling of Networked C2 Processes. In *Proc. 13th International Command and Control Research and Technology Symposium (ICCRTS)*. Washington, DC: CCRP Press. Retrieved from www.dodccrp.org/events/13th_iccrts_2008/CD/html/papers/180.pdf

Kalloniatis, A., Macleod, I., & Kohn, E. (2010). Agility in an Extended Space of Constructible Organisations. In *Proc. 15th International Command and Control Research and Technology Symposium (ICCRTS)*. Washington, DC: CCRP Press. Retrieved from www.dodccrp.org/events/15th_iccrts_2010/papers/069.pdf

Kalloniatis, A. (2010). From incoherence to synchronicity in the network Kuramoto model. *Physical Review E: Statistical, Nonlinear, and Soft Matter Physics*, *82*(6), 066202. doi:10.1103/PhysRevE.82.066202 PMID:21230718

Kang, S.-C., Morris, S. S., & Snell, S. A. (2007). Relational Archetypes, Organizational Learning, and Value Creation: Extending the Human Resource Architecture. *Academy of Management Review*, *32*(1), 236–256. doi:10.5465/AMR.2007.23464060

Kapucu, N., Arslan, T., & Collins, M. L. (2010). Examining Intergovernmental and Interorganizational Response to Catastrophic Disasters: Toward a Network-Centered Approach. *Administration & Society*, *42*(2), 222–247. doi:10.1177/0095399710362517

Kearns, M., Suri, S., & Montfort, N. (2006). An Experimental Study of the Coloring Problem on Human Subject Networks. *Science*, *313*(11), 824–827. doi:10.1126/science.1127207 PMID:16902134

Keating, C. B., Sousa-Poza, A., & Kovacic, S. (2008). System of Systems Engineering: An Emerging Multi-discipline. *International Journal of System of Systems Engineering, 1*(1/2). doi:10.1002/9780470403501.ch7

Kennedy, J., Ashmore, J., Babister, E., & Kelman, I. (2008). The Meaning of 'Build Back Better': Evidence From Post-Tsunami Aceh and Sri Lanka. *Journal of Contingencies and Crisis Management, 16*(1), 24–36. doi:10.1111/j.1468-5973.2008.00529.x

Kitzen, M., Rietjens, S. J. H., & Osinga, F. P. B. (2012). Soft Power, the Hard Way: Adaptation by the Netherlands' Task Force Uruzgan. In T. Farrell, F. P. B. Osinga, & J. A. Russell (Eds.), *Fighting the Afghanistan War*. Stanford, CA: Stanford University Press.

Klapwijk, P., & Rothkrantz, L. J. M. (2006). Topology based infrastructure for crisis situations. In *Proceedings of the 3rd International Conference on Information Systems for Crisis Response and Management* (pp. 288-297). Academic Press.

Klein, G., & Klinger, D. (1987). Naturalistic Decision Making. *Human Systems IAC GATEWAY, 11*(3).

Kleindorfer, P. R., & Wind, Y. (2009). The Network Imperative: Community or Contagion? In P. R. Kleindorfer, & Y. Wind (Eds.), *The Network Challenge: Strategy, Profit, and Risk in an Interlinked World*. Upper Saddle River, NJ: Wharton School Publishing.

Klein, G. (1999). *Sources of Power: How People Make Decisions*. Cambridge, MA: MIT Press.

Koch, R. (2011). Towards next-generation intrusion detection. In *Proceedings of the 3rd International Conference on Cyber Conflict (ICCC 2011)*. Tallinn, Estonia: NATO CCD COE Publications.

Kovács, G., & Spens, K. M. (2007). Humanitarian Logistics in Disaster Relief Operations. *International Journal of Physical Distribution and Logistics Management, 37*(2), 99–114. doi:10.1108/09600030710734820

Krepinevich, A. F. (2002). The Army and Land Warfare: Transforming the Legions. *Joint Force Quarterly,* (32), 76-82.

Kuramoto, Y. (1948). *Chemical Oscillations, Waves, and Turbulence*. Berlin, Germany: Springer.

Laity, M. (2012). The Latest Test for NATO. *RUSI Journal, 157*(1), 52–58. doi:10.1080/03071847.2012.664372

Lakhtaria, K. I. (Ed.). (2012). *Technological Advancements and Applications in Mobile Ad-Hoc Networks: Research Trends*. Hershey, PA: IGI Global. doi:10.4018/978-1-46660-321-9

Lam, L. (2013, June 14). Edward Snowden: US government has been hacking Hong Kong and China for years. *South China Morning Post*.

Langlois, R. N. (2000). Capabilities and Vertical Disintegration in Process Technology: The Case of Semiconductor Fabrication Equipment. In N. J. Foss, & P. L. Robertson (Eds.), *Resources, Technology, and Strategy*. London: Routledge.

Langlois, R. N. (2002). Modularity in Technology and Organization. *Journal of Economic Behavior & Organization, 49*(1), 19–37. doi:10.1016/S0167-2681(02)00056-2

Langlois, R. N., & Robertson, P. L. (1992). Networks and Innovation in a Modular System: Lessons From the Microcomputer and Stereo Component Industries. *Research Policy, 21*, 297–313. doi:10.1016/0048-7333(92)90030-8

Langner, R. (2011). Stuxnet: Dissecting a Cyberwarfare Weapon. *IEEE Security & Privacy Magazine, 9*(3), 49–51. doi:10.1109/MSP.2011.67

Lee, S., & Lister, R. (2008). Experiments in the Dynamics of Phase Coupled Oscillators When Applied to Graph Colouring. In *Proceedings of the 31st Australasian Computer Science Conference* (ACSC). Wollongong, Australia: ACSC.

Lewis, J. A. (2010, June 24). Cyberwarfare and Its Impact on International Security. *UNODA Occasional Papers*. New York, NY: United Nations.

Lewis, T. G. (2009). *Network Science: Theory and applications*. Hoboken, NJ: John Wiley & Sons. doi:10.1002/9780470400791

Liaropoulos, A. (2006). Revolution in Warfare: Theoretical Paradigms and Historical Evidence - the Napoleonic and First World War Revolutions. *The Journal of Military History, 70*, 363–384. doi:10.1353/jmh.2006.0106

Lindahl, D., & Wedlin, M. (2003, December). IT Weapons in a Laboratory Environment. *User Report FOI-R--1056--SE*. Linköping, Sweden: Swedish Defence Research Agency.

Lindell, M. K., Perry, R. W., Prater, C., & Nicholson, W. C. (2006). Community Disaster Recovery. In *Proceedings of Fundamentals of emergency management* (pp. 308–345). FEMA.

Lind, W. S. (2004, September-October). Understanding Fourth Generation War. *Military Review*, 12–16.

Lipshitz, R., & Strauss, O. (1997). Coping with Uncertainty: A Naturalistic Decision-Making Analysis. *Organizational Behavior and Human Decision Processes, 69*(2), 149–163. doi:10.1006/obhd.1997.2679

Little, R. L., & Krannich, R. S. (1988). A model for assessing the social impacts of natural utilization on resource-dependent communities. *Impact Assessment, 6*(2), 21–35. doi:10.1080/07349165.1988.9725633

Loch, C. H., Terwiesch, C., & Thomke, S. (2001). Parallel and Sequential Testing of Design Alternatives. *Management Science, 45*(5), 663–678. doi:10.1287/mnsc.47.5.663.10480

Luiijf, E. A. M., Nieuwenhuijs, A. H., Klaver, M. H. A., van Eeten, M., & Cruz, E. (2008). *Empirical Findings on Critical Infrastructure Dependencies in Europe*. Paper presented at the 3rd International Workshop on Critical Information Infrastructures Security. Frascati, Italy.

Luiijf, E. A. M., & Klaver, M. H. A. (2006). Protection of the Dutch critical infrastructures. *International Journal of Critical Infrastructures, 2*(2/3), 201–214. doi:10.1504/IJCIS.2006.009438

Lynch, C. J., Diallo, S. Y., & Tolk, A. (2013). Representing the ballistic missile defense system using agent-based modeling. In *Proceedings of the Military Modeling & Simulation Symposium* (pp. 3-12). San Diego, CA: Society for Computer Simulation International.

MacKay, N. (2006). Lanchester combat models. *Mathematics Today, 42*(5), 170–173.

Maindonald, J., & Braun, J. (2007). *Data Analysis and Graphics Using R: An Example-Based Approach* (2nd ed.). Cambridge, UK: Cambridge University Press.

Malcolm, W. P. (2004). *On The Character and Complexity of Certain Defensive Resource Allocation Problems*. Report DSTO-TR-1570. Edinburgh, Australia: DSTO.

Mandiant Corp. (2013, February 18). *APT1: Exposing One of China's Cyber Espionage Units*. Retrieved from http://intelreport.mandiant.com

Mannes, P. (2013). *GRIP op CRISISCOMMUNICATIE - Onderzoek naar de Maatschappelijke impact op Crisiscommunicatie*. [Grip on crisis communication - Research on the societal impact on crisis communication]. (Master Thesis). VU University, Amsterdam, The Netherlands.

Manso, M., & Manso, B. (2010, June). *N2C2M2 Experimentation and Validation: Understanding Its C2 Approaches and Implications*. Paper presented at the 15th ICCRTS. Santa Monica, CA.

Manso, M., & Moffat, J. (2011). *Defining and Measuring Cognitive Entropy and Cognitive Self-Synchronization* Paper presented at 16th ICCRTS. Quebec, Canada.

Maslow, A. H. (1943). A theory of human motivation. *Psychological Review, 50*(4), 370. doi:10.1037/h0054346

Matheus, C. J., & Ulicny, B. (2007). On the Automated Generation of an OWL Ontology based on the Joint C3 Information Exchange Data Model. In *Proceedings of the 12th International Command & Control Research & Technology Symposium* (ICCRTS). ICCRTS.

Mattis, J. N. (2008). USJFCOM Commander's Guidance for Effects-based Operations.[JFQ]. *Joint Force Quarterly, 51*, 105–109.

Maxwell, D. T. (2000). An Overview of the Joint Warfare System (JWARS). *Phalanx, 33*(3), 12–14.

McChrystal, S. A. (2013). *Lesson from Iraq: It Takes a Network to Defeat a Network*. Retrieved from http://www.linkedin.com/today/post/article/20130621110027-86145090-lesson-from-iraq-it-takes-a-network-to-defeat-a-network

McChrystal, S. A. (2011, March-April). It Takes a Network: The new frontline of modern warfare. *Foreign Policy 1-6*.

Messemaker, M., Wolbers, J. J., Treurniet, W., & Boersma, F. K. (2013). *Shaping societal impact: between Control and Cooperation.* Paper presented at the 10th International ISCRAM Conference. Baden-Baden.

Miller, N. R. (1980). A new solution set for tournaments and majority voting: further graph-theoretical approaches to the theory of voting. *American Journal of Political Science, 24,* 68–96. doi:10.2307/2110925

Ministerie van Veiligheid en Justitie. (2013). *Nationaal Handboek Crisisbesluitvorming* [National Handbook Crisis Decision-making]. Den Haag: Author.

Mintzberg, H. (1980). Structure in 5's: A Synthesis of the Research on Organization Design. *Management Science, 26*(3), 322–341. doi:10.1287/mnsc.26.3.322

Mintzberg, H. (1983). *Structure in fives: designing effective organizations.* Englewood Cliffs, NJ: Prentice-Hall.

Mintzberg, H. (1995). The Structuring of Organizations. In H. Mintzberg, J. B. Quinn, & S. Ghoshal (Eds.), *The Strategy Process.* London: Prentice-Hall.

Moffat, J. (2003). *Complexity Theory and Network Centric Warfare.* Washington, DC: US DoD CCRP.

Mohrman, S. A., Cohen, S. G., & Mohrman, A. M. (1995). *Designing Team-Based Organizations: New Forms of Knowledge Work.* San Francisco, CA: Jossey-Bass Publishers.

Monsuur, H. (2011). Cyber Operaties: een Operations Research perspectief. *Intercom,* (4): 37–38.

Monsuur, H., Grant, T. J., & Janssen, R. H. P. (2011). Network Topology of Military Command & Control Systems: Where axioms and action meet. In *Computer Science, Technology, and Applications* (Vol. 3, pp. 1–27). Hauppauge, NY: Nova Science Publishers, Inc.

Monsuur, H., Kooij, R. E., & Van Mieghem, P. F. A. (2012). Analysing and modelling the interconnected cyberspace. In *Cyber warfare: Critical perspectives* (pp. 165–183). The Hague: Asser Press.

Monsuur, H., & Storcken, T. (2004). Centers in connected undirected graphs: An axiomatic approach. *Operations Research, 52,* 54–64. doi:10.1287/opre.1030.0082

Moynihan, D. P. (2007). *From Forest Fires to Hurricane Katrina: Case Studies of Incident Command Systems. Networks and Partnerships Series.* Washington, DC: IBM Center for The Business of Government.

MSB. (2011, December). A Functioning Society in a Changing World. *Report.* Swedish Civil Contingencies Agency. Retrieved from https://www.msb.se/RibData/Filer/pdf/26084.pdf

*MSC - COE maritime security conference.* (2011). Retrieved January 01, 2014, from http://maritimesecurityconference.org

*MSC - COE maritime security conference.* (2012). Retrieved January 01, 2014, from http://maritimesecurityconference.org

Mukunda, G., & Troy, W. J. (2009). Caught in the Net: Lessons from the Financial Crisis for a Networked Future. *Parameters, 39*(2), 63–76.

Mullender, S. (1993). *Distributed Systems* (2nd ed.). New York, NY: ACM Press.

Munich Re. (2012, January 4). *Review of natural catastrophes in 2011: Earthquakes result in record loss year.* Retrieved from http://www.munichre.com/en/media_relations/press_releases/2012/2012_01_04_press_release.aspx

Nagel, E. (1979). *The structure of science: Problems in the logic of scientific explanation.* Indianapolis, IN: Hackett Publishing Company.

Nakagawa, Y., & Shaw, R. (2004). Social Capital: A Missing Link to Disaster Recovery. *International Journal of Mass Emergencies and Disasters, 22*(1), 5–34.

Nakashima, E. (2013, January 27). *Pentagon to boost cybersecurity force.* Retrieved from http://articles.washingtonpost.com/2013-01-27/world/36583575_1_cyber-protection-forces-cyber-command-cybersecurity

National Commission on Terrorist Attacks Upon the United States (NCTAUUS). (2004). *The 9/11 Commission Report.* US Government. Retrieved from govinfo.library.unt.edu/911/report

National Research Council. (2005). *Network Science: Report of the Committee on Network Science for Future Army Applications*. Washington, DC: The National Academies Press.

*NATO Code of Best Practice for C2 Assessment*. (2002). Command and Control Research Program (CCRP) Press.

NATO SAS-050 Research Task Group. (2007). *Exploring New Command and Control Concepts and Capabilities* (RTO Technical Report TR-SAS-050). Neuilly-sur-Seine Cedex, France: NATO Research and Technology Organisation.

NATO SAS-065 Research Task Group. (2010). *NATO NEC C2 Maturity Model*. Washington, DC: CCRP.

NATO. (2006). Exploring New Command and Control Concepts and Capabilities. NATO RTO SAS Task Group 050 Final Report prepared for NATO. *US DoD CCRP*. Retrieved 28 May 2013, from www.dodccrp.org

NATO. (2009). *Whitepaper on NNEC Maturity Levels. Working draft v2, dated 22 April 2009*. NATO.

NATO. (2010). *NATO NEC C2 Maturity Model*. Washington, DC: CCRP Press. Retrieved from www.dodccrp.org/files/N2C2M2_Web_optimized.pdf

NATO. (2011). Strategic Analysis of the Comprehensive Approach in NATO Operation Unified Protector. *NATO Unclassified, draft 1 July 2011*.

NC3A. (2005). *NATO NEC Feasibility Study Executive Summary v 2.0*. NATO Communications and Information Agency.

Neaga, E. I., & Henshaw, M. (2011). A Stakeholder-Based Analysis of the Benefits of Networked Enabled Capability. *Defense & Security Analysis*, *27*(2), 119–134. doi:10.1080/14751798.2011.578716

Nelson, C. B., Steckler, B. D., & Stamberger, J. A. (2011). The Evolution of Hastily Formed Networks for Disaster Response: Technologies, Case Studies, and Future Trends. In *Proceedings of the 2011 IEEE Global Humanitarian Technology Conference (GHTC)* (pp. 467-475). Seattle, WA: IEEE.

Netherlands Ministry of Defence. (2012, September). *The Defence Cyber Strategy*. The Hague, The Netherlands: Ministry of Defence.

Newman, M. E. J. (2003). The Structure and Function of Complex Networks. *SIAM Review*, *45*(2), 167–256. doi:10.1137/S003614450342480

Newman, M., & Watts, D. (1999). Renormalization Group Analysis of the Small-World Network Model. *Elsevier Physics Letters A*, *263*, 341–346. doi:10.1016/S0375-9601(99)00757-4

NOAA. (2012, December 20). *Preliminary Info on 2012 U.S. Billion-Dollar Extreme Weather/Climate Events*. Retrieved from http://www.ncdc.noaa.gov/news/preliminary-info-2012-us-billion-dollar-extreme-weatherclimate-events

*Northrop Grumman MQ-4C Triton*. (2013), Retrieved January 01, 2014, from http://www.northropgrumman.com/triton

Noy, N. F., & McGuiness, D. L. (2001). *Ontology Development 101: A guide to creating your first ontology*. Stanford Knowledge Systems Laboratory Technical Report KSL-01-5 and Stanford Medical Informatics Technical Report SMI-2001-0880.

NSC. (2014). *USMA West Point Network Science Center: About Us*. Retrieved February 6, 2014, from http://www.westpoint.edu/nsc/SitePages/About.aspx

NS-CTA. (2014). *Network Science Collaborative Technology Alliance, US Army Research Laboratory*. Retrieved February 6, 2014, from http://www.ns-cta.org/ns-cta-blog/

O'Mahony, S., & Bechky, B. A. (2008). Boundary Organizations: Enabling Collaboration among Unexpected Allies. *Administrative Science Quarterly*, *53*(3), 422–459. doi:10.2189/asqu.53.3.422

O'Hair, H. D., Kelley, K. M., & Williams, K. L. (2011). Managing Community Risks Through a Community-Communication Infrastructure Approach. In H. E. Canary, & R. D. McPhee (Eds.), *Communication and Organizational Knowledge: Contemporary Issues for Theory and Practice*. New York: Routledge.

O'Reilly, C. A., & Tushman, M. L. (2008). Ambidexterity as a Dynamic Capability: Resolving the Innovator's Dilemma. *Research in Organizational Behavior*, *28*, 185–206. doi:10.1016/j.riob.2008.06.002

Orr, R. J., & Nissen, M. E. (2006). Hypothesis Testing of Edge Organizations: Simulating Performance under Industrial Era and 21$^{st}$ Century Conditions. In *Proceedings of the 11$^{th}$ International Command and Control Research and Technology Symposium (ICCRTS)*. Washington, DC: CCRP Press. Retrieved from www.dodccrp.org/events/11th_ICCRTS/html/papers/057.pdf

Orton, J. D., & Weick, K. E. (1990). Loosely Coupled Systems: A Reconceptualization. *Academy of Management Review, 15*(2), 203–223.

Oshri, I., Pan, S. L., & Newell, S. (2005). Trade-offs between Knowledge Exploitation and Exploration Activities. *Knowledge Management Research & Practice, 3*, 10–23. doi:10.1057/palgrave.kmrp.8500042

Osinga, F. P. B. (2007). On Boyd, Bin Laden, and Fourth Generation Warfare as String Theory. In J. Olson (Ed.), On New Wars. Oslo, Norway: Oslo Files on Defence and Security no 4/2007.

Osinga, F. (2007). *Science, Strategy and War. The Strategic Theory of John Boyd*. London: Routledge.

Pahl, G., Beitz, W., Feldhusen, J., & Grote, K. H. (2007). *Engineering Design: A Systematic Approach* (3rd ed.). London: Springer. doi:10.1007/978-1-84628-319-2

Peabody, D. (2005). The Challenges of Doing Good Work: The Development of Canadian Forces CIMIC Capability and NGOs. In *Proceedings of CDAI Conference*. CDAI.

Penrose, R. (2010). *Cycles of Time*. London, UK: The Bodley Head.

Perlroth, N. (2013, January 31). Hackers in China Attacked The Times for Last 4 Months. *The New York Times*, p. A1.

Perry, W., & Moffat, J. (2004). *Information Sharing Among Military Headquarters, The Effects on Decision-Making*. Santa Monica, CA: The RAND Corporation.

Pestana, G., Rebelo, I., Duarte, N., & Couronné, S. (2012). Adressing Stakeholders Coordination for Airport Efficiency and Decision-Support Requirements. *Journal of Aerospace Operations, 1*(3), 267–280.

Pidcock, W. (2010). *What are the Differences Between a Vocabulary, a Taxonomy, a Thesaurus, an Ontology, and a Meta-Model?* Retrieved from http://www.metamodel.com/article.php

Pigeau, R., & McCann, C. (2002, Spring). Re-conceptualizing command and control. *Canadian Military Journal*, 53-64.

Pitsis, T. S., Kornberger, M., & Clegg, S. R. (2004). The Art of Managing Relationships in Interorganizational Collaboration. *M@n@gement, 7*(3), 47-67.

Politis, I., Tsagkaropoulos, M., & Kotsopoulos, S. (2007). Video Transmission over TETRA. In P. Stavroulakis (Ed.), *Terrestrial trunked radio - TETRA: A global security tool* (pp. 133–190). Berlin: Springer-Verlag. doi:10.1007/3-540-71192-9_5

Powell, W. W. (1990). Neither Market nor Hierarchy: Network Forms of Organization. In L. L. Cummings, & B. M. Staw (Eds.), *Research in Organizational Behavior* (Vol. 12, pp. 295–336). Greenwich, CT: JAI Press.

Provan, K. G., Fish, A., & Sydow, J. (2007). Interorganizational Networks at the Network Level: A Review of the Empirical Literature on Whole Networks. *Journal of Management, 33*, 479–516. doi:10.1177/0149206307302554

Provan, K. G., & Kenis, P. (2008). Modes of Network Governance: Structure, Management, and Effectiveness. *Journal of Public Administration: Research and Theory, 18*(1), 229–252.

Putnam, R. D. (1995). Bowling alone: America's declining social capital. *Journal of Democracy, 6*(1), 65–78. doi:10.1353/jod.1995.0002

Quarantelli, E. L., & Dynes, R. R. (1985). Community Response to Disasters. In *Disasters and Mental Health Selected Contemporary Perspectives*. Academic Press.

Rao, A. S., & Georgeff, M. P. (1995). BDI agents: From theory to practice. In V. Lesser & L. Gasser (Eds.), *Proceedings of the first international conference on multiagent systems*. MIT Press.

Rasmussen, J. (1985). The role of hierarchical knowledge representation in decision making and system management. *IEEE Transactions on Systems, Man, and Cybernetics, 15*(2), 234–243. doi:10.1109/TSMC.1985.6313353

Rebovich, G. Jr. (2005). Enterprise Systems Engineering[*Systems Thinking for the Enterprise: New and Emerging Perspectives*. The MITRE Corporation.]. *Theory into Practice, 2*.

Rentenaar, M. (Forthcoming). Blue on Blue: Civil-Military Interaction during the Libya Operations. In G. Lucius, & S. J. H. Rietjens (Eds.), *The Soldier's Handbook on Civil-Military Interaction in Peace Operations*. Berlin: Springer.

Reynolds, C. W. (1987). Flocks, Herds, and Schools: A Distributed Behavioral Model. *Computer Graphics, 21*(4), 25–34. doi:10.1145/37402.37406

Rietjens, S. J. H., van Fenema, P. C., & Essens, P. (2013). 'Train as you Fight' Revisited: Preparing for a Comprehensive Approach. *PRISM, 4*(2).

Rietjens, S. J. H., & Bollen, M. (2008). *Managing Civil-Military Cooperation: A 24/7 Joint Effort for Stability*. London: Ashgate. doi:10.1163/ej.9789004163270.i-253

Rietjens, S. J. H., Bollen, M. T. I. B., Khalil, M., & Wahidi, S. F. (2009). Enhancing the Footprint: Stakeholders in Afghan Reconstruction. *Parameters, 39*(1), 22–39.

Rietjens, S. J. H., Kampen, T., & Grant, T. J. (2010). Logistics Planning and Control: Lessons Learned in Afghanistan. In J. M. M. L. Soeters, P. C. van Fenema, & R. Beeres (Eds.), *Managing Military Organizations: Theory and Practice*. London: Routledge.

Rietjens, S. J. H., Soeters, J. M. M. L., & Klumper, W. (2010). Measuring Performance in Today's Missions: The Effects-based Approach to Operations. In J. M. M. L. Soeters, P. C. van Fenema, & R. Beeres (Eds.), *Managing Military Organizations: Theory and Practice*. London: Routledge.

Rietjens, S. J. H., Soeters, J. M. M. L., & van Fenema, P. C. (2013). Learning from Afghanistan: Towards a Compass for Civil–Military Coordination. *Small Wars & Insurgencies*. doi:10.1080/09592318.2013.778027

Rietjens, S. J. H., Voordijk, H., & De Boer, S. J. (2007). Coordinating Humanitarian Operations in Peace Support Missions. *Disaster Prevention and Management, 16*(1), 56–69. doi:10.1108/09653560710729811

Rivkin, J. W., & Siggelkow, N. (2003). Balancing Search and Stability: Interdependencies Among Elements of Organizational Design. *Management Science, 49*(3), 290–311. doi:10.1287/mnsc.49.3.290.12740

Roelofsen, G. (2000). TETRA Security. *Information Security Technical Report, 5*(3), 44–54. doi:10.1016/S1363-4127(00)03006-5

Rosenthal, U., Boin, A., & Comfort, L. K. (2001). *Managing crises: Threats, dilemmas, opportunities*. Charles C Thomas Springfield.

Rothkrantz, L. J. M. (2013). Crisis Management Using Multiple Camera Surveillance Systems. In *Proceedings of the 3rd International Conference on Information Systems for Crisis Response and Management* (pp. 617-626). Academic Press.

Rothkrantz, L. J. M., & Scholte, K. (2013). A Surveillance System of a Military Harbour Using an Automatic Identification System. In B. Rachev & A. Smrikarov (Eds.), *International Conference on Computer Systems and Technologies* (pp. 95-102). Academic Press.

Rothkrantz, L. J. M., Yang, Z., Jepson, M., Datcu, D., & Wiggers, P. (2009). A bottom-up approach of fusion of events in surveillance systems. In B. Rachev & A. Smrikarov (Eds.), *Proceedings of the 2009 International Conference on Computer Systems and Technologies* (art. 29). Academic Press.

Rothkrantz, L. J. M., Takapoui, R., Datcu, D., & Yang, Z. (2010). AUV Localisation using floating smart dust. In *Contributions in Military-Technology*. Swedish National Defence College.

Rowley, J. (2007). The Wisdom Hierarchy: Representations of the DIKW hierarchy. *Journal of Information Science, 33*(2), 163–180. doi:10.1177/0165551506070706

Rubbini, R., & Vindua, A. (2012). By Sea, Air, and Land. Plausible Responsibility to React Scenarios and Their Military Requirements. *Canadian Centre for the Responsibility to Protect*. Retrieved from http://ccr2p.org/wp-content/uploads/2013/01/SeaAirLand.pdf

Ruddy, M. (2007, June). *ELICIT – The Experimental Laboratory for Investigating Collaboration, Information-sharing and Trust*. Paper presented at 12th ICCRTS. Newport, RI.

Ruddy, M., & Nissen, M. (2008). *New Software Platform Capabilities and Experimentation Campaign for ELICIT*. Paper presented at 13th ICCRTS. Seattle, WA.

RUSI. (2011). Accidental Heroes: Britain, France and the Libya Operation. *Interim RUSI Campaign Report, September 2011*.

*Saab - Maritime surveillance. State of the art.* (2013). Retrieved January 01, 2014, from http://www.saabgroup.com

Sanchez, R. (1995). Strategic Flexibility in Product Competition. *Strategic Management Journal, 16*, 135–159. doi:10.1002/smj.4250160921

Sanchez, R. (2003). Commentary. In R. Garud, A. Kumaraswamy, & R. N. Langlois (Eds.), *Managing in the Modular Age*. Malden, MA: Blackwell Publishers.

Sanchez, R., & Mahoney, J. T. (1996). Modularity, Flexibility, and Knowledge Management in Product and Organization Design. *Strategic Management Journal, 17*, 77–91.

*ScanEagle, Ministry of Dutch Defence.* (2013). Retrieved January 01, 2014, from http://www.defensie.nl

Schilling, M. A., & Paparone, C. R. (2005, August-November). Modularity: An Application of General Systems Theory to Military Force Development. *Defense Acquisition Review Journal*, 278-293.

Schilling, M. A. (2000). Toward a General Modular Systems Theory and its Application to Interfirm Product Modularity. *Academy of Management Review, 25*(2), 312–334.

Schilling, M. A., & Steensma, H. K. (2001). The Use of Modular Organizational Forms: An Industry-Level Analysis. *Academy of Management Journal, 44*(6), 1149–1168. doi:10.2307/3069394

Schneier, B. (2010, July 7). *Threat of 'cyberwar' has been hugely hyped.* Retrieved from http://Ed.cnn.com/2010/OPINION/07/07/schneier.cyberwar.hyped/

Scholte, K. (2013). *Detecting suspicious behavior in Marine traffic using the Automatic Identification System.* (Unpublished doctoral dissertation). Delft University of Technology, Delft, The Netherlands.

Sclove, R. (2010). *Reinventing Technology Assessment: A 21st Century Model. Science and Technology Innovation Program Report.* Washington, DC: Woodrow Wilson International Center for Scholars.

Seifert, M., DiLego, T., Hitchings, J., Sterling, J., Hawks, K., & Griffith, D. (2005). JASMAD: Meeting Current and Future Combat Airspace Requirements. *Report AFRL-IF-RS-TP-2006-3*. Retrieved from http://www.dtic.mil/cgi-bin/GetTRDoc?AD=ADA451880

Seiple, C. (1996). *The US Military/NGO Relationship in Humanitarian Interventions.* Carlisle Barracks, PA: Peacekeeping Institute Centre for Strategic Leadership, U.S. Army War College.

Shimko, K. L. (2010). *The Iraq Wars and America's Military Revolution.* New York, NY: Cambridge University Press. doi:10.1017/CBO9780511845277

Siggelkow, N., & Levinthal, D. A. (2003). Temporarily Divide to Conquer: Centralized, Decentralized, and Reintegrated Organizational Approaches to Exploration and Adaptation. *Organization Science, 14*(6), 650–669. doi:10.1287/orsc.14.6.650.24840

Sigholm, J. (2010). Reconfigurable Radio Systems: Towards Secure Collaboration for Peace Support and Public Safety. In *Proceedings of the 9th European Conference on Information Warfare and Security (ECIW)* (pp. 268-274). Thessaloniki, Greece: ACPI Ltd.

Sigholm, J., & Raciti, M. (2012). Best-Effort Data Leakage Prevention in Inter-Organizational Tactical MANETs. In *Proceedings of the 2012 IEEE Military Communications Conference (MILCOM)* (pp. 1143-1149). Orlando, FL: IEEE.

Simon, H. A. (1962). The Architecture of Complexity. *Proceedings of the American Philosophical Society, 106*(6), 467–482.

Simon, H. A. (1996). *The Sciences of the Artificial* (3rd ed.). Cambridge, MA: MIT Press.

Singer, P. W. (2009). *Wired for War: The Robotics Revolution and Conflict in the 21st Century.* New York, NY: Penguin Books.

Sinha, K. K., & Van de Ven, A. H. (2005). Designing Work Within and Between Organizations. *Organization Science, 16*(4), 389–408. doi:10.1287/orsc.1050.0130

SIPRI. (2013). *Stockholm International Peace Research Institute. Yearbook 2013: Armaments, Disarmament and International Security*. Oxford, UK: Oxford University Press.

Sirmon, D. G., Hitt, M. A., & Ireland, R. D. (2007). Managing Firm Resources in Dynamic Environments to Create Value: Looking Inside the Black Box. *Academy of Management Review*, *32*(1). doi:10.5465/AMR.2007.23466005

Smith, M.K., Welty, C., & McGuinness, D.L. (2004). *OWL Web Ontology Language Guide*. W3C Recommendation, 10 February 2004.

Smith, D. (2013). Life's certainties: death, taxes and APTs. *Network Security*, (2): 19–20. doi:10.1016/S1353-4858(13)70033-3

Snijders, T. A. B., Van de Bunt, G. G., & Steglich, C. E. G. (2010). Introduction to stochastic actor-based models for network dynamics. *Social Networks*, *32*(1), 44–60. doi:10.1016/j.socnet.2009.02.004

Snook, S. A. (2000). *Friendly Fire: The Accidental Shootdown of U.S. Black Hawks over Northern Iraq*. Princeton, NJ: Princeton University Press.

Soeters, J. M. M. L. (2000). Culture in Uniformed Organizations. In N. M. Ashkanasy, C. P. M. Wilderom, & M. F. Peterson (Eds.), *Handbook of Organizational Culture and Climate* (pp. 465–480). Thousand Oaks, CA: Sage.

Soeters, J. M. M. L., & Manigart, P. (2008). *Military Cooperation in Multinational Peace Operations: Managing Cultural Diversity and Crisis Response*. London: Routledge.

Soeters, J., Van Fenema, P. C., & Beeres, R. (2010). Introducing Military Organizations. In J. Soeters, P. C. Van Fenema, & R. Beeres (Eds.), *Managing Military Organizations: Theory and Practice*. London: Routledge.

Sood, A. K., & Enbody, R. J. (2013). Targeted Cyberattacks: A Superset of Advanced Persistent Threats. *IEEE Security & Privacy Magazine*, *11*(1), 54–61.

Sørensen, L., & Skouby, K. E. (Eds.). (2009, July). User Scenarios 2020 - A Worldwide Wireless Future. Outlook, 4.

Spaans, M., Spoelstra, M., Douze, E., Pieneman, R., & Grisogono, A. M. (2009). *Learning to be Adaptive*. Paper presented at the 14th International Command and Control Research and Technology Symposium (ICCRTS). New York, NY.

Stanton, N. A., Baber, C., & Harris, D. (2008). *Modelling command and control: Event analysis of systemic teamwork*. Aldershot, UK: Ashgate.

Starkey, K., Barnatt, C., & Tempest, S. (2000). Beyond Networks and Hierarchies: Latent Organizations in the U.K. Television Industry. *Organization Science*, *11*(3), 299–305. doi:10.1287/orsc.11.3.299.12500

Stenumgaard, P. (2011, May). Interference susceptibility of civilian wireless consumer technology. *User Report FOI-R--3216--SE*. Linköping, Sweden: Swedish Defence Research Agency.

Stern, E. K. (2003). Crisis Studies and Foreign Policy Analysis: Insights, Synergies, and Challenges. *International Studies Review*, *5*(2), 155–202. doi:10.1111/1521-9488.5020016

Stern, E. K. (2009). Crisis Navigation: Lessons from History for the Crisis Manager in Chief. *Governance: An International Journal of Policy, Administration and Institutions*, *22*(2), 189–202. doi:10.1111/j.1468-0491.2009.01431.x

Stevens, W., Myers, G., & Constantine, L. (1974). Structured Design. *IBM Systems Journal*, *13*(2), 115–139. doi:10.1147/sj.132.0115

Stoddard, A. (2006). *Humanitarian Alert: NGO Information and its Impact on US Foreign Policy*. Sterling, VA: Kumarian Press.

Strange, J. (1996). *Centers of Gravity and Critical Vulnerabilities: Building on the Clausewitzian Foundation So That We Can All Speak the Same Language* (2nd ed.). Quantico, VA: Marine Corps University.

Stringer, K. D. (2010, March-April). Interagency Command and Control at the Operational Level: A Challenge in Stability Operations. *Military Review*, 54–62.

Strogatz, S. (2000). From Kuramoto to Crawford: exploring the onset of synchronization in populations of coupled oscillators. *Physica D. Nonlinear Phenomena, 143*, 1–20. doi:10.1016/S0167-2789(00)00094-4

Strogatz, S. (2003). *Sync: The Emerging Science of Spontaneous Order*. New York, NY: Hyperion.

Tatham, P., & Rietjens, S. J. H. (Manuscript submitted for publication). Integrated Disaster Relief Logistics: A Stepping Stone Towards Viable Civil-Military Networks? *Disasters*. PMID:21702893

Tatomir, B., Klapwijk, P., & Rothkrantz, L. J. M. (2006). Topology based infrastructure for medical emergency coordination. *International Journal of Intelligent Control and Systems, 11*(4), 228–237.

Thibodeau, P. (2010, March 24). *Cyberattacks an 'existential threat' to U.S., FBI says*. Retrieved from http://www.computerworld.com/s/article/9173967/Cyberattacks_an_existential_threat_to_U.S._FBI_says

Thunholm, P., Chong, N. E., Cheah, M., Kin Yong, T., Chua, N., & Ching Lian, C. (2009). Exploring Alternative Edge versus Hierarchy C2 Organizations using the ELICIT Platform with Configurable Chat System. *The International C2 Journal, 3*(2), 1-52.

Tolk, A. (Ed.). (2012). *Engineering principles of combat modeling and distributed simulation*. Hoboken, NJ: Wiley. doi:10.1002/9781118180310

Tolk, A., Adams, K. M., & Keating, C. B. (2011). Towards Intelligence-based Systems Engineering and System of Systems Engineering. In *Intelligence-based Systems Engineering* (pp. 1–22). Springer. doi:10.1007/978-3-642-17931-0_1

Tönnies, F. (2012). *Gemeinschaft und gesellschaft* [Community and Society]. Springer. doi:10.1007/978-3-531-94174-5

Topper, C. M., & Carley, K. M. (1999). A structural perspective on the emergence of network organizations. *The Journal of Mathematical Sociology, 24*(1), 67–96. doi:10.1080/0022250X.1999.9990229

Törnqvist, E., Sigholm, J., & Nadjm-Tehrani, S. (2009). Hastily Formed Networks for Disaster Response: Technical Heterogeneity and Virtual Pockets of Local Order. In *Proceedings of the 6th International Conference on Information Systems for Crisis Response and Management (ISCRAM2009)*. Gothenburg, Sweden: ISCRAM.

Traynor, I., & Norton-Taylor, R. (2011, April 5). *Nato lacking strike aircraft for Libya campaign*. Retrieved from http://www.guardian.co.uk/world/2011/apr/05/nato-lacking-strike-aircraft-libya

Treurniet, W., van Buul-Besseling, K., & Wolbers, J. J. (2012). *Collaboration awareness - a necessity in crisis response coordination*. Paper presented at the 9th International ISCRAM Conference. Vancouver, Canada.

Trist, E., & Bamforth, K. (1951). Some Social and Psychological Consequences of the Longwall Method of Coal Getting. *Human Relations, 4*, 3–38. doi:10.1177/001872675100400101

U.S. Department of Defense. (2011, May). *Technology Readiness Assessment (TRA) Guidance*. Washington, DC: U.S. Department of Defense.

Uiterwijk, D. J. W. B., Soeters, J. M. M. L., & van Fenema, P. C. (2013). Aligning National 'Logics' in a European Military Helicopter Program. *Defense & Security Analysis, 29*(1), 54–67. doi:10.1080/14751798.2013.760248

Ulrich, K. (1995). The Role of Product Architecture in the Manufacturing Firm. *Research Policy, 24*(3), 419–440. doi:10.1016/0048-7333(94)00775-3

United Nations Office for the Coordination of Humanitarian Affairs. (2013). *Humanitarianism in the Network Age, including world humanitarian data and trends 2012. UN Office for the Coordination of Humanitarian Affairs*. OCHA.

US DoD JP 1-02. (2013). *US Department of Defense Dictionary of Military and Associated Terms, Joint Publication 1-02, 8 November 2010 as amended through 15 December 2013*. Retrieved February 6, 2014, from http://www.dtic.mil/doctrine/dod_dictionary/

Uschold, M., & Jasper, R. (1999). A Framework for Understanding and Classifying Ontology Applications. In *Proceedings, 12ᵗʰ international workshop on Knowledge Acquisition, Modelling, and Management*, (vol. 99, pp. 16-21). Academic Press.

Van Creveld, M. (1985). *Command in War*. Cambridge, MA: Harvard University Press.

Van de Ven, A. H., Delbecq, A. L., & Koenig, R. Jr. (1976). Determinants of Coordination Modes Within Organizations. *American Sociological Review*, *41*, 322–338. doi:10.2307/2094477

van der Laan, E., de Brito, M. P., van Fenema, P. C., & Vermaesen, S. (2009). Managing Information Cycles for Intra-organizational Co-ordination of Humanitarian Logistics. *International Journal of Services Technology and Management*, *12*(4), 362–390. doi:10.1504/IJSTM.2009.025814

van der Wal, A. J. (2010). Self-organization and emergent behaviour: distributed fuzzy decision making through phase synchronization. In *Computational Intelligence, Foundations and Applications* (pp. 263–268). Singapore: World Scientific Publishing. doi:10.1142/9789814324700_0038

Van Diggelen, J., Bradshaw, J. M., Grant, T. J., Johnson, M., & Neerincx, M. (2009). Policy-Based Design of Human-Machine Collaboration in Manned Space Missions. In *Proceedings, 3ʳᵈ IEEE international conference on Space Mission Challenges for Information Technology 2009* (SMC-IT09). Pasadena, CA: SMC.

Van Ettinger, F. (2008). NATO Network Enabled Capabilities: Can it work? *Carre*, *11*, 22–26.

van Fenema, P. C. (2012). National Crisis Response Networks (NCRN) and Military Organizations: Revisiting the Katrina Case. In G. Kümmel, & J. M. M. L. Soeters (Eds.), *New Wars, New Militaries, New Soldiers: Conflicts, the Armed Forces and the Soldierly Subject* (Vol. 19, pp. 111–130). London: Emerald. doi:10.1108/S1572-8323(2012)0000019011

Van Fenema, P., Rietjens, S., & Besters, B. (2014This volume). *De-conflicting Civil-Military Networks*.

Ventre, D. (2012). *Cyber Conflict: Competing National Perspectives*. Hoboken, NJ: John Wiley & Sons. doi:10.1002/9781118562666

Verizon. (2013, April). *2013Data Breach Investigations report*. Retrieved from http://www.verizonenterprise.com/DBIR/2013/

*Vessel tracking and Automatic Transmitter Identification System (marine)*. (2013). Retrieved January 01, 2014, from http://en.wikipedia.org/wiki/Automatic_Identification_System

Vogel, S. (2009, August 27). For Intelligence Officers, A Wiki Way to Connect Dots. *The Washington Post*.

VSAM Home page, Carnegie Mellon University. (1996). *Video Surveillance and Monitoring Homepage*. Retrieved January 01, 2014, from http://www.cs.cmu.edu/~vsam/OldVsamWeb/vsamhome.html

Warden, J. (1995). The Enemy as a System. *Airpower Journal*, *14*(1), 40–55.

Warne, L., Bopping, D., Ali, I., Hart, D., & Pascoe, C. (2005). The Challenge of the Seamless Force: The Role of Informal Networks in Battlespace. In *Proceedings of the 10ᵗʰ International Command and Control Research and Technology Symposium (ICCRTS)*. Washington, DC: CCRP Press. Retrieved from www.dodccrp.org/events/10th_ICCRTS/CD/papers/215.pdf

Warren, R. (1972). *The Community in America*. Rand McNally.

Wasserman, S., & Faust, K. (1994). *Social network analysis: Methods and applications*. Cambridge, UK: Cambridge University Press. doi:10.1017/CBO9780511815478

Watts, D. (2000). *Santa Fe Working Paper 00-12-062*. Santa Fe Institute.

Watts, D. (1999). *Small Worlds, The Dynamics of Networks between Order and Randomness*. Princeton, NJ: Princeton University Press.

Watts, D. J. (2003). *Six Degrees: The Science of a Connected Age*. London, UK: William Heinemann.

Watts, D. J., & Strogatz, S. H. (1998). Collective dynamics of 'small world' networks. *Nature*, *393*, 440–442. doi:10.1038/30918 PMID:9623998

Weick, K. E. (1976). Educational organizations as loosely coupled systems. *Administrative Science Quarterly*, *21*, 1–19. doi:10.2307/2391875

Weick, K. E. (1979). *The social psychology of organizing*. Addison-Wesley Publishing Company, Inc.

Weick, K. E. (2004). Rethinking Organizational Design. In R. J. Boland, & F. Collopy (Eds.), *Managing as Designing* (pp. 36–53). Stanford, CA: Stanford University Press.

Weimann, G. (2004, May). Cyberterrorism: How Real is the Threat?. *Special Report*. Washington, DC: United States Institute of Peace.

Weiner, S. (1984). Systems and technology. In *Ballistic Missile Defense* (pp. 49–97). Brookings Inst Press.

Wentz, L. (2010). Haiti Information and Communications Observations: Trip Report for Visit 18 February to 1 March 2010. *Center for Technology and National Security Policy*. Washington, DC: National Defense University.

Whelan, C. (2012). *Networks and National Security: Dynamics, Effectiveness and Organisation*. Surrey, UK: Ashgate Publishing Limited.

White, B. E. (2006). Fostering Intra-Organizational Communication of Enterprise Systems Engineering Practices. In *Proceedings of NDIA, 9th Annual Systems Engineering Conference*. The MITRE Corporation.

Wiggers, P., Mertens, B., & Rothkrantz, L. J. M. (2011). Dynamic Bayesian Networks for Situational Awareness in the Presence of Noisy Data. In *Proceedings of International Conference on Computer Systems and Technologies* (pp. 411-416). Academic Press.

World Bank. (2013, November). Building Resilience: Integrating Climate and Disaster Risk into Development. *The World Bank Group Experience*. Washington, DC: World Bank Publications.

Worren, N., Moore, K., & Cardona, P. (2002). Modularity, Strategic Flexibility, and Firm Performance: A Study of the Home Appliance Industry. *Strategic Management Journal*, *23*, 1123–1140. doi:10.1002/smj.276

Wyld, A., & Rodgers, G. (2007). Models for Random Graphs with Variable Strength Edges. *Physica A*, *374*, 491–500. doi:10.1016/j.physa.2006.07.002

Yaziji, M., & Doh, J. (2009). *NGOs and Corporations: Conflict and Collaboration*. Cambridge, UK: Cambridge University Press. doi:10.1017/CBO9780511626708

Yost, D. S. (1982). Ballistic Missile Defense and the Atlantic Alliance. *International Security*, *7*(2), 143–174. doi:10.2307/2538436

Zins, C. (2007). Conceptual Approaches for Defining Data, Information, and Knowledge. *Journal of the American Society for Information Science and Technology*, *58*(4), 479–493. doi:10.1002/asi.20508

Zollo, M., & Winter, S. G. (2002). Deliberate Learning and the Evolution of Dynamic Capabilities. *Organization Science*, *13*(3), 339–351. doi:10.1287/orsc.13.3.339.2780

# About the Contributors

**T.J Grant** is retired but an active scientific researcher in the fields of network-enabled Command and Control (C2) systems, offensive cyber operations, sense-making in novel and unexpected situations, and agent-based simulation. He has a Bachelor of Science in Aeronautical Engineering (Bristol University, UK), a Masters-level Defence Fellowship (Brunel University, UK), and a PhD in Artificial Intelligence (Maastricht University, NL). Tim's working career covered 20 years as a military officer in the (British) Royal Air Force, 17 years consultancy experience in Atos (a global IT services supplier), and 10 years experience in academia (including a visiting professorship at the University of Pretoria, South Africa). His last appointment was as the Professor of Operational ICT and Communications within the Faculty of Military Sciences at the Netherlands Defence Academy (NLDA), where he led a team of five lecturers. He become a Professor Emeritus on 1 July 2012, when he founded Retired But Active Researchers (R-BAR) . He collaborates with other researchers and subject matter experts worldwide, and currently supervises two PhD students working on coalition and civil-military information sharing. More details about Tim's career can be found at http://www.linkedin.com/pub/tim-grant/7/605/3a3. E-mail: tim.grant.work@gmail.com

**R.H.P. Janssen** is an Assistant Professor of Mathematics and Operations Research within the Faculty of Military Sciences at the Netherlands Defence Academy (NLDA) and member of the Board of the Expertise Centre Military Operations Research. In this Expertise Centre he coaches officers facing operational and logistic problems that may benefit from a quantitative or Operations Research approach. His work concentrates on modeling and simulation of networks within the military domain with a focus on uncertainty and complexity. Dr.ir. Janssen teaches courses such as stochastic processes, optimization (with a focus on meta-heuristics), and simulation. E-mail: RHP.Janssen@mindef.nl

**H. Monsuur** is an Associate Professor of Mathematics and Operations Research (OR) at the Netherlands Defence Academy (NLDA), and is responsible for research and education on Military OR. He is also Head of the Expertise Centre Military Operations Research and member of the board of the Dutch OR Society (NGB). His research focuses on network science and C2, decision and planning tools, game-theoretic risk analysis of security threats, and quantitative operational logistics. Results of this research shows the advantage of applying an analytic approach to (military) operational problems. E-mail: H.Monsuur@mindef.nl

\* \* \*

**B. Besters**, Lieutenant-colonel, is a Logistics Officer of the NLD Army. After his military education at the Royal Military Academy, he served in several Logistics and Movement positions in national and international environments. As of 2006, he worked at the Sealift Coordination Centre (SCC) and the Movement Coordination Centre Europe (MCCE), both at Eindhoven Airbase. Subsequently he served as a Staff Officer Movements at SHAPE, the supreme Military NATO HQ, and has been deeply involved in Movement Operations in recent and current NATO operations (e.g. ISAF, OUP, and KFOR), but also for the Pakistan Flood Relief Operation in 2010. In his previous job, he was Lecturer for Logistics at the Netherlands Defence Academy (2012-2013). Currently, he is Chief Movement Coordination Centre (MCC) at NLD MoD. E-mail: bf.besters@mindef.nl

**S. Bowling** is the Dean of the School of Engineering Technology and Computer Science of Bluefield State College. In the past, Dr. Bowling taught courses in systems engineering and engineering management such as operations research, systems dynamics, agent-based modeling, and optimization methods. His research includes the modeling of complex systems using different modeling paradigms. He is an associate editor for the *International Journal of Experimental Design and Process Optimization*. E-mail: sbowling@bluefieldstate.edu

**A.H. Dekker** obtained his PhD from the University of Tasmania in 1991. Following a number of years teaching computer science at universities in Australia and Singapore, he joined the Australian Defence Science and Technology Organisation (DSTO), where his interests included knowledge management, agent-based simulation, and network theory. This work supported advice to the Australian Department of Defence on a range of topics, including headquarters organizational structure, human decision-making, and networked operations. Since 2013, Anthony has been an independent consultant. He is also a Fellow of the Modelling and Simulation Society of Australia and New Zealand, and an Honorary Research Fellow at the University of Ballarat. E-mail: dekker@acm.org

**S. Deller** is a 25-year Army veteran and a 1988 graduate of the United States Military Academy in West Point, New York. He served in the Aviation Branch for the first ten years of his career before becoming an Operations Research officer in 1997. Sean has extensive experience with leading assessments in support of capabilities development for both the United States Army and the Joint Staff. He received his doctorate in engineering management at Old Dominion University in 2009, and his research focused on the quantitative analysis of the connectivity value of networked operations. Sean's interests include game design and development and he has contributed to a number of commercially published games over the past fifteen years. He is now the Director of Operations Research and Analysis for Textron Systems, Weapons & Sensor Systems. E-mail: deller.sean@gmail.com

**B. Drabble** is the Chief Technical Officer of DMM Ventures, Inc. and also holds a Visiting faculty position at the Artificial Intelligence Applications Institute (AIAI) at the University of Edinburgh. Brian Drabble is a former Senior Research Associate and Director of Computational Intelligence Research Laboratory (CIRL) at the University of Oregon. Brian Drabble received his undergraduate degree from Staffordshire University, UK (1980-84) and his Ph.D. from Aston University UK (1984-1988). Brian Drabble has extensive experience in the development and application of planning, dependency analysis, resource allocation, and ontology and process management technologies. He was a PI on DARPA's Planning and Decision Aids, Advanced ISR Management (AIM) and Control of Agent Based Systems (CoABS) programs and was also a PI on AFRL's Effects Based Operations (EBO) program that developed and evaluated the basic dependency based technology. He was also a key member of the Lockheed Martin team that developed USSTRATCOM's ISPAN system where his expertise was used to design the core plan representation schemes, optimization architecture and develop its approach to EBO. E-mail: bdrabble1@gmail.com

**P.C. van Fenema** holds the chair of military logistics and information systems at the Netherlands Defence Academy. Previously he was affiliated with the Rotterdam School of Management, Tilburg University and Florida International University. He published extensively in the field of organization studies, network value creation, and information management in journals such as *MIS Quarterly, International Journal of Physical Distribution and Logistics Management, PRISM, Information Systems Journal, Information & Management, Defence and Security Analysis*, and *Journal of International Business Studies*. He co-edited a number of international volumes, including *Managing Military Organizations* (Routledge, 2010). For more details, please see: www.paulcvanfenema.com. E-mail: pc.v.fenema@mindef.nl

**E. Jensen** holds a PhD in psychology from Örebro University, and a MSc in Electrical Engineering from Chalmers University of Technology. She is employed by the Swedish National Defence College since 2004, where she has primarily been studying military command and control. Dr. Jensen is, however, presently working on a project funded by the Swedish Civil Contingencies Agency in collaboration with researchers from Lund University and FOI (the Swedish research institute in the areas of defence and security). The project aims to develop methods to assess the capability for successful command, control and cooperation in the partaking members of the Swedish crises management system. E-mail: eva.jensen@fhs.se

**J. Moffat** is a Senior Fellow of the Defence Science and Technology Laboratory, UK, a Fellow of the Operational Research Society, a Fellow of the Institute of Mathematics and its Applications, and a Fellow of the Royal Aeronautical Society. He is a visiting Professor at Cranfield University and has worked for the past 30 years or so on defence related operational analysis, systems engineering, and aerospace technology research. He has a BSc (Summa Cum Laude) in Mathematics, and a PhD in Quantum Operator Theory. His current research interests are in building tools, models and theories that capture the key effects of human decision-making and other aspects of Information Age conflict. He has published extensively in the peer reviewed open literature. His most recent works include the books *Command and Control in the Information Age: Representing its Impact* (The Stationery Office, London, UK, 2002), *Complexity Theory and Network Centric Warfare* (CCRP, Dept of Defense, USA, 2003), *The Agile Organisation* (CCRP, Dept of Defense, USA, 2005), and *Adapting Modelling and Simulation for Network Enabled Operations* (CCRP, Dept of Defense, USA, 2011). He has won the awards: Napier Medal (Edinburgh University), Carnegie Scholarship, President's Medal of the Operational Research Society, Enduring Achievement Award US DoD Command and Control Research Programme, US Defense and Government Award for best contribution to the advancement of NCW theory. E-mail: JMOFFAT@dstl.gov.uk

**G. Rabadi** is an Associate Professor at the Engineering Management and Systems Engineering Department at Old Dominion University. His research interest includes Operations Research, Simulation, Scheduling, and Meta-Heuristics. He teaches graduate courses in Operations Research, Applied Optimization, and Supply Chain Management. He is currently the Editor-in-Chief for the *International Journal of Planning and Scheduling*. E-mail: GRabadi@odu.edu

**S. Rietjens**, an engineer by training, is an associate professor at the Netherlands Defence Academy, and a reserve major in the Netherlands Army. He has done extensive fieldwork in military operations and has published accordingly in international journals and books. His main focus of interest is in civil-military cooperation, effectiveness of military operations, as well as military logistics and information management. He co-edited a volume on civil-military cooperation (Ashgate, 2008), and a special issue on defense logistics (*International Journal of Physical Distribution and Logistics Management*, 2013). E-mail: sjh.rietjens.01@mindef.nl

**L.J.M. Rothkrantz** studied Mathematics at the University of Utrecht from 1967-1971 and Psychology at the University of Leiden from 1980-1990. He did his PhD study Mathematics at the University of Amsterdam and graduated in 1980. From 1980-1992 he was working as teacher Mathematics at a Polytechnical School and as student counsellor at Delft University of Technology (DUT). Since 1992 he was appointed as Assistant/Associate Professor Artificial Intelligence at Delft University of Technology. Since 2007 he worked as a Professor Sensor Systems at The Netherlands Defence Academy (NLDA). In 2011 he retired from DUT and in 2013 also from the NLDA. He is honoured with golden medals from the Technical University of Prague and the Military Academy from Brno. E-mail: l.j.m.rothkrantz@tudelft.nl

**J. Sigholm**, Captain, is a lecturer in Military Science at the Swedish National Defence College in Stockholm, Sweden. He has a background as an officer of military intelligence and security in the Swedish Armed Forces, and holds a Master of Science degree in Computer Science and Engineering from Linköping University, Sweden. His research is currently focused on studying how emerging information and communications technology can be used to support and facilitate work for military personnel engaging in inter-organizational collaboration, and how to design an efficient cross-sector cyber defense capability. E-mail: johan.sigholm@fhs.se

**A. Tolk** is the Chief Scientist at SimIS Incorporated in Portsmouth, VA. He is also Adjunct Professor for Systems Engineering, Engineering Management, and Modeling, Simulation, and Visualization Engineering at Old Dominion University in Norfolk, VA. He received the Technical Merit Award of the Simulation Interoperability Standards Organization and the Outstanding Professional Contribution Award by the Society for Modeling and Simulation. E-mail: andreas.tolk@simisinc.com

**W. Treurniet** received his MSc degree in informatics from the Technical University of Delft in 1989. In the 1990s, he became involved in a TNO research programme on Command & Control, studying the feasibility of substantial reduction of frigate-level command team. From 2000 on, he has been the lead author of the C4I Policy of the Royal Netherlands Navy and as an Information Architect he has been co-authoring the corporate Information Architecture of the Dutch MoD. As a Programme Manager of several Command and Control research programmes, he has been responsible for the development of a vision on Command and Control in future military operations. In 2009 Treurniet made a switch to the application domain of crisis management. In this domain he continued to apply and develop his experience in Information Management and Netcentric Operations. From 2012 onwards – in addition to his position at TNO – Treurniet became a PhD student at the VU University Amsterdam (Faculty of Social Sciences, Department of Organization Sciences), studying trustworthiness of networked organizations. E-mail: willem.treurniet@tno.nl

**E.J. de Waard** is an assistant professor of management and organization studies at the Netherlands Defence Academy. Strategic management, organization design, and project management are his key areas of interest. He has published on these topics in *Financial Accountability and Management*, *International Journal of Project Management*, *European Security*, *Journal of Management and Organization*, *Journal of Organization Design*, and in several books with renowned publishers. E-mail: EJ.D.WAARD.01@ mindef.nl

**A.J. van der Wal** has a Ph.D. in Solid State Physics and has held several professorships in physics and electronics. Currently he is an Associate Professor of Signal Analysis and Artificial Intelligence at the Netherlands Defence Academy (NLDA). His research interests include the modeling of uncertainty with fuzzy logic, neural networks and evolutionary computing, the thermodynamics of multi-particle systems and the occurrence of synchronization in multi-agent systems, both analytically and by simulation. E-mail: AJ.vd.Wal@mindef.nl

# Index